Lecture Notes in Computer Scien

T0238427

Commenced Publication in 1973
Founding and Former Series Editors:
Gerhard Goos, Juris Hartmanis, and Jan van Leeuwen

Serge Vaudenay (Ed.)

Public Key Cryptography – PKC 2005

8th International Workshop
on Theory and Practice in Public Key Cryptography
Les Diablerets, Switzerland, January 23-26, 2005
Proceedings

Volume Editor

Serge Vaudenay
Ecole Polytechnique Fédérale de Lausanne
School of Computer and Communication Sciences
Security and Cryptography Laboratory
1015 Lausanne, Switzerland
E-mail: serge.vaudenay@epfl.ch

Library of Congress Control Number: 2004117654

CR Subject Classification (1998): E.3, F.2.1-2, C.2.0, K.4.4, K.6.5

ISSN 0302-9743
ISBN 3-540-24454-9 Springer Berlin Heidelberg New York

Springer is a part of Springer Science+Business Media

springeronline.com

Typesetting: Camera-ready by author, data conversion by Olgun Computergrafik
Printed on acid-free paper   SPIN: 11376477   06/3142   5 4 3 2 1 0

Preface

The 2005 issue of the International Workshop on Practice and Theory in Public Key Cryptography (PKC 2005) was held in Les Diablerets, Switzerland during January 23–26, 2005. It followed a series of successful PKC workshops which started in 1998 in Pacifico Yokohama, Japan. Previous workshops were successively held in Kamakura (Japan), Melbourne (Australia), Cheju Island (South Korea), Paris (France), Miami (USA), and Singapore. Since 2003, PKC has been sponsored by the International Association for Cryptologic Research (IACR). As in previous years, PKC 2005 was one of the major meeting points of worldwide research experts in public-key cryptography. I had the honor to co-chair the workshop together with Jean Monnerat and to head the program committee. Inspired by the fact that the RSA cryptosystem was invented on ski lifts, we decided that the best place for PKC was at a ski resort. Jean Monnerat and I hope that this workshop in a relaxed atmosphere will lead us to 25 more years of research fun.

PKC 2005 collected 126 submissions on August 26, 2004. This is a record number. The program committee carried out a thorough review process. In total, 413 review reports were written by renowned experts, program committee members as well as external referees. Online discussions led to 313 additional discussion messages and 238 emails. The review process was run using email and the Webreview software by Wim Moreau and Joris Claessens. Every submitted paper received at least 3 review reports. We selected 28 papers for publication on October 28, 2004. Authors were then given a chance to revise their submission over the following two weeks. This proceedings includes all the revised papers. Due to time constraints the revised versions could not be reviewed again.

Double submissions, where authors send the same or almost the same paper to multiple conferences that explicitly prohibit such practices, is an increasing problem for the research community worldwide. I do regret that we had to reject 6 such submissions without consideration of their scientific merits. I would like to thank the program chairs of other events who collaborated in this effort, in particular Anne Canteaut, Joe Kilian, Choonsik Park, and Seongtaek Chee.

With the approval of the IACR Board of Directors, PKC 2005 delivered the PKC Best Paper Award for the first time. The purpose of the award is to formally acknowledge authors of outstanding papers and to recognize excellence in the cryptographic research fields. Committee members were invited to nominate papers for this award. A poll then yielded a clear majority. This year, we were pleased to deliver the PKC Best Paper Award to Yevgeniy Dodis and Aleksandr Yampolskiy for their brilliant paper "A Verifiable Random Function with Short Proofs and Keys." This paper concluded the workshop.

I would like to thank Jean Monnerat who accepted the responsibility to co-chair the PKC 2005 workshop. I would like to thank the PKC steering committee for their support and trust. The program committee and external reviewers worked extremely hard under a tight schedule. I heartily thank them for this volunteer work. Acknowledgments also go to the authors of submitted papers and the speakers who made the real meat of PKC 2005. I am grateful to Antoine Junod and Julien Brouchier for their support with the Webreview software. I also thank my assistants Pascal Junod, Thomas Baignères, Yi Lu, Gildas Avoine, and Matthieu Finiasz for their help in the PKC 2005 organization. Special thanks to Martine Corval who orchestrated the PKC 2005 logistics. We appreciate the kind help of Christian Cachin in the advertising and registration process. We also owe our gratitude to Kevin McCurley for spending a substantial amount of his valuable time to set up the online registration website. We thank our generous sponsors Gemplus and personally David Naccache, and HP Labs and personally Wenbo Mao, for supporting PKC 2005. We also thank EPFL and IACR for sponsoring this event. It was a very pleasant experience. Crypto is fun!

Lausanne, November 19, 2004   Serge Vaudenay

PKC Steering Committee (as of November 2004)

Yvo Desmedt	University College London, UK
Hideki Imai (Chair)	University of Tokyo, Japan
Kwangjo Kim	Information and Communications University, South Korea
David Naccache	Gemplus, France, and Royal Holloway, University of London, UK
Jacques Stern	Ecole Normale Supérieure, France
Moti Yung	Columbia University, USA
Yuliang Zheng (Secretary)	University of North Carolina at Charlotte, USA
Ronald Cramer	CWI and Leiden University, The Netherlands
Tatsuaki Okamoto	NTT Labs, Japan

Organizing Committee

General Co-chairs	Jean Monnerat
	Serge Vaudenay
Local Organization	Martine Corval
Assistants	Gildas Avoine
	Thomas Baignères
	Matthieu Finiasz
	Pascal Junod
	Yi Lu

Program Committee

Carlisle Adams	University of Ottawa, Canada
Feng Bao	Institute for Infocomm Research, Singapore
Yvo Desmedt	University College London, UK
Juan Garay	Bell Labs – Lucent Technologies, USA
Martin Hirt	ETH Zurich, Switzerland
Kwangjo Kim	Information and Communications University, South Korea
Kaoru Kurosawa	Ibaraki University, Japan
Anna Lysyanskaya	Brown University, USA
Wenbo Mao	HP Labs Bristol, UK
David Naccache	Gemplus, France and Royal Holloway, University of London, UK
Kaisa Nyberg	Nokia, Finland
Tatsuaki Okamoto	NTT Labs, Japan
Josef Pieprzyk	Macquarie University, Australia
David Pointcheval	CNRS-ENS, France
Reihaneh Safavi-Naini	University of Wollongong, Australia
Kazue Sako	NEC, Japan
Claus-Peter Schnorr	University of Frankfurt am Main, Germany
Berry Schoenmakers	Technische Universiteit Eindhoven, The Netherlands
Nigel Smart	University of Bristol, UK
Edlyn Teske	University of Waterloo, Canada
Serge Vaudenay	EPFL, Switzerland
Moti Yung	University of Columbia, USA
Yuliang Zheng	University of North Carolina at Charlotte, USA

External Reviewers

Masayuki Abe
Ben Adida
Gildas Avoine
Joonsang Baek
Thomas Baignères
Mihir Bellare
Daniel Bleichenbacher
Colin Boyd
Emmanuel Bresson
Eric Brier
Duncan Buell
Srdjan Capkun
Dario Catalano
Liqun Chen
Benoît Chevallier-Mames
Jean-Sébastien Coron
Ronald Cramer
Jean-François Dhem
Christophe Doche
Atsushi Fujioka
Eiichiro Fujisaki
Jun Furukawa
Steven Galbraith
Pierrick Gaudry
Louis Granboulan
Rob Granger
Jaime Gutierrez
Darrel Hankerson
Anwar Hasan
Alex Healy
Jason Hinek
Susan Hohenberger
Thomas Holenstein
Heng Swee Huay

Toshiyuki Isshiki
Kouichi Itoh
Michael Jacobson
Marc Joye
Pascal Junod
Charanjit Jutla
Jonathan Katz
Tetsutaro Kobayashi
Robert König
Byoungcheon Lee
Arjen Lenstra
Moses Liskov
Javier Lopez
Yi Lu
John Malone-Lee
Toshihiko Matsuo
Noel McCullagh
Anton Mityagin
Atsuko Miyaji
Jean Monnerat
Waka Nagao
Phong Q. Nguyễn
Satoshi Obana
Takeshi Okamoto
Katsuyuki Okeya
Dan Page
Pascal Paillier
Jacques Patarin
Kenneth Paterson
Chris Peikert
Krzysztof Pietrzak
Bartosz Przydatek
Tal Rabin
Peter Roelse

Hans-Georg Rueck
Ryuichi Sakai
Takakazu Satoh
Katja Schmidt-Samoa
Michael Scott
Hovav Shacham
Andrey Sidorenko
Johan Sjödin
Martijn Stam
Andreas Stein
Ron Steinfeld
Makoto Sugita
Willy Susilo
Koutarou Suzuki
Tsuyoshi Takagi
Keisuke Tanaka
Isamu Teranishi
Jacques Traoré
Shigenori Uchiyama
Frederik Vercauteren
Duong Quang Viet
Jorge L. Villar
Guilin Wang
Huaxiong Wang
Stephen Weis
Claire Whelan
Christopher Wolf
Go Yamamoto
Chung-Huang Yang
Danfeng Yao
Sung-Ming Yen
Huafei Zhu

Table of Contents

RSA Cryptography

Multivariate Asymmetric Cryptography

Signature Schemes

Identity-Based Cryptography

Best Paper Award

A New Related Message Attack on RSA

Oded Yacobi[1] and Yacov Yacobi[2]

[1] Department of Mathematics, University of California San Diego,
9500 Gilman Drive, La Jolla, CA 92093, USA
oyacobi@math.ucsd.edu
[2] Microsoft Research, One Microsoft Way, Redmond, WA 98052, USA
yacov@microsoft.com

Abstract. Coppersmith, Franklin, Patarin, and Reiter show that given two RSA cryptograms $x^e \bmod N$ and $(ax + b)^e \bmod N$ for known constants $a, b \in \mathbb{Z}_N$, one can compute x in $O(e \log^2 e)$ $\mathbb{Z}_N$-operations with some positive error probability. We show that given e cryptograms $c_i \equiv (a_i x + b_i)^e \bmod N$, $i = 0, 1, ...e - 1$, for any known constants $a_i, b_i \in \mathbb{Z}_N$, one can deterministically compute x in $O(e)$ $\mathbb{Z}_N$-operations that depend on the cryptograms, after a pre-processing that depends only on the constants. The complexity of the pre-processing is $O(e \log^2 e)$ $\mathbb{Z}_N$-operations, and can be amortized over many instances. We also consider a special case where the overall cost of the attack is $O(e)$ $\mathbb{Z}_N$-operations. Our tools are borrowed from numerical-analysis and adapted to handle formal polynomials over finite-rings. To the best of our knowledge their use in cryptanalysis is novel.

1 Introduction

Messages with known relations may occur for example if an attacker pretends to be the recipient in a protocol that doesn't authenticate the recipient, and in addition the message is composed of the content concatenated with a serial number. In that case the attacker can claim that she didn't receive the transmission properly and ask that it be sent again. The next transmission will have the same content as the original but an incremented serial number. If the increment is known we have a known relation. Other examples appear in [4].

Related message attacks can be avoided all together if before RSA-encryption the message M is transformed using e.g. the OAEP function ([3]; There are other methods and some issues are not settled yet, see [5]). This transformation destroys the relations between messages and increases the message length.

Nevertheless it is useful to know the ramifications in case for some reason one chooses not to use OAEP or similar methods (even though it is highly recommended). For example RFID tags may pose tough engineering challenges of creating very compact cryptosystems, and the trade-off must be known precisely.

In [4] it was shown that given two RSA cryptograms $x^e \bmod N$, and $(ax + b)^e \bmod N$ for any known constants $a, b \in \mathbb{Z}_N$ one can compute x in $O(e \log^2 e)$ $\mathbb{Z}_N$-operations with some small error probability.

S. Vaudenay (Ed.): PKC 2005, LNCS 3386, pp. 1–8, 2005.

We show that given e cryptograms $c_i \equiv (a_i x + b_i)^e \bmod N$, $i = 0, 1, ...e-1$, for any known constants $a_i, b_i \in \mathbb{Z}_N$, one can deterministically compute x in $O(e)$ $\mathbb{Z}_N$-operations, after doing $O(e \log^2 e)$ pre-computations that depend only on the known constants. The descriptions of the protocol and the attack determine the values of these constants. For example the attack described at the beginning of this section has for all i $a_i = b_i = 1$. The cost of the pre-computations can be amortized over many instances of the problem.

Our problem could be solved by using the Newton expansion of $c_i \equiv (a_i x + b_i)^e \bmod N$, renaming $z_j = x^j$ and using linear algebra to find z_1. However, our method is more efficient.

We also show that in the special case where $c_i \equiv (ax + b \cdot i)^e \bmod N$, $i = 0, 1, ...e - 1$, for any known constants $a, b \in \mathbb{Z}_N$, where $\gcd(a, N) = \gcd(b, N) = \gcd(e!, N) = 1$, one can deterministically compute x in overall $O(e)$ $\mathbb{Z}_N$-operations using

$$x \equiv a^{-1} b[(b^e e!)^{-1} \sum_{i=0}^{e-1} \binom{e-1}{i} \cdot c_i \cdot (-1)^{e-1+i} - \frac{e-1}{2}] \bmod N$$

If any of the above gcd conditions do not hold then the system is already broken.

It remains an open problem whether the new approach can improve the general case of implicit linear dependence, i.e., suppose for known constants a_i, $i = 0, 1, 2, ...k$, there is a known relation $\sum_{i=1}^{k} a_i x_i = a_0$ among messages $x_1, x_2, ...x_k$. The current complexity of attacking this problem is $O(e^{k/2} k^2)$ [4].

Our major attack-tools are divided-differences and finite-differences. These tools are borrowed from numerical-analysis, and adapted to handle formal polynomials over finite-rings. To the best of our knowledge their use in cryptanalysis is novel.

For a survey of the work on breaking RSA see [2].

2   Main Result

2.1   Divided Differences

We borrow the concept of *divided-differences* from numerical analysis and adapt it to handle formal polynomials over finite rings. This will allow us to extract the message from a string of e cryptograms whose underlying messages are linearly related. We specialize our definitions to the ring of integers modulo N, a product of two primes (the "RSA ring"). All the congruences in this paper are taken mudulo N.

Definition 1. *Let h be a polynomial defined over the ring of integers modulo N, and let $x_0, x_1, ...x_n$ be distinct elements of the ring such that $(x_0 - x_i)^{-1} \bmod N$ exist for $i = 0, 1, ...n$. The nth divided-difference of h relative to these elements is defined as follows:*

$$[x_i] \equiv h(x_i),$$

$$[x_0, x_1] \equiv \frac{[x_0] - [x_1]}{x_0 - x_1},$$

$$[x_0, x_1, ...x_n] \equiv \frac{[x_0, x_1, ...x_{n-1}] - [x_1, x_2, ...x_n]}{x_0 - x_n}.$$

Let x be an indeterminate variable, and for $i = 0, 1, ...n$, let $x_i \equiv x + b_i$ for some known constants b_i (these are the general explicit linear relations that we assume later). We can now view the above divided differences as univariate polynomials in x defined over $\mathbb{Z}_N$.

The following lemma is true for the divided difference of any polynomial mod N, but for our purposes it is enough to prove it for the RSA polynomial $x^e \bmod N$. Related results are stated in [8]. Before beginning the proof we introduce some notation borrowed from [7]. Let $\pi_k(y) \equiv \prod_{i=0}^{k} (y - x_i)$. Then taking the derivative of π_k with respect to y we have for $i \leq k$

$$\pi'_k(x_i) \equiv \prod_{\substack{0 \leq j \leq k \\ j \neq i}} (x_i - x_j)$$

By induction on k the following equality easily follows

$$[x_0, ..., x_k] \equiv \sum_{i=0}^{k} \frac{h(x_i)}{\pi'_k(x_i)} \tag{1}$$

Let $C_t(p)$ denote the t_{th} coefficient of the polynomial p, starting from the leading coefficients (the coefficients of the highest powers). We use $C_t[x_0, ..x_k]$ as a shorthand for $C_t([x_0, ..x_k])$.

Lemma 1. *Let $[x_0, ..., x_n]$ be the nth divided difference relative to the RSA polynomial $h(x) \equiv x^e \bmod N$, and let $x_0, x_1, ...x_n$ be distinct elements of the ring such that $(x_0 - x_i)^{-1} \bmod N$ exist for $i = 0, 1, ...n$. Then (i) for $0 \leq n \leq e$, if $\binom{e}{e-n} \neq 0 \bmod N$ then $\deg[x_0, ..., x_n] = e - n$. (ii) $C_{e-n}[x_0, x_1, .., x_n] \equiv \binom{e}{e-n}$ (an important special case is $C_1[x_0, x_1, .., x_{e-1}] \equiv e \bmod N$).*

Comment: In practice the condition in claim (i) always holds, since $e << N$.

Proof. The claim is trivial for $n = 0$. For $n \geq 1$ we prove the equivalent proposition that $C_t[x_0, ..., x_n] = 0$ for $t = e, e - 1, ..., e - n + 1$ and $C_{e-n}[x_0, ..., x_n]$ is independent of the b_i and is not congruent to 0. We use the notations $1/b$ and b^{-1} interchangeably. We induct on n. When $n = 1$

$$[x_0, x_1] \equiv \frac{(x + b_0)^e - (x + b_1)^e}{b_0 - b_1} \equiv \frac{\sum_{i=0}^{e} \binom{e}{i} x^i [b_0^{e-i} - b_1^{e-i}]}{b_0 - b_1}$$

Note that by our assumption $(b_0 - b_1)^{-1} \bmod N$ exist. So $C_e[x_0, x_1] \equiv 0$ and $C_{e-1}[x_0, x_1] \equiv e$ and indeed our claim is true for $n = 1$. For the inductive hypothesis let $n = k - 1$ and assume that $C_t[x_0, ..., x_{k-1}] \equiv 0$ for $t = e, e -$

$1, ..., e - (k - 1) + 1$ and $C_{e-(k-1)}[x_0, ..., x_{k-1}]$ is independent of the b_i and is not congruent to 0. We want to show that when $n = k$, $C_t[x_0, ..., x_k] \equiv 0$ for $t = e, e - 1, ..., e - k + 1$ and $C_{e-k}[x_0, ..., x_k]$ is independent of the b_i and is not congruent to 0.

The fact that $C_t[x_0, ..., x_k] \equiv 0$ for $t = e, e-1, ..., e-k+1$ follows immediately from the inductive hypothesis and Definition 1. It takes a little more work to show that $C_{e-k}[x_0, ..., x_k]$ is independent of the b_i.

Using (1):

$$[x_0, x_1, ..., x_k] \equiv \sum_{i=0}^{k} \frac{(x + b_i)^e}{\pi'_k(x_i)} \equiv \sum_{j=0}^{e} \binom{e}{j} x^j \left[\frac{b_0^{e-j}}{\pi'_k(x_0)} + \frac{b_1^{e-j}}{\pi'_k(x_1)} + ... + \frac{b_k^{e-j}}{\pi'_k(x_k)} \right]$$

We want to show that $C_{e-k}[x_0, x_1, ..., x_k]$ is independent of the b_i.

$$C_{e-k}[x_0, x_1, .., x_k] \equiv \binom{e}{e-k} \left[\frac{b_0^k}{\pi'_k(x_0)} + \frac{b_1^k}{\pi'_k(x_1)} + ... + \frac{b_k^k}{\pi'_k(x_k)} \right] \tag{2}$$

So now it is sufficient to show that

$$(-1)^0 \frac{b_0^k}{(b_0 - b_1) \cdots (b_0 - b_k)} + ... + (-1)^k \frac{b_k^k}{(b_0 - b_k) \cdots (b_{k-1} - b_k)} \tag{3}$$

is independent of the b_i.

We first multiply (3) by the necessary terms to get a common denominator. We introduce some compact notation that will simplify the process. For a given set of constants $b_0, b_1, ... b_k$ define

$$\delta(h, i) \equiv (b_h - b_i)$$
$$\delta(h, i, j) \equiv (b_h - b_i)(b_h - b_j)\delta(i, j)$$
$$\vdots$$
$$\delta(i_0, ..., i_k) \equiv (b_{i_0} - b_{i_1})(b_{i_0} - b_{i_2}) \cdots (b_{i_0} - b_{i_k})\delta(i_1, ..., i_k)$$

Similarly we can also define $\delta_j \equiv \delta(0, 1, ..., \bar{j}, ..., k)$ where the bar denotes that the index is missing (so if $k = 4$ then $\delta_3 = \delta(0, 1, 2, 4,)$). Then (3) becomes:

$$\frac{b_0^k \delta_0 - b_1^k \delta_1 + \cdots + (-1)^k b_k^k \delta_k}{\delta(0, 1, ..., k)} \tag{4}$$

We want to show that (4) is independent of the b_i. In fact it equals 1. To see this consider the Vandermonde matrix:

$$V \equiv \begin{bmatrix} 1 & b_0 & b_0^2 & \cdots & b_0^k \\ 1 & b_1 & b_1^2 & \cdots & b_1^k \\ \vdots & \vdots & \vdots & \ddots & \vdots \\ 1 & b_k & b_k^2 & \cdots & b_k^k \end{bmatrix}$$

We conclude from (2) that $C_{e-k}[x_0, x_1, .., x_k] \equiv \binom{e}{e-k}$, which is certainly independent of the b_i. This also implies that $C_{e-k}[x_0, x_1, .., x_k]$ is not congruent to 0 when $k \le e$. By induction we are done.

2.2 Related-Messages Attack

Here we consider the general case where for $i = 0, 1, ...e-1$, $x_i \equiv a_i x + b_i \bmod N$. $N = pq$ is an RSA composite (p and q are large primes, with some additional restrictions which are irrelevant in the current discussion), and the constants a_i, b_i are known. Of course it is sufficient to consider just the case where $x_i \equiv x + b_i$. We now show how to deterministically compute x in $O(e)$ $\mathbb{Z}_N$-operations after some pre-computation that depends only on the known constants. If the constants b_i hold for many unknown values of cryptograms x^e then the cost of pre-computations can be amortized and discarded. We show that the cost of the additional computations that depend on the value of x is $O(e)$.

Specifically, $\pi'_n(x_k)$ is independent of y and of x, hence for all k these coefficients can be computed in advance. In that case the cost of computing $[x_0, x_1, ...x_{e-1}] \equiv ux + v \equiv w(x)$ is $O(e)$.

For each particular value x we know how to compute the value $w(x)$ without knowing x using Lemma 1 and Formula (1). More explicitly, Let $c_i \equiv (x + b_i)^e \bmod N$, $i = 0, 1, 2, ...e - 1$, be the given cryptograms, whose underlying messages are linearly related, and let $\pi'_{e-1}(x_k) \equiv \prod_{\substack{i=0 \\ i \neq k}}^{e-1} (b_k - b_i)$. We use p_k as a shorthand for $\pi'_{e-1}(x_k)$. Then

$$w(x) \equiv \sum_{k=0}^{e-1} \frac{[x_k]}{\pi'_{e-1}(x_k)} \equiv \sum_{k=0}^{e-1} \frac{c_k}{p_k}.$$

Here we assume that the inverses $(b_k - b_i)^{-1} \bmod N$ exist. Note that if for some k, i this isn't true then we can factor the RSA-modulus N, by computing $\gcd(N, (b_k - b_i))$.

From Lemma 1 (ii) we know that $u = e$. Note also that $w(0) \equiv v \equiv \sum_{k=0}^{e-1} b_k^e \cdot p_k^{-1} \bmod N$, and we can compute it in the pre-computation phase (before intercepting the cryptograms). So we can find $x \equiv (w(x) - v)e^{-1} \bmod N$.

The following algorithm summarizes the above discussion:

Algorithm 1

Given cryptograms $c_i \equiv (x+b_i)^e \bmod N$, $i = 0, 1, 2, ...e-1$, with known constants b_i, find x.

Method:

1. Pre computation:

   For $k = 0, ...e-1$, compute $p_k^{-1} \equiv \prod_{\substack{i=0 \\ i \neq k}}^{e-1} (b_k - b_i)^{-1}$; (If for some k, i, $(b_k - b_i)^{-1}$ does not exist then factor N using $\gcd(b_k - b_i, N)$ and halt);
   $v \equiv \sum_{k=0}^{e-1} b_k^e \cdot p_k^{-1} \bmod N$;

2. Real-time computation: $x \equiv e^{-1} \cdot ((\sum_{k=0}^{e-1} c_k p_k^{-1}) - v) \bmod N$.

The complexity of the pre-computation is $O(e \log^2(e))$ (see Appendix), and the complexity of the real time computations is $O(e)$.

3 Special Case

3.1 Finite Differences

We now consider the special case where the e cryptograms are of the form $c_i \equiv (ax + b \cdot i)^e \bmod N$, $i = 0, 1, ...e - 1$, for any known constants $a, b \in \mathbb{Z}_N$, where $\gcd(a, N) = \gcd(b, N) = \gcd(e!, N) = 1$. The special linear relations among these cryptograms allows us to deterministically compute x in overall $O(e)$ $\mathbb{Z}_N$-operations. As before x denotes an indeterminate variable.

Definition 2. *For h a polynomial over any ring let $\Delta^{(0)}(x) \equiv h(x)$, and let*

$$\Delta^{(i)}(x) \equiv \Delta^{(i-1)}(x+1) - \Delta^{(i-1)}(x), i = 1, 2, ...$$

It is easy to see that the degree of the polynomials resulting from this simpler process keep decreasing as in the case of divided-differences. More precisely:

Lemma 2. *In the special case where $x_i \equiv x+i$, and $\gcd(n!, N) = 1$, $[x_0, x_1, ...x_n] \equiv \Delta^{(n)}(x)/n!$*

A similar relation can be derived when $x_i \equiv ax + ib$, for known constants a, b. The next two lemmas are stated for general polynomials $h(x)$, although eventually we use them for $h(x) \equiv x^e \bmod N$. Let $m = \deg(h)$, and $0 \le k \le m$. By induction on k:

Lemma 3. $\Delta^{(k)}(x) \equiv \sum_{i=0}^{k} \binom{k}{i} \cdot h(x+i) \cdot (-1)^{k-i} \bmod N$.

For the algorithm we will need explicit formulas for the two leading terms of $\Delta^{(k)}(x)$. Let $h(x) = \sum_{i=0}^{m} a_i x^i$ and let $T_{a_m, a_{m-1}}^{(k)}(x)$ denote the two leading terms of $\Delta^{(k)}(x)$.

Lemma 4. $T_{a_m, a_{m-1}}^{(k)}(x) \equiv \frac{(m-1)!}{(m-k)!} x^{m-k-1}(a_m m(x + k(m-k)/2) + a_{m-1}(m-k))$.

Proof. We induct on k. The basis step is trivial. We verify one more step that is needed later.

$$T_{a_m, a_{m-1}}^{(1)}(x) \equiv x^{m-2}(a_m m(x + \frac{m-1}{2}) + a_{m-1}(m-1)) \tag{5}$$

$\Delta^{(1)}(x) \equiv h(x+1) - h(x)$, whose two leading terms are indeed equal to $T_{a_m, a_{m-1}}^{(1)}(x)$ above. Now assume that the two leading terms of $\Delta^{(k-1)}(x)$ are

$$T_{a_m, a_{m-1}}^{(k-1)}(x) \equiv \alpha x^{m-k+1} + \beta x^{m-k}, \text{ where } \alpha \equiv \frac{(m-1)!}{(m-k)!} a_m m, \text{ and}$$
$$\beta \equiv \frac{(m-1)!}{(m-k)!}[a_m mk(m-k)/2 + a_{m-1}(m-k)].$$

The proof can be completed by showing that $T_{\alpha, \beta}^{(1)}(x) \equiv T_{a_m, a_{m-1}}^{(k)}(x)$. This can be done by computing the first difference of $T_{a_m, a_{m-1}}^{(k-1)}(x)$, substituting α for a_m and β for a_{m-1} in equation (5) to get the claim.

3.2   Related-Messages Attack with Lowered Complexity

Using the results of section 3.1 we consider the special case where $x_i \equiv x + i$ (or likewise $x_i \equiv ax + bi$, for known a, b) and use the simpler finite-differences to yield overall complexity $O(e)$.

In lemmas 3 and 4 let $h(x) \equiv x^e \bmod N$, where $e \geq 3$. Thus $a_n \equiv 1, a_{n-1} \equiv 0$, and $T_{1,0}^{(e-1)} \equiv e!(x + (e - 1)/2)(\bmod N)$. Lemmas 1 and 2 imply that after the $e - 1$ finite difference we have a linear congruence $ux + v \equiv w$. Then lemma 4 gives us the values of u and v, and lemma 3 tells us how to compute w given the e cryptograms.

Specifically $u \equiv e!$, $v \equiv e!(e - 1)/2$ and $w \equiv \sum_{i=0}^{e-1} \binom{e-1}{i} \cdot c_i \cdot (-1)^{e-1+i}$ where $c_i \equiv (x + i)^e$ (all the congruences are taken $\bmod N$). This equation is solvable iff $e!^{-1} \bmod N$ exists, which holds for practical (small) values of e. The computation of w dominates, and takes $O(e)$ operations in $\mathbb{Z}_N$ (since $\binom{e-1}{i}$ can be computed from $\binom{e-1}{i-1}$ using one multiplication and one division).

If $x_i \equiv ax + bi \bmod N$, $i = 0, 1, 2 \ldots e - 1$, for known a and b, with $\gcd(a, N) = \gcd(b, N) = 1$, we can likewise compute x. Given cryptogram $c_i \equiv (ax + b \cdot i)^e \bmod N$ we can transform it into $c_i' \equiv c_i \cdot b^{-e} \equiv (z + i)^e \bmod N$, where $z \equiv xab^{-1} \bmod N$. So

$$x \equiv a^{-1}b[b^e e!]^{-1} \sum_{i=0}^{e-1} \binom{e-1}{i} \cdot c_i \cdot (-1)^{e-1+i} - \frac{e-1}{2}] \bmod N.$$

which is computable in $O(e)$ $\mathbb{Z}_N$ operations.

4   Conclusions

We have shown new attacks on RSA-encryption assuming known explicit linear relations between the messages. Our attacks require more information (i.e., intercepting more cryptograms), but they run faster than previously published attacks. In some practical cases they run three orders of magnitudes faster than previous attacks. This should be taken into consideration when designing very compact cryptosystems (e.g., for RFID tags), although the default should be using some form of protection like OAEP+ to destroy such known relations. Our attack tools are borrowed from numerical analysis and adapted to handle formal polynomials defined over finite rings.

Open problems: Can these or similar tools be used to attack other cases of known relations, such as implicit linear relations or explicit non-linear relations?

Acknowledgements

Special thanks go to Gideon Yuval who suggested looking into divided differences, and to Peter Montgomery who made numerous valuable suggestions and corrections. We also thank Don Coppersmith, Kamal Jain, Adi Shamir, and Venkie (Ramarathnam Venkatesan), for helpful discussions on earlier applications of the finite difference technique. Finally, we thank PKC'05 reviewers who made valuable suggestions that improved this paper.

References

1. Aho Hopcroft and Ullman: "The Design and Analysis of Computer Algorithms", Addison Wesley, 1974, ISBN 0-201-00029-6.
2. D. Boneh: "Twenty Years of Attacks on the RSA Cryptosystem", in Notices of the American Mathematical Society (AMS), Vol. 46, No. 2, pp. 203–213, 1999.
3. M. Bellare and P. Rogaway: "Optimal asymmetric encryption", Eurocrypt'94: 92-111.
4. Don Coppersmith, Matthew Franklin, Jacques Patarin, Michael Reiter: "Low-Exponent RSA with related Messages", Proc. of Eurocrypt'96, LNCS 1070, pp. 1-9.
5. E. Fujisaki, T. Okamoto, D. Pointcheval, J. Stern: "RSA-OAEP Is Secure Under the RSA Assumption", J. Crypt. Vo. 17, No.2, March'04, pp. 81-104 (Springer Verlag).
6. Ronald Rivest, Adi Shamir, Leonard M. Adleman: "A Method for Obtaining Digital Signatures and Public-Key Cryptosystems", CACM 21(2): 120-126 (1978).
7. Volkov, E.A., "Numerical Methods". New York: Hemisphere Publishing Corporation, pp.48, 1987.
8. Whittaker, E. T. and Robinson, "The Calculus of Observations: A Treatise on Numerical Mathematics", 4th ed. New York: Dover, pp. 20-24, 1967.

Appendix: The Complexity of the Pre-processing

The following algorithm, due to Peter Montgomery, computes the pre-processing phase of Algorithm 1 in $O(e \log^2 e)$ time. We currently do not know of a better algorithm for the general case.

For $k = 0, ...e - 1$, we need to compute $p_k = \pi'_k(y) \equiv \prod_{\substack{i=0 \\ i \neq k}}^{e-1} (b_k - b_i)$. We use the

observation stated before Formula (1). The algorithm proceeds as follows (time complexity for each step is included in the brackets):

1. Expand the formal polynomial $\pi(y) \equiv \prod_{i=0}^{e-1} (y - x_i)$ in indeterminate variable y ($O(e \log^2 e)$, as explained below).
2. Compute the formal derivative of $\pi(y)$ ($O(e)$).
3. Simultaneously evaluate the value of the derivative in the given points b_i, $i = 0, 1, ...e - 1$ ($O(e \log^2 e)$, see [1] pp. 294, Corollary 2).

Expanding step (1) above:
Suppose we have a polynomial multiplication algorithm that works in time $O(n \log n)$, where n is the degree of the polynomials. Multiply pairs (there are $n/2$ many pairs). Then multiply the resulting $n/4$ pairs at cost $O(2 \log 2)$ each. And so on. There are $\log e$ many levels. Let $e = 2^k$. The total cost is $e \sum_{i=0}^{k} i = O(e \log^2 e)$.

Note that if the b_i happen to be some powers of one primitive n_{th} root of unity, $w \in Z_N$, then we can use DFT in $O(n \log n)$. However, for arbitrary $b'_i s$ chances to have this condition with $n = O(e)$ are negligible.

Breaking a Cryptographic Protocol with Pseudoprimes

Daniel Bleichenbacher

Bell Labs, Lucent Technologies

Abstract. The Miller-Rabin pseudo primality test is widely used in cryptographic libraries, because of its apparent simplicity. But the test is not always correctly implemented. For example the pseudo primality test in GNU Crypto 1.1.0 uses a fixed set of bases. This paper shows how this flaw can be exploited to break the SRP implementation in GNU Crypto. The attack is demonstrated by explicitly constructing pseudoprimes that satisfy the parameter checks in SRP and that allow a dictionary attack. This dictionary attack would not be possible if the pseudo primality test were correctly implemented.

Often important details are overlooked in implementations of cryptographic protocols until specific attacks have been demonstrated. The goal of the paper is to demonstrate the need to implement pseudo primality tests carefully. This is done by describing a concrete attack against GNU Crypto 1.1.0. The pseudo primality test of this library is incorrect. It performs a trial division and a Miller-Rabin test with a fixed set of bases. Because the bases are known in advance an attacker can find composite numbers that pass the primality test with probability 1. A protocol implemented in GNU Crypto that requires a reliable primality test is SRP. The security of SRP depends on a group for which computing DL is hard. In SRP the server chooses the group parameters and sends them to the client. It is then important that the client verifies that computing DLs in the chosen group is indeed hard. Otherwise, the client could expose his password to a dictionary attack. This paper shows that the flaw in the GNU Crypto primality test indeed weakens the SRP implementation by explicitly constructing weak parameters for SRP. The weakness would not exist if a reliable primality test were implemented.

1 The Miller-Rabin Pseudo-primality Test

A well-known Theorem by Fermat states that if n is a prime and b is coprime to n then

$$b^{n-1} \equiv 1 \pmod{n} \tag{1}$$

Hence if Equation (1) is not satisfied for a pair (b, n) that is coprime then n is composite. Unfortunately, there also exist pairs (b, n) that satisfy Equation (1), but where n is composite. Composite numbers n that satisfy Equation (1) for all b coprime to n are called Carmichael numbers. Korselt proposed the following criterion for such numbers [7].

S. Vaudenay (Ed.): PKC 2005, LNCS 3386, pp. 9–15, 2005.

Korselt's Criterion. A composite number n is a Carmichael number if and only if n is squarefree and all prime divisors p of n satisfy

$$p - 1 | n - 1.$$

Because of the existence of Carmichael numbers [4] Equation (1) alone cannot be used to distinguish composites from primes. Miller and Rabin proposed a stronger test based on the following observation. Let n be an odd integer and write $n = u2^v + 1$ with u odd. Then for every odd prime n and every base $1 \leq b < n$ one of the following two conditions is satisfied:

$$b^u \equiv 1 \pmod{n} \tag{2}$$

or there exists $0 \leq i < v$ such that

$$b^{u2^i} \equiv -1 \pmod{n} \tag{3}$$

A composite n is called a *strong pseudoprime* for the base b if one of the conditions is satisfied. Rabin showed that if n is composite n is a strong pseudoprime for less than $n/4$ bases $b \in [2, n-1]$ [10]. Thus any composite number n can be recognized as composite with probability at least $1 - (1/4)^k$ by selecting k random bases and testing whether n fails the test for at least one base.

Damgard, Landrock, and Pomerance prove a bound much lower than $(1/4)^k$ on the average probability that a composite number passes a Miller-Rabin test with k bases [5]. This result, however, cannot be applied in cryptographic protocols for a parameter verification. If a party has to verify that a received integer is prime, then the party should assume the worst case, i.e., that the integer might have been chosen to maximize the probability of passing a Miller-Rabin test.

2 SRP

GNU Crypto implements SRP-6 [11]. The goal of the SRP protocol is to avoid offline dictionary attacks and thus increase the security of password based authentications in the case that the clients password has not much entropy. In particular, a server that does not know the clients password or a value v, which is derived from it should only be able to confirm or reject one password guess per login. This section reviews one version of the SRP protocol and describes why it is important that the client performs a proper parameter verification in step 2.

Client	Server
1.	$\xrightarrow{\;I\;}$ (lookup s, v, g, N)
2. (verify g, N)	$\xleftarrow{s,g,N}$
$\quad x = \mathrm{H}(s, I, P)$	
3. (choose random a)	(choose random b)
4. $A = g^a \bmod N$	$\xrightarrow{\;A\;} B = 3v + g^b \bmod N$
5. $u = \mathrm{H}(A, B)$	$\xleftarrow{\;B\;} u = \mathrm{H}(A, B)$
6. $S = (B - 3g^x)^{a+ux} \bmod N$	$S = (Av^u)^b \bmod N$
7. $M_1 = \mathrm{H}(A, B, S)$	$\xrightarrow{M_1}$ (verify M_1)
8. (verify M_2)	$\xleftarrow{M_2} M_2 = \mathrm{H}(A, M_1, S)$
9. $K = \mathrm{H}(S)$	$K = \mathrm{H}(S)$

In step 1 the client sends its identity I to the server and the server looks up the corresponding values s, v, g, N, where s is a salt value, g is a generator of $\mathbb{Z}/(N)^*$ and v is encryption of the clients password defined by $v = g^{\mathrm{H}(s,I,P)} \bmod N$.

In step 2 s and optional g and N are sent to the client. The client must verify that N is a strong prime $> 2^{512}$, i.e. N and $(N-1)/2$ are both prime and that g has order $N - 1$ in $\mathbb{Z}/(N)^*$.

In step 3 both client and server choose some random values a and b respectively and derive two values A and B, which are then exchanged in step 4 and 5. Both server and client can now compute a mutual secret S. This value S is subsequently used for a mutual authentication in step 7 and 8.

An outsider, or even a malicious server not knowing v should not be able to verify the correctness of a guessed password P from the values observed during a protocol run.

Attacking SRP with Bogus Parameters. MacKenzie noticed that Tom Wu's SRP implementations before version 1.6.0 are susceptible to an offline dictionary attack [8]. In particular, MacKenzie noticed that while the SRP documentation requires that N and $(N-1)/2$ are primes the implementation does not perform any primality checks when a client receives new parameters from a server. But these checks are crucial for the protocol.

If an attacker posing as a server is able to submit parameters g, N, such that computing the discrete logarithm of $g^x \bmod N$ is computable then the following attack is possible.

Client	Attacker
1.	$\xrightarrow{\;I\;}$ (select s, g, N)
2. (verify g, N)	$\xleftarrow{s,g,N}$
$\quad x = \mathrm{H}(s, I, P)$	
3. (choose random a)	
4. $A = g^a \bmod N$	$\xrightarrow{\;A\;}$ (choose any B)
5. $u = \mathrm{H}(A, B)$	$\xleftarrow{\;B\;} u = \mathrm{H}(A, B)$
6. $S = (B - 3g^x)^{a+ux} \bmod N$	
7. $M_1 = \mathrm{H}(A, B, S)$	$\xrightarrow{M_1}$ (abort)

Hence after aborting the protocol in step 7 the attacker has now enough information for an offline dictionary attack. SRP was designed to prevent such attacks. From the assumption that DLs mod N are computable follows that the server can compute a such that $g^a = A$ mod N. Now, the attacker can perform an offline dictionary attack by first guessing P', computing $x' = H(s, I, P)$ and $S' = (B - 3g^x)^{a+ux}$ mod N. Finally if $H(A, B, S')$ equals M_1 then P' is likely the client's password.

3   GNU Crypto

An analysis of the primality test in GNU Crypto 1.1.0 shows a serious flaw. The primality test, first performs a trial division test and then calls the routine gnu.util.prime.passEulerCriterion. This routine is a Miller-Rabin with the primes up to 41 as bases. Since the bases are fixed it is possible to find counter examples that pass the test with probability 1.

4   Constructing Pseudoprimes

Requirements. Composite numbers that pass the GNU Crypto 1.1.0 primality test are well known. For example Arnault has previously constructed a composite 337 digit number that is a strong pseudoprime for the 200 smallest prime bases [3]. The construction that Arnault used generates integers that are the product of a small (i.e. 2 or 3) number of large primes. While these number would incorrectly pass the parameter checks they cannot be used to break SRP.

The goal of this paper is to find parameters that pass the checks for the SRP in GNU Cryptos implementation and allow a server to find a users password. This requires to construct a triple (g, N, q) such that computing discrete logarithms of $g^x \pmod{N}$ is easy, $N = 2q + 1 > 2^{512}$, both N and q pass the primality test, $N > 2^{512}$, and $g^q \equiv -1 \pmod{N}$.

The construction given in this paper constructs q such that it is the product of small primes. Then computing DLs modulo $N = 2q + 1$ is easy, because the algorithm by Pohlig and Hellman [9] can be applied.

Description of the Method. The method used here is based on an idea by Erdös [6] to estimate the distribution of Carmichael numbers. Erdös suggested to construct Carmichael numbers as follows. First choose an even integer M that has many divisors. Let R be the set of primes r such that $r - 1$ is a divisor of M. If a subset $T \subset R$ can be found such that

$$C = \prod_{r \in T} r \equiv 1 \pmod{M}, \tag{4}$$

then C is a Carmichael number, because C satisfies Korselt's criterion. One can hope to find such sets T if R contains more than about $\log_2 M$ primes.

Erdös estimates were only heuristic. But Alford, Granville and Pomerance extended his idea and were able to prove that there exist infinitively many

Carmichael numbers [2]. The main difficulty of this proof was to show that for suitably chosen integers M the corresponding set of primes R is large enough to guarantee that Equation 4 can be solved for a subset $T \subset R$.

Additionally, a Carmichael number C is a strong pseudoprime for a base b if the order of b modulo r is divisible by the same power of 2 for all primes factors r of C. If all prime factors r are congruent 3 modulo 4 then this condition is satisfied when b is a quadratic residue modulo either all prime factors r or none at all, because in that case the order of b modulo r is either even or odd for all r. In particular, it is possible to construct a Carmichael number that is strong pseudoprime for a set of bases B as follows: Choose a suitable integer M. Then find a set R of primes, such that for all bases $b_i \in B$ there exists $c_i \in \{-1, 1\}$ with $\left(\frac{b_i}{r}\right) = c_i$ for all $r \in R$. Finally, find a subset $T \subset R$ can be found that satisfies Equation 4.

The results by Alford, Granville and Pomerance are strong enough to show that even under these restrictions large enough sets R can be found. In particular, they showed the existence of infinitively many counter examples to a Miller-Rabin test with a fixed set of bases [1].

To pass the parameter checks in GNU Crypto the pseudoprime C needs the additional property that $2C + 1$ is prime or pseudoprime. Because of this additional property it appears difficult to prove the existence of counter examples for arbitrary sets of bases.

However, the goal of this paper is to construct a pseudoprime for a given set of bases only, i.e. the set $B = \{2, 3, 5, 7, 11, 13, 17, 19, 23, 29, 31, 37, 41\}$ that is used in GNU Crypto. To do so let

$$M = 2 \cdot 5^3 \cdot 7^2 \cdot 11^2 \cdot 13 \cdot 17 \cdot 19 \cdot 23 \cdot 29 \cdot 31 \cdot 37 \cdot 41 \cdot 61.$$

Next a set R of all integers r satisfying

$$256 < r < 2^{60},$$
$$r - 1 \mid M,$$
$$r \quad \text{is prime},$$
$$\left(\frac{b_i}{r}\right) = c_i \text{ for all } 1 \leq i \leq 13,$$

where the pairs (b_i, c_i) are defined as follows:

i	1	2	3	4	5	6	7	8	9	10	11	12	13
b_i	2	3	5	7	11	13	17	19	23	29	31	37	41
c_i	-1	1	1	-1	-1	1	1	-1	-1	1	-1	1	1

The values c_i should are chosen in such a way that $\left(\frac{b_i}{r}\right) = c_i$ is possible for primes $r \equiv 1 \pmod{b_i}$. The set R can be found efficiently, by first constructing all divisors d of M and checking if $r = d + 1$ satisfies the remaining conditions.

The set of integers satisfying all these conditions contains 64 primes $R = \{r_1, \ldots r_{64}\}$. Next find subsets $T \subset R$ with at least 2 elements satisfying Equation 4, i.e., $\prod_{r \in T} r \equiv 1 \pmod{M}$. These subsets T can be found using a meet-in-the-middle approach. I.e., R is divided into two distinct subsets R_1 and R_2.

The values $(\prod_{r \in T_1} r)^{-1} \bmod M$ are precomputed for all $T_1 \subseteq R_1$ and stored in a table. Then for all $T_2 \subseteq R_2$ the value $\prod_{r \in T_2} r \bmod M$ is computed. If this value is contained in the table then set $T = T_1 \cup T_2$ and $C = \prod_{r \in T} r$. If furthermore $N = 2C + 1$ is prime and $N > 2^{512}$ then N passes the parameter test for SRP in GNU Crypto. This is shown in the next paragraph.

Correctness of the Construction. Since N is prime it remains to show that C passes the primality test. The assumption $256 < r$ implies that no prime factor of C is found during the trial division test. Thus it is sufficient to show that C is a strong pseudoprime for the bases b_i where $1 \le i \le 13$.

Since $r - 1$ divides M and $C \equiv 1 \pmod{M}$ it follows that $r - 1$ divides $C - 1$ for all prime factors r of C. Thus by Korselt's criterion C is a Carmichael number [7]. Because of $\left(\frac{2}{r}\right) = -1$ we have $r \equiv 3 \pmod{4}$ for all primes factor r of C. Moreover, from $\left(\frac{b_i}{r}\right) = c_i$ for all $1 \le i \le 13$ follows that b_i is either a quadratic residue for all prime factors r or a quadratic nonresidue for all prime factors r. Hence it follows that C is a strong pseudoprime for the base b_i.

Results. An implementation of the algorithm needed less than 10 days on a 250 MHz CPU to find about 30 examples that pass the parameter checks in GNU crypto. One example is the 1095 bit number

$C = 398462957079251 \cdot 28278016308851 \cdot 268974870654491 \cdot 1239515532971 \cdot$
$12941222544251 \cdot 2825874899 \cdot 182200861571 \cdot 480965007251 \cdot 8028415890251 \cdot$
$761874633627251 \cdot 10326412038251 \cdot 105324823451 \cdot 7128348371 \cdot 29542620251 \cdot$
$251906132167691 \cdot 64654312451 \cdot 226698699371 \cdot 130685132579 \cdot 9167201891 \cdot$
$432876391197251 \cdot 3077983389251 \cdot 17767646051 \cdot 9371850251 \cdot 954045342251 \cdot$
$112810627931 \cdot 6297653304192251 \cdot 20842025454251$

5   GNU Crypto 2.0.1

The authors of GNU Crypto were informed in January 2004 about the flaws in the primality test. Most of the problems have been fixed in version 2.0.1. However, an analysis of the source code reveals that GNU Crypto implementation of SRP still calls the function gnu.util.prime.passEulerCriterion and that this function has not been changed. Therefore the attack presented in this paper still exists more than 8 month after the authors have been notified. The next implementation error can be found just 2 lines later where SRP accepts $g \equiv -1 \pmod{N}$ as a generator of $\mathbb{Z}/(N)^*$ allowing a simple impersonation attack. Consequently, I do not recommend the use of GNU Crypto.

6   Proposed Parameter Verification for SRP

To verify that $N > 2^{512}$ is a safe prime (that is both N and $q = (N - 1)/2$ are prime) and g is a generator of $\mathbb{Z}/(N)^*$ with an error probaility $< 2^{-2k}$ one can perform the following tests:

- Check $N > 2^{512}$.
- Test the primality of q with k rounds of Miller-Rabin with random bases.
- Test that $1 < g < N - 1$ and $g^q \equiv -1 \pmod{N}$.

The k rounds of Miller-Rabin guarantee that a composite q is detected with a probability $> 1 - 2^{-2k}$. Assuming that q is indeed prime $g^q \equiv -1 \pmod{N}$ now implies that the order of g modulo N is even and divides $2q$. Hence the order is either 2 or $2q$. But $g^2 \equiv 1 \pmod{N}$ would imply $g \equiv g^q \equiv -1 \pmod{N}$ which is impossible because of $1 < g < N - 1$. Thus the order of g must be $2q$ and $N = 2q + 1$ must be prime. Hence no primality test for N is needed here.

References

1. W. R. Alford, A. Granville, and C. Pomerance. On the difficulty of finding reliable witnesses. In *Algorithmic number theory*, volume 877 of *Lecture Notes in Computer Science*, pages 1–16, Berlin, 1994. Springer Verlag.
2. W. R. Alford, A. Granville, and C. Pomerance. There are infinitely many Carmichael numbers. *Annals of Mathematics*, 140(3):703–722, 1994.
3. F. Arnault. Rabin-Miller primality test: Composite numbers which pass it. *Mathematics of Computation*, 64(209):355–361, Jan. 1995.
4. R. D. Carmichael. On composite numbers P which satisfy the Fermat congruence $a^{P-1} \equiv 1 \bmod P$. *American Math. Monthly,*, 19:22–27, 1912.
5. I. Damgård, P. Landrock, and C. Pomerance. Average case error estimates for the strong probable prime test. *Mathematics of Computation*, 61(203):177–194, 1993.
6. P. Erdös. On pseudoprimes and Carmichael numbers. *Publ. Math. Debrecen*, 4:201–206, 1956.
7. A. Korselt. Problème chinois. *L'intermédiaire des mathématiciens*, 6:142–143, 1899.
8. P. MacKenzie. Personal communications.
9. S. C. Pohlig and M. E. Hellman. An improved algorithm for computing logarithms over $GF(p)$ and its cryptographic significance. *IEEE Trans. Inform. Theory*, IT-24:106–110, Jan. 1978.
10. M. Rabin. Probabilistic algorithms for testing primality. *J. Number Theory*, 12:128–138, 1980.
11. T. Wu. SRP-6: Improvements and refinements to the secure remote password protocol. `http://srp.stanford.edu/doc.html`, Oct. 2002.

Experimenting with Faults, Lattices and the DSA

David Naccache[1,2,*], Phong Q. Nguyễn[3,*],
Michael Tunstall[2,4], and Claire Whelan[5,**]

[1] Gemplus Card International, Applied Research & Security Centre,
34 rue Guynemer, Issy-les-Moulineaux, F-92447, France
david.naccache@gemplus.com
[2] Royal Holloway, University of London, Information Security Group,
Egham, Surrey TW20 0EX, UK
david.naccache@rhul.ac.uk
[3] CNRS/École normale supérieure, Département d'Informatique,
45 rue d'Ulm, F-75230 Paris Cedex 05, France
Phong.Nguyen@di.ens.fr
http://www.di.ens.fr/~pnguyen
[4] Gemplus Card International, Applied Research & Security Centre,
Avenue des Jujubiers, La Ciotat, F-13705, France
michael.tunstall@gemplus.com
[5] School of Computing, Dublin City University,
Ballymun, Dublin 9, Ireland
cwhelan@computing.dcu.ie

Abstract. We present an attack on DSA smart-cards which combines physical fault injection and lattice reduction techniques. This seems to be the first (publicly reported) physical experiment allowing to concretely pull-out DSA keys out of smart-cards. We employ a particular type of fault attack known as a *glitch attack*, which will be used to actively modify the DSA nonce k used for generating the signature: k will be tampered with so that a number of its least significant bytes will flip to zero. Then we apply well-known lattice attacks on El Gamal-type signatures which can recover the private key, given sufficiently many signatures such that a few bits of each corresponding k are known. In practice, when one byte of each k is zeroed, 27 signatures are sufficient to disclose the private key. The more bytes of k we can reset, the fewer signatures will be required. This paper presents the theory, methodology and results of the attack as well as possible countermeasures.

Keywords: DSA, fault injection, glitch attacks, lattice reduction.

* The work described in this paper has been supported in part by the European Commission through the IST Programme under Contract IST-2002-507932 ECRYPT. The information in this document reflects only the authors' views, is provided as is and no guarantee or warranty is given that the information is fit for any particular purpose. The user thereof uses the information at its sole risk and liability.
** Supported by the Irish Research Council for Science, Engineering and Technology (IRCSET).

S. Vaudenay (Ed.): PKC 2005, LNCS 3386, pp. 16–28, 2005.

1   Introduction

Over the past few years fault attacks on electronic chips have been investigated and developed. The theory developed was used to challenge public key cryptosystems [4] and symmetric ciphers in both block [3] and stream [8] modes.

The discovery of fault attacks (1970s) was accidental. It was noticed that elements naturally present in packaging material of semiconductors produced radioactive particles which in turn caused errors in chips [11]. These elements, while only present in extremely minute parts (two or three parts per million), were sufficient to affect the chips' behaviour, create a charge in sensitive silicon areas and, as a result, cause bits to flip. Since then various mechanisms for fault creation and propagation have been discovered and researched. Diverse research organisations such as the aerospace industry and the security community have endeavoured to develop different types of fault injection techniques and devise corresponding preventative methods. Some of the most popular fault injection techniques include variations in supply voltage, clock frequency, temperature or the use of white light, X-ray and ion beams.

The objectives of all these techniques is generally the same: corrupt the chip's behaviour. The outcomes have been categorised into two main groups based on the long term effect that the fault produced. These are known as *permanent* and *transient* faults. Permanent faults, created by purposely inflicted defects to the chip's structure, have a permanent effect. Once inflicted, such destructions will affect the chip's behavior permanently. In a transient fault, silicon is locally ionized so as to induce a current that, when strong enough, is falsely interpreted by the circuit as an internal signal. As ionization ceases so does the induced current (and the resulting faulty signal) and the chip recovers its normal behavior.

Preventive measures come in the form of software and hardware protections (the most cost-effective solution being usually a combination of both). Current research is also looking into fault detection where, at stages through the execution of the algorithm, checks are performed to see whether a fault has been induced [10]. For a survey of the different types of fault injection techniques and the various software and hardware countermeasures that exist, we refer the reader to [2].

In this paper we will focus on a type of fault attack known as a glitch attack. Glitch attacks use transient faults where the attacker deliberately generates a voltage spike that causes one or more flip-flops to transition into a wrong state. Targets for insertion of such 'glitches' are generally machine instructions or data values transferred between registers and memory. Results can include the replacement of critical machine instructions by almost arbitrary ones or the corruption of data values.

The strategy presented in this paper is the following: we will use a glitch to reset some of the bytes of the nonce k, used during the generation of DSA signatures. As the attack ceases, the system will remain fully functional. Then, we will use classical lattice reduction techniques to extract the private signature key from the resulting glitched signatures (which can pass the usual verification process). Such lattice attacks (introduced by Howgrave-Graham and Smart [9], and improved by Nguyễn and Shparlinski [14]) assume that a few bits of k are known for sufficiently many signatures, without addressing how these bits could be obtained. In [14], it was reported that in practice, the lattice attack required as few as three bits of k, provided that about a hundred of such signatures were available. Surprisingly, to the authors' knowledge, no fault attack had previously exploited those powerful lattice attacks.

The paper is organised as follows: In section 2 we will give a brief description of DSA, we will also introduce the notations used throughout this paper. An overview of the attack's physical and mathematical parts will be given in section 3. In section 4 we will present the results of our attack while countermeasures will be given in section 5.

Related Work: In [1] an attack against DSA is presented by Bao *et al.*, this attack is radically different from the one presented in this paper and no physical implementation results are given. This attack was extended in [6] by Dottax. In [7], Knudsen and Giraud introduce another fault attack on the DSA. Their attack requires around 2300 signatures (*i.e.* 100 times more than the attack presented here). The merits of the present work are thus twofold: we present a new (*i.e.* unrelated to [7, 1, 6]) efficient attack and describe what is, to the authors' best knowledge, the first (publicly reported) physical experiment allowing to concretely pull-out DSA keys out of smart-cards. The present work shows that the hypotheses made in the lattice attacks [9, 14] can be realistic in certain environments.

2   Background

In this section we will give a brief description of the DSA.

2.1   DSA Signature and Verification

The system parameters for DSA [12] are $\{p, q, g\}$, where p is prime (at least 512 bits), q is a 160-bit prime dividing $p - 1$ and $g \in \mathbb{Z}_p^*$ has order q. The private key is an integer $\alpha \in \mathbb{Z}_q^*$ and the public key is the group element $\beta = g^\alpha \pmod{p}$.

Signature: To sign a message m, the signer picks a random $k < q$ and computes:

$$r \leftarrow (g^k \pmod{p}) \pmod{q} \quad \text{and} \quad s \leftarrow \frac{\text{SHA}(m) + \alpha r}{k} \pmod{q}$$

The signature of m is the pair: $\{r, s\}$.

Verification: To check $\{r, s\}$ the verifier ascertains that:

$$r \overset{?}{=} (g^{wh} \beta^{wr} \pmod{p}) \pmod{q} \quad \text{where} \quad w \leftarrow \frac{1}{s} \pmod{q} \quad \text{and} \quad h \leftarrow \text{SHA}(m)$$

3 Attack Overview

The attack on DSA proceeds as follows: we first generate several DSA signatures where the random value generated for k has been modified so that a few of k's least[1] significant bytes are reset[2]. This faulty k will then be used by the card to generate a (valid) DSA signature. Using lattice reduction, the secret key α can be recovered from a collection of such signatures (see [14, 9]). In this section we will detail each of these stages in turn, showing first how we tamper with k in a closed environment and then how we apply this technique to a complete implementation.

3.1 Experimental Conditions

DSA was implemented on a chip known to be vulnerable to Vcc glitches. For testing purposes (closed environment) we used a separate implementation for the generation of k.

A 160-bit nonce is generated and compared to q. If $k \geq q - 1$ the nonce is discarded and a new k is generated. This is done in order to ascertain that k is drawn uniformly in $\mathbb{Z}_q^*$ (assuming that the source used for generating the nonce is perfect). We present the code fragment (modified for simplicity) that we used to generate k:

```
PutModulusInCopro(PrimeQ);
RandomGeneratorStart();

status = 0;
do {
  IOpeak();
  for (i=0; i<PrimeQ[0]; i++) {
    acCoproMessage[i+1] = ReadRandomByte();
  }
  IOpeak();

  acCoproMessage[0] = PrimeQ[0];
  LoadDataToCopro(acCoproMessage);

  status = 1;
  for (j=0; j<(PrimeQ[0]+1); j++) {
    if (acCoproResult[j] != acCoproMessage[j]) {
      status = 0;
    }
  }
}
while (status == 0);
RandomGeneratorStop();
```

---

[1] It is also possible to run a similar attack by changing the most significant bytes of k. This is determined by the implementation.

[2] It would have also been possible to run a similar attack if these bytes were set to FF.

Note that IOpeaks[3], featured in the above code was also included in the implementation of DSA. The purpose of this is to be able to easily identify the code sections in which a fault can be injected to produce the desired effect. This could have been done by monitoring power consumption but would have greatly increased the complexity of the task.

The tools used to create the glitches can be seen in figure 1 and figure 2. Figure 1 is a modified CLIO reader which is a specialised high precision reader that allows one glitch to be introduced following any arbitrarily chosen number of clock cycles after the command sent to the card. Figure 2 shows the experimental set up of the CLIO reader with the oscilloscope used during our experiments. A BNC connector is present on the CLIO reader which allows the I/O to be easily read; another connector produces a signal when a glitch is applied (in this case used as a trigger). Current is measured using a differential probe situated on top of the CLIO reader.

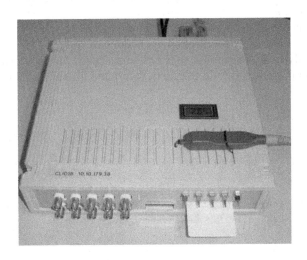

Fig. 1. A Modified CLIO Reader.

3.2 Generating a Faulty k

The command that generated k was attacked in every position between the two IOpeaks in the code. It was found that the fault did not affect the assignment of k to the RAM i.e. the instruction acCoproMessage[i+1] = ReadRandomByte(); which always executed correctly. However, it was possible to change the evaluation of i during the loop. This enabled us to select the number of least significant bytes to be reset. In theory, this would produce the desired fault in k with probability $q/2^{160}$, as if the modified k happens to be larger than q, it is discarded

---

[3] The I/O peak is a quick movement on the I/O from one to zero and back again. This is visible on an oscilloscope but is ignored by the card reader.

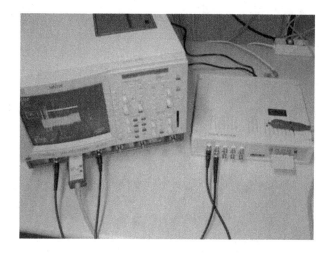

Fig. 2. Experimental Set Up.

anyway. In practice this probability is likely to be lower as it is unusual for a fault to work correctly every time.

An evaluation of a position that resetted the last two bytes was performed. Out of 2000 attempts 857 were corrupted. This is significantly less than what one would expect, as the theoretical probability is $\simeq 0.77$. We expected the practical results to perform worse than theory due to a slight variation in the amount of time that the smart card takes to arrive at the position where the data corruption is performed. There are other positions in the same area that return k values with the same fault, but not as often.

3.3   The Attack: Glitching k During DSA Computations

The position found was equated to the generation of k in the command that generates the DSA signature. This was done by using the last I/O event at the end of the command sent as a reference point and gave a rough position of where the fault needs to be injected.

As changes in the value of k were not visible in the signature, results would only be usable with a certain probability. This made the attack more complex, as the subset signatures having faulty k values had to be guessed amongst those acquired by exhaustive search.

To be able to identify the correct signatures the I/O and the current consumption signals were monitored during the attacks. An example of such a monitoring is given in figure 3. The object of these acquisitions was to measure the time T elapsed between the end of the command sent to the card and the beginning of the calculation of r. This can be seen in the current consumption, as the chip will require more energy when the crypto-coprocessor is ignited. If we denote by t the time that it takes to reach the start of the calculation of r knowing that the picked k was smaller that q (*i.e.* that it was not necessary to restart

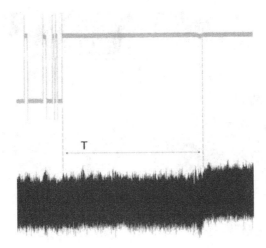

Fig. 3. I/O and Current Consumption (Beginning of the Trace of the Command Used to Generate Signatures).

the picking process) then, if $T = t$ we know that the command has executed properly and that k was picked correctly the first time. If $T > t$ then any fault targeting k would be a miss (as k was regenerated given that the value of k originally produced was greater than q). Signatures resulting from commands that feature such running times can be discarded as the value of k will not present any exploitable weaknesses. When $T < t$ we know that the execution of the code generating k has been cut short, so some of the least significant bytes will be equal to zero. This allows signatures generated from corrupted k values to be identified *a posteriori*.

As the position where the fault should be injected was only approximately identified, glitches were injected in twenty different positions until a position that produced signatures with the correct characteristics (as described above) was found. The I/O peaks left in the code were used to confirm these results. Once the correct position identified, more attacks were conducted at this position to acquire a handful of signatures. From a total of 200 acquisitions 38 signatures where $T < t$ were extracted.

This interpretation had to be done by a combination of the I/O and the current consumption, as after the initial calculation involving k the command no longer takes the same amount of time. This is because $0 < k \leq q$ and therefore k does not have a fixed size; consequently any calculations k is involved in will not always take the same amount of time.

3.4   Use of Lattice Reduction to Retrieve α

We are now in a position to apply the well-known lattice attacks of [9, 14] on El Gamal-type signature schemes: given many DSA signatures for which a few bits of the corresponding k are known, such attacks recover the DSA signer's private key. In our case, these known bits are in fact 0 bits, but that does not matter for the lattice attack. We recall how the lattice attacks work, using the presentation of Nguyễn and Shparlinski [14]. Roughly speaking, lattice attacks focus on the linear part of DSA, that is, they exploit the congruence $s \leftarrow \frac{\text{SHA}(m) + \alpha r}{k}$ (mod q) used in the signature generation, not the other congruence $r \leftarrow \left(g^k \pmod{p}\right)$ (mod q) which is related to a discrete log problem. When no information on k is available, the congruence reveals nothing, but if partial information is available, each congruence discloses something about the private key α: by collecting sufficiently many signatures, there will be enough information to recover α. If ℓ bits of k are known for a certain number of signatures, we expect that about $160/\ell$ signatures will suffice to recover α. Here is a detailed description of the attack.

For a rational number z and $m \geq 1$ we denote by $\lfloor z \rfloor_m$ the unique integer a, $0 \leq a \leq m - 1$ such that $a \equiv z$ (mod m) (provided that the denominator of z is relatively prime to m). The symbol $|.|_q$ is defined as $|z|_q = \min_{b \in \mathbb{Z}} |z - bq|$ for any real z.

Assume that we know the ℓ least significant bits of a nonce $k \in \{0, \ldots, q-1\}$ which will be used to generate a DSA signature (for the case of other bits, like most significant bits or bits in the middle, see [14]).

That is, we are given an integer a such that $0 \leq a \leq 2^\ell - 1$ and $k - a = 2^\ell b$ for some integer $b \geq 0$. Given a message m (whose SHA hash is h) signed with the nonce k, the congruence

$$\alpha r \equiv sk - h \pmod{q},$$

can be rewritten for $s \neq 0$ as:

$$\alpha r 2^{-\ell} s^{-1} \equiv (a - s^{-1}h)2^{-\ell} + b \pmod{q}. \tag{1}$$

Now define the following two elements

$$t = \lfloor 2^{-\ell} r s^{-1} \rfloor_q,$$
$$u = \lfloor 2^{-\ell}(a - s^{-1}h) \rfloor_q$$

and remark that both t and u can easily be computed by the attacker from the publicly known information. Recalling that $0 \leq b \leq q/2^\ell$, we obtain

$$0 \leq \lfloor \alpha t - u \rfloor_q < q/2^\ell.$$

And therefore:

$$|\alpha t - u - q/2^{\ell+1}|_q \leq q/2^{\ell+1}. \tag{2}$$

Thus, the attacker knows an integer t and a rational number $v = u + q/2^{\ell+1}$ such that:

$$|\alpha t - v|_q \leq q/2^{\ell+1}.$$

In some sense, we know an approximation of αt modulo q. Now, suppose we can repeat this for many signatures, that is, we know d DSA signatures $\{r_i, s_i\}$ of hashes h_i (where $1 \leq i \leq d$) such that we know the ℓ least significant bits of the corresponding nonce k_i. From the previous reasoning, the attacker can compute integers t_i and rational numbers v_i such that:

$$|\alpha t_i - v_i|_q \leq q/2^{\ell+1}.$$

The goal of the attacker is to recover the DSA private key α. This problem is very similar to the so-called hidden number problem introduced by Boneh and Venkatesan in [5]. In [5,14], the problem is solved by transforming it into a lattice closest vector problem (for background on lattice theory and its applications to cryptography, we refer the reader to the survey [16]; a similar technique was recently used in [13]).

More precisely, consider the $(d+1)$-dimensional lattice L spanned by the rows of the following matrix:

$$\begin{pmatrix} q & 0 & \cdots & 0 & 0 \\ 0 & q & \ddots & \vdots & \vdots \\ \vdots & \ddots & \ddots & 0 & \vdots \\ 0 & \cdots & 0 & q & 0 \\ t_1 & \cdots & \cdots & t_d & 1/2^{\ell+1} \end{pmatrix}. \tag{3}$$

The inequality $|v_i - \alpha t_i|_q \leq q/2^{\ell+1}$ implies the existence of an integer c_i such that:

$$|v_i - \alpha t_i - q c_i| \leq q/2^{\ell+1}. \tag{4}$$

Notice that the row vector $\boldsymbol{c} = (\alpha t_1 + q c_1, \ldots, \alpha t_d + q c_d, \alpha/2^{\ell+1})$ belongs to L, since it can be obtained by multiplying the last row vector by α and then subtracting appropriate multiples of the first d row vectors. Since the last coordinate of this vector discloses the hidden number α, we call $\boldsymbol{c}$ the *hidden vector*. The hidden vector is very close to the (publicly known) row vector $\boldsymbol{v} = (v_1, \ldots, v_d, 0)$. By trying to find the closest vector to $\boldsymbol{v}$ in the lattice L, one can thus hope to find the hidden vector $\boldsymbol{c}$ and therefore the private key α. The article [14] presents provable attacks of this kind, and explains how the attack can be extended to bits at other positions. Such attacks apply to DSA but also to any El Gamal-type signature scheme (see for instance [15] for the case of ECDSA).

In our case, we simply build the previously mentioned lattice and the target vector $\boldsymbol{v}$, and we try to solve the closest vector problem with respect to $\boldsymbol{v}$, using the so-called embedding technique that heuristically reduces the lattice closest vector problem to the shortest vector problem (see [14] for more details). From each close vector candidate, we derive a candidate y for α from its last coordinate, and we check that the public key satisfies $\beta = g^y \pmod{p}$.

4 Results

As already mentioned in Section 3.3, using a glitch attack, we were able to generate 38 DSA signatures such that the least significant byte of the corresponding

k was expected to be zero. Next, we applied the lattice attack of Section 3.4, using NTL's [18] implementation of Schnorr–Euchner's BKZ algorithm [17] with block size 20 as our lattice basis reduction algorithm. Out of the 38 signatures, we picked 30 at random to launch the lattice attack, and those turned out to be enough to disclose the DSA private key α after a few seconds on an Apple PowerBook G4. We only took 30 because we guessed from past experiments that 30 should be well sufficient.

Table 1. Experimental Attack Success Rates: n is the Number of Bytes Reset in k, and d is the Number of Signatures.

$n \downarrow$	Number d of Signatures															
	2	3	4	5	6	7	8	10	11	12	22	23	24	25	26	27
1											0%	10%	39%	63%	87%	100%
2								0%	69%	100%						
3					0%	69%	100%									
4				0%	100%											
5		0%	2%	100%												
6		0%	100%													
7	0%	96%	100%													
10	6%	100%														
11	100%															

To estimate more precisely the efficiency of the lattice attack, we computed success rates, by running the attack 100 times with different parameters. Results can be seen in Table 1. Because the number of signatures is small, the lattice dimension is relatively small, which makes the running time of the lattice attack negligible: for instance, on an Apple PowerBook G4, the lattice attack takes about 1 second for 25 signatures, and 20 seconds for 38 signatures. Table 1 shows how many signatures are required in practice to make the lattice attack work, depending on the number of least significant bytes reset in k. Naturally, there will be a tradeoff between the fault injection and the lattice reduction: when generating signatures with nonces with more reset bytes, the lattice phase of the attack will require less signatures. When only one signature is available, the lattice attack cannot work because there is not enough information in the single congruence used. However, if ever that signature is such that k has a large proportion of zero bytes, it might be possible to compute k by exhaustive search (using the congruence $\leftarrow \left(g^k \pmod{p}\right) \pmod{q}$), and then recover α. From Table 1, we see that when two signatures are available, the lattice attack starts working when 11 bytes are reset in each k. When only one byte is reset in k, the lattice attack starts working (with non-negligible probability) with only 23 signatures.

It should be stressed that the lattice attack does not tolerate mistakes. For instance, 27 signatures with a single byte reset in k are enough to make the attack successful. But the attack will not work if for one of those 27 signatures, k has no reset bytes. It is therefore important that the signatures input to the lattice attack satisfy the assumption about the number of reset bytes. Hence, if ever one is able to obtain many signatures such that the corresponding k is expected (but not necessarily all the time) to have a certain number of reset bytes, then one should not input all the signatures to the lattice attack. Instead, one should pick at random a certain number of signatures from the whole set of available signatures, and launch the lattice attack on this smaller number of signatures: Table 1 can be used to select the minimal number of signatures that will make the lattice attack successful. This leads to a combination of exhaustive search and lattice reduction.

5   Countermeasures

The heart of this attack lies with the ability to induce faults that reset some of k's bits. Hence, any strategy allowing to avoid or detect such anomalies will help thwart the attacks described in this paper. Note that checking the validity of the signature after generation will not help, contrary to the case of fault attacks on RSA signatures [4]: the faulty DSA signatures used here are valid signatures which will pass the verification process. We recommend to use *simultaneously* the following tricks that cost very little in terms of code-size and speed:

- *Checksums* can be implemented in software. This is often complementary to hardware checksums, as software CRCs can be applied to buffers of data (sometimes fragmented over various physical addresses) rather than machine words.
- *Execution Randomization:* If the order in which operations in an algorithm are executed is randomized it becomes difficult to predict what the machine is doing at any given cycle. For most fault attacks this countermeasure will only slow down a determined adversary, as eventually a fault will hit the desired instruction. This will however thwart attacks that require faults in specific places or in a specific order.
  For instance, to copy 256 bytes from buffer a to buffer b, copy

  $$b[f(i)] \leftarrow a[f(i)] \quad \text{for} \quad i = 0, \ldots, 255$$

  where $f(i) = (x \times (i \oplus w) + y \pmod{256}) \oplus z$ and $\{x, y, z, w\}$ are four random bytes (x odd) unknown to the attacker.
- *Ratification Counters and Baits:* baits are small (< 10 byte) code fragments that perform an operation and test its result. A typical bait writes, reads and compares data, performs xors, additions, multiplications and other operations whose results can be easily checked. When a bait detects an error it increments an NVM counter and when this counter exceeds a tolerance limit (usually three) the card ceased to function.
- *Repeated Refreshments:* refresh k by generating several nonces and exclusive-or them with each other, separating each nonce generation from the previous by a random delay. This forces the attacker to inject multiple faults at randomly shifting time windows in order to reset specific bits of k.

Finally, it may also be possible to have a real time testing of the random numbers being generated by the smart card, such as that proposed in the FIPS140-2.

However, even if this is practical it may be of limited use as our attack requires very few signatures to be successful. Consequently, our attack may well be complete before it gets detected.

What is very important is that no information on k is leaked, and that k is cryptographically random.

6 Conclusion

We described a method for attacking a DSA smart card vulnerable to fault attacks. Similar attacks can be mounted on any other El Gamal-type signature scheme, such as ECDSA and Schnorr's signature. The attack consisted of two stages. The first stage dealt with fault injection. The second involved forming a lattice for the data gathered in the previous stage and solving a closest vector problem to reveal the secret key.

The attack was realised in the space of a couple of weeks and was made easier by the inclusion of peaks on the I/O. This information could have been derived by using power or electromagnetic analysis to locate the target area, but would have taken significantly longer. The only power analysis done during this attack was to note when the crypto-coprocessor started to calculate a modular exponentiation.

References

1. F. Bao, R. Deng, Y Han, A. Jeng, A. Narasimhalu and T. Hgair, Breaking Public Key Cryptosystems and Tamper Resistant Devices in the Presence of Transient Faults, 5-th Security Protocols Workshop, Springer-Verlag, LNCS 1361, pp. 115–124, 1997.
2. H. Bar-El, H. Choukri, D. Naccache, M. Tunstall and C. Whelan, *The Sorcerers Apprentice Guide to Fault Attacks*, Workshop on Fault Diagnosis and Tolerence in Cryptography in association with DSN 2004 – The International Conference on Dependable Systems and Networks, pp. 330–342, 2004.
3. E. Biham and A. Shamir, *Differential Fault Analysis of Secret Key Cryptosystems*, Advances in Cryptology - CRYPTO'97, Springer-Verlag, LNCS 1294, pp. 513–525, 1997.
4. D. Boneh, R. DeMillo and R. Lipton, *On the Importance of Checking Cryptographic Protocols for Faults*, Journal of Cryptology, Springer-Verlag, nol. 14, no. 2, pp. 101–119, 2001.
5. D. Boneh and R. Venkatesan, *Hardness of Computing the Most Significant Bits of Secret Keys in Diffie-Hellman and Related Schemes*, Advances in Cryptology – CRYPTO'96, Springer-Verlag, LNCS 1109, pp. 126–142, 1996.
6. E. Dottax, *Fault Attacks on NESSIE Signature and Identification Schemes*, NESSIE Technical Report, October 2002.
7. C. Giraud and E. Knudsen, *Fault Attacks on Signature Schemes*, Workshop on Fault Diagnosis and Tolerence in Cryptography in association with DSN 2004 – The International Conference on Dependable Systems and Networks, 2004.
8. J. Hoch and A. Shamir, *Fault Analysis of Stream Ciphers*, Cryptographic Hardware and Embedded Systems – CHES 2004, Springer-Verlag, LNCS 3156, pp. 240–253, 2004.

9. N.A. Howgrave-Graham and N.P. Smart, *Lattice Attacks on Digital Signature Schemes*, Design, Codes and Cryptography, vol. 23, pp. 283–290, 2001.

10. N. Joshi, K. Wu and R. Karri, *Concurrent Error Detection Schemes for involution Ciphers*, Cryptographic Hardware and Embedded Systems – CHES 2004, Springer-Verlag, LNCS 3156, pp. 400-412, 2004.

11. T. May and M. Woods, *A New Physical Mechanism for Soft Errors in Dynamic Memories*, Proceedings of the 16-th International Reliability Physics Symposium, April, 1978.

12. National Institute of Standards and Technology, FIPS PUB 186-2: Digital Signature Standard, 2000.

13. P.Q. Nguyễn, *Can we trust Cryptographic Software? Cryptographic Flaws in GNU Privacy Guard v1.2.3*, Advances in Cryptology – EUROCRYPT 2004, Springer-Verlag, LNCS 3027, pp. 555–570, 2004.

14. P.Q. Nguyễn and I.E. Shparlinski, *The Insecurity of the Digital Signature Algorithm with Partially Known Nonces*, Journal of Cryptology, vol. 15, no. 3, pp. 151–176, Springer, 2002.

15. P.Q. Nguyễn and I.E. Shparlinski, *The Insecurity of the Elliptic Curve Digital Signature Algorithm with Partially Known Nonces*, Design, Codes and Cryptography, vol. 30, pp. 201–217, 2003.

16. P.Q. Nguyễn and J. Stern, *The two faces of lattices in cryptology*, Cryptography and Lattices – CALC'01), Springer-Verlag, LNCS 2146, pp. 146–180, 2001.

17. C.P. Schnorr and M. Euchner, *Lattice basis reduction: improved practical algorithms and solving subset sum problems*, Math. Programming, vol. 66, pp. 181–199, 1994.

18. V. Shoup, *Number Theory C++ Library (NTL)*, http://www.shoup.net/ntl/

Securing RSA-KEM via the AES

Jakob Jonsson[1] and Matthew J.B. Robshaw[2]

[1] Department of Mathematics, KTH
SE-100 44 Stockholm, Sweden
jakobj@math.kth.se
[2] Information Security Group,
Royal Holloway, University of London,
Egham, Surrey, TW20 0EX, UK
m.robshaw@rhul.ac.uk

Abstract. RSA-KEM is a popular key encapsulation mechanism that combines the RSA trapdoor permutation with a key derivation function (KDF). Often the details of the KDF are viewed as orthogonal to the RSA-KEM construction and the RSA-KEM proof of security models the KDF as a random oracle. In this paper we present an AES-based KDF that has been explicitly designed so that we can appeal to currently held views on the ideal behaviour of the AES when proving the security of RSA-KEM. Thus, assuming that encryption with the AES provides a permutation of 128-bit input blocks that is chosen uniformily at random for each key k, the security of RSA-KEM against chosen-ciphertext attacks can be related to the hardness of inverting RSA.

Keywords: RSA-KEM, AES, key derivation function.

1 Introduction

The RSA [16] public key cryptosystem has been used for more than twenty years and, during that time, a good understanding of how we might best use the basic encryption primitive has evolved [3, 17, 18]. One recent addition to the literature is the *RSA Key Encapsulation Method (RSA-KEM)* due to Shoup [18]; see [2, 8, 11, 20] for similar constructions. Two attractive features of RSA-KEM are its natural simplicity and its excellent security properties. Very loosely, we can summarise the encapsulation process in the following way:

1. Generate an input w (of appropriate size) at random.
2. Encrypt w using RSA for transport to the recipient.
3. Generate keying material $y = \text{KDF}(w)$ for use in the subsequent symmetric-based session encryption.

It is clear that the intended recipient can recover w from the received ciphertext and then generate y so that both sender and receiver can agree on the same symmetric key. When the underlying key derivation function (KDF) is modelled as a random oracle or a black box, the security of RSA-KEM (in a chosen-ciphertext attack model) can be provably related to the hardness of inverting the RSA primitive.

In this paper we consider the role of the KDF. The properties of the KDF are such that a hash function is often used to build the KDF and there are

S. Vaudenay (Ed.): PKC 2005, LNCS 3386, pp. 29–46, 2005.

many dedicated and thoroughly suitable designs. However, since we are likely to appeal to the AES [12] for any subsequent symmetric-based session encryption, it might be preferable to build our KDF out of the AES rather than support an additional algorithm. Furthermore, it might be desirable to have a design based on the AES which would provide some immunity from continued cryptanalysis of current hash function proposals [4, 19].

Of course, it is well-known that a hash function can be built out of a block cipher [5, 9] and, at first sight, it appears that one of these constructions might suffice. However, our work is further motivated by the following goal. Instead of modelling the KDF as a random oracle, we would like to provide an explicit KDF construction that allows us to demonstrate the security of RSA-KEM based upon reasonable assumptions about the underlying block cipher (i.e. the AES). Thus our goal is to obtain a security proof for RSA-KEM under the assumption that the block cipher used in our KDF construction acts as an ideal family of random permutations indexed by the choice of key. Such an assumption on the block cipher is often referred to as the *Shannon, ideal cipher*, or *black-box* model and it is used widely (see for example Black et al. [5]).

Now our goal is not difficult to achieve for a block cipher with a sufficiently large block length (say at least twice the desired security level in bits). However, we would particularly like to use the AES, and the only block length permitted for the AES is 128 bits (even though the original cipher Rijndael [6] offered more flexibility in this regard). This is a problem since typical approaches for a block cipher-based KDF appear to be at the mercy of birthday attacks; the security level is bound by only half the block length (i.e., 64 bits in the case of a 128-bit block cipher). Since the standardized block ciphers at our disposal have a block length of either 64 or 128 bits, the security level attained using such mechanisms might not be viewed as adequate. While these birthday attacks may not immediately break the security of the full scheme RSA-KEM, they do seem to make it difficult to achieve a sufficiently-tight security proof.

So the goal of our work has been to achieve the level of security offered by conventional constructions that use a 256-bit block cipher, but to do so via a construction built around a 128-bit block cipher. More generally, in the ideal cipher model and using our construction built around a block cipher with block size k_b, an adversary making q oracle queries should not be able to exploit any weakness with a probability better than

$$\frac{c \cdot q^2}{2^{2k_b}} \tag{1}$$

for some reasonably small constant c. This is approximately as hard as finding collisions for an ideal hash function with output $2k_b$ bits. Our trick in accomplishing this with a 128-bit block cipher is to use an encryption key that is twice the length of the input block; i.e. to use a 128-bit block cipher with a 256-bit key. Thus, our specific construction is valid for the AES and all AES finalists, as well as a range of block ciphers that use 64- and 128-bit block lengths[1].

---

[1] Though the security level for 64-bit block lengths is unlikely to be appropriate.

2   Notation and Specification

Establishing some of the machinery that we need in our construction might initially appear to be somewhat complicated. However the description of the scheme itself is straightforward and can be found in Section 2.2.

2.1   Pre-requisites

Our particular key derivation function KDF_E is defined in terms of any block cipher E with the property that the key length is at least twice the block length. Let E be a block cipher with block length k_b bits and key length at least $2k_b$ bits. We will assume that the key length is exactly $2k_b$; in the case of a longer key only the first $2k_b$ bits will be used and the other bits will be fixed to some prescribed value. Moreover, we will assume that k_b is a multiple of 8. For each integer $k > 0$ let $\{0,1\}^k$ denote the set of bit-strings of length k. For integers $j \geq 0$ and $k > 0$ with $j < 2^k$, let $(j)_k$ be the k-bit big-endian representation of j (e.g., $(13)_6 = 001101$). The concatenation of two bit-strings X and Y will be denoted $X\|Y$. For two bit-strings r_1 and r_2 of the same length, $r_1 \oplus r_2$ denotes the bitwise exclusive-or of r_1 and r_2. In situations where a bit-string r of length k and an integer $j < 2^k$ are combined, the expression $r \oplus j$ denotes the sum $r \oplus (j)_k$. We also use the following notational shorthand. For an integer m and a bit-string $s = v_0\|v_1$ consisting of 2 blocks v_0 and v_1, each of length k, we set $s \uplus m = (v_0 \oplus m)\|(v_1 \oplus m)$.

In our specification of KDF_E we will appeal to a function δ that "tweaks" the most significant two bits of a string in the following way. Given a bit-string r of length k_b, write $r = (a)_2\|r'$ (clearly $a \in \{0,1,2,3\}$ and $r' \in \{0,1\}^{k_b-2}$) and define $\delta(r) = \delta((a)_2\|r') = ((a+1) \bmod 4)_2\|r'$. The effect of δ is summarized in the following table:

r	$00\|r'$	$01\|r'$	$10\|r'$	$11\|r'$
$\delta(r)$	$01\|r'$	$10\|r'$	$11\|r'$	$00\|r'$

2.2   Definition of KDF_E

Formally, we define KDF_E as $\text{KDF}_E(w, L)$ with two input arguments w and L. The first argument w is the secret input, while the second argument L is an optional label to be associated with the key. Let Valid be the set of valid input pairs (w, L) to KDF_E. To process a pair $(w, L) \in$ Valid, we need to apply a deterministic *encoding function* β to (w, L) to give an input string of an appropriate form (i.e., a sequence of blocks, each of bit length k_b). We also need to generate an initial value of bit length k_b from (w, L) using a deterministic *IV generator* $\tau :$ Valid $\rightarrow \{0,1\}^{k_b}$.

The output from the encoding function β is a string $R = (r_1, \ldots, r_n)$ of blocks r_i, each of bit length k_b. We assume that there is an upper bound $n_{\max}$ on the maximum number of blocks in an output $(r_1, \ldots, r_n) = \beta(w, L)$ with $(w, L) \in$ Valid. We require that it be computationally straightforward to recover

w and L in an unambiguous and unique manner from $\beta(w, L)$ and the initial value $t_0 = \tau(w, L)$. Our recommended encoding function $\beta(w, L)$ is specified as $\beta(w, L) = w\|L\|0^{k_1}\|(l(L))_{64}$; k_1 is the minimum value such that the bit length of $\beta(w, L)$ becomes a multiple of k_b.

The initial value $t_0 = \tau(w, L)$ should contain the length in octets of w (even in applications where the length is fixed) along with a "KDF Mode" indicator.

The output from KDF_E will be a sequence $U = (u_1, \ldots, u_\lambda)$ of blocks u_i, each of bit length k_b. We fix the number λ of blocks to be a constant. For a shorter output, we just truncate U to the desired number of bits.

The specification of $\mathrm{KDF}_E(w, L)$ now follows and consists of two stages. This process is illustrated in Figure 1 provided in Appendix A.

1. Apply the encoding rule to give $\beta(w, L) = (r_1, \ldots, r_n)$ and set the initial value $t_0 = \tau(w, L)$.
2. Extend t_0 to a *padded* initial value $s_0 = t_0\|t_0$ of length $2k_b$.
3. Process the blocks $r_1, \ldots, r_n$ as follows with i running from 1 to n:

$$t_{i,0} = E_{s_{i-1}}(r_i) \oplus r_i \; ;$$
$$t_{i,1} = E_{s_{i-1}}(\delta(r_i)) \oplus r_i \; ;$$
$$s_i = t_{i,0}\|t_{i,1} \; . \tag{2}$$

4. Generate λ blocks of output from s_n as follows:

$$u_m = E_{s_n \uplus m}(m) \quad (1 \le m \le \lambda) \tag{3}$$

(the k_b-bit representation of m is encrypted). The output is the string

$$U = u_1\|u_2\|\ldots\|u_\lambda \; ,$$

which can be truncated to a smaller number of bits if desired.

2.3   Properties of KDF_E

Our construction has some similarity to mechanisms for providing double block-length hash functions out of a block cipher [9]. Schemes such as MDC-2 [10] were designed to give a collision-resistant hash function when using the block cipher DES [13] (with its short block and key sizes as well as unusual complementation and weak key properties) as a building block. While the underlying motivation – to gain a level of security greater than the block size initially allows – is common to both applications, our KDF construction differs in many important ways, not least in how the chaining variables are specified and used.

To gauge the performance of our proposal, we observe that to produce λ blocks of output from n blocks of input, KDF_E requires $2n + \lambda$ applications of E with $n + \lambda$ different keys. The computation can be carried out on $p \ge 2$ parallel processors, each applying the block cipher at most $n + \lceil \lambda/p \rceil$ times. The last λ applications of E are fully parallelizable, whereas the first $2n$ applications are inherently serial with only two computations performed in parallel.

We note that while the AES is a fast cipher, the rate of encryption [7] for the AES with a 256-bit key (which is what we require in our construction) is comparable to the hashing rate of SHA-256 [14] (the NIST hash function that offers a similar level of security to that offered in our construction). Since two invocations of the AES are required at each step of the first stage of KDF_E, we would expect our construction to compare reasonably well to one based on a standardized hash function. Further, since the AES has a particularly lightweight key schedule, even though there is considerable re-keying, we would not expect the overhead to be too significant. Of course, it should also be stressed that if KDF_E is used as a component within RSA-KEM, then the RSA operation is already likely to be a dominating factor (particularly the RSA private key operation) in an application.

2.4   Design Rationale

An overall goal has been to design KDF_E in a manner that puts minimal constraints on the encoding method β; the security of KDF_E should not rely on how inputs are encoded as long as β is reversible. Here we give our rationale behind other aspects to the design of KDF_E.

THE FIRST STAGE IN KDF_E
The purpose of the first stage of the algorithm is to translate the input into a secret s_n in a collision-resistant manner. Specifically, it should be hard to find two distinct inputs (w, L), (w', L') such that the corresponding outputs s_n, $s'_{n'}$ from the first stage are equal. This is to provide a high level of assurance that different sets of keys are used in the second stage of the algorithm for different inputs. Note that it is easy to find inputs such that the outputs are related in a prescribed manner. Specifically, if we replace the last block r_n in the first stage with $\delta(r_n)$, then the rightmost k_b bits of the new output key coincide with the rightmost k_b bits of the old output key, except that the two leftmost positions in each block may differ. Yet in the ideal cipher model, such a correlation cannot be exploited in a useful manner by an adversary.

In round i of the first stage, the same key s_{i-1} is used for both encryptions. This introduces an effect that we may actually benefit from. Namely, we can control the behaviour of the output key s_i in such a way that collisions with padded initial values are impossible. Indeed, s_i cannot be equal to a padded initial value since this would imply that $E_{s_{i-1}}(r_i) = E_{s_{i-1}}(\delta(r_i))$, which is impossible. The same is true for $s_n \uplus m$; if $E_{s_{n-1}}(r_n) \oplus r_n \oplus m = E_{s_{n-1}}(\delta(r_n)) \oplus r_n \oplus m$, then we would again have $E_{s_{n-1}}(r_n) = E_{s_{n-1}}(\delta(r_n))$, which is impossible. If such collisions had been possible then it would have been difficult to achieve our desired security bound (1) without putting undesirable restrictions on the size of the set of possible initial values.

THE SECOND STAGE IN KDF_E
In the second stage we use different keys to derive the blocks u_m and our approach has some similarity to the counter mode of operation for a block

cipher [15]. If we were to use a single key, then we would see a small bias in the output due to the non-existence of collisions $E_s(r) = E_s(r')$. This would result in a violation of (1). Indeed, in applications where plenty of output is desirable, the security bound would be weak enough to be a concern in practice.

To minimize the probability of reusing a key, we derive the mth key from s_n by adding a simple counter m to s_n. In this manner, if

$$s_n \uplus m = s'_{n'} \uplus m' \qquad (4)$$

for some $m, m' \in \{0, \ldots, \lambda\}$, then

$$s_n = s'_{n'} \uplus (m' \oplus m) = s'_{n'} \uplus m''$$

for some $m'' \in \{0, \ldots, \hat{\lambda}\}$, where

$$\hat{\lambda} = \begin{cases} 0 & \text{when } \lambda = 0; \\ 2^{\lfloor \log_2 \lambda \rfloor + 1} - 1 & \text{otherwise.} \end{cases} \qquad (5)$$

Consequently, while there are $(1 + \lambda)^2$ pairs $(s_n \uplus m, s'_{n'} \uplus m')$ to be considered in (4), there are only $1 + \hat{\lambda}$ values on $s'_{n'}$ for each s_n that give a collision in (4). In particular, the constant c in our security bound (1) will turn out to be proportional to λ rather than to λ^2.

The keys in the second stage are obtained from s_n by adding the same counter value to each of the two blocks in s_n. This is to ensure that the derived blocks do not collide with padded initial values. The counter starts at 1 to avoid undesirable collisions between keys used in the first stage and keys used in the second stage. For instance, there may be two inputs for which, in the first case, s_n is used as a key in some round $n + 1$ of the first stage, while in the second case, the same s_n is used in the second stage[2]. It seems worth taking the precaution to provide this separation.

THE USE OF THE FUNCTION δ

The function δ is chosen so that $\delta(\delta(r)) \neq r$. Otherwise a function δ' (e.g. one that maps r to $r \oplus d$ for some d) would suffer from the property that if $E_{s_{i-1}}(r_i) \oplus r_i = E_{s_{i-1}}(\delta'(r_i)) \oplus \delta'(r_i)$, then r_i and $\delta'(r_i)$ both yield the same intermediate s_i in (2). This would result in a violation of our bound (1) and a modified security bound would contain a term of the form $c \cdot q/2^{k_b}$.

We have chosen δ to be simple, modifying only two bits of the input. As well as having little impact on efficiency this facilitates the security analysis. To see this, consider the *order* of an element r defined as the smallest integer j such that $r = \delta^j(r)$, where δ^j is shorthand for δ applied j times. Clearly the order of any element r with respect to δ is only four. While it seems that any order larger than two would result in a security bound of the form we require (1), analysis could be harder. The reason is as follows.

We say that an input pair (s, r) to the block cipher E is *of relevance* in the ith round of the first stage if $(s, r) = (s_{i-1}, r_i)$ or $(s, r) = (s_{i-1}, \delta(r_i))$. This

---

[2] Essentially the set of possible sequences $(r_1, \ldots, r_n)$ is not necessarily "prefix-free".

means that the pair (s, r) is related to the two pairs $(s, \delta(r))$ and $(s, \delta^{-1}(r))$ in an obvious manner. Similarly, $(s, \delta(r))$ is related to $(s, \delta^2(r))$, $(s, \delta^2(r))$ is related to $(s, \delta^3(r))$, and so on and so forth. Consequently, if the order of r were large, then we would have a long chain of related input pairs. This would make it hard to analyse dependencies between pairs of inputs in the first stage of KDF_E, which we require in the context of RSA-KEM. Thus the main benefit of δ as we have defined it is to ensure that the corresponding chain of pairs is short; for the given choice of δ, any set of the form $\{(s, r), (s, \delta(r)), (s, \delta^2(r)), (s, \delta^3(r))\}$ has the property that each pair in the set is only related to other pairs in the set and not to any pairs outside the set. This property makes it easier to obtain stream-lined security proofs.

2.5 Some Related Applications

While an AES-based key derivation function (KDF) for use within RSA-KEM is the focus of our work, we have actually designed something more flexible. Very simple variants and extensions of our KDF design could be used as a *mask generating function* MGF_E, a block-cipher based hash function construction, and as a block-cipher based message authentication code. However, these may compare unfavourably with other, more established, mechanisms [9].

For instance, it is easy to modify $\text{KDF}_E(w, L)$ for use as a hash function and we define the hash function $\text{Hash}_E(M)$ as

$$\text{Hash}_E(M) = \text{KDF}_E(M, \phi) ,$$

where ϕ is the empty string. However, we need to make a few minor changes. First, we change the encoding function and set

$$\beta_{\text{HASH}}(M) = \beta(M, \phi) = M \| 0^{k_1} \| (l(M))_{64} .$$

Here, $l(M)$ is the length in bits (or bytes) of the message M and k_1 is the minimum value such that the bit length of $\beta_{\text{HASH}}(M)$ becomes a multiple of k_b. Second, we fix the initial value t_0, which should contain a "Hash Mode" indicator, and we set $\lambda = 2$, which would give a hash function with a 256-bit output.

$\text{KDF}_E(w, L)$ can also be used as the basis for a message authentication code. Let the first argument w be the secret key and let the second argument L be the message M to be authenticated (possibly a concatenation of the message and other data). We can define the message authentication code $\text{MAC}_E(w, M)$ as

$$\text{MAC}_E(w, M) = \text{KDF}_E(w, M) ,$$

using the same encoding function β as in key derivation mode;

$$\beta_{\text{MAC}}(w, M) = w \| M \| 0^{k_1} \| (l(M))_{64} .$$

The initial value t_0 should be fixed and include the length in octets of w (even in applications where the length is fixed) and also a "MAC Mode" indicator. A typical parameter choice would be $\lambda = 1$ or 2 (the latter if collision-resistance is desired). Of course, another possibility would be to define a message authentication code as HMAC [1] with Hash_E as the underlying hash function.

3   KDF$_E$ Within RSA-KEM (and f-KEM)

KDF$_E$ is intended for use as an AES-based key derivation function within RSA-KEM [2, 18, 20]. However, to make the discussion as general as possible, we consider an arbitrary trapdoor permutation $f : X_f \to X_f$; see below for a formal treatment of trapdoor permutations. We briefly discuss even more general encryption schemes at the end of Section 4. Let

$$\mathrm{KDF} : X_f \times \mathcal{L} \to \{0,1\}^*$$

be a key derivation function, where $\mathcal{L}$ is a set of *labels* and $\{0,1\}^*$ is the set of all finite bit-strings. Then f-KEM is defined as follows, where the input to f-KEM is a label $L \in \mathcal{L}$.

1. Generate an element $w \in X_f$ uniformly at random.
2. Compute $y = f(w)$.
3. Compute $U = \mathrm{KDF}(w, L)$.
4. Output y, the *ciphertext*, and U, the *derived secret*.

In Section 4 we will analyse f-KEM in the special case that the underlying KDF is KDF$_E$.

For a security parameter k, let $\mathcal{F}_k$ be a finite family of pairs (f, f^{-1}) with the property that f is a permutation with inverse f^{-1}; f takes as input an element x in a set $X = X_f$ and returns an element y in the same set X. We assume that the running time of each of f and f^{-1} is polynomial in k. Let $\mathcal{G}$ be a probabilistic polynomial-time (PPT) algorithm that on input 1^k (i.e., k uniformly random bits) outputs a pair $(f, f^{-1}) \in \mathcal{F}_k$. $\mathcal{G}$ is a *trapdoor permutation generator*. An f-*inverter* $\mathcal{I}$ is an algorithm that on input (f, y) tries to compute $f^{-1}(y)$ for a random $y \in X$. $\mathcal{I}$ has success probability $\epsilon = \epsilon(k)$ and running time $T = T(k)$ if

$$\Pr\left((f, f^{-1}) \leftarrow \mathcal{G}(1^k), y \stackrel{\mathrm{R}}{\leftarrow} X_f : \mathcal{I}(f,y) = f^{-1}(y) \right) \geq \epsilon$$

and the running time for $\mathcal{I}$ is at most T. In words, $\mathcal{I}$ should be able to compute $f^{-1}(y)$ with probability ϵ within time T, where (f, f^{-1}) is derived via the trapdoor permutation generator and y is random. $\mathcal{I}$ solves the f *problem*.

$\mathcal{F}_k$ is a *trapdoor permutation family* with respect to (ϵ, T) if there is no f-inverter with success probability ϵ within running time T. The individual permutation f is referred to as a *trapdoor permutation*.

4   Security Analysis

In this section we prove the security of f-KEM based on KDF$_E$.

With the random oracle assumption on KDF it is straightforward to prove that f-KEM based on KDF is secure against a chosen-ciphertext adversary if f is a secure trapdoor permutation; see Shoup [18] for details. The purpose of this section is to analyse f-KEM when KDF$_E$ (see Section 3) is used as the underlying KDF. Our goal is to show that the security of f-KEM can be related to the hardness of inverting f if the block cipher E is modelled as an indexed family of random permutations.

The attack model against f-KEM is defined as follows and aligns with the security model for key encapsulation schemes defined in Shoup [18]. The adversary is given free access to a *decryption oracle* that on input (y, L) decrypts y and outputs the corresponding secret $U = \text{KDF}_E(f^{-1}(y), L)$. This means that we consider the family of adaptive chosen-ciphertext attacks (typically referred to as CCA2). The adversary also has free access to an E-oracle and a D-oracle simulating encryption and decryption with the block cipher E.

The task for the adversary is to distinguish a secret U_0 corresponding to a certain *challenge ciphertext* (y^*, L^*) from a random string. To make the challenge nontrivial, we do not allow the adversary to query the challenge ciphertext (y^*, L^*) at the decryption oracle after the challenge ciphertext has been published. However, there are no other restrictions on decryption queries; the adversary may well include either of y^* and L^* in a decryption query as long as the query does not include both.

The attack experiment runs as follows. First, the adversary is given a trapdoor permutation f generated at random. The adversary is allowed to send queries to her oracles during the entire attack and they may be chosen in an adaptive manner depending on responses to previous queries. At any time of the attack – but only once – the adversary sends a label L^* to a *challenge generator*. The challenge generator applies the f-KEM operation, producing a ciphertext y^* and a secret output U_0. In addition, the generator selects a uniformly random string U_1 and flips a fair coin b. The generator returns y^* and U_b; thus the response depends on b.

At the end, the adversary outputs a bit b'. The *distinguishing advantage* ϵ of the adversary is defined as

$$\epsilon = \Pr(b' = b) - \Pr(b' \neq b) = 2\Pr(b' = b) - 1$$

where the probability is computed over all possible trapdoor permutations. The adversary is referred to as an *IND-CCA2* adversary. The main result now follows.

Theorem 1. *Let $\mathcal{A}$ be an IND-CCA2 adversary against f-KEM based on KDF_E making q_E queries to the E- and D-oracles and q_f queries to the decryption oracle (including one query to the challenge generator). Let*

$$q = q_E + (n_{\max} + \lambda) \cdot q_f,$$

where $n_{\max}$ is defined in Section 2.1. Assume that $q \leq 2^{k_b}/24$. Moreover, assume that the distinguishing advantage of $\mathcal{A}$ is ϵ' and that the running time is bounded by T'. Then, viewing the block cipher E in the ideal cipher model, there is an f-inverter $\mathcal{I}$ with success probability ϵ and running time T such that

$$\epsilon = \epsilon' - \frac{18(\hat{\lambda} + 1) \cdot q^2}{2^{2k_b}} - \frac{q_f}{|X_f|} \tag{6}$$

with $\hat{\lambda}$ defined in (5) and

$$T = T' + O(q \cdot T_f) + O(\lambda \cdot q_f) , \tag{7}$$

where T_f is the time needed to compute f on a given input.

The proof of Theorem 1 is given in Appendix B. Here we comment on the security bounds in Theorem 1.

First, consider the difference $\epsilon' - \epsilon$ in success probabilities for the adversary and the inverter. For typical applications, λ will be quite small, say at most 100; this would give $100k_b$ bits of (symmetric) key material as output. Assuming that $\hat{\lambda} = 2^7 - 1$ and $q = 2^{k_b - \mu} \leq T'$ for some μ, the significant term in (6) is equal to

$$\frac{18 \cdot 2^7}{2^{2\mu}} < \frac{2^{12}}{2^{2\mu}} = 2^{12 - 2\mu} .$$

Defining a success probability of an algorithm to be "negligible" if the time-success ratio (time/probability) of the algorithm is at least 2^{k_b}, we may conclude that $\epsilon' - \epsilon$ is "negligible" as long as q is at most $2^{k_b - 12}$; the running time of the adversary is assumed to be at least q.

Next, consider the running time of the adversary in terms of the inverter. A close examination of the proof of Theorem 1 yields that the term $O(q \cdot T_f)$ in (7) is approximately $4T_f \cdot q \leq 4T_f \cdot T'$. Namely, for each application of the E-oracle simulation, the inverter applies f up to four times. As a consequence, T'/T is approximately $1/(4T_f)$. We may ignore the rightmost term $O(\lambda \cdot q_f)$ in (7) as q_f is typically bounded by a fairly small value such as 2^{48}. Note that the factor T_f is not due to the specific KDF_E construction but rather it is a generic factor that is also present when the entire key derivation function is modelled as a random oracle; see Shoup [18]. Hence, only the factor 4 is actually related to the specifics of KDF_E. To conclude, we lose approximately two bits of tightness with respect to running time when replacing the random oracle with KDF_E.

Remark. While we only consider trapdoor permutations, we conjecture that the proof might extend to general deterministic public-key encryption algorithms [8].

5   Conclusion

In this paper we have introduced and analysed a new key derivation function KDF_E. Defined in terms of a block cipher E, KDF_E has been specifically designed as an AES-based key derivation function for use within the key encapsulation mechanism RSA-KEM [18]. However the KDF_E construction could also be used as the basis for a mask generating function, a hash function, or a message authentication code. While the KDF_E construction might be somewhat unusual, there is considerable value in considering designs that allow us to demonstrate the security of RSA-KEM under reasonable assumptions on the behaviour of AES rather than the black-box behaviour of some *ad-hoc* construction. We leave the definition of alternative proposals as a matter for further research.

References

1. M. Bellare, R. Canetti, and H. Krawczyk. Keying hash functions for message authentication. In N. Koblitz, editor, *Advances in Cryptology – Crypto '96*, LNCS 1109, pp. 1–15, Springer-Verlag, 1996.

2. M. Bellare and P. Rogaway. Random Oracles are Practical: A Paradigm for Designing Efficient Protocols. *Proceedings of the First Annual Conference on Computer and Communications Security.* ACM, 1993.

3. M. Bellare and P. Rogaway. Optimal Asymmetric encryption - How to Encrypt with RSA. In A. De Santis, editor, *Advances in Cryptology – Eurocrypt'94*, LNCS 950, pp. 92–111, Springer-Verlag, 1995.

4. E. Biham and R. Chen. Near-collisions in SHA-0. In M. Franklin, editor, *Advances in Cryptology – Crypto '04*, LNCS 3152, pp. 290–305, Springer-Verlag, 2004.

5. J. Black, P. Rogaway, and T. Shrimpton. Block-Box Analysis of the Block-Cipher-Based Hash-Function Constructions from PGV. In M. Yung, editor, *Advances in Cryptology – Crypto '02*, LNCS 2442, pp. 320–335, Springer-Verlag, 2002.

6. J. Daemen and V. Rijmen. AES Proposal: Rijndael. Version 2. 1999.

7. W. Dai. Performance figures. Available via www.eskimo.com/~weidai/.

8. A. Dent. A Designer's Guide to KEMs. In K. Paterson, editor, 9th *IMA Conference on Coding and Cryptography*, LNCS 2898, 133–151, Springer-Verlag, 2004.

9. A. Menezes, P. van Oorschot, and S. Vanstone. Handbook of Applied Cryptography. CRC Press. 1997.

10. C.H. Meyer and M. Schilling. Secure program load with manipulation detection code. In Proceedings of SECURICOM '88, pp. 111–130, 1998.

11. T. Okamoto and D. Pointcheval. REACT: Rapid Enhanced-security Asymmetric Cryptosystem Transform. In D. Naccache, editor, *Topics in Cryptology – CT-RSA 2001*, LNCS 2020, pp. 159–175. Springer-Verlag, 2001.

12. National Institute of Standards and Technology. FIPS 196: The Advanced Encryption Standard. October, 2001. Available via csrc.nist.gov.

13. National Institute of Standards and Technology. FIPS 46-2: The Data Encryption Standard. December, 1993. Available via www.itl.nist.gov/fipspubs/.

14. National Institute of Standards and Technology. FIPS 180-2: The Secure Hash Standard. August, 2002. Available via csrc.nist.gov.

15. National Institute of Standards and Technology. Special Publication SP-800-38A: Recommondation for Block Cipher Modes of Operation – Methods and Techniques. December, 2001. Available via csrc.nist.gov.

16. R. Rivest, A. Shamir, and L. Adleman. A Method for Obtaining Digital Signatures and Public-Key Cryptosystems. *Communications of the ACM*, 21 (2), 120–126, February 1978.

17. RSA Laboratories. PKCS #1 v2.1: RSA Cryptography Standard. June 14, 2002. Available via www.rsasecurity.com.

18. V. Shoup. *A Proposal for an ISO Standard for Public Key Encryption.* Preprint, December 2001. Available via eprint.iacr.org/2001/112.

19. X. Wang, D. Feng, X. Lai, and H. Yu. Collisions for hash functions MD4, MD5, Haval-128 and RIPEMD. Available via http://eprint.iacr.org/2004/199.

20. Y. Zheng and J. Seberry. Practical Approaches to Attaining Security Against Adaptively Chosen Ciphertext Attacks. In E.F. Brickell, editor, *Advances in Cryptology – Crypto '92*, LNCS 740,pp. 292-304. Springer-Verlag, 1992.

A   Pictorial Representation of KDF$_E$

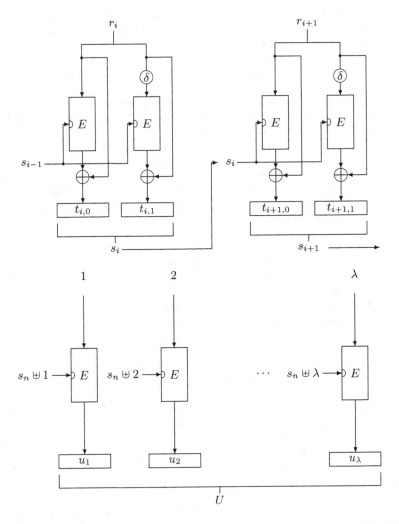

Fig. 1. The two stages of KDF$_E$; E represents a k_b-bit block cipher with a $2k_b$-bit key.

B   Proof of Theorem 1

Theorem 1. Let $\mathcal{A}$ be an IND-CCA2 adversary against f-KEM based on KDF_E making q_E queries to the E- and D-oracles and q_f queries to the decryption oracle (including one query to the challenge generator). Let

$$q = q_E + (n_{\max} + \lambda) \cdot q_f,$$

where $n_{\max}$ is defined in Section 2.1. Assume that $q \leq 2^{k_b}/24$. Moreover, assume that the distinguishing advantage of $\mathcal{A}$ is ϵ' and that the running time is bounded by T'. Then, viewing the block cipher E in the ideal cipher model, there is an f-inverter $\mathcal{I}$ with success probability ϵ and running time T such that

$$\epsilon = \epsilon' - \frac{18(\hat{\lambda}+1) \cdot q^2}{2^{2k_b}} - \frac{q_f}{|X_f|}$$

with $\hat{\lambda}$ defined in (5) and

$$T = T' + O(q \cdot T_f) + O(\lambda \cdot q_f),$$

where T_f is the time needed to compute f on a given input.

Let $\mathcal{A}$ be the adversary. We will define an inverter $\mathcal{I}$ in terms of $\mathcal{A}$ where $\mathcal{I}$ stores information on several lists:

1. f-List: Entries of the form (y, w) (with $y = f(w)$), sorted in alphabetic order with respect to y. Refer to an entry starting with y as a y-entry.
2. KEM-List: Entries of the form (y, L, U) where L, $w = f^{-1}(y)$, and U satisfy $\mathrm{KDF}_E(w, L) = U$. The entries are sorted alphabetically with respect to y and then L. Refer to an entry starting with y as a y-entry.
3. History List: Entries of the form $(s_i; (s_0, r_1, \ldots, r_i))$, sorted with respect to s_i where s_i is derived from s_0 and $r_1, \ldots, r_i$ via $i < n_{\max}$ rounds of (2). Refer to an entry starting with s_i as an s_i-entry.
4. E- and D-List: Entries of the form $(s, (r_1, v_1), \ldots, (r_d, v_d))$ where $v_i = E_s(r_i)$ sorted with respect to s. Within each entry pairs are sorted with respect to r_i on the E-list and with respect to v_i on the D-list. Refer to an entry starting with s as an s-entry. Since the E- and D-lists are essentially the same, we suppress the D-list. Whenever $\mathcal{I}$ requires an output value v, it is implicitly assumed that $\mathcal{I}$ looks on the D-list rather than on the E-list.

Let S_0 be the set of possible padded initial values s_0. Introduce additional sets S_1 and S_2 as follows. S_1 is the set of elements s such that there is an s-entry on the history list, whereas S_2 is the set of elements queried to the E- and D-oracles (by either $\mathcal{A}$ or $\mathcal{I}$) that are *not* contained in S_0 or S_1. At the beginning of the experiment, all lists and all sets except S_0 are empty.

Suppose that $\mathcal{A}$ sends a decryption query (y, L). Then $\mathcal{I}$ proceeds as follows.

F1 If (y, L) is on KEM-list, output the corresponding U and exit.

F2 If no (y, L) is found on KEM-list, check if there is some y-entry on f-list to examine whether $w = f^{-1}(y)$ is known. If w is known, simulate the encryption oracle as specified below to compute $U = \text{KDF}_E(w, L)$, output U, and exit.

F3 In the case that w is unknown, generate a string U as the concatenation of λ uniformly random blocks of length k_b, add (y, L, U) to KEM-list, output U, and exit.

At some point during the attack, the adversary $\mathcal{A}$ requests a challenge ciphertext, providing as input a label L^*. $\mathcal{I}$ proceeds as follows; y^* is the value that he wants to invert.

C1 If (y^*, L^*) is a previous decryption query, output ERROR and exit.

C2 Generate uniformly random strings U_0 and U_1 of length λk_b. Add (y^*, L^*, U_0) to KEM-list, flip coin b, output (y^*, U_b, U_{1-b}), and exit.

Suppose that $\mathcal{A}$ sends an E-query (s, r). Say that $E_s(r) = v$ is *consistent* if there is no conflict between this assignment and the pairs (r_i, v_i) within the s-entry on E-list. $\mathcal{I}$ proceeds as follows.

E1 If $v = E_s(r)$ is already known, output v and exit.

E2 If $s \notin S_0 \cup S_1$, generate a uniformly random v such that the assignment $v = E_s(r)$ is consistent. Add the pair (r, v) to the s-entry on E-list (introduce the entry if necessary), output v, and exit.

E3 If $s \in S_0 \cup S_1$, for each $j \in \{0, 1, 2, 3\}$ generate a uniformly random string v_j such that the four assignments $v_j = E_s(\delta^j(r))$ are consistent. Add the pairs $(\delta^j(r), v_j)$ to the s-entry on E-list (introduce the entry if necessary).

E4 For $0 \le j \le 3$, let $s^j = (v_j \oplus \delta^j(r)) \| (v_{(j+1) \bmod 4} \oplus \delta^j(r))$. The simulation fails if any of the $4(1 + \lambda)$ elements in

$$\{s^j \uplus m : 0 \le j \le 3, 0 \le m \le \lambda\} \tag{8}$$

are contained in $S_1 \cup S_2$ or collide with each other. Let E4-Err be the event that this failure occurs at some point during the attack.

E5 If $s \in S_1$, there is a (unique) s-entry $(s = s_i; (s_0, r_1, \ldots, r_i))$ on the history list. If $s \in S_0$, consider the "empty" entry $(s; (s, -))$ and let $i = 0$ and $s_0 = s$. If $i + 1 < n_{\max}$, then add the entries $(s^j, (s_0, r_1, \ldots, r_i, \delta^j(r)))$ to the history list.

E6 For each $j \in \{0, 1, 2, 3\}$, check whether s_0 and $(r_1, \ldots, r_i, \delta^j(r))$ correspond to a valid input (w, L) to KDF_E (meaning that s_0 is the padded initial value corresponding to (w, L) and $\beta(w, L) = (r_1, \ldots, r_i, \delta^j(r))$). If this is the case:
  1. Compute $y = f(w)$ and add (y, w) to f-list (if not present).
  2. If there is an entry (y, L, U) on KEM-list, then $\text{KDF}_E(w, L)$ has already been defined (implicitly) as $U = u_1 \| u_2 \| \ldots \| u_\lambda$. If this is the case, for $1 \le m \le \lambda$ assign

$$E_{s^j \uplus m}(m) = u_m . \tag{9}$$

  For each m introduce an $(s^j \uplus m)$-entry on E-list, add (m, u_m) to the $(s^j \uplus m)$-entry, and remove (y, L, U) from KEM-list.

E7 Output $v_0 = E_s(r)$ and exit.

The s-entry in step E5 being unique follows from the fact that E5 is the only step where we add new entries to the history list; if some of the added keys s^j were already there (thus already contained in the set S_1), the error E4-Err would have occurred in step E4. The assignments in (9) are trivially consistent; arriving at step E6 means that no error occurred in step E4, which implies that $s^j \uplus m$ has never been used as a key before.

Now consider a D-query (s, v) by $\mathcal{A}$. $\mathcal{I}$ proceeds as follows.

D1 If $r = D_s(v)$ is already known, output r and exit.
D2 Generate a random string r such that the assignment $r = D_s(v)$ is consistent and add (r, v) to the s-entry on E-list (introduce the entry if necessary).
D3 Check whether $s \in S_0 \cup S_1$. If this is *not* the case, output r, and exit.
D4 Proceed with steps E3-E6 in the simulation above with s and r, keeping in mind in step E3 that $E_s(r)$ has already been defined as v.
D5 Output $r = D_s(v)$ and exit.

We need to analyse what could go wrong in this simulation. First, we have a possible error in step C1, but this error occurs only if the adversary picks y^* in one of her decryption queries preceding the challenge ciphertext query; denote this event as C1-Err. Since the adversary has no prior information about y^*, $\Pr(\text{C1-Err}) \leq q_f / |X_f|$. Note that this value is an extremely small value if f is RSA with key size at least 1024 bits.

The remaining source of error is related to how $\mathcal{I}$ simulates the E- and D-oracles. Besides the event E4-Err in step E4, we also have the potential error that the uniformly random strings generated in steps C2 and F3 may not be consistent with other values. To analyse the probability of this error, we introduce an auxiliary algorithm $\mathcal{J}$ that can compute inverses of f. To make $\mathcal{J}$ indistinguishable from $\mathcal{I}$ for the adversary, we let $\mathcal{J}$ do exactly what $\mathcal{I}$ does during the whole experiment until the adversary exits. At the very end, we add a *checking phase*, where $\mathcal{J}$ proceeds with each entry (y, L, U) on KEM-list, computes $w = f^{-1}(y)$, and simulates the encryption oracle as specified above on all inputs necessary to compute $\text{KDF}_E(w, L)$ (keeping in mind as specified in step E6 that the end result should be U).

Now $\mathcal{J}$, and hence $\mathcal{I}$, will provide a perfect simulation unless an error occurs in step C1 or the error E4-Err occurs in step E4, either during the original experiment or during the additional checking phase. Namely, as long as all responses are consistent and chosen uniformly at random, there is no way for the adversary to distinguish the two simulations.

Before we can estimate the probability of the error E4-Err, we need to count the number of keys s for which $\mathcal{J}$ ever provides some assignment $v = E_s(r)$. Now, while $\mathcal{J}$ simulates the E-oracle on some inputs not queried by $\mathcal{A}$, the underlying key is always part of some other explicit or implicit query from $\mathcal{A}$. This implies that the total number of keys is at most $q = q_E + (n_{\max} + \lambda) \cdot q_f$; the latter term $(n_{\max} + \lambda) \cdot q_f$ estimates the total number of keys used when responding to the decryption queries and the challenge ciphertext query. In particular, the size of S_2 is at most q, as is the number of applications of each of the steps E1-E7.

We also need an upper bound on the total number of assignments $v = E_s(r)$ for any fixed key s. Such a bound is given by $4q$. Namely, each E- and D-query results in at most four assignments, whereas each decryption query and the challenge ciphertext query results in at most $4n_{\max}$ assignments in the first stage and at most λ assignments in the second stage. For the last claim, note that step E6.2 is applied at most once for each entry on KEM-list; the number of entries on this list is bounded by q_f.

In step E3, there are four assignments $v_j = E_s(\delta^j(r))$. We refer to the set $Q = \{(s, \delta^j(r)) : 0 \le j \le 3\}$ as a *4-set* and to a pair of the form $\{(s, r), (s, \delta(r))\}$ as a *window*. Within a 4-set Q there are four windows $\{(s, \delta^j(r)), (s, \delta^{j+1}(r))\}$ for $0 \le j \le 3$.

To estimate $\Pr(\mathsf{E4\text{-}Err})$, consider a set of assignments to be made in step E3 (steps D2 and E3 in case of a decryption query) corresponding to a 4-set Q and let s be the underlying key. Since $s \in S_0 \cup S_1$ and since it is impossible for a key once in S_2 to end up in S_1 (this would result in an error in step E4), each previous application of the key s must have been an assignment of values for a full 4-set (as opposed to an assignment of a single value as would have been the case if $s \in S_2$). As a consequence, the four values $E_s(\delta^i(r))$ all remain to be assigned.

First, assume that the underlying query was not a decryption query; we did not arrive at step E3 from step D4. For $i \in \{0, 1, 2, 3\}$, the adversary cannot predict the two values $v_j = E_s(\delta^j(r))$ and $v_{j+1} = E_s(\delta^{j+1}(r))$, and hence not the value s^j, with probability better than

$$\frac{1}{(2^{k_b} - 4q)^2} < \frac{1}{2^{2k_b}} \cdot \frac{1}{1 - 8q/2^{k_b}} \le \frac{1}{2^{2k_b}} \cdot \frac{1}{1 - 1/3} = \frac{3}{2^{2k_b+1}} =: \rho \ . \tag{10}$$

The value $4q$ in the denominator is the upper bound derived above on the number of previous queries with the key s; each such query corresponds to a value $E_s(r')$ that must be different from all $E_s(\delta^i(r))$. The second inequality follows from the assumption $q \le 2^{k_b}/24$.

Next, assume that we arrived at step E3 from step D4. Thus the first of the four queries in step E3 is a new D-query (s, v_0). As in (10), the adversary cannot predict any two of the four values

$$r = D_s(v_0), v_1 = E_s(\delta(r)), v_2 = E_s(\delta^2(r)), v_3 = E_s(\delta^3(r))$$

with probability better than ρ, not even if the two other values were revealed. In particular, since the adversary needs at least two of these values to determine any s^j, no s^j can be determined with probability better than ρ.

We may now easily compute a bound on the probability that we have a collision between some element in the set (8) and some element in S_2; refer to this event as E4-Err2. Specifically, for any j and m, $s^j \uplus m$ collides with any fixed element in S_2 with probability at most ρ. Since there are a total of at most $4(\lambda + 1) \cdot q$ values in (8) to be considered during the entire experiment and since $|S_2| \le q$, we have that

$$\Pr(\mathsf{E4\text{-}Err2}) \le \rho \cdot 4(\lambda + 1) \cdot q^2 = \frac{3 \cdot 4(\lambda + 1) \cdot q^2}{2^{2k_b+1}} \le \frac{6(\hat{\lambda} + 1) \cdot q^2}{2^{2k_b}} \ ; \tag{11}$$

$\hat{\lambda}$ was defined in (5).

Next, consider the probability of a collision either between two of the elements in the set (8) or between one of these elements and some element in the set S_1; refer to this event as E4-Err1. In such an eventuality, we have distinct (s, r) and (s', r') such that

$$\begin{cases} E_s(r) \oplus r = E_{s'}(r') \oplus r' \oplus m \\ E_s(\delta(r)) \oplus r = E_{s'}(\delta(r')) \oplus r' \oplus m \end{cases} \qquad (12)$$

for some integer m (with $0 \le m \le \hat{\lambda}$). Now, each element in S_1 corresponds to a 4-set generated in a previous application of steps E3 and E4. This means that we are effectively looking for collisions of the kind (12) with both keys in $S_0 \cup S_1$ and we have up to q different 4-sets among which we want to find a collision.

For any fixed previously known window W, and for each of the four windows within the 4-set Q under consideration, the probability that the two windows satisfy (12) is at most $(\hat{\lambda} + 1) \cdot \rho$; use (10) and the fact that there are $\hat{\lambda} + 1$ possibilities for m. At the end of the experiment, there are a total of at most $4^2 q(q - 1)/2 = 8q(q - 1)$ pairs of known windows from *different* 4-sets. This implies that the probability that (12) holds for some pair of this kind is bounded by

$$(\hat{\lambda} + 1) \cdot \rho \cdot 8q(q - 1) . \qquad (13)$$

Next, we turn our attention to windows within the same 4-set. Let W_i be the window $\{(s, \delta^i(r)), (s, \delta^{i+1}(r))\}$. For $0 \le i \le 3$, the pair (W_i, W_{i+1}) (indices computed modulo 4) cannot satisfy (12). Namely, if

$$\begin{cases} v_i \oplus \delta^i(r) = v_{i+1} \oplus \delta^{i+1}(r) \oplus m \\ v_{i+1} \oplus \delta^i(r) = v_{i+2} \oplus \delta^{i+1}(r) \oplus m , \end{cases}$$

then $v_i = v_{i+2}$, which is impossible. The remaining two cases (W_0, W_2) and (W_1, W_3) both result in the same system of equations

$$\begin{cases} v_2 = v_0 \oplus c \oplus m \\ v_3 = v_1 \oplus c \oplus m ; \end{cases}$$

$c = r \oplus \delta^2(r) = \delta(r) \oplus \delta^3(r) = 100 \ldots 0$. By (10), the left-hand side cannot be predicted with probability better than ρ even if the right-hand side (i.e., v_0 and v_1) is known. As a consequence, since there are at most q known 4-sets and since m can be chosen in $\hat{\lambda} + 1$ ways, the probability that (12) holds for some pair of known windows from the same 4-set is bounded by

$$(\hat{\lambda} + 1) \cdot \rho \cdot q . \qquad (14)$$

Combining (13) and (14), we obtain that

$$\Pr(\text{E4-Err1}) \le (\hat{\lambda} + 1) \cdot \rho \cdot 8q(q - 1) + (\hat{\lambda} + 1) \cdot \rho \cdot q$$
$$< 8(\hat{\lambda} + 1) \cdot \rho \cdot q^2 = \frac{12(\hat{\lambda} + 1) \cdot q^2}{2^{2k_b}} . \qquad (15)$$

Summing (11) and (15), we conclude that

$$
\begin{aligned}
\Pr(\text{E4-Err}) &\leq \Pr(\text{E4-Err1}) + \Pr(\text{E4-Err2}) \\
&\leq \frac{12(\hat{\lambda}+1)\cdot q^2}{2^{2k_b}} + \frac{6(\hat{\lambda}+1)\cdot q^2}{2^{2k_b}} = \frac{18(\hat{\lambda}+1)\cdot q^2}{2^{2k_b}} \ .
\end{aligned} \tag{16}
$$

Now return to the original inverter $\mathcal{I}$. Assume that $\mathcal{A}$ is able to guess the bit b with advantage ϵ' in a perfect simulation model. In the model provided by $\mathcal{I}$, the advantage of $\mathcal{A}$ is at least

$$
\epsilon = \epsilon' - \Pr(\text{E4-Err}) - \Pr(\text{C1-Err}) \geq \epsilon' - \frac{18(\hat{\lambda}+1)\cdot q^2}{2^{2k_b}} - \frac{q_f}{|X_f|} \ ,
$$

the subtracted terms bounding the probability that $\mathcal{J}$ fails, in which case $\mathcal{I}$ does not necessarily provide a perfect simulation. To demonstrate that ϵ is at least the success probability of $\mathcal{I}$, note that the only situation where the interactions between $\mathcal{I}$ and $\mathcal{A}$ depend on b is in step E6 when the underlying values y and L coincide with y^* and L^*. Namely, this is the only place where U_0 is used in a way distinguishable from U_1. However, if $\mathcal{I}$ obtains y^* in step E6, then by construction $\mathcal{I}$ obtains it from $w^* = f^{-1}(y^*)$; hence $\mathcal{I}$ wins.

One-Time Verifier-Based
Encrypted Key Exchange

Michel Abdalla[1], Olivier Chevassut[2], and David Pointcheval[1]

[1] Dépt d'informatique, École normale supérieure, 75230 Paris Cedex 05, France
{Michel.Abdalla,David.Pointcheval}@ens.fr
http://www.di.ens.fr/users/{mabdalla,pointche}
[2] Lawrence Berkeley National Laboratory, Berkeley, CA 94720, USA
OChevassut@lbl.gov
http://www.itg.lbl.gov/~chevassu

Abstract. "Grid" technology enables complex interactions among computational and data resources; however, to be deployed in production computing environments "Grid" needs to implement additional security mechanisms. Recent compromises of user and server machines at Grid sites have resulted in a need for secure password-authentication key-exchange technologies. AuthA is an example of such a technology considered for standardization by the IEEE P1363.2 working group. Unfortunately in its current form AuthA does not achieve the notion of forward-secrecy in a provably-secure way nor does it allow a Grid user to log into his account using an un-trusted computer. This paper addresses this void by first proving that AuthA indeed achieves this goal, and then by modifying it in such a way that it is secure against attacks using captured user passwords or server data.

1 Introduction

Motivation. Next generation distributed infrastructures integrate the ongoing work in Web Services (WS) with the state-of-the-art in distributed systems to enable seamless interaction among computational and data resources. "Grid" technology for example links computers, storage systems, and other devices through common interfaces and infrastructure to create powerful distributed computing capabilities [9, 11]. In this model of distributed computing, researchers and businesses not only plug into a global network of computer systems to access information but also to access distributed processing power. In parallel with the growth of Grid concepts and software in the scientific communities, commercial interests have been developing Web Services (WS) for the next generation business-to-business applications. Interest in both communities has grown to combine the techniques and concepts of Grid computing with the functionality of WS. This has led to the development of the Web Service Resource Framework (WSRF) specification and other elements of the Open Grid Services Architecture (OGSA) within several standard bodies such as the OASIS [19] and the Global Grid Forum (GGF) [13].

S. Vaudenay (Ed.): PKC 2005, LNCS 3386, pp. 47–64, 2005.

Security is one of the major requirements of Grid computing. Any Grid deployment must provide the security services of authentication, authorization, and secure session establishment. These services are provided by the Grid security infrastructure which was initially built upon the Transport Layer Security (TLS) protocol [10] and with the migration towards Web Services is now being built upon the WS-security primitives [9]. The current implementation of the Grid security infrastructure is based on public-key certificates. Recent security hacks of Grid sites due to the compromise of client and server machines, however, have led to a trend where many Grid sites are changing their security policies. The new policy prohibits long-term private keys from being stored on the Grid user's machines but requires that the keys are stored on servers in data centers where their integrity can be better protected. Grid users will authenticate to the data centers using a (one-time) human-memorable password and be issued short-lived certificates. Human-memorable passwords are short strings (e.g, 4 decimal digits) chosen from a relatively small dictionary so that they can be remembered easily.

The unique requirement of Grid provides security researchers with the opportunity to design and develop "provably-secure" cryptographic technologies that will play an essential role in securing next generation distributed infrastructures. The most immediate cryptographic need is certainly a "provably-secure" One-time Password-authentication and Key-eXchange technology (OPKeyX) for two-party [8].

Contributions. This paper is the third tier in the treatment of *Encrypted Key Exchange* (EKE), where the Diffie-Hellman key-exchange flows are encrypted using a password, in the direct model of Bellare-Pointcheval-Rogaway [1]. The first tier showed that under the computational Diffie-Hellman (CDH) assumption the AuthA password-authenticated key-exchange protocol is secure in both the random-oracle and ideal-cipher models [6]; the encryption primitive used is a password-keyed symmetric cipher. The second tier provided a very "elegant" and compact proof showing that under the CDH assumption the AuthA protocol is secure in the random-oracle model only [7]; the encryption primitive used is a mask generation function. In the present paper, we propose a slightly different variant of AuthA, where both flows are encrypted using separate mask generation functions, similarly to [18]. This *Two-Mask Encrypted Key Exchange* (EKE– both flows are encrypted) was not created for the sake of having one more variant, but simply because it allows us to provide the first complete proof of forward-secrecy for AuthA. The forward-secrecy of AuthA was indeed explicitly stated as an open problem in [2, 18]. Our result shows that under the Gap Diffie-Hellman assumption [20] this variant of AuthA is forward-secure in the random-oracle model. This is a significant achievement over other works which we hope will leverage our work to obtain tighter and more meaningful security measurements for the forward-secrecy of their EKE-like protocols.

We have furthermore augmented the *Two-Mask* protocol with two cryptographic mechanisms to reduce the risk of corruption of the server and the client. Corruption of a server occurs when an attacker gains access to the server's local database of passwords. If client's passwords are stored directly in the database, then the attacker can immediately use any of these passwords to impersonate these clients. Fortunately, there is a means to prevent an attacker from doing just that: *verifier-based password-authentication*. Of course, this mechanism will not prevent an adversary from mounting (off-line) dictionary attacks but it will slow him or her down and thus give the server's administrator time to react appropriately and to inform its clients. Corruption of a client occurs when a client is using an un-trusted machine which happens frequently these days as hackers run password sniffers on the Internet. There is a means to prevent a client's password from being captured: *one-time password-based authentication*. Passwords sniffed by hackers are of no use since users' passwords change from one session to the other. The end result is a "provably-secure" One-time Password-authentication and Key-eXchange (OPKeyX) technology for Grid computing.

The remainder of the paper is organized as follows. We first present the related work. In Section 2, we define the formal security model which we use through the rest of the paper. In Section 3, we present the computational assumptions upon which the security of *Two-Mask* and, thus, our OPKeyX technology are based upon. In Section 4, we describe the *Two-Mask* protocol itself and prove that the latter is forward-secure via a reduction from the *Two-Mask* protocol to the Gap Diffie-Hellman problem. In Section 5, we augment the *Two-Mask* protocol to reduce the risk of stolen server databases and captured client passwords to construct a technology for OPKeyX.

Related Work. The seminal work in this area is the *Encrypted Key Exchange* (EKE) protocol proposed by Bellovin and Merritt in [3, 4]. EKE is a classical Diffie-Hellman key exchange wherein either or both flows are encrypted using the password as a common symmetric key. The encryption primitive can be instantiated via either a password-keyed symmetric cipher or a mask generation function computed as the product of the message with the hash of a password. Bellare et al. sketched a security proof for the flows at the core of the EKE protocol in [1], and specified a EKE-structure (called the AuthA protocol) in [2]. Boyko et al. proposed very similar EKE-structures (called the PAK suite) and proved them secure in Shoup's simulation model [5, 18]. The PPK protocol in the PAK suite is similar to our *Two-Mask Encrypted Key Exchange* protocol; however, arguments in favor of forward-secrecy under the computational Diffie-Hellman (CDH) assumption do not give many guarantees on its use in practice [18]. The KOY protocol [16] is also proved to be forward-secure but it is not efficient enough to be used in practice.

The PAK suite is in the process of being standardization by the IEEE P1363.2 Standard working group [15]. Server machines store images of the password under a one-way function instead of a plaintext password when the "augmented" versions of the PAK suite are used. "Augmented" EKE-like protocols indeed limit the damage due to the corruption of a server machine, but do not protect against attacks replaying captured users' passwords. On the other hand, One-Time Password (OTP) systems protect against the latter kind of attacks but provide neither privacy of transmitted data nor protection against active attacks such as session hijacking [14]. The present paper designs and develops a cryptographic protocol for one-time "augmented" password-authenticated key exchange.

2   Password-Based Authenticated Key Exchange

In this section, we recall the security model of Bellare *et al.* [1] for password-based authenticated key exchange protocol.

2.1   Overview

A password-based authenticated key exchange protocol P is a protocol between two parties, a client $A \in$ client and a server $S \in$ server. Each participant in a protocol may have several *instances*, called oracles, involved in distinct, possibly concurrent, executions of P. We let U^i denote the instance i of a participant U, which is either a client or a server.

Each client $A \in$ client holds a password pw_A. Each server $S \in$ server holds a vector $pw_S = \langle pw_S[A] \rangle_{A \in \text{client}}$ with an entry for each client, where $pw_S[A]$ is the derived-password defined in [1]. In the symmetric model, $pw_S[C] = pw_C$, but they may be different in general, as in our verifier-based scheme. pw_C and pw_S are also referred to as the long-lived keys of client C and server S. Each password pw_A is considered to be a low-entropy string, drawn from the dictionary Password according to the distribution $\mathcal{PW}$. As in [7], we let $\mathcal{PW}(q)$ denote the probability to be in the most probable set of q passwords:

$$\mathcal{PW}(q) = \max_{P \subseteq \text{Password}} \left\{ \Pr_{pw \in \mathcal{PW}}[pw \in P \mid \#P \leq q] \right\}.$$

Note that, if we denote by $\mathcal{U}_N$ the uniform distribution among N passwords, then $\mathcal{U}_N(q) = q/N$.

2.2   The Security Model

The interaction between an adversary $\mathcal{A}$ and the protocol participants occurs only via oracle queries, which model the adversary capabilities in a real attack (see literature for more details [1, 7].) The types of oracles available to the adversary are as follows:

- Execute(A^i, S^j): The output of this query consists of the messages exchanged during the honest execution of the protocol.
- Reveal(U^i): This query is only available to $\mathcal{A}$ if the attacked instance actually "holds" a session key and it releases the latter to $\mathcal{A}$.
- Send(U^i, m): The output of this query is the message that the instance U^i would generate upon receipt of message m. A query Send(A^i, Start) initializes the key exchange protocol, and thus the adversary receives the initial flow that client instance A^i would send to the server S.

2.3   Security Notions

In order to define a notion of security for the key exchange protocol, we consider a game in which the protocol P is executed in the presence of the adversary $\mathcal{A}$. In this game, we first draw a password pw from Password according to the distribution $\mathcal{PW}$, provide coin tosses and oracles to $\mathcal{A}$, and then run the adversary, letting it ask any number of queries as described above, in any order.

AKE Security. In order to model the privacy (semantic security) of the session key, we consider a new game $\mathbf{Game}^{\mathsf{ake}}(\mathcal{A}, P)$, in which an additional oracle is available to the adversary: the $\mathsf{Test}(U^i)$ oracle.

– $\mathsf{Test}(U^i)$: This query tries to capture the adversary's ability to tell apart a real session key from a random one. In order to answer it, we first flip a (private) coin b and then forward to the adversary either the session key sk held by U^i (i.e., the value that a query $\mathsf{Reveal}(U^i)$ would output) if $b = 1$ or a random key of the same size if $b = 0$.

The Test-oracle can be queried at most once by the adversary $\mathcal{A}$ and is only available to $\mathcal{A}$ if the attacked instance U^i is **Fresh** (which roughly means that the session key is not "obviously" known to the adversary). When playing this game, the goal of the adversary is to guess the hidden bit b involved in the Test-query, by outputting a guess b'. Let Succ denote the event in which the adversary is successful and correctly guesses the value of b. The **AKE advantage** of an adversary $\mathcal{A}$ is then defined as $\mathsf{Adv}_P^{\mathsf{ake}}(\mathcal{A}) = 2\Pr[\mathsf{Succ}] - 1$. The protocol P is said to be (t, ε)-**AKE-secure** if $\mathcal{A}$'s advantage is smaller than ε for any adversary $\mathcal{A}$ running with time t. Note that the advantage of an adversary that simply guesses the bit b is 0 in the above definition due to the rescaling of the probabilities.

Forward-Secrecy. One additional security property to consider is that of forward secrecy. A key exchange protocol is said to be forward-secure if the security of a session key between two participants is preserved even if one of these participants is later compromised. In order to consider forward secrecy, one has to account for a new type of query, the Corrupt-query, which models the compromise of a participant by the adversary. This query is defined as follows:

– $\mathsf{Corrupt}(U)$: This query returns to the adversary the long-lived key pw_U for participant U. As in [1], we assume the weak corruption model in which the internal states of all instances of that user are not returned to the adversary.

In order to define the success probability in the presence of this new type of query, one should extend the notion of freshness so as not to consider those cases in which the adversary can trivially break the security of the scheme. In this new setting, we say that a session key sk is **FS-Fresh** if all of the following hold: (1) the instance holding sk has accepted, (2) no Corrupt-query has been asked since the beginning of the experiment; and (3) no Reveal-query has been asked to the instance holding sk or to its partner (defined according to the session identification). In other words, the adversary can only ask Test-queries to instances which had accepted before the Corrupt query is asked.

Let Succ denote the event in which the adversary successfully guesses the hidden bit b used by Test oracle. The **FS-AKE advantage** of an adversary $\mathcal{A}$ is then defined as $\mathsf{Adv}_P^{\mathsf{ake-fs}}(\mathcal{A}) = 2\Pr[\mathsf{Succ}] - 1$. The protocol P is said to be (t, ε)-**FS-AKE-secure** if $\mathcal{A}$'s advantage is smaller than ε for any adversary $\mathcal{A}$ running with time t.

Verifier-Based and One-Time-Password Protocols. In order to mitigate the amount of damage that can be caused by corruptions in the server and in the client, we consider two extensions to the standard notion of EKE protocols which we call *Verifier-Based* and *One-Time-Password* protocols.

In a Verifier-Based protocol, the goal is to keep the attacker capable of corrupting the server from obtaining the password for all the clients in the system. To achieve this goal, we need to adopt the asymmetric model in which the server no longer knows the password of a user, but only a function of it, which we call the verifier. In other words, only the client should know its password in a verifier-based protocol. Even though off-line dictionary attacks cannot be avoided in this case, the main idea of such protocols is to force an adversary who breaks into a server to have to perform an off-line dictionary attack for each password that it wants to crack based on its verifier. Therefore, the security of verifier-based protocols is directly related to the difficulty of recovering the original password from the verifier. In a One-Time-Password protocol, on the other hand, the goal is to limit the damage caused by an attacker who breaks into a client's machine or sniffs the password. This is achieved by forcing the user to use a different password in each session. That is, passwords are good for one session only and cannot be reused.

3   Algorithmic Assumptions

The arithmetic is in a finite cyclic group $\mathbb{G} = \langle g \rangle$ of order a ℓ-bit prime number q, where the operation is denoted multiplicatively. We also denote by $\mathbb{G}^{\star}$ the subset $\mathbb{G}\backslash\{1\}$ of the generators of $\mathbb{G}$.

A (t, ε)-$\mathsf{CDH}_{g,\mathbb{G}}$ attacker, in a finite cyclic group $\mathbb{G}$ of prime order q with g as a generator, is a probabilistic machine Δ running in time t such that its success probability $\mathsf{Succ}_{g,\mathbb{G}}^{\mathsf{cdh}}(\Delta)$, given random elements g^x and g^y to output g^{xy}, is greater than ε:

$$\mathsf{Succ}_{g,\mathbb{G}}^{\mathsf{cdh}}(\Delta) = \Pr[\Delta(g^x, g^y) = g^{xy}] \geq \varepsilon.$$

We denote by $\mathsf{Succ}_{g,\mathbb{G}}^{\mathsf{cdh}}(t)$ the maximal success probability over every adversaries running within time t. The CDH-Assumption states that $\mathsf{Succ}_{g,\mathbb{G}}^{\mathsf{cdh}}(t) \leq \varepsilon$ for any t/ε not too large.

A (t, n, ε)-$\mathsf{GDH}_{g,\mathbb{G}}$ attacker is a (t, ε)-$\mathsf{CDH}_{g,\mathbb{G}}$ attacker, with access to an additional oracle: a DDH-oracle, which on any input (g^x, g^y, g^z) answers whether $z = xy \bmod q$. Its number of queries is limited to n. As usual, we denote by

$$pw \in \mathsf{Password}, \mathsf{PW}^{\mathsf{as}} = \mathcal{G}(A\|S\|pw), \mathsf{PW}^{\mathsf{sa}} = \mathcal{G}(S\|A\|pw) \in \mathbb{G}$$

Client		Server
accept $\leftarrow$ false		accept $\leftarrow$ false
$x \xleftarrow{R} \mathbb{Z}_q$		$y \xleftarrow{R} \mathbb{Z}_q$
$X \leftarrow g^x$		$Y \leftarrow g^y$
$X^\star \leftarrow X \times \mathsf{PW}^{\mathsf{as}}$	$\xrightarrow{\quad A, X^\star \quad}$	$X \leftarrow X^\star/\mathsf{PW}^{\mathsf{as}}$
$Y \leftarrow Y^\star/\mathsf{PW}^{\mathsf{sa}}$	$\xleftarrow{\quad S, Y^\star \quad}$	$Y^\star \leftarrow Y \times \mathsf{PW}^{\mathsf{sa}}$
$sk = \mathcal{H}(A\|S\|X^\star\|Y^\star\|pw\|Y^x)$		$sk = \mathcal{H}(A\|S\|X^\star\|Y^\star\|pw\|X^y)$
accept $\leftarrow$ true		accept $\leftarrow$ true

Fig. 1. An execution of the EKE protocol.

$\mathsf{Succ}^{\mathsf{gdh}}_{g,\mathbb{G}}(t)$ the maximal success probability over every adversaries running within time t. The GDH-Assumption states that $\mathsf{Succ}^{\mathsf{gdh}}_{g,\mathbb{G}}(t) \leq \varepsilon$ for any t/ε not too large.

4   The EKE Protocol: Encrypted Key Exchange

4.1   Description of the Scheme

A hash function from $\{0,1\}^\star$ to $\{0,1\}^\ell$ is denoted $\mathcal{H}$. While $\mathcal{G}$ denotes a full-domain hash function from $\{0,1\}^\star$ into $\mathbb{G}$. As illustrated on Figure 1 (with an honest execution of the EKE protocol), the protocol runs between two parties A and S, and the session-key space **SK** associated to this protocol is $\{0,1\}^\ell$ equipped with a uniform distribution. It works as follows. The client chooses at random a private random exponent x and computes its Diffie-Hellman public value g^x. The client encrypts the latter value using a password-based mask, as the product of a Diffie-Hellman value with a full-domain hash of the password, and sends it to the server. The server in turn chooses at random a private random exponent y and computes its Diffie-Hellman public value g^y which it encrypts using another password-based mask[1]. The client (resp. server) then decrypts the flow it has received and computes the session key.

4.2   Security Result

In this section, we assert that under the intractability of the Diffie-Hellman problem, the EKE protocol, securely distributes session keys: the key is semantically secure. The proof, which is an improvement of [7], can be found in the full version of this paper.

---

[1] This differs from the classical EKE protocol, which uses a common mask [7]. But this helps to improve the security result.

Theorem 1 (AKE Security). *Let us consider the above* EKE *protocol, over a group of prime order q, where* Password *is a dictionary equipped with the distribution* $\mathcal{PW}$. *Let* $\mathcal{A}$ *be an adversary against the AKE security within a time bound t, with less than* q_s *active interactions with the parties (*Send-*queries) and* q_p *passive eavesdroppings (*Execute-*queries), and, asking* q_g *and* q_h *hash queries to* $\mathcal{G}$ *and* $\mathcal{H}$ *respectively. Then we have*

$$\mathsf{Adv}^{\mathsf{ake}}_{\mathsf{eke}}(\mathcal{A}) \leq 2 \times \mathcal{PW}(q_s) + 4q_h^2 \times \mathsf{Succ}^{\mathsf{cdh}}_{g,\mathbb{G}}(t + 5\tau_e) + \frac{(q_p + q_s)^2 + 3(q_g + q_h)^2}{2q},$$

where τ_e *denotes the computational time for an exponentiation in* $\mathbb{G}$.

Let us now enhance the result to cover forward-secrecy. The proof will be different from previous proofs for EKE-like protocols since the simulation still must be independent of any password (so that we can say that the adversary has a minute of chance to guess the correct one), while after a corruption the adversary will be able to check the consistency. To reach this aim, we will need to rely on a stronger assumption: the Gap Diffie-Hellman problem. The Decisional Diffie-Hellman oracle will be used to identify the public random oracle $\mathcal{H}$ to the private one $\mathcal{H}'$ when the input is a valid Diffie-Hellman value.

Theorem 2 (FS-AKE Security). *Let us consider the above* EKE *protocol, over a group of prime order q, where* Password *is a dictionary equipped with the distribution* $\mathcal{PW}$. *Let* $\mathcal{A}$ *be an adversary against the FS-AKE security within a time bound t, with less than* q_s *active interactions with the parties (*Send-*queries) and* q_p *passive eavesdroppings (*Execute-*queries), and, asking* q_g *and* q_h *hash queries to* $\mathcal{G}$ *and* $\mathcal{H}$ *respectively. Then we have*

$$\mathsf{Adv}^{\mathsf{ake-fs}}_{\mathsf{eke}}(\mathcal{A}) \leq 2 \times \mathcal{PW}(q_s) + 4 \times \mathsf{Succ}^{\mathsf{gdh}}_{g,\mathbb{G}}(q_h, t + 5\tau_e) + \frac{(q_p + q_s)^2 + 3(q_g + q_h)^2}{2q},$$

where τ_e *denotes the computational time for an exponentiation in* $\mathbb{G}$.

Proof. As usual, we incrementally define a sequence of games starting at the real game $\mathbf{G}_0$ and ending up at $\mathbf{G}_5$. We are interested in the event S, which occurs if the adversary correctly guesses the bit b involved in the Test-query. Let us remember that in this attack game, the adversary is provided with the Corrupt-query.

GAME $\mathbf{G}_0$: This is the real protocol, in the random-oracle model. By definition of event S_0, which means that the adversary correctly guesses the bit b involved in the Test-query, we have

$$\mathsf{Adv}^{\mathsf{ake-fs}}_{\mathsf{eke}}(\mathcal{A}) = 2\Pr[S_0] - 1.$$

GAME $\mathbf{G}_2$: In this game, we simulate the hash oracles ($\mathcal{G}$ and $\mathcal{H}$, but also an additional hash function $\mathcal{H}' : \{0,1\}^\star \to \{0,1\}^\ell$ that will appear in the Game $\mathbf{G}_3$) as usual by maintaining hash lists $\Lambda_\mathcal{G}$, $\Lambda_\mathcal{H}$ and $\Lambda_{\mathcal{H}'}$ (see Figure 2). Except that

$\mathcal{G}$ and $\mathcal{H}$ oracles

For a hash-query $\mathcal{G}(q)$ such that a record $(q, r, \star)$ appears in $\Lambda_{\mathcal{G}}$, the answer is r. Otherwise the answer r is defined according to the following rule:

▶**Rule $\mathcal{G}^{(1)}$**

  Choose a random element $r \in \mathbb{G}$. The record $(q, r, \perp)$ is added to $\Lambda_{\mathcal{G}}$.

Note: the third component of the elements of this list will be explained later.

For a hash-query $\mathcal{H}(q)$ such that a record (q, r) appears in $\Lambda_{\mathcal{H}}$, the answer is r. Otherwise, q is parsed as $(A\|S\|X^\star\|Y^\star\|pw\|K)$, one first asks for $\mathcal{G}(A\|S\|pw)$ and $\mathcal{G}(S\|A\|pw)$, using the above simulation, then the answer r is defined according to the following rule:

▶**Rule $\mathcal{H}^{(1)}$**

  Choose a random element $r \in \{0,1\}^\ell$.

One adds the record (q, r) to $\Lambda_{\mathcal{H}}$.

For a hash-query $\mathcal{H}'(q)$, such that a record (q, r) appears in $\Lambda_{\mathcal{H}'}$, the answer is r. Otherwise, one chooses a random element $r \in \{0,1\}^\ell$, answers with it, and adds the record (q, r) to $\Lambda_{\mathcal{H}'}$.

Fig. 2. Simulation of the EKE protocol (random oracles)

we query $\mathcal{G}(A\|S\|pw)$ and $\mathcal{G}(S\|A\|pw)$ as soon as A, S and pw appear in a $\mathcal{H}$-query. This just increases the number of $\mathcal{G}$ queries. We also simulate all the instances, as the real players would do, for the Send-queries and for the Execute, Reveal, Test and Corrupt-queries (see Figure 3).

From this simulation, we easily see that the game is perfectly indistinguishable from the real attack.

GAME $\mathbf{G_2}$: First, we cancel games in which some collisions appear:

- collisions on the transcripts $((A, X^\star), (S, Y^\star))$;
- collisions on the output of $\mathcal{G}$.

$$\Pr[\mathsf{Coll}_2] \leq \frac{(q_p + q_s)^2}{2q} + \frac{(q_g + q_h)^2}{2q}.$$

GAME $\mathbf{G_3}$: In this game, we do not compute the session key sk using the oracle $\mathcal{H}$, but using the private oracle $\mathcal{H}'$ so that the value sk is completely independent not only from $\mathcal{H}$, but also from pw and thus from both K_A and K_S. We reach this aim by using the following rule:

▶**Rule A3/S3$^{(3)}$**

  Compute the session key $sk_{A/S} = \mathcal{H}'(A\|S\|X^\star\|Y^\star)$.

Since we do no longer need to compute the values K_A and K_S, we can also simplify the second rules:

▶**Rule A2/S2$^{(3)}$**

  Do nothing.

Send-queries to A

We answer to the Send-queries to an A-instance as follows:

- A $\mathsf{Send}(A^i, \mathtt{Start})$-query is processed according to the following rule:
  ▶**Rule A1**$^{(1)}$
  | Choose a random exponent $\theta \in \mathbb{Z}_q$, compute $X = g^\theta$ and $X^\star = X \times \mathsf{PW}^{\mathsf{as}}$.

  Then the query is answered with $(A, X^\star)$, and the instance goes to an expecting state.
- If the instance A^i is in an expecting state, a query $\mathsf{Send}(A^i, (S, Y^\star))$ is processed by computing the session key. We apply the following rules:
  ▶**Rule A2**$^{(1)}$
  | Compute $Y = Y^\star/\mathsf{PW}^{\mathsf{sa}}$ and $K_A = Y^\theta$.

  ▶**Rule A3**$^{(1)}$
  | Compute the session key $sk_A = \mathcal{H}(A\|S\|X^\star\|Y^\star\|pw\|K_A)$.

  Finally the instance accepts.

Send-queries to S

We answer to the Send-queries to a S-instance as follows:

- A $\mathsf{Send}(S^j, (A, X^\star))$-query is processed according to the following rules:
  ▶**Rule S1**$^{(1)}$
  | Choose a random exponent $\varphi \in \mathbb{Z}_q$, compute $Y = g^\varphi$ and $Y^\star = Y \times \mathsf{PW}^{\mathsf{sa}}$.

  Then the query is answered with $(S, Y^\star)$, and the instance applies the following rules.
  ▶**Rule S2**$^{(1)}$
  | Compute $X = X^\star/\mathsf{PW}^{\mathsf{as}}$ and $K_S = X^\varphi$.

  ▶**Rule S3**$^{(1)}$
  | Compute the session key $sk_S = \mathcal{H}(A\|S\|X^\star\|Y^\star\|pw\|K_S)$.

  Finally, the instance accepts.

Other queries

An $\mathsf{Execute}(A^i, S^j)$-query is processed using successively the above simulations of the Send-queries: $(A, X^\star) \leftarrow \mathsf{Send}(A^i, \mathtt{Start})$ and $(S, Y^\star) \leftarrow \mathsf{Send}(S^j, (A, X^\star))$, and outputting the transcript $((A, X^\star), (S, Y^\star))$.

A $\mathsf{Reveal}(U)$-query returns the session key (sk_A or sk_S) computed by the instance I (if the latter has accepted).

A $\mathsf{Test}(U)$-query first gets sk from $\mathsf{Reveal}(U)$, and flips a coin b. If $b = 1$, we return the value of the session key sk, otherwise we return a random value drawn from $\{0, 1\}^\ell$.

A $\mathsf{Corrupt}(U)$-query returns password pw of the user U.

Fig. 3. Simulation of the EKE protocol (Send, Reveal, Execute, Test and Corrupt queries)

The games $\mathbf{G}_3$ and $\mathbf{G}_2$ are indistinguishable unless $\mathcal{A}$ queries the hash function $\mathcal{H}$ on either $A\|S\|X^\star\|Y^\star\|pw\|K_A$ or $A\|S\|X^\star\|Y^\star\|pw\|K_S$, for some execution transcript $((A, X^\star), (S, Y^\star))$. We hope to prove that for all the transcripts of accepted sessions, the probability of such an event is negligible. However, there is no hope for proving it about sessions accepted *after* the corruption of the password, since the adversary may know the x and thus K_A (or y and K_S). One should note that sessions accepted *after* the corruption may have been started *before*. There is no way in our simulation to anticipate different answers for the Send-queries according to that. Therefore, we have to make answers from $\mathcal{H}$ and $\mathcal{H}'$ (when they correspond to the same query, which can be checked with the DDH-oracle) to be the same for sessions accepted after the corruption of the password:

▶**Rule $\mathcal{H}^{(3)}$**

- Before the corruption, randomly choose $r \in \{0,1\}^\ell$.
- After the corruption, knowing the correct password, if
  - pw is the correct password;
  - $A, S, X^\star, Y^\star$ corresponds to the session ID of a session accepted after the corruption;
  - $K = \mathsf{CDH}_{g,\mathbb{G}}(X^\star/\mathsf{PW}^{\mathsf{as}}, Y^\star/\mathsf{PW}^{\mathsf{sa}})$ (checked using the DDH-oracle);

  then r is set to $\mathcal{H}'(A\|S\|X^\star\|Y^\star)$.
  Else, choose a random element $r \in \{0,1\}^\ell$.

This new rule for the simulation of $\mathcal{H}$ just replaces some random values by other random values. The games $\mathbf{G}_3$ and $\mathbf{G}_2$ are now indistinguishable unless $\mathcal{A}$ queried the hash function $\mathcal{H}$ on either $A\|S\|X^\star\|Y^\star\|pw\|K_A$ or $A\|S\|X^\star\|Y^\star\|pw\|K_S$, for some accepted-session transcript $((A, X^\star), (S, Y^\star))$, *before* corrupting the password: event AskHbC. This means that, for *some transcript* $((A, X^\star), (S, Y^\star))$, the tuple $(A, S, X^\star, Y^\star, pw, \mathsf{CDH}_{g,\mathbb{G}}(X^\star/\mathsf{PW}^{\mathsf{as}}, Y^\star/\mathsf{PW}^{\mathsf{sa}}))$ lies in the list $\Lambda_\mathcal{H}$.

On the other hand, the session key (associated to a session accepted *before* the corruption) is computed with a random oracle that is private to the simulator, then one can remark that it cannot be distinguished by the adversary unless the same transcript $((A, X^\star), (S, Y^\star))$ appeared in another session, for which a Reveal-query has been asked (which event has been excluded in the previous game). The adversary correctly guesses the bit b involved in the Test-query (event S_3) only by chance: $\Pr[\mathsf{S}_3] = 1/2$.

Actually, one does not need the Diffie-Hellman values K_A or K_S for computing sk, but the password: we can formally simplify again some rules but thus without modifying anything w.r.t. the probabilities:

▶**Rule A1$^{(3)}$**

| Choose a random element $x \in \mathbb{Z}_q$ and compute $X^\star = g^x$.

▶**Rule S1$^{(3)}$**

| Choose a random element $y \in \mathbb{Z}_q$ and compute $Y^\star = g^y$.

GAME $\mathbf{G}_4$:   In order to evaluate the probability of event AskHbC, let us modify the simulation of the oracle $\mathcal{G}$, with two random elements $P, Q \in \mathbb{G}\backslash\{1\}$ (which are thus generators of $\mathbb{G}$, since the latter has a prime order q). The simulation introduces values in the third component of the elements of $\Lambda_\mathcal{G}$, but does not use it. It would let the probabilities unchanged, but we exclude the cases $\mathsf{PW}^{\mathsf{as}} = 1$ or $\mathsf{PW}^{\mathsf{sa}} = 1$:

► **Rule** $\mathcal{G}^{(4)}$

- If $q = \text{"}A\|S\|\star\text{"}$, randomly choose $k \in \mathbb{Z}_q^\star$, and compute $r = P^{-k}$;
- If $q = \text{"}S\|A\|\star\text{"}$, randomly choose $k \in \mathbb{Z}_q^\star$, and compute $r = Q^{-k}$;
- Else, choose a random element $r \in \mathbb{G}$, and set $k = \perp$.

The record (q, r, k) is added to $\Lambda_\mathcal{G}$.

Since we just exclude $k = 0$, we have:

$$|\Pr[\mathsf{AskHbC_4}] - \Pr[\mathsf{AskHbC_3}]| \le \frac{q_g + q_h}{q}.$$

GAME $\mathbf{G_5}$: It is now possible to evaluate the probability of the event AskHbC. Indeed, one can remark that the password is never used during the simulation, before the corruption. It thus does not need to be chosen in advance, but at the time of the corruption (or at the very end only). At that time, one can check whether the event AskHbC happened or not. To make this evaluation easier, we cancel the games wherein for some pair $(X^\star, Y^\star) \in \mathbb{G}^2$, involved in a communication, there are two passwords pw such that the tuple $(A, S, X^\star, Y^\star, pw, \mathsf{CDH}_{g,\mathbb{G}}(X^\star/\mathsf{PW}^{as}, Y^\star/\mathsf{PW}^{sa}))$ is in $\Lambda_\mathcal{H}$ (which event is denoted $\mathsf{CollH_5}$). Hopefully, event $\mathsf{CollH_5}$ can be upper-bounded, granted the following Lemma:

Lemma 1. *For any pair $(X^\star, Y^\star)$ involved in a communication, there is at most one password pw such that $(A, S, X^\star, Y^\star, pw, \mathsf{CDH}_{g,\mathbb{G}}(X^\star/\mathsf{PW}^{as}, Y^\star/\mathsf{PW}^{sa}))$ is in $\Lambda_\mathcal{H}$, unless one can solve the Diffie-Hellman problem:*

$$\Pr[\mathsf{CollH_5}] \le \mathsf{Succ}_{g,\mathbb{G}}^{gdh}(q_h, t + 5\tau_e).$$

Proof. Assume there exist $(X^\star = g^x, Y^\star = g^y) \in \mathbb{G}^2$ involved in a communication, $\mathsf{PW}_0^{as} = P^{-k_0} \ne 1$, $\mathsf{PW}_0^{sa} = Q^{-k_0'} \ne 1$, and $\mathsf{PW}_1^{as} = P^{-k_1} \ne 1$, $\mathsf{PW}_1^{sa} = Q^{-k_1'} \ne 1$ such that the two following tuples (for $i = 0, 1$) are in $\Lambda_\mathcal{H}$:

$$(A, S, X^\star, Y^\star, pw_i, Z_i = \mathsf{CDH}_{g,\mathbb{G}}(X^\star/\mathsf{PW}_i^{as}, Y^\star/\mathsf{PW}_i^{sa})).$$

Then, $Z_i = \mathsf{CDH}_{g,\mathbb{G}}(X^\star \times P^{k_i}, Y^\star \times Q^{k_i'})$. Since $(X^\star, Y^\star) \in \mathbb{G}^2$ has been involved in a communication (either from Send-queries or an Execute-query), one of $X^\star = g^x$ or $Y^\star = g^y$, has been simulated: at least one of x or y is known. Without loss of generality, we can assume we know x:

$$Z_i = (Y^\star \times Q^{k_i'})^x \times \mathsf{CDH}_{g,\mathbb{G}}(Y^\star, P)^{k_i} \times \mathsf{CDH}_{g,\mathbb{G}}(P, Q)^{k_i k_i'}$$

$$Z_1^{k_0}/Z_0^{k_1} = \left(Y^{\star k_0 - k_1} \times \mathsf{PW}_0^{sa\,k_1}/\mathsf{PW}_1^{sa\,k_0}\right)^x \times \mathsf{CDH}_{g,\mathbb{G}}(P, Q)^{k_0 k_1(k_1' - k_0')}$$

$$\mathsf{CDH}_{g,\mathbb{G}}(P, Q) = \left(((\mathsf{PW}_1^{sa}/Y^\star)^x Z_1)^{k_0}/((\mathsf{PW}_0^{sa}/Y^\star)^x Z_0)^{k_1}\right)^u,$$

where u is the inverse of $k_0 k_1(k_1' - k_0')$ in $\mathbb{Z}_q$. The latter exists since PW_0^{as}, PW_0^{sa}, PW_1^{as}, $\mathsf{PW}_1^{sa} \ne 1$, and they are all distinct from each other (we have excluded collisions for $\mathcal{G}$). Since we have access to a DDH-oracle, one can find the two useful $\mathcal{H}$-queries. □

For a more convenient analysis, we can split the event AskHbC in two disjoint sub-cases:

1. AskHbC-Passive, where the transcript $((A, X^\star), (S, Y^\star))$ involved in the crucial $\mathcal{H}$-query comes as an answer from an Execute-query;
2. AskHbC-Active, the other cases.

About the active case (the event AskHbC-Active$_5$), the above Lemma 1 applied to games where the event CollH$_5$ did not happen states that for each pair $(X^\star, Y^\star)$ involved in an active transcript, there is at most one pw such that the corresponding tuple is in $\Lambda_\mathcal{H}$:

$$\Pr[\mathsf{AskHbC\text{-}Active}_5] \leq \mathcal{PW}(q_s).$$

Moreover, in the particular case of passive transcripts, one can state a stronger result:

Lemma 2. *For any pair $(X^\star, Y^\star) \in \mathbb{G}^2$, involved in a passive transcript, there is no password pw such that $(A, S, X^\star, Y^\star, pw, \mathsf{CDH}_{g,\mathbb{G}}(X^\star/\mathsf{PW}^{as}, Y^\star/\mathsf{PW}^{sa}))$ is in $\Lambda_\mathcal{H}$, unless one can solve the Diffie-Hellman problem:*

$$\Pr[\mathsf{AskHbC\text{-}Passive}_5] \leq \mathsf{Succ}^{\mathsf{gdh}}_{g,\mathbb{G}}(q_h, t + 4\tau_e).$$

Proof. Assume there exist $(X^\star = g^x, Y^\star = g^y) \in \mathbb{G}^2$ involved in a passive transcript, and values $\mathsf{PW}^{as} = P^{-k} \neq 1$, $\mathsf{PW}^{sa} = Q^{-k'} \neq 1$ such that the tuple

$$(A, S, X^\star, Y^\star, pw, Z = \mathsf{CDH}_{g,\mathbb{G}}(X^\star/\mathsf{PW}^{as}, Y^\star/\mathsf{PW}^{sa}))$$

is in $\Lambda_\mathcal{H}$. Then, as above (but with x and y known),

$$\mathsf{CDH}_{g,\mathbb{G}}(P, Q) = \left(Z \times \mathsf{PW}^{sa\,x} \times \mathsf{PW}^{as\,y}/g^{xy}\right)^u,$$

where u is the inverse of kk' in $\mathbb{Z}_q$. By using the DDH-oracle, one easily gets the crucial $\mathcal{H}$-query. □

As a conclusion,

$$\Pr[\mathsf{AskHbC}_5] \leq \mathsf{Succ}^{\mathsf{gdh}}_{g,\mathbb{G}}(q_h, t + 4\tau_e) + \mathcal{PW}(q_s).$$

Combining all the above equations, one gets

$$\mathsf{Adv}^{\mathsf{ake\text{-}fs}}_{\mathsf{eke}}(\mathcal{A}) \leq 2 \times \left(\begin{array}{c} \mathcal{PW}(q_s) + \mathsf{Succ}^{\mathsf{gdh}}_{g,\mathbb{G}}(q_h, t + 4\tau_e) + \mathsf{Succ}^{\mathsf{gdh}}_{g,\mathbb{G}}(q_h, t + 5\tau_e) \\ + \dfrac{q_g + q_h}{q} + \dfrac{(q_g + q_h)^2}{2q} + \dfrac{(q_p + q_s)^2}{2q} \end{array} \right).$$

□

5   The OPKeyX Protocol

The basic EKE protocol withstands password corruption, by providing forward-secrecy. But this just protects the secrecy of session keys established before the corruption. Nothing is guaranteed for future sessions. We can even show that one easily breaks the semantic security of their session keys, by simply impersonating one of the parties with the knowledge of the password.

In the above protocol, the password can be extracted from both machines: the server and the client. And moreover, the server stores many passwords (since its is aimed at establishing sessions with many clients), then the corruption of the server does not just leak one password, but a huge number of them. This would be quite useful to be able to reduce the damages of such a corruption. We propose below two different ways to achieve this task.

5.1   Stealing the Server Database

In a verifier-based protocol, the client owns a password, but the server just knows a verifier of the latter (which is actually a hash value, or the image by a one-way function), not the password itself. Hence, the corruption of the server just reveals this verifier. Of course, an off-line dictionary attack thereafter leads to the password. Such an exhaustive search cannot be prevented but should be the most efficient one: by including salts (sent back to the client by the server in the first flow) would reduce even more the impact of the corruption, since a specific dictionary attack should be performed towards each specific user, and could not be generic.

A verifier-based enhancement of EKE is proposed on Figure 4. It is basically the previous EKE scheme using first the verifier as common password. Then, the client furthermore proves his knowledge of the password which matches the password-verifier relation. In our proposal, the relation is the pairs (x, g^x), and thus the proof is a Schnorr-like proof of knowledge of a discrete logarithm [21], with a multi-collision resistant function f [12]. To prevent dictionary attacks, we introduce the Diffie-Hellman secret in the hash input to get the challenge e, so that the latter can be computed by the two parties only: it is semantically secure for external adversaries for exactly the same reasons the session key is. Because of this semantic security, dictionary attacks are still prevented, since the additional proof of knowledge does not reveal any information: the verification relation is actually secret, because of the secrecy of e. As a consequence, the private property of e makes that the proof does not leak any information about both the password and the verifier to external parties. The zero-knowledge property of this proof makes that even the server does not learn any additional information about the password.

To improve efficiency, we also swapped the flows, so that the protocol remains a 2-pass one. Indeed, the client has to be the last, since it has to send its proof of knowledge of the password. By swapping the two flows of the basic EKE protocol, the latter proof of knowledge can be concatenated to the last flow, which does not increase the communication cost.

$$
\begin{array}{cc}
\underline{\textit{Client}} & \underline{\textit{Server}}
\end{array}
$$

$$
\begin{array}{cc}
\mathsf{pw} \in \mathbb{Z}_q & pw = g^{\mathsf{pw}}
\end{array}
$$

$$
\mathsf{PW}^{\mathsf{as}} = \mathcal{G}(A\|S\|pw), \mathsf{PW}^{\mathsf{sa}} = \mathcal{G}(S\|A\|pw) \in \mathbb{G}
$$

$$
\begin{array}{cc}
\mathsf{accept} \leftarrow \mathsf{false} & \mathsf{accept} \leftarrow \mathsf{false}
\end{array}
$$

$$
\begin{array}{ccc}
x \xleftarrow{R} \mathbb{Z}_q, X \leftarrow g^x & & y \xleftarrow{R} \mathbb{Z}_q, Y \leftarrow g^y \\
Y \leftarrow Y^\star / \mathsf{PW}^{\mathsf{sa}} & \xleftarrow{\ S, Y^\star\ } & Y^\star \leftarrow Y \times \mathsf{PW}^{\mathsf{sa}} \\
X^\star \leftarrow X \times \mathsf{PW}^{\mathsf{as}} & &
\end{array}
$$

$$
r \xleftarrow{R} \mathbb{Z}_q, R \leftarrow g^r, \rho = f(R)
$$

$$
e = \mathcal{H}_1(A\|S\|X^\star\|Y^\star\|\rho\|pw\|Y^x)
$$

$$
\begin{array}{ccc}
s = r - e \cdot \mathsf{pw} \bmod q & \xrightarrow{\ A, X^\star, \rho, s\ } & X \leftarrow X^\star / \mathsf{PW}^{\mathsf{as}} \\
& & e = \mathcal{H}_1(A\|S\|X^\star\|Y^\star\|\rho\|pw\|Y^x) \\
& & \text{if } \rho = f(g^s pw^e), \\
& & \qquad \text{then } \mathsf{accept} \leftarrow \mathsf{true}
\end{array}
$$

$$
\begin{array}{cc}
sk = \mathcal{H}(A\|S\|X^\star\|Y^\star\|\rho\|pw\|Y^x) & sk = \mathcal{H}(A\|S\|X^\star\|Y^\star\|\rho\|pw\|X^y)
\end{array}
$$

$$
\mathsf{accept} \leftarrow \mathsf{true}
$$

Fig. 4. An execution of the VB-EKE protocol.

From a more practical point of view, this inversion better suits the Transport Layer Security (TLS) protocol [22]. The flows of the VB-EKE protocol thus have to comply with the key-exchange phase, which happens right after the *hello* flows (the first is from the client to the server, then the second goes back from the server to the client) and precedes the *finish* phase (the first *finish* message is again from the client to the server). In short, the first message of the VB-EKE protocol would simply map to the *ServerKeyExchange* flows while the second message to the *ClientKeyExchange* message.

5.2   Capturing the Client Password

The above modified scheme does not really increase the communication cost, since additional data can be concatenated to existing flows. But both parties have more computation to do, and namely a few exponentiations. The password-verifier relation can be more efficient, using any one-way function. However, for such a general function, a zero-knowledge proof of knowledge of the password may not be easy to perform. But the zero-knowledge property is not required, if we move to the one-time password scenario: $f(pw)$ is first used as a common password, then the client eventually reveals the password, which will thereafter be the future common data (or verifier) if $pw = f^n(\mathsf{seed})$ [17]. The computation of $f^n(pw)$ is performed by a one-time password generator which derives

$$\begin{array}{cc}
\underline{Client} & \underline{Server} \\
\end{array}$$

pw $\in$ Password, $n, pw_n = f^n(\text{pw})$ $\qquad n, pw = f(pw_n)$

$\text{PW}^{\text{as}} = \mathcal{G}(A\|S\|pw), \text{PW}^{\text{sa}} = \mathcal{G}(S\|A\|pw) \in \mathbb{G}$

accept $\leftarrow$ false $\qquad\qquad\qquad$ accept $\leftarrow$ false

$x \xleftarrow{R} \mathbb{Z}_q, X \leftarrow g^x \qquad\qquad y \xleftarrow{R} \mathbb{Z}_q, Y \leftarrow g^y$

n correct? $\xleftarrow{\quad S, Y^\star, n \quad} Y^\star \leftarrow Y \times \text{PW}^{\text{sa}}$

$Y \leftarrow Y^\star / \text{PW}^{\text{sa}}$

$X^\star \leftarrow X \times \text{PW}^{\text{as}}$

$s = \mathcal{H}_1(A\|S\|X^\star\|Y^\star\|pw\|Y^x)$

$c = E_s(pw_n) \xrightarrow{\quad A, X^\star, c \quad} X \leftarrow X^\star / \text{PW}^{\text{as}}$

$\qquad\qquad\qquad\qquad\qquad s = \mathcal{H}_1(A\|S\|X^\star\|Y^\star\|pw\|Y^x)$

$\qquad\qquad\qquad\qquad\qquad p = D_s(c), \text{if } pw = f(p),$

$\qquad\qquad\qquad\qquad\qquad \text{then } pw \leftarrow p, n \leftarrow n - 1,$

$\qquad\qquad\qquad\qquad\qquad \text{accept} \leftarrow \text{true}$

$sk = \mathcal{H}(A\|S\|X^\star\|Y^\star\|pw\|Y^x) \qquad sk = \mathcal{H}(A\|S\|X^\star\|Y^\star\|pw\|X^y)$

accept $\leftarrow$ true

Fig. 5. An execution of the OPKeyX protocol.

successive passwords from a seed. Since one-time password generators do not require reader devices they are much more adapted for the Grid environment than contact tokens (e.g, smart-card, USB tokens). This discussion leads to the One-time Password-enhanced version of VB-EKE which is proposed on Figure 5. The communication of the password has indeed to be sent in a private way, since it will become the future common data, hence the use of an ephemeral session key, which is trivially semantically secure (due to Theorem 2).

6   Conclusion

This paper provides strong security arguments to support the EKE-like protocols being standardized by the IEEE P1363.2 Standard working group (namely the PPK series). We have reached this aim by slightly modifying the original AuthA protocol (the two encryption primitives are instantiated using separate mask generation functions but derived from a unique shared password) to be able to achieve the security notion of forward-secrecy in a provably-secure way. Our result is a slight departure from previously known results on EKE-like structures since the security of AuthA is now based on the Gap Diffie-Hellman problem. Moreover, we have extended AuthA into a One-time Password-authentication and Key eXchange (OPKeyX) technology which allows a user to securely log into his account using a remote un-trusted computer and limits the damages of corruption of the server.

Acknowledgments

The authors would like to thanks Frank Siebenlist for invaluable discussions related to Grid computing. The first and third authors have been supported in part by the European Commission through the IST Programme under Contract IST-2002-507932 ECRYPT. The second author was supported by the Director, Office of Science, Office of Advanced Scientific Computing Research, Mathematical Information and Computing Sciences Division, of the U.S. Department of Energy under Contract No. DE-AC03-76SF00098. This document is report LBNL-56212. Disclaimer available at http://www-library.lbl.gov/disclaimer.

References

1. M. Bellare, D. Pointcheval, and P. Rogaway. Authenticated Key Exchange Secure Against Dictionary Attacks. In *Eurocrypt '00*, LNCS 1807, pages 139–155. Springer-Verlag, Berlin, 2000.
2. M. Bellare and P. Rogaway. The AuthA Protocol for Password-Based Authenticated Key Exchange. Contributions to IEEE P1363. March 2000.
3. S. M. Bellovin and M. Merritt. Encrypted Key Exchange: Password-Based Protocols Secure against Dictionary Attacks. In *Proc. of the Symposium on Security and Privacy*, pages 72–84. IEEE, 1992.
4. S. M. Bellovin and M. Merritt. Augmented Encrypted Key Exchange: A Password-Based Protocol Secure against Dictionary Attacks and Password File Compromise. In *Proc. of the 1st CCS*, pages 244–250. ACM Press, New York, 1993.
5. V. Boyko, P. MacKenzie, and S. Patel. Provably Secure Password Authenticated Key Exchange Using Diffie-Hellman. In *Eurocrypt '00*, LNCS 1807, pages 156–171. Springer-Verlag, Berlin, 2000.
6. E. Bresson, O. Chevassut, and D. Pointcheval. Security proofs for an efficient password-based key exchange. In *Proc. of the 10th CCS*, pages 241–250. ACM Press, New York, 2003.
7. E. Bresson, O. Chevassut, and D. Pointcheval. New Security Results on Encrypted Key Exchange. In *PKC '04*, LNCS, pages 145–159. Springer-Verlag, Berlin, 2004.
8. L. Fang, S. Meder, O. Chevassut, and F. Siebenlist. Secure Password-based Authenticated key Exchange for Web Services In *Proc. of the ACM Workshop on Secure Web Services*, 2004.
9. I. Foster and C. Kesselman. *The Grid 2: Blueprint for a New Computing Infrastructure*. Morgan Kaufmann, 2004.
10. I. Foster, C. Kesselman, G. Tsudik, and S. Tuecke. Security Architecture for Computational Grids. In *Proc. of the 5th CCS*, pages 83–92. ACM Press, New York, 1998.
11. I. Foster, C. Kesselman, and S. Tuecke. The Anatomy of the Grid: Enabling Scalable Virtual Organizations. *International J. Supercomputer Applications*, 15(3), 2001.
12. M. Girault and J. Stern. On the Length of Cryptographic Hash-Values used in Identification Schemes. In *Crypto '94*, LNCS 839, pages 202–215. Springer-Verlag, Berlin, 1994.
13. The Global Grid Forum (GGF). http://www.ggf.org.
14. N. Haller, C. Metz, P. Nesser, and M. Straw. *RFC 2289: A One-Time Password System*. Internet Activities Board, February 1998.

15. IEEE Standard 1363.2 Study Group. Password-Based Public-Key Cryptography. http://grouper.ieee.org/groups/1363/passwdPK.
16. J. Katz, R. Ostrovsky, and M. Yung. Forward secrecy in password-only key exchange protocols. In *SCN'02*, LNCS 2576, pages 29–44. Springer-Verlag, Berlin, 2002.
17. L. Lamport. Password Authentication with Insecure Communication. *Communications of the ACM 24*, 11:770–771, November 1981.
18. P. D. MacKenzie. The PAK suite: Protocols for password-authenticated key exchange. Technical Report 2002-46, DIMACS, 2002.
19. The Oasis standard body. http://www.oasis-open.org.
20. T. Okamoto and D. Pointcheval. The Gap-Problems: a New Class of Problems for the Security of Cryptographic Schemes. In *PKC '01*, LNCS 1992. Springer-Verlag, Berlin, 2001.
21. C. P. Schnorr. Efficient Signature Generation by Smart Cards. *Journal of Cryptology*, 4(3):161–174, 1991.
22. M. Steiner, P. Buhler, T. Eirich, and M. Waidner. Secure Password-Based Cipher Suite for TLS. *ACM Transactions on Information and System Security (TISSEC)*, 4(2):134–157, 2001.

Password-Based Authenticated Key Exchange in the Three-Party Setting

Michel Abdalla, Pierre-Alain Fouque, and David Pointcheval

Departement d'Informatique
École normale supérieure
45 Rue d'Ulm, 75230 Paris Cedex 05, France
{Michel.Abdalla,Pierre-Alain.Fouque,David.Pointcheval}@ens.fr
http://www.di.ens.fr/users/{mabdalla,fouque,pointche}

Abstract. Password-based authenticated key exchange are protocols which are designed to be secure even when the secret key or password shared between two users is drawn from a small set of values. Due to the low entropy of passwords, such protocols are always subject to on-line guessing attacks. In these attacks, the adversary may succeed with non-negligible probability by guessing the password shared between two users during its on-line attempt to impersonate one of these users. The main goal of password-based authenticated key exchange protocols is to restrict the adversary to this case only. In this paper, we consider password-based authenticated key exchange in the three-party scenario, in which the users trying to establish a secret do not share a password between themselves but only with a trusted server. Towards our goal, we recall some of the existing security notions for password-based authenticated key exchange protocols and introduce new ones that are more suitable to the case of generic constructions. We then present a natural generic construction of a three-party protocol, based on any two-party authenticated key exchange protocol, and prove its security without making use of the Random Oracle model. To the best of our knowledge, the new protocol is the first provably-secure password-based protocol in the three-party setting.

Keywords: Password, authenticated key exchange, key distribution, multi-party protocols.

1   Introduction

Motivation. A fundamental problem in cryptography is how to communicate securely over an insecure channel, which might be controlled by an adversary. It is common in this scenario for two parties to encrypt and authenticate their messages in order to protect the privacy and authenticity of these messages. One way of doing so is by using public-key encryption and signatures, but the cost associated with these primitives may be too high for certain applications. Another way of addressing this problem is by means of a key exchange protocol, in which users establish a common key which they can then use in their applications.

S. Vaudenay (Ed.): PKC 2005, LNCS 3386, pp. 65–84, 2005.

In practice, one finds several flavors of key exchange protocols, each with its own benefits and drawbacks. Among the most popular ones is the 3-party *Kerberos* authentication system [25]. Another one is the 2-party SIGMA protocol [17] used as the basis for the signature-based modes of the Internet Key Exchange (IKE) protocol. Yet another flavor of key exchange protocols which has received significant attention recently are those based on passwords.

PASSWORD-BASED KEY EXCHANGE. Password-based key exchange protocols assume a more realistic scenario in which secret keys are not uniformly distributed over a large space, but rather chosen from a small set of possible values (a four-digit pin, for example). They also seem more convenient since human-memorable passwords are simpler to use than, for example, having additional cryptographic devices capable of storing high-entropy secret keys. The vast majority of protocols found in practice do not account, however, for such scenario and are often subject to so-called *dictionary* attacks. Dictionary attacks are attacks in which an adversary tries to break the security of a scheme by a brute-force method, in which it tries all possible combinations of secret keys in a given small set of values (i.e., the dictionary). Even though these attacks are not very effective in the case of high-entropy keys, they can be very damaging when the secret key is a password since the attacker has a non-negligible chance of winning. Such attacks are usually divided in two categories: *off-line* and *online* dictionary attacks.

To address this problem, several protocols have been designed to be secure even when the secret key is a password. The goal of these protocols is to restrict the adversary's success to on-line guessing attacks only. In these attacks, the adversary must be present and interact with the system in order to be able to verify whether its guess is correct. The security in these systems usually relies on a policy of invalidating or blocking the use of a password if a certain number of failed attempts has occurred.

3-PARTY PASSWORD-BASED KEY EXCHANGE. Passwords are mostly used because they are easier to remember by humans than secret keys with high entropy. Consequently, users prefer to remember very few passwords but not many. However, in scenarios where a user wants to communicate with many other users, then the number of passwords that he or she would need to remember would be linear in the number of possible partners. In order to limit the number of passwords that each user needs to remember, we consider in this paper password-based authenticated key exchange in the 3-party model, where each user only shares a password with a trusted server. The main advantage of this solution is that it provides each user with the capability of communicating securely with other users in the system while only requiring it to remember a single password. This seems to be a more realistic scenario in practice than the one in which users are expected to share multiple passwords, one for each party with which it may communicate privately. Its main drawback is that the server is needed during the establishment of all communication as in the Needham and Schroeder protocol.

KEY PRIVACY. One potential disadvantage of a 3-party model is that the privacy of the communication with respect to the server is not always guaranteed. Since we want to trust as little as possible the third party, we develop a new notion called key privacy which roughly means that, even though the server's help is required to establish a session key between two users in the system, the server should not be able to gain any information on the value of that session key. Here we assume that the server is honest but curious. Please note that key distribution schemes usually do *not* achieve this property.

INSIDER ATTACKS. One of the main differences between the 2-party and the 3-party scenarios is the existence of insider attacks. To better understand the power of these attacks, consider the protocol in Figure 1, based on the encrypted key exchange of Bellovin and Merritt[9], in which the server simply decrypts the message it receives and re-encrypts it under the other user's password. In this protocol, it is easy to see that one can mount an off-line dictionary by simply playing the role of one of the involved parties. Notice that both A and B can obtain the necessary information to mount an off-line dictionary attack against each other simply by eavesdropping on the messages that are sent out by the server. More specifically, A and B can respectively learn the values $X_S^\star = \mathcal{E}_{PW_B}(X_S)$ and $Y_S^\star = \mathcal{E}_{PW_A}(Y_S)$ and mount a dictionary attack against each other using the fact that $X_S = X_A$ and $Y_S = Y_B$. Insider attacks do not need be considered explicitly in the case of 2-party protocols due to the independence among the passwords shared between pairs of honest users and those shared with malicious users.

A NEW SECURITY MODEL. In order to analyze the security of 3-party password-based authenticated key exchange protocols, we put forward a new security model and define two notions of security: semantic security of the session key and key privacy with respect to the server. The first of these notions is the usual one and is a straight-forward generalization of the equivalent notion in the 2-party

Public information: $\mathbb{G}, g, p, \mathcal{E}, \mathcal{D}, H$

Client A	Server	Client B
$pw_A \in$ Password	$pw_A, pw_B \in$ Password	$pw_B \in$ Password

$$x \xleftarrow{R} Z_p \; ; \; X_A \leftarrow g^x$$
$$X_A^\star \leftarrow \mathcal{E}_{pw_A}(X_A)$$

$$\xrightarrow{\quad X_A^\star \quad}$$

$$y \xleftarrow{R} Z_p \; ; \; Y_B \leftarrow g^y$$
$$Y_B^\star \leftarrow \mathcal{E}_{pw_B}(Y_B)$$

$$\xleftarrow{\quad Y_B^\star \quad}$$

$$X_S \leftarrow \mathcal{D}_{pw_A}(X_A^\star)$$
$$Y_S \leftarrow \mathcal{D}_{pw_B}(Y_B^\star)$$
$$Y_S^\star \leftarrow \mathcal{E}_{pw_A}(Y_S)$$
$$X_S^\star \leftarrow \mathcal{E}_{pw_B}(X_S)$$

$$\xleftarrow{\quad Y_S^\star \quad}$$

$$\xrightarrow{\quad X_S^\star \quad}$$

$$Y_A \leftarrow \mathcal{D}_{pw_A}(Y_S^\star)$$
$$K_A \leftarrow Y_A^x$$
$$SK_A \leftarrow H(A \| B \| S \| K_A)$$

$$X_B \leftarrow \mathcal{D}_{pw_B}(X_S^\star)$$
$$K_B \leftarrow X_B^y$$
$$SK_B \leftarrow H(A \| B \| S \| K_B)$$

Fig. 1. An insecure 3-party password-based encrypted key exchange protocol.

password-based authenticated key exchange model. The second one is new and particular to the new setting, and captures the privacy of the key with respect to the trusted server to which all passwords are known.

A GENERIC CONSTRUCTION. In this paper, we consider a generic construction of 3-party password-based protocol. Our construction is a natural one, building upon existing 2-party password-based key exchange and 3-party symmetric key distribution schemes, to achieve provable security in the strongest sense. Moreover, our construction is also modular in the sense that it can be broken into two parts, a 3-party password-based key distribution protocol and 2-party authenticated key exchange. The second part is only needed if key privacy with respect to the server is required.

THE NEED FOR NEW SECURITY NOTIONS. Surprisingly, the proof of security for the new scheme *does not* follow from the usual security notions for the underlying schemes as one would expect and requires a *new* and *stronger* notion of security for the underlying 2-party password-based scheme (see Section 2). In fact, this new security notion is not specific to password-based schemes and is one of the main contributions of this paper. Fortunately, we observe that most existing 2-party password-based schemes do in fact satisfy this new property [11, 13, 16, 21]. More specifically, only a few small changes are required in their proof in order to achieve security in the new model. The bounds obtained in their proof remain essentially unchanged.

Contributions. In this paper, we consider password-based (implicitly) authenticated key exchange in the 3-party model, where each user only shares a password with a trusted server.

NEW SECURITY MODELS. Towards our goal, we put forth a new formal security model that is appropriate for the 3-party password-based authenticated key exchange scenario and give precise definitions of what it means for it to be secure. Our model builds upon those of Bellare and Rogaway [7, 8] for key distribution schemes and that of Bellare, Pointcheval, and Rogaway [5] for password-based authenticated key exchange.

NEW SECURITY NOTIONS. We also present a new and stronger model for 2-party authenticated key exchange protocols, which we call the Real-Or-Random model. Our new model is provably stronger than the existing model, to which we refer to as the Find-Then-Guess model, in the sense that a scheme proven secure in the new model is also secure in the existing model. However, the reverse is not necessarily true due to an unavoidable non-constant factor loss in the reduction. Such losses in the reduction are extremely important in the case of password-based protocols.

A GENERIC CONSTRUCTION IN THE STANDARD MODEL. We present a generic and natural framework for constructing a 3-party password-based authenticated key exchange protocol from any secure 2-party password-based one. We do so by combining a 3-party key distribution scheme, an authenticated Diffie-Hellman key exchange protocol, and the 2-party password-based authenticated key exchange protocol. The proof of security relies solely on the security properties of underlying primitives it uses and does not assume the Random Oracle model [6]. Hence, when appropriately instantiated, this construction yields a secure protocol in the standard model.

A SEPARATION BETWEEN KEY DISTRIBUTION AND KEY EXCHANGE. In addition to semantic security of the session key, we present a new property, called key privacy, which is specific to key exchange protocols. This new notion captures in a quantitative way the idea that the session key shared between two instances should be only known to these two instances and no one else, including the trusted server.

Related Work. Password-based authenticated key exchange has been extensively studied in the last few years [5, 10–15, 18–20, 23, 26], with a portion of the work dealing with the subject of group key exchange and the vast majority dealing with different aspects of 2-party key exchange. Only a few of them (e.g., [12, 18, 26]) consider password-based protocols in the 3-party setting, but none of their schemes enjoys provable security. In fact, our generic construction seems to be the first provably-secure 3-party password-based authenticated key exchange protocol.

Another related line of research is authenticated key exchange *in the 3-party setting*. The first work in this area is the protocol of Needham and Schroeder [22], which inspired the *Kerberos* distributed system. Later, Bellare and Rogaway introduced a formal security model in this scenario along with a construction of the first provably-secure symmetric-key-based key distribution scheme [8]. In this paper, we consider the special but important case in which the secret keys are drawn from a small set of values.

Organization. In Section 2, we recall the existing security model for 2-party password-based authenticated key exchange and introduce a new one. Next, in Section 3, we introduce new models for 3-party password-based authenticated key exchange. Section 4 then presents our generic construction of a 3-party password-based authenticated key exchange protocol, called GPAKE, along with the security claims and suggestions on how to instantiate it. Some future extensions of this work are presented in Section 5. In Appendix A, we describe the cryptographic primitives and assumptions on which GPAKE is based. We conclude by presenting some results in Appendix B regarding the relation between the existing security notions and the new ones being introduced in this paper.

2   Security Models
for 2-Party Password-Based Key Exchange

A secure 2-party password-based key exchange is a 2PAKE protocol where the parties use their password in order to derive a common session key sk that will be used to build secure channels. Loosely speaking, such protocols are said to be secure against *dictionary attacks* if the advantage of an attacker in distinguishing a real session key from a random key is less than $O(n/|\mathcal{D}|) + \varepsilon(k)$ where $|\mathcal{D}|$ is the size of the dictionary $\mathcal{D}$, n is the number of active sessions and $\varepsilon(k)$ is a negligible function depending on the security parameter k.

In this section, we recall the security model for 2-party password-based authenticated key exchange protocols introduced by Bellare, Pointcheval, and Rogaway (BPR) [5] and introduce a new one. For reasons that will soon become apparent, we refer to the new model as the Real-Or-Random (ROR) model and to the BPR model as the Find-Then-Guess (FTG) model, following the terminology of Bellare *et al.* for symmetric encryption schemes [4].

2.1   Communication Model

PROTOCOL PARTICIPANTS. Each participant in the 2-party password-based key exchange is either a client $C \in \mathcal{C}$ or a server $S \in \mathcal{S}$. The set of all users or participants $\mathcal{U}$ is the union $\mathcal{C} \cup \mathcal{S}$.

LONG-LIVED KEYS. Each client $C \in \mathcal{C}$ holds a password pw_C. Each server $S \in \mathcal{S}$ holds a vector $pw_S = \langle pw_S[C] \rangle_{C \in \mathcal{C}}$ with an entry for each client, where $pw_S[C]$ is the transformed-password, as defined in [5]. In a symmetric model, $pw_S[C] = pw_C$, but they may be different in some schemes. pw_C and pw_S are also called the long-lived keys of client C and server S.

PROTOCOL EXECUTION. The interaction between an adversary A and the protocol participants occurs only via oracle queries, which model the adversary capabilities in a real attack. During the execution, the adversary may create several concurrent instances of a participant. These queries are as follows, where U^i denotes the instance i of a participant U:

- *Execute*(C^i, S^j): This query models passive attacks in which the attacker eavesdrops on honest executions between a client instance C^i and a server instance S^j. The output of this query consists of the messages that were exchanged during the honest execution of the protocol.
- *Send*(U^i, m): This query models an active attack, in which the adversary may intercept a message and then either modify it, create a new one, or simply forward it to the intended participant. The output of this query is the message that the participant instance U^i would generate upon receipt of message m.

2.2   Security Definitions

PARTNERING. We use the notion of partnering based on session identifications (*sid*), which says that two instances are partnered if they hold the same non-null *sid*. In practice, the *sid* is taken to be the partial transcript of the conversation between the client and the server instances before the acceptance.

FRESHNESS. In order to properly formalize security notions for the session key, one has to be careful to avoid cases in which adversary can trivially break the security of the scheme. For example, an adversary who is trying to distinguish the session key of an instance U^i from a random key can trivially do so if it obtains the key for that instance through a *Reveal* query (see definition below) to instance U^i or its partner. Instead of explicitly defining a notion of freshness and mandating the adversary to only perform tests on *fresh* instances as in previous work, we opted to embed that notion inside the definition of the oracles.

Semantic Security in the Find-Then-Guess Model. This is the definition currently being used in the literature. In order to measure the semantic security of the session key of user instance, the adversary is given access to two additional oracles: the *Reveal* oracle, which models the misuse of session keys by a user, and the *Test* oracle, which tries to capture the adversary's ability (or inability) to tell apart a real session key from a random one. Let b be a bit chosen uniformly at random at the beginning of the experiment defining the semantic security in the Find-Then-Guess model. These oracles are defined as follows.

- *Reveal*(U^i): If a session key is not defined for instance U^i or if a *Test* query was asked to either U^i or to its partner, then return $\perp$. Otherwise, return the session key held by the instance U^i.
- *Test*(U^i): If no session key for instance U^i is defined or if a *Reveal* query was asked to either U^i or to its partner, then return the undefined symbol $\perp$. Otherwise, return the session key for instance U^i if $b = 1$ or a random of key of the same size if $b = 0$.

The adversary in this case is allowed to ask multiple queries to the *Execute*, *Reveal*, and *Send* oracles, but it is restricted to ask only a *single* query to the *Test* oracle. The goal of the adversary is to guess the value of the hidden bit b used by the *Test* oracle. The adversary is considered successful if it guesses b correctly.

Let SUCC denote the event in which the adversary is successful. The **ftg-ake-advantage** of an adversary $\mathcal{A}$ in violating the semantic security of the protocol P in the Find-Then-Guess sense and the **advantage function** of the protocol P, when passwords are drawn from a dictionary $\mathcal{D}$, are respectively

$$\mathbf{Adv}_{P,\mathcal{D}}^{\text{ftg}-\text{ake}}(\mathcal{A}) = 2 \Pr[\,\text{SUCC}\,] - 1 \text{ and } \mathbf{Adv}_{P,\mathcal{D}}^{\text{ftg}-\text{ake}}(t, R) = \max_{\mathcal{A}} \{\, \mathbf{Adv}_{P,\mathcal{D}}^{\text{ftg}-\text{ake}}(\mathcal{A}) \,\},$$

where the maximum is over all $\mathcal{A}$ with time-complexity at most t and using resources at most R (such as the number of queries to its oracles). The definition of time-complexity that we use henceforth is the usual one, which includes the maximum of all execution times in the experiments defining the security plus the code size [1]. Note that the advantage of an adversary that simply guesses the bit b is 0 in the above definition due to the rescaling of the probabilities.

Semantic Security in the Real-Or-Random Model. This is a new definition. In the Real-Or-Random model, we only allow the adversary to ask *Execute*, *Send*, and *Test* queries. In other words, the *Reveal* oracle that exists in the Find-Then-Guess model is no longer available to the adversary. Instead, we allow the adversary to ask as many *Test* queries as it wants to different instances. All *Test* queries in this case will be answered using the same value for the hidden bit b that was chosen at the beginning . That is, the keys returned by the *Test* oracle are either all real or all random. However, in the random case, the same random key value should be returned for *Test* queries that are asked to two instances which are partnered. *Please note that the Test oracle is the oracle modeling the misuse of keys by a user in this case.* The goal of the adversary is still the same: to guess the value of the hidden bit b used to answer *Test* queries. The adversary is considered successful if it guesses b correctly.

Let SUCC denote the event in which the adversary is successful. The **ror-ake-advantage** $\mathbf{Adv}_{P,\mathcal{D}}^{\mathrm{ror-ake}}(\mathcal{A})$ of an adversary $\mathcal{A}$ in violating the semantic security of the protocol P in the Real-Or-Random sense and the **advantage function** $\mathbf{Adv}_{P,\mathcal{D}}^{\mathrm{ror-ake}}(t, R)$ of the protocol P are then defined as in the previous definition.

Relation Between Notions. As we prove in Appendix B, the Real-Or-Random (ROR) security model is actually stronger than the Find-Then-Guess (FTG) security model. More specifically, we show that proofs of security in the ROR model can be easily translated into proofs of security in the FTG model with only a 2 factor loss in the reduction (see Lemma 1). The reverse, however, is not necessarily true since the reduction is not security preserving. There is a loss of non-constant factor in the reduction (see Lemma 2). Moreover, the loss in the reduction cannot be avoided as there exist schemes for which we can prove such a loss in security exists (see Proposition 1).

To better understand the gap between the two notions, imagine a password-based scheme that was proven secure in the FTG model. By definition, the advantage of any adversary is at most $O(n/|\mathcal{D}|) + \varepsilon(k)$, where n is the number of active sessions and $\varepsilon(k)$ is a negligible term. By applying the reduction, we can show that no adversary can do better than $O(n^2/|\mathcal{D}|) + n \cdot \varepsilon(k)$, which is not enough to guarantee the security of the same scheme in the ROR model. Note that such a gap is not as important in the case where high-entropy keys are used since both terms in the expression would be negligible.

As a consequence, we cannot take for granted the security of the existing schemes and new proofs of security need be provided. Fortunately, we would like to point out here that the security proof for several of the existing schemes can be easily modified to meet the new security goals with essentially the same bounds. The reason for that is that the security proofs of most existing password-based schemes in fact prove something stronger than what is required by the security model. More specifically, most proofs generally show that not only the session key being tested looks random, but all the keys that may be involved in a reveal query also look random to an adversary that does not know the secret password, thus satisfying the security requirements of our new model. In particular, this is the case for the KOY protocol [16] and its generalization [13], and some other schemes based on the encrypted key exchange scheme of Bellovin and Merritt [9] (e.g., [11, 21]).

Since most existing password-based schemes do seem to achieve security in the new and stronger security model and since the latter appears to be more applicable to situations in which one wishes to use a password-based key exchange protocol as a black box, we suggest the use of our new model when proving the security of new password-based schemes.

3   Security Models
for 3-Party Password-Based Key Exchange

In this section, we put forward new formal security models for 3-party password-authenticated key exchange and key distribution protocols. Our models are generalizations of the model of Bellare and Rogaway [8] for 3-party key distribution schemes to the password case and that of Bellare, Pointcheval, and Rogaway [5] for 2-party password-based authenticated key exchange.

3.1   Protocol Syntax

PROTOCOL PARTICIPANTS. Each participant in a 3-party password-based key exchange is either a client $U \in \mathcal{U}$ or a trusted server $S \in \mathcal{S}$. The set of clients $\mathcal{U}$ is made up of two disjoint sets: $\mathcal{C}$, the set of honest clients, and $\mathcal{E}$, the set of malicious clients. For simplicity, and without loss of generality[1], we assume the set $\mathcal{S}$ to contain only a single trusted server.

The inclusion of the malicious set $\mathcal{E}$ among the participants is one the main differences between the 2-party and the 3-party models. Such inclusion is needed in the 3-party model in order to cope with the possibility of insider attacks. The set of malicious users did not need to be considered in the 2-party due to the independence among the passwords shared between pairs of honest participants and those shared with malicious users.

LONG-LIVED KEYS. Each participant $U \in \mathcal{U}$ holds a password pw_U. Each server $S \in \mathcal{S}$ holds a vector $\mathsf{pw}_S = \langle pw_S[U] \rangle_{U \in \mathcal{U}}$ with an entry for each client, where $pw_S[U]$ is the transformed-password, following the definition in [5]. In a symmetric model, $pw_S[U] = pw_U$, but they may be different in some schemes. The set of passwords pw_E, where $E \in \mathcal{E}$, is assumed to be known by the adversary.

3.2   Communication Model

The interaction between an adversary A and the protocol participants occurs only via oracle queries, which model the adversary capabilities in a real attack. These queries are as follows:

- *Execute*$(U_1^{i_1}, S^j, U_2^{i_2})$: This query models passive attacks in which the attacker eavesdrops on honest executions among the client instances $U_1^{i_1}$ and $U_2^{i_2}$ and trusted server instance S^j. The output of this query consists of the messages that were exchanged during the honest execution of the protocol.
- *SendClient*(U^i, m): This query models an active attack, in which the adversary may intercept a message and then modify it, create a new one, or simply forward it to the intended client. The output of this query is the message that client instance U^i would generate upon receipt of message m.
- *SendServer*(S^j, m): This query models an active attack against a server. It outputs the message that server instance S^j would generate upon receipt of message m.

---

[1] This is so because we are working in the concurrent model and because all servers in the general case know all users' passwords.

3.3 Semantic Security

The security definitions presented here build upon those of Bellare and Rogaway [7, 8] and that of Bellare, Pointcheval, and Rogaway [5].

NOTATION. Following [7, 8], an instance U^i is said to be *opened* if a query $Reveal(U^i)$ has been made by the adversary. We say an instance U^i is *unopened* if it is not *opened*. Similarly, we say a participant U is *corrupted* if a query $Corrupt(U)$ has been made by the adversary. A participant U is said to be *uncorrupted* if it is not *corrupted*. We say an instance U^i has *accepted* if it goes into an accept mode after receiving the last expected protocol message.

PARTNERING. Our definition of partnering follows that of [5], which uses session identifications (*sid*). More specifically, two instances U_1^i and U_2^j are said to be partners if the following conditions are met: (1) Both U_1^i and U_2^j accept; (2) Both U_1^i and U_2^j share the same session identifications; (3) The partner identification for U_1^i is U_2^j and vice-versa; and (4) No instance other than U_1^i and U_2^j accepts with a partner identification equal to U_1^i or U_2^j. In practice, as in the 2-party case, the *sid* could be taken to be the partial transcript before the acceptance of the conversation among all the parties involved in the protocol, a solution which may require the forwarding of messages.

FRESHNESS. As in the 2-party case, we opted to embed the notion of freshness inside the definition of the oracles.

Semantic Security in Find-Then-Guess Model. This definition we give here is the straight-forward generalization of that of Bellare, Pointcheval, and Rogaway [5] for the 2-party case, combined with ideas of the model of Bellare and Rogaway [8] for 3-party key distribution. As in the 2-party case, we also define a *Reveal* oracle to model the misuse of session keys and a *Test* oracle to capture the adversary's ability to distinguish a real session key from a random one. Let b be a bit chosen uniformly at random at the beginning of the experiment defining the semantic security in the Find-Then-Guess model. These oracles are defined as follows:

- $Reveal(U^i)$: If a session key is not defined for instance U^i or if a *Test* query was asked to either U^i or to its partner, then return $\perp$. Otherwise, return the session key held by the instance U^i.
- $Test(U^i)$: If no session key is defined for instance U^i or if the intended partner of U^i is part of the malicious set or if a *Reveal* query was asked to either U^i or to its partner, then return the invalid symbol $\perp$. Otherwise, return either the session key for instance U^i if $b = 1$ or a random of key of the same size if $b = 0$.

Consider an execution of the key exchange protocol P by an adversary $\mathcal{A}$, in which the latter is given access to the *Reveal*, *Execute*, *SendClient*, *SendServer*, and *Test* oracles and asks a single *Test* query, and outputs a guess bit b'. Such an adversary is said to win the experiment defining the semantic security if $b' = b$, where b is the hidden bit used by the *Test* oracle.

Let SUCC denote the event in which the adversary wins this game. The **ftg-ake-advantage $\mathbf{Adv}_{P,\mathcal{D}}^{\mathrm{ftg-ake}}(\mathcal{A})$** of an adversary $\mathcal{A}$ in violating the semantic security of the protocol P in the Find-Then-Guess sense and the **advantage function** $\mathbf{Adv}_{P,\mathcal{D}}^{ftg-ake}(t, R)$ of the protocol P are then defined as in previous definitions.

We say a 3-party password-based key exchange protocol P is semantically secure in the Find-Then-Guess sense if the advantage $\mathbf{Adv}_{P,\mathcal{D}}^{ftg-ake}$ is only negligibly larger than $kn/|\mathcal{D}|$, where n is number of active sessions and k is a constant. Note that $k = 1$ in the best scenario since an adversary that simply guesses the password in each of the active sessions has an advantage of $n/|\mathcal{D}|$.

Semantic Security in Real-Or-Random Model. This is a new definition. In the Real-Or-Random model, *Reveal* queries are no longer allowed and are replaced by *Test* queries. In this case, however, the adversary is allowed to ask as many *Test* queries as it wants.

The modifications to the *Test* oracle are as follows. If a *Test* query is asked to a client instance that has not *accepted*, then return the undefined $\perp$. If a *Test* query is asked to an instance of an honest client whose intended partner is dishonest or to an instance of a dishonest client, then return the real session key. Otherwise, the *Test* query returns either the real session key if $b = 1$ and a random one if $b = 0$, where b is the hidden bit selected at random prior to the first call. However, when $b = 0$, the same random key value should be returned for *Test* queries that are asked to two instances which are partnered. The goal of the adversary is still the same: to guess the value of the hidden bit used by the *Test* oracle. The adversary is considered successful if it guesses b correctly.

Consider an execution of the key exchange protocol P by an adversary A, in which the latter is given access to the *Execute*, *SendClient*, *SendServer*, and *Test* oracles, and outputs a guess bit b'. Such an adversary is said to win the experiment defining the semantic security in the ROR sense if $b' = b$, where b is the hidden bit used by the *Test* oracle. Let Succ denote the event in which the adversary wins this game. The **ror-ake-advantage** $\mathbf{Adv}_{P,\mathcal{D}}^{ror-ake}(\mathcal{A})$ of an adversary $\mathcal{A}$ in violating the semantic security of the protocol P in the Real-Or-Random sense and the **advantage function** $\mathbf{Adv}_{P,\mathcal{D}}^{ror-ake}(t, R)$ of the protocol P are then defined as in previous definitions.

3.4   Key Privacy with Respect to the Server

Differently from previous work, we define the notion of key privacy to capture, in a quantitative way, the idea that the session key shared between two instances should only be known to these two instances and no one else, including the trusted server. The goal of this new notion is to limit the amount of trust put into the server. That is, even though we rely on the server to help clients establish session keys between themselves, we still want to guarantee the privacy of these session keys with respect to the server. In fact, this is the main difference between a key distribution protocol (in which the session key is known to the server) and a key exchange protocol (for which the session key remains unknown to the server).

In defining the notion of key privacy, we have in mind a server which knows the passwords for all users, but that behaves in an honest but curious manner.

For this reason, we imagine an adversary who has access to all the passwords as well as to the *Execute* and *SendClient* oracles but not to a *Reveal* oracle or to a *SendServer* oracle, since the latter can be easily simulated using the passwords. To capture the adversary's ability to tell apart the real session key shared between any two instances from a random one, we also introduce a new type of oracle, called *TestPair*, defined as follows, where b is a bit chosen uniformly at random at the beginning of the experiment defining the notion of key privacy.

- *TestPair*(U_1^i, U_2^j): If client instances U_1^i and U_2^j do not share the same key, then return the undefined symbol $\perp$. Otherwise, return the real session key shared between client instances U_1^i and U_2^j if $b = 1$ or a random key of the same size if $b = 0$.

Consider an execution of the key exchange protocol P by an adversary A with access to the *Execute*, *SendClient*, and *TestPair* oracles and the passwords of all users, and let b' be its output. Such an adversary is said to win the experiment defining the key privacy if $b' = b$, where b is the hidden bit used by the *TestPair* oracle. Let SUCC denote the event in which the adversary guesses b correctly. We can then define the **kp-advantage** $\mathbf{Adv}_{P,\mathcal{D}}^{\mathrm{kp-ake}}(\mathcal{A})$ of $\mathcal{A}$ in violating the key privacy of the key exchange protocol P and the **advantage function** $\mathbf{Adv}_{P,\mathcal{D}}^{\mathrm{kp-ake}}(t, R)$ of P as in previous definitions.

Finally, we say an adversary $\mathcal{A}$ succeeds in breaking the key privacy of a protocol P if $\mathbf{Adv}_{P,\mathcal{D}}^{\mathrm{kp-ake}}(\mathcal{A})$ is non-negligible.

4   A Generic Three-Party Password-Based Protocol

In this section, we introduce a generic construction of a 3-party password-based key exchange protocol in the scenario in which we have an *honest-but-curious* server. It combines a 2-party password-based key exchange, a secure key distribution protocol and a 2-party MAC-based key exchange and has several attractive features. First, it does not assume the Random Oracle (RO) model [6]. That is, if the underlying primitives do not make use of the RO model, neither does our scheme. Hence, by using schemes such as the KOY protocol [16] for the 2-party password-based key exchange and the 3-party key distribution scheme in [8], one gets a 3-part password-based protocol whose security is in the standard model. Second, if 2-party password-based key exchange protocols already exist between the server and its users in a distributed system, they can be re-used in the construction of our 3-party password-based key exchange.

Description of the Generic Solution. Our generic construction can be seen as a form of compiler transforming any secure 2-party password-based key exchange protocol P into a secure password-based 3-party key exchange protocol P' in the *honest-but-curious* security model using a secure key distribution KD, a secure MAC scheme, and generic number-theoretic operations in a group $\mathbb{G}$ for which the DDH assumption holds (see Appendix A).

The compiler, depicted in Figure 2, works as follows. First, we use the protocol P between a user A and the server S to establish a secure high-entropy

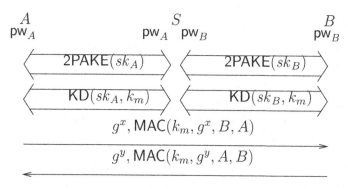

Fig. 2. GPAKE: a generic three-party password-based key exchange.

session key sk_A. Second, we use the protocol P between the server S and the user B in order to establish a session key sk_B. Third, using a key distribution KD, we have the server S first select a MAC key k_m, using the key generation of the latter, and then distribute this key to A and B using the session keys sk_A and sk_B, respectively, generated in the first two steps. Finally, A and B use a MAC-based key exchange to establish a session key CDH in an authenticated way.

Semantic Security in the Real-Or-Random Model. As the following theorem states, the generic scheme GPAKE depicted in Figure 2 is a secure 3-party password-based key exchange protocol as long as the Decisional Diffie-Hellman assumption holds in $\mathbb{G}$ and the underlying primitives it uses are secure. The proof can be found in the full version of this paper [2].

Theorem 1. *Let* 2PAKE *be a secure 2-party password-based Key Exchange,* KD *be a secure key distribution, and* MAC *be a secure MAC algorithm. Let* q_{exe} *and* q_{test} *represent the number of queries to Execute and Test oracles, and let* q_{send}^A, q_{send}^B, q_{kd}, *and* q_{ake} *represent the number of queries to the SendClient and SendServer oracles with respect to each of the two* 2PAKE *protocols, the* KD *protocol, and the final* AKE *protocol. Then,*

$$\mathbf{Adv}_{\mathsf{GPAKE},\mathcal{D}}^{\mathrm{ror-ake}}(t, q_{exe}, q_{test}, q_{send}^A, q_{send}^B, q_{kd}, q_{ake}) \leq$$

$$4 \cdot (q_{exe} + q_{kd}) \cdot \mathbf{Adv}_{\mathsf{KD}}^{\mathrm{ftg-kd}}(t, 1, 0) + 2 \cdot q_{ake} \cdot \mathbf{Adv}_{\mathsf{MAC}}^{\mathrm{euf-cma}}(t, 2, 0)$$

$$+ 2 \cdot \mathbf{Adv}_{\mathbb{G}}^{\mathrm{ddh}}(t + 8(q_{exe} + q_{ake})\tau_e) + 4 \cdot \mathbf{Adv}_{\mathsf{2PAKE},\mathcal{D}}^{\mathrm{ror-ake}}(t, q_{exe}, q_{exe} + q_{send}^A, q_{send}^A)$$

$$+ 4 \cdot \mathbf{Adv}_{\mathsf{2PAKE},\mathcal{D}}^{\mathrm{ror-ake}}(t, q_{exe}, q_{exe} + q_{send}^B, q_{send}^B) ,$$

where τ_e *denotes the exponentiation computational time in* $\mathbb{G}$.

Key Privacy with Respect to the Server. As the following theorem states, whose proof can be found in the full version of this paper [2], the generic scheme GPAKE depicted in Figure 2 has key privacy with respect to the server as long as the Decisional Diffie-Hellman assumption holds in $\mathbb{G}$.

Theorem 2. *Let* GPAKE *be the 3-party password-based authenticated key exchange scheme depicted in Figure 2. Then,*

$$\mathbf{Adv}_{\mathsf{GPAKE},\mathcal{D}}^{\mathsf{kp-ake}}(t, q_{\mathrm{exe}}, q_{\mathrm{test}}, q_{\mathrm{send}}^{A}, q_{\mathrm{send}}^{B}, q_{\mathrm{kd}}, q_{\mathrm{ake}}) \leq 2 \cdot \mathbf{Adv}_{\mathbb{G}}^{\mathsf{ddh}}(t') ,$$

where $t' = t + 8 \cdot (q_{\mathrm{exe}} + q_{\mathrm{ake}}) \cdot \tau_e$ and the other parameters are defined as in Theorem 1.

Instantiations. Several practical schemes can be used in the instantiation of the 2-party password-based key exchange of our generic construction. Among them are the KOY protocol [16] and its generalization [13], the PAK suite [21], and several other schemes based on the encrypted key exchange scheme of Bellovin and Merritt [9] (e.g., [11]).

In the instantiation of the key distribution scheme, one could use the original proposal in [8] or any other secure key distribution scheme. In particular, the server could use a chosen-ciphertext secure symmetric encryption scheme to distribute the keys to the users. Independently of the choice, one should keep in mind that the security requirements for the key distribution scheme are very weak. It only needs to provide security with respect to one session.

For the instantiation of the MAC, any particular choice that makes the MAC term in Theorem 1 negligible will do. Possible choices are the HMAC [3] or the CBC MAC.

It is important to notice that, in order for GPAKE to be secure, the underlying 2-party password-based protocol *must* be secure in the ROR model. In view of the computational gap that exists between the ROR and the FTG models (see Proposition 1), a 2-party password-based secure in the FTG model does not suffice to prove the security of GPAKE.

5   Concluding Remarks

AUTHENTICATION. In order to take (explicit) authentication into account, one can easily extend our model using definitions similar to those of Bellare *et al.* [5] for unilateral or mutual authentication. In their definition, an adversary is said to break authentication if it succeeds in making any oracle instance terminate the protocol without a partner oracle. Likewise, one could also use their generic transformation to enhance our generic construction so that it provides unilateral or mutual authentication. The drawback of using their generic transformation is that it requires the random oracle model.

MORE EFFICIENT CONSTRUCTIONS. Even though the generic construction presented in this paper is quite practical, more efficient solutions are possible. One example of such an improvement is a generic construction in which the key distribution and the final key exchange phases are combined into a single phase. One can easily think of different solutions for this scenario that are more efficient that the one we give. However, the overall gain in efficiency would not be very significant since the most expensive part of these two phases, the Diffie-Hellman protocol, seems to be necessary if key privacy with respect to the server is to be achieved. Perhaps the best way to improve the efficiency of 3-party password-based schemes is to adapt specific solutions in the 2-party model to the 3-party model, instead of treating these schemes as black boxes.

RELATION TO SIMULATION MODELS. In [24], the Find-Then-Guess model of [8] is shown to be equivalent to simulation models in the sense that a scheme that is proven secure in one model is also secure in the other model. By closely examining their proof, one can easily see that the equivalence does not apply to the case of password-based protocols due to the non-security-preserving reduction. It seems, however, that their proof of equivalence can be adapted to show the equivalence between the simulation model and the Real-Or-Random model that we introduce in this paper in the case of password-based protocols. This is also the subject of ongoing work.

Acknowledgements

The work described in this document has been supported in part by the European Commission through the IST Programme under Contract IST-2002-507932 ECRYPT.

References

1. M. Abdalla, M. Bellare, and P. Rogaway. The oracle Diffie-Hellman assumptions and an analysis of DHIES. In *CT-RSA 2001*, LNCS 2020, Springer-Verlag, Apr. 2001.
2. M. Abdalla, P.-A. Fouque, and D. Pointcheval. Password-based authenticated key exchange in the three-party setting. Full version of current paper. Available from authors' web pages.
3. M. Bellare, R. Canetti, and H. Krawczyk. Keying hash functions for message authentication. In *CRYPTO'96*, LNCS 1109, Springer-Verlag, Aug. 1996.
4. M. Bellare, A. Desai, E. Jokipii, and P. Rogaway. A concrete security treatment of symmetric encryption. In *38th FOCS*, Oct. 1997.
5. M. Bellare, D. Pointcheval, and P. Rogaway. Authenticated key exchange secure against dictionary attacks. In *EUROCRYPT 2000*, LNCS 1807, Springer-Verlag, May 2000.
6. M. Bellare and P. Rogaway. Random oracles are practical: A paradigm for designing efficient protocols. In *ACM CCS 93*, Nov. 1993.
7. M. Bellare and P. Rogaway. Entity authentication and key distribution. In *CRYPTO'93*, LNCS 773, Springer-Verlag, Aug. 1994.
8. M. Bellare and P. Rogaway. Provably secure session key distribution – the three party case. In *28th ACM STOC*, May 1996.
9. S. M. Bellovin and M. Merritt. Encrypted key exchange: Password-based protocols secure against dictionary attacks. In *1992 IEEE Symposium on Security and Privacy*, May 1992.
10. V. Boyko, P. MacKenzie, and S. Patel. Provably secure password-authenticated key exchange using Diffie-Hellman. In *EUROCRYPT 2000*, LNCS 1807, Springer-Verlag, May 2000.
11. E. Bresson, O. Chevassut, and D. Pointcheval. New security results on encrypted key exchange. In *PKC 2004*, LNCS 2947, Springer-Verlag, Mar. 2004.
12. J. W. Byun, I. R. Jeong, D. H. Lee, and C.-S. Park. Password-authenticated key exchange between clients with different passwords. In *ICICS 02*, LNCS 2513, Springer-Verlag, Dec. 2002.
13. R. Gennaro and Y. Lindell. A framework for password-based authenticated key exchange. In *EUROCRYPT 2003*, LNCS 2656, Springer-Verlag, May 2003.

14. O. Goldreich and Y. Lindell. Session-key generation using human passwords only. In *CRYPTO 2001*, LNCS 2139, Springer-Verlag, Aug. 2001.

15. S. Halevi and H. Krawczyk. Public-key cryptography and password protocols. In *ACM Transactions on Information and System Security*, pages 524–543. ACM, 1999.

16. J. Katz, R. Ostrovsky, and M. Yung. Efficient password-authenticated key exchange using human-memorable passwords. In *EUROCRYPT 2001*, LNCS 2045, Springer-Verlag, May 2001.

17. H. Krawczyk. SIGMA: The "SIGn-and-MAc" approach to authenticated Diffie-Hellman and its use in the ike protocols. In *CRYPTO 2003*, LNCS 2729, Springer-Verlag, Aug. 2003.

18. C.-L. Lin, H.-M. Sun, and T. Hwang. Three-party encrypted key exchange: Attacks and a solution. *ACM SIGOPS Operating Systems Review*, 34(4):12–20, Oct. 2000.

19. P. MacKenzie, S. Patel, and R. Swaminathan. Password-authenticated key exchange based on RSA. In *ASIACRYPT 2000*, LNCS 1976, Springer-Verlag, Dec. 2000.

20. P. MacKenzie, T. Shrimpton, and M. Jakobsson. Threshold password-authenticated key exchange. In *CRYPTO 2002*, LNCS 2442, Springer-Verlag, Aug. 2002.

21. P. D. MacKenzie. The PAK suite: Protocols for password-authenticated key exchange. Contributions to IEEE P1363.2, 2002.

22. R. Needham and M. Schroeder. Using encryption for authentication in large networks of computers. *Communications of the ACM*, 21(21):993–999, Dec. 1978.

23. M. D. Raimondo and R. Gennaro. Provably secure threshold password-authenticated key exchange. In *EUROCRYPT 2003*, LNCS 2656, Springer-Verlag, May 2003.

24. V. Shoup. On formal models for secure key exchange. Technical Report RZ 3120, IBM, 1999.

25. J. G. Steiner, B. C. Neuman, and J. L. Schiller. Kerberos: An authentication service for open networks. In *Proceedings of the USENIX Winter Conference*, pages 191–202, 1988.

26. M. Steiner, G. Tsudik, and M. Waidner. Refinement and extension of encrypted key exchange. *ACM SIGOPS Operating Systems Review*, 29(3):22–30, July 1995.

A   Building Blocks

Decisional Diffie-Hellman Assumption: DDH. The DDH assumption states, roughly, that the distributions (g^u, g^v, g^{uv}) and (g^u, g^v, g^w) are computationally indistinguishable when u, v, w are drawn at random from $\{1, \ldots, |\mathbb{G}|\}$. This can be made more precise by defining two experiments, $\mathbf{Exp}_{\mathbb{G}}^{\text{ddh-real}}(\mathcal{A})$ and $\mathbf{Exp}_{\mathbb{G}}^{\text{ddh-rand}}(\mathcal{A})$. In both experiments, we compute two values $U = g^u$ and $V = g^v$ to be given to $\mathcal{A}$. But in addition to that, we also provide a third input, which is g^{uv} in $\mathbf{Exp}_{\mathbb{G}}^{\text{ddh-real}}(\mathcal{A})$ and g^z for a random z in $\mathbf{Exp}_{\mathbb{G}}^{\text{ddh-rand}}(\mathcal{A})$. The goal of the adversary is to guess a bit indicating the experiment it thinks it is in. We define the **advantage** of $\mathcal{A}$ in violating the DDH assumption, $\mathbf{Adv}_{\mathbb{G}}^{\text{ddh}}(\mathcal{A})$, as $\Pr[\mathbf{Exp}_{\mathbb{G}}^{\text{ddh-real}}(\mathcal{A}) = 1] - \Pr[\mathbf{Exp}_{\mathbb{G}}^{\text{ddh-rand}}(\mathcal{A}) = 1]$. The **advantage function** of the group, $\mathbf{Adv}_{\mathbb{G}}^{\text{ddh}}(t)$ is then defined as the maximum value of $\mathbf{Adv}_{\mathbb{G}}^{\text{ddh}}(\mathcal{A})$ over all $\mathcal{A}$ with time-complexity at most t.

Message Authentication Codes (MAC). A Message Authentication Code
MAC = (Key, Tag, Ver) is defined by the following three algorithms: (1) A *MAC
key generation algorithm* Key, which on input 1^k, produces a ℓ-bit secret-key sk
uniformly distributed in $\{0,1\}^\ell$; (2) A *MAC generation algorithm* Tag, possibly
probabilistic, which given a message m and a secret key $sk \in \{0,1\}^\ell$, produces
an authenticator μ; and (3) A *MAC verification algorithm* Ver, which given an
authenticator μ, a message m, and a secret key sk, outputs 1 if μ is a valid
authenticator for m under sk and 0 otherwise.

Like in signature schemes, the classical security level for a MAC is to prevent
existential forgeries, even for an adversary which has access to the generation
and verification oracles. We define the **advantage** of $\mathcal{A}$, $\mathbf{Adv}_{\mathsf{MAC}}^{\mathsf{euf-cma}}(\mathcal{A})$, as

$$\Pr\left[sk \leftarrow \{0,1\}^\ell, (m,\mu) \leftarrow \mathcal{A}^{\mathsf{Tag}(sk;\cdot),\mathsf{Ver}(sk;\cdot,\cdot)}() : \mathsf{Ver}(sk;m,\mu) = 1\right],$$

and the **advantage function** of the MAC, $\mathbf{Adv}_{\mathsf{MAC}}^{\mathsf{euf-cma}}(t, q_g, q_s)$, as the maximum value of $\mathbf{Adv}_{\mathsf{MAC}}^{\mathsf{euf-cma}}(\mathcal{A})$ over all $\mathcal{A}$ that asks up to q_g and q_v queries to
the generation and verification oracles, respectively, and with time-complexity
at most t. Note that $\mathcal{A}$ wins the above experiment only if it outputs a *new* valid
authenticator.

3-Party Key Distribution. A secure key distribution protocol KD is a 3-party
protocol between 2 parties and a trusted server S where S picks a session key at
random and securely sends it to the users. The security model, formally introduced in [8], is a generalization of that for 2-party authenticated key exchange
protocols, to which a new oracle was added to represent the trusted server.
Their security is in the Find-Then-Guess model, using the terminology that we
introduced for key exchange protocols.

In our generic construction, we only need a KD secure with respect to a
single session since the symmetric keys used as input to the key distribution
protocol differ from session to session. They are the session keys obtained from
the 2-party password-based authenticated key exchange protocols between the
server and each of the two parties. Since in this case, both the Find-Then-Guess
and Real-Or-Random notions are equivalent, we opted to use their definition
(i.e. FTG) adapted to our terminology. That is, we define $\mathbf{Adv}_{\mathsf{KD}}^{\mathsf{ftg-kd}}(\mathcal{A})$ as the
advantage of adversary $\mathcal{A}$ in violating the semantic security of a key distribution
KD in the FTG sense, and $\mathbf{Adv}_{\mathsf{KD}}^{\mathsf{ftg-kd}}(t, s, r)$ as the **advantage function** of KD,
which is the maximum value of $\mathbf{Adv}_{\mathsf{KD}}^{\mathsf{ftg-kd}}(\mathcal{A})$ over all $\mathcal{A}$ with time-complexity
at most t, asking *Send* queries with respect to at most s sessions and asking at
most r *Reveal* queries.

B   Relations Between Notions

In this section, we prove the relation between the Find-Then-Guess (FTG) and
Real-Or-Random (ROR) notions of security for authenticated key exchange protocols. The relation is not specific to password-based schemes, but its implica-
tions are more important in that scenario. We do not present proofs for the

forward-secure case as these proofs can be easily derived from the proofs in the non-forward-secure case.

Lemma 1. *For any* AKE, $\mathbf{Adv}_{\mathsf{AKE}}^{\mathrm{ftg-ake}}(t, q_{\mathrm{send}}, q_{\mathrm{reveal}}, q_{\mathrm{exe}}) \leq 2 \cdot \mathbf{Adv}_{\mathsf{AKE}}^{\mathrm{ror-ake}}(t,$ $q_{\mathrm{send}}, q_{\mathrm{reveal}} + 1, q_{\mathrm{exe}}).$

Proof. In order to prove this lemma, we show how to build an adversary $\mathcal{A}_{\mathrm{ror}}$ against the semantic security of an authenticated key exchange AKE protocol in the ROR model given an adversary $\mathcal{A}_{\mathrm{ftg}}$ against the semantic security of the same protocol AKE in the FTG model. We know that $\mathcal{A}_{\mathrm{ftg}}$ has time-complexity at most t and that it asks at most q_{send}, q_{reveal}, and q_{exe} queries to its *Send*, *Reveal*, and *Execute* oracles, respectively.

The description of $\mathcal{A}_{\mathrm{ror}}$ is as follows. $\mathcal{A}_{\mathrm{ror}}$ starts by choosing a bit b uniformly at random and starts running $\mathcal{A}_{\mathrm{ftg}}$. If $\mathcal{A}_{\mathrm{ftg}}$ asks a *Send* query, then $\mathcal{A}_{\mathrm{ror}}$ asks the corresponding query to its *Send* oracle. If $\mathcal{A}_{\mathrm{ftg}}$ asks a *Execute* query, then $\mathcal{A}_{\mathrm{ror}}$ asks the corresponding query to its *Execute* oracle. If $\mathcal{A}_{\mathrm{ftg}}$ asks a *Reveal* query, then $\mathcal{A}_{\mathrm{ror}}$ asks a *Test* query to its *Test* oracle and uses the answer it receives as the answer to the *Reveal* query. If $\mathcal{A}_{\mathrm{ftg}}$ asks a *Test* query, then $\mathcal{A}_{\mathrm{ror}}$ asks the corresponding query to its *Test* oracle. If $b = 1$, then $\mathcal{A}_{\mathrm{ror}}$ uses the answer it received as the answer to the *Test* query. Otherwise, it returns a random key to $\mathcal{A}_{\mathrm{ftg}}$. Let b' be the final output of $\mathcal{A}_{\mathrm{ftg}}$. If $b' = b$, then $\mathcal{A}_{\mathrm{ror}}$ outputs 1. Otherwise, it outputs 0.

Note that $\mathcal{A}_{\mathrm{ror}}$ has time-complexity at most t and asks at most q_{send}, $q_{\mathrm{reveal}} + 1$, and q_{exe} queries to its *Send*, *Test*, and *Execute* oracles, respectively.

In order to analyze the advantage of $\mathcal{A}_{\mathrm{ror}}$, first consider the case in which its *Test* oracle returns random keys. It is easy to see that, in this case, $\mathcal{A}_{\mathrm{ftg}}$ cannot gain any information about the hidden bit b used to answer its single *Test* query. Therefore, the probability that $\mathcal{A}_{\mathrm{ror}}$ outputs 1 is exactly $\frac{1}{2}$. Now consider the case in which its *Test* oracle returns the actual sessions keys. In this case, the simulation of *Reveal* is perfect and $\mathcal{A}_{\mathrm{ror}}$ runs $\mathcal{A}_{\mathrm{ftg}}$ exactly as in the experiment defining the semantic security of $\mathcal{A}_{\mathrm{ftg}}$ in the FTG model. Therefore, the probability that $\mathcal{A}_{\mathrm{ror}}$ outputs 1 is exactly $\frac{1}{2} + \frac{1}{2}\mathbf{Adv}_{\mathsf{AKE}}^{\mathrm{ftg-ake}}(\mathcal{A}_{\mathrm{ftg}})$ and, as a result, $\mathbf{Adv}_{\mathsf{AKE}}^{\mathrm{ftg-ake}}(\mathcal{A}_{\mathrm{ftg}}) \leq 2 \cdot \mathbf{Adv}_{\mathsf{AKE}}^{\mathrm{ror-ake}}(\mathcal{A}_{\mathrm{ror}}) \leq \mathbf{Adv}_{\mathsf{AKE}}^{\mathrm{ror-ake}}(t, q_{\mathrm{send}}, q_{\mathrm{reveal}} + 1, q_{\mathrm{exe}})$. The lemma follows easily. □

Lemma 2. *For any* AKE, $\mathbf{Adv}_{\mathsf{AKE}}^{\mathrm{ror-ake}}(t, q_{\mathrm{send}}, q_{\mathrm{test}}, q_{\mathrm{exe}}) \leq q_{\mathrm{test}} \cdot \mathbf{Adv}_{\mathsf{AKE}}^{\mathrm{ftg-ake}}(t,$ $q_{\mathrm{send}}, q_{\mathrm{test}} - 1, q_{\mathrm{exe}}).$

Proof. In order to prove this lemma, we show how to build a sequence of adversaries $\mathcal{A}_{\mathrm{ftg}}^{i}$ against the semantic security of an authenticated key exchange AKE protocol in the FTG model given an adversary $\mathcal{A}_{\mathrm{ror}}$ against the semantic security of the same protocol AKE in the ROR model. We know that $\mathcal{A}_{\mathrm{ror}}$ has time-complexity at most t and that it asks at most q_{send}, q_{test}, and q_{exe} queries to its *Send*, *Test*, and *Execute* oracles, respectively.

The proof uses a standard hybrid argument, in which we define a sequence of $q_{\mathrm{test}} + 1$ hybrid experiments V_i, where $0 \leq i \leq q_{\mathrm{test}}$. In experiment V_i, the first $i-1$ queries to the *Test* oracle are answered using a random key and all remaining *Test* queries are answered using the real key. Please note that the hybrid experiments at the extremes correspond to the real and random experiments in the definition of semantic security in the ROR model. Hence, in order to prove the bound in the lemma, it suffices to prove that the difference in probability that adversary $\mathcal{A}_{ror}$ returns 1 between any two consecutive experiments V_i and V_{i-1} is at most $\mathbf{Adv}_{AKE}^{ftg-ake}(t, q_{send}, q_{test}-1, q_{exe})$. This is achieved by building a sequence of q_{test} adversaries $\mathcal{A}_{ftg}^i$, as described below.

Let $\mathcal{A}_{ftg}^i$ be a distinguisher $\mathcal{A}_{ftg}^i$ for experiments V_i and V_{i-1}, where $1 \leq i \leq q_{test}$. $\mathcal{A}_{ftg}^i$ starts running $\mathcal{A}_{ror}$ answering to its queries as follows. If $\mathcal{A}_{ror}$ asks a Send or Execute query, then $\mathcal{A}_{ftg}$ answers it using its corresponding oracle. If $\mathcal{A}_{ror}$ asks a Test query, then $\mathcal{A}_{ftg}$ answers it with a random key if this query is among the first $i-1$. If this is the i-th Test, then $\mathcal{A}_{ftg}$ uses its Test oracle to answer it. All remaining Test queries are answered using the output of the Reveal query. $\mathcal{A}_{ftg}$ finishes its execution by outputting the same guess bit b outputted by $\mathcal{A}_{ror}$.

Note that $\mathcal{A}_{ftg}^i$ has time-complexity at most t and asks at most q_{send}, $q_{test}-1$, and q_{exe} queries to its Send, Reveal, and Execute oracles, respectively.

In order to analyze the advantage of $\mathcal{A}_{ftg}^i$, first notice that when Test oracle returns a random key, $\mathcal{A}_{ftg}^i$ runs $\mathcal{A}_{ror}$ exactly as in the experiment V_i. Next, notice that when Test oracle returns the real key, $\mathcal{A}_{ftg}^i$ runs $\mathcal{A}_{ror}$ exactly as in the experiment V_i. It follows that the difference in probability that adversary $\mathcal{A}_{ror}$ returns 1 between experiments V_i and V_{i-1} is at most $\mathbf{Adv}_{AKE}^{ftg-ake}(\mathcal{A}_{ror}) \leq \mathbf{Adv}_{AKE}^{ftg-ake}(t, q_{send}, q_{test}-1, q_{exe})$. The lemma follows easily.   □

Even though the reduction in Lemma 2 is not security-preserving (i.e., there is a non-constant factor loss in the reduction), it does not imply that a gap really exists – there might exist a tight reduction between the two notions that we have not yet found. In order to prove that the non-constant factor loss in the reduction is indeed intrinsic, we need to show that there exist schemes for which the gap does exist.

To achieve this goal, one can use techniques similar to those used to prove that a gap exists between the Left-Or-Right and Find-Then-Guess notions of security for symmetric encryption schemes [4]. In that paper, they show how to construct a new symmetric encryption scheme $\mathcal{E}'$ from a secure encryption scheme $\mathcal{E}$ such that $\mathcal{E}'$ exhibits the gap. $\mathcal{E}'$ was constructed in such a way that its encryption function works like the encryption function of $\mathcal{E}$ most of the time, except in a few cases (which are easily identifiable) in which the ciphertext it generates contains the plaintext. The probability in which such bad cases happen in their construction is exactly $1/q$, where q is the non-constant factor in the reduction.

A similar technique can be applied to authenticated key exchange protocols. Imagine a secure authenticated key exchange protocol AKE exists. For simplicity, assume $q_{test} = 2^l$, for some integer l. We can construct a new scheme AKE' such that the session key k that it generates equals the one generated by AKE most of the time except when the first l bits are 0. In this case, we just make $k = 0$. Using a proof technique similar to that used in [4], one can prove the the gap in Lemma 2 cannot be avoided and we thus omit the detail. But before stating our proposition, we make a final remark that when the underlying scheme AKE is a password-based key exchange, not every choice of parameters will yield the desired result claimed in the proposition. However, there are (easy) choices of parameters for which the gap does exist and that suffices for the purpose of the proposition. We are now ready to state our claim.

Proposition 1. *The gap exhibited in Lemma 2 is intrinsic and cannot be avoided.*

On the Optimization of Side-Channel Attacks
by Advanced Stochastic Methods

Werner Schindler

Bundesamt für Sicherheit in der Informationstechnik (BSI),
Godesberger Allee 185–189,
53175 Bonn, Germany
Werner.Schindler@bsi.bund.de

Abstract. A number of papers on side-channel attacks have been published where the side-channel information was not exploited in an optimal manner, which reduced their efficiency. A good understanding of the source and the true risk potential of an attack is necessary to rate the effectiveness of possible countermeasures. This paper explains a general approach to optimize the efficiency of side-channel attacks by advanced stochastic methods. The approach and its benefits are illustrated by examples.

Keywords: Side-channel attack, Montgomery's multiplication algorithm, stochastic process, statistical decision problem, optimal decision strategy.

1   Introduction

At Crypto 1996 and Crypto 1998 Kocher, resp. Kocher et al., introduced timing and power attacks [5, 8]. Since then side-channel attacks have attracted enourmous attention in the scientific community and the smart card industry as they constitute serious threats against cryptosystems. Their targets are usually smart cards but also software implementations may be vulnerable, even against remote attacks ([1, 2] etc.). In a side-channel attack the attacker guesses the secret key portion by portion. The correctness of the partial guesses cannot be verified (at least not with certainty) until all parts of the key have been guessed. If the verification of the whole key guess fails (e.g. by checking a digital signature) this does not provide the position(s) of the wrong guess(es).

A large number of research papers on timing attacks, power attacks, radiation attacks and combined timing / power attacks have been published. A variety of countermeasures have been proposed that shall prevent these attacks.

In 'real life' the number of measurements is often limited, or it is at least costly to perform a large number of measurements. From the attacker's point of view it is hence desirable to minimize the error probabilities for the guesses of the particular key parts (for a given number of measurements) or vice versa, to minimize the number of measurements which is necessary for a successful attack. If the outcome of the previous guesses has an impact on the guessing strategy of

S. Vaudenay (Ed.): PKC 2005, LNCS 3386, pp. 85–103, 2005.

the present key part it is additionally desirable to have criteria with which the correctness of the previous guesses can be verified with reasonable probability.

In order to achieve these goals the side-channel information should be exploited in an optimal manner. Many papers present ingenious ideas but lack of sound mathematical methods. As a consequence, only a fraction of the overall side-channel information is indeed used which in turn lowers the efficiency of the attack. As a consequence it may even be difficult to rate the true risk potential of these attacks and to assess the effectiveness of the proposed countermeasures. By applying appropriate stochastic methods it was possible to increase the efficiency of a number of known attacks considerably ([12, 14–16]; Sects. 4, 6, 7 in this paper), in one case even by factor 50. Moreover, some attacks were generalized, and new attacks were detected due to the better understanding of the situation ([13, 16, 17], Sects. 5, 6 in this paper).

The focus of this paper are the applied mathematical methods themselves but not new attacks. This shall put the reader into the position to apply and to adjust these methods when considering side-channel attacks that are tailored to a specific target. An individual treatment should in particular be necessary for most of the power and radiation attacks. Often the (timing, power, radiation) behaviour of the attacked device can be modelled as a stochastic process, and the attack can be interpreted as a sequence of statistical decision problems. Roughly speaking, in a statistical decision problem the optimal decision strategy minimizes the expected loss which primarily depends on the probabilities for wrong guesses but also on the a priori information and the consequences of errors. In fact, depending on the concrete situation particular types of errors may be easier to detect and correct than others (e.g., in the examples explained in Sects. 6 and 7).

We refer readers who are generally interested in stochastic and statistical applications in cryptography to ([10]) and to various papers of Meier and Staffelbach, Golic, Vaudenay and Junod, for instance.

Our paper is organized as follows: In Section 2 we introduce the concept of statistical decision theory, and in Section 3 we exemplarily work out a stochastic model for Montgomery's multiplication algorithm. Then we illustrate our approach by various examples and give final conclusions.

2   A Survey on Statistical Decision Theory

We interpret side-channel measurements as realizations of random variables, i.e. as values assumed by these random variables. The relevant part of the information is covered by noise but an attacker clearly aims to exploit all of the available information in an optimal way. Therefore, he interprets the side-channel attack as a sequence of statistical decision problems. Each decision problem corresponds to the guessing of a particular key part. Previous guesses may have an impact on the present guess (cf. Sects. 4, 5), or all guesses may be independent (cf. Sect. 6). Statistical decision theory quantifies the impact of the particular pieces of information on the decision so that the search for the optimal decision strategy can be formalized. In this section we introduce the concept of statistical decision theory as far it is relevant for our purposes, namely to improve the efficiency of side-channel attacks.

Formally, a statistical decision problem is defined by a 5-tuple $(\Theta, \Omega, s, \mathcal{D}, A)$. The statistician (in our context: the attacker) observes a sample $\omega \in \Omega$ that he interprets as a realization of a random variable X with unknown distribution p_θ. On basis of this observation he estimates the parameter $\theta \in \Theta$ where Θ denotes the *parameter space*, i.e., the set of all admissible hypotheses (= possible parameters). Further, the set Ω is called the *observation space*, and the letter A denotes the set of all admissible alternatives the statistician can decide for. In the following we assume $\Theta = A$ where Θ and A are finite sets.

Example 1. (i) Assume that the attacker guesses a single RSA key bit and that his decision is based upon N timing or power measurements. Then $\Theta = A = \{0,1\}$, $\Omega = \mathbb{R}^N$.
(ii) Consider a power attack on a DES implementation where the attacker guesses a particular 6-bit-subkey that affects a single S-box in the first round. Then $\Theta = A = \{0,1\}^6$.

A deterministic decision strategy is given by a mapping $\tau: \Omega \to A$ (cf. Remark 1 (ii)). If the statistician applies the decision strategy τ he decides for $\tau(\omega) \in A = \Theta$ whenever he observes $\omega \in \Omega$.

Finally, the *loss function* $s: \Theta \times A \to [0, \infty)$ quantifies the harm of a wrong decision, i.e., $s(\theta, a)$ gives the loss if the statistician decides for $a \in A$ although $\theta \in \Theta = A$ is the correct parameter. In our context this quantifies the efforts (time, money etc.) to detect, to localize and to correct a wrong decision, i.e. a wrong guess of a key part. Clearly, $s(\theta, \theta) := 0$ since a correct guess does not cause any loss. For some attacks (as in Sects. 6, 7) specific types of errors are easier to correct than others. The optimal decision strategy takes such phenomena into account.

Assume that the statistician uses the deterministic decision strategy $\tau: \Omega \to A$ and that θ is the correct parameter. The expected loss (= average loss if the hypothesis θ is true) is given by the *risk function*

$$r(\theta, \tau) := \int_\Omega s(\theta, \tau(\omega)) \, p_\theta(d\omega). \tag{1}$$

Our goal clearly is to apply a decision strategy that minimizes this term. Unfortunately, usually there does not exist a decision strategy that is simultaneously optimal for all admissible parameters $\theta \in \Theta$. However, in the context of side-channel attacks one can usually determine (at least approximate) probabilities with which the particular parameters occur. This is quantified by the so-called *a priori distribution* η, a probability measure on the parameter space Θ.

Example 2. (i) (Continuation of Example 1(i)) Assume that k exponent bits remain to be guessed and that the attacker knows that r of them equal 1. If the secret key was selected randomly then it is reasonable to assume that the present bit is 1 with probability $\eta(1) = r/k$.
(ii) (Continuation of Example 1(ii)) Here $\eta(x) = 2^{-6}$ for all $x \in \{0,1\}^6$.

Assume that η denotes the a priori distribution. If the statistician applies the deterministic decision strategy $\tau \colon \Omega \to A$ the expected loss equals

$$R(\eta, \tau) := \sum_{\theta \in \Theta} r(\theta, \tau) \eta(\theta) = \sum_{\theta \in \Theta} \int_{\Omega} s(\theta, \tau(\omega))\, p_\theta(d\omega)\, \eta(\theta). \tag{2}$$

A decision strategy τ' is optimal against η if it minimizes the right-hand term. Such a decision strategy is also called a *Bayes strategy* against η.

Remark 1. (i) For specific decision problems (e.g. minimax problems) it is reasonable to consider the more general class of *randomized decision strategies* where the statistician decides randomly (quantified by a probability measure) between various alternatives when observing a particular ω ([20]). In our context we may restrict our attention to the deterministic decision strategies (cf. Theorem 1). We point out that deterministic decision strategies can be viewed as specific randomized decision strategies.
(ii) Theorem 1 is tailored to our situation. It provides concrete formulae that characterize the optimal decision strategy. Although Theorem 1 can be deduced from more general theorems (e.g., Hilfssatz 2.137 and Satz 2.138(i) in [20] immediately imply assertion (i)) we give an elementary proof (cf. Theorem 2.48 in [20] for the special case $t = 2$) in order to illustrate the background. We restricted our attention to the case $|\Theta| < \infty$ and left out mathematical difficulties as the concept of σ-algebras and measurability. We mention that the optimal decision strategy τ from Theorem 1 is measurable.

Theorem 1. *Assume that $(\Theta, \Omega, s, \mathcal{D}, A)$ describes a statistical decision problem with finite parameter space $\Theta = \{\theta_1, \ldots, \theta_t\} = A$ where $\mathcal{D}$ contains the deterministic decision strategies. Further, let μ denote a σ-finite measure on Ω with $p_{\theta_i} = f_{\theta_i} \cdot \mu$, i.e. p_{θ_i} has μ-density f_{θ_i}, for each $i \le t$.*
(i) The deterministic decision strategy $\tau \colon \Omega \to A$,

$$\tau(\omega) := a \quad \text{if} \quad \sum_{i=1}^{t} s(\theta_i, a) \eta(\theta_i) f_{\theta_i}(\omega) = \min_{a' \in A} \left\{ \sum_{i=1}^{t} s(\theta_i, a') \eta(\theta_i) f_{\theta_i}(\omega) \right\} \tag{3}$$

is optimal against the a priori distribution η. (If the minimum is attained for several decisions, we chose $a \in A$ according to any (fixed) order on A.)
(ii) If $\Theta = \{0, 1\}$ and $s(0, 1), s(1, 0) > 0$ the indicator function

$$\tau(\omega) := 1_{f_0(\omega)/f_1(\omega) \le s(1,0)\eta(1)/s(0,1)\eta(0)}(\omega) \tag{4}$$

is optimal against η. (We set $\tau(\omega) := 1$ if $f_0(\omega) = f_1(\omega) = 0$ or $f_0(\omega) = f_1(\omega) = \infty$.)
(iii) Assume that $C \subseteq \Omega$ with $p_{\theta_i}(C) = p > 0$ for all $\theta_i \in \Theta$. Then (i) and (ii) remain valid if f_θ is replaced by the conditional density $f_{\theta|C}$.

Proof. Let $\kappa \colon \Omega \times \mathcal{P}(A) \to [0, 1]$ denote any randomized decision strategy (cf. [20], for instance). Fubini's Theorem implies

$$R(\eta, \kappa) = \sum_{i=1}^{t} \left(\int_{\Omega} \sum_{j=1}^{t} s(\theta_i, \theta_j) \kappa(\omega, \theta_j) f_{\theta_i}(\omega)\, \mu(d\omega) \right) \eta(\theta_i)$$

$$\int_{\Omega} \left(\sum_{i=1}^{t} \sum_{j=1}^{t} s(\theta_i, \theta_j) \kappa(\omega, \theta_j) f_{\theta_i}(\omega) \eta(\theta_i) \right) \mu(d\omega).$$

Since $\kappa(\omega, \cdot)$ is a probability measure, reordering the integrand yields

$$\sum_{j=1}^{t} \kappa(\omega, \theta_j) \sum_{i=1}^{t} s(\theta_i, \theta_j) f_{\theta_i}(\omega) \eta(\theta_i) \geq \min_{a' \in A} \left\{ \sum_{i=1}^{t} s(\theta_i, a') f_{\theta_i}(\omega) \eta(\theta_i) \right\}$$

which proves (3). Assertion (ii) is an immediate consequence from (i) since $f_0(\omega) = f_1(\omega) = 0$ and $f_0(\omega) = f_1(\omega) = \infty$ occur only with probability zero. Assertion (iii) is a corollary from (i) and (ii) since $f_{\theta|C} = f_\theta / p$.

Remark 2. (i) A σ-finite measure μ on Ω with the properties claimed in Theorem 1 does always exist (e.g. $\mu = p_{\theta_1} + \cdots + p_{\theta_t}$).
(ii) For $\Omega = \mathbb{R}^n$ the well-known Lebesgue measure λ_n is σ-finite (The Lebesgue measure on $\mathbb{R}^n$ is given by $\lambda_n([a_1, b_1] \times \cdots [a_n, b_n]) = \prod_{i=1}^{n}(b_i - a_i)$ if $b_i \geq a_i$ for all $i \leq n$.) If Ω is finite or countable the counting measure μ_C is σ-finite. The counting measure is given by $\mu_C(\omega) = 1$ for all $\omega \in \Omega$. In particular, the probabilities $\text{Prob}_\theta(X = \omega) = p_\theta(\omega)$ can be interpreted as densities with respect to μ_C.
(iii) The examples mentioned in (ii) and combinations thereof cover the cases that are relevant in the context of side-channel attacks.

With regard to Theorem 1 we will restrict our attention to decision problems of the type

$$(\Theta, \Omega, s, \mathcal{DS}, A = \Theta) \quad \text{with finite } \Theta = A \tag{5}$$

where $\mathcal{DS}$ denotes the set of all deterministic decision strategies. At first the attacker has to define the sets $\Theta = A$ and an appropriate loss function s. Then he determines the a priori distribution η and, in particular, the probability densities p_{θ_i} for all $i \leq t$. In our context the latter will be the most difficult part but gives the most significant impact on the decision strategy. For timing attacks on public key algorithms, for instance, these distributions depend essentially on the implemented arithmetic algorithms, for power and radiation attacks on the internal activity within the attacked device or specific areas thereof when the measurements are taken. Finally, the attacker applies Theorem 1 to determine an optimal decision strategy τ (= Bayes strategy against the a priori distribution η). In specific situations the attacker may also be interested in the value $R(\eta, \tau)$.

3   Montgomery's Modular Multiplication Algorithm

In this section we investigate the timing behaviour of Montgomery's modular multiplication algorithm ([9], Alg. 14.36) as it is implemented in most of the smart cards that compute modular exponentiations (e.g., RSA-based digital signatures).

3.1   Algebraic Background and Montgomery's Algorithm

In this subsection we briefly describe the algebraic background and formulate the multiprecision variant of Montgomery's algorithm. We begin with a definition.

Definition 1. As usually, $Z_M := \{0, 1, \ldots, M-1\}$, and for an integer $b \in Z$ the term $b(\mathrm{mod}\, M)$ denotes the unique element of Z_M that is congruent to b modulo M.

In order to compute $y^d(\mathrm{mod}\, M)$ a sequence of modular multiplications and squarings have to be carried out. If 'ordinary' modular multiplication algorithms are used this requires a large number of time-consuming integer divisions by the modulus M. Montgomery's multiplication algorithm saves these operations.

In the following we assume that M is an odd modulus (e.g., an RSA modulus or a prime factor) and that $R := 2^x > M$ is a power of two (e.g. $x = 512$). The elementary variant of Montgomery's algorithm transfers the modular multiplications from the modulus Z_M to Z_R. The term $R^{-1} \in Z_M$ denotes the multiplicative inverse of R in Z_M, i.e. $RR^{-1} \equiv 1 \pmod{M}$. The integer $M^* \in Z_R$ satisfies the integer equation $RR^{-1} - MM^* = 1$. For input $a, b \in Z_M$ Montgomery's multiplication algorithm returns $\mathrm{MM}(a, b; M) := abR^{-1}(\mathrm{mod}\, M)$. We point out that the mappings $\Psi, \Psi_*: Z_M \to Z_M$, given by $\Psi(x) := xR \,(\mathrm{mod}\, M)$ and $\Psi_*(x) := xR^{-1} \,(\mathrm{mod}\, M)$, induce inverse operations on Z_M.

Usually, a time-efficient multiprecision variant of Montgomery's algorithm is implemented which is tailored to the device's hardware architecture. Assume that ws denotes the word size for the arithmetic operations (e.g. $ws = 32$) and that ws divides the exponent x. Then $r := 2^{ws}$ and $R = r^v$ with $v = x/ws$ (Example: $x = 512$, $ws = 32$, $v = 16$). For the moment let further $a = (a_{v-1}, \ldots, a_0)_r$, $b = (b_{v-1}, \ldots, b_0)_r$, and $s = (s_{v-1}, \ldots, s_0)_r$ denote the r-adic representations of a, b and s, resp., and let $m' := M^*(\mathrm{mod}\, r)$.

Algorithm 1: Montgomery's Algorithm (Multiprecision Variant)

```
1.) s:=0
2.) for i=0 to v-1 do {
        u_i:= (s_0+a_i*b_0)m' (mod r)
        s:= (s+a_ib+u_iM) /r }
3.) if s≥M then s:=s-M
4.) return s  ( = MM(a,b;M) = abR^{-1} (mod M) )
```

In the following we assume that for fixed parameters M, R and r the run times needed for Step 1 and Step 2 are identical for all pairs of operands. (This assumption is reasonable, in particular for smart cards. Software implementations may process small operands (i.e., those with leading zero-words) faster due to optimizations of the integer multiplication algorithms. This is absolutely negligible for the attacks considered in Sects. 4 and 6 but may cause additional difficulties for particular chosen-input attacks as described in Sect. 5, for instance (cf. [1]).) Timing differences are caused by the fact whether in Step 3 the subtraction, the so-called *extra reduction*, has to be carried out. Hence

$$\mathrm{Time}\,(MM(a, b; M)) \in \{c, c + c_{\mathrm{ER}}\} \qquad (6)$$

where the time c is required iff no extra reduction is necessary. The constant c_{ER} quantifies the time needed for an integer subtraction by M. The values of the constants c and c_{ER} surely depend on the concrete implementation. Lemma 1 below (cf. [13] (Remark 1) or [11] (Lemma 1)) says that the fact whether an extra reduction is necessary does only depend on a, b, M and R but not on the word size ws.

Lemma 1. *For each word size ws the intermediate result after Step 2 equals $s = (ab + uM)/R$ with $u = abM^*(\mathrm{mod}\,R)$.*

3.2 The Stochastic Model

In this subsection we study the timing behaviour of Montgomery's multiplication algorithm within modular exponentiation algorithms. It will turn out that the probability for an extra reduction (ER) in a squaring operation differs from the probabiliy for an extra reduction in a multiplication with a particular value $a \in Z_M$. The latter depends linearly on the ratio a/M. We point out that the probabilities, or more general, the stochastic properties of random extra reductions do not depend on the size of the modulus M but on the ratio M/R.

Lemma 2. *(i)* $\frac{\mathrm{MM}(a,b;M)}{M} = \left(\frac{a}{M}\frac{b}{M}\frac{M}{R} + \frac{abM^* \ (\mathrm{mod}\,R)}{R}\right)(\mathrm{mod}\,1).$ *That is, an extra reduction is carried out iff the sum within the bracket is ≥ 1 iff $\frac{\mathrm{MM}(a,b;M)}{M} < \frac{a}{M}\frac{b}{M}\frac{M}{R}$.*
(ii) Assume that the random variable B is equidistributed on Z_M. Then the intermediate result in Algorithm 1 before the ER step is (in good approximation) distributed as

$$\frac{M}{R}\frac{a}{M}U + V \qquad \textit{for } \mathrm{MM}(a, B; M) \tag{7}$$

$$\frac{M}{R}U^2 + V \qquad \textit{for } \mathrm{MM}(B, B; M). \tag{8}$$

where U and V denote independent random variables that are equidistributed on $[0, 1)$.

Sketch of the Proof. Assertion (i) follows immediately from Lemma 1. For a proof of (ii) we refer the interested reader to [12], Lemma A.3. The central idea is that a small deviation of B/M causes 'vast' deviations in the second summand and that the distribution of the second summand is close to the equidistribution on $[0, 1]$ for nearly all values of a. An alternate proof for a related assertion is given in [11]. (Both proofs use plausible heuristic arguments (Assumption DIS in [11]). We further mention that (7) and (8) yield probabilities for extra reductions (cf. (11)) which were confirmed by a large number of simulation experiments.

Modular exponentiation algorithms initialize a variable (in the following denoted with temp) with the base y or, in case of table methods, with a power of y. A sequence of modular squarings of temp and multiplications of temp with particular table values are carried out until temp equals $y^d(\bmod M)$. Pseudoalgorithm 2 below combines modular exponentiation algorithms with Montgomery's multiplication algorithm. The modular exponentiation algorithm may be the 'square and multiply' algorithm ([9], Alg. 14.79; cf. Sect. 4), a table method (e.g. left-to right b-ary exponentiation, cf. [9], Alg. 14.82 and Sect. 6) or the sliding windows exponentiation algorithm ([9], Alg. 14.85). In Pseudoalgorithm 2 the table values equal $(y^j R)(\bmod M)$ (unlike $(y^j)(\bmod M)$ if 'ordinary' modular multiplication algorithms are used) and hence temp $= y^d R (\bmod M)$ after Step 2.

Pseudoalgorithm 2: Modular Exponentiation with Montgomery's Multiplication Algorithm

```
1.) \bar y_{1}:=MM(y,R^2;M)     (= yR (mod M))
2.) Modular Exponentiation algorithm
      a) table initialization (if necessary)
      b) exponentiation phase
         (Replace modular squarings and multiplications in
         2a) and 2b) with the respective Montgomery operations)
3.) return temp:=MM(temp,1;M)   (=y^d (mod M))
```

We interpret the normalized intermediate values $\text{temp}_0/M, \text{temp}_1/M, \dots$ from the exponentiation phase as realizations of $[0, 1)$-valued random variables $S_0, S_1,$ $\dots$. Consequently, the time needed for the ith Montgomery operation (squaring or multiplication of temp with a particular table value), is interpreted as a realization of $c + W_i \cdot c_{\text{ER}}$, where W_i is a $\{0,1\}$-valued random variable, assuming 1 iff an extra reduction is necessary. The understanding of the stochastic process $W_1, W_2, \dots$ will turn out to be necessary to determine the optimal decision strategies in the following sections.

From Lemma 2 we deduce the following relations where the right-hand sides denote the possible types of the ith Montgomery operation within the exponentiation phase.

$$S_{i+1} := \begin{cases} \frac{M}{R} S_i^2 + V_{i+1}(\bmod 1) & \text{for MM(temp, temp; } M) \\ \frac{\bar{y}_j}{M} \frac{M}{R} S_i + V_{i+1}(\bmod 1) & \text{for MM(temp, } \bar{y}_j; M) \end{cases} \quad (9)$$

The term $\bar{y}_j$ denotes the jth table entry ($j \equiv 1$ for the square & multiply algorithm). With regard to Lemma 2(ii) we may assume that the random variables $V_1, V_2, \dots$ are iid equidistributed on $[0, 1)$. As an immediate consequence, the random variables $S_1, S_2, \dots$ are also iid equidistributed on $[0, 1)$. From the random variables $S_0, S_1, \dots$ one derives the random variables $W_1, W_2, \dots$ that describe the (random) timing behaviour of the Montgomery operations within the exponentiation phase. To be precise, from Lemma 2(i) we conclude

$$W_i := \begin{cases} 1_{S_i < S_{i-1}^2(M/R)} & \text{for MM(temp, temp; } M) \\ 1_{S_i < S_{i-1}(\bar{y}_j/M)(M/R)} & \text{for MM(temp, } \bar{y}_j; M). \end{cases} \quad (10)$$

We mention that the sequence $W_1, W_2, \dots$ is neither independent nor identically distributed but W_i and W_{i+1} are negatively correlated. On the other hand, the tuples $(W_i, W_{i+1}, \ldots, W_{i+j})$ and $(W_k, W_{k+1}, \ldots, W_{k+t})$ (but not their components!) are independent if $k > i + j + 1$. In particular, (10) implies

$$E(W_i) = \begin{cases} \frac{1}{3}\frac{M}{R} & \text{for MM}(\text{temp}, \text{temp}; M) \\ \frac{1}{2}\frac{\bar{y}_j}{M}\frac{M}{R} & \text{for MM}(\text{temp}, \bar{y}_j; M). \end{cases} \tag{11}$$

Remark 3. In this section we have derived a stochastic process $W_1, W_2, \ldots$ that models the timing behaviour of the Montgomery multiplications within modular exponentiation algorithms. Clearly, a similar approach is at least principally feasible for other arithmetic algorithms, too.

4   Timing Attacks on RSA Without CRT

A timing attack on RSA implementations was first described (and experimentally verified) in [5]. Two years later a successful timing attack on a preliminary version of the Cascade chip was presented at the Cardis conference ([4]). Kocher's attack was generalized and optimized in [12]. In this section we consider the attack presented in [4]. Our approach improves its efficiency by factor 50.

4.1   The Optimal Decision Strategy

In this section we assume that the attacked smart card (e.g., a preliminary version of the Cascade chip) calculates the modular exponentiations $y \mapsto y^d (\text{mod } n)$ with the square & multiply algorithm, combined with Montgomery's algorithm (cf. Pseudoalgorithm 2). We assume further that the secret exponent d (target of the attack) remains fixed for all observed exponentiations and that no blinding techniques are applied (cf. Remark 4) so that repetitions with identical bases require equal running times. The binary representation of the secret exponent d reads $(d_{v-1}, \ldots, d_0)_2$, and in Phase 2b of Pseudoalgorithm 2 the exponent bits are processed from the left to the right.

In a pre-step the attacker measures the exponentiation times $\tilde{t}_{(j)} :=$ Time$(y_{(j)}^d (\text{mod } n)) + t_{\text{Err}(j)}$ for a sample $y_{(1)}, \ldots, y_{(N)}$ where $t_{\text{Err}(j)}$ denotes the measurement error for sample j. To be precise, we have

$$\tilde{t}_{(j)} = t_{\text{Err}(j)} + t_{S(j)} + (v + \text{ham}(d) - 2)c + \left(w_{(j)1} + \ldots + w_{(j)v + \text{ham}(d) - 2}\right)c_{\text{ER}} \tag{12}$$

where $w_{(j)i} \in \{0, 1\}$ equals 1 iff the ith Montgomery operation requires an extra reduction for sample j and 0 else. The term $t_{S(j)}$ summarizes the time needed for all operations apart from the Montgomery multiplications (input, output, handling the loop variable, evaluating the if-statements, pre- and post-multiplication). We may assume that the attacker knows $t_{S(j)}$ exactly as possible errors can be interpreted as part of the measurement error $t_{\text{Err}(j)}$. We may further assume that the attacker had guessed the parameters v, ham(d), c and c_{ER} in a pre-step of the attack (cf. [14], Sect. 6).

The exponent bits are guessed from the left to the right. For the moment we assume that the most significant exponent bits $d_{v-1}, \ldots, d_{k+1}$ have already been guessed, and that all guesses $\tilde{d}_{v-1}, \ldots, \tilde{d}_{k+1}$ are correct. Our goal is to derive an optimal decision strategy to guess the exponent bit d_k. At first the attacker subtracts the time needed to process the (correctly) guessed exponent bits $d_{v-1}, \ldots, d_{k+1}$ from the measured exponentiation time in order to obtain the time needed for the remaining bits $d_k, \ldots, d_0$ (beginning with 'if $(d_k = 1)$ then $\text{MM}(\text{temp}_{(j)}, \bar{y}_{1(j)}; n)$'), and from $\text{ham}(d)$ he further computes the number m of remaining Montgomery multiplications with $\bar{y}_{1(j)}$. If the random exponent d has been selected randomly it is reasonable to assume that $\eta(1) := \text{Prob}(d_k = 1) = (m-1)/k$ since $d_0 = 1$. That is, the a priori distribution is given by $(\eta(0), \eta(1)) = ((k+1-m)/k, (m-1)/k)$. Clearly, $\Theta = A = \{0, 1\}$. Since the differences of the running times are caused by the number of extra reductions (and maybe by measurement errors) we consider the 'normalized' remaining time

$$\tilde{t}_{d,rem(j)} := \frac{\tilde{t}_{(j)} - t_{S(j)} - (v + \text{ham}(d) - 2)c}{c_{\text{ER}}} - \sum_{i=1}^{v+\text{ham}(d)-2-k-m} w_{i(j)} \quad (13)$$

$$= t_{dErr(j)} + \sum_{i=v+\text{ham}(d)-k-m-1}^{v+\text{ham}(d)-2} w_{i(j)}.$$

where the last sum equals the number of extra reductions in the remaining Mongomery multiplications. The remaining Montgomery operations are labelled by the indices $v + \text{ham}(d) - k - m - 1, \ldots, v + \text{ham}(d) - 2$. The normalized measurement error $t_{dErr(i)} = t_{Err(i)}/c_{\text{ER}}$ is assumed to be a realization of an $N(0, \alpha^2(= \sigma_{Err}^2/c_{\text{ER}}^2))$-distributed random variable that is independent of $W_1, W_2, \ldots$ (cf. [12], Sect. 6).

The attacker bases his decision on the $4N$-tuple

$$\left(\tilde{t}_{\text{drem}(j)}, u_{M(j)}, u_{S(j)}, t_{S(j)} \right)_{j \leq N}$$

('observation') where $u_{M(j)}, u_{S(j)}, t_{S(j)} \in \{0, 1\}$ quantify the timing of sample j until the next decision (i.e., when guessing d_{k-1}). To be precise, $u_{M(j)} = 1$ (resp. $u_{S(j)} = 1$, resp. $t_{S(j)} = 1$) iff $\theta = 1$ and the next multiplication with $\bar{y}_{1(j)}$ (resp., iff $\theta = 1$ and the subsequent squaring, resp. iff $\theta = 0$ and the next squaring) requires an extra reduction. That is, $u_{M(j)}$ and $u_{S(j)}$ are summands of the right-hand side of (13) if $\theta = 1$ whereas $t_{S(j)}$ is such a summand if $\theta = 0$. Next, we study the stochastic process $W_{1(j)}, W_{2(j)}, \ldots$ that quantifies the (random) timing behaviour of these Montgomery multiplications. Although these random variables are neither independent nor stationary distributed they yet meet the central limit theorem ([12], Lemma 6.3(iii)). Since $W_{i(j)}$ and $W_{r(j)}$ are independent if $|i - r| > 1$ (cf. Subsection 3.2) we conclude

$$\text{Var}\left(W_{1(j)} + \ldots + W_{t(j)} \right) = \sum_{i=1}^{t} \text{Var}(W_{i(j)}) + 2 \sum_{i=1}^{t-1} \text{Cov}(W_{i(j)}, W_{i+1(j)}) \quad (14)$$

Concerning the variances we have to distinguish between two cases (squaring, multiplication with $\bar{y}_{(j)}$; cf. (11)), for the covariances between three cases, namely that $W_{i(j)}$ and $W_{i+1(j)}$ correspond to two squarings (cov$_{SS}$), resp. to a squaring followed by a multiplication with $\bar{y}_{(j)}$ (cov$_{SM(j)}$), resp. to a multiplication with $\bar{y}_{(j)}$ followed by a squaring (cov$_{MS(j)}$). Exploiting (10) and (9) the random vector $(W_{i(j)}, W_{i+1(j)})$ can be expressed as a function of the iid random variables $S_{i-1(j)}, S_{i(j)}, S_{i+1(j)}$. For instance, $\text{Cov}_{MS}(W_i W_{i+1}) =$

$$\int_{[0,1)^3} 1_{\{s_i < s_{i-1}\bar{y}_j/R\}} \cdot 1_{\{s_{i+1} < s_i^2 n/R\}} (s_{i-1}, s_i, s_{i+1})\, ds_{i-1} ds_i ds_{i+1} - \frac{\bar{y}_{(j)}}{2R} \cdot \frac{n}{3R} \quad (15)$$

Careful but elementary computations yield

$$\text{cov}_{MS(j)} = 2p_j^3 p_* - p_j p_*, \quad \text{cov}_{SM(j)} = \frac{9}{5}p_j p_*^2 - p_j p_* \quad (16)$$

$$\text{cov}_{SS} = \frac{27}{7}p_*^4 - p_*^2 \quad \text{with } p_j := \frac{\bar{y}_{(j)}}{2R} \text{ and } p_* := \frac{n}{3R}.$$

Since the random variables $W_{1(j)}, W_{2(j)}, \ldots$ are not independent the distribution of $W_{i+1(j)} + \cdots + W_{t(j)}$ depends on the preceding value $w_{i(j)}$. Theorem 2 considers this fact (cf. [12]). We first introduce some abbreviations.

Notation. $hn(0, j) := (k-1)p_*(1-p_*) + mp_j(1-p_j) + 2(m-1)\text{cov}_{MS(j)} + 2(m-1)\text{cov}_{SM(j)} + 2(k-m-1)\text{cov}_{SS} + 2\frac{k-m}{k-1}\text{cov}_{SM(j)} + 2\frac{m-1}{k-1}\text{cov}_{SS} + \alpha^2$,
$hn(1, j) := (k-1)p_*(1-p_*) + (m-1)p_j(1-p_j) + 2(m-2)\text{cov}_{MS(j)} + 2(m-2)\text{cov}_{SM(j)} + 2(k-m)\text{cov}_{SS} + 2\frac{k-m+1}{k-1}\text{cov}_{SM(j)} + 2\frac{m-2}{k-1}\text{cov}_{SS} + \alpha^2$,
$ew(0, j \mid b) := (k-1)p_* + mp_j + \frac{k-m}{k-1}(p_{*S(b)} - p_*) + \frac{m-1}{k-1}(p_{jS(b)} - p_j)$,
$ew(1, j \mid b) := (k-1)p_* + (m-1)p_j + \frac{k-m+1}{k-1}(p_{*S(b)} - p_*) + \frac{m-2}{k-1}(p_{jS(b)} - p_j)$ with
$p_{*S(1)} := \frac{27}{7}p_*^3$, $p_{*S(0)} := \frac{p_* - p_* p_{*S(1)}}{1 - p_*}$, $p_{jS(1)} := \frac{9}{5}p_* p_j$ and $p_{jS(0)} := \frac{p_j - p_* p_{jS(1)}}{1 - p_*}$.

A false guess $\tilde{d}_k \neq d_k$ implies wrong assumptions about the intermediate temp values for both hypotheses $d_t = 0$ and $d_t = 1$ for all the forthcoming decisions (when guessing d_t for $t < k$). Consequently, these guesses cannot be reliable, and hence we use the loss function $s(0, 1) = s(1, 0) = 1$. (For this setting the expected loss $R(\eta, \tau)$ equals the error probability $\text{Prob}(d_k \neq \tilde{d}_k)$.) For a complete proof of Theorem 2 we refer the interested reader to [12], Theorem 6.5 (i).

Theorem 2. *(Optimal decision strategy) Assume that the guesses $\tilde{d}_{v-1}, \ldots, \tilde{d}_{k+1}$ are correct and that* $\text{ham}(d_k, \ldots, d_0) = m$. *Let*

$$\psi_{N,d} : (\mathbb{R} \times \{0,1\}^3)^N \to \mathbb{R}, \qquad \psi_{N,d}((\tilde{t}_{\text{drem}(1)}, u_{M(1)}, \ldots, u_{S(N)}, t_{S(N)})) :=$$

$$-\frac{1}{2}\sum_{j=1}^{N}\left(\frac{(\tilde{t}_{\text{drem}(j)} - t_{S(j)} - ew(0, j \mid t_{S(j)}))^2}{hn(0, j)} - \right.$$

$$\left. \frac{(\tilde{t}_{\text{drem}(j)} - u_{M(j)} - u_{S(j)} - ew(1, j \mid u_{S(j)}))^2}{hn(1, j)}\right).$$

Then the deterministic decision strategy $\tau_d : (\mathbb{R} \times \{0,1\}^3)^N \to \{0,1\}$, defined by

$$\tau_d = 1_{\psi_{N,d} < \log(\frac{m-1}{k-m+1}) + \frac{1}{2}\sum_{j=1}^{N}\log(1+c_j)} \quad \text{with } c_j := \frac{hn(0, j) - hn(1, j)}{hn(1, j)} \quad (17)$$

is optimal (i.e., a Bayes strategy against the a priori distribution η).

Sketch of the Proof. To apply Theorem 1(ii), (iii) we first have to determine the conditional probability densities $h_{\theta,*j|C_j}(\tilde{t}_{\mathrm{drem}(j)}, u_{M(j)}, u_{S(j)}, t_{S(j)})$ (normal distribution) of the random vectors $X_j := (\tilde{T}_{\mathrm{drem}(j)}, U_{M(j)}, U_{S(j)}, T_{S(j)})$ for $\theta = 0, 1$ and $j \leq N$ with $C_j = (U_{M(j)} = u_{M(j)}, U_{S(j)} = u_{S(j)}, T_{S(j)} = t_{S(j)})$. (We point out that the X_j are independent but not their components.) The products $\prod_{j=1}^{N} h_{\theta,*j|C_j}(\cdot)$ are inserted in (4), and elementary computations complete the proof of Theorem 2.

The overall attack is successful iff all the guesses $\tilde{d}_{v-1}, \ldots, \tilde{d}_0$ are correct. Theorem 6.5 (ii) in [12] quantifies the probability for individual wrong guesses. In particular, guessing errors will presumably only occur in the first phase of the attack since the variance of the sum $W_{v+\mathrm{ham}(d)-k-m-1(j)} + \cdots + W_{v+\mathrm{ham}(d)-2(j)}$ decreases as k tends to 0. Due to the lack of space we skip this aspect but give a numerical example.

Example 3. Assume that the guesses $\tilde{d}_{v-1}, \ldots, \tilde{d}_{k+1}$ have been correct. For randomly chosen bases $y_{(1)}, \ldots, y_{(N)}$, for $n/R = 0.7$, $\alpha^2 = 0$, $N \geq 5000$, and ...

(a) ... $(k, m) = (510, 255)$ we have $\mathrm{Prob}(\tilde{d}_k \neq d_k) \leq 0.014$.

(b) ... $(k, m) = (440, 234)$ we have $\mathrm{Prob}(\tilde{d}_k \neq d_k) \leq 0.010$.

(c) ... $(k, m) = (256, 127)$ we have $\mathrm{Prob}(\tilde{d}_k \neq d_k) \leq 0.001$.

4.2   Error Detection, Error Location and Error Correction

In order to guess the secret exponent d the attacker considers a sequence of statistical decision problems (one for each exponent bit). The $\psi_{N,d}$-values themselves can be interpreted as realizations of random variables $Z_{v-1}, Z_{v-2}, \ldots$ with the pleasant property that their distributions change noticeably after the first wrong guess. For instance, the decision strategy from Theorem 2 then yields the guess 1 only with a probability of about 0.20 (The exact probability depends on the concrete parameters; cf. [12], Theorem 6.5(iii)). The interested reader is referred to Section 3 of [15] where a new stochastic strategy was introduced to detect, locate and correct guessing errors, which additionally reduces the sample size by about 40%.

4.3   Practical Experiments/Efficiency of the Optimized Attack

Reference [15] distinguishes two cases. In the *ideal* case it is assumed that the time measurements are exact, that the attacker knows the constants and parameters c, c_{ER}, v and $\mathrm{ham}(d)$ and that he is able to determine the setup time $t_{(S)}$ exactly. For the 'real-life' case the timing measurements were performed using an emulator which predicts the running time of a program in clock cycles. The code we used was the ready-for-transfer version of the Cascade library, i.e. with critical routines directly written in the card's native assemble language. Since the emulator is designed to allow implementors to optimize their code before 'burning' the actual smart cards, its predictions should match almost perfectly. In the 'real-life' case the attacker did not know $c, c_{\mathrm{ER}}, v, \mathrm{ham}(d)$, and $t_{(S)}$. Instead, these values were guessed in a pre-step ([14], Sect. 6).

Applying the optimized decision strategy and the error detection strategy mentioned in the previous subsection we obtained for sample size $N = 5000$ success rates of 85% (ideal case) and 74% ('real-life' case). For $N = 6000$ we obtained success rates of 95% and 85%, respectively. The original attack ([4]) yet required $200.000 - 300.000$ measurements. In other words: The optimized decision strategy from Theorem 2, combined with an efficient new error detection strategy, improved the efficiency of the original attack by factor 50. Moreover, the success rates for the ideal and the 'real-life' case are of the same size, which additionally underlines that our stochastic model is very appropriate.

Remark 4. (Countermeasures). The attacker exploits that the secret exponent d is the same for each exponentiation and that he knows both the bases and the modulus. In fact, this type of timing attack can be prevented with exponent blinding or base blinding techniques ([5]; Sect. 10). The latter is yet not sufficient to prevent combined timing and power attacks (cf. Sect. 6). Constant processing times for all Montgomery operations clearly is an alternative countermeasure. This goal can be reached by omitting all extra reductions within the exponentiation phase at cost of a larger modulus $R > 4M$ ([18]). Alternatively, an integer subtraction may be carried out in each Montgomery operation. (The dummy subtractions should be implemented carefully since otherwise the compiler might ignore them.)

5   A Timing Attack on RSA with CRT

In the previous section we considered a timing attack on RSA implementations that do not use the CRT. It was essential that the attacker knew the base y, the modulus n and the intermediate results of the computation. These requirements are obviously not fulfilled if the CRT is used. Consequently, it had been assumed for some years that CRT implemenations were not vulnerable to timing attacks. In [13] a new type of timing attack against RSA with CRT and Montgomery's multiplication algorithm was introduced (adaptive chosen-input attack). Unlike the attack from the previous section it does not guess the secret exponent d bit by bit but factorizes the modulus $n = p_1 p_2$. The attack would not have been detected without the understanding of the stochastic behaviour of Montgomery's multiplication algorithm. We point out that also this timing attack can be prevented with the countermeasures mentioned in Remark 4.

If the CRT is applied $x_i := (y(\bmod p_i))^{d_i} \equiv y^d(\bmod p_i)$ is computed for $i = 1, 2$ with $d_i = d(\bmod (p_i - 1))$. Finally, $y^d(\bmod n)$ is computed from these intermediate results. We assume that the square & multiply exponentiation algorithm and Montgomery's algorithm are used to calculate x_1 and x_2. As in the previous section $R > p_i$ denotes the Montgomery constant (which is assumed to be the same for p_1 and p_2), while R^{-1} stands for the multiplicative inverse of R in Z_n. For input $y := uR^{-1}(\bmod n)$ the constant factor in the computation of x_i equals $\bar{y}_{i;1} = yR \equiv u(\bmod p_i)$ (cf. Step 1 of Pseudoalgorithm 2).

Let $0 < u_1 < u_2 < n$ with $u_2 - u_1 \ll p_1, p_2$. Three cases are possible: The 'interval set' $\{u_1 + 1, \ldots, u_2\}$ contains no multiple of p_1 and p_2 (Case A), resp. contains a multiple of p_1 or p_2 but not of both (Case B), resp. contains multiples of both p_1 and p_2 (Case C). The computation of x_i requires about $\log_2(n)/2$ squarings and $\log_2(n)/4$ multiplications with $\bar{y}_{i;1}$. The running time for input $y := uR^{-1} \pmod{n}$, denoted with $T(u)$, is interpreted as a realization of a normally distributed random variable X_u (cf. [13]), and from (11) we obtain

$$E(X_{u_2} - X_{u_1}) \approx \begin{cases} 0 & \text{for Case A} \\ -\frac{c_{\mathrm{ER}}}{8} \frac{\sqrt{n}}{R} & \text{for Case B} \\ -\frac{c_{\mathrm{ER}}}{4} \frac{\sqrt{n}}{R} & \text{for Case C.} \end{cases} \tag{18}$$

where '$E(\cdot)$' denotes the expectation of a random variable. This observation can be used for a timing attack that factorizes the modulus n. In Phase 1 the attacker determines an 'interval set' $\{u_1 + 1, \dots, u_2\}$ with $u_2 - u_1 \approx 2^{-6}p_1, 2^{-6}p_2$ that contains a multiple of p_1 or p_2. The attacker is convinced that this is the case iff $T(u_2) - T(u_1) > -c_{\mathrm{ER}}\sqrt{n}/16R$. (There is no need to distinguish between Case B and Case C.) Starting with this interval $\{u_1 + 1, \dots, u_2\}$ in Phase 2 he applies the same decision rule to decide whether its upper halve contains a multiple of p_1 or p_2, and he replaces current interval by that halve (upper halve or lower halve) that contains a multiple of p_1 or p_2. In the elementary form of the attack this process is continued until the actual subset $\{u_1 + 1, \dots, u_2\}$ is sufficiently small so that it is feasible to calculate $\gcd(u, n)$ for all u within this subset (Phase 3). If all decisions within Phase 1 and Phase 2 have been correct the final subset indeed contains a multiple of p_1 or p_2, and Phase 3 yields the factorization of n.

At any instant within Phase 2 the attacker can verify with high probability whether his decisions have been correct so far, i.e. whether a given interval $\{u_1 + 1, \dots, u_2\}$ really contains a multiple of p_1 or p_2. He just applies the decision rule to the time difference required for neighboured values of u_1 and u_2, for instance to $T(u_2 - 1) - T(u_1 + 1)$. If this confirms the preceding decisions it is verified with overwhelming probability that the interval $\{u_1 + 1, \dots, u_2\}$ truly contains a multiple of p_1 or p_2. Consequently, we then call $\{u_1 + 1, \dots, u_2\}$ a *confirmed interval*. Otherwise, the attacker evaluates a further time difference (e.g. $T(u_2 - 2) - T(u_1 + 2)$). Depending on this difference he either finally confirms the interval $\{u_1 + 1, \dots, u_2\}$ or restarts the attack at the preceding confirmed interval, denoted with $\{u_{1;c} + 1, \dots, u_{2;c}\}$, using values u_1' and u_2' that are close to $u_{1;c}$ and $u_{2;c}$, respectively.

Under ideal conditions (no measurement errors) this attack required 570 time measurements to factorize 1024 bit moduli $n \approx 0.7 \cdot 2^{1024}$. Confirmed intervals were tried to establish after each 42 steps ([13]). When attacking a prime p_i directly (instead of any multiple) it suffices to reconstruct the upper half of the bit representation of p_1 or p_2 ([3]). For the parameters from above this reduces the number of time measurements from 570 to 300.

Also this attack may be interpreted as a sequence of decision problems with $|\Theta| = 2$, $s(1, 0) = s(0, 1) = 1$ and $\eta(0) = \eta(1) = 0.5$. However, the loss function and the a priori distribution do not yield any additional information in this case. We point out that this attack can be generalized to table methods ([13]) although its efficiency decreases due to a lower signal-to-noise ratio. In [1] this attack was modified to attack OpenSSL implementations over local networks.

6   A Combined Timing and Power Attack

In this section we assume that the attacked device computes modular exponentiations $y \mapsto y^d (\mathrm{mod}\, n)$ with a modular exponentiation algorithm that uses a b-bit-table ([9], Alg. 14.82) and Montgomery's multiplication algorithm (cf. Pseudoalgorithm 2). The b-bit table stores the values $\bar{y}_1, \ldots, \bar{y}_{2^b-1}$ with $\bar{y}_{j+1} = \mathrm{MM}(\bar{y}_j, \bar{y}_1; M)$ (cf. Sect. 3). We assume that the attacked device is resistant against pure power attacks but that the power measurements (SPA; cf. [16], Remark 3) enable the attacker to identify the beginning and the end of the particular Montgomery multiplications, i.e., whether an extra reduction is carried out. Due to base blinding (which prevents pure timing attacks) the attacker does not any of the table values, that is, the operands of the Montgomery multiplications. (If the attacker knew the table entries the attack was indeed elementary ([19], Subsect. 3.3).) In [19] only the special case $b = 2$ was considered. In [16] this attack was optimized and generalized to arbitrary b. Reference [17] treats the sliding windows exponentiation algorithm ([9], Alg. 14.85) with a modified variant of Montgomery's exponentiation algorithm where an extra reduction is carried out iff $s \geq R$ (cf. Sect. 3, Alg. 1). Although the general approach remains the same this increases the mathematical difficulties considerably.

The attack falls into four phases. At first the attacker measures the power consumption for a sample $y_1, \ldots, y_N$, and therefrom he determines those Montgomery operations that require extra reductions. On basis of this information he guesses the types ('S', 'M'_1', $\ldots$, 'M'_{2^b-1}') of all Montgomery operations within the exponentiation phase. The attacker guesses blocks of $f \geq 1$ consecutive Montgomery operations independently. (The attack becomes more efficient for $f > 1$ since the extra reductions of consecutive Montgomery multiplications are not independent. At the same time the computations become more complex.) Finally, the attacker tries to correct possible guessing errors and checks the resulting guess $\tilde{d}$ for the secret exponent d (e.g. by a known digital signature).

Theorem 3 specifies the optimal decision strategy. The $\{0, 1\}$-valued random variables $W_{1(k)}, W_{2(k)}, \ldots$ describe the random timing behaviour of the Montgomery multiplications in the exponentiation phase (see Sect. 3) where '(k)' indicates sample k. Equation (11) quantifies the probabilities for extra reductions which yet depend on the unknown table values. The 'source' of the attack is the initialization phase where the table values $\bar{y}_{1(k)}, \ldots, \bar{y}_{2^b-1(k)}$ computed. Although the attacker does not know the particular operands he at least knows the type of these operation ($\bar{y}_{j+1(k)} = \mathrm{MM}(\bar{y}_{j(k)}, \bar{y}_{1(k)}; M)$). The random timing behaviour in the initialization phase is quantified by another stochastic process $W'_{1(k)}, \ldots, W'_{2^b-1(k)}$ (cf. [16], Equation (3)). Theorem 3 uses Theorem 1(iii). For its proof we refer the interested reader to [16].

Theorem 3. Let $\tau_{opt}\Big((w_{i(k)}, \ldots, w_{i+f-1(k)}, w'_{1(k)}, \ldots, w'_{2^b-1(k)})_{1 \leq k \leq N} \Big) := \theta^*$ if

$$\sum_{\theta \in \Theta} s(\theta, \theta') \eta(\theta) \prod_{k=1}^{N} \mathrm{Prob}_\theta \big(W_{i(k)} = w_{i(k)}, \ldots, W_{i+f-1(k)} = w_{i+f-1(k)} \,|$$

$$W'_{r(k)} = w'_{r(k)}, r = 1, \ldots, 2^b - 1 \big)$$

is minimal for $\theta' = \theta^*$. *The decision strategy* τ_{opt} *is optimal among all the decision strategies that guess the types* $T(i), \ldots, T(i+f-1)$ *simultaneously.*

Apart from additional technical difficulties the conditional probabilities $\text{Prob}_\theta(\cdot \mid \cdot)$ are computed in a similar manner as in (15). We refer the interested reader to Section 4 of [16]. Due to the lack of space we restrict our attention to the a priori distribution and the loss function where we exclusively consider the case $f = 1$. (The general case $f \geq 1$ is treated in [16], Sect. 5.) In particular, $\Theta = \{`S', `M_1' \ldots, `M_{2^b-1}'\}$. In the exponentiation phase $\approx \log_2(d)$ squarings and $\approx \log_2(d)/(b2^b)$ multiplications with any particular table entry $\bar{y}_j$ are carried out. This yields the a priori distribution

$$\eta(`M_1') = \cdots = \eta(`M_{2^b-1}') = \frac{\frac{1}{b2^b}}{\frac{2^b-1}{b2^b}+1} = \frac{1}{b2^b(2^b-1)}, \quad \eta(`S') = \frac{b2^b}{b2^b(2^b-1)}. \quad (19)$$

The following example underlines that unlike in Sects. 4 and 5 it is reasonable to distinguish between different types of guessing errors.

Example 4. Let $b = 4$ and let the correct type sequence be given by
. $\ldots, `S', `M_3', `S', `S', `S', `S', \quad `M_{12}', `S', `S', `S', `S', `M_1', `S', \ldots$
whereas a), b) and c) are possible guesses.
a) $\ldots, `S', `M_3', `S', `S', `S', `M_{11}', `M_{12}', `S', `S', `S', `S', `M_1', `S', \ldots$
b) $\ldots, `S', `M_3', `S', `S', `S', `S', \quad `S', \quad `S', `S', `S', `S', `M_1', `S', \ldots$
c) $\ldots, `S', `M_3', `S', `S', `S', `S', \quad `M_{14}', `S', `S', `S', `S', `M_1', `S', \ldots$

Each of the subsequences a), b), and c) contains exactly one wrong guess. The error in Sequence a) ('M_{11}') is obvious as the number of squarings between two multiplications with table entries must be a multiple of $b = 4$. *Type-a errors* ('M_j' instead of 'S') are easy to detect and to correct if they occur isolated, i.e. if there are no further type-a or *type-b errors* ('S' instead of 'M_j'; cf. Sequence b)) in their neighbourhood. The correction of type-b-errors is not as obvious as that of type-a errors. (Reasonably, the attacker tries that alternative $a \in \Theta \setminus \{`S'\}$ that yields the second lowest expected loss.) The detection and location of type-a errors and type-b errors can be interpreted as a decoding problem. (Therefore, 'S' is replaced by 0 and 'M_j' by 1. Valid code words consist of isolated 1s and subsequences of 0s with lengths that are multiples of b.) Most cumbersome are the *type-c errors* ('M_j' instead of 'M_t') as not even their detection is obvious. Clearly, the attacker wants to avoid false guesses. However, the optimal decision strategy need not minimize the total number of errors (which was achieved by defining $s(\theta_i, \theta_j) := 1$ for all $\theta_i \neq \theta_j \in \Theta$) but should 'favour' type-a and type-b errors in comparison with type-c errors. Consequently, it is reasonable to choose a loss function that punishes type-c errors more than type-a and type-b errors, In our practical experiments we used for $b = 4$, for instance, the values $s(`S', `M_j') = 1$, $s(`M_j', `S') = 1.5$, $s(`M_t', `M_j') = 8$ (cf. [16]). We point out that the attack can be prevented with suitable exponent blinding or constant processing times for all Montgomery operations in the exponentiation phase (cf. Remark 4 and [16], Sect. 11) but not with base blinding.

Recall that whether a Montgomery operation requires an extra reduction neither depends on the concrete hardware platform nor on the used multiprecision variant of Montgomery's multiplication algorithm but only on d, n, R and the base $y_{(k)}$ (cf. Subsect. 3.1). Hence we emulated the modular exponentiations on a computer, outputting which Montgomery operations required extra reductions. This clearly corresponds with an attack under ideal conditions (also considered in [19] and [16]) where the attacker knows definitely whether a particular Montgomery operation needs an extra reduction. We point out that the attack, though less efficient, will also work under less favourable conditions. An attack was counted as successful iff the closest code word yielded the location of all type-a and type-b errors, and if there was at most one type-c error. For RSA without CRT, $b = 2$, $n/R \approx 0.99$, $\log_2(d) \approx 384$ and $(f = 3, N = 200)$ we obtained a success rate of about 90% whereas the attack in [19] required $N = 1000$ samples. (The efficiency of the attack increases as the ratio n/R increases.) For $b = 4$, $n/R \approx 0.70$ (average case), $\log_2(d) \approx 512$ and $(f = 1, N = 550)$ about of 94% of the attacks were successful. We point out that also CRT implementations are vulnerable to this attack (cf. [16], Sect. 10).

For $b = 4$, $n/R \approx 0.70$, $\log_2(d) \approx 512$ and $(f = 1, N = 550)$, resp. $(f = 1, N = 450)$ the optimal decision strategy was successful in about 94%, resp. 67% of the trials. Neglecting the a priori distribution and the different classes of errors, i.e. when using the maximum-likelihood estimator, the success rates decreased to 74% and 12%, resp., for these two parameter sets. For the optimal decision strategy the average numbers of type-c errors per trial were about 0.3 and 0.8, respectively. When using the maximum-likelihood estimator about 0.8, resp. 2.4, type-c errors occurred per trial in average.

These results underline that the probabilities p_θ have the most significant impact on the efficiency of the decision rule. Depending on the concrete situation, however, also the a priori distribution and the definition of an appropriate loss function may have non-negligible impact on the efficiency of the decision statrategy, especially for small sample sizes.

7   A Timing Attack on a Weak AES Implementation

Reference [7] considers a timing attack on a careless AES implementation. In the MixColumn transformation multiplications over $GF(2^8)$ by '02' and '03' = '01' + '02' are carried out. Essentially, only the multiplications by '02' need to be calculated, and this is done by shifting the respective state byte by one position to the left. If a carry occurs the hexadecimal constant '1B' is XORed to the shifted value. In the attacked implementation these conditional operations caused differences in the encryption times since the other AES transformations required identical time for all input values. In [7] the key bytes $k_1, k_2, \ldots, k_{16}$ were treated independently, and all combinations of key byte candidates were checked by a known plaintext/ciphertext pair.

Clearly, the larger the candidate sets the more time-consuming is the checking phase. On the other hand, if a correct key byte is rejected the attack must fail.

In [15] the efficiency of this attack was increased noticeably by interpreting the encryption times as realizations of random variables and by applying statistical decision theory. The candidate sets for the particular key bytes were reduced in two steps, considering one further key byte in each step. Each reduction step itself consists of many decisions, tolerating errors in some of these individual decision problems. Due to the lack of space we omit details and refer the interested reader to [15]. We merely point out that the sample size was reduced from 48000 to 4000 with a success rate of more than 90%. Moreover, this two-step sieving process can be adjusted to other side-channel attacks (e.g., to power attacks) where different parts of the key influence the measurements simultaneously.

8   Final Remarks

This paper proposes a general method to optimize the efficiency of side-channel attacks by advanced stochastic methods, especially by applying the calculus of stochastic processes and statistical decision theory. The proposed method is not a 'ready-to-use' tool for any application but requires some work to apply it to specific problems. We yet believe that the above examples have illustrated the central principles. We emphasize that a good understanding of the potential power of an attack is necessary to be able to rate its true risk potential and to design adequate and reliable countermeasures.

References

1. D. Brumley, D. Boneh: Remote Timing Attacks are Practical. In: Proceedings of the 12th Usenix Security Symposium, 2003.
2. B. Canvel, A. Hiltgen, S. Vaudenay, M. Vuagnoux: Password Interception in a SSL/TSL Channel. In: D. Boneh (ed.): Crypto 2003, Lecture Notes in Computer Science 2729, Springer, Heidelberg (2003), 583–599.
3. D. Coppersmith: Small Solutions to Polynomial Equations, and Low Exponent RSA Vulnerabilities. J. Cryptology 10 (no. 4) (1997) 233–260.
4. J.-F. Dhem, F. Koeune, P.-A. Leroux, P.-A. Mestré, J.-J. Quisquater, J.-L. Willems: A Practical Implementation of the Timing Attack. In: J.-J. Quisquater and B. Schneier (eds.): Smart Card – Research and Applications, Springer, Lecture Notes in Computer Science 1820, Berlin (2000), 175–191.
5. P. Kocher: Timing Attacks on Implementations of Diffie-Hellman, RSA, DSS and Other Systems. In: N. Koblitz (ed.): Crypto 1996, Springer, Lecture Notes in Computer Science 1109, Heidelberg (1996), 104–113.
6. K. Gandolfi, C. Mourtel, F. Olivier: Electromagnetic Analysis: Concrete Results. In: Ç.K. Koç, D. Naccache, C. Paar (eds.): Cryptographic Hardware and Embedded Systems – CHES 2001, Springer, Lecture Notes in Computer Science 2162, Berlin (2001), 251–261.
7. F. Koeune, J.-J. Quisquater: A Timing Attack against Rijndael. Catholic University of Louvain, Crypto Group, Technical report CG-1999/1, 1999.
8. P. Kocher, J. Jaffe, B. Jub: Differential Power Analysis. In: M. Wiener (ed.): Crypto 1999, Springer, Lecture Notes in Computer Science 1666, Berlin (1999), 388–397.

9. A.J. Menezes, P.C. van Oorschot, S.C. Vanstone: Handbook of Applied Cryptography, Boca Raton, CRC Press (1997).

10. D. Neuenschwander: Probabilistic and Statistical Methods in Cryptology. An Introduction by Selected Topics. Springer, Lecture Notes in Computer Science **3028**, Berlin (2004).

11. H. Sato, D. Schepers, T. Takagi: Exact Analysis of Montgomery Multiplication. TU Darmstadt, Technical Report TI-6/04.

12. W. Schindler: Optimized Timing Attacks against Public Key Cryptosystems. Statist. Decisions **20** (2002), 191–210.

13. W. Schindler: A Timing Attack against RSA with the Chinese Remainder Theorem. In: Ç.K. Koç, C. Paar (eds.): Cryptographic Hardware and Embedded Systems – CHES 2000, Springer, Lecture Notes in Computer Science **1965**, Berlin (2000), 110–125.

14. W. Schindler, F. Koeune, J.-J. Quisquater: Unleashing the Full Power of Timing Attack. Catholic University of Louvain, Technical Report CG-2001/3.

15. W. Schindler, F. Koeune, J.-J. Quisquater: Improving Divide and Conquer Attacks Against Cryptosystems by Better Error Detection / Correction Strategies. In: B. Honary (ed.): Cryptography and Coding – IMA 2001, Springer, Lecture Notes in Computer Science **2260**, Berlin (2001), 245–267.

16. W. Schindler: A Combined Timing and Power Attack. In: P. Paillier, D. Naccache (eds.): Public Key Cryptography – PKC 2002, Springer, Lecture Notes in Computer Science **2274**, Berlin (2002), 263–279.

17. W. Schindler, C. Walter: More Detail for a Combined Timing and Power Attack against Implementations of RSA. In: K.G. Paterson (ed.): Cryptography and Coding – IMA 2003, Springer, Lecture Notes in Computer Science **2898**, Berlin (2003), 245–263.

18. C.D. Walter: Precise Bounds for Montgomery Montgomery Modular Multiplication and Some Potentially Insecure RSA Moduli. In: B. Preneel (ed.): Topics in Cryptology – CT-RSA 2002, Springer, Lecture Notes in Computer Science **2271**, Berlin (2002), 30–39.

19. C.D. Walter, S. Thompson: Distinguishing Exponent Digits by Observing Modular Subtractions. In: D. Naccache (ed.): Topics in Cryptology – CT-RSA 2001, Springer, Lecture Notes in Computer Science **2020**, Berlin (2001), 192–207.

20. H. Witting.: Mathematische Statistik I, Stuttgart, Teubner (1985).

Symmetric Subgroup Membership Problems

Kristian Gjøsteen

Department of Matematical Sciences,
Norwegian University of Science and Technology, 7491 Trondheim, Norway
kristian.gjosteen@math.ntnu.no

Abstract. We define and discuss symmetric subgroup membership problems and their properties, including a relation to the Decision Diffie-Hellman problem. We modify the Cramer-Shoup framework, so that we can derive a chosen ciphertext secure cryptosystem in the standard model from symmetric subgroup membership problems. We also discuss how chosen ciphertext secure hybrid cryptosystems based on a symmetric subgroup membership can be constructed in the standard model, giving a very efficient cryptosystem whose security relies solely on the symmetric subgroup membership problem.

Keywords: public key encryption, hybrid encryption, standard model, subgroup membership problem.

1 Introduction

Public key cryptography was first proposed by Diffie and Hellman [5]. The most general security notion for public key cryptosystems is security against adaptive chosen ciphertext attacks (CCA) [10]. While many efficient schemes achieve this in the random oracle model, Cramer and Shoup [2,4] designed the first efficient scheme to achieve this security level in the standard model.

The security proofs for many public key cryptosystems essentially rely on subgroup membership problems. The most famous subgroup membership problem is the Decision Diffie-Hellman problem [1], on which the Cramer-Shoup cryptosystem relies. Yamamura and Saito [11] catalogued many subgroup membership problems that have appeared in the literature. Cramer and Shoup [3] gave a framework for turning general subgroup membership problems into secure cryptosystems, generalising their previous work and giving several new instances with interesting properties.

We study *symmetric subgroup membership problems* (Sect. 2), and show how they relate to the Decision Diffie-Hellman problem (Sect. 3). We also extend the framework of Cramer and Shoup to make efficient use of symmetric subgroup membership problems, giving very efficient cryptosystems secure against chosen ciphertext attacks in the standard model (Sect. 4). Finally, we discuss new developments in hybrid encryptions (Sect. 5) and construct a very efficient cryptosystem provably chosen ciphertext secure in the standard model, relying solely on the symmetric subgroup membership problem.

S. Vaudenay (Ed.): PKC 2005, LNCS 3386, pp. 104–119, 2005.

1.1 Notation

If S is a non-empty finite set, we denote by $\mathbb{N}_S$ the set $\{0, \ldots, |S| - 1\}$.

Let X be a distribution on a set S. We denote by $x \leftarrow X$ the act of sampling x from S according to the distribution X. The notation $x \leftarrow S$ is used to denote sampling x from S according to the uniform distribution. We denote by $x \leftarrow s$ the assignment of the value s to x.

We use the following notation to describe new distributions. Let $X_1, \ldots, X_n$ be distributions on sets $S_1, \ldots, S_n$, and let $f : S_1 \times \cdots \times S_n \to S$ be a function. Then by

$$X = \{f(x_1, \ldots, x_n) \mid x_1 \leftarrow X_1, \ldots, x_n \leftarrow X_n\}$$

we denote the distribution on S defined by

$$\Pr[x = s \mid x \leftarrow X] = \Pr[f(x_1, \ldots, x_n) = s \mid x_1 \leftarrow X_1, \ldots, x_n \leftarrow X_n] .$$

The distance between two distributions X and Y on a set S is

$$\mathrm{Dist}(X, Y) = \frac{1}{2} \sum_{s \in S} |\Pr[X = s] - \Pr[Y = s]| .$$

We say that two distributions X and Y are δ-close if $\mathrm{Dist}(X, Y) \leq \delta$.

2 Symmetric Subgroup Membership Problem

A subgroup membership problem consists of a finite abelian group G along with a proper, non-trivial subgroup K. The problem is to decide if a group element $x \in G$ is in K or in $G \setminus K$. We denote this subgroup membership problem by $\mathcal{SM}_{(G,K)}$, and the advantage of an adversary A is

$$\mathrm{Adv}_A^{\mathcal{SM}_{(G,K)}} = |\Pr[A(G, K, x) = 1 \mid x \leftarrow K] - \Pr[A(G, K, x) = 1 \mid x \leftarrow G \setminus K]| .$$

Let G be a finite abelian group, and let K and H be subgroups of G such that $K \cap H = \{1\}$ and $G = KH$. Then $K \times H \simeq G$, and the isomorphism is simply the group operation: $(k, h) \mapsto kh$. If $\gcd(|K|, |H|) = 1$, then if $d \equiv |H|^{-1}$ (mod $|K|$), we get that $c \mapsto (c^{|H|d}, c^{1-|H|d})$ is the inverse map. So anyone who knows $|K|$ and $|H|$ can compute the reverse isomorphism.

The *symmetric subgroup membership problem* $\mathcal{SSM}_{(G,K,H)}$ is the subgroup membership problem $\mathcal{SM}_{(G \times G, K \times H)}$. It is easy to show that distinguishing $K \times H$ is equivalent to distinguishing either K or H or both, and that considering maximum advantages for algorithms using some fixed amount of resources, we get

$$\mathrm{Adv}^{\mathcal{SM}_{(G,K)}} - \frac{|K| - 1}{|G| - 1} \leq \mathrm{Adv}^{\mathcal{SSM}_{(G,K,H)}} \leq \mathrm{Adv}^{\mathcal{SM}_{(G,K)}} + \mathrm{Adv}^{\mathcal{SM}_{(G,H)}} .$$

We shall assume that there are efficient algorithms available for sampling the subgroups K and H from a distribution that is δ-close to the uniform distribution, for some negligible $\delta \geq 0$. Typically, these algorithms simply choose a random exponent and exponentiate a generator for the subgroup. If δ cannot be zero, it is always easy to make δ arbitrarily small.

We describe two instances of the symmetric subgroup membership problem.

Let $n = pq$ be an RSA modulus, and let G be a group of order n. Let K be the subgroup of order p and let H be the subgroup of order q. Then we have a symmetric subgroup membership problem $\mathcal{SSM}_{(G,K,H)}$.

If $p' = 2n + 1$ is prime, the set of quadratic residues in $GF(p')^*$ is exactly such a group structure, and it seems plausible that it gives a hard symmetric subgroup membership problem. It was discussed in [8] and [9]. We could also consider $p' = 2sn + 1$ for some small integer s, with little additional complexity.

As an alternative, let a, b, c, d, $p = 2ab + 1$ and $q = 2cd + 1$ be primes, let $n = pq$, and let G be the subgroup of $\mathbb{Z}_n^*$ with Jacobi symbol 1. Let K be the subgroup of order $2ac$ and H be the subgroup of order bd. It is plausible that the resulting symmetric subgroup membership problem is hard. Note also that ac can be made much smaller than bd.

To see how this group structure can be used, we briefly describe a key encapsulation method (KEM) [4], and show that it is secure against passive attacks if and only if the symmetric subgroup membership problem is hard.

The key generation algorithm simply selects a suitable symmetric subgroup membership problem $\mathcal{SSM}_{(G,K,H)}$, and outputs a public key (G, K, H). The private key is $(G, |K|, |H|)$.

To sample a symmetric key and encipher it, $(x, y) \in G \times G$ is sampled (almost) uniformly at random from $K \times H$, using the sampling algorithms for $\mathcal{SSM}_{(G,K,H)}$. The key is (x, y) and the ciphertext is the product xy.

To decipher $c \in G$, the knowledge of $|K|$ and $|H|$ is used to compute $(x, y) \in K \times H$ such that $c = xy$, as described above.

It is clear that distinguishing the decryption (x, y) of a ciphertext c from a random pair $(x', y') \in G \times G$ such that $x'y' = c$ is equivalent to deciding the symmetric subgroup membership $\mathcal{SSM}_{(G,K,H)}$.

To discuss the efficiency of the above KEM, we shall compare it with three other schemes. The first is the cryptosystem proposed in [9] (NBD), the second is Diffie-Hellman in G (DH/G), and the third is Diffie-Hellman in the subgroup K (DH/K).

It was shown in [9] that NBD is secure if the symmetric subgroup membership problem is hard. Sect. 3 will show that Diffie-Hellman in G is not less secure than the above KEM. Sect. 4 will show that Diffie-Hellman in K can be turned into a cryptosystem with messages in G that is secure if the symmetric subgroup membership problem is hard.

DH/G requires two exponentiations in G to encrypt, and one to decrypt. DH/K requires two exponentiations in K to encrypt, and one to decrypt. NBD requires one exponentiation in K and one in H to encrypt, and approximately 1.3 exponentiations in G to decrypt. Our KEM requires essentially one exponentiation in K and one in H, both to encrypt and decrypt.

As we can see, Diffie-Hellman in K is the best option, especially if exponentiations in K can be made cheaper than exponentiations in H.

3   The Decision Diffie-Hellman Problem

We keep the notation introduced in Sect. 2. Let x be a generator for G. The *Decision Diffie-Hellman* (DDH) problem is to distinguish the two distributions $\{(x, x^u, x^v, x^{uv}) \mid u, v \leftarrow \mathbb{N}_G\}$ and $\{(x, x^u, x^v, x^w) \mid u, v, w \leftarrow \mathbb{N}_G\}$. Some definitions require $w \not\equiv uv \pmod{|G|}$, but the difference is negligible. The advantage of an algorithm A taking four group elements as input and answering 0 or 1 against DDH is defined to be

$$\text{Adv}_A^{\mathcal{DDH}_G} = \frac{1}{2} |\Pr[A(x, x^u, x^v, x^{uv}) \mid u, v \leftarrow \mathbb{N}_G]-$$

$$\Pr[A(x, x^u, x^v, x^w) \mid u, v, w \leftarrow \mathbb{N}_G]| .$$

We shall need the following result later on, so we state it as a separate lemma.

Lemma 1. *Let G be a finite cyclic group, and let K and H be non-trivial subgroup of G such that $K \cap H = \{1\}$ and $G = KH$. Let g be a generator for K. Consider the two distributions given by $U = \{(g^u, y, y^u) \mid u \leftarrow \mathbb{N}_G, y \leftarrow G \setminus K\}$ and $V = \{(g^u, y, y^u z \mid u \leftarrow \mathbb{N}_G, y \leftarrow G \setminus K, z \leftarrow H\}$. Then*

$$\text{Dist}(U, V) \leq \frac{|H| - \phi(|H|)}{|H|} .$$

Proof. Let $u_1 = u \bmod |K|$ and $u_2 = u \bmod |H|$, and let $y = y_1 y_2$ with $y_1 \in K$, $y_2 \in H$. It is easy to see that

$$U = \{(g^{u_1}, y_1^{u_1} y_2^{u_2}) \mid u_1 \leftarrow \mathbb{N}_K, u_2 \leftarrow \mathbb{N}_H, y_1 \leftarrow K, y_2 \leftarrow H \setminus \{1\}\}$$

and

$$V = \{(g^{u_1}, y_1^{u_1} y_2^{u_2} z) \mid u_1 \leftarrow \mathbb{N}_K, u_2 \leftarrow \mathbb{N}_H, y_1 \leftarrow K, y_2 \leftarrow H \setminus \{1\}, z \leftarrow H\} .$$

With $U' = \{y_2^{u_2} \mid u_2 \leftarrow \mathbb{N}_H, y_2 \leftarrow H \setminus \{1\}\}$ and $V' = \{y_2^{u_2} z \mid u_2 \leftarrow \mathbb{N}_H, y_2 \leftarrow H \setminus \{1\}, z \leftarrow H\}$, it is clear that

$$\text{Dist}(U, V) = \text{Dist}(U', V')$$

and that V' is exactly the uniform distribution on H. If y_2 is a generator, then U' is also uniformly distributed on H. It follows that

$$\text{Dist}(U', V') \leq \frac{|H| - \phi(|H|)}{|H|},$$

which concludes the proof. $\qquad\qquad\qquad\qquad\qquad\qquad\qquad\qquad\qquad\square$

Theorem 1. *Let $\mathcal{SSM}_{(G,K,H)}$ be a symmetric subgroup membership problem such that G is cyclic, and suppose that the sampling algorithms for K and H are δ-close to uniform. Let A be an algorithm that decides the Decision Diffie-Hellman problem in G. Then for any $\delta' > 0$ there are algorithms A_1, A_2 and A_3*

that use A once as an oracle and otherwise do $O(\log 1/\delta')$ exponentiations in G, such that

$$\mathrm{Adv}_A^{\mathcal{DDH}_G} \leq \mathrm{Adv}_{A_1}^{\mathcal{SM}_{(G,K)}} + \mathrm{Adv}_{A_2}^{\mathcal{SM}_{(G,K)}} + \mathrm{Adv}_{A_3}^{\mathcal{SM}_{(G,H)}} +$$
$$\frac{|G| - \phi(|G|)}{|G| - |K|} + \frac{|K| - \phi(|K|)}{|K|} + \frac{|H| - \phi(|H|)}{|H|} + \frac{|G| - \phi(|G|)}{|G| - |H|} +$$
$$7\delta' + 4\delta .$$

Proof. We shall need the following three experiments.

Experiment 1	**Experiment 2**	**Experiment 3**
Input: A, G, $x \in G$	Input: A, G, $y \in G$	Input: A, G, $h \in G$
1. $u, v, w \leftarrow \mathbb{N}_G$.	1. $u, v \leftarrow \mathbb{N}_G$.	1. $u, v \leftarrow \mathbb{N}_G$.
2. $y \leftarrow x^v$.	2. $x \leftarrow K$.	2. $x \leftarrow K$, $y \leftarrow G \setminus K$.
3. $b \leftarrow \{0,1\}$.	3. $b \leftarrow \{0,1\}$.	3. $b \leftarrow \{0,1\}$.
4. If $b = 1$, then $z \leftarrow y^u$, otherwise $z \leftarrow x^w$.	4. If $b = 1$, then $z \leftarrow y^u$, otherwise $z \leftarrow y^w$.	4. If $b = 1$, then $z \leftarrow y^u h$, otherwise $z \leftarrow y^w$.
5. $b' \leftarrow A(x, x^u, y, z)$.	5. $b' \leftarrow A(x, x^u, y, z)$.	5. $b' \leftarrow A(x, x^u, y, z)$.
6. If $b = b'$, output 1, otherwise output 0.	6. If $b = b'$, output 1, otherwise output 0.	6. If $b = b'$, output 1, otherwise output 0.
Output: 0 or 1.	Output: 0 or 1.	Output: 0 or 1.

In each experiment, Step 1 and 2 requires sampling certain elements from certain uniform distributions. It may be impossible to implement these steps, but we can implement approximations.

For Step 1, we note that the numbers sampled are used as exponents. Therefore, we can sample uniformly from a larger set to get an element distribution close to uniform. The cost is exponentiating to the larger exponent, but it is easy to show that for any $\delta' > 0$, $O(1/\log \delta')$ extra work suffices for a δ'-close to uniform distribution.

For Step 2, we simply use the algorithms provided by the subgroup membership problem, which are δ-close to uniform.

Consider first Experiment 1. If the input x is a generator for G, then this experiment measures the advantage of A against DDH. Let T_1 denote the event that the experiment outputs 1 when the input x is sampled from $G \setminus K$. An easy computation shows that

$$\mathrm{Adv}_A^{\mathcal{DDH}_G} \leq |\Pr[T_1] - 1/2| + \frac{|G| - \phi(|G|)}{|G| - |K|} . \qquad (1)$$

Let T_1' denote the event that the Experiment 1 outputs 1 when the input x is sampled from K. By the comments above, we can use Experiment 1 to construct a distinguisher A_1 for K, and

$$|\Pr[T_1] - \Pr[T_1']| \leq \mathrm{Adv}_{A_1}^{\mathcal{SM}_{(G,K)}} + 3\delta' . \qquad (2)$$

Next, we consider Experiment 2. Let T_2' be the event that Experiment 2 outputs 1 when the input y is sampled from K. Suppose the input x to Experiment 1 and y to Experiment 2 are sampled uniformly from K. In either case, if the x sampled generates K, the two experiments proceed identically. In other words,

$$|\Pr[T_1'] - \Pr[T_2']| \leq \frac{|K| - \phi(|K|)}{|K|} . \tag{3}$$

Let T_2 be the event that Experiment 2 outputs 1 when the input y is sampled from $G \setminus K$. As above, we can use Experiment 2 to construct a distinguisher A_2 for K, and

$$|\Pr[T_2] - \Pr[T_2']| \leq \mathrm{Adv}_{A_2}^{\mathcal{SM}(G,K)} + 2\delta' + \delta . \tag{4}$$

Then we consider Experiment 3. Let T_3' be the event that the experiment outputs 1 when the input h is sampled from H. When the input y to Experiment 2 is sampled from $G \setminus K$ and the input h to Experiment 3 is sampled from H, Lemma 1 shows that

$$|\Pr[T_2] - \Pr[T_3']| \leq \frac{|H| - \phi(|H|)}{|H|} . \tag{5}$$

Let T_3 be the event that the experiment outputs 1 when the input h is sampled from $G \setminus H$. As above, we can use Experiment 3 to construct a distinguisher A_3 for H, and

$$|\Pr[T_3] - \Pr[T_3']| \leq \mathrm{Adv}_{A_3}^{\mathcal{SM}(G,H)} + 2\delta' + 3\delta . \tag{6}$$

To conclude, we need only observe that in Experiment 3, when the input h is sampled from $G \setminus H$ and y is a generator, the distribution of z is independent of b, and therefore

$$|\Pr[T_3] - 1/2| \leq \frac{|G| - \phi(|G|)}{|G| - |H|} . \tag{7}$$

Combining equations (1)–(7) proves the theorem.   □

4   Chosen Ciphertext Security

4.1   Hash Proof Systems

We give a brief presentation of hash proof systems. It is only superficially different from [3], so we refer the reader there for further details.

Let G be a set, and let K be a subset of G. We say that W is a *witness set* for K if there is an easily computable bijection $\rho : W \to K$. This bijection allows one to prove that an element $x \in G$ really is in K by presenting an element $w \in W$ such that $\rho(w) = x$. This obviously assumes that it is easy to recognise elements of W.

For two sets S, S', denote by $\mathrm{Map}(S, S')$ the set of maps from S to S'. Let L be a group. We are interested in looking at maps from G to L. There is a natural map $\mathrm{Map}(G, L) \to \mathrm{Map}(K, L)$ given by restriction. From ρ we get a bijection $\rho^* : \text{Map}(K, L) \to \text{Map}(W, L)$. We also denote the natural map $\text{Map}(G, L) \to \text{Map}(W, L)$ by ρ^*.

A *projective hash family* is a tuple (G, K, L, W, ρ, M), where G is a set, K is a subset of G, L is a group, W is a witness set for K with isomorphism ρ, M is a subset of $\text{Map}(G, L)$, and for any $f \in M$, the image of K under f is a subgroup of L. We also suppose that L has a subgroup L', such that $L' \cap f(K) = \{1\}$ and $L = L'f(K)$. This gives us a subgroup membership problem $\mathcal{SM}_{(L,L')}$. (This corresponds to the definition sketched in Section 8.2.4 of [3].)

Let (G, K, L, W, ρ, M) be a projective hash family. The projective hash family is ϵ-*universal* if for any $f' \in \rho^*(M)$, $x \in G \setminus K$ and $y \in L$, we have that

$$\Pr[f(x) = y \wedge \rho^*(f) = f' | f \leftarrow M] \leq \epsilon \Pr[\rho^*(f) = f' | f \leftarrow M] .$$

The projective hash family is ϵ-*universal-2* if for any $f' \in \rho^*(M)$, $x_0 \in G \setminus K$, $x \in G \setminus (K \cup \{x_0\})$ and $y, y_0 \in L$, we have that

$$\Pr[f(x) = y \wedge f(x_0) = y_0 \wedge \rho^*(f) = f' | f \leftarrow M]$$
$$\leq \epsilon \Pr[f(x_0) = y_0 \wedge \rho^*(f) = f' | f \leftarrow M] .$$

It is clear that ϵ-universal follows from ϵ-universal-2.

Let (G, K, L, W, ρ, M) be a projective hash family. Define the two distributions

$$U = \{(x, \rho^*(f), f(x)) \mid x \leftarrow G \setminus K, f \leftarrow M\},$$
$$V = \{(x, \rho^*(f), f(x)y) \mid x \leftarrow G \setminus K, f \leftarrow M, y \leftarrow L'\} .$$

We say that the projective hash family is ϵ-*smooth* if

$$\text{Dist}(U, V) \leq \epsilon .$$

A *hash proof system* Π for a subgroup membership problem $\mathcal{SM}_{(G,K)}$ is a projective hash family (G, K, L, W, ρ, M), along with efficient algorithms for sampling W and M δ'-close to uniform, and for evaluating the hash functions on points in G and W.

An *extended hash proof system* $\hat{\Pi}$ for $\mathcal{SM}_{(G,K)}$ is a projective hash family $(G \times S, K \times S, \hat{L}, W, \hat{\rho}, \hat{M})$, where S is some set depending on G, along with efficient algorithms for sampling W and $\hat{M}$ δ'-close to uniform, and for evaluating the hash functions on points in $G \times S$ and $W \times S$.

A (extended) hash proof system Π ($\hat{\Pi}$) is ϵ-smooth (ϵ-universal-2) if the projective hash family is ϵ-smooth (ϵ-universal-2).

Let $\mathcal{SSM}_{(G,K,H)}$ be a symmetric subgroup membership problem such that G is cyclic, and suppose that a generator g is available for K. We shall describe a hash proof system Π and an extended hash proof system $\hat{\Pi}$ for $\mathcal{SSM}_{(G,K,H)}$. The group L will be G, and $L' = H$.

Let $W = \mathbb{Z}_{|K|}$ and $\rho([w]) = g^w$. Let $L = G$ and let $L' = H$. Since G is cyclic, the homomorphism group $\text{Hom}(G, G)$ is isomorphic to $\mathbb{Z}_{|G|}$, and we let $M = \text{Hom}(G, G)$. For any $f \in M$, a useful description of the function $\rho^*(f)$

is the group element $f(g)$, since for any $[w] \in W$, $f(g^w) = f(g)^w$. The projective hash family is $(G, K, G, \mathbb{Z}_{|K|}, \rho, \mathrm{Hom}(G, G))$, with the obvious sampling and evaluation algorithms.

By Lemma 1, this hash proof system is ϵ-smooth, for $\epsilon = 1 - \phi(|H|)/|H|$.

The extended hash proof system $\hat{\Pi}$ is slightly more complicated. Let ℓ be the smallest prime dividing $|H|$. We shall suppose that for some sufficiently large l, a 1-1 function $h : G \times G \to \{0, \dots, \ell - 1\}^l$ is available. Then $\hat{M}$ is the set of functions of the form

$$\hat{f}(x, e) = f_0(x) \prod_{i=1}^{l} f_i(x)^{\gamma_i},$$

where $h(x, e) = (\gamma_1, \dots, \gamma_l)$, and $f_i \in \mathrm{Hom}(G, G)$.

The witness set for $K \times G$ is $\mathbb{Z}_{|K|} \times G$, and the map $\hat{\rho}$ is given by $\hat{\rho}([w], e) = (g^w, e)$, where g is a generator for K. It is clear that

$$\hat{\rho}^*(\hat{f})([w], e) = f_0(g)^w \prod_{i=1}^{l} f_i(g)^{w\gamma_i},$$

where $h(g^w, e) = (\gamma_1, \dots, \gamma_l)$. So a useful description of the function $\hat{\rho}^*(\hat{f})$ is the tuple $(s_0, s_1, \dots, s_l) = (f_0(g), f_1(g), \dots, f_l(g))$.

By Theorem 3 of [3], the extended hash proof system $\hat{\Pi}$ described above is $1/\ell$-universal-2. Just as in [4], it is possible to replace the 1-1 function h with a collision resistant hash function, to get a computationally secure construction with $l = 1$.

4.2   The Cryptosystem

The standard goal for a public key cryptosystem is indistinguishability of ciphertexts against a adaptive chosen ciphertext adversary. We consider adversaries A consisting of a pair of algorithms (A_1, A_2), where A_1 receives the public key and outputs a pair of messages (m_0, m_1). A_2 then receives an encryption of one of the messages and must decide which one. Both A_1 and A_2 are allowed to have arbitrary ciphertexts decrypted (the challenge ciphertext excepted, obviously). If T is the event that A decides correctly, we say that A wins the game, and its advantage is defined to be

$$\mathrm{Adv}_A^{CCA} = |\Pr[T] - 1/2|.$$

Suppose we have a subgroup membership problem $\mathcal{SM}_{(G,K)}$, a hash proof system Π for $\mathcal{SM}_{(G,K)}$, and an extended hash proof system $\hat{\Pi}$ for $\mathcal{SM}_{(G,K)}$ such that the projective hash families are (G, K, L, W, ρ, M) and $(G \times L, K \times L, \hat{L}, W, \hat{\rho}, \hat{M})$, respectively.

We derive the cryptosystem CS' described in Fig. 1 from the two hash proof systems. Note that M, $\hat{M}$ and W are sampled using the algorithms from the hash proof systems.

The security analysis closely follows the analysis in [3].

Key Generation
Input: $\mathcal{SM}_{(G,K)}$, Π, $\hat{\Pi}$.

1. $f \leftarrow M$, $\hat{f} \leftarrow \hat{M}$.
2. $sk \leftarrow (G, L, \hat{L}, f, \hat{f})$.
3. $pk \leftarrow (G, W, L, \hat{L}, \rho,$
   $\rho^*(f), \hat{\rho}^*(\hat{f}))$.

Output: (pk, sk).

Encryption
Input: pk, $m \in L$.

1. $w \leftarrow W$.
2. $x \leftarrow \rho(w)$.
3. $y \leftarrow \rho^*(f)(w)$.
4. $e \leftarrow ym$.
5. $\hat{y} \leftarrow \rho^*(\hat{f})(w, e)$.

Output: $(x, e, \hat{y})$.

Decryption
Input: sk, $(x, e, \hat{y})$.

1. $\hat{y}' \leftarrow \hat{f}(x, e)$.
2. If $\hat{y}' \neq \hat{y}$, output $\perp$.
3. $y \leftarrow f(x)$.
4. $m \leftarrow ey^{-1}$.
5. Output m.

Output: A message m or $\perp$.

Fig. 1. The cryptosystem CS'.

Key Generation
Input: $\mathcal{SSM}_{(G,K,H)}$, $g \in K$.

1. $(k, k_0, k_1, \ldots, k_l) \leftarrow \{0, \ldots, |G| - 1\}^{l+2}$.
2. $(s, s_0, s_1, \ldots, s_l) \leftarrow (g^k, g^{k_0}, g^{k_1}, \ldots, g^{k_l})$.
3. $pk \leftarrow (G, g, s, s_0, s_1, \ldots, s_l, h)$.
4. $sk \leftarrow (G, k, k_0, k_1, \ldots, k_l, h)$.

Output: (pk, sk).

Encryption
Input: pk, $m \in G$.

1. $w \leftarrow \{0, \ldots, |K| - 1\}$.
2. $x \leftarrow g^w$.
3. $y \leftarrow s^w$.
4. $e \leftarrow ym$.
5. $(\gamma_1, \ldots, \gamma_l) \leftarrow h(x, e)$.
6. $\hat{y} \leftarrow s_0^w \prod_{i=1}^l s_i^{w\gamma_i}$.

Output: $(x, e, \hat{y}) \in G \times G \times G$.

Decryption
Input: sk, $(x, e, \hat{y}) \in G \times G \times G$.

1. $(\gamma_1, \ldots, \gamma_l) \leftarrow h(x, e)$.
2. $\hat{y}' \leftarrow x^{k_0} \prod_{i=1}^l x^{k_i \gamma_i}$.
3. If $\hat{y} \neq \hat{y}'$, then output $\perp$.
4. $y \leftarrow x^k$.
5. $m \leftarrow ey^{-1}$.

Output: A message $m \in G$ or $\perp$.

Fig. 2. The cryptosystem CS' instantiated with a symmetric subgroup membership problem $\mathcal{SSM}_{(G,K,H)}$.

Suppose that Π is ϵ-smooth, that $\hat{\Pi}$ is ϵ'-universal-2, that the sampling algorithms for Π and $\hat{\Pi}$ are δ'-close to uniform, and that the sampling algorithms for the subgroup membership problems are δ-close to uniform.

Suppose $A = (A_1, A_2)$ is a chosen ciphertext adversary against CS'. We shall use the following experiment to construct a distinguisher A' for (G, K). Again, note that M and $\hat{M}$ are sampled using the algorithms from the hash proof systems.

Experiment 4
Input: $A = (A_1, A_2)$, (G, K), Π, $\hat{\Pi}$, $x_0 \in G$.

1. $f \leftarrow M$, $\hat{f} \leftarrow \hat{M}$.
2. $sk \leftarrow (G, L, \hat{L}, f, \hat{f})$.
3. $pk \leftarrow (G, W, L, \hat{L}, \rho, \rho^*(f), \hat{\rho}^*(\hat{f}))$.
4. Initialise decryption oracle $\mathcal{D}_{sk}$.
5. $(m_0, m_1, s) \leftarrow A_1(pk)$, giving A_1 access to $\mathcal{D}_{sk}$.
6. $b \leftarrow \{0, 1\}$.
7. $y_0 \leftarrow f(x_0)$, $e_0 \leftarrow y_0 m_b$, $\hat{y}_0 \leftarrow \hat{f}(x_0, e_0)$.
8. Initialise restricted decryption oracle $\mathcal{D}'_{sk}$.
9. $b' \leftarrow A_2(pk, m_0, m_1, s, x_0, e_0, \hat{y}_0)$, giving A_2 access to $\mathcal{D}'_{sk}$.
10. If $b = b'$, output 1, otherwise output 0.

Output: 0 or 1.

Note that Steps 1–3 do exactly as the key generation algorithm would do.

Let T' be the event that Experiment 4 outputs 1 when the input x_0 is in K. Since Step 7 produces exactly the same result as the encryption algorithm when the input $x_0 \in K$, it is clear that the only difference between Experiment 4 and a real attack is that x_0 has been sampled uniformly from K, and not via the sampling algorithm for W. Since Experiment 4 outputs 1 when the adversary wins, we have that

$$\mathrm{Adv}_A^{CCA} \leq |\Pr[T'] - 1/2| + \delta', \tag{8}$$

since the sampling algorithm for W is δ'-close to uniform.

Let T be the event that Experiment 4 outputs 1 when the input x_0 is in $G \setminus K$. It is clear that from Experiment 4 we can derive an algorithm A' for distinguishing K from $G \setminus K$ such that

$$|\Pr[T'] - \Pr[T]| \leq \mathrm{Adv}_{A'}^{\mathcal{SM}_{(G,K)}} . \tag{9}$$

To analyse the event T, we shall make a series of modifications to Experiment 4. We number the modified experiments as $4'$, $4''$, etc. Note that these modifications need not be efficiently implementable.

First Modification. We change Step 1 so that f and $\hat{f}$ are sampled from the uniform distribution, and not using the algorithms provided by the hash proof systems.

Let T_1 be the event that Experiment $4'$ outputs 1 when the input x_0 is in $G \setminus K$. Since the algorithms provided by the hash proof systems were δ'-close to uniform, we obviously have that

$$|\Pr[T] - \Pr[T_1]| \leq 2\delta' . \tag{10}$$

Second Modification. We change the decryption oracles so that they refuse to decrypt a ciphertext $(x, e, \hat{y})$ if $x \notin K$. Let T_2 be the event that Experiment $4''$ outputs 1 when the input x_0 is in $G \setminus K$.

It is clear that this modification only affects the outcome if the adversary produces a valid ciphertext $(x', e', \hat{y}')$ with $x \notin K$, so $|\Pr[T_2] - \Pr[T_1]|$ is upper-bounded by the probability of this happening.

Since $\hat{\Pi}$ is ϵ'-universal-2, we can show, using the same arguments as in [3], that if A_1 and A_2 make Q decryption queries in total, then

$$|\Pr[T_2] - \Pr[T_1]| \leq Q\epsilon' . \tag{11}$$

Third Modification. We change Step 7 to be

7. $y' \leftarrow L'$, $y_0 \leftarrow f(x_0)$, $e_0 \leftarrow y_0 m_b y'$, $\hat{y}_0 \leftarrow \hat{f}(x_0, e_0)$.

Let T_3 be the event that Experiment $4'''$ outputs 1 when the input x_0 is in $G \setminus K$.

Since A_1 and A_2 cannot query the decryption oracle with ciphertexts $(x, e, \hat{y})$ where $x \notin K$, their only information about f is $\rho^*(f)$. Since Π is ϵ-smooth, we get that

$$|\Pr[T_3] - \Pr[T_2]| \leq \epsilon . \tag{12}$$

Fourth Modification. We change Step 7 to be

7. $y' \leftarrow L \setminus L'$, $y_0 \leftarrow f(x_0)$, $e_0 \leftarrow y_0 m_b y'$, $\hat{y}_0 \leftarrow \hat{f}(x_0, e_0)$.

Let T_4 be the event that Experiment $4''''$ outputs 1 when the input x_0 is in $G \setminus K$.

It is quite clear that if y' had been sampled uniformly from L, then there would be no information about m_b present in the ciphertext, and the probability that Experiment $4''''$ output 1 when the input x_0 was in $G \setminus K$ would be $1/2$. Since Experiment $4''''$ samples from $L \setminus L'$, we get that

$$|\Pr[T_4] - 1/2| \leq \frac{2|L'|}{|L|} . \tag{13}$$

We need to bound $|\Pr[T_4] - \Pr[T_3]|$. To do this, we introduce another experiment.

Experiment 5
Input: $A = (A_1, A_2)$, (G, K), Π, $\hat{\Pi}$, $y' \in L$.

Steps 1–6 are as in Experiment 4.
7. $x_0 \leftarrow G \setminus K$, $y_0 \leftarrow f(x_0)$, $e_0 \leftarrow y_0 m_b y'$, $\hat{y}_0 \leftarrow \hat{f}(x_0, e_0)$.
Steps 8–10 are as in Experiment 4.

Output: 0 or 1.

It is quite clear that we can repeat the two first modifications to Experiment 4 on Experiment 5, and the analysis remains the same. Let R' be the event that Experiment $5''$ outputs 1 when the input y' is in L', and let R be the event that Experiment $5''$ outputs 1 when the input y' is in $L \setminus L'$.

If the input y' to Experiment $5''$ is in L', then it behaves exactly as Experiment $4'''$. Hence, $\Pr[R'] = \Pr[T_3]$.

If the input y' to Experiment $5''$ is in $L \setminus L'$, then it behaves exactly as Experiment $4''''$. Hence, $\Pr[R] = \Pr[T_4]$.

It is clear that we from Experiment 5 can derive an algorithm A'' to distinguish L' from $L \setminus L'$, by sampling x_0 not uniformly from $G \setminus K$, but via the subgroup membership problem's algorithms, and that

$$|\Pr[T_4] - \Pr[T_3]| = |\Pr[R] - \Pr[R']| \leq \mathrm{Adv}_{A''}^{\mathcal{SM}_{(L,L')}} + 2\delta' + \delta + Q\epsilon' . \quad (14)$$

Summing Up. Combining (8)–(14), we have proved the following theorem.

Theorem 2. *Let CS' be the cryptosystem described above, based on a subgroup membership problem $\mathcal{SM}_{(G,K)}$ and hash proof systems Π and $\hat{\Pi}$. Let L be the group associated to G by Π, and let L' be the subgroup of L. Suppose that Π is ϵ-smooth, that $\hat{\Pi}$ is ϵ'-universal-2, that the sampling algorithms for Π and $\hat{\Pi}$ are δ'-close to uniform, and that the sampling algorithms for the subgroup membership problem are δ-close to uniform. Then for any chosen ciphertext adversary A against CS', we have that*

$$\mathrm{Adv}_A^{CCA} \leq \mathrm{Adv}_{A'}^{\mathcal{SM}_{(G,K)}} + \mathrm{Adv}_{A''}^{\mathcal{SM}_{(L,L')}} + 5\delta' + \delta + 2Q\epsilon' + \epsilon + \frac{2|L'|}{|L|},$$

where A' and A'' are algorithms that invoke each stage of A once, and Q is the number of decryption queries made by A

It is clear that when instantiated with the hash proof systems described in Sect. 4.1, then if the extended hash proof system is removed, the cryptosystem CS' reduces to Diffie-Hellman in K, and the above proof is easily modified to show that it is secure, as was claimed in Sect. 2.

Finally, we briefly discuss the performance of the scheme when instantiated with the hash proof systems described in Sect. 4.1 (using a hash function instead of a 1-1 function) and the symmetric subgroup membership problems discussed in Sect. 2.

Two things should be noted. For encryption, three exponentiations in CS' are in K, while the fourth exponent has bit length equal to the length of the hash value used. Second, when $\mathbb{Z}_n^*$ is used, K can be made very small compared to G. It is not unreasonable that for a t bit security level, $\log_2 |K| \approx 4t$ is sufficient.

The length of the hash should be $2t$. This means that the work required for an exponentiation corresponds roughly to one exponentiation with exponent bit length $14t$. For 80 bit security level this is 1120, and 1792 for 128 bit security level. This compares well with the corresponding modulus lengths 1024 and 3096.

For decryption, slightly more than two exponentiations in G are required (exactly two if $GF(2n + 1)^*$ is used and $|G| = n$ is known). If the order of K is known to the private key holder, then roughly three exponentiations in K are required, but since they are all to the same base, the actual cost is smaller, say roughly equivalent to two exponentiations. For $\mathbb{Z}_n^*$, this corresponds to one exponentiation in G with exponent bit length $8t$.

Of course, if $\mathbb{Z}_n^*$ is used and the factorisation of n is known to the private key holder, Chinese remainder tricks are also available.

Compared to the instantiations of the Cramer-Shoup construction given in [3], our two instantiations are significantly faster, except for the elliptic curve variants of Cramer-Shoup. Asymptotically, they are faster than our variants, but at 80 bit security level, our variants would seem to have an advantage, at least for encryption.

5   Hybrid Encryption

When a key encapsulation method is all that is required, the Cramer-Shoup key encapsulation method [4] using a subgroup of a finite field will be faster than our two constructions in the previous section. However, recent advances in [7] and [6] show that it is possible to construct secure hybrid encryption schemes from key encapsulation methods that are by themselves not secure.

The basic idea is that an ϵ-universal-2 hash proof system by itself will do, when its output is split into two bit strings, where one is used as a key for a symmetric cryptosystem, and the other is used as a key to a message authentication code.

We sketch a variant of this construction based on the symmetric subgroup membership problem in $\mathbb{Z}_n^*$. We do not believe that it will be faster than other instantiations, but we believe it is possible to construct a very fast cryptosystem based only on the hardness of the subgroup membership problem, which is in itself interesting.

The basic scheme requires five parts, a subgroup membership problem, a key derivation function, a MAC, a symmetric encryption scheme, and a hash function. Note that there are information theoretically secure MACs and symmetric encryption schemes.

The subgroup membership problem is based on $\mathbb{Z}_n^*$, where $n = (2ab+1)(2cd+1)$ as described in Sect. 2. To simplify things, G shall be the subgroup of quadratic residues. (It may be possible to use the subgroup with Jacobi symbol 1 instead.) We are given a generator g for K, of order ac.

The key derivation function $\kappa : G \rightarrow \{0,1\}^{l_1} \times \{0,1\}^{l_2}$ should return bit strings indistinguishable from random when applied to group elements sampled uniformly at random from certain subsets of G. Universal hashing techniques should provide an information-theoretically secure key derivation function.

The interesting point, however, is the hash function. What we need is a hash function $h : G \rightarrow \text{Hom}(G, G)$ that is target collision resistant, where we count as a collision two homomorphisms that happen to be the same on any subgroup of G (this is why we restrict to the quadratic residues, and why $GF(2n + 1)^*$ cannot be used).

Note that $\text{Hom}(G, G) \simeq \mathbb{Z}_{\phi(n)/2}$. The hash function is simply $h(x) = x$, since $x \in G$ can be represented by an integer in the set $\{1, \ldots, n-1\}$ (we will consider the group elements to be integers when convenient). We claim that the advantage of any collision finder against this hash function is less than $\text{Adv}^{\mathcal{SSM}(G,K,H)}$.

So suppose we have some algorithm that on input of G and g outputs distinct x_1, x_2 such that $h(x_1)$ and $h(x_2)$ collide on some subgroup of G. We consider all possibilities in turn.

If they collide on G itself, this means that $x_1 \equiv x_2 \pmod{abcd}$, or that $abcd$ divides $x_1 - x_2$. Let z be any element with Jacobi symbol -1. Then $z^{x_1 - x_2}$ must be congruent to 1 modulo p and -1 modulo q, or vice versa. In other words, $z^{x_1 - x_2}$ gives a factorisation of n.

If they collide on K or H, but not both, then ac or bd divides $x_1 - x_2$, but not both. This may not lead to a factorisation of n, but it is clear that any multiple of $ac = |K|$ or $bd = |H|$ can be used to distinguish K or H.

If they collide modulo a, but not modulo c, or vice versa, we use the subgroup membership problems sampling algorithm to get an element $z \in K$. Unless we by chance have already got a factorisation of n, $z^{x_1 - x_2}$ will give us one. Likewise, for b and d.

This proves the claim. (Note that we prove collision resistance, which is stronger than target collision resistance.)

The key generation algorithm takes as input G and g. It samples k_0, k_1 uniformly at random from $\{1, \ldots, \lfloor n/4 \rfloor\}$. The public key is $(G, g, s_0, s_1) = (g^{k_0}, g^{k_1})$, the private key is (G, k_0, k_1).

The encryption algorithm takes the public key as input, as well as a message encoded as a bit string. It samples w uniformly at random from $\{1, \ldots, N\}$ (where N is sufficiently much larger than $|K|$). It computes $x = g^w$, $x' = s_0^{2w} s_1^{2wh(x)}$. Then it applies the key derivation function to x' to get encryption and MAC keys. It uses the encryption key to encrypt the message into ciphertext e and the MAC key to compute a tag t for e. The ciphertext is (x, e, t).

The decryption algorithm computes $x^{2(k_0 + h(x)k_1)}$ and applies the key derivation function to the result. It checks the tag t with the derived MAC key, and if it is correct, decrypts the ciphertext e with the encryption key and outputs the result.

Key Generation	**Encryption**	**Decryption**
Input: $G \subseteq \mathbb{Z}_n^*, g \in G$.	Input: $pk, m \in G$.	Input: $sk, (x, e, t)$.
1. $(k_0, k_1) \leftarrow$ $\{0, \ldots, \lfloor n/4 \rfloor\}^2$.	1. $w \leftarrow \{0, \ldots, |K| - 1\}$.	1. $x' \leftarrow x^{2(k_0 + h(x)k_1)}$.
2. $(s_0, s_1) \leftarrow (g^{k_0}, g^{k_1})$.	2. $x \leftarrow g^w$.	2. $(\kappa_1, \kappa_2) \leftarrow kdf(x')$.
3. Select kdf.	3. $x' \leftarrow s_0^{2w} s_1^{2wh(x)}$.	3. $t' \leftarrow \mathcal{T}(\kappa_2, e)$.
4. $pk \leftarrow (G, g, s_0, s_1, kdf)$.	4. $(\kappa_1, \kappa_2) \leftarrow kdf(x')$.	4. If $t \neq t'$, output $\bot$.
5. $sk \leftarrow (G, k_0, k_1, kdf)$.	5. $e \leftarrow \mathcal{E}(\kappa_1, m)$.	5. $m \leftarrow \mathcal{D}(\kappa_1, e)$.
	6. $t \leftarrow \mathcal{T}(\kappa_2, e)$.	6. Output m.
Output: (pk, sk).	Output: (x, e, t).	Output: A message m or $\bot$.

Fig. 3. The hybrid cryptosystem using a symmetric cryptosystem $(\mathcal{E}, \mathcal{D})$ and MAC algorithm $\mathcal{T}$.

The security analysis for this scheme should be essentially the same as in [6], which is very similar to the proof in Sect. 4. Note that the extra squaring makes the cryptosystem benignly malleable, in the sense that (x, e, t) and $(-x, e, t)$ both decrypt to the same message. This is not a security problem.

Compared to the scheme described in Sect. 4, the encryption cost measured in total exponent length is $8t + \log_2 n$. For 80 bit security level, this is roughly 1664, and 4120 for 128 bit security level. The decryption cost is roughly 480 and 768, respectively. The advantage is that we only depend on the subgroup membership problem.

6   Concluding Remarks

We have defined and discussed symmetric subgroup membership problems. The main result of the theoretic discussion is a relation between the Decision Diffie-Hellman problem and the symmetric subgroup membership problem.

Then we have designed and analysed a chosen ciphertext secure public key cryptosystem based on a symmetric subgroup membership problem, by extending the framework of Cramer and Shoup. The resulting scheme is quite efficient compared to other instances of the Cramer-Shoup framework, although it requires a new hardness assumption.

Finally, we have sketched how to design a hybrid cryptosystem with chosen ciphertext security based only on a symmetric subgroup membership problem. In the immediate aftermath of CRYPTO'04, not relying on a target collision resistant hash function seems to be a conservative move. The full security proof for this cryptosystem will appear at a later time.

References

1. D. Boneh. The Decision Diffie-Hellman problem. In *Proceedings of the Third Algorithmic Number Theory Symposium*, volume 1423 of *LNCS*, pages 48–63. Springer-Verlag, 1998.
2. Ronald Cramer and Victor Shoup. A practical public key cryptosystem secure against adaptive chosen cipher text attacks. In Hugo Krawczyk, editor, *Proceedings of CRYPTO '98*, volume 1462 of *LNCS*, pages 13–25. Springer-Verlag, 1998.
3. Ronald Cramer and Victor Shoup. Universal hash proofs and a paradigm for adaptive chosen ciphertext secure public-key encryption. In Lars R. Knudsen, editor, *Proceedings of EUROCRYPT 2002*, volume 2332 of *LNCS*, pages 45–64. Springer-Verlag, 2002.
4. Ronald Cramer and Victor Shoup. Design and analysis of practical public-key encryption schemes secure against adaptive chosen ciphertext attack. *SIAM Journal on Computing*, 33(1):167–226, 2003.
5. W. Diffie and M. E. Hellman. New directions in cryptography. *IEEE Transactions on Information Theory*, 22:644–654, 1976.
6. Rosario Gennaro and Victor Shoup. A note on an encryption scheme of Kurosawa and Desmedt. Cryptology ePrint Archive, Report 2004/194, 2004. http://eprint.iacr.org/.

7. K. Kurosawa and Y. Desmedt. A new paradigm of hybrid encryption scheme. In Matt Franklin, editor, *Proceedings of CRYPTO 2004*, volume 3152 of *LNCS*. Springer-Verlag, 2004.

8. W. Mao. Fast Monte-Carlo primality evidence shown in the dark. Technical Report HPL-1999-30R1, HP Laboratories, October 1999.

9. Juan Manuel González Nieto, Colin Boyd, and Ed Dawson. A public key cryptosystem based on the subgroup membership problem. In S. Quing, T. Okamoto, and J. Zhou, editors, *Proceedings of ICICS 2001*, volume 2229 of *LNCS*, pages 352–363. Springer-Verlag, 2001.

10. C. Rackoff and D. Simon. Non-interactive zero-knowledge proof of knowledge and chosen ciphertext attack. In Joan Feigenbaum, editor, *Proceedings of CRYPTO '91*, volume 576 of *LNCS*, pages 433–444. Springer-Verlag, 1992.

11. Akihiro Yamamura and Taiichi Saito. Private information retrieval based on the subgroup membership problem. In V. Varadharajan and Y. Mu, editors, *Proceedings of ACISP 2001*, volume 2119 of *LNCS*, pages 206–220. Springer-Verlag, 2001.

Optimizing Robustness
While Generating Shared Secret Safe Primes

Emil Ong and John Kubiatowicz

University of California, Berkeley

Abstract. We develop a method for generating shared, secret, safe primes applicable to use in threshold RSA signature schemes such as the one developed by Shoup. We would like a scheme usable in practical settings, so our protocol is robust and efficient in asynchronous, hostile environments. We show that the techniques used for robustness need special care when they must be efficient. Specifically, we show optimizations that minimize the number and size of the proofs of knowledge used. We also develop optimizations based on computer arithmetic algorithms, in particular, precomputation and Montgomery modular multiplication.

Keywords: Distributed key generation, safe primes, threshold RSA signatures.

1   Introduction

Shoup's scheme [1] for threshold RSA signatures was a great leap forward in making threshold signature schemes practical. Its ability to avoid interaction while signing makes the scheme efficient and easy to implement. Unfortunately, Shoup's scheme required the use of a safe prime product modulus for its proof of correctness. Moreover, the scheme assumes a trusted dealer to create and distribute this modulus and the private key shares. Since the development of Shoup's scheme, several works ([2–4]) have been published to try to eliminate the single dealer, but none have shown the costs associated with a robust solution.

In this paper, we show the cost required for a robust implementation of a distributed safe prime generation scheme. We follow the basic form of the algorithm in [2], but we also show that the changes necessary for robustness are non-trivial if we want efficiency. We develop several techniques for reducing the number of proofs of knowledge while maintaining security. Our methods are based on computer arithmetic, number theory, and simple protocol analysis to reduce redundancy.

1.1   Algorithm Overview

Before diving into the details of our safe prime generation algorithm, we will give a high-level overview. Our approach to prime finding is very familiar: effectively we generate candidate numbers and test them until we find a safe prime. First we use the usual techniques for improving our search – we make sure that our

S. Vaudenay (Ed.): PKC 2005, LNCS 3386, pp. 120–137, 2005.

---

1. Find a candidate number ϕ which has no small prime factors and has the property $\phi \equiv 3 \mod 4$.
2. If the number 2 is a Miller-Rabin witness to the compositeness of ϕ or $\frac{\phi-1}{2}$, return to step 1.
3. Run the Miller-Rabin test repeatedly on ϕ with random inputs a sufficient number of times to ensure primality with a small error probability.

Fig. 1. Algorithm Overview.

candidate prime is not composed of small prime factors. However instead of doing trial division, we produce our candidate in a constructive way following the lead of Malkin, Wu, and Boneh [5]. We modify their algorithm however by making it robust through contributing several zero-knowledge proofs. This method is detailed in Section 3.

After finding such a candidate, we then proceed to do more rigorous tests. Specifically, we follow the techniques outlined by Cramer and Shoup in [6]. The procedure recommended in that work involves two specialized Miller-Rabin tests followed by a generic Miller-Rabin test of compositeness. To do Miller-Rabin compositeness tests, we have to perform modular exponentiation. In our case the modulus is secret, a fact which is the main source of difficulty in our algorithm. Sections 4.1 and 4.2 are dedicated to optimizing the performance of this type of modular exponentiation. Specifically, we generalized the modular exponentiation method given in [2] and provided a new modular multiplication algorithm based on Montgomery multiplication. The high-level algorithm is summarized in Figure 1.

1.2 Application: RSA Signatures

After successfully generating two shared, safe primes with this algorithm, the players can simply multiply their shares of these primes together and reveal the result. The factorization of the composite number is not revealed because the VSS and multiplication schemes conceal. At this point, the players have all generated a public RSA modulus for which no player knows the factors. Moreover, the players can compute secret shares of the Euler totient function of the modulus. This fact allows them to use the algorithm of Catalano et al. [7] to compute secret shares of an RSA private key. These key shares are then immediately usable for Shoup's RSA signature scheme [1].

1.3 Related Work

Shoup's proof of correctness required the use of safe primes in the RSA modulus (i.e. $n = pq$ where p, q are primes of the form $p = 2p' + 1, q = 2q' + 1$ with p', q' also being primes). [3, 4] noted that this requirement is a bit strong and replaced it with assumptions relating to the computational difficulty of certain operations in RSA groups. Safe primes meet and exceed the requirements set by [3, 4] and these works both showed RSA moduli with lesser constraints are suitable for Shoup's scheme. The assumptions made are non-standard, but reasonable.

Works by Boneh et al. [8, 5] developed ways to generate and verify RSA moduli and inverses, but do not necessarily produce primes suitable to Shoup's threshold scheme. Moreover, these schemes are secure only in the honest-but-curious setting. An optimization in [5], called *distributed sieving*, however is very useful and we will develop a robust version in section 3.

Frankel, MacKenzie, and Yung [9] developed a robust method for RSA key generation, but also do not produce safe prime product moduli. Many of their techniques will be very useful in our protocol, however.

Algesheimer, Camenish, and Shoup [2] were the first to suggest an algorithm for distributively generating safe primes and we follow their exposition closely. Our work expands on their algorithm by making it robust and optimizing within this robust framework.

1.4   Contributions

Our contributions to this field are three-fold:

- We provide a robust version of the Malkin, Wu, and Boneh [5] distributed sieving algorithm,
- We improve the Miller-Rabin algorithm of Algesheimer, Camenish, and Shoup [2] by (1) generalizing the modular exponentiation method and (2) introducing Montgomery multiplication into a distributed computational framework for faster modular arithmetic.

2   Preliminaries: Model and Commitments

We deal with two preliminaries before proceeding to our algorithm, the computational and network models and the commitment and verified secret sharing schemes we use.

2.1   Model

We assume an asynchronous network only offering point-to-point messages. We view the network as an adversary that can choose to drop or delay the messages sent between two parties. The protocols we use require authenticated messages however, so we will assume that there exists some way of ensuring the integrity of messages which are delivered. We rely on the work of Goldwasser and Lindell [10] which provides a broadcast protocol which is simpler than full, authenticated Byzantine agreement, but is sufficient for both serial and parallel composition of secure computation.

For the secrecy and binding of our commitment and secret sharing protocols, we rely on the assumption that computing discrete logarithms is difficult. We will build our protocols to be secure in the random oracle model since we intend them to be used for Shoup's RSA signature scheme [1], which uses a random oracle for non-interactivity. This assumption can be removed by reintroducing additional interactivity, though at significant cost, as usual.

In describing these multiparty protocols, we will borrow the notation of [2] for secret sharing. We assume familiarity with both additive and polynomial secret sharing (also known as Shamir secret sharing [11]). Our algorithms will only involve polynomial secret sharing and we shall denote player j's polynomial share of a as $[a]_j^p \in \mathbb{Z}_p$. In general, we will use these notations to show the format of the input and output values of our multiparty protocols, but refer to the shared value directly in the body of the protocol for clarity.

2.2 Commitments

We will need a commitment scheme where the properties of the *integers* hold because we may need to deal with negative numbers to prove relative primality. We will also need a verifiable secret sharing scheme that works using integer commitments. This property will give us the ability to prove statements about the numbers we share. These two primitives are the basis for robustness in our algorithm.

We will use a scheme discussed in [7] which uses a prime finite field of very large order and relies on the discrete logarithm problem. In truth, these are not commitments over the integers, but the finite field on which they are defined is large enough that relations we are trying to prove also hold in these fields. We prefer this technique over that of [12] in our case. A more complete explanation of the differences is available in the extended version of this paper[1].

Setup. The prime number that we use needs to be larger than any term we will use in our commitments and computations. Since our goal is to create an RSA modulus by multiplying shared primes, the players can agree to a specific RSA key size *a priori* and this size will determine the maximum size of our committed numbers. For example, if we are trying to generate a key of size 1024, we can set the bound for candidate safe prime numbers at $B = 2^{512}$.

There are two computations for which we need to be careful: those involved in verifiable secret sharing (VSS) and the proofs of k-roughness. For VSS, if we create a t-out-of-n sharing using a method similar to Pedersen's VSS [13], then we are creating a random polynomial of degree t which will be evaluated at the integers $\{1, 2, ..., n\}$. In order to make Lagrange interpolation calculations remain in the integers, we will need to multiply our secret by $n!$ and choose the coefficients of this polynomial to be bound by $\pm Bn!$. As a consequence, no shared point on the polynomial should exceed $2Btn^tn!$. We choose prime $p > 2Btn^tn!$ and work over the field $GF(p)$. [7] contains a VSS protocol in which obeying this bound is a requirement for secret share verification. This protocol is the one we will use to share secrets.

We will give a brief discussion here of k-roughness proofs in order to develop our commitment scheme with full details to follow in Section 3.1. We say that a number a is k-rough if it has no small prime factors less than k. Let $M_b = \sum_{i \leq b} p_i$, where p_i is the ith prime. The proof that a number is p_{b+1}-rough involves showing that a is relatively prime to M_b. Specifically, we will compute

---

[1] Visit http://oceanstore.cs.berkeley.edu for the extended version.

Setup

INPUT: A bound B on the size of prime candidates, a number b such that $M_b = \prod_{i \leq b} p_i < B$, and a bound β for the prime p (usually either $\beta = 2Btn^t n!$ or $\beta = 2BM_b$).

1. Perform three β-bit joint coin-flipping protocols in parallel. Call the results x, y, and z.
2. Let p be the smallest prime greater than x.
3. Let $g = y \mod p$ and $h = z \mod p$.

Making commitments

To make a commitment to $x \in \mathbb{Z}_p$, a party chooses $r_x \in_R \mathbb{Z}_p$ and the commitment is $g^x h^{r_x} \mod p$.

Fig. 2. The integer commitment scheme.

and commit to x and y such that $ax + M_b y = 1$. We need to make sure that our commitment scheme is sufficient to contain ax and $M_b y$, both of which are bounded by BM_b. Since we will never use ax or $M_b y$ in conjunction with VSS however, we can set the bounds for the prime field in our commitment scheme to be $p > 2B \max(M_b, tn^t n!)$.

Usually, the M_b term will dominate the $tn^t n!$ term, unless there are a large number of players. Because of the way that we create the prime candidates, we must choose b such that $M_b < B$ to ensure that the candidates are not too large. Choosing a large b means that we will be more likely to find a safe prime quickly, but increases our commitment size. However, if the number of players in our generation scheme is large, we can use a large b without this difficulty because of the $tn^t n!$ term. As an example, suppose we are trying to generate a 1024-bit RSA key with factors of size 512-bits. Thus $B = 2^{512}$. We can choose $b = 71$, which makes the bit size of M_b be $|M_b|_2 = 475$. Suppose $t = 5$ and $n = 11$. Then $|tn^t n!)|_2 = 45$. In this case p must be greater than 2^{988} since $475 > 45$.

As an optimization, after we prove the k-roughness of a number a, we can use the secret share conversion methods of [2] to reshare a over a prime field of size p with $2Btn^t n! < p < 2BM_b$. This step will reduce the size of messages for the more communication intensive modular multiplication protocol.

A summary of the commitment scheme is given in Figure 2.

3 Distributed Sieving

In this section, we show how to generate safe prime candidates in a robust way. We begin with a technique by Malkin, Wu, and Boneh [5] called distributed sieving which aims to improve the efficiency of distributed random prime generation. Specifically, the technique constructively produces numbers without small prime factors, *rough numbers*. Using such numbers is a common approach in classical prime number generation. The technique described in [2] to find rough numbers is distributed trial division on random candidates. Unfortunately this approach is probabilistic and may take many iterations. Distributed sieving requires only

INPUT: A bound, B, for generated prime candidates. Let $M_b = \prod_{i \leq b} p_i < B$ be a product of the first b primes.

OUTPUT: A number $a + rM_b$ relatively prime to M_b.

1. Each server sieves to find a random integer a_i relatively prime to M_b. In other words, each server finds a random integer with no prime factors smaller than p_b. The a_i are multiplicative shares of a (i.e. $a = \prod_{i=1..n} a_i$). Note that a also has no prime factors less than p_b.

2. The servers produce an additive sharing of a such that each server has a share b_i with $a = \sum_{i=1..n} b_i$.

3. The servers choose a random number $r_i \in_R [0..\frac{B}{M_b}]$, then locally compute $b_i + r_i M_b$. At this point, each server has an additive share of $a + rM_b$ (where $r = \sum_{i=1..n} r_i$) which is also relatively prime to M_b.

Fig. 3. Malkin, Wu, and Boneh Distributed Sieving in the Honest-but-Curious Model.

a small constant number of multiparty computations. The algorithm of Malkin, Wu, and Boneh is listed in Figure 3.

The empirical experiments of [5] showed a factor of 10 improvement in the speed of prime generation using this method. However this protocol is secure only in the honest-but-curious model. Specifically, there is no check that the multiplicative shares a_i are being produced correctly. In other words, if even one of the servers chooses a number with a prime factor less than or equal to p_b, the protocol will *never* find a prime number as the sum $a + rM_b$ will always be divisible by that prime. Moreover, unverified additive sharing is central in this protocol and thus requires that a fixed threshold set of the servers be available and honest throughout the protocol.

Thus we need a way to prove and verify that each a_i is relatively prime to M_b using a non-interactive zero-knowledge argument (assuming the random oracle model[2]). After these proofs, we will create a verifiable polynomial sharing of a (resistant to failing or malicious servers) that allows easy computation of $a + rM_b$ and with comparable efficiency to the scheme used in [5].

3.1 Proving a Number is k-Rough

In order for distributed sieving to work correctly, each player needs to produce a number which is relatively prime to M_b (equivalently, we say that the number is p_{b+1}-rough or has no prime factors less than p_{b+1}, where p_i is the ith prime number). The protocol of [5] assumes honesty on the part of the players, but this assumption may not always be acceptable.

Using the properties of integer commitment and the multiplication proof protocol of [12], we can prove that a number is relatively prime to M_b. Note that showing relatively primality of a and M_b is equivalent to showing that there exist integers x, y such that $ax + M_b y = 1$. Since we are actually working in a finite field however, we also need to make sure that none of a, x, or y is 0 since a

---

[2] Shoup's RSA signature scheme already invokes the random oracle model, so we lose no security in making this assumption.

Step	Bits
Find integers x_i, y_i such that $a_i x_i + M_b y_i = 1$ holds using the extended Euclidean algorithm.	–
Prove that $x_i \neq 0$, $y_i \neq 0$, and $a_i \neq 0$.	$33\|p\|_2$
Produce $g^{a_i} h^{r_{a_i}}$, $g^{x_i} h^{r_{x_i}}$, $g^{y_i} h^{r_{y_i}}$, and $g^{a_i x_i} h^{r_{a_i x_i}}$, integer commitments to a_i, x_i, y_i, and $a_i x_i$, respectively.	$4\|p\|_2$
Show the multiplicative relationship between the commitments of a_i, x_i and $a_i x_i$.	$8\|p\|_2$
Prove $a_i x_i + M_b y_i$ to be 1 by showing knowledge of the discrete logarithm $log_h g^{-1}(g^{a_i x_i} h^{r_{a_i x_i}})(g^{y_i} h^{r_{y_i}})^{M_b}$.	$2\|p\|_2$
Total	$47\|p\|_2$

Fig. 4. Proof that a_i is p_{b+1}-rough. Sizes given are for the random oracle, non-interactive proof versions. See the extended version of this paper for more information.

dishonest prover could make $y = M_b^{-1} \mod p$ and $x = 0$ to prove $ax + M_b y = 1$ while making a of any form the prover desires. A protocol for this proof is given in the extended version of the paper. Thus each player distributing an a_i proves its p_b-roughness by the protocol in Figure 4. If we invoke the random oracle model, we can do all of these proofs without interaction.

Although the integer commitments that we are using are homomorphic and are the basis of our VSS scheme, we will not use the commitment of a_i directly in the sharing. Recall that because we want to make Lagrange interpolation easier, we multiply the secret in our VSS scheme by $n!$. Thus, we commit to a_i and prove the properties we need, then share $n!a_i$ and prove the multiplicative relationship between the two commitments. As mentioned in Section 2.2, the commitment scheme we use for this proof may be larger than the one we need for the rest of the computations. We may choose to reshare $a + rM_b$ over a smaller finite field after its computation.

At this point, each player should also prove that $2a_i + 1$ is relatively prime to M_b as well. This fact will assure us that $2(a + rM_b) + 1$ is also p_{b+1}-rough – a helpful optimization when we later test for safe primality. Each proof of relative primality requires a message of size $47\|p\|_2$ in addition to the commitment of a_i, so each player will need to send messages of size $95\|p\|_2$ for each a_i. If we consider the example from Section 2.2 where $\|p\|_2 = 988$, the message size is $95\|p\|_2 \approx 11732$ bytes ≈ 11kB.

3.2   Computing the Primality Candidate

The previous section showed how to produce a polynomial secret sharing of p_{b+1}-rough number a_i. Now we need to multiply the a_i together to produce a. Note of course that we do not need all the a_i of the previous section to create a p_{b+1}-rough number for primality testing – any subset of $\{a_i\}$ will do.

This fact is convenient if one of the players was malicious or unavailable in the previous sharing round. The classic technique for multiplying a number shared polynomially was shown in [14]. This method simply multiplies two polynomial shares together, rerandomizes the new (double degree) polynomial, then reduces the degree of the polynomial through a linear transformation. We will need to do this step once for each remaining good player. This multiplication requires the same amount of communication as the multiplication scheme in [5], but produces a polynomial (instead of additive) sharing of a at the conclusion.

Finally, each player chooses a random number $r_i \in_R [0..\frac{B}{M_b}]$. The players all share and commit to these numbers, then each player multiplies their share by M_b and adds the result to their share of a. This arithmetic is all done non-interactively. Now each player has a polynomial share of $a + rM_b$. Note that each player should prove that their r_i is within the range $[0..\frac{B}{M_b}]$ so that the final prime is of the appropriate size. To this end, will use Mao's proof of bit length [15]. This proof requires $\frac{B}{M_b}(6|p|_2 + 1)$ bits in the non-interactive form.

3.3   Ensuring $a + rM_b \equiv 3 \mod 4$

We would like to use an algorithm from [2] for safe primality testing, however this algorithm makes one additional requirement on $a + rM_b$: it must be congruent to 3 mod 4. Going back to the distribution of the a_i, each player needs to produce a claim and a proof of each $a_i \mod 4$ in addition to the proofs of relative primality of a_i and M_b. The proofs for $a_i \mod 4$ ensure that no player can force $a + rM_b \not\equiv 3 \mod 4$, thus avoiding progress in the safe primality generation. A full description of this technique is given in the extended paper.

A similar procedure must be performed for the r_i. Then all the players can compute $a + rM_b \mod 4$ and if $a + rM_b \equiv 3 \mod 4$, they do nothing, otherwise they add 2 to their share of $a + rM_b$.

Notice that the proof of congruence   mod 4 serves another purpose: it proves that the length of a_i is correct. Thus although the proof seems expensive, it is actually necessary and dual use.

3.4   Communication Efficiency

We now summarize the efficiency of the robust distributed sieving protocol. Specifically we address the size of all the messages sent by a single player. The proofs necessary for each players a_i are the roughness proofs ($95|p|_2$ bits), the bit length proof of r_i ($\frac{B}{M_b}(6|p|_2 + 1)$ bits), the claims of congruence   mod 4 ($((|B|_2(|p|_2 + 1) - 9|p|_2) + (4|p|_2 + \frac{B}{M_b}(6|p|_2 + 1) + 2)$ bits), and the proofs of equivalence of the commitment of a_i to the VSS commitment of $a_i n!$ ($2|p|_2$). Using the example numbers from Section 2.2 ($B = 2^{512}$ and $p > 2^{988}$), we see that the proof size is approximately 418267 bytes or about 408kB. These proofs must be broadcast.

We also have to share a_i and r_i using VSS. Sharing two values requires us to broadcast $2t|p|_2$ bits to all players. We can reasonably assume[3] that there is a

---

[3] Practical Byzantine broadcast schemes can use secure hashes of the message to verify correct transmission.

small constant c such that $n(2t|p|_2 + c)$ is cost of this broadcast to n players. The remaining messages[4] are point-to-point and total $2 \cdot 2n|p|_2$ bits. Assuming the player and threshold numbers from Section 2.2 ($t = 5$ and $n = 11$) along with $c = $ 1kB, we see that each player will broadcast about 24.3kB and send about 5.3kB in point-to-point messages. Broadcasting the proofs above costs approximately 4.3MB and dominates the communication costs. This number is large, but as we will see in Section 4.3, we can amortize the cost with a reuse trick.

We also have to multiply the a_i together. Recall from [14] that the communication required for multiplication is simply a secret sharing with a polynomial of order $2t$. We need n such random polynomials. The broadcast cost for these larger polynomials is again 24.3kB, but we only need 2.7kB in point-to-point messages.

In terms of round efficiency, we have only two concerns: the secret sharing of a_i and r_i and the multiplication of the a_i. Thus the number of communication rounds that we use is $2 + n$. Section 4.3 also shows how to parallelized this procedure to use only 1 round of multi-secret VSS.

3.5   Application in Safe Prime Finding

We performed a simulation of this algorithm to get an empirical estimate on the number of iterations required to find a safe prime. When we constructed 4858 1024-bit prime candidates of the form $a + rM_{128}$, we found that the median number of iterations between finding safe primes is approximately 45,000 and the mean is approximately 63,000. When using purely random numbers, we found that the mean number of iterations was about 436,000 and the median was 275,000. Safe primes are unfortunately less dense than unrestricted primes, but distributed sieving seems to be a great help in finding them. Based on our experiment, sieving requires only about 15% of the time required by random searching.

4   Optimizing the Distributed Miller-Rabin Test

In this section, we describe the distributed Miller-Rabin test we will use to check for safe primes. We also give two improvements which improve on the performance of the test, namely optimization of modular exponentiation and multiplication.

The algorithm for our distributed Miller-Rabin test is given in Figure 5. On the whole, the test is not significantly different than the version given in [2], so we will not discuss it thoroughly. The main differences between our version and the original is our preparation for the modular exponentiation step. Instead of converting from additive shares of the candidate to polynomial shares of the bits, we convert from polynomial shares of the candidate to polynomial shares

---

[4] We ignore the size of complaint messages, which are relatively small.

INPUT: Shares of the prime candidate ϕ.

1. Locally compute $e = \frac{\phi-1}{2}$ (recall that since $\phi \equiv 3 \mod 4$, we can do the division correctly in the finite field).
2. Compute shares of the base-η representation of e, $[e^{\eta_0}]_j^p, [e^{\eta_1}]_j^p, \cdots, [e^{\eta_\omega - 1}]_j^p$.
3. Precompute the values needed for modular exponentiation and multiplication.
4. Repeat the following step m times (in parallel):

   (a) Choose $[r]_j^p \in_R \{0, 1\}^{2B}$ and set $[g]_j^p = \text{MOD}([r]_j^p, [\phi]_j^p, [\tilde{\phi}]_j^p)$
   (b) Compute $g^e \mod q$
   (c) If $g^e \mod q \notin \{-1, 1\}$ (using the SETMEM algorithm of [2]), output failure.

5. Output success.

Fig. 5. Distributed Miller-Rabin Algorithm.

INPUT: $[g]_j^p, [e]_j^p, [\phi]_j^p$.
OUTPUT: $[g^e \mod \phi]_j^p$.

1. Reshare the bits of e as $\beta_1, ..., \beta_n$ where β_n is the most significant bit.
2. $c = (g - 1) * \beta_n + 1$
3. For $i = n - 1$ downto 1, Do

   (a) $d = (g - 1) * \beta_i + 1$
   (b) $c = ((c^2 \mod \phi) * d) \mod \phi$

4. Output c.

Fig. 6. Algesheimer et al. Modular Exponentiation.

of the base-η representation. We also do precomputations of the values needed for the modular exponentiation and multiplication procedures. In the next few sections, we describe our optimizations to algorithms used by the Miller-Rabin test.

4.1 Optimizing Modular Exponentiation

The modular exponentiation method of [2], shown in Figure 6, uses the familiar square-and-multiply technique with a clever trick to decide when to square and when to multiply. Suppose that $\beta_1, ..., \beta_n$ are the bits of the exponent e and are shared polynomially among the players (the details of how to perform this sharing are given in Section 5.4). The algorithm uses the observation that $g^{\beta_i} = (g - 1) * \beta_i - 1$ to decide when to square and when to multiply.

We generalize this algorithm to improve the running time by a constant factor. Suppose we think of step 3a as a lookup instead of a algebraic manipulation – when β_i is 0, we assign d the value 1 and when β_i is 1, we assign d the value g. Thus the modular exponentiation procedure is based on (albeit very immediate) precomputations of the values 1 and g which are referenced based on the value of β_i. We can extend this idea of a precomputed lookup table. Suppose that instead of a shared binary representation of e, we have a shared base-η representation

INPUT: $[\kappa]_j^p$ and $[g^0 \mod \phi]_j^p$, $[g^1 \mod \phi]_j^p, \cdots, [g^{\eta-1} \mod \phi]_j^p$.
OUTPUT: $[g^\kappa \mod \phi]_j^p$.

1. In parallel:
   For $i = 0$ to $\eta - 1$, Do
   $\qquad \sigma_i = 1 - ||\kappa - i||$
2. In parallel:
   For $i = 0$ to $\eta - 1$, Do
   $\qquad \rho_i = \sigma_i * (g^i \mod \phi)$
3. Locally compute $\sum_{i=0..\eta-1} \rho_i$.

Fig. 7. Lookup.

INPUT: $[g]_j^p, [e]_j^p, [\phi]_j^p$.
OUTPUT: $[g^e \mod \phi]_j^p$.

1. Reshare e in base-η: $e^{(\eta_0)}, ..., e^{(\eta_{\omega-1})}$ where $e^{(\eta_{\omega-1})}$ is the most significant digit.
2. $c = \text{LOOKUP}(e^{(\eta_{\omega-1})})$
3. For $i = \omega - 2$ downto 0, Do
   (a) $d = \text{LOOKUP}(e^{(\eta_i)})$
   (b) $c = ((c^\eta \mod \phi) * d) \mod \phi$
4. Output c.

Fig. 8. Revised Modular Exponentiation.

and we precompute the values $g^0 \mod q, g^1 \mod q, \cdots, g^{\eta-1} \mod q$. Then we can use the algorithm in Figure 7 to perform a lookup of these values.

Note that in this algorithm, we use a "normalization" procedure defined simply as:

$$||x|| = \begin{cases} 0 & \text{if } x = 0, \\ 1 & \text{otherwise} \end{cases}$$

The implementation of this procedure is given later in Section 5.1.

With this lookup procedure, we can now rewrite the modular exponentiation algorithm of Algesheimer et al. to use generic lookups. The revised algorithm is shown in Figure 8. (The technique for resharing a secret in a different base is given in Section 5.4.) Clearly, this approach uses a smaller number of outer loops, but there is still one concern in step 3b. Specifically, this step requires exponentiating by η in $\mathbb{Z}_q$ and would appear at first glance to remove the advantage of the reduced outer loop. There are however two reasons that this step saves time. First, we are exponentiating by a known, public constant. Thus no extra lookups are necessary in this step. Second, we still only have to perform ω lookups and multiplications by d. Overall we have reduced the number of modular multiplications from $2|e|_2$ to $|e|_2 + \omega$.

Our generic lookup procedure is clearly more expensive than the special case used in [2]. Specifically, it requires η normalizations. However, we use it only ω times during the loop. Moreover, the normalization protocol of Section 5.1 is simpler than modular multiplication, though it requires larger message sizes.

4.2 Optimizing Modular Multiplication

We present an alternative algorithm for modular multiplication which is based on the Montgomery method [16]. In [17], Bajard et al. modified Montgomery multiplication to work by manipulating representations in two different residue number systems (RNS's). We use a highly specialized case of this technique in which the two RNS's are simply prime finite fields. Although this approach requires us to do some pre- and post-computations, we are able to parallelize slightly more than with the algorithm of [2] and we also avoid some additional zero-knowledge proofs in the robust case. The algorithm is listed in Figure 9.

Let p be the prime associated with our VSS scheme. Let p' be the smallest prime greater than p.
INPUT: $[A]_j^p$, $[B]_j^p$, and $[\phi]_j^p$.
OUTPUT: $[ABp^{-1} \mod \phi]_j^p$.

Precomputation

1. Reshare A, B, and ϕ over $\mathbb{Z}_{p'}$.
2. Compute shares of $\phi^{-1} \mod p$ and $\phi^{-1} \mod p'$.

Multiplication

1. Compute $-A * B \mod p$ and $A * B \mod p'$ simultaneously.
2. Compute $q = (-A * B \mod p) * (\phi^{-1} \mod p)$.
3. Convert q to a sharing over p'.
4. Compute $q * \phi \mod p'$.
5. Locally compute $r = (A * B \mod p') + (q * \phi \mod p') * (p^{-1} \mod p')$.
6. Convert r to shares over p.

Fig. 9. Modular Multiplication.

Most of the operations performed during the multiplication are familiar: they are modular multiplication and addition in the same field as our shared secrets. These steps are performed relatively quickly. The conversion steps 3 and 6 are new. To convert a sharing over $\mathbb{Z}_p$ to a sharing over $\mathbb{Z}_{p'}$, we use the method of [2] which entails converting the polynomial sharing over $\mathbb{Z}_p$ to an additive sharing over $\mathbb{Z}_p$, converting that sharing to an additive sharing over the integers, converting that sharing to an additive sharing over $\mathbb{Z}_{p'}$, and finally converting that additive sharing to a polynomial sharing over $\mathbb{Z}_p$. This approach is complicated and expensive, but the best way known.

In comparing the algorithm here to the one in [2], we notice that the latter has a much simpler form. Specifically, the algorithm of Algesheimer et al. simply multiplies in the finite field, then takes the remainder of the product mod ϕ. The complexity of the algorithm is in the remainder functionality. Taking a remainder requires two multiplications, a subtraction, and two truncation operations. The truncations involve converting a polynomial sharing   mod p to an additive sharing over the integers, shifting the additive shares right by some number of bits, then resharing the shifted shares as polynomial shares   mod p. Our algorithm has the same number of multiplication and addition rounds, but we avoid this additional bit shifting. In the honest-but-curious model, the bit shifting is a local operation, so at first it may seem cheap. However since we are in the robust setting, each player must produce a proof of correctness of their truncated share, so we do end up saving some processing time[5].

Moreover, more of the multiplications in this algorithm are grouped together, rather than being split by conversions as in the [2] algorithm. As mentioned

---

[5] We are not able to avoid truncation proofs entirely – truncation is necessary for the algorithm to convert from additive shares over a finite field to additive shares over the integers [2]. We provide an interactive proof for truncation correctness in the extended paper.

in [14], we can multiply polynomial shares together several times before reran-
domizing so long as the degree of the polynomial does not exceed the number
of players. The closeness of the multiplications makes this optimization feasible
here, but not in [2].

Note that we are doing Montgomery multiplication in this algorithm; the
output is actually $(ABp^{-1} \mod \phi)$, the Montgomery product. When we do exponentiation, we will work with Montgomery products and then at the end, we
will convert this product by removing the p^{-1} factor [18]. This step requires
one additional Montgomery multiplication at the beginning and the end of the
exponentiation.

4.3   Parallel Optimizations

There are (at least) two parallelization tricks that we can employ to improve the
speed of our algorithm. The most obvious trick is to generate and test several
k-rough candidates simultaneously. Unfortunately, the message sizes required for
robustness in the distribute sieving algorithm can grow to be quite large when
trying to generate safe primes suitable for RSA.

Thus we suggest that each player can generate and share some small number
of k-rough components (i.e. the a_i). The proofs will be large initially, but once
the players have shared these numbers, they can recombine them in different
ways to produce new candidates. Specifically, let the number of players be l and
have each player share m different k-rough numbers. Then if we require that
each player gets to contribute one component rough number to each primality
candidate, then there are l^m different combinations possible. Recombinations
can proceed in the usual lexigraphical order, for example. A more thorough
exploration of these and other parallel techniques is available in the full paper.

5   Multiparty Arithmetic Circuits

This section develops the multiparty circuits that we will need to convert a
polynomial secret sharing into a sharing of the same number in base-η. Proofs
of secrecy and correctness for the protocols in this section are straightforward
since they are the composition of secure protocols.

INPUT: $[x]_j^p$.
OUTPUT: $[||x||]_j^p$.

1. Generate p^2 shared secret pairs $(r_i, s_i) \in \mathbb{Z}_p \times \mathbb{Z}_p$
2. Compute in parallel for each pair $u_i = r_i * (1 - r_i * s_i)$ and $v_i = s_i * (1 - s_i * r_i)$
3. Reveal all the u_i and v_i
4. For every i such that $u_i = v_i = 0$, compute and reveal $x - r_i$
5. Let $s = s_i$ where i is the smallest index such that $x - r_i = 0$ or return to step 1 and
   try again if no such i exists
6. Output $||x|| = x * s$

Fig. 10. Normalization based on Bar-Ilan and Beaver's algorithm.

5.1   Normalization

Recall the normalization procedure we used previously in Section 4.1. Note that the output from this procedure is a *shared secret* containing $||x||$; $||x||$ is neither public nor revealed. We derive our algorithm for normalization from Bar-Ilan and Beaver's algorithm for "extended inverses" [19]. Their method computes either the inverse $x^{-1} \in \mathbb{Z}_p$ of an element $x \in \mathbb{Z}_p$ if $x \neq 0$ and 0 otherwise. We compute this value as well, then multiply x by x^{-1} or 0, respectively, to obtain $||x||$. The full procedure is given in Figure 10. Note that we optimistically generate only p^2 shared secret pairs in step 1, a reduction from the suggested p^4 of [19].

We usually expect we will need only one iteration of this algorithm to calculate $||x||$. During one iteration, we must generate and share $2p^2$ random numbers, do $4p^2$ multiplications, and reveal between $2p^2$ and $4p^2$ numbers. While this complexity may seem high at first, we are saved by the fact that p will quite small in practice.

Notice that these multiplications and random number generations can be batched in advance (as described in Section 4.3) and the addition and scalar multiplications are local operations. All the revelations can be done in parallel.

We will consider the bandwidth required by one normalization. Suppose we choose $p = 37$ (for reasons we will see in the next few sections). We will need to share $p^2 = 1369$ random pairs and do $4p^2 + 1 = 5477$ multiplications with upto $4p^2 = 5476$ revelations. The random pairs and multiplications are simply VSS operations, which we can batch. Each random number we share requires broadcasting $t|p|_2$ bits and sending $2n|p|_2$ bits point-to-point. Batching makes the broadcast costs much smaller (since in practice, confirmation messages are secure hashes of the broadcast message), so we will generously assume there is a 1kB per player overhead for this operation. Random secret sharing for multiplication requires a polynomial of degree $2t$, so broadcast costs are higher, but point-to-point bits remain the same. For $p = 37$, $|p|_2 = 6$, so we arrive at a total of $5477 \cdot n \cdot |p|_2(2t + 2) + 1369 \cdot n \cdot |p|_2(t + 2) + 1024n$ bits. If we again use the example $t = 5$ and $n = 11$ from Section 2.2, we need to send about 608kB.

We also need to account for the revelations. Each revelation requires broadcasting 2 numbers to all parties. We can batch these revelations, but we need two steps instead of one because of a dependency in the normalization algorithm. Each batch of revelations requires broadcasting (at most) $2 * 2p^2 = 5476$ numbers. The total, with broadcast costs, is $n(5476 * |p|_2 + 1024) \approx 55$kB for the revelations. To summarize our example, each normalization requires sending about 718kB over 3 rounds. This primitive is our most expensive.

INPUT: $[x]_j^p$ and a publicly known set $S \subset \mathbb{Z}_p$.
OUTPUT: $[0]_j^p$ if $x \notin S$ and $[1]_j^p$ otherwise.

1. $\delta = \prod_{s \in S}(x - s)$
2. Output $1 - ||\delta||$.

Fig. 11. Secret set membership protocol.

5.2 Secret Set Membership

In this section, we describe an algorithm for "secret set membership." Given $x \in \mathbb{Z}_p$ and $S \subset \mathbb{Z}_p$, this algorithm outputs a shared secret containing 1 if $x \in S$ and a shared secret containing 0 otherwise. We denote this method as computing $x \in_? S$. Readers familiar with the SETMEM algorithm in [2] should notice that our algorithm is much simpler than SETMEM. This reduction is possible because we do not test whether a shared secret is congruent to a member of S modulo another shared secret modulus p' – we need only test congruence modulo p, which is public. See Figure 11.

Computation of the product in step 1 requires $|S|$ multiplications which we must do in serial. Note of course that we can share all the rerandomizing polynomials for this step in advance, so we only incur one round of secret sharing. The secret set membership algorithm is dominated by the cost of the normalization in step 2. See Section 5.1 for the complexity of that step.

5.3 Base-η Addition Circuit

Assume we have shared base-η representations of two numbers x and y. We will show how to add these numbers together via the normal "elementary school algorithm." While there are more advanced circuits to perform this addition, we describe this simple addition to show the underlying mechanisms at play. Smaller depth circuits may be possible using these mechanisms.

We draw inspiration from the classic binary-coded-decimal addition algorithm. Since we can easily do arithmetic on shared secrets over fields a prime $p > 2\eta$, this model makes sense. See Figure 12 for the full details.

We now give an example to illustrate the costs associated with the protocol. Suppose we have 512-bit numbers x and y with $\eta = 16$. Then we may choose $p = 37$ since two base-16 digits with carry can add to at most 31. All the additions and subtractions are local operations, so we ignore them. Choosing the initial carry bit in step 1 requires one degree t secret sharing and the multiplication in step 2c requires us to do $\omega = 128$ degree $2t$ secret sharings.

INPUT:

– A radix $\eta = 2^\nu$ which is a power of 2
– Numbers x and y shared in base-η representation over $\mathbb{Z}_p$. Let $x = \sum_{i=0}^{\omega-1} x^{(\eta_i)} \eta^i$ and $y = \sum_{i=0}^{\omega-1} y^{(\eta_i)} \eta^i$.

Assume without loss of generality that $|x|_2 = |y|_2$, $\nu || x|_2$, and $\omega = \frac{|x|_2}{\nu}$.

OUTPUT: Shares of $z^{(\eta_i)}$ for $i = 0, \cdots, \omega - 1$, where $z = x + y$.

1. Generate shared zero $c_0 = 0$
2. For $i = 0$ to $\omega - 1$ Do

    (a) $z^{(\eta_i)} = x^{(\eta_i)} + y^{(\eta_i)} + c_i$
    (b) $c_{i+1} = z^{(\eta_i)} \in_? \{\eta, \eta + 1, ..., 2\eta - 1\}$
    (c) $z^{(\eta_i)} = z^{(\eta_i)} + (p - \eta) * c_{i+1}$

Fig. 12. Addition in base-η representation.

INPUT:

- A radix $\eta = 2^\nu$ which is a power of 2
- Polynomial shares of secret x.

Assume without loss of generality that $\nu | |x|_2$ and and $\omega = \frac{|x|_2}{\nu}$.

OUTPUT: Polynomial shares of the base-η representation of x, $[x^{(\eta_0)}]_j^p, \cdots, [x^{(\eta_{\omega-1})}]_j^p$.

1. Convert the polynomial shares of x to additive shares such that $x = \sum_{j=1..n} x_j$. (Recall that we also have verifiers for the additive shares when we use the poly-to-sum protocol of [20].)

2. Reshare each ν-bit block of x_j in polynomial form as $x_j^{(\eta_0)}, x_j^{(\eta_1)}, \cdots, x_j^{(\eta_{\omega-1})}$.

    (a) Prove that these numbers are the base-η form of x_j by showing that the commitment, $g^{x_i} h^{r_{x_i}}$, to x_i contains the same value as $\prod_{i=0..\omega-1} (g^{x_j^{(\eta_i)}} h^{r_{x_j^{(\eta_i)}}})^{\eta^i}$.

    (b) Prove that $|x_j^{(\eta_i)}|_2 = \nu$ for each $i = 0, \cdots, \omega - 1$.

3. Convert all the shares $x_j^{(\eta_i)}$ over p to shares over a smaller prime (e.g. the smallest prime $p' > 2\eta$).

4. Add all the base-eta shares of the x_j together.

Fig. 13. Conversion to base-η representation.

Clearly the cost of the set membership to compute the carry bit in step 2b dominates this algorithm. Our set has size $\eta - 1 = 15$, so we must perform this many multiplications in each round. We must also perform 128 total normalizations. Thus we end up doing 1 degree t secret sharing, $15 * 128 + 128 = 2048$ degree $2t$ secret sharings, and 128 normalizations. The normalizations dwarf the other costs. With $t = 5$ and $n = 11$ as before, the messages sent for the whole protocol will total between 70MB and 80MB, depending on the random factors in the normalization algorithm.

5.4   Converting a Number to Base-η Representation

We now have all the tools that we need to convert a polynomial secret sharing of a number x to its base-η representation. The method we use is inspired by the one from [2] which produces the binary representation of a number. The basic idea is that the secret is reshared as an additive secret, each η digit is reshared as a polynomial, then we use the addition circuit to add all the numbers together in base-η. The conversion algorithm is detailed in Figure 13.

Most of the cost of this algorithm is in the addition step which we addressed in the previous section. The proofs in step 2 are non-trivial, however. Step 2a is relatively simple because of the homomorphic commitment scheme – it requires only $2|p|_2$ additional bits to be broadcast. Step 2b requires a proof of size proportional to the size of x. Specifically, each base-η digit requires a proof of size $\eta(6|p|_2 + 1)$ (See the extended paper for more details). Since we have ω of these digits, the proof expands to $\omega\eta(6|p|_2 + 1) = |x|_2(6|p|_2 + 1)$.

6 Summary

We presented a robust algorithm to generate shared secret, safe prime numbers. Our algorithm owes much to the work of [2] and [5] in the general form. Using this framework, we developed efficient zero-knowledge proofs of knowledge making the algorithm robust. We also borrowed ideas ([17]) from the computer arithmetic world that reduced the number of such proofs we have to transmit during the algorithm. We generalized the modular exponentiation algorithm of [2] to general precomputed lookup tables. We believe our techniques make shared generation of a safe prime much more feasible in the robust setting. Using this primitive and the works of Catalano et al. [7], Shoup's RSA scheme is much closer to practical use without a trusted dealer.

References

1. Shoup, V.: Practical Threshold Signatures. Lecture Notes in Computer Science **1807** (2000)
2. Algesheimer, J., Camenisch, J., Shoup, V.: Efficient computation modulo a shared secret with application to the generation of shared safe-prime products. In: Proceedings of CRYPTO 2002, Springer Verlag (2002) 417–432
3. Fouque, P.A., Stern, J.: Fully distributed threshold RSA under standard assumptions. In: Proceedings of Asiacrypt. (2001) 310–330
4. Damgård, I.B., Koprowski, M.: Practical Threshold RSA Signatures Without a Trusted Dealer. Technical Report RS-00-30, Basic Research in Computer Science, University of Aarhus (2000)
5. Malkin, M., Wu, T., Boneh, D.: Experimenting with Shared Generation of RSA keys. In: Symposium on Network and Distributed System Security. (1999) 43–56
6. Cramer, R., Shoup, V.: Signature Schemes Based on the Strong RSA Assumption. ACM Transactions on Information and System Security **3** (2000) 161–185
7. Catalano, D., Gennaro, R., Halevi, S.: Computing inverses over a secret shared modulus. In: EUROCRYPT 2000. Volume 1807 of LNCS., Springer-Verlag (2000) 190–207
8. Boneh, D., Franklin, M.: Efficient generation of shared RSA keys. Journal of the ACM (JACM) **48** (2001) 702–722
9. Frankel, Y., MacKenzie, P.D., Yung, M.: Robust Efficient Distributed RSA-Key Generation. In: Annual ACM Symposium on Theory of Computing. (1998)
10. Goldwasser, S., Lindell, Y.: Secure Multi-Party Computation Without Agreement. In: 16th International Symposium on DIStributed Computing. Volume 2508 of LNCS. (2002) 17–32
11. Shamir, A.: How to share a secret. Communications of the ACM **22** (1979)
12. Damgård, I., Fujisaki, E.: A Statistically-Hiding Integer Commitment Scheme Based on Groups with Hidden Order. In: ASIACRYPT. (2002) 125–142
13. Pedersen, T.: Non-interactive and information-theoretic secure verifiable secret sharing. In: CRYPTO 1991. Volume 576 of LNCS. (1991) 129–140
14. Ben-Or, M., Goldwasser, S., Wigderson, A.: Completeness theorems for non-cryptographic fault-tolerant distributed computation. In: Annual ACM Symposium on Theory of Computing. (1988) 1–10

15. Mao, W.: Guaranteed Correct Sharing of Integer Factorization with Off-line Shareholders. In: Public Key Cryptography. Volume 1431 of LNCS. (1998) 60–71
16. Montgomery, P.L.: Modular Multiplication Without Trial Division. Mathematics of Computation **44** (1985) 519–521
17. Bajard, J.C., Didier, L.S., Kornerup, P.: Modular Multiplication and Base Extensions in Residue Number Systems. In: Proceedings of the 15th IEEE Symposium on Computer Arithmetic. (2001) 59–65
18. Ç.K. Koç, Acar, T.: Fast Software Exponentiation in $GF(2^k)$. In: Symposium on Computer Arithmetic. (1997) 225–231
19. Bar-Ilan, J., Beaver, D.: Non-Cryptographic Fault-Tolerant Computing in a Constant Number of Rounds of Interaction. In: 8th ACM Symposium on Principles of Distributed Computation. (1989) 201–209
20. Frankel, Y., MacKenzie, P., Yung, M.: Adaptively secure distributed public-key systems. Theoretical Computer Science **287** (2002) 535–561

Fast Multi-computations
with Integer Similarity Strategy*

Wu-Chuan Yang[1], Dah-Jyh Guan[2], and Chi-Sung Laih[1]

[1] Department of Electrical Engineering, National Cheng Kung University,
Tainan, Taiwan 701, R.O.C.
[2] Department of Computer Science, National Sun Yat Sen University,
Kaohsiung, Taiwan 804, R.O.C.
wcyang77@ms32.hinet.net, guan@cse.nsysu.edu.tw, laihcs@eembox.ncku.edu.tw

Abstract. Multi-computations in finite groups, such as multiexponentiations and multi-scalar multiplications, are very important in ElGamal-like public key cryptosystems. Algorithms to improve multi-computations can be classified into two main categories: precomputing methods and recoding methods. The first one uses a table to store the precomputed values, and the second one finds a better binary signed-digit (BSD) representation. In this article, we propose a new integer similarity strategy for multi-computations. The proposed strategy can aid with precomputing methods or recoding methods to further improve the performance of multi-computations. Based on the integer similarity strategy, we propose two efficient algorithms to improve the performance for BSD sparse forms. The performance factor can be improved from 1.556 to 1.444 and to 1.407, respectively.

Keywords: ElGamal-like public key cryptosystems, binary signed-digit (BSD) representations, sparse forms, multi-computations, multiexponentiations, multi-scalar multiplications

1 Introduction

Multi-computations in finite groups, such as multiexponentiations, e.g. $c = a^x b^y$, and multi-scalar multiplications, e.g. $C = xA + yB$ (A, B, and C denote points in one elliptic curve), are very important in many ElGamal-like public key cryptosystems [8, 21, 9]. In addition to the algorithms for single computations (some good surveys can be found in [13, 5, 10]), the performance of multi-computations can be improved by the concept of multiexponentiation [8, Section V.B]. This concept was generalized to the small window methods by Yen, Laih, and Lenstra [23].

Based on the concept of multiexponentiations, many algorithms have been proposed to improve the performance of multi-computations. In general, these

---

* This work was supported by the National Science Council, Taiwan, under contract NSC 92-2213-E-232-002.

S. Vaudenay (Ed.): PKC 2005, LNCS 3386, pp. 138–153, 2005.

algorithms can be classified into two categories: precomputing methods and recoding methods. Precomputing methods use a large table to store the precomputed values, such as the BGMW method [4] and the Lim-Lee method [14]. Precomputing methods are very suitable for memory sufficient environment and have the better performance indeed. Since the binary signed-digit (BSD) representation of an integer is not unique, recoding methods try to recode the BSD representations of x and y such that their joint Hamming weight $w(x, y)$ is as minimal as possible [7, 22]. The joint Hamming weight can be defined by the number of digit pairs, at least one of which is nonzero. Recoding methods are very useful in memory limited environments, such as IC cards or smart consumer electronic devices. Recently, this topic has been discussed in many articles [15, 18, 2, 3, 16, 19].

In this article, we focus on the memory limited environment and introduce a new integer similarity strategy to improve the performance of multi-computations. When computing $c = a^x b^y$ or $C = xA + yB$, the recoding methods match the zeros or nonzeros as possible by **recoding** x and y in advance, therefore the performance of multi-computations can be improved. Instead of recoding x and y, the new strategy is by **deleting** or **inserting** some digits in x and y, such that x and y have as much similarity as possible. For example, if $x = 010101011_2$ and $y = 101010101_2$, we can match the zeros by deleting the first zero in x and inserting a zero before the last digit in y as follows.

	x	0 1 0 1 0 1 0 1	1	
Original computation	y	1 0 1 0 1 0 1 0	1	$w(x, y) = 9$

	x	0 1 0 1 0 1 0 1	1	
adjusted computation	y	1 0 1 0 1 0 1	01	$w(x, y) = 5$
		↑	↑	
		deleted	inserted	

Obviously, the computation must be modified for evaluating the correct result if some digits in x or y were deleted or inserted. As the above example, we only compute the deleted digit which is the beginning digit of x. Afterwards the digit with the same value can be computed simultaneously. Finally, the inserted digit in y should be computed with the last digit pair. Different from the recoding methods, our proposed methods improve the performance by **shifting** the digits. Thus our methods are very promising ones to improve performance in memory limited environments.

Since the performance of the multi-computation algorithms is determined by the computations of nonzero columns, we use a performance factor, ρ, to evaluate the performance of multi-computations. The performance factor can be defined as follows, note that "1" refers to the necessary computations of square (in multiexponentiation) or double (in multi-scalar multiplication).

$$\rho = 1 + \frac{\text{number of nonzero digit pairs}}{\text{number of total digit pairs}}.$$

The performance of multi-computations by BSD representations can be described as follows: $\rho = 1.556$ by using sparse forms directly [13], $\rho' = 1.534$ [7] by using the Dimitrov-Jullien-Miller method, and $\rho'' = 1.500$ [22] by using joint sparse forms, respectively. The proposed integer similarity strategy has practical applications for the above BSD methods. Based on the integer similarity strategy, we propose two efficient algorithms to improve the performance for BSD sparse forms; the performance factor can be reduced from 1.556 to 1.444 and to 1.407, respectively. The proposed strategy can also be used in binary representations since it does not recode the representation. Based on the proposed strategy, ρ can be reduced from 1.75 to 1.667 in binary method.

The rest of this article is organized as follows. In Section 2, we first review the basic multi-computation algorithms. The concept of integer similarity strategy and the proposed algorithms are illustrated in Section 3. And we also prove the performance of the proposed algorithms. In Section 4, we compare the performances of some well-known recoding methods and our proposed methods. Besides, the application of the proposed strategy to binary representations is also discussed in Section 4. Finally, our conclusion is presented in Section 5.

2   Preliminaries of Multi-computations

To simplify the description, the integer similarity strategy is described by multi-scalar multiplication, $C = xA + yB$, with BSD representations only. Note that our strategy can also be applied to multiexponentiation, $c = a^x b^y$, with binary representations [11]. The notations used in this article are described as follows. The uppercase alphabet, such as A or B, denotes the discrete point in elliptic curve public key cryptosystems. The lowercase alphabet, such as x or y, denotes an n-bit integer. Because the minimal weight BSD representations need an extra BSD, x can be represented by $n + 1$ BSDs as follows ($\bar{1}$ denotes -1).

$$x = \sum_{i=0}^{n} x_i 2^i = (x_n x_{n-1} \cdots x_1 x_0)_2, \text{ where } x_i \in \{\bar{1}, 0, 1\}.$$

Symbol $|x|$ represents the bit-length of x, $\omega(x)$ represents the Hamming weight of x, i.e. the number of nonzero digits. In multi-computation, we put our emphasis on whether the digit is zero or not. Therefore we use "o" to denote zero value, and "ι" to denote the nonzero values. Hence the digits can be classified into two sets: the zero set S_o and the nonzero set S_ι. $x_i \sim y_i$ denotes $x_i, y_i \in S_o$ or $x_i, y_i \in S_\iota$. The expression $x_i \nsim y_i$ denotes $x_i \in S_o$, $y_i \in S_\iota$ or $x_i \in S_\iota$, $y_i \in S_o$.

For integer pairs, $|(x, y)| = \max(|x|, |y|)$, the joint Hamming weight $\omega(x, y)$ is defined by the total number of $(x_i, y_i) \neq (0, 0)$, for all i. Thus, the performance factor ρ can be simplified to $\rho = 1 + \frac{\omega(x,y)}{|(x,y)|}$.

2.1   The Basic BSD Method for Multi-scalar Multiplications

The expected $\omega(x)$ in minimal weight BSD representations is $\frac{1}{3}n$ [1]. Many algorithms can be used to recode the binary representation or any BSD representation to minimum weight BSD representation [20, 11, 12]. Notice that an integer may have many minimal weight BSD representations, the most famous one is called the sparse form since no two consecutive digits are both nonzeros. Sparse forms are also called canonical forms or non-adjacent forms [10]. Minimal weight BSD representations are especially suitable for elliptic curve scalar multiplications since the inverse of a point is easy to compute. The basic BSD method for multi-scalar multiplications is shown in *Algorithm 1*. Symbol O denotes the identity element of the elliptic curve, this point is also called "point at infinity." The value of all possible $x_i A + y_i B$ must be precomputed in Line 6 of *Algorithm 1*. Therefore it needs 5 registers to store the value of A, B, $A + B$, $A - B$, and C. The inverse value $-A$, $-B$, $-A - B$ and $-A + B$ are easily to obtain from the precomputed table, so we do not need to precompute these value. The performance factor of *Algorithm 1*, ρ_1, is equal to 1.556. The proof is shown in Theorem 1.

Algorithm 1. The Basic BSD Method for multi-computations

I/P: A, B, x, y

O/P: $C = xA + yB$

1: Recode x and y to the minimum weight BSD representations;

2: Prepare the following values: $A, B, A \pm B$;

3: $C = O$;

4: **for** $i = n$ **downto** 0 **do** {

5:     $C = 2C$;

6:     **if** $(x_i, y_i) \neq (0, 0)$ **then** $C = C + (x_i A + y_i B)$;

7: }

Theorem 1. *The performance factor of Algorithm 1 is* $\rho_1 = 1\frac{5}{9} \simeq 1.556$.

Proof. In Line 6, the probability of $(x_i, y_i) \neq (0, 0)$ is $1 - (\frac{2}{3})^2 = \frac{5}{9}$. Therefore the performance factor $\rho_1 = 1 + \frac{5}{9} \simeq 1.556$.   □

2.2   The Recoding Methods for BSD Representations

Since there are many minimal weight BSD representations, the result of *Algorithm 1* can be improved by recoding the representations. Dimitrov, Jullien, and Miller proposed 8 reduction rules to recode x and y (called the DJM method in this article) [7]. In their method, if the scanned segment of three consecutive digits matches one of the upper part of Table 1, the algorithm recode the segment to the corresponding lower part. The performance factor can be reduced from 1.556 to 1.534 by using the DJM method.

On the view of sparse form for the single integer, Solinas proposed the concept of joint sparse form (JSF) for pairs of integers, the properties of JSF are illustrated as follows [22]:

Table 1. The DJM reduction rules.

Original digits	$x_{i+2}x_{i+1}x_i$	010	010	$0\bar{1}0$	$0\bar{1}0$	$10\bar{1}$	$10\bar{1}$	$\bar{1}01$	$\bar{1}01$
	$y_{i+2}y_{i+1}y_i$	$10\bar{1}$	$\bar{1}01$	$10\bar{1}$	$\bar{1}01$	010	$0\bar{1}0$	010	$0\bar{1}0$
After	$x'_{i+2}x'_{i+1}x'_i$	010	010	$0\bar{1}0$	$0\bar{1}0$	011	011	$0\bar{1}\bar{1}$	$0\bar{1}\bar{1}$
Adjusted	$y'_{i+2}y'_{i+1}y'_i$	011	$0\bar{1}\bar{1}$	011	$0\bar{1}\bar{1}$	010	$0\bar{1}0$	010	$0\bar{1}0$

1. Of any 3 consecutive digits, at least one is double zeros.
2. Adjacent digits do not have opposite signs.
3. If $x_{i+1}x_i \neq 0$, then $y_{i+1} \neq 0$ and $y_i = 0$.
   If $y_{i+1}y_i \neq 0$, then $x_{i+1} \neq 0$ and $x_i = 0$.

Solinas also proposed two efficient recoding algorithms to generate the joint sparse form from binary representation and sparse form, respectively. The performance factor can be improved to 1.500 when n approaches infinite, and this value is the minimum of all the recoding methods.

3   The Integer Similarity Strategy

By observing above recoding methods, we find two major limitations in those method. First, they can not recode the binary representations since the binary representation for an integer is unique. Second, they cannot recode the digits with the same signs, such as 101 or $\bar{1}0\bar{1}$, because they are unique minimum weight form. For example, if $x = (10101010)_2$ and $y = (01010101)_2$, all recoding methods cannot improve the computation. Based on the observation, we propose a totally new strategy, the integer similarity strategy, to improve the performance of multi-computations. Our idea is to shift some digits by **deleting** and **inserting** so that two different integers can be as much similarity as possible. For example $x = (01010101)_2$ and $y = (10101010)_2$, x can be adjusted by deleting the first zero and inserting a zero in the end. When the digit of x or y is deleted or inserted, the corresponding computation must be defined for evaluating the correct result. In order to use the proposed strategy for multi-computations, the following items must be taken into consideration.

1. *The Condition for Deleting or Inserting*
   For improving the performance, we have to define the condition to let the integers be as much similarity as possible. The condition depends on both integer representations and memory space.
2. *The Corresponding Computation of Deletion or Insertion*
   In computing $C = xA + yB$, $C = 2C + x_i A$ is computed when deleting x_i and $C = 2(C + y_{i+1}B) + (x_i A + y_i B)$ when inserting y_i.
3. *The Computation After Deletion or Insertion*
   After deletion, the corresponding digits of x and y will be shifted, that is the corresponding digits of x_{i-1} is y_i after deleting x_i. The corresponding computation after deletion is $C = 2C + (x_{i-1}A + y_i 2B)$.

The simplest case of the integer similarity strategy is that one insertion in an integer follows one deletion in another integer, we name it the single-stage version. The deletion can be acted on only one integer, called the single-integer version, and it can be also acted on both the integers, call double-integer version. In this article, in order to point out the essence of the integer similarity strategy, two basic methods are taken into consideration. The first one, called the **single-stage single-integer (1S1I)** method, is to delete one digit in x then to insert another digit in y at an appropriate position. The second one, called the **single-stage double-integer (1S2I)** method, is to delete one digit in x or y and insert another digit in its opposite integer. The single stage can be generalized to multistage. However, we do not discuss the generalization of 1S1I and 1S2I method in this article due to the page limitation.

3.1   The 1S1I Method for Sparse Forms

The BSD sparse form has an important property – of any 2 consecutive digits, at least one is zero. According to this property, if we want to match the zeros and nonzeros, $x_i \nsim y_i$ is a suitable condition to delete one digit in x. When one digit in x is deleted, the computation should be modified, which is called "Delete x" state, denoted by Dx. On the contrary, if the computation is the same with the original algorithm, the state can be called the "Normal" state, denoted by Nr. Thus the state diagram of the 1S1I method is shown in Fig. 1.

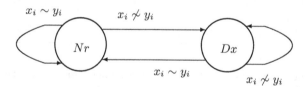

Fig. 1. The state diagram of the 1S1I method.

Consider the following condition, x_u is deleted in x and y_v is inserted in y.

$$x = (x_n \cdots \not{x_u}\, x_{u-1} \cdots \qquad x_v\, x_{v-1} \cdots x_0)_2$$
$$y = (y_n \cdots \qquad y_u \qquad \cdots y_{v+1}y_v\, y_{v-1} \cdots y_0)_2$$

Before deleting x_u and after inserting y_v ($i > u$ or $i < v$), the computation is $2C + (x_i A + y_{i+1} B)$. It is the same as *Algorithm 1*. When deleting x_u ($i = u$), the computation is $2C + x_u A$. After deleting x_u and before inserting y_v ($u > i > v$), the computation is $2C + (x_i A + y_{i+1} 2B)$ and the state is transferred into Dx. When inserting y_v ($i = v$), the computation is $C = 2(C + y_{v+1}B) + (x_v A + y_v B)$. The corresponding digits are (x_i, y_i) in Nr, and (x_i, y_{i+1}) in Dx. Therefore, the corresponding computations can be illustrated in Table 2. To summarize the above, *Algorithm 1* can be modified to the following *Algorithm 2*.

Table 2. The corresponding computations of the proposed algorithm.

State	Corresponding computation
Nr	$C = 2C + (x_i A + y_i B)$
$Nr \rightarrow Dx$	$C = 2C + x_i A$
Dx	$C = 2C + (x_i A + y_{i+1} 2B)$
$Dx \rightarrow Nr$	$C = 2(C + y_{i+1} B) + (x_i A + y_i B)$

Algorithm 2. The 1S1I method for sparse forms

I/P: A, B, $x = (x_{n-1}, \cdots, x_1, x_0)_2$, $y = (y_{n-1}, \cdots, y_1, y_0)_2$

O/P: $C = xA + yB$

1: Prepare the value of $A, B, A \pm B, A \pm 2B$;
2: $C = O$, *State* = Nr;
3: **for** $i = n$ **downto** 0 **do** {
4:   **if** $(State = Nr)$ {
5:     **if** $(x_i \sim y_i)$ **then** $C = 2C + (x_i A + y_i B)$;
6:     **else** *State* = Dx, $C = 2C + x_i A$;
7:   }
8:   **else** {
9:     **if** $(x_i \not\sim y_i)$ **then** $C = 2C + (x_i A + y_{i+1} 2B)$;
10:    **else** *State* = Nr, $C = 2(C + y_{i+1} B) + (x_i A + y_i B)$;
11: }
12: }

The rules in Fig. 1 are very simple and efficient. Theorem 2 proves that *Algorithm 2* is guaranteed to further improvement of the performance of *Algorithm 1* with BSD sparse forms.

Theorem 2. *Let ρ_1 and ρ_2 be the performance factor of Algorithm 1 and Algorithm 2, respectively. If x and y are both sparse forms, then $\rho_2 \leq \rho_1$.*

Proof. The performance factor is analyzed by considering the computation of Nr and of Dx.

First, we consider the computation in state Nr of *Algorithm 2*. In Line 5, it is the same with *Algorithm 1*. In Line 6, if y_i is zero, ρ will be decreased by 1, otherwise ρ remains the same with *Algorithm 1*.

Then we consider the computation of state Dx. if $x_i \not\sim y_i$ for $u \geq i \geq v$, therefore Dx is occurred for $(u - 1) \geq i \geq (v - 1)$, thus the corresponding computation digits are shown as follows.

Nr	$Nr \rightarrow Dx$	Dx	$\cdots$	Dx	Dx	$Dx \rightarrow Nr$
x_{u+1}	$\not{x}_u$	x_{u-1}	$\cdots$	x_{v+1} x_v		x_{v-1}
y_{u+1}		y_u	$\cdots$	y_{v+2}	y_{v+1}	$y_v y_{v-1}$

Suppose the length of the above interval of Dx is k, then $k = u - v + 1$. We can get $x_i \sim y_{i+1}$ for $(u - 1) \geq i \geq v$, because of the property of sparse forms and $x_i \not\sim y_i$ for $u \geq i \geq v$. Thus ρ can be considered into the following 4 conditions:

1. Led by deleting o and ended by inserting ι: $\rho = \frac{3k+1}{2}$, $k = 1, 3, 5, \cdots$.
2. Led by deleting ι and ended by inserting o: $\rho = \frac{3k+1}{2}$, $k = 1, 3, 5, \cdots$.
3. Led by deleting o and ended by inserting o: $\rho = \frac{3k}{2}$, $k = 2, 4, \cdots$.
4. Led by deleting ι and ended by inserting ι: $\rho = \frac{3k}{2} + 1$, $k = 2, 4, \cdots$.

ρ will be decreased by $\frac{k-1}{2}$, $\frac{k-1}{2}$, $\frac{k}{2}$, and $\frac{k}{2} - 1$ for the above 4 conditions, respectively, because $\rho = 2k$ in *Algorithm 1*. Thus ρ will never be increased either in Dx.

For the above discussion, $\rho_2 \leq \rho_1$. $\square$

According to the proof of Theorem 2, the computation cost will not be increased even if in the worst case. The average performance of *Algorithm 2* is analyzed as follows. We now concern the conditional probability of x_i when x_{i+1} is given. We know $P_o = \frac{2}{3}$ and $P_\iota = \frac{1}{3}$ in sparse forms have been proved in [20]. Lemma 1 illustrates the conditional probability $P_{x_i|x_{i+1}}$, and it can be extended to pairs of integers, $P_{x_i y_i | x_{i+1} y_{i+1}}$, as described in Lemma 2.

Lemma 1. *Let $P_{x_i|x_{i+1}}$ be the conditional probability of x_i given x_{i+1}. Then $P_{o|o} = P_{\iota|o} = \frac{1}{2}$, $P_{o|\iota} = 1$, and $P_{\iota|\iota} = 0$ in BSD sparse forms.*

Proof. Since no two consecutive digits are nonzero, $P_{o|\iota} = 1$ and $P_{\iota|\iota} = 0$.
Let $P_{o|o} = p$ and $P_{\iota|o} = 1 - p$.
$P_o = P_o \cdot P_{o|o} + P_\iota P_{o|\iota}$, therefore $\frac{2}{3} = \frac{2}{3} \cdot p + \frac{1}{3} \cdot 1 \to p = \frac{1}{2}$.
We can get $P_{o|o} = p = \frac{1}{2}$ and $P_{\iota|o} = 1 - p = \frac{1}{2}$. $\square$

Lemma 2. *Let $P_{x_i y_i | x_{i+1} y_{i+1}}$ be the conditional probability of $x_i y_i$ given $x_{i+1} y_{i+1}$. Then $P_{oo|\iota\iota} = 1$, $P_{oo|o\iota} = P_{\iota o|o\iota} = P_{oo|\iota o} = P_{o\iota|\iota o} = \frac{1}{2}$, $P_{oo|oo} = P_{o\iota|oo} = P_{\iota o|oo} = P_{\iota\iota|oo} = \frac{1}{4}$, $P_{o\iota|\iota\iota} = P_{\iota o|\iota\iota} = P_{\iota\iota|\iota\iota} = P_{o\iota|o\iota} = P_{\iota\iota|o\iota} = P_{\iota o|\iota o} = P_{\iota\iota|\iota o} = 0$.*

Proof. Because the digits in x and y are independent, the probability $P_{x_i y_i | x_{i+1} y_{i+1}} = P_{x_i | x_{i+1}} \times P_{y_i | y_{i+1}}$. Thus the proof of this Lemma is completed. $\square$

According to Lemma 3, the corresponding computations and their probabilities of *Algorithm 2* are illustrated in Table 3, where the symbols "P.S." and "N.S." stand for "Present state" and "Next state", respectively. The items "computations," "$n_{x_i y_i}$," "$P_{x_{i+1} x_i y_{i+1} y_i}$," and "Line" denote the corresponding computations, the number of additions, the probability of the computation of this row, and the corresponding line number in *Algorithm 2*. In Theorem 3, we show that the performance factor ρ_2 of *Algorithm 2* is 1.444. In comparison with 5 registers in *Algorithm 1*, *Algorithm 2* needs 2 extra registers to store the value of $A \pm 2B$.

Lemma 3. *Among the 16 possible $x_{i+1} x_i y_{i+1} y_i$, there are 9 nonzero $P_{x_{i+1} x_i y_{i+1} y_i}$, i.e. $P_{oooo}, P_{ooo\iota}, P_{o\iota oo}, P_{o\iota o\iota}, P_{\iota o\iota o}, P_{oo\iota o}, P_{o\iota\iota o}, P_{\iota ooo}$, and $P_{\iota oo\iota}$, and all of them are all equal to $\frac{1}{9}$.*

Table 3. Performance Analysis of *Algorithm 2*.

P.S.	$x_{i+1}y_{i+1}$	x_iy_i	N.S. computations	$n_{x_iy_i}$	$P_{x_{i+1}x_iy_{i+1}y_i}$	Line
Nr	oo	$\underline{o}\underline{o}$	Nr $C = 2C$	1	1/9	5
Nr	oo	$o\underline{\iota}$	Dx $C = 2C$	1	1/9	6
Nr	oo	$\underline{\iota}o$	Dx $C = 2C \pm A$	2	1/9	6
Nr	oo	$\underline{\iota}\underline{\iota}$	Nr $C = 2C \pm (A \pm B)$	2	1/9	5
Nr	$\iota\iota$	$\underline{o}\underline{o}$	Nr $C = 2C$	1	1/9	5
Dx	$o\underline{\iota}$	$\underline{o}\underline{o}$	Nr $C = 2(C \pm B)$	2	1/9	10
Dx	$o\underline{\iota}$	$\underline{\iota}o$	Dx $C = 2C \pm (A \pm 2B)$	2	1/9	9
Dx	$\iota\underline{o}$	$\underline{o}\underline{o}$	Nr $C = 2C$	1	1/9	10
Dx	$\iota\underline{o}$	$o\underline{\iota}$	Dx $C = 2C$	1	1/9	9

Proof. The value of P_{x_i} is $P_o = \frac{2}{3}$ and $P_\iota = \frac{1}{3}$, then the value of $P_{x_iy_i}$ is $P_{oo} = \frac{4}{9}$, $P_{o\iota} = P_{\iota o} = \frac{2}{9}$, and $P_{\iota\iota} = \frac{1}{9}$.

The value of $P_{x_{i+1}x_iy_{i+1}y_i}$ is equal to $P_{x_{i+1}y_{i+1}} \times P_{x_iy_i|x_{i+1}y_{i+1}}$. Thus, according to Lemma 2 and the above fact, all the nonzero $P_{x_{i+1}x_iy_{i+1}y_i}$ are as shown in this Lemma, and the values are all $\frac{1}{9}$. □

Theorem 3. *The performance factor of Algorithm 2 is $\rho_2 = 1\frac{4}{9} \simeq 1.444$.*

Proof. The performance factor is computed by $\sum (n_{x_iy_i} \times P_{x_{i+1}x_iy_{i+1}y_i})$.
According to Table 3,
$$\rho_2 = \frac{1 \cdot 1 + 1 \cdot 1 + 1 \cdot 2 + 1 \cdot 1 + 1 \cdot 2 + 1 \cdot 2 + 1 \cdot 1 + 1 \cdot 1}{9} = \frac{13}{9} \simeq 1.444.$$ □

3.2   The 1S2I Method for Sparse Forms

When the deleted digit is equal to zero, it only needs one computation. Therefore if $x_i = \iota$ and $y_i = o$, it is more suitable to delete y_i instead of x_i. When we delete y_i, the state is transferred into the state "Delete y," denote by Dy. In this subsection, we propose a method which deletes one digit of x_i or y_i rather than deletes x_i only. The method is called the 1s2I method. The corresponding

Table 4. The corresponding computations of the 1S2I algorithm.

State	Corresponding computations
Nr	$C = 2C + (x_iA + y_iB)$
$Nr \rightarrow Dx$	$C = 2C$
$Nr \rightarrow Dy$	$C = 2C$
Dx	$C = 2C + (x_iA + y_{i+1}2B)$
$Dx \rightarrow Nr$	$C = 2(C + y_{i+1}B) + (x_iA + y_iB)$
Dy	$C = 2C + (x_{i+1}2A + y_iB)$
$Dy \rightarrow Nr$	$C = 2(C + x_{i+1}A) + (x_iA + y_iB)$

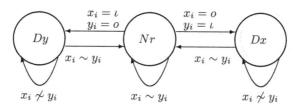

Fig. 2. The state diagram for the 1S2I method.

computation is illustrated in Table 4 and the state diagram of the 1S2I method is shown in Fig. 2. Thus *Algorithm 2* can be modified in the 1S2I method, as shown in *Algorithm 3*.

Algorithm 3. The 1S2I method for sparse forms

I/P: A, B, $x = (x_{n-1}, \cdots, x_1, x_0)_2$, $y = (y_{n-1}, \cdots, y_1, y_0)_2$
O/P: $C = xA + yB$

1: Prepare the value of A, B, $A \pm B$, $A \pm 2B$, $2A \pm B$;
2: $C = O$, $State = Nr$;
3: **for** $i = n$ **downto** 0 **do** {
4: **if** $(State = Nr)$ {
5:   **if** $(x_i \sim y_i)$ **then** $C = 2C + (x_iA + y_iB)$;
6:   **else if** $(x_i = o$ **and** $y_i = \iota)$ **then** $State = Dx$, $C = 2C$;
7:   **else** $State = Dy$, $C = 2C$;
8: }
9: **else if** $(State = Dx)$ {
10:   **if** $(x_i \not\sim y_i)$ **then** $C = 2C + (x_iA + y_{i+1}2B)$;
11:   **else** $State = Nr$, $C = 2(C + y_{i+1}B) + (x_iA + y_iB)$;
12: }
13: **else** {
14:   **if** $(x_i \not\sim y_i)$ **then** $C = 2C + (x_{i+1}2A + y_iB)$;
15:   **else** $State = Nr$, $C = 2(C + x_{i+1}A) + (x_iA + y_iB)$;
16: }
17: }

The performance analysis of *Algorithm 3* is similar to *Algorithm 2*. In order to get the performance analysis table like Table 3, we compute the probability of all the state beforehand. We first find that the deleted digit is always zero and the corresponding digit is always nonzero. Therefore, the state Dx is separated into Dx' ($x_i = o$ and $y_i = \iota$) and Dx'' ($x_i = \iota$ and $y_i = o$); the state Dy is separated into Dy' ($x_i = \iota$ and $y_i = o$) and Dy'' ($x_i = o$ and $y_i = \iota$). Then according to Lemma 1 and Lemma 2, the probability of the state diagram is

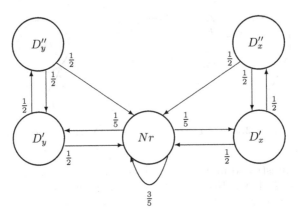

Fig. 3. The detail state probability of *Algorithm 3*.

illustrated as Fig. 3. The probability of state Nr, Dx', Dx'', Dy', and Dy'' are illustrated in Lemma 4. Thus the performance analysis is illustrated in Table 5. In Theorem 4, the performance factor ρ_3 is proved to be 1.407. In comparison with 5 registers in *Algorithm 1*, *Algorithm 3* needs 4 extra registers to store the value of $A \pm 2B$ and $2A \pm B$.

Lemma 4. *Suppose p_0, p_1', p_1'', p_2', and p_2'' denote the probabilities of state Nr, Dx', Dx'', Dy', and Dy'', respectively. Then $p_0 = \frac{5}{9}$, $p_1' = \frac{4}{27}$, $p_1'' = \frac{2}{27}$, $p_2' = \frac{4}{27}$, and $p_2'' = \frac{2}{27}$*

Proof. Consider the probability in Fig. 2, we can get

$p_2'' = \frac{1}{2}p_2' \rightarrow p_2' = 2p_2''$,

$p_2' = \frac{1}{5}p_0 + \frac{1}{2}p_2'' \rightarrow p_0 = \frac{15}{2}p_2''$,

$p_1'' = \frac{1}{2}p_1' \rightarrow p_1' = 2p_1''$,

$p_1' = \frac{1}{5}p_0 + \frac{1}{2}p_1'' \rightarrow p_0 = \frac{15}{2}p_1''$,

Suppose $p_2'' = p_1'' = a$, and $p_2' = p_1' = 2a, p_0 = \frac{15}{2}a$,

We can get $(1 + 1 + 2 + 2 + \frac{15}{2})a = 1 \rightarrow a = \frac{2}{27}$,

Therefore $p_0 = \frac{5}{9}$, $p_1' = \frac{4}{27}$, $p_1'' = \frac{2}{27}$, $p_2' = \frac{4}{27}$, and $p_2'' = \frac{2}{27}$. $\qquad\square$

Theorem 4. *The performance factor of Algorithm 3 is $\rho_3 = 1\frac{11}{27} \simeq 1.407$.*

Proof. The performance factor is computed by $\sum (n_{x_i y_i} \times P_{x_{i+1} x_i y_{i+1} y_i})$.
According to Table 5,
$$\rho_3 = \frac{1 \cdot 1 + 1 \cdot 1 + 1 \cdot 1 + 1 \cdot 2 + 1 \cdot 1}{9} + \frac{2 \cdot 2 + 2 \cdot 2 + 1 \cdot 1 + 1 \cdot 1 + 2 \cdot 2 + 2 \cdot 2 + 1 \cdot 1 + 1 \cdot 1}{27} = \frac{38}{27} \simeq 1.407. \qquad\square$$

4   Comparison and Discussion

The performance of multi-computations can be improved by integer similarity strategy. Consider the 1S1I and 1S2I methods with sparse forms, $\rho_1 = 1.556$ is improved to $\rho_2 = 1.444$ and $\rho_3 = 1.407$. The performance of the proposed algorithm seems to be further improve by combining with recoding methods.

Table 5. Performance analysis of *Algorithm 3*.

P.S.	$x_{i+1}y_{i+1}$	x_iy_i	N.S. computations	$n_{x_iy_i}$	$P_{x_{i+1}x_iy_{i+1}y_i}$	Line
Nr	oo	$\underline{oo}$	Nr $C = 2C$	1	1/9	5
Nr	oo	$\underline{o\iota}$	Dx $C = 2C$	1	1/9	6
Nr	oo	$\iota\underline{o}$	Dx $C = 2C$	1	1/9	7
Nr	oo	$\underline{\iota\iota}$	Nr $C = 2C \pm (A \pm B)$	2	1/9	5
Nr	$\iota\iota$	$\underline{oo}$	Nr $C = 2C$	1	1/9	5
Dx	$o\underline{\iota}$	$\underline{oo}$	Nr $C = 2(C \pm B)$	2	2/27	11
Dx	$o\underline{\iota}$	$\iota\underline{o}$	Dx $C = 2C \pm (A \pm 2B)$	2	2/27	10
Dx	$\iota\underline{o}$	$\underline{oo}$	Nr $C = 2C$	1	1/27	11
Dx	$\iota\underline{o}$	$o\underline{\iota}$	Dx $C = 2C$	1	1/27	10
Dy	$\underline{o\iota}$	$\underline{oo}$	Nr $C = 2C$	1	1/27	15
Dy	$\underline{o\iota}$	$\iota\underline{o}$	Dy $C = 2C$	1	1/27	14
Dy	$\underline{\iota o}$	$\underline{oo}$	Nr $C = 2(C \pm A)$	2	2/27	15
Dy	$\underline{\iota o}$	$o\underline{\iota}$	Dy $C = 2C \pm (2A \pm B)$	2	2/27	14

Thus, using recoding methods in *Algorithm 2* and *Algorithm 3* is an interesting approach. As described in proof of Theorem 2, the computation in Dx can be divided into 4 conditions, and the performance factor can be increased in each condition. Thus our proposed methods will also improve the performance when combined with recoding methods. Unfortunately, the performance is poorer than directly using sparse forms. The reason is that zeros (or nonzeros) have been aligned between x and y in recoding methods. If we try to apply our method to the recoded BSD representations, the ratio of the improvement is less than the ratio that we apply the method on sparse forms. In our simulation (10000 pairs of 1024-bit integers generated by java.security.SecureRandom object in Java 2 platform), the performance factor is shown in Table 6. Thus the proposed strategy is suitable for spars forms especially. We illustrate improvement of the 1S1I method of the by given instance in Example 1. Furthermore, the proposed strategy seems to be similar to the width-w nonadjacent form (w-NAF) encoding method [6, 17]. In order to achieve the unique w-NAF, the digits in w-NAF should be zero or odds. If the digits is in $\{-2, -1, 0, 1, 2\}$, the effect is very near to the proposed integer similarity strategy, but the integer will be many representations. It does not exist an exact method to find a good "w-NAF(-2,-1,0,1,2)" for multi-computations. Based on the proposed strategy, *Algorithm 2* and *Algorithm 3* exactly define the rules of deleting or inserting digits. However, the w-NAF encoding is a very interesting research topic in multi-computations.

Example 1. Let $x = (10\bar{1}0\bar{1}010101010\bar{1}0)_2$ and $y = (01010\bar{1}0\bar{1}0\bar{1}010\bar{1}00)_2$. The performance factor of the combination with recoding methods and the 1s1I method is shown as follows. In this example, we first find that $\rho_1 = 1.938$ is improved to $\rho'_1 = \rho''_1 = 1.563$ by using the DJM method and JSF, respectively. Second, we find that $\rho_1 = 1.938$ is improved to $\rho_2 = 1.500$ by using the 1S1I method. Finally, ρ_2 can not be improved by using the DJM method and JSF.

Table 6. The comparison of some algorithms.

Performance Factor	Original	with 1S1I	with 1S2I
Sparse Forms	1.556	1.444	1.407
recode by DJM	1.534	1.453	1.414
recode to JSF	1.500	1.469	1.438

Sparse forms	$1\ 0\ \bar{1}\ 0\ \bar{1}\ \ 0\ 1\ 0\ 1\ \ 0\ \ 1\ 0\ \bar{1}\ 0\ \bar{1}\ 0$
	$0\ 1\ 0\ \ 1\ 0\ \ \bar{1}\ 0\ \bar{1}\ 0\ \bar{1}\ \ 0\ 1\ 0\ \bar{1}\ \ 0\ \ 0\ \rho_1 = 1.938$
with 1S1I	$\not{1}\ 0\ \bar{1}\ \ 0\ \bar{1}\ \ 0\ 1\ 0\ 1\ 0\ \ 1\ 0\ \bar{1}\ 0\ \bar{1}\ 0$
	$0\ \ 1\ 0\ 1\ \ 0\ \bar{1}\ 0\ \bar{1}\ 0\ \ \bar{1}\ 0\ 1\ 0\ \ \bar{1}\ 0\ 0\ \rho_2 = 1.500$

recode by DJM	$0\ \bar{1}\ \ \bar{1}\ \ 0\ \bar{1}\ \ 0\ 1\ 0\ 1\ 0\ \ 0\ 1\ 0\ 1\ \ 1\ 0$
	$0\ 1\ 0\ \ 0\ 1\ \ 0\ 1\ 0\ 1\ 1\ \ 0\ 1\ 0\ \bar{1}\ \ 0\ \ 0\ \rho'_1 = 1.563$
with 1S1I	$0\ \bar{1}\ \not{1}\ \ 0\ \bar{1}\ \ 0\ 1\ 0\ 1\ \not{0}\ \ 0\ 1\ 0\ 1\ \not{1}\ 0$
	$0\ 1\ \ \ \ 0\ 0\ \ 1\ \ 0\ 1\ 0\ 1\ \ \ \ 1\ 0\ 1\ 0\ \bar{1}\ \ \ \ 0\ 0\ \rho'_2 = 1.563$

recode to JSF	$0\ 1\ 0\ \ 1\ \ 1\ \ 0\ 1\ 0\ 1\ 0\ \ 0\ 1\ 0\ 1\ \ 1\ 0$
	$0\ 1\ 0\ \ 1\ 0\ \ 0\ 1\ 0\ 1\ 1\ \ 0\ 1\ 0\ \bar{1}\ \ 0\ \ 0\ \rho''_1 = 1.563$
with 1S1I	$0\ 1\ 0\ \ 1\ \not{1}\ \ 0\ 1\ 0\ 1\ \not{0}\ \ 0\ 1\ 0\ 1\ \not{1}\ 0$
	$0\ 1\ 0\ \ 1\ \ \ \ 0\ 0\ 1\ 0\ 1\ \ \ \ 1\ 0\ 1\ 0\ \bar{1}\ \ \ 0\ 0\ \rho''_2 = 1.563$

Besides, our proposed strategy can also be applied to multiexponentiation with binary representations. With regard to state Dx, the corresponding digits are (x_i, y_{i+1}), $x_i \neq y_{i+1}$ is suitable to insert y_i. But the value of $(c \times b^{y_{i+1}})^\beta \times a^{x_i}b^{y_i}$ must be computed by inserting y_i. The computation needs 1 square and 2 multiplications. Therefore, the condition, $x_i = y_i$ and $y_i \neq y_{i+1}$ (denoted by $x_i = y_i \neq y_{i+1}$) is more suitable. Since the number of multiplication can be reduced by 1. The conditions of deletion and insertion for binary representations are shown in Fig. 4. Apply the strategy to the binary method (the square-and-multiply method), the modified algorithm is shown in *Algorithm 4*. The performance factor can be reduced from 1.75 to 1.667 and only increase one extra register to store ab^2.

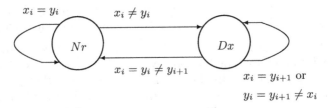

Fig. 4. The state diagram for binary representations.

Algorithm 4 Apply the integer similarity strategy to binary methods

I/P: a, b, $x = (x_{n-1} \cdots x_1 x_0)_2$, $y = (y_{n-1} \cdots y_1 y_0)_2$

O/P: $c = a^x b^y$

1: Precompute and store the values of a, b, ab, and ab^2.

2: $c = 1$, $state = Nr$;

3: **for** $i = n - 1$ **downto** 0 **do** {

4:   **if** $(state = Nr)$ {

5:     **if** $(x_i \neq y_i)$ **then** $state = Dx$, $c = c^2 \times a^{x_i}$;

6:     **else** $c = c^2 \times (a^{x_i} b^{y_i})$;

7:   }

8:   **else** {

9:     **if** $(x_i \neq y_{i+1})$ **then** {

10:       **if** $(x_i = y_i)$ **then** $state = Nr$, $c = (c \times b^{y_{i+1}})^2 \times (a^{x_i} b^{y_i})$;

11:       **else** $c = (c \times b^{y_{i+1}})^2 \times a^{x_i}$;

12:     }

13:     **else** $c = c^2 \times (a^{x_i} b^{2y_i})$;

14:   }

15: }

---

5 Conclusion

In this article, we propose a totally new strategy, the integer similarity strategy, for multi-computations. In order to match zeros and nonzeros in multi-computation, the proposed strategy modifies the computing sequences by deleting and inserting some digits. According to the strategy, we propose two efficient algorithms, named the 1S1I and 1S2I method for multi-scalar multiplications with BSD sparse forms. The performance factor is improved from 1.556 to 1.444 and to 1.407, respectively. The memory space only required 2 and 4 extra registers, respectively. Thus the proposed algorithms is suitable for memory limited environments.

Our proposed algorithms can also be combined with recoding methods, including the DJM method and joint sparse forms. However, this way turns out to be far from desirable. Besides, the proposed strategy can be still used in binary representations. In binary methods for multiexponentiation, the performance factor can be improved form 1.75 to 1.667 with only one extra register.

Based on the integer similarity strategy, all the proposed methods are all single stage in this article, that is one insertion must appear after one deletion. In general case, the deletion and insertion should be appeared without any limitations. The multi-stage version of the proposed strategy is an interesting work in the future.

References

1. S. Arno and F. S. Wheeler. Signed digit representations of minimal hamming weight. *IEEE Trans. Computers*, 42(8):1007–1010, 1993.
2. R. M. Avanzi. On multi-exponentiation in cryptography. *IACR Cryptology ePrint Archive 2002/154, http://eprint.iacr.org*, 2002.
3. D. J. Bernstein. Pippenger's exponentiation algorithm. *http://cr.yp.to/antiforgery.html*, 2002.
4. E. F. Brickelland, D. M. Gordon, K. S. McCurley, and D. Wilson. Fast exponentiation with precomputation. *Advances in Cryptology-EUROCRYPT'92, LNCS 658, Springer-Verlag*, pages 200–207, 1992.
5. Ç. K. Koç. High-speed RSA implementations. *RSA Laboratories, Technique Notes TR201, http://www.rsasecurity.com/rsalabs*, pages 9–32, Nov. 1994.
6. H. Cohen, A. Miyagi, and T. Ono. Efficient elliptic curve exponentiation using mixed coordinates. *Advances in Cryptology-AISACRYPT'98, LNCS 1514, Springer-Verlag*, pages 51–65, 1998.
7. V. S. Dimitrov, G. A. Jullien, and W. C. Miller. Complexity and fast algorithms for multiexponentiation. *IEEE Trans. Computers*, 49(2):141–147, Feb. 2000.
8. T. ElGamal. A public key cryptosystem and a signature scheme based on discrete logarithms. *IEEE Trans. Information Theory*, 31(4):469–472, Jul. 1985.
9. FIPS186-2. Digital signature standard(DSS). *NIST Computer Security FIPS page, http://csrc.nist.gov/publications/fips/*, 2001.
10. D. M. Gordon. A survey of fast exponentiation methods. *Journal of Algorithms*, 27:129–146, 1998.
11. J. Jedwab and C. J. Mitchell. Minimum weight modified signed-digit representations and fast exponentiation. *Electronics Letters*, 25(17):1171–1172, 1989.
12. M. Joye and S. M. Yen. Optimal left-to-right binary signed-digit recoding. *IEEE Trans. Computers*, 49(7):740–748, 2000.
13. D. E. Knuth. *The Art of Computer Programming, Seminumerical Algorithms*, volume 2. Addison-Wesley, 3rd edition, 1998.
14. C. H. Lim and P. J. Lee. More flexible exponentiation with precomputation. *Advances in Cryptology-CRYPTO'94, LNCS 839, Springer-Verlag*, pages 95–107, 1994.
15. B. Möller. Algorithms for multi-exponentiations. *8th Annual Workshop on Selected Areas in Cryptography -SAC 2001, LNCS 2259, Springer-Verlag*, pages 165–180, 2001.
16. P. K. Mishra. Scalar multiplication in elliptic curve cryptosystems: Pipelining with pre-computations. *IACR Cryptology ePrint Archive 2004/191, http://eprint.iacr.org*, 2004.
17. J. Muir and D. Stinson. Minimality and other properties of the width-w nonadjacent form. *Technique Report CORR 2004-08, http://www.cacr.math.uwaterloo.ca*, 2004.
18. K. Okeya and K. Sakurai. Fast multi-scalar multiplication methods on elliptic curves with precomputation using montgomery trick. *4th International Workshop on Cryptographic Hardware and Embedded Systems - CHES 2002, LNCS 2523, Springer-Verlag*, pages 564–578, 2003.
19. K. Okeya, K. Schmidt-Samoa, C. Spahn, and T. Takagi. Signed binary representations revisited. *IACR Cryptology ePrint Archive 2004/195, http://eprint.iacr.org*, 2004.
20. G. W. Reitwiesner. Binary arithmetic. *Advance in computers*, pages 231–308, 1960.

21. C. P. Schnorr. Efficient identification and signatures for smart cards. *Advances in Cryptology-CRYPTO'89, LNCS 435, Springer-Verlag*, pages 239–252, 1989.
22. J. A. Solinas. Low-weight binary representations for pairs of integers. *Technique Report CORR 2001-41, http://www.cacr.math.uwaterloo.ca*, 2001.
23. S. M. Yen, C. S. Laih, and A. K. Lenstra. Multiexponentiation. *IEE Proc., Computers and Digital Techniques*, 141(6):325–326, 1994.

Efficient Proofs of Knowledge
of Discrete Logarithms and Representations
in Groups with Hidden Order

Endre Bangerter[1], Jan Camenisch[1], and Ueli Maurer[2]

[1] IBM Research, Zurich Research Lab, CH-8803 Rueschlikon, Switzerland
{eba,jca}@zurich.ibm.com
[2] Departement of Computer Science, ETH Zurich, CH-8092 Zurich, Switzerland
maurer@inf.ethz.ch

Abstract. For many one-way homomorphisms used in cryptography, there exist efficient zero-knowledge proofs of knowledge of a preimage. Examples of such homomorphisms are the ones underlying the Schnorr or the Guillou-Quisquater identification protocols.

In this paper we present, for the first time, efficient zero-knowledge proofs of knowledge for exponentiation $\psi(x_1) \doteq h_1^{x_1}$ and multi-exponentiation homomorphisms $\psi(x_1, \ldots, x_l) \doteq h_1^{x_1} \cdot \ldots \cdot h_l^{x_l}$ with $h_1, \ldots, h_l \in H$ (i.e., proofs of knowledge of discrete logarithms and representations) where H is a group of hidden order, e.g., an RSA group.

1 Introduction

Consider mappings $\psi : G \to H$, where the domain is the group $(G, +)$ and the co-domain is $(H, \cdot)$. A mapping ψ is called a *homomorphism* if $\psi(g + g') = \psi(g) \cdot \psi(g')$ for all g and g' from G. A *proof of knowledge of a preimage under a homomorphism* is a two-party protocol between a prover and a verifier. The parties' common input is a homomorphism ψ and an element $y \in H$. As a result of the protocol the verifier either accepts or rejects. Informally speaking, a proof of knowledge has the property that if a prover succeeds in making the verifier accept with a probability larger than some threshold probability (the *knowledge error*), then the prover must "know" a preimage x of y, i.e., an element $x \in G$ such that $y = \psi(x)$. That is, there exists an algorithm (the *knowledge extractor*) for the protocol that can compute a preimage x of y given rewinding oracle access to such a prover.

For all (computable) homomorphisms there exists a proof of knowledge: the well known commitment-challenge-response protocol, often called Σ-protocol [17, 18], with binary challenges. Due to the binary challenges, the protocol has a knowledge error of $1/2$ and therefore it needs to be repeated sequentially sufficiently many times to achieve a reasonably small knowledge error (i.e., a small success probability for a cheating prover). However, some homomorphisms allow one to use the Σ-protocol with larger challenges, which results in a smaller knowledge error. Thus, the protocol needs to be repeated only a few times or

S. Vaudenay (Ed.): PKC 2005, LNCS 3386, pp. 154–171, 2005.

just once, which is an order of magnitude more efficient. Examples of homomorphisms for which this is known to be possible are for instance those underlying the Schnorr and the Guillou-Quisquater identification schemes [32, 27]. In fact, Cramer [17] remarks that all the homomorphisms for which this is the case allow one to compute some information (e.g., the order of the group) from their description that enables the knowledge extractor, together with the information extracted from a convincing prover, to compute a preimage. Cramer calls such homomorphisms *special*.

Unfortunately, many homomorphisms widely used in cryptographic protocols are not known to be special and hence the most efficient proofs of knowledge known for them is the Σ-protocol with binary challenges. Prominent examples of such homomorphisms are exponentiations $\psi(x_1) \doteq h_1^{x_1}$ and multi-exponentiations $\psi(x_1, \ldots, x_l) \doteq h_1^{x_1} \cdot \ldots \cdot h_l^{x_l}$ with $h_1, \ldots, h_l \in H$ in hidden order groups H, e.g., where H is a class group [7, 22] or an RSA group. Such homomorphisms are for instance the basis of recent group signature and identity escrow schemes, credential systems, and fair exchange protocols [2, 1, 8–10, 28, 5, 25, 11]. In fact in these schemes, the authors often employ the Σ-protocol with non-binary challenges, sometimes wrongly relying on them to be proofs of knowledge in this setting as well.

Related Work. Girault [26] suggests an efficient proof of knowledge for discrete logarithms in the RSA group based on the Σ-protocol. His approach is to publish the order of the sub-group in which the images lies. This requires, on the one hand, that the RSA modulus has a special form and, on the other hand, the non-standard assumption that giving away the order of the sub-group does not allow one to factor the RSA modulus. Also, one can no longer make use of the RSA-trapdoor for this subgroup with this approach.

Poupard and Stern [30] describe an identification scheme based on the Σ-protocol, where the private key is a discrete logarithm of a generator of a sub-group of the RSA group. They show that from an adversary that breaks the identification scheme, a discrete logarithm can be extracted. While their construction is appropriate to prove the security of their identification scheme, their protocol is not a proof of knowledge of a discrete logarithm in the RSA group.

The most relevant work in the field is that by Damgård and Fujisaki [21] (based on work by Fujisaki and Okamoto [24]). They show that the Σ-protocol can be used in certain cases to demonstrate knowledge of a discrete logarithm (or representation) in hidden order groups provided that the prover is not given the group's order. Let us refer in the following to the Damgård and Fujisaki scheme as the DF scheme. As pointed out and explained in detail by its authors [21], the DF scheme is *not* a (computational) proof of knowledge according to the standard definition [4]. Rather, it only works in a stronger definitional setting resulting in "weak proofs of knowledge". Technically, the DF scheme demonstrates knowledge only over a suitable probability distribution of (multi-) exponentiations. This distribution is enforced in a setup phase prior to the proof protocol. While for some applications this is appropriate, it often leads to complicated and error-prone proofs of security as one can no longer consider each proof protocol separately (as one could with standard proofs of knowledge) but has to analyze all of them in conjunction with each other. In fact, many authors seem not to be aware of this fact and correspondingly the security analysis of their applications using the DF scheme are incomplete or false.

Our Results. In this paper we provide two independent, new methods to obtain, for the first time, efficient zero-knowledge proofs of knowledge for (multi-) exponentiations in hidden order groups H, where the order H is not known to at least the verifier.

Our first method is based on the Σ-protocol. It relies on the new idea to provide auxiliary information to the verifier (and thus to the knowledge extractor) to obtain proofs of knowledge for homomorphisms for which the Σ-protocol is not known to work otherwise. The method applies to (multi-) exponentiation homomorphisms in hidden order groups H, provided that the prover (but not the verifier) knows the order H. The method relies on the hardness of a new computational problem, which we call the *pseudo-preimage problem*. We prove the pseudo-preimage problem to be hard under standard assumptions, e.g., the RSA assumption. This result is of potential independent interest for the construction of new cryptographic schemes.

Our second method is based on a new protocol, which we call the Σ^+-protocol. The Σ^+-protocol yields efficient proofs of knowledge for any (multi-) exponentiation homomorphism in groups H with hidden order. The efficiency of the proof depends on the smallest factor of the order of the homomorphism's image. Thus, we obtain for instance efficient proofs for discrete logarithm-based homomorphisms in RSA groups whose modulus is a product of two safe primes. Technically, we apply the ideas underlying the DF scheme and extend them to obtain standard proofs of knowledge. As a consequence one can *always* use our protocol instead of the DF scheme to obtain standard proofs of knowledge. Yet, compared to the DF scheme, our protocol is applicable to a wider number of settings and is also more efficient in certain application scenarios.

A Remark on the Presentation. We formulate all our new results for multi-exponentiation $\psi_M : \mathbb{Z}^l \to H$ in hidden order groups H, i.e., mappings $\psi_M(x_1, \ldots, x_l) \doteq h_1^{x_1} \cdot \ldots \cdot h_l^{x_l}$ with $h_1, \ldots, h_l \in H$. We would like to emphasize that the results (trivially) specialize to the practically relevant cases such as when H is an RSA group or a class group and also to simple exponentiations $\psi_M(x) = h^x$. We recall that what we call a proof of knowledge for a multi-exponentiation homomorphism is often referred to as a proof of knowledge of a representation.

Outline. The remainder of this paper is structured as follows: In § 2 we introduce the basic concepts and the notation we use. In § 3 we introduce the notion of a pseudo-preimage and the related pseudo-preimage problem, which we prove to be hard under standard assumptions. In § 4 we review the Σ-protocol and its properties and then making use of the hardness of the pseudo-preimage problem we discuss the first of our new methods, i.e., the one based on the Σ-protocol where the verifier is given auxiliary information. In § 5 we discuss our second method which is based on the Σ^+-protocol.

2   Preliminaries

Let M be an algorithm. By $y \leftarrow M(x)$, we denote that y was obtained by running M on input x. If M is deterministic, then this y is unique; if M is probabilistic, then y is a random variable.

By k we denote an integer *security parameter*. A *negligible function* is a function that, asymptotically in k, is smaller than one divided by any polynomial in k.

We call a computational problem *hard* if there is a probability ensemble $\mathcal{D}(k)$ on problem instances such that for any probabilistic polynomial-time algorithm, the probability of solving the problem over choices according to $\mathcal{D}(k)$ is negligible. If there is a probabilistic polynomial-time algorithm that is successful over choices $\mathcal{D}(k)$ with probability $1 - \nu(k)$, where $\nu(k)$ is a negligible function, we call the problem *easy*.

Let $(G, +)$ and $(H, \cdot)$ be abelian groups, with their identity elements denoted 0 and 1, respectively. By $|H|$ we denote the order of the group H, and by $|h|$ the order of the element $h \in H$. We say that a group H has *hidden order* if there is a description of H such that it is hard to compute a non-zero multiple of $|H|$. A *(group) homomorphism* ψ is a mapping $\psi : G \to H$ such that $\psi(g_1 + g_2) = \psi(g_1) \cdot \psi(g_2)$ for all $g_1, g_2 \in G$. We recall that the image of a homomorphism, denoted $\text{image}(\psi)$, is a subgroup of its co-domain H. In the following we assume that H is a finite group. Throughout the paper ψ_M stands for a multi-exponentiation homomorphism $\psi_M : \mathbb{Z}^l \to H$, where $\psi_M(x_1, \ldots, x_l) = h_1^{x_1} \cdot \ldots \cdot h_l^{x_l}$ and $h_1, \ldots, h_l \in H$. We always assume that groups and homomorphisms are computationally tractable. That is, there shall be descriptions of groups and homomorphisms such that in (probabilistic) polynomial-time one can evaluate the group operation, invert group elements, test membership in the group, uniformly choose an element from the group (for finite groups), and evaluate a homomorphism.

By a *collection of homomorphisms* Ψ we refer to a (finite or infinite) set of homomorphisms together with a probability ensemble $\mathcal{D}_\Psi(k)$ on Ψ. We assume that there is a probabilistic polynomial-time algorithm that allows one to chose homomorphisms ψ according to $\mathcal{D}_\Psi(k)$. Also, we consider sequences of sets $\Psi(k) \doteq \{\psi : \psi \in \Psi, \psi : G \to H, \text{ and } \lceil \log(|H|) \rceil = k\}$. The notion of a collection of homomorphisms Ψ comprises as special cases sequences of homomorphisms, where Ψ is an infinite set of homomorphisms indexed by the security parameter, and single homomorphisms, i.e., $\Psi = \{\psi\}$.

Given a binary relation $\mathcal{R}$, we denote the corresponding language by $\mathcal{L}_\mathcal{R}$. Homomorphism collections give rise to what we call a *homomorphism relation*

$$\mathcal{R}[\Psi] \doteq \{((\psi, y), x) : \psi \in \Psi, \psi : G \to H, x \in G, y \doteq \psi(x)\} \quad \text{or}$$

$$\mathcal{R}[\Psi(k)] \doteq \{((\psi, y), x) : \psi :\in \Psi(k), \psi : G \to H, x \in G, y \doteq \psi(x)\} \ .$$

Our results on (computational) proofs of knowledge are formulated with respect to the corresponding definitions put forth by Bellare and Goldreich [4].

3   The Pseudo-preimage Problem

In this section we introduce the notion of a *pseudo-preimage* of a homomorphism and a related computational problem termed the *pseudo-preimage problem*. While the pseudo-preimage problem has not been explicitly considered in existing work, it is implicit in the construction of all known knowledge extractors for the Σ-protocol. In fact, these constructions crucially rely on the existence of easy instances of the pseudo-preimage problem. In the following we prove that for a large class of multi-exponentiation homomorphisms the pseudo-preimage problem is hard.

Definition 1 (Pseudo-preimage). *Consider a homomorphism $\psi : G \to H$ and $y \in H$. A pseudo-preimage of y under ψ is a pair (v, w) such that $y^v = \psi(w)$, where v is a non-zero integer and $w \in G$. We refer to v as the* exponent *of the pseudo-preimage (v, w).*

Note that when ψ is not surjective, then there are pseudo-preimages (v, w) of $y \in H$ under ψ even for elements $y \notin \text{image}(\psi)$.

Definition 2 (Pseudo-preimage Problem). *The* pseudo-preimage (PP) problem *for a homomorphism ψ is to compute a preimage x of y under ψ given a pseudo-preimage (v, w) of y under ψ, with $y \in \text{image}(\psi)$.*

For homomorphisms that are easy to invert, the PP problem trivially is easy. More interestingly, the PP problem is also easy for certain one-way homomorphisms. In fact, as we will see in § 4.1, the existence of easy instances of the PP problem for one-way homomorphisms is key for the construction of knowledge extractors for the Σ-protocol. Examples of such one-way homomorphisms are the ones underlying the Schnorr and the Guillou-Quisquater schemes.

In the following we show that the PP problem is hard for multi-exponentiations in groups for which the ROOT problem, i.e., computing roots, is hard. Let us introduce concepts and notation used for the formulation of this result. We recall the ROOT problem for an arbitrary abelian group H. It is to compute a $h \in H$ such that $h^e = u$ given an integer $e > 1$ and a group element $u \in H$. Next, we define generators $\mathcal{D}_\mathcal{R}$ and $\mathcal{D}_\mathcal{P}$ for the ROOT and PP problem, respectively. Let H be an arbitrary multiplicative abelian group and let l be an arbitrary integer parameter. The generator $\mathcal{D}_\mathcal{R}(H)$ works as follows: 1) Choose $u \in_U H$ and an integer $e > 1$ such that $\gcd(|H|, e) = 1$, whereas the distribution of e may be arbitrary. 2) Output the ROOT problem instance (u, e).

In the definition of the generator for the PP problem we use as a subroutine a probabilistic polynomial-time algorithm $\tilde{\mathcal{D}}(H, l)$ with the following properties. The algorithm $\tilde{\mathcal{D}}(H, l)$ outputs tuples $(v, (w_1, \ldots, w_l), (e_1, \ldots, e_l))$, where v is an integer and $(w_1, \ldots, w_l)$ and $(e_1, \ldots, e_l)$ are elements of $\mathbb{Z}^l$, such that $v \nmid (e_1 w_1 + \ldots + e_l w_l)$ and $\gcd(|H|, v) = 1$. Apart from this, the tuples may be distributed arbitrarily. Note that the latter condition can be fulfilled by $\tilde{\mathcal{D}}(H, l)$ without being given $|H|$. It suffices if one can compute a $\lambda^+ \geq |H|$ from the description of H. Then one can, for instance, choose a v as a prime $\geq \lambda^+$.

Now, the generator $\mathcal{D}_P(H, |H|, l)$ is as follows: 1) Choose $(v, (w_1, \ldots, w_l),$ $(e_1, \ldots, e_l)) \leftarrow \tilde{\mathcal{D}}(H, l)$ and an element $h \in_U H$. 2) Set $h_1 \doteq h^{e_1}, \ldots, h_l \doteq h^{e_l}$ and define the homomorphism $\psi_M : \mathbb{Z}^l \to H$ by $\psi_M(x_1, \ldots, x_l) \doteq h_1^{x_1} \cdot \ldots \cdot h_l^{x_l}$. 3) Set $(z_1, \ldots, z_l) \doteq (w_1 v^{-1} \pmod{|H|}, \ldots, w_l v^{-1} \pmod{|H|}))$ and let $y \doteq \psi_M(z_1, \ldots, z_l) = h_1^{z_1} \cdot \ldots \cdot z_l^{z_l}$. (Note that by construction $(v, (w_1, \ldots, w_l))$ is a pseudo-preimage of y under ψ_M.) 4) Output the PP problem instance $((v, (w_1, \ldots, w_l)), y, \psi_M)$.

Let be given computational problems P_1 and P_2 and the respective generators $\mathcal{D}_1$ and $\mathcal{D}_2$. We say P_2 is reducible to P_1, if given a probabilistic polynomial-time solver M with non-negligible success probability for P_1 over choices of $\mathcal{D}_1$, one can construct a probabilistic polynomial-time solver given black box access to M that has non-negligible success probability for P_2 over choices of $\mathcal{D}_2$. We denote this by $P_1[\mathcal{D}_1] \geq P_2[\mathcal{D}_2]$.

Theorem 1. *For the generators $\mathcal{D}_\mathcal{R}(H)$ and $\mathcal{D}_P(H, |H|, l)$ (as defined above) we have $PP[\mathcal{D}_P(H, |H|, l)] \geq ROOT[\mathcal{D}_\mathcal{R}(H)]$.*

Proof. Let M denote a probabilistic polynomial-time solver of the PP problem that is successful with non-negligible probability over choices of $\mathcal{D}_P$.

Given an instance of the ROOT problem $(u, e) \leftarrow \mathcal{D}_\mathcal{R}(H)$ we construct an instance of the PP problem as follows. Choose $(v', (w'_1, \ldots, w'_l), (e'_1, \ldots, e'_l)) \leftarrow \tilde{\mathcal{D}}(H, l)$. Then we set $h' \doteq u^v$, $h'_1 \doteq h'^{e'_1}, \ldots, h'_l \doteq h'^{e'_l}$ and define the homomorphism $\psi'_M : \mathbb{Z}^l \to H$ by $\psi'_M(x_1, \ldots, x_l) \doteq h_1'^{x_1} \cdot \ldots \cdot h_l'^{x_l}$. We set $y' \doteq u^{(e'_1 w'_1 + \ldots + e'_l w'_l)}$. It is easy to see that we have constructed an instance $(v', (w'_1, \ldots, w'_l), y', \psi'_M)$ of the PP problem.

Now, we invoke M on input $(v', (w'_1, \ldots, w'_l), y', \psi'_M)$ and let us assume that M outputs a preimage $(z_1, \ldots, z_l)$ of y' under ψ'_M. Thus we have $y'^{v'} = (h_1'^{z_1} \cdot \ldots \cdot h_l'^{z_l})^{v'} = h'^{(e'_1 z_1 + \ldots + e'_l z_l) v'}$ and $y'^{v'} = h_1'^{w'_1} \cdot \ldots \cdot h_l'^{w'_l} = h'^{(e'_1 w'_1 + \ldots + e'_l w'_l)}$. Using $\lambda \doteq (e'_1 w'_1 + \ldots + e'_l w'_l) - (e'_1 z_1 + e'_2 z_2 + \ldots + e'_l z_l) v'$ we have $h'^\lambda = 1$. By assumption $v \nmid (e'_1 w'_1 + \ldots + e'_l w'_l)$ and thus $\lambda \neq 0$, i.e., λ is a non-zero multiple of the order of h'. As h' and u have the same order, λ is also a multiple of the order of u. This allows us to compute the e-th root of u as follows. We note that λ is not necessarily co-prime to e. However, we have by assumption $\gcd(e, |H|) = 1$. Thus we can easily find a multiple λ' of $|u|$ that is co-prime to e, if we set $\lambda' \doteq \lambda$ and compute $\lambda' \doteq \lambda' / \gcd(e, \lambda')$ until $\gcd(e, \lambda') = 1$. Finally we compute $1/e$ modulo λ' to obtain $u^{1/e}$.

It remains to show that the distribution of instances $(v', (w'_1, \ldots, w'_l), y', \psi'_M)$ of the PP problem constructed above is equal to the distribution of instances generated by $\mathcal{D}_P(H, |H|, l)$. From $y^v = \psi_M(w_1, \ldots, w_l)$ and $\gcd(v, |H|) = 1$ we have that the image element y is uniquely determined by ψ_M and $(v, (w_1, \ldots, w_l))$ and the same is true for $((v', (w'_1, \ldots, w'_l)), y', \psi'_M)$. Hence, it suffices to show that the distribution of v', $(w'_1, \ldots, w'_l)$, and ψ'_M is indistinguishable from the distribution of the corresponding quantities chosen by $\mathcal{D}_P(H, |H|, l)$. By construction the distribution of tuples $(v', (w'_1, \ldots, w'_l), (e'_1, \ldots, e'_l))$ chosen above is the same as the one of those output by $\mathcal{D}_P(H, |H|, l)$. It remains to see that ψ'_M and ψ_M have the same distribution. To this end, note that $h' = u^v$, where u

is a uniform random element of H. From $\gcd(v, |H|) = 1$ it follows that h' is uniformly distributed in H, and thus has the same distribution as the element h chosen by the generator $\mathcal{D}_{\mathcal{P}}(H, |H|, l)$. The claim now follows immediately, as the homomorphism ψ'_M is constructed from h' in the same way as is ψ_M from h by the generator $\mathcal{D}_{\mathcal{P}}(H, |H|, l)$. $\qquad\square$

Theorem 1 implies that the PP problem is hard for multi-exponentiations in groups for which the ROOT problem is hard. This is widely assumed to be the case for RSA groups [31] and class groups [7]. Moreover, Damgård and Koprowski [22] have shown that if a group has hidden order and if the order of that group contains a large prime factor, then the ROOT problem is hard for generic algorithms.

Corollary 1. *There is a probabilistic polynomial-time algorithm M such that the probability distributions $((v, (w_1, \ldots, w_l)), y, \psi_M) \leftarrow \mathcal{D}_{\mathcal{P}}(H, |H|, l)$ and $((v, (w_1, \ldots, w_l)), y, \psi_M) \leftarrow M(H, l)$ are equal.*

Corollary 1 follows from the proof of Theorem 1. It implies that instances of the PP problem as output by $\mathcal{D}_{\mathcal{P}}(H, |H|, l))$ do not reveal any computational information on the order of H.

4   Efficient Proofs of Knowledge Using Auxiliary Pseudo-preimages

This section presents a new technique that uses the hardness of the pseudo-preimage problem to yield proofs of knowledge for multi-exponentiations ψ_M in groups for which the ROOT problem is hard (e.g., RSA groups and class groups). The proofs are based on the Σ-protocol. The technique requires that the honest prover is given the order of H, while it ensures that the verifier does not learn the order of H. The resulting proofs are efficient, they achieve in fact an arbitrarily small knowledge error in a single execution of the Σ-protocol.

4.1   Preliminaries: The Σ-Protocol and Its Properties

In this section we review known properties of the Σ-protocol. For a detailed discussion we refer to Cramer [17] and Damgård [20].

Definition 3 (Σ-Protocol). *Let Ψ be a collection of homomorphisms with a finite domain and let $((\psi, y), x) \in \mathcal{R}[\Psi(k)]$. Let (P, V) be a pair of interactive machines with common input (ψ, y), the private input of P being x. A Σ-protocol with challenge set $\mathcal{C} \doteq \{0, \ldots, c^+(k)\}$ is (P, V) performing the following joint computation.*

1. *P: Choose $r \in_U G$, compute $t \doteq \psi(r)$, and send t to V.*
2. *V: Choose $c \in_U \mathcal{C}$ and send c to P.*
3. *P: Set $s \doteq r + cx$ and send s to V.*
4. *V: If $\psi(s) = ty^c$ output 1; otherwise output 0.*

The Σ-protocol is honest-verifier zero-knowledge but not known to be zero-knowledge unless the cardinality of $\mathcal{C}$ is polynomially bounded in k. In case one requires real zero-knowledge or the even stronger notion of concurrent zero-knowledge, one can apply one of numerous constructions, e.g., [19, 23, 15]. Most notably, the technique by Damgård [19] achieves concurrent zero-knowledge at almost no computational and communicational overhead. In Definition 3, the Σ-protocol is only defined for homomorphisms with a finite domain. However, there is a standard variant of the Σ-protocol that is defined for multi-exponentiations $\psi_M : \mathbb{Z}^l \to H$ (which have an infinite domain). That variant of the protocol is statistical zero-knowledge instead of perfect zero-knowledge; apart from this, the above comments and results stated in the following are valid for both variants of the Σ-protocol.

We call Ψ a (collection of) *special homomorphisms*, if there is a probabilistic polynomial-time algorithm M that on input any $(\psi, y) \in \mathcal{L}_{\mathcal{R}[\Psi]}$ outputs a pseudo-preimage (v, w) of y under ψ. The algorithm M is called a *pseudo-preimage finder (for Ψ)*. An example of a special homomorphism is the one used in the Schnorr protocol, i.e., the mapping $\psi : \mathbb{Z}_q \to \mathbb{Z}_p^*$ defined by $\psi(x) \doteq h^x$ with $q \mid (p-1)$ and $|h| = q$. From the description of this mapping, the pseudo-preimage finder can derive $(q, 0)$. Now $y^q = 1 = \psi(0)$ for all $y \in \text{image}(\psi)$ and therefore the pair $(q, 0)$ is a pseudo-preimage of y under ψ. More generally, homomorphisms $\psi : G \to H$ for which a multiple of the order image(ψ) can be efficiently computed from the description of ψ are easily seen to be special. An example of a special homomorphism with hidden order co-domain is the mapping $\psi : \mathbb{Z}_n^* \to \mathbb{Z}_n^*$ given by $\psi(x) \doteq x^e$, where e is an integer, which is used in the Guillou and Quisquater [27] scheme. For such mappings we have $y^e = \psi(y)$ and hence (y, e) is a pseudo-preimage of y under ψ.

To simplify the subsequent discussion we make the following assumption on collections Ψ and pseudo-preimage finders M. For $(\psi, y) \in \mathcal{L}_{\mathcal{R}[\Psi(k)]}$ and $(v, w) \leftarrow M(\psi, y)$ we assume that the exponents v are all equal for a given value of the security parameter k, i.e., that $v = v(k)$. It is straightforward to generalize our discussion and results to the setting where this assumption is not made. Moreover, all known examples of (collections of) special homomorphisms fulfill this assumption.

Theorem 2. *The Σ-protocol with challenge set $\mathcal{C} = \{0, \ldots, c^+(k)\}$ is a proof of knowledge for $\mathcal{R}[\Psi]$,*

(a) with knowledge error $1/2$ if $c^+(k) = 1$.

(b) with knowledge error $1/(c^+ + 1)$ if Ψ is a collection of special homomorphisms and $c^+(k) < p(k)$, where $p(k)$ is the smallest prime dividing the pseudo-preimage exponent $v(k)$ output by a pseudo-preimage finder M for Ψ.

Pseudo-preimages have the property that given two (appropriate) pseudo-preimages of y under ψ one can compute a preimage of y as follows.

Lemma 1 (Shamir's Trick). *Let be given two pseudo-preimages (v_1, w_1) and (v_2, w_2) of y for ψ. If $\gcd(v_1, v_2) = 1$, then $x = aw_1 + bw_2$ is a preimage of y under ψ, where a and b are integers (computed using the extended Euclidean algorithm) such that $av_1 + bv_2 = 1$.*

Proof (Theorem 2). Let us describe a knowledge extractor for the Σ-protocol. Let P^* be an arbitrary prover that is successful in the Σ-protocol on common input $(\psi, y) \in \mathcal{L}_{\mathcal{R}[\Psi]}$ and arbitrary private input with probability $\epsilon > \kappa \doteq 1/(c^+ + 1)$. It is well known that given rewinding access to P^*, one can obtain a pair of tuples (t, c, s) and (t', c', s') that fulfill the verification equation in step 4 of the Σ-protocol, with $t = t'$ and $c \neq c'$. We refer to this property of the Σ-protocol as the *collision extractibility* property. For a detailed analysis of this property we refer to Damgård [20]. Now, using $\triangle c \doteq c' - c$ and $\triangle s \doteq s - s'$, where wlog we assume $\triangle c > 0$, one gets

$$y^{\triangle c} = \psi(\triangle s). \tag{1}$$

In the case where the challenge set is $\mathcal{C} = \{0, 1\}$ we have $\triangle c = 1$ and thus $y = \psi(\triangle s)$. This proves part (a) of the theorem. To prove part (b) we may assume that ψ is special. Now, we in invoke a pseudo-preimage finder for ψ on input (ψ, y) to obtain a pseudo-preimage (v, w) of ψ under y. Using that $\triangle c \leq c^+(k)$ and the assumption $c^+(k) < p(k)$, it follows that $\gcd(v, \triangle c) = 1$, and by Lemma 1 we can compute a preimage of y under ψ. $\square$

We call the knowledge extractor described in the proof of Theorem 2 the *standard knowledge extractor (for the Σ-protocol)*. The standard knowledge extractor, informally speaking, is the "only knowledge extractor that is known for the Σ-protocol". More precisely, Cramer [17] points out that all existing knowledge extractors for the Σ-protocol with a challenge set of cardinality larger than two use the collision extractability property, the existence of pseudo-preimage finders for special homomorphisms, and Shamir's trick to compute a preimage.

It is worthwhile to note that the standard knowledge extractor is only successful when the instances (1) of the PP problem (obtained from the prover P^*) are easy to solve. In fact, we can distinguish two classes of PP instances that are easy to solve. One class consists of PP problem instances $((v, w), y, \psi)$ with $v = 1$, where w is a preimage of y under ψ, in which case the PP problem is trivial to solve. The other class consists of easy PP problem instances for special homomorphisms. In fact, let ψ be a special homomorphism, $y \in \text{image}(\psi)$, and (v, w) be the pseudo-preimage output by a pseudo-preimage finder for ψ. Then by Lemma 1 all instances $((v', w'), y, \psi)$ of the PP problem with $\gcd(v, v') = 1$ are easy. The former class of easy instances underlies the proof of part (a) and the latter the proof of part (b) of Theorem 2.

For non-special homomorphisms, such as multi-exponentiations in groups with hidden order, the PP problem instances (1) extracted from the Σ-protocol with non-binary challenge set are not known to be easy. Hence, the standard knowledge extractor does not work for non-special homomorphisms.

4.2 Σ-Protocol with Auxiliary Pseudo-preimages: Basic Idea

Our idea in the following is to enhance the common input of the Σ-protocol by a pseudo-preimage. That is, we consider the Σ-protocol on common input (ψ, y) and a pseudo-preimage (v, w) (of y under ψ). The prover's private input remains to be a preimage x (of y under ψ). This allows us to obtain proofs of knowledge for non-special homomorphisms using the Σ-protocol with challenge sets of cardinality larger than two.

Let us refer to the pseudo-preimage in the common input as an "auxiliary pseudo-preimage". In fact, auxiliary pseudo-preimages enable us to use the standard knowledge extractor for non-special homomorphisms. This claim is easy to verify: The common input and thus the auxiliary pseudo-preimage is by definition given to the knowledge extractor [4]. We recall that the standard knowledge extractor (described in §4.1) first computes a pseudo-preimage $(\triangle c, \triangle s)$ from the prover P^*. It then uses a second pseudo-preimage to compute the desired preimage using Shamir's trick. For special homomorphisms the second pseudo-preimage can be obtained using a corresponding pseudo-preimage finder. In our approach, this second preimage is the auxiliary preimage contained in the common input. In the following we formalize this idea and discuss under what conditions it can be used to obtain practically useful proofs of knowledge.

Definition 4. *Let $v(k)$ be an arbitrary integer parameter and Ψ a collection of homomorphisms. We call $\mathcal{R}^{(v)}[\Psi] \doteq \{((\psi, y, (v(k), w)), x) : \psi \in \Psi(k), \psi : G \to H, x \in G, y = \psi(x),$ and $(v(k), w)$ is a pseudo-preimage of y under $\psi\}$ a pseudo-preimage relation.*

Note that while in Definition 3 we describe the Σ-protocol only for homomorphism relations, it is clear it is also defined for pseudo-preimage relations $\mathcal{R}^{(v)}[\Psi]$ (i.e., where the common input is $(\psi, y, (v, w)) \in \mathcal{L}_{\mathcal{R}^{(v)}[\Psi]}$).

Corollary 2. *The Σ-protocol with challenge set $\mathcal{C} \doteq \{0, \ldots, c^+(k)\}$ is a proof of knowledge for the pseudo-preimage relation $\mathcal{R}^{(v)}[\Psi]$ if the smallest prime factor of $v(k)$ is larger than $c^+(k)$. The knowledge error is $1/(c^+(k) + 1)$.*

Corollary 2 follows from the proof of Theorem 2. Let us consider a collection of homomorphisms Ψ, a homomorphism relation $\mathcal{R}[\Psi]$, and the pseudo-preimage relation $\mathcal{R}^{(v)}[\Psi]$. We observe that a proof of knowledge for a $((\psi, y), x) \in \mathcal{R}[\Psi]$ and a proof of knowledge for $((\psi, y, (v, w)), x) \in \mathcal{R}^{(v)}[\Psi]$ both are proofs of knowledge of a preimage x of y under ψ (possibly with different knowledge errors). Thus to prove knowledge of a preimage under a homomorphism one can use proofs of knowledge for pseudo-preimage relations. In the following we pursue this idea of using pseudo-preimage relations for proving knowledge of a preimage of a homomorphism. We refer to a proof of knowledge for a collection of homomorphisms Ψ using a pseudo-preimage relation $\mathcal{R}^{(v)}[\Psi]$ as a *proof of knowledge in the auxiliary setting* and call $\mathcal{R}^{(v)}[\Psi]$ an *auxiliary relation*.

A desirable property of the auxiliary setting is that it allows one to obtain very efficient proofs of knowledge for *any* homomorphism collection Ψ. In fact, using the Σ-protocol in the auxiliary setting, we can achieve an arbitrary small knowledge error for any Ψ. Therefore, we use the auxiliary relation $\mathcal{R}^{(v)}[\Psi]$, where $v(k)$ is prime, and the Σ-protocol with the challenge set $\mathcal{C} \doteq \{0, \ldots, (v(k) - 1)\}$. By Corollary 2, the resulting knowledge error is $1/v(k)$, which can be made arbitrarily small by choosing $v(k)$ appropriately. This is in contrast to existing proofs of knowledge for homomorphisms (i.e., not in the auxiliary setting) based on Σ-protocol, where the knowledge error can not be made arbitrarily small and is in fact often quite large (see Theorem 2).

Our discussion so far was focused on obtaining proofs of knowledge of a preimage. We have seen that within this focus proofs in the auxiliary setting and conventional proofs (i.e., proofs for homomorphism relations without using auxiliary pseudo-preimages) are equivalent and thus one can use the former instead of the latter. However, if we widen our focus, then the auxiliary setting is in general not equivalent to the conventional setting. The reason is that providing auxiliary pseudo-preimages might reveal information that is not available otherwise. For instance, the auxiliary pseudo-preimage could suddenly allow a verifier to compute a preimage from the common input to the Σ-protocol. Thus, in the following we need to additionally consider what (computational) information the prover and the verifier obtain from an auxiliary pseudo-preimage.

4.3 Σ-Protocol with Auxiliary Pseudo-preimages: Applied to Multi-exponentiations in Hidden Order Groups

In the following we look at proofs of knowledge in the auxiliary setting for multi-exponentiations $\psi_M : \mathbb{Z}^l \to H$ in groups H for which the ROOT problem is hard. In particular, we consider the information the prover and the verifier can derive from an auxiliary pseudo-preimage. It turns out that, on the one hand, the verifier does not get any additional (computational) information on $|H|$ and the preimage x. On the other hand, we see that $|H|$ is required by the (honest) prover.

Let us first consider a (possibly dishonest) verifier in the auxiliary setting. The results from §3 allow us to exclude that the verifier can either compute a preimage or information about the order of H from an auxiliary pseudo-preimage. In fact, by Theorem 1 (under the ROOT assumption) it is impossible for the verifier to compute a preimage from a pseudo-preimage, i.e., to solve the PP problem. Concerning the order of H, Corollary 1 implies that instances of the PP problem for multi-exponentiations in a group H, and thus the common input to the Σ-protocol in the auxiliary setting, can be generated without knowing the order of H. Hence, an auxiliary pseudo-preimage gives the verifier no advantage in computing the order of H either. Finally, as the Σ-protocol is (honest verifier) zero-knowledge (c.f. §4.1), the verifier does not get an advantage in computing a preimage or information on the order of H from running the protocol with the prover.

Next, we consider the information the (honest) prover learns on $|H|$ in the auxiliary setting. We note that the prover in addition to the common input is also given a preimage as private input. It is easy to see that from the honest prover's input $(\psi_M, y, (v, w), x) \in \mathcal{R}^{(v)}$ (where $\psi_M(z) = h^z$), one can compute the order of h (assuming $v \nmid w$). Moreover, in certain groups, such as RSA groups with moduli being a safe-prime product, this allows one to factor the modulus and to obtain the group's order. For the case where ψ_M is a multi-exponentiation, we don't know how to show that the (honest) prover obtains information on $|H|$. But neither can we prove that it does not get information on $|H|$. Thus, unless we want to put forth a corresponding (and "rather questionable") computational assumption, we should expect that the prover can compute $|H|$. Moreover, we only know how to generate the protocol's input in the auxiliary setting, i.e., $(\psi_M, y, (v, w), x)$ when the order of H is given. (For a possible way to generate the input we refer to the description of the PP instance generator $\mathcal{D_P}$ in §3.) Thus, in the context of an application where the input to the Σ-protocol in the auxiliary setting is generated by the (honest) prover, then the (honest) prover explicitly needs to be privy to $|H|$.

Finally, we note that if one uses our auxiliary setting to obtain a proof of knowledge as a sub-protocol in some application, one needs to consider the information an auxiliary pseudo-preimage reveals in the context of the whole system—in the same way one has to do this for the image y itself. Such an analysis, however, must be outside the scope of this paper.

A property of practical interest of proofs of knowledge in the auxiliary setting is that one can use techniques from groups with known order for proving relations among preimages of different multi-exponentiations [6, 14]. As an example one can prove knowledge of two discrete logarithms of two different group elements with respect to different bases and also that the discrete logarithms are equal. That is, using notation introduced by Camenisch and Stadler [13], on can realize a proof $PK(\{\alpha_1, \alpha_2\} : y_1 = h_1^{\alpha_1} \wedge y_2 = h_2^{\alpha_2} \wedge \alpha_1 = \alpha_2\})$. The approach to obtain such an equality proof in the auxiliary setting is to choose the auxiliary pseudo-preimage (v, w) to be the *same* for $(y_1, \psi_{M,1}(x_1) = h_1^{x_1})$ and for $(y_2, \psi_{M,2}(x_2) = h_2^{x_2})$. Using this approach it is straightforward to verify that the knowledge extractor indeed is able to find a value $x = \log_{h_1} y_1 = \log_{h_2} y_2$.

5   The Σ^+-Protocol

In this section we introduce a new protocol that we call the Σ^+-protocol. The Σ^+-protocol is a an efficient zero-knowledge (computational) proof of knowledge for multi-exponentiations ψ_M in arbitrary groups H and, in particular, in groups with hidden order. The knowledge error of the Σ^+-protocol is governed by the smallest prime in $|\,\text{image}(\psi_M)|$. The computational validity property of the Σ^+-protocol holds under the Strong RSA assumption [3, 24] and under the computational binding property of the commitment scheme used in the protocol. The Σ^+-protocol is a proof of knowledge regardless of whether the prover or the verifier knows the order of H.

Technically, the construction of the Σ^+-protocol takes up and extends ideas underlying the DF scheme (c.f. § 1) to obtain standard proofs of knowledge according to [4]. In fact, the Σ^+-protocol can *always* be used to replace the DF scheme to obtain standard proofs of knowledge.

Yet, compared to the DF scheme, the Σ^+-protocol works under weaker conditions and hence can be used more broadly. In fact, when applied to a multi-exponentiation $\psi_M : \mathbb{Z}^l \to H$, the DF scheme requires that H is a group (with hidden order) for which the generalized root assumption[1] holds, and that the

---

[1] The assumption is that given $h \in_U H$ it is hard to compute an integer $e \neq 1$ and $u \in H$ such that $u^e = h$.

prover must not know the order of H. The Σ^+-protocol needs neither of these requirements. Additionally, in certain application scenarios the Σ^+-protocol is more efficient than the DF scheme. We recall that the DF scheme consists of two parts. A rather inefficient setup part that is run once and an efficient proof of knowledge part using the Σ-protocol, which is typically executed several times. The computational cost of the Σ^+-protocol, which is an atomic protocol, is roughly three times the cost of the Σ-protocol. As a consequence, the Σ^+-protocol is more efficient than the DF protocol in settings when few proofs of knowledge are required, while the DF scheme is more efficient when one requires many proofs of knowledge.

5.1   Preliminaries

The Strong RSA assumption [3, 24] states that there is a generator $\mathcal{D}_\mathcal{S}(k)$ such that given $(n,g) \leftarrow \mathcal{D}_\mathcal{S}(k)$, with $g \in \mathbb{Z}_n^*$, it is hard to compute a $u \in \mathbb{Z}_n^*$ and an integer $e > 1$ fulfilling $u^e = g$. In the following we assume that $n = (2p+1)(2q+1)$ with p, q, $(2p+1)$, and $(2q+1)$ being primes, and that $g \in \mathrm{QR}_n$, where QR_n is the subgroup of quadratic residues of $\mathbb{Z}_n^*$.

We define a generator $\mathcal{D}_\vartheta(l,k)$ that outputs multi-exponentiations $\vartheta : \mathbb{Z}^l \to \mathrm{QR}_n$ as follows: 1) Choose $(n,g) \leftarrow \mathcal{D}_\mathcal{S}(k)$. 2) For $i = 1, \ldots, (l-1)$ choose $\rho_i \in_U [0, 2^k \lfloor n/4 \rfloor]$. 3) Set $g_i \doteq g^{\rho_i}$. 4) Define the multi-exponentiation $\vartheta(x_1, \ldots, x_l) \doteq g_1^{x_1} \cdot \ldots \cdot g_{l-1}^{x_{l-1}} \cdot g^{x_l}$. 5) Output (ϑ, n). Using this notation the following holds.

Theorem 3. *Under the Strong RSA assumption, it is hard given $(n, \vartheta) \leftarrow D_\vartheta(l,k)$ to compute a $y \in \mathbb{Z}_n^*$ and a pseudo-preimage $(v, (w_1, \ldots, w_l))$ of y under ϑ such that $v \neq 1$ and $v \nmid w_i$ for some $i \in \{1, \ldots, l\}$.*

Theorem 3 underlies the construction of the knowledge extractor of the DF scheme as well as the one for our Σ^+-protocol. A similar statement was recently proved by Camenisch and Shoup [12, Theorem 3].

Let $\mathrm{commit}(\cdot, \cdot)$ be a computationally binding and statistically hiding commitment scheme such as the one by Pedersen [29]. To commit to value γ, one computes $C \leftarrow \mathrm{commit}(\gamma, r)$, where r is a random value. To open the commitment C, one reveals γ and r to a verifier, who checks that $C = \mathrm{commit}(\gamma, r)$.

5.2   The Σ^+-Protocol and Its Properties

In this section we define the Σ^+-protocol. For simplicity, we describe the protocol only for simple-exponentiations $\psi_M(x) \doteq h^x$ with $h \in H$. This allows us to focus on the key ideas underlying the protocol construction. It is a straightforward exercise to extend the definition of the protocol and the results given below to multi-exponentiations $\psi_M(x_1, \ldots, x_l) \doteq h_1^{x_1} \cdot \ldots \cdot h_l^{x_l}$ with $h_1, \ldots, h_l \in H$. Let $\triangle x \doteq \triangle x(k)$ and $l_z \doteq l_z(k)$ denote integer parameters.

Definition 5 (Σ^+-Protocol). *Let Ψ be a collection of simple-exponentiation homomorphisms and $((\psi_M, y), x) \in \mathcal{R}[\Psi]$ with $x \in [-\triangle x, +\triangle x]$. Let (P, V) be a pair of interactive Turing machines with common input (ψ_M, y), the private input of P being x. A Σ^+-protocol with challenge set $\mathcal{C} \doteq \{0, \ldots, c^+\}$ consists of (P, V) performing the joint computation described in Fig. 1.*

Note that $x \in [-\triangle x, +\triangle x]$ in Definition 5 is necessary for the Σ^+-protocol to be statistical zero-knowledge (i.e., one needs to know how large x can be to blind x in the messages sent by the prover). The tightness of the statistical zero-knowledge property of the Σ^+-protocol is controlled by the parameter l_z.

Next, we sketch the key features underlying the proof of knowledge and zero-knowledge property of the Σ^+-protocol. Let us therefore consider the Σ^+-protocol on input $((\psi_M, y), x)$.

First, we look at the proof of knowledge property, i.e., the features that allow us to construct a knowledge extractor. In step 1, the verifier chooses a multi-exponentiation $\vartheta(\cdot, \cdot)$ by executing the steps of the generator $\mathcal{D}_\vartheta(2, k)$ (as defined in the previous section). The description of $\vartheta(\cdot, \cdot)$ is sent to the prover. In step 2, the prover first computes $\mathsf{y} \doteq \vartheta(x, \mathsf{x})$, where x is the preimage of y under ψ_M and x is random value to ensure that y does not reveal information about x. Now, we observe that the remainder of step 2 and steps 3, 4, and 7 essentially correspond to two Σ-protocols run in parallel for each of the homomorphisms ψ and ϑ. (For the matter of this observation, we may forget about the commitment commit$(\cdot, \cdot)$ used in steps 2 and 7, and assume that the message sent at the end of step 2 is (t, t).) These two Σ-protocols are run in parallel as one would do in a proof of equality in groups of known order to demonstrate that the preimage of y equals the first component of the preimage of y (cf. [16]). In fact, in all evaluations of ψ_M and ϑ (see steps 2 and 7) the argument of ψ_M and the first argument of ϑ are equal. This allows us to obtain a knowledge extractor for the Σ^+-protocol as follows. As the Σ-protocol uses essentially the same verification equations (step 7) as the Σ^+-protocol, the knowledge extractor can retrieve from a convincing prover a pseudo-preimage $(\triangle c, \triangle s)$ of y under ψ_M and a pseudo-preimage $(\triangle c, (\triangle s, \triangle \mathsf{s}))$ of y under ϑ. That is, we have

$$y^{\triangle c} = \psi_M(\triangle s) = h^{\triangle s} \tag{2}$$

$$\mathsf{y}^{\triangle c} = \vartheta(\triangle s, \triangle \mathsf{s}) = g^{\triangle s} g_1^{\triangle \mathsf{s}}. \tag{3}$$

As we run the two Σ-protocols in parallel as described above, the same integers $\triangle c$ and $\triangle s$ occur in (2) and (3). Now, as ϑ was chosen according to $\mathcal{D}_\vartheta(2, k)$, Theorem 3 implies that in (3) we must have $\triangle c \mid \triangle s$ and $\triangle c \mid \triangle \mathsf{s}$. Thus, (if we, e.g., additionally assert that $\gcd(\triangle c, |\text{image}(\psi_M)|) = 1$) the knowledge extractor can compute a preimage $x \doteq \triangle s / \triangle c$ of y under ψ_M. Finally we note, that the Σ^+-protocol is not a proof of knowledge for the multi-exponentiation ϑ; the role of ϑ is just to enable the construction of the knowledge extractor for ψ_M.

It remains to discuss the statistical zero-knowledge property of the Σ^+-protocol. We have seen that for the knowledge extractor to work, the prover needs to provide to the verifier the values (t, s) and $(\mathsf{t}, (s, \mathsf{s}))$ that fulfill the verification equations in step 7. As these are the same verification equations as for the Σ-protocol, we can use the standard zero-knowledge simulation technique for the Σ-protocol, i.e., given (ψ_M, y) and (ϑ, y) we can simulate tuples (t, c, s) and $(\mathsf{t}, c, (s, \mathsf{s}))$ fulfilling the respective verification equations. This approach works fine for *given* (ψ_M, y) and (ϑ, y), respectively. However, in the Σ^+-protocol (ϑ, y) are chosen within the protocol. Thus, for the Σ^+-protocol to be zero-knowledge,

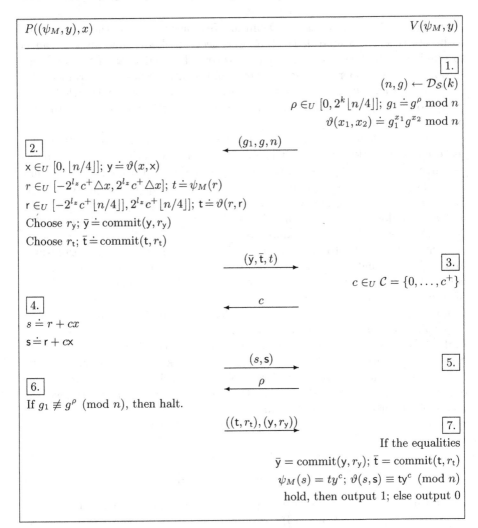

Fig. 1. Description Σ^+-Protocol.

we additionally need to simulate the choices of y. Choices of y can be easily simulated when $\vartheta(x_1, x_2) = g_1^{x_1} g^{x_2}$ is formed correctly, i.e., $g_1 \in \langle g \rangle$. Then, over the choices of x, y $= \vartheta(x, \mathsf{x}) = g_1^x g^{\mathsf{x}}$ is a uniform random element in $\langle g \rangle$ (we recall that x $\in_U [0, \lfloor n/4 \rfloor]$ is statistically close to uniform on $\mathbb{Z}_{|g|}$). However, a dishonest verifier could choose a malformed ϑ such that y $= \vartheta(x, \mathsf{x})$ would leak information about the preimage x and thus ruin the zero-knowledge property of the Σ^+-protocol. To overcome this problem, we use the commitment scheme commit$(\cdot, \cdot)$ as follows. In step 2, the prover does not know whether ϑ is correctly chosen, and thus only sends the commitments to t and y instead of these values themselves. Then, in steps 5 and 6 the verifier convinces the prover that ϑ is correctly formed., i.e., that $g_1 \in \langle g \rangle$. To this end, it sends the discrete logarithm

ρ of g_1 with respect to g to the prover. Finally, when the prover is convinced of the correctness of ϑ, it opens the commitments from step 2 and reveals the values t and y. It is important that the verifier reveals the discrete logarithm ρ only after the prover has answered the challenge (steps 3 and 4). This is because for Theorem 3 to be applicable in the construction of the knowledge extractor, $\triangle s$ and $\triangle$s in (3) and thus s and s in step 4 of the protocol need to be computed by the prover without being given the discrete logarithm ρ. (In fact, Theorem 3 does not hold when one is given the discrete logarithms (with respect to some base element) of the g_i defining ϑ).

Note that the simulator sketched above only works when the cardinality of $\mathcal{C}$ is bounded by some polynomial in the security parameter. This is because the simulator needs to be able to guess the challenge value for which it computes the simulated view. However, applying Damgård's technique [19], we turn the Σ^+-protocol into a concurrent-zero knowledge protocol simply by additionally committing to t in step 2 and correspondingly open the commitment in step 6.

Now, along the lines sketched above one can prove the following theorem.

Theorem 4. *Let Ψ be a collection of simple-exponentiation homomorphisms and $c^+(k)$ be a positive integer parameter such that for any $\psi_M \in \Psi(k)$, $c^+(k)$ is smaller than the smallest prime dividing $|\,\mathrm{image}(\psi_M)|$. Then the Σ^+-protocol with challenge set $\mathcal{C} \doteq \{0,\ldots,c^+(k)\}$ is a computational proof of knowledge for $\mathcal{R}[\Psi]$. The computational validity property holds under the computational binding property of the commitment scheme and the Strong RSA assumption. The knowledge error is $1/|\mathcal{C}| + 1/p(k)$, where $p(\cdot)$ is an arbitrary polynomial.*

Let us conclude with a technical remark. Consider the DF scheme and the Σ^+-protocol computed for, e.g., common input a simple-exponentiation $\psi_M(x) = h^x$ and an image element y. We note that the knowledge extractors of both schemes rely on obtaining a pseudo-preimage $(\triangle c, \triangle s)$ of y under ψ_M, i.e., $y^{\triangle c} = h^{\triangle s}$ such that the divisibility $\triangle c \mid \triangle s$ (which allows one to compute a preimage of y) holds. (In fact, the Σ^+-protocol can guarantee the divisibility under weaker conditions.) Technically, this is the reason why the Σ^+-protocol works in all cases where the DF scheme is known to work. In particular, the Σ^+-protocol can also be used to obtain so called interval or range proofs [5]. Finally, the DF scheme is often considered under different conditions than formulated in Theorem 4, allowing one, e.g., only to prove that one knows b and z such that $y = bh^z$ with $b^2 = 1$. Given the foregoing observation, it is clear that such proofs can also be obtained using the Σ^+-protocol.

References

1. G. Ateniese. Efficient verifiable encryption (and fair exchange) of digital signatures. In *Proc. 6th ACM Conference on Computer and Communications Security*, pp. 138–146. ACM press, Nov. 1999.
2. G. Ateniese, J. Camenisch, M. Joye, and G. Tsudik. A practical and provably secure coalition-resistant group signature scheme. In *Advances in Cryptology – CRYPTO 2000*, vol. 1880 of *Lecture Notes in Computer Science*, pp. 255–270. Springer Verlag, 2000.

3. N. Barić and B. Pfitzmann. Collision-free accumulators and fail-stop signature schemes without trees. In *Advances in Cryptology – EUROCRYPT '97*, vol. 1233 of *LNCS*, pp. 480–494. Springer Verlag, 1997.
4. M. Bellare and O. Goldreich. On defining proofs of knowledge. In *Advances in Cryptology – CRYPTO '92*, vol. 740 of *Lecture Notes in Computer Science*, pp. 390–420. Springer-Verlag, 1992.
5. F. Boudot. Efficient proofs that a committed number lies in an interval. In *Advances in Cryptology – EUROCRYPT 2000*, vol. 1807 of *Lecture Notes in Computer Science*, pp. 431–444. Springer Verlag, 2000.
6. S. Brands. Rapid demonstration of linear relations connected by boolean operators. In *Advances in Cryptology – EUROCRYPT '97*, vol. 1233 of *Lecture Notes in Computer Science*, pp. 318–333. Springer Verlag, 1997.
7. J. Buchmann and H. C. Williams. A key-exchange system based on imaginary quadratic fields. *Journal Of Cryptology*, 1(2):107 – 118, 1998.
8. J. Camenisch and A. Lysyanskaya. Efficient non-transferable anonymous multishow credential system with optional anonymity revocation. In *Advances in Cryptology – EUROCRYPT 2001*, vol. 2045 of *LNCS*, pp. 93–118. Springer Verlag, 2001.
9. J. Camenisch and A. Lysyanskaya. An identity escrow scheme with appointed verifiers. In *Advances in Cryptology – CRYPTO 2001*, vol. 2139 of *LNCS*, pp. 388–407. Springer Verlag, 2001.
10. J. Camenisch and A. Lysyanskaya. Dynamic accumulators and application to efficient revocation of anonymous credentials. In *Advances in Cryptology – CRYPTO 2002*, vol. 2442 of *LNCS*, pp. 61–76. Springer Verlag, 2002.
11. J. Camenisch and M. Michels. A group signature scheme with improved efficiency. In *Advances in Cryptology – ASIACRYPT '98*, vol. 1514 of *LNCS*, pp. 160–174. Springer Verlag, 1998.
12. J. Camenisch and V. Shoup. Practical verifiable encryption and decryption of discrete logarithms. In *Advances in Cryptology – CRYPTO 2003*, vol. 2729 of *LNCS*, pp. 126–144, 2003.
13. J. Camenisch and M. Stadler. Efficient group signature schemes for large groups. In *Advances in Cryptology – CRYPTO '97*, vol. 1296 of *Lecture Notes in Computer Science*, pp. 410–424. Springer Verlag, 1997.
14. J. L. Camenisch. *Group Signature Schemes and Payment Systems Based on the Discrete Logarithm Problem*. PhD thesis, ETH Zürich, 1998. Diss. ETH No. 12520, Hartung Gorre Verlag, Konstanz.
15. R. Canetti, O. Goldreich, S. Goldwasser, and S. Micali. Resettable zero-knowledge. pp. 235–244. ACM Press, 2000.
16. D. Chaum and T. P. Pedersen. Wallet databases with observers. In *Advances in Cryptology – CRYPTO '92*, vol. 740 of *Lecture Notes in Computer Science*, pp. 89–105. Springer-Verlag, 1993.
17. R. Cramer. *Modular Design of Secure yet Practical Cryptographic Protocol*. PhD thesis, University of Amsterdam, 1997.
18. R. Cramer and I. Damgård. Zero-knowledge proof for finite field arithmetic, or: Can zero-knowledge be for free? In *Advances in Cryptology – CRYPTO '98*, vol. 1642 of *Lecture Notes in Computer Science*, pp. 424–441, Berlin, 1998. Springer Verlag.
19. I. Damgård. Efficient concurrent zero-knowledge in the auxiliary string model. In *Advances in Cryptology – EUROCRYPT 2000*, vol. 1807 of *Lecture Notes in Computer Science*, pp. 431–444. Springer Verlag, 2000.

20. I. Damgård. On sigma-protocols. *Lecture Notes*, 2002.
21. I. Damgård and E. Fujisaki. An integer commitment scheme based on groups with hidden order. In *Advances in Cryptology – ASIACRYPT 2002*, vol. 2501 of *LNCS*. Springer, 2002.
22. I. Damgård and M. Koprowski. Generic lower bounds for root extraction and signature schemes in general groups. In *Advances in Cryptology – EUROCRYPT'02*, vol. 2332 of *Lecture Notes in Computer Science*, pp. 256–271 Springer Verlag, 2002.
23. C. Dwork, M. Naor, and A. Sahai. Concurrent zero knowledge. In *Proc. 30th Annual ACM Symposium on Theory of Computing (STOC)*, 1998.
24. E. Fujisaki and T. Okamoto. Statistical zero knowledge protocols to prove modular polynomial relations. In *Advances in Cryptology – CRYPTO '97*, vol. 1294 of *Lecture Notes in Computer Science*, pp. 16–30. Springer Verlag, 1997.
25. E. Fujisaki and T. Okamoto. A practical and provably secure scheme for publicly verifiable secret sharing and its applications. In *Advances in Cryptology – EUROCRYPT '98*, vol. 1403 of *LNCS*, pp. 32–46. Springer Verlag, 1998.
26. M. Girault. An identity-based identification scheme based on discrete logarihtms modulo a composite number. In *Advances in Cryptology – EUROCRYPT '90*, vol. 473 of *Lecture Notes in Computer Science*, pp. 481–486. Springer-Verlag, 1991.
27. L. C. Guillou and J.-J. Quisquater. A practical zero-knowledge protocol fitted to security microprocessor minimizing both transmission and memory. In *Advances in Cryptology – EUROCRYPT '88*, vol. 330 of *Lecture Notes in Computer Science*, pp. 123–128. Springer Verlag, 1988.
28. P. MacKenize and M. K. Reiter. Two-party generation of DSA signatures. In *Advances in Cryptology – CRYPTO 2001*, vol. 2139 of *LNCS*, pp. 137–154. Springer Verlag, 2001.
29. T. P. Pedersen. Non-interactive and information-theoretic secure verifiable secret sharing. In *Advances in Cryptology – CRYPTO '91*, vol. 576 of *Lecture Notes in Computer Science*, pp. 129–140. Springer Verlag, 1992.
30. G. Poupard and J. Stern. Security analysis of a practical "on the fly" authentication and signature generation. In *Advances in Cryptology – EUROCRYPT '98*, vol. 1403 of *Lecture Notes in Computer Science*, pp. 422–436. Springer Verlag, 1998.
31. R. Rivest, A. Shamir, and L. Adleman. A method for obtaining digital signatures and public-key cryptosystems. *Communications of the ACM*, 21(2):120–126, Feb. 1978.
32. C. P. Schnorr. Efficient signature generation for smart cards. *Journal Of Cryptology*, 4(3):239–252, 1991.

Efficient k-Out-of-n Oblivious Transfer Schemes with Adaptive and Non-adaptive Queries

Cheng-Kang Chu and Wen-Guey Tzeng

Department of Computer and Information Science,
National Chiao Tung University,
Hsinchu, Taiwan 30050
{ckchu,tzeng}@cis.nctu.edu.tw

Abstract. In this paper we propose efficient two-round k-out-of-n oblivious transfer schemes, in which R sends $O(k)$ messages to S, and S sends $O(n)$ messages back to R. The computation cost of R and S is reasonable. The choices of R are unconditionally secure. For the basic scheme, the secrecy of unchosen messages is guaranteed if the Decisional Diffie-Hellman problem is hard. When $k = 1$, our basic scheme is as efficient as the most efficient 1-out-of-n oblivious transfer scheme. Our schemes have the nice property of *universal parameters*, that is each pair of R and S need neither hold any secret key nor perform any prior setup (initialization). The system parameters can be used by all senders and receivers without any trapdoor specification. Our k-out-of-n oblivious transfer schemes are the most efficient ones in terms of the communication cost, in both rounds and the number of messages.

Moreover, one of our schemes can be extended in a straightforward way to an *adaptive k-out-of-n* oblivious transfer scheme, which allows the receiver R to choose the messages one by one adaptively. In our adaptive-query scheme, S sends $O(n)$ messages to R in one round in the commitment phase. For each query of R, only $O(1)$ messages are exchanged and $O(1)$ operations are performed. In fact, the number k of queries need not be pre-fixed or known beforehand. This makes our scheme highly flexible.

Keywords: k-out-of-n Oblivious Transfer, Adaptive Oblivious Transfer

1 Introduction

Oblivious transfer (OT) is an important primitive used in many cryptographic protocols [GV87,Kil88]. An oblivious transfer protocol involves two parties, the sender S and the receiver R. S has some messages and R wants to obtain some of them via interaction with S. The security requirement is that S wants R to obtain the message of his choice only and R does not want S to know what he chooses. The original OT was proposed by Rabin [Rab81], in which S sends a message to R, and R gets the message with probability 0.5. On the other hand, S does not know whether R gets the message or not. Even, et al. [EGL85] suggested a more general scheme, called 1-out-of-2 OT (OT_2^1). In this scheme, S

S. Vaudenay (Ed.): PKC 2005, LNCS 3386, pp. 172–183, 2005.

has two messages m_1 and m_2, and would like R to obtain exactly one of them. In addition, S remains oblivious to R's choice. Brassard, et al. [BCR86] further extended OT_2^1 to 1-out-of-n OT (OT_n^1) for the case of n messages.

Oblivious transfer has been studied extensively and in many flavors. Most of them consider the case that R chooses one message. In this paper we are concerned about the case that R chooses many messages at the same time. A k-out-of-n OT (OT_n^k) scheme is an OT scheme in which R chooses k messages at the same time, where $k < n$. A straightforward solution for OT_n^k is to run OT_n^1 k times independently. However, this needs k times the cost of OT_n^1. The communication cost is two-round, $O(k)$ messages from R to S, and $O(kn)$ messages from S to R even using the most efficient OT_n^1 schemes [NP01,Tze02].

Oblivious transfer with adaptive queries (Adpt-OT) allows R to query the messages one by one adaptively [NP99a]. For the setting, S first commits the messages to R in the commitment phase. Then, in the transfer phase, R makes queries of the messages one by one. The cost is considered for the commitment and transfer phases, respectively. It seems that the adaptive case implies the non-adaptive case. But, the non-adaptive one converted from an adaptive one usually needs more rounds (combining the commitment and transfer phases), for example, the scheme in [OK02]. Since our scheme needs no trapdoors, there is no entailed cost due to conversion. Adaptive OT_n^k is natural and has many applications, such as oblivious search, oblivious database queries, private information retrieval, etc.

In this paper we propose efficient two-round OT_n^k schemes, in which R sends $O(k)$ messages to S, and S sends $O(n)$ messages back to R. The computation cost of R and S is reasonable. The choices of R are unconditionally secure. For the basic scheme, the secrecy of unchosen messages is guaranteed if the Decisional Diffie-Hellman (DDH) problem is hard. When $k = 1$, our scheme is as efficient as the one in [Tze02]. Our schemes have the nice property of universal parameters, that is, each pair of R and S need neither hold any secret key nor perform any prior setup (initialization). The system parameters can be used by all senders and receivers without any trapdoor specification. Our OT_n^k schemes are the most efficient one in terms of the communication cost, either in rounds or the number of messages.

Moreover, one of our schemes can be extended in a straightforward way to an Adpt-OT_n^k scheme. In our adaptive-query scheme, S sends $O(n)$ messages to R in one round in the commitment phase. For each query of R, only $O(1)$ messages are exchanged and $O(1)$ operations are performed. In fact, the number k of queries need not be fixed or known beforehand. This makes our scheme highly flexible.

1.1   Previous Work and Comparison

Rabin [Rab81] introduced the notion of OT and presented an implementation to obliviously transfer one-bit message, based on quadratic roots modulo a composite. Even, Goldreich and Lempel [EGL85] proposed an extension of bit-OT_2^1, in which m_1 and m_2 are only one-bit. Brassard, Crépeau and Robert [BCR86] proposed OT_n^1 soon after in the name "all-or-nothing disclosure of secrets" (ANDOS). After that, OT_n^1 has become an important research topic in cryptographic protocol design. Some OT_n^1 schemes are built by invoking basis OT_2^1 several times [BCR87,BCS96,NP99b], and the others are constructed directly from basic cryptographic techniques [SS90,NR94,Ste98,NP01,Tze02]. Some OT_n^1 schemes derived from computational private information retrieval (CPIR) have polylogarithmic communication cost [Lip04]. Nevertheless, the privacy of the receiver's choice is computationally secure. Besides, there are various oblivious transfer schemes developed in different models and applications, such as OT in the bounded storage model [CCM98,Din01], distributed OT [NP00,BDSS02], Quantum OT [BBCS91,CZ03], and so on. Lipmaa [Lip] provided a good collection of these works.

For OT_n^k, Bellare and Micali [BM89] proposed an OT_n^{n-1} scheme. Naor and Pinkas [NP99b] proposed a non-trivial OT_n^k scheme. The scheme invokes a basis OT_2^1 scheme $O(wk \log n)$ times, where $w > \log \delta / \log(k^4/\sqrt{n})$ and δ is the probability that R can obtain more than k messages. The scheme works only for $k \le n^{1/4}$. After then, they also took notice of adaptive queries and provided some Adpt-OT_n^k schemes [NP99a]. In one scheme (the two-dimensional one), each query needs invoke the basis $OT_{\sqrt{n}}^1$ scheme twice, in which each invocation of $OT_{\sqrt{n}}^1$ needs $O(\sqrt{n})$ initialization work. In another scheme, each adaptive query of messages need invoke the basis OT_1^2 protocol $\log n$ times. Mu, Zhang, and Varadharajan [MZV02] presented some efficient OT_n^k schemes[1]. These schemes are designed from cryptographic functions directly. The most efficient one is a non-interactive one. To be compared fairly, the setup phase of establishing shared key pairs of a public-key cryptosystem should be included. Thus, the scheme is two-round and R and S send each other $O(n)$ messages. However, the choices of R cannot be made adaptive since R's choices are sent to S first and the message commitments are dependent on the choices. Recently, Ogata and Kurosawa [OK02] proposed an efficient adaptive OT scheme based on the RSA cryptosystem. Each S needs a trapdoor (the RSA modulus) specific to him. The scheme is as efficient as our Adpt-OT_n^k scheme. But, if the adaptive OT scheme is converted to a non-adaptive one, it needs 3 rounds (In the first round, S sends the modulus N to R).

Ishai, Kilian, Nissim and Petrank [IKNP03] proposed some efficient protocols for extending a small number of OT's to a large number of OT's. Chen and Zhu [CZ03] provided an OT_n^k in the quantum computation model. We won't compare these schemes with ours since they are in different categories.

In Table 1 we summarize the comparison of our, Mu, Zheng, and Varadharajan's, and Naor and Pinkas's OT_n^k schemes. In Table 2 we summarize the comparison of our and Naor and Pinkas's Adpt-OT_n^k schemes.

---

[1] Yao, Bao, and Deng [YBD03] pointed out some security issues in [MZV02].

Table 1. Comparison of OT_n^k schemes in communication cost.

	Ours (this paper)	Mu, et al. [MZV02]	Naor, et al. [NP99b]
rounds	2	2	$O(wk \log n)$
messages $(R \rightarrow S)$	$O(k)$	$O(n)$	$O(wk \log n))$
messages $(S \rightarrow R)$	$O(n)$	$O(n)$	$O(n + wk \log n)$
universal parameters	Yes	Yes	No (need setup)
made to adaptiveness	Yes $(OT_n^k\text{-II})$	No	Yes

Table 2. Comparison of Adpt-OT_n^k schemes in communication cost.

		Ours (this paper)	2-dimensional one, Naor, et al. [NP99a]	OT_n^k, Ogata, et al.[OK02]
commitment	rounds	1	1	1
phase	messages	$O(n)$	$O(n)$	$O(n)$
transfer	rounds	2	3*	2
phase	messages	$O(1)$	$O(\sqrt{n})$**	$O(1)$

* Two invocations of $OT_{\sqrt{n}}^1$ in parallel.

** Use the most round-efficient $OT_{\sqrt{n}}^1$ scheme as the basis.

2 Preliminaries

Involved Parties. The involved parties of an OT scheme is the sender and receiver. Both are polynomial-time-bounded probabilistic Turing machines (PPTM). A party is semi-honest (or passive) if it does not deviate from the steps defined in the protocol, but tries to compute extra information from received messages. A party is malicious (or active) if it can deviate from the specified steps in any way in order to get extra information.

A malicious sender may cheat in order or content of his possessed messages. To prevent the cheat, we can require the sender to commit the messages in a bulletin board. When the sender sends the encrypted messages to the receiver during execution of an OT scheme, he need tag a zero-knowledge proof of showing equality of committed messages and encrypted messages. However, in most applications, the sender just follows the protocol faithfully. Therefore, we consider the semi-honest sender only and the semi-honest/malicious receiver.

Indistinguishability. Two probability ensembles $\{X_i\}$ and $\{Y_i\}$, indexed by i, are (computationally) indistinguishable if for any PPTM D, polynomial $p(n)$ and sufficiently large i, it holds that

$$|\Pr[D(X_i) = 1] - \Pr[D(Y_i) = 1]| \leq 1/p(i).$$

Correctness of a Protocol. An OT scheme is correct if the receiver obtains the messages of his choices when the sender with the messages and the receiver with the choices follow the steps of the scheme.

Security Model. Assume that S holds n messages $m_1, m_2, \ldots, m_n$ and R's k choices are $\sigma_1, \sigma_2, \ldots, \sigma_k$. Note that only semi-honest sender is considered. We say that two sets C and C' are different if there is x in C, but not in C', or vice versa. An OT_n^k scheme with security against a semi-honest receiver should meet following requirements:

1. Receiver's privacy – indistinguishability: for any two different sets of choices $C = \{\sigma_1, \sigma_2, \ldots, \sigma_k\}$ and $C' = \{\sigma_1', \sigma_2', \ldots, \sigma_k'\}$, the transcripts, corresponding to C and C', received by the sender are indistinguishable. If the received messages of S for C and C' are identically distributed, the choices of R are unconditionally secure.
2. Sender's security – indistinguishability: for any choice set $C=\{\sigma_1, \sigma_2, \ldots, \sigma_k\}$, the unchosen messages should be indistinguishable from the random ones.

An OT_n^k scheme with security against a malicious receiver should meet following requirements:

1. Receiver's privacy – indistinguishability: the same as the case of the semi-honest receiver.
2. Sender's security – compared with the Ideal model: in the Ideal model, the sender sends all messages and the receiver sends his choices to the trusted third party (TTP). TTP then sends the chosen messages to the receiver. This is the securest way to implement the OT_n^k scheme. The receiver R cannot obtain extra information from the sender S in the Ideal model. We say that the sender's security is achieved if for any receiver R in the real OT_n^k scheme, there is another PPTM R' (called simulator) in the Ideal model such that the outputs of R and R' are indistinguishable.

Computational Model. Let G_q be a subgroup of Z_p^* with prime order q, and $p = 2q+1$ is also prime. Let g be a generator of G_q. We usually denote $g^x \bmod p$ as g^x, where $x \in Z_q$. Let $x \in_R X$ denote that x is chosen uniformly and independently from the set X.

Security Assumptions. For our OT_n^k schemes against semi-honest and malicious receiver, we assume the hardness of Decisional Diffie-Hellman (DDH) problem and Chosen-Target Computational Diffie-Hellman (CT-CDH) problem, respectively.

Assumption 1 (Decisional Diffie-Hellman (DDH)). *Let $p = 2q + 1$ where p, q are two primes, and G_q be the subgroup of Z_p^* with order q. The following two distribution ensembles are computationally indistinguishable:*

- $Y_1 = \{(g, g^a, g^b, g^{ab})\}_{G_q}$, *where g is a generator of G_q, and $a, b \in_R Z_q$.*
- $Y_2 = \{(g, g^a, g^b, g^c)\}_{G_q}$, *where g is a generator of G_q, and $a, b, c \in_R Z_q$.*

For the scheme against malicious receiver, we use the assumption introduced by Boldyreva [Bol03], which is analogous to the chosen-target RSA inversion assumption defined by Bellare, et al. [BNPS01].

- System parameters: (g, h, G_q);
- S has messages: $m_1, m_2, \ldots, m_n$;
- R's choices: $\sigma_1, \sigma_2, \ldots, \sigma_k$;

1. R chooses two polynomials $f(x) = a_0 + a_1 x + \cdots + a_{k-1} x^{k-1} + x^k$ and $f'(x) = b_0 + b_1 x + \cdots + b_{k-1} x^{k-1} + x^k$ where $a_0, a_1, \ldots, a_{k-1} \in_R Z_q$ and $b_0 + b_1 x + \cdots + b_{k-1} x^{k-1} + x^k \equiv (x - \sigma_1)(x - \sigma_2) \cdots (x - \sigma_k) \bmod q$.
2. $R \longrightarrow S : A_0 = g^{a_0} h^{b_0}, A_1 = g^{a_1} h^{b_1}, \ldots, A_{k-1} = g^{a_{k-1}} h^{b_{k-1}}$.
3. S computes $c_i = (g^{k_i}, m_i B_i^{k_i})$ where $k_i \in_R Z_q^*$ and $B_i = g^{f(i)} h^{f'(i)} = A_0 A_1^i \cdots A_{k-1}^{i^{k-1}} (gh)^{i^k} \bmod p$, for $i = 1, 2, \ldots, n$.
4. $S \longrightarrow R$: $c_1, c_2, \ldots, c_n$.
5. Let $c_i = (U_i, V_i)$, R computes $m_{\sigma_i} = V_{\sigma_i} / U_{\sigma_i}^{f(\sigma_i)} \bmod p$ for each σ_i.

Fig. 1. OT_n^k-I: k-out-of-n OT against semi-honest receiver.

Assumption 2 (Chosen-Target Computational Diffie-Hellman (CT-CDH)). *Let G_q be a group of prime order q, g be a generator of G_q, $x \in_R Z_q^*$. Let $H_1 : \{0,1\}^* \to G_q$ be a cryptographic hash function. The adversary A is given input (q, g, g^x, H_1) and two oracles: target oracle $T_G(\cdot)$ that returns a random element $w_i \in G_q$ at the i-th query and helper oracle $H_G(\cdot)$ that returns $(\cdot)^x$. Let q_T and q_H be the number of queries A made to the target oracle and helper oracle respectively. The probability that A outputs k pairs $((v_1, j_1), (v_2, j_2), \ldots, (v_k, j_k))$, where $v_i = (w_{j_i})^x$ for $i \in \{1, 2, \ldots, k\}$, $q_H < k \le q_T$, is negligible.*

3 k-Out-of-n OT Schemes

We first present a basic OT_n^k scheme for the semi-honest receiver in the standard model. Then, we modify the scheme to be secure against the malicious receiver in the random oracle model. Due to the random oracle model, the second scheme is more efficient in computation.

3.1 k-Out-of-n OT Against Semi-honest Receiver

The sender S has n secret messages $m_1, m_2, \ldots, m_n$. Without loss of generality, we assume that the message space is G_q, that is, all messages are in G_q. The semi-honest receiver R wants to get $m_{\sigma_1}, m_{\sigma_2}, \ldots, m_{\sigma_k}$. The protocol OT_n^k-I with security against the semi-honest receiver is depicted in Figure 1.

For system parameters, let g, h be two generators of G_q where $\log_g h$ is unknown to all, and G_q be the group with some descriptions. These parameters can be used repeatedly by all possible senders and receivers as long as the value $\log_g h$ is not revealed. Therefore, (g, h, G_q) are universal parameters.

The receiver R first constructs a k-degree polynomial $f'(x)$ such that $f'(i) = 0$ if and only if $i \in \{\sigma_1, \ldots, \sigma_k\}$. Then R chooses another random k-degree polynomial $f(x)$ to mask the chosen polynomial $f'(x)$. The masked choices $A_0, A_1, \ldots, A_{k-1}$ are sent to the sender S.

When S receives these queries, he first computes $B_i = g^{f(i)}h^{f'(i)}$ by computing $A_0 A_1^i \cdots A_{k-1}^{i^{k-1}}(gh)^{i^k} \bmod p$. Because of the random polynomial $f(x)$, S does not know which $f'(i)$ is equal to zero, for $i = 1, 2, \ldots, n$. Then S treats B_i as the public key and encrypts each message m_i by the ElGamal cryptosystem. The encrypted messages $c_1, c_2, \ldots, c_n$ are sent to R.

For each $c_i, i \in \{\sigma_1, \sigma_2, \ldots, \sigma_k\}$, since $B_i = g^{f(i)}h^{f'(i)} = g^{f(i)}h^0 = g^{f(i)}$, R can get these messages by the decryption of ElGamal cryptosystem with secret key $f(i)$. If $i \notin \{\sigma_1, \sigma_2, \ldots, \sigma_k\}$, since R can not compute $(g^{f(i)}h^{f'(i)})^{k_i}$ with the knowledge of g^{k_i} and $f(i), f'(i)$ only, the message m_i is unknown to R.

Correctness. Let $c_i = (U_i, V_i)$, we can check that the chosen messages m_{σ_i}, $i = 1, 2, \ldots, k$, are computed as

$$V_{\sigma_i}/U_{\sigma_i}^{f(\sigma_i)} = m_{\sigma_i} \cdot (g^{f(\sigma_i)}h^{f'(\sigma_i)})^{k_{\sigma_i}}/g^{k_{\sigma_i}f(\sigma_i)}$$
$$= m_{\sigma_i} \cdot (g^{f(\sigma_i)} \cdot 1)^{k_{\sigma_i}}/g^{k_{\sigma_i}f(\sigma_i)}$$
$$= m_{\sigma_i}.$$

Security Analysis. We now prove the security of OT_n^k-I.

Theorem 1. *For scheme OT_n^k-I, R's choices are unconditionally secure.*

Proof. For every tuple $(b_0', b_1', \ldots, b_{k-1}')$ representing the choices $\sigma_1', \sigma_2', \ldots, \sigma_k'$, there is a tuple $(a_0', a_1', \ldots, a_{k-1}')$ that satisfies $A_i = g^{a_i'}h^{b_i'}$ for $i = 0, 1, \ldots, k-1$. Thus, the receiver R's choices are unconditionally secure.   □

Theorem 2. *Scheme OT_n^k-I meets the sender's security requirement. That is, by the DDH assumption, if R is semi-honest, he gets no information about messages $m_i, i \notin \{\sigma_1, \sigma_2, \ldots, \sigma_k\}$.*

Proof. We show that for all $i \notin \{\sigma_1, \sigma_2, \ldots, \sigma_k\}$, c_i's look random if the DDH assumption holds. First, we define the random variable for the unchosen messages

$$C = (g, h, (g^{k_{i_1}}, m_{i_1}(g^{f(i_1)}h^{f'(i_1)})^{k_{i_1}}), \ldots, (g^{k_{i_{n-k}}}, m_{i_{n-k}}(g^{f(i_{n-k})}h^{f'(i_{n-k})})^{k_{i_{n-k}}})),$$

where $k_{i_1}, k_{i_2}, \ldots, k_{i_{n-k}} \in_R Z_q^*$. Since the polynomial $f(x)$ and $f'(x)$ are chosen by the receiver, and $f'(i_1), \ldots, f'(i_{n-k}) \neq 0$, we can simplify C as

$$C' = (g, h, (g^{k_{i_1}}, h^{k_{i_1}}), \ldots, (g^{k_{i_{n-k}}}, h^{k_{i_{n-k}}}))$$

Since the indistinguishability is preserved under multiple samples, we just need to show that if the following two distributions

- $\tilde{C} = (g, h, g^r, h^r)$, where $h \neq 1, r \in_R Z_q^*$
- $\tilde{X} = (g, h, x_1, x_2)$, where $h \neq 1, x_1, x_2 \in_R G_q$

are distinguishable by a polynomial-time distinguisher $\mathcal{D}$, we can construct another polynomial-time machine $\mathcal{D}'$, which takes $\mathcal{D}$ as a sub-routine, to solve the DDH problem:

- System parameters: (g, H_1, H_2, G_q);
- S has messages: $m_1, m_2, \ldots, m_n$;
- R's choices: $\sigma_1, \sigma_2, \ldots, \sigma_k$;

1. R computes $w_{\sigma_j} = H_1(\sigma_j)$ and $A_j = w_{\sigma_j} g^{a_j}$, where $a_j \in_R Z_q^*$ and $j = 1, 2, \ldots, k$.
2. $R \longrightarrow S$: $A_1, A_2, \ldots, A_k$.
3. S computes $y = g^x$, $D_j = (A_j)^x$, $w_i = H_1(i)$, and $c_i = m_i \oplus H_2(w_i^x)$, where $x \in_R Z_q^*, i = 1, 2, \ldots, n$, and $j = 1, 2, \ldots, k$.
4. $S \longrightarrow R$: $y, D_1, D_2, \ldots, D_k, c_1, c_2, \ldots, c_n$
5. R computes $K_j = D_j / y^{a_j}$ and gets $m_{\sigma_j} = c_{\sigma_j} \oplus H_2(K_j)$ for $j = 1, 2, \ldots, k$.

Fig. 2. OT_n^k-II: k-out-of-n OT against malicious receiver.

Machine $\mathcal{D}'$

Input: (g, u, v, w) (either from Y_1 or Y_2 in DDH)
Output: $\mathcal{D}(g, u, v, w)$

If $\mathcal{D}$ distinguishes $\tilde{C}$ and $\tilde{X}$ with non-negligible advantage ε (Should be $\epsilon(n, t)$, we omit the security parameter n and t here for simplicity, where t is the security parameter.), $\mathcal{D}'$ distinguishes Y_1, Y_2 in the DDH problem with at least non-negligible advantage $\varepsilon - 2/q$, where $dist(\tilde{C}, Y_1) = 1/q$ and $dist(\tilde{X}, Y_2) = 1/q$.

$\square$

Complexity. The scheme uses two rounds (steps 2 and 4), the first round sends $k + 1$ messages and the second round sends $2n$ messages. For computation, R computes $3k + 2$ and S computes $(k + 2)n$ modular exponentiations.

3.2 k-Out-of-n OT Against Malicious Receiver

A malicious player may not follow the protocol dutifully. For example, in scheme OT_n^k-I, a malicious R might send some special form of A_i's in step 2 such that he is able to get extra information, such as the linear combination of two messages (even though we don't know how to do such attack). So, we present another scheme OT_n^k-II that is provable secure against the malicious R. The scheme is depicted in Figure 2.

Let G_q be the subgroup of Z_p^* with prime order q, g be a generator of G_q, and $p = 2q + 1$ is also prime. Let $H_1 : \{0, 1\}^* \to G_q, H_2 : G_q \to \{0, 1\}^l$ be two collision-resistant hash functions. Let messages be of l-bit length. Assume that CT-CDH is hard under G_q.

Correctness. We can check that the chosen messages $m_{\sigma_j}, j = 1, 2, \ldots, k$, are computed as

$$c_{\sigma_j} \oplus H_2(K_j) = m_{\sigma_j} \oplus H_2(w_{\sigma_j}^x) \oplus H_2(w_{\sigma_j}^x)$$
$$= m_{\sigma_j}.$$

Security Analysis. We need the random oracle model in this security analysis.

Theorem 3. *In OT_n^k-II, R's choice meets the receiver's privacy.*

Proof. For any $A_j = w_j g^{a_j}$ and w_l, $l \neq j$, there is an a_l' that satisfies $A_j = w_l g^{a_l'}$. For S, A_j can be a masked value of any index. Thus, the receiver's choices are unconditionally secure. □

Theorem 4. *Even if R is malicious, the scheme OT_n^k-II meets the requirement for the sender's security assuming hardness of the CT-CDH problem the random oracle model.*

Proof. Since we treat H_2 as a random oracle, the malicious R has to know $K_i = w_i^x$ in order to query the hash oracle to get $H_2(w_i^x)$. For each possible malicious R, we construct a simulator R^* in the Ideal model such that the outputs of R and R^* are indistinguishable.

R^* works as follows:

1. R^* simulates R to obtain $A_1^*, A_2^*, \ldots, A_k^*$. When R queries H_1 on index i, we return a random w_i^* (consistent with the previous queries.)
2. R^* simulates S (externally without knowing m_i's) on inputs $A_1^*, A_2^*, \ldots, A_k^*$ to obtain x^*, y^*, $D_1^*, D_2^*, \ldots, D_k^*$.
3. R^* randomly chooses $c_1^*, c_2^*, \ldots, c_n^*$.
4. R^* simulates R on input $(y^*, D_1^*, D_2^*, \ldots, D_k^*, c_1^*, c_2^*, \ldots, c_n^*)$ and monitors the queries closely. If R queries H_2 on some $v_j = (w_j^*)^{x^*}$, R^* sends j to the TTP T to obtain m_j and returns $c_j^* \oplus m_j$ as the hash value $H_2((w_j^*)^{x^*})$, otherwise, returns a random value (consistent with previous queries).
5. Output $(A_1^*, A_2^*, \ldots, A_k^*, y^*, D_1^*, D_2^*, \ldots, D_k^*, c_1^*, c_2^* \ldots, c_n^*)$.

If R obtains $k + 1$ decryption keys, R^* does not know which k indices are really chosen by R. The simulation would fail. Therefore we show that R can obtain at most k decryption keys by assuming the hardness of chosen-target CDH problem: In the above simulation, if R queries H_1, we return a random value output by the target oracle. When R^* simulates S on input $A_1^*, A_2^*, \ldots, A_k^*$, we forward these queries to the helper oracle, and return the corresponding outputs. Finally, if R queries H_2 on legal v_{j_i} for all $1 \leq i \leq k + 1$, we can output $k + 1$ pairs (v_{j_i}, j_i), which contradicts to the CT-CDH assumption. Thus, R obtains at most k decryption keys.

Let $\sigma_1, \sigma_2, \ldots, \sigma_k$ be the k choices of R. For the queried legal v_{σ_j}'s, c_{σ_j} is consistent with the returned hash values, for $j = 1, 2, \ldots, k$. Since no other $(w_l^*)^{x^*}$, $l \neq \sigma_1, \sigma_2, \ldots, \sigma_k$, can be queried to the H_2 hash oracle, c_l has the right distribution (due to the random oracle model). Thus, the output distribution is indistinguishable from that of R. □

Complexity. OT_n^k-II has two rounds. The first round sends k messages and the second round sends $n + k + 1$ messages. For computation, R computes $2k$, and S computes $n + k + 1$ modular exponentiations.

- System parameters: (g, H_1, H_2, G_q);
- S has messages: $m_1, m_2, \ldots, m_n$;
- R's choices: $\sigma_1, \sigma_2, \ldots, \sigma_k$;

Commitment Phase

1. S computes $c_i = m_i \oplus H_2(w_i^x)$ for $i = 1, 2, \ldots, n$, and $y = g^x$ where $w_i = H_1(i)$, and $x \in_R Z_q^*$.
2. $S \longrightarrow R : y, c_1, c_2, \ldots, c_n$.

Transfer Phase

For each σ_j, $j = 1, 2, \ldots, k$, R and S execute the following steps:

1. R chooses a random $a_j \in Z_q^*$ and computes $w_{\sigma_j} = H_1(\sigma_j)$, $A_j = w_{\sigma_j} g^{a_j}$.
2. $R \longrightarrow S : A_j$.
3. $S \longrightarrow R : D_j = (A_j)^x$.
4. R computes $K_j = D_j / y^{a_j}$ and gets $m_{\sigma_j} = c_{\sigma_j} \oplus H_2(K_j)$.

Fig. 3. Adpt-OT$_n^k$: Adaptive OT$_n^k$.

4 k-Out-of-n OT with Adaptive Queries

The queries of R in our schemes can be adaptive. In our schemes, the commitments c_i's of the messages m_i's of S to R are independent of the key masking. Therefore, our scheme is adaptive in nature. Our Adpt-OT$_n^k$ scheme, which rephrases the OT$_n^k$-II scheme, is depicted in Figure 3.

The protocol consists of two phases: the commitment phase and the transfer phase. The sender S first commits the messages in the commitment phase. In the transfer phase, for each query, R sends the query A_j to S and obtains the corresponding key to decrypt the commitment c_j.

Correctness of the scheme follows that of OT$_n^k$-II.

Security Analysis. The security proofs are almost the same as those for OT$_n^k$-II. We omit them here.

Complexity. In the commitment phase, S needs $n + 1$ modular exponentiations for computing the commitments c_i's and y. In the transfer phase, R needs 2 modular exponentiations for computing the query and the chosen message. S needs one modular exponentiation for answering each R's query. The commitment phase is one-round and the transfer phase is two-round for each adaptive query.

5   Conclusion

We have presented two very efficient OT$_n^k$ schemes against semi-honest receivers in the standard model and malicious receivers in the random oracle model. Our schemes possess other interesting features, such as, it can be non-interactive and needs no prior setup or trapdoor. We also proposed an efficient Adpt-OT$_n^k$ for adaptive queries. The essential feature allowing this is the reversal of the orders of key commitment and message commitment. In most previous schemes (including OT_n^k-I), the key commitments (for encrypting the chosen messages) are sent to S first. The message commitments are dependent on the key commitments. Nevertheless, in our scheme OT_n^k-II the message commitments are independent of the key commitment. Thus, the message commitments can be sent to R first.

References

[BBCS91] Charles H. Bennett, Gilles Brassard, Claude Crépeau, and Marie-Hélène Skubiszewska. Practical quantum oblivious transfer. In *Proceedings of Advances in Cryptology - CRYPTO '91*, volume 576 of *LNCS*, pages 351–366. Springer-Verlag, 1991.

[BCR86] Gilles Brassard, Claude Crépeau, and Jean-Marc Robert. All-or-nothing disclosure of secrets. In *Proceedings of Advances in Cryptology - CRYPTO '86*, volume 263 of *LNCS*, pages 234–238. Springer-Verlag, 1986.

[BCR87] Gilles Brassard, Claude Crépeau, and Jean-Marc Robert. Information theoretic reductions among disclosure problems. In *Proceedings of 28th Annual Symposium on Foundations of Computer Science (FOCS '87)*, pages 427–437. IEEE, 1987.

[BCS96] Gilles Brassard, Claude Crépeau, and Miklós Sántha. Oblivious transfers and intersecting codes. *IEEE Transactions on Information Theory*, 42(6):1769–1780, 1996.

[BDSS02] Carlo Blundo, Paolo D'Arco, Alfredo De Santis, and Douglas R. Stinson. New results on unconditionally secure distributed oblivious transfer. In *Proceedings of Selected Areas in Cryptography - SAC '02*, volume 2595 of *LNCS*, pages 291–309. Springer-Verlag, 2002.

[BM89] Mihir Bellare and Silvio Micali. Non-interactive oblivious transfer and applications. In *Proceedings of Advances in Cryptology - CRYPTO '89*, volume 435 of *LNCS*, pages 547–557. Springer-Verlag, 1989.

[BNPS01] Mihir Bellare, Chanathip Namprempre, David Pointcheval, and Michael Semanko. Power of rsa inversion oracles and the security of Chaum's RSA-based blind signature scheme. In *Proceedings of Financial Cryptography (FC '01)*, pages 319–338. Springer-Verlag, 2001.

[Bol03] Alexandra Boldyreva. Threshold signatures, multisignatures and blind signatures based on the gap-diffie-hellman-group signature scheme. In *Proceedings of the Public-Key Cryptography (PKC '03)*, pages 31–46. Springer-Verlag, 2003.

[CCM98] Christian Cachin, Claude Crepeau, and Julien Marcil. Oblivious transfer with a memory-bounded receiver. In *Proceedings of 39th Annual Symposium on Foundations of Computer Science (FOCS '98)*, pages 493–502. IEEE, 1998.

[CZ03] Zhide Chen and Hong Zhu. Quantum m-out-of-n oblivious transfer. Technical report, arXiv:cs.CR/0311039, 2003.

[Din01] Yan Zong Ding. Oblivious transfer in the bounded storage model. In *Proceedings of Advances in Cryptology - CRYPTO '01*, volume 2139 of *LNCS*, pages 155–170. Springer-Verlag, 2001.

[EGL85] Shimon Even, Oded Goldreich, and Abraham Lempel. A randomized protocol for signing contracts. *Communications of the ACM*, 28(6):637–647, 1985.

[GV87]   Oded Goldreich and Ronen Vainish. How to solve any protocol problem
            - an efficiency improvement. In *Proceedings of Advances in Cryptology -
            CRYPTO '87*, volume 293 of *LNCS*, pages 73–86. Springer-Verlag, 1987.

[IKNP03]   Yuval Ishai, Joe Kilian, Kobbi Nissim, and Erez Petrank. Extending
            oblivious transfers efficiently. In *Proceedings of Advances in Cryptology
            - CRYPTO '03*, volume 2729 of *LNCS*, pages 145–161. Springer-Verlag,
            2003.

[Kil88]   Joe Kilian. Founding cryptography on oblivious transfer. In *Proceedings
            of the 20th Annual ACM Symposium on the Theory of Computing (STOC
            '88)*, pages 20–31. ACM, 1988.

[Lip]   Helger Lipmaa. Oblivious transfer.
            http://www.tcs.hut.fi/~helger/crypto/link/protocols/oblivious.html.

[Lip04]   Helger Lipmaa. An oblivious transfer protocol with log-squared commu-
            nication. Technical report, Cryptology ePrint Archive: Report 2004/063,
            2004.

[MZV02]   Yi Mu, Junqi Zhang, and Vijay Varadharajan. m out of n oblivious transfer.
            In *Proceedings of the 7th Australasian Conference on Information Security
            and Privacy (ACISP '02)*, volume 2384 of *LNCS*, pages 395–405. Springer-
            Verlag, 2002.

[NP99a]   Moni Naor and Benny Pinkas. Oblivious transfer and polynomial evalua-
            tion. In *Proceedings of the 31th Annual ACM Symposium on the Theory of
            Computing (STOC '99)*, pages 245–254. ACM, 1999.

[NP99b]   Moni Naor and Benny Pinkas. Oblivious transfer with adaptive queries.
            In *Proceedings of Advances in Cryptology - CRYPTO '99*, volume 1666 of
            LNCS, pages 573–590. Springer-Verlag, 1999.

[NP00]   Moni Naor and Benny Pinkas. Distributed oblivious transfer. In *Proceedings
            of Advances in Cryptology - ASIACRYPT '00*, volume 1976 of *LNCS*, pages
            200–219. Springer-Verlag, 2000.

[NP01]   Moni Naor and Benny Pinkas. Efficient oblivious transfer protocols. In
            *Proceedings of the 12th Annual Symposium on Discrete Algorithms (SODA
            '01)*, pages 448–457. ACM/SIAM, 2001.

[NR94]   Valtteri Niemi and Ari Renvall. Cryptographic protocols and voting. In
            Results and Trends in Theoretical Computer Science, volume 812 of *LNCS*,
            pages 307–317. Springer-Verlag, 1994.

[OK02]   Wakaha Ogata and Kaoru Kurosawa. Oblivious keyword search. Technical
            report, Cryptology ePrint Archive: Report 2002/182, 2002.

[Rab81]   Michael O. Rabin. How to exchange secrets by oblivious transfer. Technical
            Report TR-81, Aiken Computation Laboratory, Harvard University, 1981.

[SS90]   Arto Salomaa and Lila Santean. Secret selling of secrets with several buy-
            ers. *Bulletin of the European Association for Theoretical Computer Science
            (EATCS)*, 42:178–186, 1990.

[Ste98]   Julien P. Stern. A new and efficient all or nothing disclosure of secrets
            protocol. In *Proceedings of Advances in Cryptology - ASIACRYPT '98*,
            volume 1514 of *LNCS*, pages 357–371. Springer-Verlag, 1998.

[Tze02]   Wen-Guey Tzeng. Efficient 1-out-n oblivious transfer schemes. In *Proceed-
            ings of the Public-Key Cryptography (PKC '02)*, pages 159–171. Springer-
            Verlag, 2002.

[YBD03]   Gang Yao, Feng Bao, and Robert Deng. Security analysis of three oblivious
            transfer protocols. Workshop on Coding, Cryptography and Combinatorics,
            Huangshan City, China, 2003.

Converse Results to the Wiener Attack on RSA

Ron Steinfeld, Scott Contini, Huaxiong Wang, and Josef Pieprzyk

Dept. of Computing, Macquarie University, North Ryde, Australia
{rons,scontini,hwang,josef}@ics.mq.edu.au
http://www.ics.mq.edu.au/acac/

Abstract. A well-known attack on RSA with low secret-exponent d was given by Wiener about 15 years ago. Wiener showed that using continued fractions, one can efficiently recover the secret-exponent d from the public key (N, e) as long as $d < N^{1/4}$. Interestingly, Wiener stated that his attack may sometimes also work when d is slightly *larger* than $N^{1/4}$. This raises the question of how much larger d can be: could the attack work with non-negligible probability for $d = N^{1/4+\rho}$ for some constant $\rho > 0$? We answer this question in the negative by proving a converse to Wiener's result. Our result shows that, for *any* fixed $\epsilon > 0$ and all sufficiently large modulus lengths, Wiener's attack succeeds with negligible probability over a random choice of $d < N^{\delta}$ (in an interval of size $\Omega(N^{\delta})$) as soon as $\delta > 1/4 + \epsilon$. Thus Wiener's success bound $d < N^{1/4}$ for his algorithm is essentially tight. We also obtain a converse result for a natural class of extensions of the Wiener attack, which are guaranteed to succeed even when $\delta > 1/4$. The known attacks in this class (by Verheul and Van Tilborg and Dujella) run in exponential time, so it is natural to ask whether there exists an attack in this class with subexponential run-time. Our second converse result answers this question also in the negative.

1 Introduction

The RSA public-key cryptosystem is one of the most popular systems in use today. Accordingly, the study of the security of special variants of RSA designed for computational efficiency is a major area of research. One natural RSA variant which is attractive for speeding up secret operations (signature generation or decryption) is *Low Secret-Exponent RSA*. In this variant the RSA secret exponent d is chosen to be small compared to the RSA modulus N. A well-known attack on RSA with low secret-exponent d was given by Wiener[10] about 15 years ago. Wiener showed that using continued fractions, one can efficiently recover the secret-exponent d from the public key (N, e) as long as $d < N^{1/4}$. Interestingly, Wiener stated that his attack may sometimes also work when d is slightly *larger* than $N^{1/4}$. This raises the question of how much larger d can be: could the attack work with non-negligible probability for $d = N^{1/4+\rho}$ for some constant $\rho > 0$?

In this paper, we answer the above question in the negative by proving a converse to Wiener's result. Our result shows that, for *any* fixed $\epsilon > 0$ and all sufficiently large modulus lengths, Wiener's attack succeeds with negligible

S. Vaudenay (Ed.): PKC 2005, LNCS 3386, pp. 184–198, 2005.

probability over a random choice of $d < N^\delta$ (in an interval of size $\Omega(N^\delta)$) as soon as $\delta > 1/4 + \epsilon$. Thus Wiener's bound $d < N^{1/4}$ for his attack is essentially tight. We also obtain a converse result for a natural class of extensions of the Wiener attack, which are guaranteed to succeed even when $\delta > 1/4$. The known attacks in this class (by Verheul and Van Tilborg [8] and Dujella [3]) run in exponential time, so it is natural to ask whether there exists an attack in this class with subexponential run-time. Our second converse result answers this question also in the negative.

Related Work. To our knowledge, the converse results in this paper provide the first *proven* evidence for the limitations of the Wiener attack [10] and its extensions by Verheul and Van Tilborg [8] and Duejlla [3]. Essentially, our results prove that when $\delta > 1/4$, the linear equation (satisfied by the secret key) which is exploited by the Wiener attack cannot lead by itself to a key-recovery attack which runs in subexponential time (because there are too many solutions). In order to obtain a subexponential attack when $\delta > 1/4$ one must exploit some other property of the secret key. Indeed, the lattice-based Boneh-Durfee attack [2] and its variant given by Blömer and May [1], exploit a non-linear equation satisfied by the secret key, which gives an attack that heuristically succeeds in polynomial-time when $\delta < 0.292$. Finding proven limitations on the Boneh-Durfee attack and its variants is currently an open problem, but we believe our results on provable limitations of the Wiener attack are a first step in this direction.

Organization of This Paper. Section 2 presents definitions and known results from number theory that we use. In Section 3, we define the standard RSA key-generation algorithm that our results apply to and review Wiener's result. In Section 4, we state and prove our converse to Wiener's result. In Section 5, we present our generalized converse result which applies to a natural class of extensions of the Wiener attack. Section 6 concludes the paper.

2 Preliminaries

2.1 Continued Fractions

Here we collect several known results that we use about continued fractions, which can be found in [5, 6].

For positive integers $a_1, \ldots, a_n$, we define the rational number

$$x \stackrel{\mathrm{def}}{=} \cfrac{1}{a_1 + \cfrac{1}{a_2 + \ldots + \frac{1}{a_n}}}.$$

For brevity, we write $x = (a_1, a_2, \ldots, a_n)$, and we call the sequence $(a_1, \ldots, a_n)$ a *continued fraction expansion of length n for x*.

Theorem 1 (Continued Fractions). *Let $x = \frac{r}{s}$ for positive integers r, s with $\gcd(r, s) = 1$ and $r < s$. Then the rational x has a* unique *continued fraction expansion $x = (a_1, \ldots, a_n)$ with $a_n > 1$, which can be computed in time $O(\log^2 s)$ by the following algorithm:*

1. *Initialize $x_0 = x$.*
2. *Compute iteratively $x_i = \frac{1}{x_{i-1} - \lfloor x_{i-1} \rfloor}$ for $i = 1, \ldots, n$, where $n \leq 2 \log(s)$ is the smallest value of i such that $\lfloor x_i \rfloor = x_i$.*
3. *Return $(a_1, \ldots, a_n)$, where $a_i = \lfloor x_i \rfloor$ for $i = 1, \ldots, n$.*

Let $(a_1, \ldots, a_n)$ denote the continued fraction expansion of rational x. For $i = 1, \ldots, n$, the rationals $y_i = \frac{r_i}{s_i} \overset{\text{def}}{=} (a_1, \ldots, a_i)$ are called the *convergents* of (the continued fraction expansion for) x. The convergents y_i to x become successively closer to x with increasing index i until the last convergent y_n which is equal to x.

Theorem 2 (Convergents). *Let $y_1, \ldots, y_n$ denote the convergents of a rational $x = \frac{r}{s}$ for positive integers r, s with $\gcd(r, s) = 1$ and $r < s$. For $i = 1, \ldots, n - 1$, let us write $y_i = \frac{r_i}{s_i}$ for integers r_i, s_i with $\gcd(r_i, s_i) = 1$. Then the following statements hold:*

(1) *For $i \in \{1, \ldots, n-1\}$, $y_i = \frac{r_i}{s_i}$ is a best approximation to x in the sense that $|s_i \cdot x - r_i| < |s' \cdot x - r'|$ for all r', s' such that $0 < s' \leq s_i$ and $\frac{r'}{s'} \neq y_i$ (note: this implies that $|\frac{r_i}{s_i} - x| < |\frac{r'}{s'} - x|$ for all r', s' such that $0 < s' \leq s_i$ and $\frac{r'}{s'} \neq y_i$).*

(2) *For $i \in \{1, \ldots, n-1\}$, $|\frac{r_i}{s_i} - x| < \frac{1}{s_i^2}$ and $s_{i+1} \geq 2 s_i$.*

(3) *Let $y = \frac{\widehat{r}}{s}$ be any rational such that $|\frac{\widehat{r}}{s} - x| < \frac{1}{2s^2}$. Then y is equal to one of the convergents of x, i.e. $y = y_i$ for some $i \in \{1, \ldots, n\}$.*

3 Review of Wiener's Attack

3.1 The RSA Key-Generation Algorithm

In this paper we assume the following natural key-generation algorithm $\mathsf{RSAKG}_{\delta, \beta_1, \beta_2}(\ell)$ for RSA, which would typically be used when the goal is to produce a modulus N in the order of 2^ℓ and a secret exponent d in the order of N^δ for some fixed $0 < \delta \leq 1$. The fixed real-valued parameters $\beta_1 > 0$ and $\beta_2 > 0$ control the size of the intervals from which the prime factors of N and the secret exponent d are chosen from (typically, we set $\beta_1 = \beta_2 = 1$, to fix a certain bit-length for p, q and d).

All the probabilities computed in this paper are evaluated over the random choices of algorithm $\mathsf{RSAKG}_{\delta, \beta_1, \beta_2}(\ell)$.

$\mathsf{RSAKG}_{\delta, \beta_1, \beta_2}(\ell)$: RSA Key-Generation Algorithm

1 Pick uniformly at random a prime $p \in \mathcal{P}_{\ell/2, \beta_1}$ (Here $\mathcal{P}_{\ell/2, \beta_1}$ denotes the set of all primes in the interval $[2^{\ell/2 - \beta_1}, 2^{\ell/2}]$ and typically we set $\beta_1 = 1$).
2 Pick uniformly at random a prime $q \in \mathcal{P}_{\ell/2, \beta_1}$.
3 Compute integers $N = pq$ and $\phi = (p-1)(q-1)$.

4 Pick uniformly at random a secret exponent $d \in \mathcal{D}_{\ell,\delta,\beta_2}(\phi)$ (Here $\mathcal{D}_{\ell,\delta,\beta_1}(\phi)$ denotes the set of all integers in the interval $[2^{\delta \cdot \ell - \beta_2}, 2^{\delta \cdot \ell}]$ which are coprime to ϕ, and typically we set $\beta_2 = 1$).

5 Compute $e = d^{-1} \bmod \phi$ (note: this implicitly defines the integer $k = (ed - 1)/\phi$).

6 Return secret-exponent d and public key (N, e).

3.2 Wiener's Attack

The idea behind Wiener's attack on RSA with small secret-exponent d is that for small d, the publicly known fraction e/N is a very good approximation to the secret fraction k/d (here $k = (ed - 1)/\phi$), and hence k/d can be found from the convergents of the continued-fraction expansion of e/N, using the results of Section 2.1.

WienAtk(N, e): Wiener Attack Algorithm

1 Compute the continued fraction convergents $\left(\frac{k_1}{d_1}, \ldots, \frac{k_n}{d_n}\right)$ of $\frac{e}{N}$ using the algorithm of Theorem 1.

2 Return $\left(\frac{k_1}{d_1}, \ldots, \frac{k_n}{d_n}\right)$.

We say that algorithm WienAtk *succeeds* on input (N, e) if it outputs $\left(\frac{k_1}{d_1}, \ldots, \frac{k_n}{d_n}\right)$ with $\frac{k_i}{d_i} = \frac{k}{d}$ for some $i \in \{1, \ldots, n\}$ (where $d = e^{-1} \bmod \phi$ and $k = (ed - 1)/\phi$).

To obtain Wiener's sufficient condition for the success of algorithm WienAtk, we observe that, from the equation $ed - 1 = k\phi$ it follows that the approximation error of k/d by e/N is given by:

$$\frac{k}{d} - \frac{e}{N} = e \cdot \left(\frac{1}{\phi} - \frac{1}{N}\right) - \frac{1}{\phi \cdot d} \tag{1}$$

$$= e \cdot \left(\frac{1}{N-s} - \frac{1}{N}\right) - \frac{1}{(N-s) \cdot d} \quad \text{where } s = p + q - 1 \tag{2}$$

$$= \left(\frac{s}{N-s}\right)\left(\frac{e}{N} - \frac{1}{d \cdot s}\right) \tag{3}$$

$$< \frac{s}{N-s} < \frac{2^{2\beta_1+1}}{2^{\ell/2}}. \tag{4}$$

The last bound uses the fact that $s < 2^{\ell/2+1}$ since p and q are not even. Note also that $\frac{k}{d} - \frac{e}{N} > 0$.

From Theorem 2 part (3), we know that k/d will be one of the convergents of the continued fraction expansion of e/N if $\frac{k}{d} - \frac{e}{N} < \frac{1}{2d^2}$. Using the above bound on $\frac{k}{d} - \frac{e}{N}$ and the fact that $d < 2^{\delta \cdot \ell}$, we conclude that a sufficient condition for success of algorithm WienAtk is that $\frac{2^{2\beta_1+1}}{2^{\ell/2}} < \frac{1}{2^{2\delta \cdot \ell + 1}}$. This immediately gives us the following result due to Wiener [10].

Theorem 3 (WienAtk Sufficient Condition). *Suppose that the key-generation parameters $(\delta, \beta_1, \beta_2, \ell)$ satisfy the condition*

$$\delta < 1/4 - \frac{\beta_1 + 1}{\ell}.$$

Then on input (N, e), where $(N, e, d) = \mathsf{RSAKG}_{\delta, \beta_1, \beta_2}(\ell)$, the Wiener attack algorithm WienAtk succeeds with probability 1.

4   A Converse to Wiener's Result

The following statement is our *necessary* condition for success of Wiener's algorithm. It shows that whenever δ exceeds the Wiener sufficiency threshold $1/4$ by any positive constant ϵ, the Wiener attack algorithm succeeds with negligible probability $2^{-c \cdot \ell}$ for some constant $c > 0$.

Theorem 4 (WienAtk Necessary Condition). *Fix positive constants $0 < \epsilon < 3/4$, β_1 and β_2, and suppose that the key-generation parameter δ satisfies the condition*

$$\delta = 1/4 + \epsilon.$$

Then there exist positive constants c and ℓ_0 (depending on ϵ, β_1 and β_2) such that on input (N, e), where $(N, e, d) = \mathsf{RSAKG}_{\delta, \beta_1, \beta_2}(\ell)$, the Wiener attack algorithm WienAtk succeeds with probability at most $2^{-c \cdot \ell}$ for all $\ell \geq \ell_0$.

Proof. By definition, if WienAtk succeeds on input (N, e), then one of the convergents $\left(\frac{k_1}{d_1}, \ldots, \frac{k_n}{d_n}\right)$ of $\frac{e}{N}$ is equal to $\frac{k}{d}$. But by Theorem 2 part (2), it follows that $\frac{k}{d} - \frac{e}{N} < \frac{1}{d^2}$. Using $d > 2^{\delta \cdot \ell - \beta_2}$ and $\delta = 1/4 + \epsilon$, we obtain the necessary success condition

$$\frac{k}{d} - \frac{e}{N} < 2^{2\beta_2 - (1/2 + 2\epsilon) \cdot \ell}. \tag{5}$$

We now show that, for any $\epsilon > 0$, the probability that (5) holds is negligible over the random choice of $d \in \mathcal{D}_{\ell, \delta, \beta_2}(\phi)$. We first reduce the problem to upper bounding the probability that $\frac{e}{N}$ is negligibly small.

Lemma 1. *Fix positive constants c_1 and η_1. Then there exist positive constants c_2 and η_2 such that*

$$\Pr\left[\frac{k}{d} - \frac{e}{N} < c_1 \cdot 2^{-(1/2 + \eta_1) \cdot \ell}\right] \leq \Pr\left[\frac{e}{N} < c_2 \cdot 2^{-\eta_2 \cdot \ell}\right].$$

Proof. Let $\Delta = \frac{k}{d} - \frac{e}{N}$. From (3) in Section 3.2 we have $\Delta = \left(\frac{s}{N-s}\right) \cdot \left(\frac{e}{N} - \frac{1}{d \cdot s}\right)$, and using $s = p + q - 1 > N^{1/2}$ we get $\Delta > N^{-1/2} \cdot \left(\frac{e}{N} - \frac{1}{dN^{1/2}}\right)$. Using $d > 2^{\delta \cdot \ell - \beta_2}$ and $N > 2^{\ell - 2\beta_1}$ we get $\Delta > N^{-1/2} \cdot \left(\frac{e}{N} - 2^{\beta_1 + \beta_2 - (1/2 + \delta) \cdot \ell}\right)$, and then using

$N < 2^\ell$ we get $\Delta > 2^{-\ell/2} \cdot \left(\frac{e}{N} - 2^{\beta_1 + \beta_2 - (1/2 + \delta) \cdot \ell} \right)$. Let $C = 2^{\beta_1 + \beta_2 - (1/2 + \delta) \cdot \ell}$. Then we have

$$\Pr\left[\Delta < c_1 \cdot 2^{-(1/2 + \eta_1) \cdot \ell} \right] \leq \Pr\left[2^{-\ell/2} \cdot \left(\frac{e}{N} - C \right) < c_1 \cdot 2^{-(1/2 + \eta_1) \cdot \ell} \right]$$

$$= \Pr\left[\frac{e}{N} < c_1 \cdot 2^{-\eta_1 \cdot \ell} + C \right]$$

$$\leq \Pr\left[\frac{e}{N} < c_2 \cdot 2^{-\eta_2 \cdot \ell} \right],$$

for positive constants $c_2 = 2\max(c_1, 2^{\beta + 1 + \beta_2})$ and $\eta_2 = \min(\eta_1, 1/2 + \delta)$, as claimed. $\qquad\square$

To bound $\Pr\left[\frac{e}{N} < c_2 \cdot 2^{-\eta_2 \cdot \ell} \right]$, we need an upper bound on the number of $d \in \mathcal{D}_{\ell, \delta, \beta_2}(\phi)$ such that $\frac{e}{N} < c_2 \cdot 2^{-\eta_2 \cdot \ell}$ holds, and a lower bound on the total size of the set $\mathcal{D}_{\ell, \delta, \beta_2}(\phi)$. These bounds are provided by the following two counting results.

Lemma 2. *Fix positive constants c_1, c_2 and δ. The size of the set M of secret-exponents $d < 2^{\delta \cdot \ell}$ such that the corresponding public exponent $e = d^{-1} \bmod \phi$ satisfies $\frac{e}{N} < c_1 \cdot 2^{-c_2 \cdot \ell}$ is bounded as follows:*

$$\#M = O\left(2^{\left(\delta - c_2 + \frac{c_3}{\log \ell} \right) \cdot \ell} \right),$$

with constant $c_3 = 2(1 + \delta)$.

Proof. For each $d \in M$, we have $e \cdot d = 1 + k \cdot \phi$ for some positive integer k, where $k < \frac{ed}{\phi} = O\left(2^{(\delta - c_2) \cdot \ell} \right)$ using the fact that $N/\phi = O(1)$. So, to get an upper bound on the number of (e, d) pairs, we only need to consider the possibilities for k, from 1 up to some integer $K = O\left(2^{(\delta - c_2) \cdot \ell} \right)$.

For each $k \in \{1, \ldots, K\}$, let $m = 1 + k \cdot \phi = O\left(2^{(1 + \delta - c_2) \cdot \ell} \right)$. The possible (e, d) pairs for this k correspond to factorizations of m as a product of two integers. The number of such factorizations is equal to $\tau(m)$, the number of divisors of m. It is known (see Theorem 317 of [4]) that $\tau(m) = O\left(2^{\frac{2 \log m}{\log \log m}} \right)$, and using the bounds $m = O(k \cdot \phi) = O\left(2^{(1 + \delta) \cdot \ell} \right)$ and $m = \Omega(N) = \Omega\left(2^\ell \right)$ we conclude that $\tau(m) = O\left(2^{\frac{2(1 + \delta)}{\log \ell} \cdot \ell} \right)$.

Thus the total number of possible (e, d) pairs satisfying the required conditions is bounded as $\#M = O(K \cdot \tau(m)) = O\left(2^{\left(\delta - c_2 + \frac{c_3}{\log \ell} \right) \cdot \ell} \right)$ where $c_3 = 2(1 + \delta)$, as required. $\qquad\square$

Lemma 3. *Fix positive constants β_1, β_2 and δ. The size of the set $\mathcal{D}_{\ell, \delta, \beta_1}(\phi)$ of all integers in the interval $[2^{\delta \cdot \ell - \beta_2}, 2^{\delta \cdot \ell}]$ which are coprime to ϕ is lower bounded as follows:*

$$\#\mathcal{D}_{\ell, \delta, \beta_1}(\phi) = \Omega\left(2^{\left(\delta - \frac{\log \log \ell}{\ell} \right) \cdot \ell} \right).$$

Proof. For an integer $d \geq 1$, we denote by $\mu(m)$ the Möbius function. We recall that $\mu(1) = 1$, $\mu(d) = 0$ if $d \geq 2$ is not square-free and $\mu(d) = (-1)^{\omega(d)}$ otherwise, where for integer d we denote by $\omega(d)$ the number of distinct prime factors of d.

Fix any integers $m, J \geq 1$. Using the Möbius function $\mu(d)$ over the divisors of q to detect the co-primality condition (see Section 3.d of Chapter 2 of [9]) and interchanging the order of summation, we obtain the Legendre formula

$$\sum_{\substack{j=1 \\ \gcd(j,m)=1}}^{J} 1 = \sum_{d|m} \mu(d) \left\lfloor \frac{J}{d} \right\rfloor = J \sum_{d|m} \frac{\mu(d)}{d} + O\left(\sum_{d|m} |\mu(d)| \right). \tag{6}$$

Observe that

$$\sum_{d|m} |\mu(d)| = \sum_{k=0}^{\omega(m)} |(-1)^k| \binom{\omega(m)}{k} = 2^{\omega(m)},$$

and recall that the Möbius function satisfies

$$\sum_{d|m} \frac{\mu(d)}{d} = \frac{\varphi(m)}{m},$$

where $\varphi(m)$ denotes Euler's phi function evaluated at m. So, for any integers $J_{max} > J_{min} \geq 1$, applying (6) to both intervals $[1, \ldots, J_{min}]$ and $[1, \ldots, J_{max}]$ and subtracting gives us

$$\sum_{\substack{J_{min} \leq j \leq J_{max} \\ \gcd(j,m)=1}} 1 = \frac{\varphi(m)}{m}(J_{max} - J_{min}) + O(2^{\omega(m)}).$$

But $2^{\omega(m)}$ is the number of square-free divisors of m, which is upper bounded by the total number $\tau(m)$ of divisors of m. It is known (see Theorem 317 of [4]) that $\tau(m) = O\left(2^{\frac{2 \log m}{\log \log m}} \right)$. Setting $m = \phi$, $J_{min} = 2^{\delta \cdot \ell}/2^{\beta_2}$ and $J_{max} = 2^{\delta \cdot \ell}$, we get

$$\#\mathcal{D}_{\ell,\delta,\beta_2}(\phi) = \Omega\left(\frac{\varphi(\phi)}{\phi} \cdot 2^{\delta \cdot \ell} \right) + O\left(2^{\frac{2 \log \phi}{\log \log \phi}} \right). \tag{7}$$

We now observe that $\phi = \Theta(2^\ell)$ so $2^{\frac{2 \log \phi}{\log \log \phi}} = O\left(2^{\frac{c_5 \ell}{\log \ell}} \right)$ for some positive constant c_5. Furthermore, it is known [7] that $\frac{\phi}{\varphi(\phi)} = O(\log \log \phi) = O(2^{\log \log \ell})$. Plugging these results in (7) and using the fact that $2^{\frac{c_5 \ell}{\log \ell}} = o\left(2^{\delta \cdot \ell - \log \log \ell} \right)$ we obtain the claimed result $\#M = \Omega\left(2^{(\delta - \frac{\log \log \ell}{\ell}) \cdot \ell} \right)$.   □

Using Lemma 1 and the fact that d is chosen uniformly at random from the set $\mathcal{D}_{\ell,\delta,\beta_2}(\phi)$, we conclude that WienAtk's success probability p is upper bounded as $p \leq \frac{\#M}{\#\mathcal{D}_{\ell,\delta,\beta_2}(\phi)}$, where M denotes the set of all secret-exponents $d < 2^{\delta \cdot \ell}$ such that the corresponding public exponent $e = d^{-1} \bmod \phi$ satisfies $\frac{e}{N} < c_2 \cdot 2^{-\eta_2 \cdot \ell}$. Taking the ratio of the bounds on $\#M$ and $\#\mathcal{D}_{\ell,\delta,\beta_2}(\phi)$ from

Lemma 2 and Lemma 3, we have that $p = O\left(2^{-\left(\eta_2 - \frac{c_3}{\log \ell} - \frac{\log \log \ell}{\ell}\right) \cdot \ell}\right)$ for some positive constants η_2 and c_3. It follows that there exists a constant ℓ_0 such that $p \leq 2^{-c \cdot \ell}$ for all $\ell \geq \ell_0$, where $c = \eta_2/2 > 0$. This completes the proof of the theorem. $\square$

5   A Converse Result for Improved Variants of Wiener Attack

Since Wiener's attack fails as soon as $\delta > 1/4$, it is natural to investigate improved variants of the Wiener attack which may succeed even in this case. In particular, Verheul and Van Tilborg (VVT) [8], and more recently Dujella [3], presented improved variants of Wiener's attack which are guaranteed to succeed even when $\delta > 1/4$. However, the run-time of these attacks when $\delta = 1/4 + \epsilon$ (for some positive constant ϵ) is exponential in $\epsilon \cdot \ell$, so these attacks are asymptotically slower than the generic attack of factoring the RSA modulus, which runs in *subexponential* time. As we explain below, both the VVT and Dujella attacks can be viewed as members of a natural class of extensions of the Wiener attack (which are all guaranteed to succeed when $\delta > 1/4$), which we call the *Wiener Search Variant* (WSV) class of attacks (essentially, a WSV attack searches an interval near the known fraction e/N for the secret fraction k/d – see below for a precise definition). It is interesting to ask whether one can substantially improve on the VVT and Dujella attacks – in particular: does there exist an attack in the WSV class which has *subexponential* run-time? In this section, we answer this question in the negative by proving the following 'converse' result: For any attack algorithm in the WSV class and any subexponential run-time bound T, the probability (over the random choices of the key generation algorithm RSAKG) that the attack halts with success after a run-time less than T is negligible whenever $\delta = 1/4 + \epsilon$ for any constant $\epsilon > 0$. Thus there are no WSV attacks which are asymptotically faster than factoring (and hence the VVT and Dujella attacks are optimal in the sense that all WSV attacks must have at least exponential run-time).

The Wiener Search Variant (WSV) Attack Class. Recall that the central idea behind Wiener's attack is that the public fraction e/N is a good approximation to the secret fraction k/d. Indeed, when $\delta < 1/4 - \epsilon$, k/d is the *best* approximation to e/N among all fractions with denominator at most d (see Theorem 2), and Wiener's continued fractions attack efficiently finds this best approximation. Our converse result in the previous section shows that when $\delta > 1/4$, k/d is likely to no longer be the *best* approximation to e/N in the set of all fractions with denominator at most d, but it is still likely to be a good approximation. So, a natural extension of the Wiener attack is to search through the set of fractions with denominator less than $2^{\delta \cdot \ell}$ (and greater than $2^{\delta \cdot \ell - \beta_2}$) in an interval close to e/N, until k/d is found. This leads to the following definition.

Definition 1 (Wiener Search Variant Attack Class – WSV). *An attack algorithm $\mathsf{A}_{\delta, \beta_2, \ell}$ is said to belong to the* Wiener Search Variant *(WSV) attack class if it has the following form.*

$A_{\delta,\beta_2,\ell}(N,e)$: WSV Attack Algorithm

1 *Enumerate a set $S(N,e)$ of approximations to $\frac{k}{d}$, where $S(N,e)$ is guaranteed to contain the set $\widehat{S}(N,e)$ of all fractions $\frac{k'}{d'}$ in the interval $[\frac{e}{N},\frac{k}{d}]$ with denominator $d' \in [2^{\delta \cdot \ell - \beta_2}, 2^{\delta \cdot \ell}]$.*

2 *Return a list containing all elements of the set $S(N,e)$.*

We note that the above definition gives rise to a class of attacks, since it allows any choice for the set $S(N,e)$ (subject to the constraint that $S(N,e)$ contains $\widehat{S}(N,e)$). As in the case of the original Wiener attack, we say that a WSV attack *succeeds* if it outputs a set of approximations $S(N,e)$ which contains the desired secret fraction k/d. From the definition, it is in fact clear that any WSV attack succeeds with probability 1 because of the requirement that $S(N,e) \supseteq \widehat{S}(N,e)$ and the fact that $k/d \in \widehat{S}(N,e)$. The central question is, therefore, how large is the running-time of the attack for $\delta = 1/4 + \epsilon$. The running-time depends on the size of the set $S(N,e)$ output by the attack, and on the efficiency by which the elements of $S(N,e)$ are enumerated.

Known WSV Attacks. The VVT [8] and Dujella [3] attacks are both members of the WSV class. Let $\delta = 1/4 + \epsilon$ with $\epsilon > 0$. In the VVT attack [8], it is shown, using continued fraction techniques, how to enumerate a set of approximations $S_{VVT}(N,e)$ (containing $\widehat{S}(N,e)$ as defined in Def. 1) of size $\#S_{VVT}(N,e) = O(A^2 \cdot 2^{2\epsilon \cdot \ell})$ in time $T_{VVT} = O(\ell^2 \# S_{VVT}(N,e))$, where the integer A is proportional to certain coefficients in the continued fraction expansion of e/N and heuristically expected to be small with high probability. The Dujella attack [3] improves on the VVT attack by using results from diophantine approximation to enumerate a smaller set $\#S_{Duj}(N,e)$ (containing $\widehat{S}(N,e)$) of size $\#S_{Duj}(N,e) = O(\log(A) \cdot 2^{2\epsilon \cdot \ell})$ in time $T_{Duj} = O(\ell^2 \# S_{Duj}(N,e))$, where the integer A is the same as in the VVT attack. Moreover, Dujella proves that $\#S_{Duj}(N,e) = O(\ell \cdot 2^{2\epsilon \cdot \ell})$.

Our Result: A Lower Bound on WSV Attack Running-Time. The known WSV attacks have exponential run-times for $\delta = 1/4 + \epsilon$ with $\epsilon > 0$. We now address the following question: Does there exist a WSV attack with *subexponential* run-time for $\delta = 1/4 + \epsilon$? The following result shows that the answer is no. Therefore, the WSV class does not contain an attack faster than factoring.

Theorem 5 (WSV Attack Lower Bound). *Let $A_{\delta,\beta_2,\ell}$ denote any 'Wiener Search Variant' (WSV) attack algorithm (see Def. 1). Let $T(\ell) = 2^{g(\ell)}$ denote any subexponential function, where $g(\ell) = o(\ell)$. Fix positive constants $0 < \epsilon < 3/4$, β_1 and β_2, and suppose that the key-generation parameter δ satisfies the condition*

$$\delta = 1/4 + \epsilon.$$

Then there exist positive constants c and ℓ_0 (depending on ϵ,β_1, β_2 and $g(\ell)$) such that on input (N,e), where $(N,e,d) = \mathsf{RSAKG}_{\delta,\beta_1,\beta_2}(\ell)$, the running-time of the WSV attack algorithm $A_{\delta,\beta_2,\ell}$ is less than $T(\ell)$ with probability at most $2^{-c \cdot \ell}$ for all $\ell \geq \ell_0$.

Proof. The set $S(N,e)$ output by $A_{\delta,\beta_2,\ell}$ is guaranteed by Def. 1 to contain the set $\widehat{S}(N,e)$, where

$$\widehat{S}(N, e) = (\mathcal{F}_{2^{\delta \cdot \ell}} \setminus \mathcal{F}_{2^{\delta \cdot \ell - \beta_2}}) \cap [\frac{e}{N}, \frac{k}{d}],$$

and for any $m > 0$, we denote by $\mathcal{F}_m$ the *Farey set of order* m which consists of all rational numbers k'/d' with $k', d' \in \mathbb{Z}$, $0 < d' \leq m$ and $0 \leq k' < d'$. So the running-time T_A of $\mathsf{A}_{\delta, \beta_2, \ell}$ on input (N, e) is certainly lower bounded as $T_A = \Omega(\#\widehat{S}(N, e))$. To prove the theorem, it therefore suffices to show that for any subexponential bound $T = 2^{g(\ell)}$ with $g(\ell) = o(\ell)$, there exist positive constants c and ℓ_0 such that

$$\Pr[\#\widehat{S}(N, e) < T] \leq 2^{-c \cdot \ell} \text{ for all } \ell \geq \ell_0. \tag{8}$$

We will first reduce this problem to several simpler problems. To do so, we introduce the following definitions. For an element $\frac{k'}{d'} \in \mathcal{F}_{2^{\delta \cdot \ell}} \setminus \mathcal{F}_{2^{\delta \cdot \ell - \beta_2}}$, we denote by $A_{\delta, \beta_2, \ell}^-(\frac{k'}{d'})$ the *adjacent* element of $\frac{k'}{d'}$ in $\mathcal{F}_{2^{\delta \cdot \ell}} \setminus \mathcal{F}_{2^{\delta \cdot \ell - \beta_2}}$ in the '$-$' direction, i.e. the largest element of $\mathcal{F}_{2^{\delta \cdot \ell}} \setminus \mathcal{F}_{2^{\delta \cdot \ell - \beta_2}}$ which is strictly less than $\frac{k'}{d'}$. We will be interested in elements $\frac{k'}{d'}$ for which the gap $\frac{k'}{d'} - A_{\delta, \beta_2, \ell}^-(\frac{k'}{d'})$ is 'large'. Accordingly, for positive $\widehat{\Delta}$, let $\widehat{S}_{\delta, \beta_2, \ell}^*(\widehat{\Delta})$ denote the set of all elements $\frac{k'}{d'}$ in $\mathcal{F}_{2^{\delta \cdot \ell}} \setminus \mathcal{F}_{2^{\delta \cdot \ell - \beta_2}}$ such that $\frac{k'}{d'} - A_{\delta, \beta_2, \ell}^-(\frac{k'}{d'}) \geq \widehat{\Delta}$.

We now have the following result.

Lemma 4. *For any $\Delta_{min} > 0$, we have*

$$\Pr[\#\widehat{S}(N, e) < T] \leq T \cdot \#\widehat{S}_{\delta, \beta_2, \ell}^* \left(\frac{\Delta_{min}}{T} \right) \cdot p^* + \Pr\left[\frac{k}{d} - \frac{e}{N} < \Delta_{min} \right], \tag{9}$$

where

$$p^* = \max_{\frac{k'}{d'} \in \mathcal{F}_{2^{\delta \cdot \ell}} \setminus \mathcal{F}_{2^{\delta \cdot \ell - \beta_2}}} \left(\Pr\left[\frac{k}{d} = \frac{k'}{d'} \right] \right).$$

Proof. For a positive integer i, let $\frac{k_i}{d_i}$ denote the ith closest element in $\mathcal{F}_{2^{\delta \cdot \ell}} \setminus \mathcal{F}_{2^{\delta \cdot \ell - \beta_2}}$ to $\frac{k}{d}$ in the '$-$' direction (if i exceeds the number of elements of $\mathcal{F}_{2^{\delta \cdot \ell}} \setminus \mathcal{F}_{2^{\delta \cdot \ell - \beta_2}}$ which are less than $\frac{k}{d}$ then we define $\frac{k_i}{d_i} = 0$). Also, we define $\frac{k_0}{d_0} = \frac{k}{d}$. Then $\#\widehat{S}(N, e) < T$ implies that $\frac{k}{d} - \frac{k_T}{d_T} > \Delta$, where $\Delta = \frac{k}{d} - \frac{e}{N}$, and hence that

$$\sum_{r=0}^{T-1} \left(\frac{k_r}{d_r} - A_{\delta, \beta_2, \ell}^- \left(\frac{k_r}{d_r} \right) \right) > \Delta.$$

It follows that there exists $r^* \in \{0, \ldots, T-1\}$ such that $\frac{k_{r^*}}{d_{r^*}} - A_{\delta, \beta_2, \ell}^-(\frac{k_{r^*}}{d_{r^*}}) > \frac{\Delta}{T}$. So, for any $\Delta_{min} > 0$:

$$\Pr[\#\widehat{S}(N, e) < T]$$
$$\leq \Pr\left[\exists r^* < T : \frac{k_{r^*}}{d_{r^*}} - A_{\delta, \beta_2, \ell}^- \left(\frac{k_{r^*}}{d_{r^*}} \right) > \frac{\Delta}{T} \right]$$
$$= \Pr\left[\left(\exists r^* < T : \frac{k_{r^*}}{d_{r^*}} - A_{\delta, \beta_2, \ell}^- \left(\frac{k_{r^*}}{d_{r^*}} \right) > \frac{\Delta}{T} \right) \text{ and } \Delta \geq \Delta_{min} \right]$$

$$+ \Pr\left[\left(\exists r^* < T : \frac{k_{r^*}}{d_{r^*}} - A^-_{\delta,\beta_2,\ell}\left(\frac{k_{r^*}}{d_{r^*}}\right) > \frac{\Delta}{T}\right) \text{ and } \Delta < \Delta_{min}\right]$$

$$\leq \Pr\left[\exists r^* < T : \frac{k_{r^*}}{d_{r^*}} - A^-_{\delta,\beta_2,\ell}\left(\frac{k_{r^*}}{d_{r^*}}\right) > \frac{\Delta_{min}}{T}\right] + \Pr[\Delta < \Delta_{min}]$$

$$\leq \left(\sum_{r=0}^{T-1} p_r\right) + \Pr[\Delta < \Delta_{min}], \tag{10}$$

where, for each $r \in \{0, \ldots, T-1\}$,

$$p_r = \Pr\left[\frac{k_r}{d_r} - A^-_{\delta,\beta_2,\ell}\left(\frac{k_r}{d_r}\right) > \frac{\Delta_{min}}{T}\right]$$

$$= \Pr\left[\frac{k_r}{d_r} \in \widehat{S}^*_{\delta,\beta_2,\ell}(\Delta_{min}/T)\right] \tag{11}$$

$$\leq \#\widehat{S}^*_{\delta,\beta_2,\ell}(\Delta_{min}/T) \cdot p^*_r, \tag{12}$$

and

$$p^*_r = \max_{\frac{k'}{d'} \in \widehat{S}^*_{\delta,\beta_2,\ell}(\Delta_{min}/T)} \left(\Pr\left[\frac{k_r}{d_r} = \frac{k'}{d'}\right]\right)$$

$$\leq \max_{\frac{k'}{d'} \in \mathcal{F}_{2^{\delta \cdot \ell}} \setminus \mathcal{F}_{2^{\delta \cdot \ell - \beta_2}}} \left(\Pr\left[\frac{k}{d} = \frac{k'}{d'}\right]\right) = p^* \text{ for all } r, \tag{13}$$

where the last inequality follows because the probability that $\frac{k_r}{d_r} = \frac{k'}{d'}$ is equal to the probability that $\frac{k}{d}$ coincides with the rth closest element in $\mathcal{F}_{2^{\delta \cdot \ell}} \setminus \mathcal{F}_{2^{\delta \cdot \ell - \beta_2}}$ to $\frac{k'}{d'}$ in the '+' direction.

Plugging (13) into (12) and the result into (10), the claimed bound on $\Pr[\#\widehat{S}(N, e) < T]$ follows immediately. □

Let us now apply Lemma 4 with the parameter $\Delta_{min} = 2^{-(1/2+\eta_2)\cdot\ell}$ for some positive constant η_2 such that $\eta_2 < 2\cdot\epsilon$ (recall that $\delta = 1/4+\epsilon$), and upper bound each of the terms on the right-hand side of (9). First, combining Lemmas 1, 2 and 3 from the proof of Theorem 4, we conclude that there exists a positive constant c_3 such that

$$\Pr\left[\frac{k}{d} - \frac{e}{N} < \Delta_{min}\right] = O\left(2^{-c_3\cdot\ell}\right). \tag{14}$$

Next, we upper bound $\#\widehat{S}^*_{\delta,\beta_2,\ell}\left(\frac{\Delta_{min}}{T}\right)$. Let us define $n = 2^{\delta\cdot\ell} = 2^{(1/4+\epsilon)\cdot\ell}$. Then we have, using $T = 2^{g(\ell)}$ with $g(\ell)/\ell = o(1)$, that there exist positive constants $\widehat{\epsilon}$ and $\widehat{\ell}_0$ such that

$$\frac{\Delta_{min}}{T} = \frac{1}{2^{(\eta_2+g(\ell)/\ell)\cdot\ell} \cdot 2^{\ell/2}}$$

$$= \frac{2^{2\epsilon\cdot\ell}}{2^{(\eta_2+g(\ell)/\ell)\cdot\ell}} \cdot \left(\frac{1}{2^{2\epsilon\cdot\ell} \cdot 2^{\ell/2}}\right)$$

$$= n^{(2\epsilon-(\eta_2+g(\ell)/\ell))/\delta} \cdot n^{-2}$$

$$\geq n^{-2\cdot(1-\widehat{\epsilon})} \text{ for all } \ell \geq \widehat{\ell}_0, \tag{15}$$

where we have used the fact that $0 < \eta_2 < 2\epsilon$ to obtain the last inequality.

The following lemma shows that 'large' gaps (exponentially larger than n^{-2}) between adjacent elements of the set $\mathcal{F}_n \setminus \mathcal{F}_{n/2^{\beta_2}}$ are very 'rare' (negligible fraction).

Lemma 5. *Fix positive constants β_2, ν, and δ. For any $n = 2^{\delta \cdot \ell}$, and any $\nu' > \nu$ we have*

$$\#\widehat{S}^*_{\delta,\beta_2,\ell}(n^{-(2-\nu')}) = O(n^{2-\nu}).$$

Proof. For brevity, in the following we let $\mathcal{F}$ denote the set $\mathcal{F}_n \setminus \mathcal{F}_{n/2^{\beta_2}}$. For each $x \in \mathcal{F}$, let $d(x) = x - A^-_{\delta,\beta_2,\ell}(x)$ denote the distance to the adjacent element to x in $\mathcal{F}$ in the '-' direction (and $d(0) = 0$). Notice that $\widehat{S}^*_{\delta,\beta_2,\ell}(n^{-(2-\nu)}) = \{x \in \mathcal{F} : d(x) > n^{-(2-\nu)}\}$.

Let X denote a random variable uniformly distributed in $\mathcal{F}$. The expected value of $d(X)$ is

$$E[d(X)] = \frac{1}{\#\mathcal{F}} \cdot \sum_{x \in \mathcal{F}} d(x) < \frac{1}{\#\mathcal{F}},$$

since $\sum_{x \in \mathcal{F}} d(x) = \max_{x \in \mathcal{F}} x < 1$. Now recall that by the Markov inequality, the probability that $d(X)$ exceeds $r \cdot E[d(X)]$ is at most $1/r$ for any $r > 0$. Hence, for any constant $c > 0$, we have:

$$\Pr\left[d(X) \geq \frac{c \cdot n^\nu}{\#\mathcal{F}}\right] \leq \Pr\left[d(X) \geq c \cdot n^\nu \cdot E[d(X)]\right] \leq c^{-1} n^{-\nu}.$$

Since X is uniformly random in $\mathcal{F}$, it follows that

$$\#\widehat{S}^*_{\delta,\beta_2,\ell}\left(c \cdot \frac{n^\nu}{\#\mathcal{F}}\right) \leq c^{-1} \cdot n^{-\nu} \cdot \#\mathcal{F} \leq c^{-1} \cdot n^{2-\nu}, \tag{16}$$

using $\#\mathcal{F} \leq n^2$. Below we will show that $\#\mathcal{F} = \Omega(n^{2-h(\ell)})$ where $h(\ell) = o(\ell)$. Plugging this in (16) we obtain $\#\widehat{S}^*_{\delta,\beta_2,\ell}\left(\frac{n^{\nu+h(\ell)}}{n^2}\right) = O(n^{2-\nu})$ and hence $\#\widehat{S}^*_{\delta,\beta_2,\ell}\left(\frac{n^{\nu'}}{n^2}\right) = O(n^{2-\nu})$ for any any $0 < \nu' < \nu$, as claimed.

It remains to show that $\#\mathcal{F} = \Omega(n^{2-h(\ell)})$ where $h(\ell) = o(\ell)$. Indeed, for every $d' \in [n/2^{\beta_2}, n]$ there are $\varphi(d')$ fractions $k'/d' \in \mathcal{F}$ with $\gcd(k',d') = 1$, and from [7] we know that $\varphi(d') = \Omega(d'/\log\log d') = \Omega(n/\log\log n)$. Since there are $\Omega(n)$ choices for d', we have $\#\mathcal{F} = \Omega(n^2/\log\log n) = \Omega(n^{2-h(\ell)})$ with $h(\ell) = \log\log \delta\ell/(\delta\ell) = o(\ell)$, as required. This completes the proof of the lemma. □

The next lemma shows that, thanks to the uniformly random choice of p and q in $\mathcal{P}_{\ell/2,\beta_1}$ and d in $\mathcal{D}_{\ell,\delta,\beta_2}(\phi)$, the resulting probability distribution of k/d is 'close' to uniform in the set $\mathcal{F}_n \setminus \mathcal{F}_{n/2^{\beta_2}}$.

Lemma 6. *Fix positive constants β_1, β_2 and set $n = 2^{\delta \cdot \ell}$. There exists a positive constant c_7 such that*

$$p^* = \max_{\frac{k'}{d'} \in \mathcal{F}_{2^{\delta \cdot \ell}} \setminus \mathcal{F}_{2^{\delta \cdot \ell - \beta_2}}} \left(\Pr\left[\frac{k}{d} = \frac{k'}{d'}\right]\right) = O\left(n^{-(2-c_7/\log\ell)}\right).$$

Proof. The algorithm RSAKG always generates k and d such that $\gcd(k, d) = 1$ and $\frac{k}{d} \in \mathcal{F}_{2^{\delta \cdot \ell}} \setminus \mathcal{F}_{2^{\delta \cdot \ell - \beta_2}}$. So, in bounding p^* it is enough to consider any fixed k' and d' with $\gcd(k', d') = 1$ and $\frac{k}{d} \in \mathcal{F}_{2^{\delta \cdot \ell}} \setminus \mathcal{F}_{2^{\delta \cdot \ell - \beta_2}}$, and we have $\Pr[k/d = k'/d'] = \Pr[k = k' \text{ and } d = d']$. But from $ed - 1 = k\phi$ we have that $k = -\phi^{-1} \bmod d$ and hence

$$
\begin{aligned}
\Pr\left[\frac{k}{d} = \frac{k'}{d'}\right] &= \Pr[-\phi^{-1} \bmod d = k' \text{ and } d = d'] \\
&= \Pr[-\phi^{-1} \bmod d' = k' \text{ and } d = d'] \\
&= \Pr[-\phi^{-1} \equiv k' \pmod{d'} \text{ and } d = d'] \\
&= \Pr[\phi \equiv (-k')^{-1} \pmod{d'} \text{ and } d = d'] \\
&= \Pr[\phi \equiv (-k')^{-1} \pmod{d'}] \cdot \Pr[d = d' | \phi \equiv (-k')^{-1} \pmod{d'}] \quad (17)
\end{aligned}
$$

We now upper bound each of the two probabilities in the right-hand side of (17). First we upper bound the probability $\Pr[d = d' | \phi \equiv (-k')^{-1} \pmod{d'}]$. To do so, observe that for any fixed ϕ' in the support of ϕ and any fixed $d' \in \mathbb{Z}$ we have

$$
\Pr[d = d' | \phi = \phi'] \leq 1/\#\mathcal{D}_{\ell, \delta, \beta_2}(\phi) \leq p, \quad (18)
$$

for some fixed $p = O\left(n^{-(1 - \frac{\log \ell}{\delta \cdot \ell})}\right)$, using Lemma 3. Letting Φ denote the set of ϕ' in the support of ϕ satisfying $\phi \equiv (-k')^{-1} \pmod{d'}$, we have

$$
\begin{aligned}
\Pr\left[d = d' | \phi \equiv (-k')^{-1} \bmod d'\right] &= \frac{\Pr[d = d' \text{ and } \phi \equiv (-k')^{-1} \pmod{d'}]}{\Pr[\phi \equiv (-k')^{-1} \pmod{d'}]} \\
&= \frac{\sum_{\phi' \in \Phi} \Pr[d = d' \text{ and } \phi = \phi']}{\Pr[\phi \equiv (-k')^{-1} \pmod{d'}]} \\
&= \frac{\sum_{\phi' \in \Phi} \Pr[d = d' | \phi = \phi'] \cdot \Pr[\phi = \phi']}{\Pr[\phi \equiv (-k')^{-1} \pmod{d'}]} \\
&\leq \frac{\sum_{\phi' \in \Phi} p \cdot \Pr[\phi = \phi']}{\Pr[\phi \equiv (-k')^{-1} \pmod{d'}]} \\
&= p = O\left(n^{-(1 - \frac{\log \ell}{\delta \cdot \ell})}\right), \quad (19)
\end{aligned}
$$

where we used (18) to get the inequality in the fourth line.

Fix $\phi' = (-k')^{-1} \bmod d'$. We now focus on upper bounding $\Pr[\phi \equiv \phi' \pmod{d'}]$. First, observe that $\phi < N < 2^\ell$. So

$$
\Pr[\phi \equiv \phi' \bmod d'] \leq \#\{\widehat{\phi} \in \mathbb{Z}_{2^\ell} : \widehat{\phi} \equiv \phi' \pmod{d'}\} \cdot \max_{2^\ell/4 < \widehat{\phi} < 2^\ell} \Pr[\phi = \widehat{\phi}].
$$

But

$$
\#\{\widehat{\phi} \in \mathbb{Z}_{2^\ell} : \widehat{\phi} \equiv \phi' \pmod{d'}\} = \#\{h \in \mathbb{Z} : h \geq 0 \text{ and } \phi' + h \cdot d' < 2^\ell\} \leq \frac{2^\ell}{d'} + 1.
$$

Now recall that $\phi = (p - 1) \cdot (q - 1)$. So, for any $\widehat{\phi} < 2^\ell$, we have using the uniform distribution of (p, q) in $\mathcal{P}^2_{\ell/2, \beta_1}$, that $\Pr[\phi = \widehat{\phi}] = \#\{(p, q) \in \mathcal{P}^2_{\ell/2, \beta_1} : (p - 1)(q - 1) = \widehat{\phi}\}/\#\mathcal{P}^2_{\ell/2, \beta_1} \leq \tau(\widehat{\phi})/\#\mathcal{P}^2_{\ell/2, \beta_1}$, where $\tau(\widehat{\phi})$ denotes the total number of divisors of $\widehat{\phi}$. It is known (see Theorem 317 of [4]) that $\tau(\widehat{\phi}) = O\left(2^{2\log(\widehat{\phi})/\log\log(\widehat{\phi})}\right) = O(n^{c_2/\log\ell})$ for some positive constant c_2, using the fact that $2^\ell/4 < \widehat{\phi} < 2^\ell$. Also, from the prime number theorem (see Theorem 6 of [4]), we have that $c_L \cdot x/\ln x < \pi(x) < c_H \cdot x/\ln x$ for any constants $c_L < 1$ and $c_H > 1$ for all sufficiently large x, where $\pi(x)$ denotes the number of primes less than or equal to x. It follows that $\#\mathcal{P}_{\ell/2,\beta_1} = \pi(2^{\ell/2}) - \pi(2^{\ell/2-\beta_1}) = \Omega(2^{\ell/2}/\ell)$ meaning that $\#\mathcal{P}^2_{\ell/2,\beta_1} = \Omega(2^\ell/\ell^2)$. So we conclude that

$$\Pr[\phi = \widehat{\phi}] = O\left(\frac{n^{c_2/\log\ell}}{2^\ell/\ell^2}\right) = O\left(\frac{n^{c_3/\log\ell}}{2^\ell}\right),$$

for some positive constant c_3. Hence, using the fact that $d' \in [n/2^{\beta_2}, n]$, we have

$$\Pr[\phi \equiv \phi' \bmod d'] = O\left((2^\ell/d' + 1) \cdot \left(\frac{n^{c_3/\log\ell}}{2^\ell}\right)\right) = O\left(n^{-(1-c_3/\log\ell)}\right). \quad (20)$$

Plugging in (19) and (20) into (17), we finally obtain

$$\Pr\left[\frac{k}{d} = \frac{k'}{d'}\right] = O\left(n^{-(2-c_7/\log\ell)}\right)$$

for some positive constant c_7, as claimed. This completes the proof of the lemma. □

Combining (15) and Lemma 5 we know that (with $n = 2^{\delta\cdot\ell}$) there exists a positive constant ν such that

$$\#\widehat{S}^*_{\delta,\beta_2,\ell}(\Delta_{min}/T) = O\left(n^{2-\nu}\right). \quad (21)$$

Using the bounds from Lemma 6 and (21) and the fact that $T = 2^{g(\ell)}$ with $g(\ell)/\ell = o(1)$, we get, for some positive constant ϵ' that

$$T \cdot \#\widehat{S}^*_{\delta,\beta_2,\ell}(\Delta_{min}/T) \cdot p^* = O\left(2^{g(\ell)} \cdot n^{2-\nu/2} \cdot n^{-(2-c_7/\log\ell)}\right) = O\left(2^{-\epsilon'\cdot\ell}\right). \quad (22)$$

Finally, plugging in the bounds from (14) and (22) into (9), we conclude that there exist positive constants c and ℓ_0 such that (8) holds. This completes the proof of the theorem. □

6   Conclusions

We obtained converse results to the Wiener attack on low secret-exponent RSA and its extensions. Our results show that the Wiener approach alone cannot lead to a subexponential-time attack when the RSA secret exponent $d > N^{1/4}$. Obtaining converse results for the lattice-based Boneh-Durfee attack and its extensions, which heuristically succeed in polynomial-time when $d < N^{0.292}$, is currently an interesting open problem. We believe our results are a first step towards a solution to this open problem.

Acknowledgements

We would like to thank Igor Shparlinski for helpful discussions and assistance with the proof of Lemma 3. This work was supported by ARC Discovery Grants DP0345366 and DP0451484.

References

1. J. Blömer and A. May. Low Secret Exponent RSA Revisited. In *CaLC 2001*, volume 2146 of *LNCS*, pages 110–125, Berlin, 2001. Springer-Verlag.
2. D. Boneh and G. Durfee. Cryptanalysis of RSA with private key d less than $N^{0.292}$. *IEEE Trans. on Info. Theory*, 46(4):1339–1349, 2000.
3. A. Dujella. Continued Fractions and RSA with Small Secret Exponents. *Tatra Mt. Math. Publ. (to appear)*, 2004. Available at
   http://www.math.hr/ duje/papers1.html.
4. G.H. Hardy and E.M. Wright. *An Introduction to the Theory of Numbers*. Oxford University Press, London, 1965.
5. W.J. LeVeque. *Fundamentals of Number Theory*. Dover Publications, New York, 1996.
6. L. Lovász. *An Algorithmic Theory of Numbers, Graphs and Convexity*. Society for Industrial and Applied Mathematics, Philadelphia, 1986.
7. J.B. Rosser and L. Schoenfeld. Approximate Formulas for Some Functions of Prime Numbers. *Illinois. J. Math.*, 6:64–94, 1962.
8. E. Verheul and H. van Tilborg. Cryptanalysis of 'Less Short' RSA Secret Exponents. *Applicable Algebra in Engineering, Communication and Computing*, 8:425–435, 1997.
9. I.M. Vinogradov. *Elements of Number Theory*. Dover Publications, New York, 1954.
10. M.J. Wiener. Cryptanalysis of Short RSA Secret Exponents. *IEEE Trans. on Information Theory*, 36:553–558, 1990.

RSA with Balanced Short Exponents
and Its Application to Entity Authentication

Hung-Min Sun[1] and Cheng-Ta Yang[2]

[1] Department of Computer Science,
National Tsing Hua University, Hsinchu, Taiwan 30055
hmsun@cs.nthu.edu.tw
[2] Department of Computer Science and Information Engineering,
National Cheng Kung University

Abstract. In typical RSA, it is impossible to create a key pair (e, d) such that both are simultaneously much shorter than $\phi(N)$. This is because if d is selected first, then e will be of the same order of magnitude as $\phi(N)$, and vice versa. At Asiacrypt'99, Sun et al. designed three variants of RSA using prime factors p and q of unbalanced size. The first RSA variant is an attempt to make the private exponent d short below $N^{0.25}$ and $N^{0.292}$ which are the lower bounds of d for a secure RSA as argued first by Wiener and then by Boneh and Durfee. The second RSA variant is constructed in such a way that both d and e have the same bit-length $\frac{1}{2} \log_2 N + 56$. The third RSA variant is constructed by such a method that allows a trade-off between the lengths of d and e. Unfortunately, at Asiacrypt'2000, Durfee and Nguyen broke the illustrated instances of the first RSA variant and the third RSA variant by solving small roots to trivariate modular polynomial equations. Moreover, they showed that the instances generated by these three RSA variants with unbalanced p and q in fact become more insecure than those instances, having the same sizes of exponents as the former, in RSA with balanced p and q. In this paper, we focus on designing a new RSA variant with balanced d and e, and balanced p and q in order to make such an RSA variant more secure. Moreover, we also extend this variant to another RSA variant in which allows a trade-off between the lengths of d and e. Based on our RSA variants, an application to entity authentication for defending the stolen-secret attack is presented.

Keywords: RSA, Short Exponent Attack, Lattice Reduction, Entity Authentication

1 Introduction

RSA [14], the most popular public key cryptosystem, was announced in 1978 by Rivest, Shamir, and Adleman at MIT. However, RSA suffers from heavy computation because it requires exponentiation operations modulo a large integer N ($N = pq$, a product of two large primes). The RSA encryption and decryption time is almost proportional to the number of bits in the exponent. In order to

S. Vaudenay (Ed.): PKC 2005, LNCS 3386, pp. 199–215, 2005.

reduce the RSA encryption (signature verification) time or decryption (signature generation) time, it is important to choose a small public exponent or a short private exponent. Generally speaking, in standard RSA, encryption are much faster than decryption because the public exponent is usually selected as $2^{16}+1$, while the private exponent is of the same order of magnitude as $\phi(N)$. In some applications, one would like to accelerate decryption process. Thus selecting a short private exponent is preferred. In such a case, the encryption will be cost-inefficient because the size of public exponent will be of the same order of magnitude as $\phi(N)$. Towards to the use of RSA with short private exponent, one must be careful with the short exponent attacks on RSA. In 1990, Wiener [21] first showed that the instances of RSA cryptosystem with short secret exponent ($d < N^{0.25}$) are insecure because one could find the short private exponent d in polynomial time by using the continued fractions algorithm. In 1999, Boneh and Durfee [2] showed how to improve the bound of Wiener up to $d < N^{0.292}$. Their attack is based on the famous L^3-lattice reduction algorithm [10] by Coppersmith [4] on finding small roots of particular bivariate modular polynomial equations.

At Asiacrypt'99, Sun, Yang, and Laih [17, 18] designed three variants of RSA using prime factors p and q of unbalanced size. The first RSA variant is an attempt to make the private exponent d short below Wiener's bound [21] and Boneh and Durfee's bound [2]. In this variant, the RSA system is constructed from p and q of different sizes in order to defend against the well-known short private exponent attacks. They claimed that when p and q are unbalanced enough, d can be even smaller than $N^{0.25}$. A suggested choice of parameters is: p of 256 bits, q of 768 bits, and d of 192 bits. Note that in this variant, e is determined as that in typical RSA, hence e is of 1024 bits. The second RSA variant is constructed in such a way that both d and e have the same bit-length $\frac{1}{2}\log_2 N + 56$ by choosing unbalanced p of $\frac{1}{2}\log_2 N - 112$ bits and q of $\frac{1}{2}\log_2 N + 112$ bits respectively. The motivation of this variant is for balancing and minimizing both public and private exponents. A suggested choice of parameters is: p of 400 bits, q of 624 bits, d of 568 bits, and e of 568 bits. The third RSA variant is constructed by such a method that allows a trade-off between the lengths of d and e (that is $\log_2 e + \log_2 d \approx \log_2 N + l_k$, where l_k is a predetermined constant, e.g., 112) under the limitation of $\log_2 p + \log_2 d \leq \log_2 N$ (assuming $p < q$). The purpose of this variant is for rebalancing the computation cost between encryption and decryption. By this method, one may shift the work from decryptor to encryptor. An illustrated instance of RSA has the parameters: p of 256 bits, q of 768 bits, d of 256 bits, and e of 880 bits. Unfortunately, Durfee and Nguyen [5] broke the illustrated instances of the first RSA variant and the third RSA variant by solving small roots to trivariate modular polynomial equations. They also showed that the instances generated by these three RSA variants with unbalanced p and q in fact become more insecure than those instances, having the same sizes of exponents as the former, in RSA with balanced p and q. In this paper, we are interested in enhancing the security of Sun et al.'s RSA variants by using balanced p and q. It is clear that for the first RSA variant, the improved one with balanced p and q is in fact the standard RSA. Hence, it is impossible to make d short below Boneh and Durfee's bound and Wiener's bound. Therefore, we will not focus on the first variant. For the second RSA variant, it is unable to make p and q balanced because p is of $\frac{1}{2}\log_2 N - 112$ bits and q is of $\frac{1}{2}\log_2 N + 112$ bits in this variant. For the third RSA variant, the possible constructed RSA with balanced p and q are only those instances of RSA with d of $\frac{1}{2}\log_2 N$ bits and e of $\frac{1}{2}\log_2 N + l_k$ bits. This is due to the limitation of $\log_2 p + \log_2 d \leq \log_2 N$. In this paper, we focus on designing a new RSA variant with balanced p and q, and balanced d and e in order to make such an RSA variant more secure against the Durfee-Nguyen attack and the other existing attacks. Moreover, we also extend our variant to another RSA variant in which p and q are balanced and $\log_2 e + \log_2 d \approx \log_2 N + l_k$. Compared with RSA using CRT-based decryption (RSA-CRT for short), our schemes seem not to provide better performance for decryption. However it is still an interesting topic like those short exponent attacks [2, 21] working on the standard RSA. Moreover, based on our schemes, we present an application to entity authentication for defending the stolen-secret attack. On the contrary, RSA-CRT can not be applied to the application. We refer the readers to Section 7.

This paper is organized as follows. In Section 2, we review the standard RSA, RSA-CRT, Sun et al.'s RSA variants, and recall some well-known attacks on RSA with short private exponent. In Section 3, we present a new RSA variant with balanced p and q, and balanced e and d; and show the flexibility for constructing such an RSA variant. In Section 4, we analyze the security of this proposed RSA variant. In Section 5, we extend the proposed RSA variant in Section 3 to another RSA variant in which p and q are balanced and $\log_2 e + \log_2 d \approx \log_2 N + l_k$. In Section 6, we show the experimental results of our implementations for our schemes. In Section 7, we compare our RSA variants with RSA-CRT, and give an application based on our RSA variants. Finally, we conclude this paper in Section 8.

2   Preliminaries

2.1   Description of Notations

The notations in Table 1 are used throughout this paper.

2.2   The Standard RSA and RSA-CRT

In standard RSA, $N = p \times q$ is the product of two large primes p and q. The public exponent e and private exponent d satisfy $e \times d \equiv 1 \bmod \phi(N)$, where $\phi(N) = (p-1)(q-1)$ is the Euler totient function of N. Here, N is called the RSA modulus. The public key is the pair (N, e) that is used for encryption (or signature verification): $c = m^e \bmod N$. The private key d is to enable decryption of ciphertext (or signature generation): $m = c^d \bmod N$. Traditionally, we select two primes (of 512 bits) p and q first, and then multiply them to obtain N (about 1024 bits). Next, we pick the public exponent e first, and then determine the

Table 1. Notations.

p, q :	The two large primes of RSA.
N :	The product of two large prime factors p and q, i.e. $N = p \times q$.
e, d :	The public exponent and private exponent, $ed \equiv 1 \bmod \phi(N)$.
Δ :	The prime difference, $\Delta = |p - q|$.
δ :	$d = N^\delta$.
ϖ :	$e = N^\varpi$.
γ :	$|p - q| = N^\gamma$.
l_X :	The bit-length of a variable X.

private exponent d by $d \equiv e^{-1} \bmod \phi(N)$, or we select the private exponent d first, and then compute the public exponent e by $e \equiv d^{-1} \bmod \phi(N)$. For the deduction mentioned above, either e or d is of the same order of magnitude as $\phi(N)$. Instead of computing $m = c^d \bmod N$, RSA-CRT computes $m_1 = c^{d_p} \bmod p$, and $m_2 = c^{d_q} \bmod q$, where $d_p = d \bmod p - 1$ and $d_q = d \bmod q - 1$, then applying the Chinese Remainder Theorem, one may easily recover m by m_1 and m_2.

2.3 Sun, Yang, and Laih's RSA Variants

At Asiacrypt'99, Sun et al. [17, 18] designed three variants of RSA using prime factors p and q of unbalanced size. The first variant of RSA is an attempt to make the private exponent d short below Wiener's bound and Durfee and Nguyen's bound. In this variant, the RSA system is designed by unbalanced p and q in order to defend against all existing attacks on short private exponent. The second variant of RSA is an attempt to balance and minimize both public and private exponents. It is constructed in such a way that both d and e have the same size of $\frac{1}{2} \log_2 N + 56$ bits by choosing unbalanced p of $\frac{1}{2} \log_2 N - 112$ bits and q of $\frac{1}{2} \log_2 N + 112$ bits respectively. The third variant of RSA is an attempt to rebalance the computation cost between encryption and decryption. By this variant, one may shift the work from decryptor to encryptor. It is constructed by such a method that allows a trade-off between the lengths of d and e (that is $\log_2 e + \log_2 d \approx \log_2 N + 112$) under the limitation of $\log_2 p + \log_2 d \leq \log_2 N$. Due to the limit of space, we describe the details of these three RSA variants in Appendix A.

Very soon, Durfee and Nguyen [5] broke the illustrated instances of the first RSA variant and the third RSA variant. Moreover, they showed that the instances generated by these three RSA variants with unbalanced p and q in fact become more insecure than those instances, having the same sizes of exponents as the former, in RSA with balanced p and q. We describe their attack later.

2.4 Attacks on RSA with Short Private Exponent

Wiener's Attack and Its Extensions. Wiener's attack [21] is based on continued fractions algorithm to find the numerator and denominator of a fraction in polynomial time when a sufficiently close estimate of the fraction is known. He showed that the RSA system can be totally broken if the private exponent is up to approximately one-quarter as many bits as the modulus under both p and q of approximately the same size. For simplicity, we slightly modify Wiener's attack in the following way. Since $ed \equiv 1 \bmod \phi(N)$, there exists a k, $\gcd(d,k) = 1$, such that $ed = k\phi(N) + 1$. So, $|\frac{e}{\phi(N)} - \frac{k}{d}| = \frac{1}{d\phi(N)}$. Hence, $\frac{k}{d}$ is an approximation of $\frac{e}{\phi(N)}$. We can rewrite the equation: $ed = k\phi(N)+1$ as: $ed = k(N-(p+q)+1)+1$. As pointed out by Pinch [12], if $p < q < 2p$ and $d < \frac{1}{3}N^{0.25}$, then $p+q-1 < 3\sqrt{N}$ and $k < d < \frac{1}{3}N^{0.25}$. Using N in place of $\phi(N)$, we obtain:

$$|\frac{e}{N} - \frac{k}{d}| = \frac{k(p+q-1-\frac{1}{k})}{dN} \leq \frac{1}{dN^{0.25}} < \frac{1}{3d^2} < \frac{1}{2d^2}.$$

Thus $\frac{k}{d}$ can be found because it is one of the $\log N$ convergents of the continued fraction for $\frac{e}{N}$.

The extension of Wiener's attack was proposed by Verheul and Tilborg [19]. When $d > N^{0.25}$, their attack needs to do an exhaustive search for about $2t + 8$ bits, where $t \approx \log_2(\frac{d}{N^{0.25}})$. In addition, Weger [20] further proposed another extension of Wiener's attack in the case when the prime difference of N, $\Delta = |p - q|$, is small. Let the prime difference $\Delta = |p - q| = N^\gamma$ for $0.25 \leq \gamma \leq 0.5$, and $d = N^\delta$. Weger showed that if $\delta < \frac{3}{4} - \gamma$, one could find the short private exponent d using Wiener's attack. Thus Weger improved Wiener's bound from $\delta < 0.25$ to $\delta < \frac{3}{4} - \gamma$.

The Boneh-Durfee Attack and Its Extension. Based on solving the small inverse problem, Boneh and Durfee [2] proposed another attack on RSA with short private exponent, which leads to a better bound than that proposed by Wiener [21]. They concluded that if $e \approx N$ and $d < N^{0.292}$, then the private exponent d can be found efficiently.

In typical RSA system, $ed = k\phi(N) + 1$, $e = N^\varpi$ and $d = N^\delta$. So, $ed = k(p-1)(q-1) + 1 = k((N+1) - (p+q)) + 1$. Let $A = N + 1$, $s = -(p+q)$, and $t = -k$. Then $ed + t(A + s) = 1$. Thus, $t(A + s) \equiv 1 \pmod{e}$ and we can bound s and t by $|t| < 3e^{1+\frac{\delta-1}{\varpi}}$ and $|s| < 2e^{\frac{1}{(2\varpi)}}$. Boneh and Durfee took $\varpi \approx 1$ and ignored small constants, and ended up with the following problem: finding integer t and s such that $t(A + s) \equiv 1 \pmod{e}$ where $|s| < e^{0.5}$ and $|t| < e^\delta$.

Now, we have a simple review of the lattice theory first. Let $v_1, ..., v_w \in Z^n$ be linearly independent vectors with $w \leq n$. A lattice L spanned by $\langle v_1, ..., v_w \rangle$ is the set of all integer combinations of $v_1, ..., v_w$. We denote by $v_1^*, ..., v_w^*$ the vectors obtained by applying the Gram-Scmidt process to the vectors $v_1, ..., v_w$. We define the determinant of the lattice L as $det(L) := \prod_{i=1}^{w} ||v_i^*||$, where $||.||$ denotes the Euclidean norm on vectors. We say that the lattice is full rank if $w = n$. For a lattice L spanned by $\langle v_1, ..., v_w \rangle$, the LLL algorithm runs in polynomial time and produces a new basis $\langle r_1, ..., r_w \rangle$ of L as $||r_1|| \leq 2^{\frac{w}{2}} det(L)^{\frac{1}{w}}$ and $||r_2|| \leq 2^{\frac{(w-1)}{2}} det(L)^{\frac{1}{(w-1)}}$, r_1 and r_2 are two shortest vectors in the new basis.

Boneh and Durfee solved the small inverse problem by using Coppersmith's approach [4]. Recall that let $h(x, y) \in Z[x, y]$ be a polynomial which is a sum of at most w monomials. Suppose that (1) $h(x_0, y_0) \equiv 0 \bmod e^m$ for some positive integer m where $|x_0| < X$ and $|y_0| < Y$, and (2) $\|h(xX, yY)\| < e^m/\sqrt{w}$, then $h(x_0, y_0) = 0$ holds over the integers.

The small inverse problem is the following: given a polynomial $f(x, y) = x(A + y) - 1$, find an (x_0, y_0) as $f(x_0, y_0) \equiv 0 \pmod e$ where $|x_0| < e^\delta$ and $|y_0| < e^{0.5}$. We would find a polynomial with a small norm that has (x_0, y_0) as a root modulo e^m for some positive integer m. Boneh and Durfee defined the polynomials $g_{i,k}(x, y) = x^i f^k(x, y)e^{m-k}$ and $h_{j,k}(x, y) = y^j f^k(x, y)e^{m-k}$, for $k = 0, ..., m$, where $g_{i,k}(x, y)$ is called x-shifts and $h_{j,k}(x, y)$ is called y-shifts. For each k, they used $g_{i,k}(xX, yY)$ for $i = 0, ..., m - k$ and used $h_{j,k}(xX, yY)$ for $j = 0, ..., t$, where t is minimized based on m. Observe that the matrix is triangular and has a dimension $\frac{(m+1)(m+2)}{2} + t(m + 1)$. The determinant of the lattice can be easily computed as the product of the diagonal entries

$$det_x = e^{m(m+1)(m+2)/3} \cdot X^{m(m+1)(m+2)/3} \cdot Y^{m(m+1)(m+2)/6}$$
$$det_y = e^{tm(m+1)/2} \cdot X^{tm(m+1)/2} \cdot Y^{t(m+1)(m+t+1)/2}.$$

Let $det(L) = det_x \cdot det_y$. By Ignoring the denominator in order to simplify the derivations, we get the condition $det(L) < e^{mw}$. Finally, on the basis of the lattice theory and Coppersmith's approach, We deduce that

$$\delta < \frac{7}{6} - \frac{1}{3}\sqrt{7 + \frac{16}{m} + \frac{4}{m^2}} + \frac{5}{6m}.$$

For large m, this converges to $\delta < \frac{7}{6} - \frac{\sqrt{7}}{3} \approx 0.285$. By working on a sub-lattice, the bound on δ can be improved to $\delta < 1 - \frac{\sqrt{2}}{2} \approx 0.292$.

Another improvement was proposed by Wager [20]. He showed that RSA is insecure when the length δ of the private exponent is in $2 - 4\gamma < \delta < 1 - \sqrt{2\gamma - \frac{1}{2}}$, where $|p - q| = N^\gamma$ and $d = N^\delta$.

The Cubic Attack. Here, we review the cubic attack in [17, 18]. In RSA, $N = pq$ and $ed = k(p - 1)(q - 1) + 1$, therefore, the modular equations are $k(p - 1)(q - 1) + 1 \equiv 0 \pmod e$ and $pq \equiv N \pmod e$. According to the above two equations, we can obtain one cubic equation with two variables k and p : $k(p - 1)(N - p) + p \equiv 0 \pmod e$. If $\log_2 k + \log_2 p < \frac{1}{3}\log_2 e$, we can solve such a cubic equation heuristically using Coppersmith's technique [4].

2.5   The Durfee-Nguyen Attack and Its Extension

Extending the Boneh-Durfee attack, Durfee and Nguyen [5] attacked Sun et al.'s RSA variants by solving small roots to trivariate modular polynomial equations using Coppersmith's lattice technique. From the RSA equation $ed = k\phi(N) + 1 = k(p - 1)(q - 1) + 1$, let $A = N + 1$, it implies $1 + k(A - p - q) \equiv 0 \pmod e$.

Table 2. Largest δ (where $d < N^{\delta}$) for which Durfee-Nguyen's attack can be completed.

	$\log_N(e)$						
	1.0	0.9	0.86	0.8	0.7	0.6	0.55
0.5	0.284	0.323	0.339	0.363	0.406	0.451	0.475
0.4	0.296	0.334	0.350	0.374	0.415	0.460	0.483_{II}
$\log_N(p)$ 0.3	0.334	0.369	0.384	0.406	0.446	0.487	0.510
0.25	0.364_{I}	0.398	0.412_{III}	0.433	0.471	0.511	0.532
0.2	0.406	0.437	0.450	0.470	0.505	0.542	0.562
0.1	0.539	0.563	0.573	0.588	0.615	0.644	0.659

They treated the above equation as a trivariate equation modular e with three unknown variables, k, p, q, with the special property that the product pq of two of them is the known quantity N. Here, the problem is regarded as given a polynomial $f(x, y, z) = x(A + y + z) - 1$, finding an integer solution (x_0, y_0, z_0) satisfying the equation $f(x_0, y_0, z_0) \equiv 0 \pmod{e}$ where $|x_0| < X$, $|y_0| < Y$, $|z_0| < Z$, and $y_0 z_0 = N$. Note that the bounds are $X \approx \frac{ed}{N}$, $Y \approx p$, and $Z \approx q$.

To search for low-norm integer linear combinations of these polynomials of the form $e^{m-v} x^{u1} y^{u2} z^{u3} \cdot f^v(x, y, z)$, they chose the polynomials $g_{k,i,b}(x, y, z) := e^{m-k} x^i y^a z^b f^k(x, y, z)$, for $k = 0..(m-1)$, $i = 1..(m-k)$, and $b = 0, 1$; and, $h_{k,j}(x, y, z) := e^{m-k} y^{a+j} f^k(x, y, z)$, for $k = 0..m$ and $j = 0..t$, then fixed an integer m, and let a and $t > 0$ be integers which would be optimized later. Following the LLL algorithm [4], they obtained two short vectors corresponding to polynomials $h_1(x, y, z)$, $h_2(x, y, z)$ that had (k, p, q) as a root over the integers; and letting $z = \frac{y}{N}$, they deduced these polynomials to bivariate polynomials $H_1(x, y)$ and $H_2(x, y)$ which had (k, p) as a solution. Taking the resultant $Res_x(H_1(x, y), H_2(x, y))$ produced an univariate polynomial $H(y)$ which had p as a root. They summarized the largest possible δ for which their attack could succeed as shown in Table 2.

From Table 2, we conclude that instances from RSA with unbalanced p and q are in fact more insecure than those from RSA with unbalanced p and q. An improvement of Durfee-Nguyen's largest δ was proposed by Hong et al. in [7]. They showed how to improve the bound from 0.483 to 0.486 when $\log_N(p) \approx 0.4$, $\log_N(e) \approx 0.55$ using Coppersmith's theorem [4]. Because their attack is very similar to the Durfee-Nguyen attack, we omit to review the details of their attack.

3   New RSA Variant with Balanced Exponents and Balanced Prime Factors

Sun et al.'s second variant is designed for balancing and minimizing both public and private exponents. An illustrated instance of this variant was given in [17, 18]. The illustrated instance has parameters: p of 400 bits, q of 624 bits, d of 568 bits, and e of 568 bits. Although this instance is still secure against the Durfee-Nguyen attack, however, as shown in Table 2, an instance of RSA with the same size of d and e, and balanced p and q is more secure than the illustrated instance in [17, 18]. Unfortunately, it is impossible to make p and q balanced in Sun et al.'s second variant because p is of $\frac{1}{2}\log_2 N - 112$ bits and q is of $\frac{1}{2}\log_2 N + 112$ bits. In this section, we present a new RSA variant in which d and e are balanced, and p and q are also balanced.

3.1   The Proposed Scheme

Our scheme is based on the Extended Euclidean algorithm [6]. Recall that for two integers $a, b > 1$, if $\gcd(a, b) = 1$, then we can find a unique pair (u_h, v_h) satisfying $au_h - bv_h = 1$, where $(h-1)b < u_h < hb$ and $(h-1)a < v_h < ha$, for any integer $h \geq 1$. Our method is as follows:

Scheme A: input: l_N and w; output: e, d, p, q and N.

Step 1. Randomly select a prime p of $\frac{1}{2}l_N$ bits.

Step 2. Randomly select a number k', such that $k'(p-1)$ is of $\frac{1}{2}l_N + w$ bits, where w is a security parameter, e.g., $w = 56$.

Step 3. Randomly select a number d of $\frac{1}{2}l_N + w$ bits, such that $\gcd(k'(p-1), d) = 1$.

Step 4. Determine u', v' such that $du' - k'(p-1)v' = 1$, where $0 < u' < k'(p-1)$ and $0 < v' < d$.

Step 5. If $l_{v'} < \frac{1}{2}l_N + w$, then assign $u' = u' + k'(p-1)$ and $v' = v' + d$.

Step 6. Try to find $v' = k''q'$, where $l_{k''} = w$ and $q' + 1$ is a prime. If this fails, go to Step 3.

Step 7. Let $e = u'$, $q = q' + 1$, and $N = pq$.

The algorithm will generate RSA instances in which both p and q are approximately $\frac{1}{2}\log_2 N$ bits long, and both e and d are approximately $(\frac{1}{2}\log_2 N + w)$ bits long. Also the resulting e and d will satisfy $ed = k'k''(p-1)(q-1)+1 = k\phi(N)+1$, where $k = k'k''$. Note that the prime p generated in Step 1 can be determined arbitrarily, e.g., by selecting a strong prime p, but the prime q generated in Step 7 cannot. Fortunately, for an RSA key the requirement that p and q are strong primes is no longer needed due to [15]. As an example, we construct an instance of RSA that p is of 512 bits, q is of 513 bits, and e and d are 568 bits (assigning $\log_2 N \approx 1024$, and $w = 56$). We show this instance in Appendix B.

3.2   Feasibility for the Algorithm

In this section, we show that the proposed algorithm in Section 3.1 is feasible. Without loss of generality, we assume $\log_2 N \approx 1024$, and $w = 56$. The critical step in the above algorithm is Step 6. Because v' is about of 568 or 569 bits, we will try to find a lower bound for the probability of that being given a random number x of 568 or 569 bits, it can be expressed in the form $x = yz$ satisfying $l_x = 568$ or 569, $l_y = 56$, $l_z = 512$ or 513 or 514, and $z + 1$ being a prime.

Theorem 1. *The probability that given a randomly selected number x of 568 or 569 bits, it can be expressed in the form $x = yz$ satisfying $l_x = 568$ or 569, $l_y = 56$, $l_z = 512$ or 513 or 514, and $z + 1$ being a prime is much higher than* $\frac{1}{387618}$.

Proof. We omit the details due to the limit of space.

Based on Theorem 1, the existence and its probability for a random number which can go through Step 6 in the proposed scheme has been evaluated. Now we consider the cost for factoring a 568-bit v' into the form: $k''q'$, where $l_{k''} = 56$, in Step 6. Given a number v', it is easy for us to find all prime factors of v' which are less than 56 bits by some well-known factoring algorithms, such as ECM algorithm [8]. Then we can try to combine these prime factors to form a 56-bit k'' in polynomial time.

4   Security Considerations

In this section, we analyze our scheme to thwart the previous well-known attacks on short private exponent, including Wiener's attack [21], the Boneh-Durfee attack [2], the Durfee-Nguyen attack [5], the cubic attack [17, 18], and their extensions [7, 19, 20].

Defending Against Wiener's Attack. We will check the security of our RSA variant according to Wiener's attack. It is clear that

$$\left| \frac{e}{N} - \frac{k}{d} \right| = \frac{k}{d} \times \frac{p + q - 1 - \frac{1}{k}}{N} > \frac{k}{d} \frac{q}{N}.$$

In our variant, p and q are about of 512 bits, and e and d are about of 568 bits, so $2^{511} \le p < 2^{512}$, $2^{111} \le k < 2^{112}$, $2^{567} \le e < 2^{568}$, $2^{567} \le d < 2^{568}$. Now, we can obtain $\left| \frac{e}{N} - \frac{k}{d} \right| > \frac{k}{d} \frac{q}{N} > \frac{2^{111}}{2^{568}} \times \frac{2^{511}}{2^{1024}} = \frac{1}{2^{970}} \gg \frac{1}{2d^2} \approx \frac{1}{2^{1136}}$. Thus, Wiener's attack does not apply to our scheme.

Defending Against the Boneh-Durfee Attack and the Durfee-Nguyen Attack. Following Boneh and Durfee's approach, let $A = N + 1$, $s = -(p + q)$, and $t = -k$. Thus $t(A + s) \equiv 1 \pmod{e}$. Let $|s| < e^\alpha$ and $|t| < e^\beta$. The sufficient condition for solving the small inverse problem is: $4\alpha(2\beta + \alpha - 1) < 3(1 - \beta - \alpha)^2$.

In our example, p and q are about of 512 bits, and e and d are about of 568 bits, therefore, $2^{511} \le p < 2^{512}$, $2^{111} \le k < 2^{112}$, $2^{567} \le e < 2^{568}$, $2^{511} \le d < 2^{512}$. We can calculate $|s| = |p + q| = e^\alpha$, $|k| = e^\beta$, i.e. $2^{512} < (2^{568})^\alpha$, $2^{112} < (2^{568})^\beta$, we can get $\alpha \approx \frac{512}{568}$, $\beta \approx \frac{112}{568}$ respectively. It is clear that $4\alpha(2\beta + \alpha - 1) = 1.06645 \gg 0.02916 = 3(1 - \beta - \alpha)^2$. So, the Boneh-Durfee attack cannot succeed.

Next, we examine the largest δ (where $d < N^\delta$) for which the Durfee-Nguyen attack [5] can succeed. Our p is of 512 bits, then $\log_N(p) \approx 0.5$; e is of 568 bits, then $\log_N(e) \approx 0.55$; and d is of 568 bits. So, we can figure out $d \approx N^{\frac{568}{1024}} \approx N^{0.55} > N^{0.475}$. So our RSA variant is secure against the Durfee-Nguyen attack.

Finally, we check the prime difference that Weger proposed.
$2 - 4\gamma = 2 - 4 \times \frac{1}{2} = 0$ and $1 - \sqrt{2\gamma - \frac{1}{2}} = 1 - \sqrt{2 \times \frac{1}{2} - \frac{1}{2}} = 1 - \sqrt{0.5} = 0.29289$. In our RSA variant, the private exponent is of 568 bits. Therefore, $\delta = \frac{568}{1024} = 0.5546875$ which is out of the range of $0 < \delta < 0.29289$. So our RSA variant is secure against Weger's attack [20].

Defending Against the Cubic Attack. According to Section 2.3.3 for the cubic attack, in our variant, k is of 112 bits, p is of 512 bits, and e is of 568 bits. It is clear that $\log_2 k + \log_2 p \approx 112 + 512 = 624 >> \frac{1}{3}\log_2 e \approx \frac{1}{3} \times 568$, In such a case, the cubic attack cannot work.

Defending Against an Exhaustive Search. One can check a guess for k since $\phi(N) = N + 1 - (p+q) \equiv (-k)^{-1} \pmod{e}$ and so $(p+q) \equiv N + 1 + k^{-1} \pmod{e}$. Since $p + q < e$, this gives $p + q$ exactly and then we can test the guess by checking whether $a^{N+1-(p+q)} \equiv 1 \pmod{N}$ for a random value a. In our proposed scheme, k is large enough (112 bits), an exhaustive search method can not work effectively.

Defending Against Other Attacks. We also consider the extensions of the above attacks, including the Verheul and Tilborg attack [19], the Weger attack [20], and Hong *et al.*' attack [7]. There is no evidence showing that the proposed scheme is insecure under these extensions. We also try to construct new polynomial equations in which we expect to solve their roots using Coppersmith's lattice technique. So far we are unable to find any useful polynomial equation to do that. Note that it is still an open problem if there exists any polynomial-time algorithm for breaking Sun et al.'s second RSA variant. This also implies that so far no feasible attacks can work well on the new RSA variant because breaking the new RSA variant would be more difficult than breaking Sun et al.'s second RSA variant.

5   New RSA Variant with Balanced Prime Factors and Trade-Off Exponents

Sun et al.'s third RSA variant is designed for rebalancing the computation cost between encryption and decryption. By this method, one may shift the work from decryptor to encryptor due to $\log_2 e + \log_2 d \approx \log_2 N + l_k$, where l_k is a predetermined constant, e.g., $l_k = 112$. However, the constructed RSA has the limitation of $\log_2 p + \log_2 d \leq \log_2 N$ (assuming $p < q$). That means that if we make both p and q have the same length, $\frac{1}{2}\log_2 N$, the instances that can be constructed by Sun et al.'s scheme are only those instances whose d are of $\frac{1}{2}\log_2 N$ bits, and e are of $\frac{1}{2}\log_2 N + l_k$ bits. Note that in the past, Sakai et al. [16] proposed a key generation algorithm for RSA which provides the similar goal as Sun et al.'s third variant. Regrettably, their algorithm is insecure due to [17, 18]. In this section, we present a new RSA variant with balanced p and q and $\log_2 e + \log_2 d \approx \log_2 N + l_k$ without any other constraint. Without loss of generality, we assume $d < e$. If $d > e$, we need only interchange them.

Scheme B: input: l_N, l_d, and l_k; output: e, d, p, q and N.

Step 1. Randomly select a prime p of $\frac{1}{2}l_N$ bits.

Step 2. Randomly select a number k' such that $k'(p-1)$ is of $l_N + l_k - l_d$ bits, where l_k is a security parameter, e.g., $l_k = 112$, and l_d is the bit-length of d.

Step 3. Randomly select a number d of l_d bits, such that $\gcd(k'(p-1), d) = 1$.

Step 4. Determine u', v' such that $du' - k'(p-1)v' = 1$, where $0 < u' < k'(p-1)$ and $0 < v' < d$.

Step 5. If $l_{v'} < l_d$, then assign $u' = u' + k'(p-1)$ and $v' = v' + d$.

Step 6. (Case I) If $l_d > \frac{1}{2}l_N$, try to find $v' = k''q'$, where $l_{k''} = (l_d - \frac{1}{2}l_N)$ and $q' + 1$ is a prime. If it fails, go to Step 3; else $e = u'$, $q = q' + 1$, and $N = pq$.

(Case II) If $l_d \leq \frac{1}{2}l_N$, try to find $k' = k''t$, where $l_{k''} = l_k$ and $tv' + 1$ is a prime. If it fails, go to Step 3; else $e = u'$, $q = tv' + 1$, and $N = pq$.

Here we omit to analyze the feasibility for this algorithm and the security for this variant because these analyses are very similar to those of Scheme A. Instead, we illustrate two instances constructed from this variant. The first instance has p and q of 512 bits, d of 540 bits, and e of 596 bits; and the other one has p and q of 512 bits primes, d of 512 bits, and e of 624 bits. These two examples are shown in Appendix C.

6   Implementations for the Proposed Schemes

In order to show that our schemes are actually feasible, we implemented our algorithms and measured the average running time for three different sizes of RSA. The main component in our implementations is the factorization method. In our implementations, we select Pollard $p - 1$ method [13] as our fundamental factorization method. Furthermore, the programming language used for our implementations is C under NTL with GMP (GNU Multi-Precision library) on Windows systems using Cygwin tools. The machine we used is a personal computer (PC) with 2.8GHz CPU and 512MB DRAM. We consider three different cases for comparisons. The first case has p and q of 512 bits, d and e of 568 bits; the second case has p and q of 512 bits, d of 540 bits, and e of 596 bits; the third case has p and q of 512 bits, d of 512 bits, and e of 624 bits.

Table 3 shows the results and conditions for generating RSA key pairs in our schemes. The item "B_Bound", a predetermined integer using the Pollard $p - 1$ method, denotes the upper bound for all prime power divisors of $p - 1$. This value is chosen by experience in our program. The item "AverageTime" denotes the average running time for each case upon testing 100 samples. The item "AverageLoopNum" counts the number of loops running from Step 3 to Step 6. Note that what we are doing in Step 6 of our implementations is only to find small factors of v' and then try to compose part of these small factors into what we need. According to our experiments, if one tries to factor v' completely, then "AverageLoopNum" will be smaller, but "AverageTime" will be longer because

Table 3. Experimental results in PC platform of 2.8GHz CPU, 512M DRAM.

	Scheme A	Scheme B	
Input (Bit-length)	$l_N = 1024$ $l_e = 568$ $l_d = 568$ $w = 56$	$l_N = 1024$ $l_e = 596$ $l_d = 540$ $l_k = 112$	$l_N = 1024$ $l_e = 624$ $l_d = 512$ $l_k = 112$
B_Bound	150	30	
AverageTime (sec)	1060.93	20.61	0.46
AverageLoopNum	290490	29273	319

the time will be dominated by the factorization. From Table 3, we know that the more balanced e and d are, the more time-consuming our algorithms are. The most time-consuming case is exactly Scheme A. The average time for generating such a key pair is about 16 minutes under our implementations. This may be heavy for the end user's use. However, it can be much improved by some parallel techniques and/or high-end computers in the case when the RSA key pair must be generated and issued by centralized control. For example, a trusted CA issues smart cards in which every user's private key, public key, and the corresponding certificate are embedded by a smart card writer.

7   Discussion and Application

Comparing with the typical RSA with small e and randomly determined d, Scheme A is about twice faster in decryption, but the public exponent e is about of $\frac{1}{2}l_N$ bits. On the other hand, RSA-CRT achieves 4 times faster and can choose small e, e.g. $e=2^{16}+1$. Thus, our variants can not provide better performance than RSA-CRT. However RSA-CRT needs to keep more secrets (d_p, d_q, p, and q) than our schemes. Besides, RSA-CRT usually brings on some additional security problems [9]. In the following, we further propose an application, based on RSA, to entity authentication for defending a type of attack, called the stolen-secret attack. It is remarked that our RSA variants can be applied to realize such an application, while RSA-CRT can not.

With two-party authentication protocols in place, it would be easy for one participant to establish trusted communication with the other. In general, there are three approaches to designing authentication protocols. The first approach is based on the public-key cryptosystem (involving signature mechanism). This approach works under PKI environment and needs a trusted CA to support. The second approach is based on a shared password which is easy to remember by user. This approach usually need to be designed to defend the dictionary attack. The third approach is based on a shared secret-key of a symmetric cryptosystem. This approach uses symmetric-key encryption to validate the identity of protocol participants. Here we consider the *stolen-secret attack* in which an adversary who has stolen the secret (a private key, or a shared password, or a shared secret-key) from one party can use it directly to masquerade as the other party. Among these three approaches, the first approach is secure against the stolen-secret attack because one party's private key leaked will not lead to a forgery of the other party. However, it is only suitable for the environment with CA and PKI supporting. For the password-based protocol, because two parties share a common password, therefore it is insecure against the stolen-secret attack. An improvement for this approach is called the verifier-based protocol in which one party (client) keeps a password and the other one (server) keeps the corresponding verifier (usually it is a hashed image of the password). Thus if the verifier is leaked, it will not lead a forgery of the client. However, if the password is leaked (on the client side), this will lead to a successful forgery of the server because the verifier can be easily computed from password. As for the third approach, it is clear that the stolen-secret attack can work well.

As mentioned above, the stolen-secret attack is a baffling problem in authentication protocols. Here we attempt to enhance the secret-key based protocol to defend the stolen-secret attack. In general, RSA system generates a key pair (e, d), where the public key e is disclosed and the private key d is disguised. If both e and d are kept secret by two parties respectively, and p and q are unknown to any one. Thus we can regard RSA as a secret-key cryptosystem. We imagine that a key distribution center generates an RSA key pair (e, d) by using the key generating algorithm in Scheme A. And then e is kept secret by Alice and d is kept secret by Bob. The RSA modulus N is public but no one knows p and q exactly. Thus, neither Alice nor Bob can obtain the secret of each other. Note that it is clear that RSA-CRT can not be used in such a situation because p and q are unknown by any party.

In 1993, Bellare and Rogaway [1] proposed two provably secure symmetric-key authentication protocols, MAP1 and MAP2. MAP1 is a mutual authentication protocol for two parties, and MAP2 allows arbitrary text strings to be authenticated along with its flows. As our examples of defending the stolen-secret attack, we modify MAP1 and MAP2 in the following. A brief outline of these two protocols and our improvements are presented in Fig. 1 and Fig. 2. Here A^a and B^a denote that Alice keeps a shared secret key a with Bob; and A^e and B^d denote that Alice keeps e and Bob keeps d, where (e, d) is a key pair of RSA using our scheme A. Let R_X denote a random challenge from X and $[x]_k = (x, f_k(x))$, where $f_k(x)$ is a pseudorandom function family specified by key k. It is commonly believed that pseudorandom functions can be well-implemented by encryption primitives in practice. Here we replace $f_k(x)$ by either a symmetric-key encryption with key k (in MAP1 and MAP2) or an encryption of RSA with exponent k (in the improved MAP1 and the improved MAP2). Here we remark that the plain RSA encryption can not be used directly for practical purpose, some padding techniques, such as PKCS #1 and OAEP, are required. We also note that although we limit our discussion to authentication protocols, there exists the even more important concept of key-distribution, often coupled with authentication. Our improvements to defend the stolen-secret attack can be also applied to those key distribution protocols whose security are based on symmetric-key encryption.

$$A^a \qquad\qquad B^a \quad A^e \qquad\qquad B^d$$

$$\xrightarrow{\quad R_A \quad} \qquad\qquad \xrightarrow{\quad R_A \quad}$$

$$\xleftarrow{[B.A.R_A.R_B]_a} \quad\Longrightarrow\quad \xleftarrow{[B.A.R_A.R_B]_d}$$

$$\xrightarrow{[A.R_B]_a} \qquad\qquad\qquad \xrightarrow{[A.R_B]_e}$$

Fig. 1. MAP1 and Improved MAP1.

$$A^a \qquad\qquad\qquad B^a \quad A^e \qquad\qquad\qquad B^d$$

$$\xrightarrow{\quad R_A.Text_1 \quad} \qquad\qquad \xrightarrow{\quad R_A.Text_1 \quad}$$

$$\xleftarrow{[B.A.R_A.R_B.Text_1.Text_2]_a} \quad\Longrightarrow\quad \xleftarrow{[B.A.R_A.R_B.Text_1.Text_2]_d}$$

$$\xrightarrow{[A.R_B.Text_3]_a} \qquad\qquad\qquad \xrightarrow{[A.R_B.Text_3]_e}$$

Fig. 2. MAP2 and Improved MAP2.

8   Conclusions

As shown by Durfee and Nguyen, the more unbalanced the prime factors are, the more insecure Sun et al.'s RSA variants are. In this paper, we propose a new RSA variant with balanced prime factors and balanced exponents. It is clear that this proposed variant is more secure than Sun et al.'s second RSA variant with unbalanced prime factors and balanced exponents. As an example, we can construct an instance of RSA with p of 512 bits, q of 513 bits, and d and e of 568 bits. In addition, for repairing the security of Sun, Yang, and Laih's third RSA variant, we also present another RSA variant with balanced prime factors and $\log_2 e + \log_2 d \approx \log_2 N + l_k$. This variant is designed for rebalancing the computation cost between encryption and decryption. It should be noted that in this variant the private exponent d must be large enough to defend against the Durfee-Nguyen attack and its extensions. Based on RSA, we also give an application to entity authentication in order to defend the stolen-secret attack. Our RSA variants can be applied to realize such an application, while RSA-CRT can not.

Acknowledgements

The authors wish to acknowledge the anonymous reviewers for valuable comments and thank helpful discussions with Chiung-Hsun Chen, Mu-En Wu and Ting-Yao Lin on several points in the paper. This research was supported in part by the National Science Council, Taiwan, under contract NSC-93-2213-E-007-102.

References

1. Bellare,M., Rogaway, P.: Entity authentication and key distribution. Proceedings of Crypto '93 , LNCS 773 (1994) 232-249
2. Boneh, D., Durfee, G.: Cryptanalysis of RSA with private key d less than $N^{0.292}$. Proceedings of Eurocrypt '99, LNCS 1592 (1999) 1–11

3. Cavallar, S., Dodson B., Lenstra, A. K., Lioen, W., Montgomery, P. L., Murphy, B., te Riele, H., Aardal, K., Gilchrist, J., Guillerm, G., Leyland, P., Marchand, J., Morain, F., Muffett, A., Putnam, C., Putnam, C., Zimmermann,P.: Factorization of 512-bit RSA key using the number field sieve. Proceedings of Eurocrypt'00, LNCS 1807 (2000) 1-18

4. Coppersmith, D.: Finding a Small Root of a Bivariate Integer Equation; Factoring with High Bits Known. Proceedings of Eurocrypt'96, LNCS 1070 (1996) 178–189

5. Durfee, G., Nguyen, P.: Cryptanalysis of the RSA Schemes with Short Secret Exponent from Asiacrypt'99. Proceedings of Asiacrypt'00, LNCS 1976 (2000) 14–29

6. Herstein, I. N.: Topics in Algebra, Xerox Corporation. (1975)

7. Hong, H. S., Lee, H. K., Lee, H. S., Lee, H. J.: The better bound of private key in RSA with unbalanced primes. Applied Mathematics and Computation, Vol. 139 (2003) 351-362

8. http://www.alpertron.com.ar/ECM.HTM

9. Joye,M., Quisquater, J. J., Yen, S. M., Yung, M.: Security paradoxes: how improving a cryptosystem may weaken it. Proceedings of the Ninth National Conference on Information Security (1999) 27-32

10. Lenstra,A., Lenstra, H., Lovasz, L.: Factoring polynomial with rational coefficients. Mathematiche Annalen, Vol. 261 (1982) 515-534

11. Lenstra Jr, H. W.: Factoring integers with elliptic curves. Annuals of Mathematics, vol. 126 (1987) 649–673

12. Pinch, R.: Extending the Wiener attack to RSA-type cryptosystems. Electronics Letters, Vol. 31 (1995) 1736-1738

13. Pollard, J.: Theorems of factorization and primality testing. Proc. Cambridge Philos. Soc., (1974) 76:521–528

14. Rivest, R. L., Shamir, A., Adleman, L. M.: A method for obtaining digital signatures and public-key cryptosystems. Comm. ACM, Vol. 21 (1987) 120-126

15. Rivest, R., Silverman, R. D.: Are strong primes needed for RSA?. The 1997 RSA Laboratories Seminar series, Seminar Proceedings (1997)

16. Sakai, R., Morii, M., Kasahara, M.: New key generation algorithm for RSA cryptosystem. IEICE Transactions on Fundamentals, Vol. E77-A (1994) 89-97

17. Sun, H. M., Yang, W. C., Laih, C. S.: On the design of RSA with short secret exponent. Proceedings of Asiacrypt'99, LNCS 1716 (1999) 150–164

18. Sun, H. M., Yang, W. C., Laih, C. S.: On the design of RSA with short secret exponent. Journal of Inforamtion Science and Engineering, Vol.18 No.1 (January 2002) 1-18

19. Verheul, E., van Tilborg, H.: Cryptanalysis of less short RSA secret exponents. Applicable Algebra in Engineering, Communication and Computing, Vol. 8 (1997) 425-435

20. de Weger, B.: Cryptanalysis of RSA with small prime difference. Applicable Algebra in Engineering, Communication and Computing, Vol. 13 (2002) 17-28

21. Wiener, M.: Cryptanalysis of short RSA secret exponents. IEEE Transactions on Information Theory, Vol. 36, no. 3 (1990) 553–558

Appendix A: Sun, Yang, and Laih's RSA Variants

Scheme(I). input: l_N, l_p, l_d, and γ; output: e, d, p, q and N.

Step 1. Select two random primes $p < q$ such that both p and N are sufficiently large to defend factorization algorithms such as ECM [11] and NFS [3].

Step 2. Randomly select the secret exponent d such that $l_d + l_p > \frac{1}{3}l_N$ and $d > 2^\gamma p^{0.5}$, where γ is the security parameter (larger than 64).

Step 3. If the public exponent e defined by $ed \equiv 1(\mathrm{mod}\phi(N))$ is not larger than $\frac{\phi(N)}{2}$, one restarts the previous step.

It is clear that for the first RSA variant, the improved one with balanced p and q is, in fact, the standard RSA. Hence, it is impossible to make d short below Boneh and Durfee's bound and Wiener's bound.

Scheme(II). input: l_N; output: e, d, p, q and N.

Step 1. Randomly select a prime p of $\frac{1}{2}l_N - 112$ bits, and a k of 112 bits.

Step 2. Randomly select a d of $\frac{1}{2}l_N + 56$ bits coprime with $k(p-1)$.

Step 3. We can unique determined two numbers u and v, such that $du - k(p-1)v = 1$,where $0 < u < k(p-1)$,$0 < v < d$.

Step 4. If $\gcd(v + 1, d) \neq 1$,then go to step 2.

Step 5. Select a number h of 56 bits until $q = v + hd + 1$ is prime.

Step 6. Let $p,q,e = u + hk(p-1),d$, and $N = pq$ are the parameters of RSA.

For the second RSA variant, it is impossible to make p and q balanced because p is of $\frac{1}{2}\log_2 N - 112$ bits and q is of $\frac{1}{2}\log_2 N + 112$ bits in this variant.

Scheme(III). input: l_N, l_p, l_d,and l_k; output: e, d, p, q and N.

Step 1. Randomly select a prime number p of length l_p, such that it is large enough to make an ECM [11] attack infeasible.

Step 2. Randomly select a number k of length l_k.

Step 3. Randomly select a number d of length l_d and $\gcd(k(p-1), d) = 1$.

Step 4. we can uniquely determine two numbers u' and v' such that $du' - k(p-1)v' = 1$, where $0 < u' < k(p-1)$ and $0 < v' < d$.

Step 5. If $\gcd(v' + 1, d) \neq 1$, then go to Step 3.

Step 6. Randomly select a number h of length $l_N - l_p - l_d$, then compute $u = u' + hk(p-1)$ and $v = v' + hd$.

Step 7. If $v + 1$ is not a prime number, go to Step 6.

Step 8. Let p, $q = v + 1$, $e = u$, d, and $N = pq$ are the parameters of RSA.

For the third RSA variant, the possibly constructed RSA with balanced p and q are only those instances of RSA with d of $\frac{1}{2}\log_2 N$ bits and e of $\frac{1}{2}\log_2 N + l_k$ bits, e.g., $l_k=112$. This is due to the limitation of $\log_2 p + \log_2 d \leq \log_2 N$.

Appendix B: An Instance of RSA with Balanced Prime Factors and Balanced Exponents

As an example for Scheme A, we construct an instance of RSA with p of 512 bits, q of 513 bits, d and e of 568 bits.

$p=$ EB73E838 FE3A755B 1B08C0A5 4070CF38 62046A3D 77E26D54 73EB8541
6662E060 25388EC1 17129F9F D3F7E81A 81CC11DC 0ED30F96 39E201C4
FAC77E73 73B75CDD

$q =$ 1   E47C6F97 82515CEE 69DA0782 A1D1DEF3 A7F15B88 F513242F
CF505867 24AB9F4F 39349987 006B5AE6 3A0FBFA7 A7BBFAC7 8D6B0BEE
04089C0C 7F82C605 85A66B79

$d =$ F34255 6EB55834 5EB2023d 33DA5792 8C373385 86B72B71 D0A19BB6
4B490155 74BBB648 287F297F 865313B7 4F17982D D854F694 82C19436
91F7FB5B B73BE6CB 66952AC4 1A416E69

$e =$ D01CD7 7DA75CA6 39247A84 45E39813 B98BF2DC 13DEEC98 D31725A4
52F83345 0647E852 0CA70032 600B582B 1B2BB83F 9DF38D6E 1F73069C
C2B05BCB 81710127 D33D9414 D5654D39

Appendix C: Two Instances of RSA with Balanced Prime Factors and Trade-off Exponents

As an example for Scheme B, we construct an instance of RSA with p and q of 512 bits, d of 540 bits, and e of 596 bits.

$p =$ DE7332C0 6DDB34F5 86598C8F 2F103983 EE86007F DFB44CBF F503F1EB
F4BCD507 23EA54EA 5E9AE43F 7FC54021 CD026D8B C23B48CD D00ECDA2
9054EBB5 C5A6D063

$q =$ 89575BE4 F0310066 113CF04C 1220DAB7 25DD3F2F DD59BA09 3CC31FAC
467D17F9 2FA38A26 72D92E32 B91333FA 88F1D013 E5EB1A74 E4DE793E
E9A299A9 A7C0D24B

$e =$ 88E33   2BF9879D 6AD5324B 6763FB22 E6D21B8D CB28E5E5 437AA101
D27D7992 42E507D3 D2639902 C58C4978 D79D5A0A CF515FA0 028662AF
5F26F0FB AF60DF38 8E4409F3 63AE6806 B2045771

$d =$ 8BB9953 6F0577AC DF1D6DB8 0F76A4CF 992F8538 FC89BEB6 5DEA50E1
124AB868 9BD989B3 D20A8EC9 B3D697AF 76F1C16F 4BD09BBC C8E53CCB
AC16B232 FD39134E 7E913009

As another example for Scheme B, we construct an instance of RSA with p and q of 512 bits primes, d of 512 bits, and e of 624 bits.

$p =$ 84A0CC27 66ACCDA9 57646FC5 924AA056 5E2AC1DA 1137B9DB AC6BE9D2
DD09FA82 193D6205 0E62C4BD 0D2A0304 037DED34 03290E3A 748C6AF4
80FB6880 828CF3A3

$q =$ B187BA5F AB9CABEC 765897BA B364DB52 D8959D5C B765A725 1A1EDCA3
19F9601D 2CE5D8A9 570386BB 1F016B40 6DDBE6C2 EBEA445F 14D48FD4
B7177E03 F4959BFF

$e =$ D260   A347D9C1 76B8BC8B DB527877 F09489C0 E634E313 4A7FAB5C
A135EB1D A6410CBC CD497FB7 092C3CB2 2BA23E7D D02201B3 ABD9E989
584ED3C7 262A3ED0 CEFD6757 00E7B6DC 414D77BA 050BF525

$d =$ 91273082 5084AB61 D38E2142 3AED897E 97FBDCEC 00081122 3FCF3B70
E3D5D8BE A5AD07F5 B0D67990 6C253F89 30A26574 F80CD0F6 A007AE0A
6C131816 E85A4B35

The Sampling Twice Technique for the RSA-Based Cryptosystems with Anonymity

Ryotaro Hayashi and Keisuke Tanaka

Dept. of Mathematical and Computing Sciences, Tokyo Institute of Technology,
2-12-1 Ookayama, Meguro-ku, Tokyo 152-8552, Japan
{hayashi9,keisuke}@is.titech.ac.jp

Abstract. We say that an encryption scheme or a signature scheme provides anonymity when it is infeasible to determine which user generated a ciphertext or a signature. To construct the schemes with anonymity, it is necessary that the space of ciphertexts or signatures is common to each user. In this paper, we focus on the techniques which can be used to obtain this anonymity property, and propose a new technique for obtaining the anonymity property on RSA-based cryptosystem, which we call "sampling twice." It generates the uniform distribution over 2^k by sampling the two elements from $\mathbb{Z}_N$ where $|N| = k$. Then, by applying the sampling twice technique, we construct the schemes for encryption, undeniable and confirmer signature, and ring signature, which have some advantage to the previous schemes.

Keywords: RSA, anonymity, encryption, undeniable and confirmer signature, ring signature

1 Introduction

We say that an encryption scheme or a signature scheme provides anonymity when it is infeasible to determine which user generated a ciphertext or a signature. A simple observation that seems to be folklore is that standard RSA encryption, namely, a ciphertext is $x^e \bmod N$ where x is a plaintext and (N, e) is a public key, does not provide anonymity, even when all moduli in the system have the same length. Suppose an adversary knows that the ciphertext y is created under one of two keys (N_0, e_0) or (N_1, e_1), and suppose $N_0 \leq N_1$. If $y \geq N_0$ then the adversary bets it was created under (N_1, e_1), else the adversary bets it was created under (N_0, e_0). It is not hard to see that this attack has non-negligible advantage. To construct the schemes with anonymity, it is necessary that the space of ciphertexts is common to each user. We can say the same thing about RSA-based signature schemes.

Bellare, Boldyreva, Desai, and Pointcheval [1] proposed a new security requirement of the encryption schemes called "key-privacy" or "anonymity." It asks that the encryption provide (in addition to privacy of the data being encrypted) privacy of the key under which the encryption was performed. In [1], they provided the key-privacy encryption scheme, RSA-RAEP, which is a variant of RSA-OAEP (Bellare and Rogaway [2], Fujisaki, Okamoto, Pointcheval,

S. Vaudenay (Ed.): PKC 2005, LNCS 3386, pp. 216–233, 2005.

and Stern [3]), and made the space of ciphertexts common to each user by repeating the evaluation of the RSA-OAEP permutation $f(x, r)$ with plaintext x and random r, each time using different r until the value is in the safe range. For deriving a value in the safe range, the number of the repetition would be very large (the value of the security parameter). In fact, their algorithm can fail to give a desired output with some (small) probability.

The anonymous encryption scheme has various applications. For example, anonymous authenticated key exchange protocol such as SKEME (Krawczyk [4]), anonymous credential system (Camenisch and Lysyanskaya [5]), and auction protocols (Sako [6]).

Chaum and Antwerpen provided undeniable signature which cannot be verified without the signer's cooperation [7, 8]. The validity or invalidity of an undeniable signature can be ascertained by conducting a protocol with the signer, assuming the signer participates. Chaum provided confirmer signature [9] which is undeniable signature where signatures may also be verified by interacting with an entity called the confirmer who has been designated by the signer. Galbraith and Mao proposed a new security notion for undeniable and confirmer signature named "anonymity" in [10]. We say that an undeniable or confirmer signature scheme provides anonymity when it is infeasible to determine which user generated the message-signature pair. In [10], Galbraith and Mao provided the undeniable and confirmer signature scheme with anonymity. They made the space of signatures common to each user by applying a standard RSA permutation to the signature and expanding it to the common domain $[0, 2^k)$ where N is a public key for each user and $|N| = k$. This technique was proposed by Desmedt [11].

Rivest, Shamir, and Tauman [12] proposed the notion of ring signature, which allows a member of an ad hoc collection of users S to prove that a message is authenticated by a member of S without revealing which member actually produced the signature. Unlike group signature, ring signature has no group managers, no setup procedures, no revocation procedures, and no coordination. The signer does not need the knowledge, consent, or assistance of the other ring members to put them in the ring. All the signer needs is knowledge of their regular public keys. They also proposed the efficient schemes based on RSA and Rabin. In their RSA-based scheme, the trap-door RSA permutations of the various ring members will have ranges of different sizes. This makes it awkward to combine the individual signatures, so one should construct some trap-door one-way permutation which has a common range for each user. Intuitively, in the ring signature scheme, Rivest, Shamir, and Tauman solved this problem by encoding the message to an N_i-ary representation and applying a standard RSA permutation f to the low-order digits where N_i is a public key for each user. This technique is considered to be essentially the same as that by Desmedt. As mentioned in [12], for deriving a secure permutation g with a common range, the range of g would be 160 bits larger than that of f.

Hayashi, Okamoto, and Tanaka [13] recently proposed the RSA family of trap-door permutations with a common domain denoted by RSACD. They showed that the θ-partial one-wayness of RSACD is equivalent to the one-wayness of RSACD for $\theta > 0.5$, and that the one-wayness of RSACD is equivalent to the one-wayness of RSA which is the standard RSA family of trap-door permutations. They also proposed the applications of RSACD to the key-privacy encryption scheme and ring signature scheme. Their schemes have some advantages to the previous schemes.

1.1   Our Contribution

In this paper, we focus on the techniques which can be used to obtain this anonymity property.

From the previous results mentioned above, we can find three techniques, repeating, expanding, and using RSACD, for anonymity of cryptosystems based on RSA.

Repeating. Repeating the evaluation of the encryption (respectively the signing) with plaintext x (resp. message m), random r, and the RSA function, each time using different r until the value is smaller than any public key N of each user.

   In [1], Bellare, Boldyreva, Desai, and Pointcheval used this technique for the encryption scheme.

Expanding. Doing the evaluation of the encryption (respectively the signing) with plaintext x (resp. message m), random r, and the RSA function, and expanding it to the common domain.

   This technique was proposed by Desmedt [11]. In [10], Galbraith and Mao used this technique for the undeniable signature scheme. In [12], Rivest, Shamir, and Tauman also used this technique for the ring signature.

RSACD. Doing the evaluation of the encryption (respectively the signing) with plaintext x (resp. message m), random r, and the RSACD function. This function was proposed by Hayashi, Okamoto, and Tanaka [13].

   In this paper, we propose a new technique for obtaining the anonymity property of RSA-based cryptosystems. We call this technique "sampling twice." In our technique, we employ an algorithm `ChooseAndShift`. It takes two numbers $x_1, x_2 \in \mathbb{Z}_N$ as input and returns a value $y \in [0, 2^k)$ where $|N| = k$, and if x_1 and x_2 are independently and uniformly chosen from $\mathbb{Z}_N$ then y is uniformly distributed over $[0, 2^k)$.

Sampling Twice. Doing the evaluation of the encryption (respectively the signing) twice with plaintext x (resp. message m), random r_1 and r_2, and the RSA function, and applying our proposed algorithm `ChooseAndShift` for the two resulting values.

   Then, by applying the sampling twice technique, we construct the schemes for encryption, undeniable and confirmer signature, and ring signature (See Figure 1.).

   We summarize the (dis)advantage of our proposed schemes.

	Sampling Twice	Repeating	Expanding	RSACD
Encryption	**this paper**	Bellare et al.	-	Hayashi et al.
Undeniable and Confirmer Signature	**this paper**	-	Galbraith et al.	-
Ring Signature	**this paper**	-	Rivest et al.	Hayashi et al.

Fig. 1. The previous and our proposed schemes.

Our proposed encryption scheme with sampling twice is efficient with respect to the size of ciphertexts and the decryption cost. It is also efficient with respect to the encryption cost in the worst case. On the other hand, that in the average case is larger than that of the previous schemes. More precisely, in our encryption scheme, the number of modular exponentiation to encrypt in the worst case is 2, while those in the previous schemes are 1 or 1.5.

Our proposed undeniable and confirmer signature scheme with sampling twice is efficient with respect to the size of signatures. On the other hand, the number of exponentiations for signing and that of computation of square roots is always 2, while those of the other schemes are 1 or 1.5 in the average case.

Our proposed ring signature scheme with sampling twice is efficient with respect to the size of signatures and the verification cost. On the other hand, the signing cost of our scheme is larger than those of the previous schemes.

If we use the RSACD function, the resulting value is calculated by applying the RSA function either once or twice. Fortunately, since applying the RSA function twice does not reduce security, we can prove that the RSACD function is one-way if the RSA function is one-way. Generally speaking, a one-way function does not always have this property, and we cannot construct a one-way functions with a common domain.

On the other hand, in the sampling twice, repeating, and expanding techniques, the resulting value is calculated by applying the RSA function once. Therefore, it might be possible to apply these techniques to other one-way functions and prove the security of the resulting schemes.

The organization of this paper is as follows. In Section 2, we review the definitions of families of functions and the standard RSA family. In Section 3, we construct the algorithm `ChooseAndShift` and propose the sampling twice technique. We propose the encryption schemes with anonymity in Section 4, the undeniable and confirmer signature schemes with anonymity in Section 5, and the ring signature schemes with anonymity in Section 6. We conclude in Section 7.

2   Preliminaries

We describe the definitions of families of functions, families of trap-door permutations, and θ-partial one-way.

Definition 1 (Families of Functions [1]). *A family of functions $F = (K, S, E)$ consists of three algorithms. The randomized key-generation algorithm K takes* *as input a security parameter $k \in \mathbb{N}$ and returns a pair (pk, sk) where pk is a public key and sk is an associated secret key. (In cases where the family is not trap-door, the secret key is simply the empty string.) The randomized sampling algorithm S takes input pk and returns a random point in a set that we call the domain of pk and denote by $\mathrm{Dom}_F(pk)$. The deterministic evaluation algorithm E takes input pk and a point $x \in \mathrm{Dom}_F(pk)$ and returns an output we denote by $E_{pk}(x)$. We let $\mathrm{Rng}_F(pk) = \{E_{pk}(x) \mid x \in \mathrm{Dom}_F(pk)\}$ denote the range of the function $E_{pk}(\cdot)$.*

Definition 2 (Families of Trap-Door Permutations [1]). *We say that F is a family of trap-door functions if there exists a deterministic inversion algorithm I that takes input sk and a point $y \in \mathrm{Rng}_F(pk)$ and returns a point $x \in \mathrm{Dom}_F(pk)$ such that $E_{pk}(x) = y$. We say that F is a family of trap-door permutations if F is a family of trap-door functions, $\mathrm{Dom}_F(pk) = \mathrm{Rng}_F(pk)$, and E_{pk} is a bijection on this set.*

Definition 3 (θ-Partial One-Way [1]). *Let $F = (K, S, E)$ be a family of functions. Let $b \in \{0, 1\}$ and $k \in \mathbb{N}$ be a security parameter. Let $0 < \theta \le 1$ be a constant. Let A be an adversary. Now, we consider the following experiments:*

> Experiment $\mathbf{Exp}_{F,A}^{\theta\text{-pow-fnc}}(k)$
> $(pk, sk) \leftarrow K(k)$
> $x \stackrel{R}{\leftarrow} \mathrm{Dom}_F(pk)$
> $y \leftarrow E_{pk}(x)$
> $x_1 \leftarrow A(pk, y)$ where $|x_1| = \lceil \theta \cdot |x| \rceil$
> if $\big(E_{pk}(x_1 \| x_2) = y$ for some $x_2\big)$ return 1 else return 0

Here " $\|$ " denotes concatenation and " $x \stackrel{R}{\leftarrow} \mathrm{Dom}_F(pk)$ " is the operation of picking an element x uniformly from $\mathrm{Dom}_F(pk)$. We define the advantages of the adversary via

$$\mathbf{Adv}_{F,A}^{\theta\text{-pow-fnc}}(k) = \Pr[\mathbf{Exp}_{F,A}^{\theta\text{-pow-fnc}}(k) = 1]$$

where the probability is taken over K, $x \stackrel{R}{\leftarrow} \mathrm{Dom}_F(pk)$, E, and A. We say that the family F is θ-partial one-way if the function $\mathbf{Adv}_{F,A}^{\theta\text{-pow-fnc}}(\cdot)$ is negligible for any adversary A whose time complexity is polynomial in k.

The "time-complexity" is the worst case execution time of the experiment plus the size of the code of the adversary, in some fixed RAM model of computation.

Note that when $\theta = 1$ the notion of θ-partial one-wayness coincides with the standard notion of one-wayness. We say that the family F is one-way when F is 1-partial one-way.

We describe the standard RSA family of trap-door permutations denoted by RSA.

Definition 4 (The Standard RSA Family of Trap-Door Permutations).
The specifications of the standard RSA family of trap-door permutations RSA = (K, S, E) are as follows. The key generation algorithm takes as input a security

parameter k and picks random, distinct primes p, q in the range $2^{\lceil k/2 \rceil - 1} < p, q < 2^{\lceil k/2 \rceil}$ and $2^{k-1} < pq < 2^k$. It sets $N = pq$. It picks $e, d \in \mathbb{Z}^*_{\phi(N)}$ such that $ed = 1 \pmod{\phi(N)}$ where $\phi(N) = (p-1)(q-1)$. The public key is N, e, k and the secret key is N, d, k. The sets $\mathrm{Dom}_{\mathsf{RSA}}(N, e, k)$ and $\mathrm{Rng}_{\mathsf{RSA}}(N, e, k)$ are both equal to $\mathbb{Z}^*_N$. The evaluation algorithm $E_{N,e,k}(x) = x^e \bmod N$ and the inversion algorithm $I_{N,d,k}(y) = y^d \bmod N$. The sampling algorithm returns a random point in $\mathbb{Z}^*_N$.

Fujisaki, Okamoto, Pointcheval, and Stern [3] showed that the θ-partial one-wayness of RSA is equivalent to the one-wayness of RSA for $\theta > 0.5$.

3   The Sampling Twice Technique

In this section, we propose a new technique for obtaining the anonymity property of RSA-based cryptosystems. We call this technique "sampling twice." In our technique, we employ the following algorithm ChooseAndShift. It takes two numbers $x_1, x_2 \in \mathbb{Z}_N$ as input and returns a value $y \in [0, 2^k)$ where $|N| = k$.

> Algorithm ChooseAndShift$_{N,k}(x_1, x_2)$
> if $(0 \le x_1, x_2 < 2^k - N)$
> $\quad$ return $\begin{cases} x_1 & \text{with probability } \frac{1}{2} \\ x_1 + N & \text{with probability } \frac{1}{2} \end{cases}$
> elseif $(2^k - N \le x_1, x_2 < N)$
> $\quad$ return x_1
> else
> $\quad y_1 \leftarrow \min\{x_1, x_2\}; \quad y_2 \leftarrow \max\{x_1, x_2\}$
> $\quad$ %%% Note that $0 \le y_1 < 2^k - N$ and $2^k - N \le y_2 < N$. %%%
> $\quad$ return $\begin{cases} y_1 & \text{with probability } (\frac{1}{2} + \frac{N}{2^{k+1}}) \times \frac{1}{2} \\ y_1 + N & \text{with probability } (\frac{1}{2} + \frac{N}{2^{k+1}}) \times \frac{1}{2} \\ y_2 & \text{with probability } \frac{1}{2} - \frac{N}{2^{k+1}} \end{cases}$

Note that $2^{k-1} < N < 2^k$ ensures $2^k - N < N$, $0 < \frac{1}{2} - \frac{N}{2^{k+1}} < 1$, and $0 < \frac{1}{2} + \frac{N}{2^{k+1}} < 1$. In order to run this algorithm, it is sufficient to prepare only $k + 3$ random bits.

We prove the following theorem on the property of ChooseAndShift.

Theorem 1. *If x_1 and x_2 are independently and uniformly chosen from $\mathbb{Z}_N$ then the output of the above algorithm is uniformly distributed over $[0, 2^k)$.*

Proof. To prove this theorem, we show that if x_1 and x_2 are independently and uniformly chosen from $\mathbb{Z}_N$ then $\Pr[\text{ChooseAndShift}(x_1, x_2) = z] = 1/2^k$ for any $z \in [0, 2^k)$. For any $z \in [0, 2^k - N)$, we have

$$\Pr[\text{ChooseAndShift}(x_1, x_2) = z]$$
$$= \Pr[x_1 = z \wedge 0 \le x_2 < 2^k - N] \times \frac{1}{2}$$
$$+ \Pr[(x_1 = z \wedge 2^k - N \le x_2 < N) \vee (x_2 = z \wedge 2^k - N \le x_1 < N)]$$
$$\times (\frac{1}{2} + \frac{N}{2^{k+1}}) \times \frac{1}{2}$$
$$= \frac{1}{N} \times \frac{2^k - N}{N} \times \frac{1}{2} + (\frac{1}{N} \times \frac{2N - 2^k}{N}) \times 2 \times (\frac{1}{2} + \frac{N}{2^{k+1}}) \times \frac{1}{2} = \frac{1}{2^k}.$$

It is clear that $\Pr[\texttt{ChooseAndShift}(x_1, x_2) = z'] = \Pr[\texttt{ChooseAndShift}(x_1, x_2)$
$= z' + N]$ for any $z' \in [0, 2^k - N)$. Therefore, for any $z \in [N, 2^k)$, we have
$\Pr[\texttt{ChooseAndShift}(x_1, x_2) = z] = 1/2^k$.

Furthermore, for any $z \in [2^k - N, N)$, we have

$$
\begin{aligned}
&\Pr[\texttt{ChooseAndShift}(x_1, x_2) = z] \\
&= \Pr[x_1 = z \wedge 2^k - N \le x_2 < N] \\
&\quad + \Pr[(x_1 = z \wedge 0 \le x_2 < 2^k - N) \vee (x_2 = z \wedge 0 \le x_1 < 2^k - N)] \\
&\quad \times (\tfrac{1}{2} - \tfrac{N}{2^{k+1}}) \\
&= \tfrac{1}{N} \times \tfrac{2N - 2^k}{N} + (\tfrac{1}{N} \times \tfrac{2^k - N}{N}) \times 2 \times (\tfrac{1}{2} - \tfrac{N}{2^{k+1}}) = \tfrac{1}{2^k}. \qquad \square
\end{aligned}
$$

By using the algorithm $\texttt{ChooseAndShift}$, we propose a new technique for obtaining the anonymity property. We call this technique "sampling twice."

Sampling Twice. Doing the evaluation of the encryption (respectively the signing) twice with plaintext x (resp. message m), random r_1 and r_2, and the RSA function, and applying our proposed algorithm $\texttt{ChooseAndShift}$ for the two resulting values.

In the following sections, by applying the sampling twice technique, we construct the schemes for encryption, undeniable and confirmer signature, and ring signature.

4   Encryption

4.1   Definitions

In [1], Bellare, Boldyreva, Desai, and Pointcheval proposed a new security requirement of encryption schemes called "key-privacy." It asks that the encryption provide (in addition to privacy of the data being encrypted) privacy of the key under which the encryption was performed. In [1], a public-key encryption scheme with common-key generation is described as follows.

Definition 5. *A public-key encryption scheme with common-key generation $\mathcal{PE}$ $= (\mathcal{G}, \mathcal{K}, \mathcal{E}, \mathcal{D})$ consists of four algorithms. The common-key generation algorithm $\mathcal{G}$ takes as input some security parameter k and returns some common key I. The key generation algorithm $\mathcal{K}$ is a randomized algorithm that takes as input the common key I and returns a pair (pk, sk) of keys, the public key and a matching secret key. The encryption algorithm $\mathcal{E}$ is a randomized algorithm that takes the public key pk and a plaintext x to return a ciphertext y. The decryption algorithm $\mathcal{D}$ is a deterministic algorithm that takes the secret key sk and a ciphertext y to return the corresponding plaintext x or a special symbol $\bot$ to indicate that the ciphertext was invalid.*

In [1], they formalized the property of "key-privacy." This can be considered under either the chosen-plaintext attack or the chosen-ciphertext attack, yielding two notions of security, IK-CPA and IK-CCA. (IK means "indistinguishability of keys.")

Definition 6 (IK-CPA, IK-CCA [1]). *Let $\mathcal{PE} = (\mathcal{G}, \mathcal{K}, \mathcal{E}, \mathcal{D})$ be an encryption scheme. Let $b \in \{0, 1\}$ and $k \in \mathbb{N}$. Let $A_{\mathrm{cpa}} = (A^1_{\mathrm{cpa}}, A^2_{\mathrm{cpa}})$, $A_{\mathrm{cca}} = (A^1_{\mathrm{cca}}, A^2_{\mathrm{cca}})$ be adversaries that run in two stages and where A_{cca} has access to the oracles $\mathcal{D}_{sk_0}(\cdot)$ and $\mathcal{D}_{sk_1}(\cdot)$. Note that si is the state information. It contains pk_0, pk_1, and so on. For atk $\in \{\mathrm{cpa}, \mathrm{cca}\}$, we consider the following experiments:*

$$\text{Experiment } \mathbf{Exp}^{\text{ik-atk-}b}_{\mathcal{PE}, A_{\mathrm{atk}}}(k)$$
$$I \leftarrow \mathcal{G}(k); \ (pk_0, sk_0) \leftarrow \mathcal{K}(I); \ (pk_1, sk_1) \leftarrow \mathcal{K}(I)$$
$$(x, \mathsf{si}) \leftarrow A^1_{\mathrm{atk}}(pk_0, pk_1); \ y \leftarrow \mathcal{E}_{pk_b}(x); \ d \leftarrow A^2_{\mathrm{atk}}(y, \mathsf{si})$$
$$\text{return } d$$

Above it is mandated that A^2_{cca} never queries $\mathcal{D}_{sk_0}(\cdot)$ and $\mathcal{D}_{sk_1}(\cdot)$ on the challenge ciphertext y. For atk $\in \{\mathrm{cpa}, \mathrm{cca}\}$, we define the advantages via

$$\mathbf{Adv}^{\text{ik-atk}}_{\mathcal{PE}, A_{\mathrm{atk}}}(k) = \left| \Pr[\mathbf{Exp}^{\text{ik-atk-1}}_{\mathcal{PE}, A_{\mathrm{atk}}}(k) = 1] - \Pr[\mathbf{Exp}^{\text{ik-atk-0}}_{\mathcal{PE}, A_{\mathrm{atk}}}(k) = 1] \right|.$$

The scheme $\mathcal{PE}$ is said to be IK-CPA secure (respectively IK-CCA secure) if the function $\mathbf{Adv}^{\text{ik-cpa}}_{\mathcal{PE}, A_{\mathrm{cpa}}}(\cdot)$ (resp. $\mathbf{Adv}^{\text{ik-cca}}_{\mathcal{PE}, A_{\mathrm{cca}}}(\cdot)$) is negligible for any adversary A whose time complexity is polynomial in k.

4.2   Encryption with Sampling Twice

In this section, we propose the encryption scheme with the sampling twice technique.

Definition 7. *The common-key generation algorithm $\mathcal{G}$ takes a security parameter k and returns parameters k, k_0 and k_1 such that $k_0(k) + k_1(k) < k$ for all $k > 1$. This defines an associated plaintext-length function $n(k) = k - k_0(k) - k_1(k)$. The key generation algorithm $\mathcal{K}$ takes k, k_0, k_1, runs the key-generation algorithm of RSA, and gets N, e, d. The public key pk is $(N, e), k, k_0, k_1$ and the secret key sk is $(N, d), k, k_0, k_1$. The other algorithms are depicted below. Let $G : \{0, 1\}^{k_0} \to \{0, 1\}^{n+k_1}$ and $H : \{0, 1\}^{n+k_1} \to \{0, 1\}^{k_0}$ be hash functions. Note that $[x]^n$ denotes the n most significant bits of x and $[x]_m$ denotes the m least significant bits of x. Note that the valid ciphertext y satisfies $y \in [0, 2^k)$ and $(y \bmod N) \in \mathbb{Z}^*_N$.*

```
Algorithm E^{G,H}_{pk}(x)                    Algorithm D^{G,H}_{sk}(y)

  r_1, r_2  ←^R  {0,1}^{k_0}                    v ← y mod N
  s_1 ← (x||0^{k_1}) ⊕ G(r_1);  t_1 ← r_1 ⊕ H(s_1)    s ← [v^d]^{n+k_1};  t ← [v^d]_{k_0}
  v_1 ← (s_1||t_1)^e mod N                      r ← t ⊕ H(s)
  s_2 ← (x||0^{k_1}) ⊕ G(r_2);  t_2 ← r_2 ⊕ H(s_2)    x ← [s ⊕ G(r)]^n;  p ← [s ⊕ G(r)]_{k_1}
  v_2 ← (s_2||t_2)^e mod N                      if (p = 0^{k_1}) z ← x else z ← ⊥
  y ← ChooseAndShift(v_1, v_2)                  return z
  return y
```

4.3   Analysis

We compare the four schemes with sampling twice, repeating, RSACD, and expanding.

Security. Bellare, Boldyreva, Desai, and Pointcheval [1] proved that the scheme with repeating (RSA-RAEP) is secure in the sense of IND-CCA2 and IK-CCA in the random oracle model assuming RSA is θ-partial one-way for $\theta > 0.5$. Hayashi, Okamoto, and Tanaka [13] proved that the encryption scheme with RSACD is also secure in the sense of IND-CCA2 and IK-CCA in the random oracle model assuming RSACD is θ-partial one-way for $\theta > 0.5$.

In order to prove that the scheme with sampling twice is secure in the sense of IK-CCA, we need the restriction as follows.

Since if c is a ciphertext of m for $pk = (N, e, k)$ and $c < 2^k - N$ then $c + N$ is also a ciphertext of m, the adversary can ask $c + N_0$ to decryption oracle $\mathcal{D}_{sk_0}$ where c is a challenge ciphertext such that $c < 2^k - N_0$ and $pk_0 = (N_0, e_0, k)$, and if the answer of $\mathcal{D}_{sk_0}$ is m, then c is encrypted by pk_0.

To prevent this attack, we add some natural restriction to the adversaries in the definitions of IK-CCA. That is, it is mandated that the adversary never queries D_{sk_0} on $(c \bmod N_0) + \beta_0 N_0$ where $\beta_0 \in \lfloor (2^k - (c \bmod N_0))/N_0 \rfloor$, and D_{sk_1} on $(c \bmod N_1) + \beta_1 N_1$ where $\beta_1 \in \lfloor (2^k - (c \bmod N_1))/N_1 \rfloor$.

Similarly, in order to prove that the scheme with sampling twice is secure in the sense of IND-CCA2, we need the same restriction. That is, in the definition of IND-CCA2, it is mandated that the adversary never queries D_{sk} on $(c \bmod N) + \gamma N$ where $\gamma \in \lfloor (2^k - (c \bmod N))/N \rfloor$.

We think these restrictions are natural and reasonable. Actually, in the case of undeniable and confirmer signature schemes, Galbraith and Mao [10] defined the anonymity on undeniable signature schemes with the above restriction.

If we add these restrictions then we can prove that the scheme with sampling twice is secure in the sense of IK-CCA in the random oracle model assuming RSA is θ-partial one-way for $\theta > 0.5$. More precisely, we can prove the following theorem.

Theorem 2. *If* RSA *is partial one-way then the encryption scheme Π with sampling twice is secure in the sense of IK-CCA in the random oracle model. More precisely, for any adversary A attacking the anonymity of our scheme under an adaptive chosen-ciphertext attack, and making at most q_{dec} decryption oracle queries, q_{gen} G-oracle queries, and q_{hash} H-oracle queries, there exists a θ-partial inverting adversary B for the* RSA *family, such that for any $k, k_0(k), k_1(k)$, and $\theta = \frac{k - k_0(k)}{k}$,*

$$\mathbf{Adv}^{\text{ik-cca}}_{\Pi,A}(k) \leq 8q_{\text{hash}} \cdot ((1 - \epsilon_1) \cdot (1 - \epsilon_2) \cdot (1 - \epsilon_3))^{-1} \cdot \mathbf{Adv}^{\theta\text{-pow-fnc}}_{\text{RSA},B}(k)$$
$$+ q_{\text{gen}} \cdot q_{\text{hash}} \cdot (1 - \epsilon_3)^{-1} \cdot 2^{-k+3}$$

where

$$\epsilon_1 = \frac{1}{2}; \quad \epsilon_2 = \frac{1}{2^{k/2-3} - 1}; \quad \epsilon_3 = \frac{2q_{\text{gen}} + q_{\text{dec}} + 2q_{\text{gen}}q_{\text{dec}}}{2^{k_0}} + \frac{2q_{\text{gen}}}{2^{k_1}} + \frac{2q_{\text{hash}}}{2^{k-k_0}},$$

and the running time of B is that of A plus $q_{\text{gen}} \cdot q_{\text{hash}} \cdot O(k^3)$.

Noticing that the range of valid ciphertexts changes, the proof is similar to that for RSA-RAEP (See Appendix C in the full version of [1].), and will be available in the full version of this paper.

	Sampling Twice	Repeating [1]	RSACD [13]	Expanding
# of mod. exp. to encrypt (average / worst)	2 / 2	1.5 / k_1	1.5 / 2	1 / 1
# of mod. exp. to decrypt (average / worst)	1 / 1	1 / 1	1.5 / 2	1 / 1
size of ciphertexts	k	k	k	$k + 160$
# of random bits to encrypt (average / worst)	$2k_0 + k + 3$ / $2k_0 + k + 3$	$1.5k_0$ / $k_1 k_0$	$1.5k_0$ / $1.5k_0$	$k_0 + 160$ / $k_0 + 160$

Fig. 2. The comparison of the encryption schemes.

We can also prove that the scheme with sampling twice is secure in the sense of IND-CCA2 in the random oracle model assuming RSA is θ-partial one-way for $\theta > 0.5$. More precisely, we can prove that if there exists a CCA2-adversary $A = (A_1, A_2)$ attacking indistinguishability of our scheme with advantage ϵ, then there exists a CCA2-adversary $B = (B_1, B_2)$ attacking indistinguishability of RSA-OAEP with advantage $\epsilon/2$. We construct B as follows.

1. B_1 gets pk and passes it to A_1. B_1 gets (m_0, m_1, si) which is an output of A_1, and B_1 outputs it.
2. B_2 gets a challenge ciphertext y and sets $y' \leftarrow y + tN$ where $t \overset{R}{\leftarrow} \{0, 1\}$. If $y' \geq 2^k$ then B_2 outputs Fail and halts; otherwise B_2 passes (y', si) to A_2. B_2 gets $d \in \{0, 1\}$ which is an output of A_2, and B_2 outputs it.

If B does not output Fail, A outputs correctly with advantage ϵ. Since $\Pr[B$ outputs Fail$] < 1/2$, the advantage of B is greater than $\epsilon/2$.

Efficiency. We show the number of modular exponentiations to encrypt and decrypt, the size of ciphertexts, and the bit-length of randomness to encrypt in Figure 2. We assume that N is uniformly distributed in $(2^{k-1}, 2^k)$.

5 Undeniable and Confirmer Signature

5.1 Definitions

Digital signatures are easily verified as authentic by anyone using the corresponding public key. This property can be advantageous for many users, but it is unsuitable for many other users. Chaum and Antwerpen provided undeniable signature which cannot be verified without the signer's cooperation [7, 8]. The validity or invalidity of an undeniable signature can be ascertained by conducting a protocol with the signer, assuming the signer participates. Chaum provided confirmer signature [9] which is undeniable signature where signatures may also be verified by interacting with an entity called the confirmer who has been designated by the signer, and many undeniable and confirmer signature schemes were proposed. We describe the definition of undeniable and confirmer signature.

Definition 8. *An undeniable signature scheme* $\mathcal{SIG}$ = (CGEN, KGEN, SIGN, CONF, DENY) *consists of three algorithms and two protocols.*

- CGEN *is a (randomized) common-key generation algorithm that takes as input some security parameter k and returns a common key I.*
- KGEN *is a (randomized) key generation algorithm that takes as input the common key I and returns a pair (pk, sk) of keys, the public key and a matching secret key.*
- SIGN *is a (randomized) signing algorithm that takes as input a secret key sk and a message m and outputs a signature s.*
- CONF *is a confirmation protocol between a signer and a verifier which takes as input a message m, a signature s, and signer's public key pk and allows the signer to prove to a verifier that the signature s is valid for the message m and the key pk.*
- DENY *is a denial protocol between a signer and a verifier which takes as input a message m, a signature s, and signer's public key pk and allows the signer to prove to a verifier that the signature s is invalid for the message m and the key pk.*

A confirmer signature scheme is essentially the same as above, except the role of confirmation and denial can also be performed by a third party called a confirmer. The significant modification is that the key generation algorithm produces a confirmation key ck which is needed for the confirmation or denial protocol.

Galbraith and Mao proposed a new security notion of undeniable and confirmer signatures named "anonymity" in [10]. We say that an undeniable or confirmer signature scheme provides anonymity when it is infeasible to determine which user generated the message-signature pair.

We slightly modify the definition of anonymity in [10] in order to put a common key generation into it explicitly.

Definition 9 ([10]). *Let $\mathcal{SIG} = (\text{CGEN}, \text{KGEN}, \text{SIGN}, \text{CONF}, \text{DENY})$ be an undeniable or confirmer signature scheme. Let $b \in \{0, 1\}$ and $k \in \mathbb{N}$ (security parameter). Let $A = (A_1, A_2)$ be adversaries that run in two stages. A has access to the oracles $\text{SIGN}_{sk_0}, \text{SIGN}_{sk_1}$ and A can execute confirmation and denial protocols $\text{CONF}_{sk_0}, \text{CONF}_{sk_1}, \text{DENY}_{sk_0}, \text{DENY}_{sk_1}$ on any message-signature pair. However, it is mandated that A_2 never execute $\text{CONF}_{sk_0}, \text{CONF}_{sk_1}, \text{DENY}_{sk_0}, \text{DENY}_{sk_1}$ on $(m', \sigma') \in EC(m, \sigma, pk_0) \cup EC(m, \sigma, pk_1)$ (EC means "equivalence class." If we get a message-signature pair (m, σ) under the key pk, then we can easily compute all elements in $EC(m, \sigma, pk)$.). Note that si be a state information. It contains common keys, public keys, and so on. Now we consider the following experiments:*

> **Experiment $\text{Exp}_{\mathcal{SIG}, A}^{\text{Anonym-}b}(k)$**
> $I \leftarrow \text{CGEN}(1^k); \ (pk_0, sk_0) \leftarrow \text{KGEN}(I); \ (pk_1, sk_1) \leftarrow \text{KGEN}(I)$
> $(m, \text{si}) \leftarrow A_1(pk_0, pk_1); \ \sigma \leftarrow \text{SIGN}_{sk_b}(m); \ d \leftarrow A_2(m, \sigma, \text{si})$
> return d

We define the advantages of the adversaries via:

$$\mathbf{Adv}_{\mathcal{SIG}, A}^{\text{Anonym}}(k) = \left| \Pr[\mathbf{Exp}_{\mathcal{SIG}, A}^{\text{Anonym-1}}(k) = 1] - \Pr[\mathbf{Exp}_{\mathcal{SIG}, A}^{\text{Anonym-0}}(k) = 1] \right|.$$

The scheme $\mathcal{SIG}$ provides anonymity if the function $\mathbf{Adv}_{\mathcal{SIG}, A}^{\text{Anonym}}(\cdot)$ is negligible for any adversary A whose time complexity is polynomial in k.

5.2   Undeniable and Confirmer Signature with Sampling Twice

In this section, we propose the undeniable and confirmer signature schemes with the sampling twice technique.

Definition 10. *The common-key generation algorithm* CGEN *takes a security parameter k and returns parameters k, k_0 and k_1 such that $k_0(k) + k_1(k) < k$ for all $k > 1$. The key generation algorithm* KGEN *takes k, k_0, k_1, runs the key-generation algorithm of* RSA, *and gets N, e, d, p, q where p, q are the safe primes (i.e. $(p-1)/2$ and $(q-1)/2$ are also primes)[1]. It picks g from $\mathbb{Z}_N^*$ and sets $h \leftarrow g^d \bmod N$. The public key pk is $(N, g, h), k, k_0, k_1$ and the secret key sk is $(N, e, d, p, q), k, k_0, k_1$. Let $G_0 : \{0,1\}^* \rightarrow \{0,1\}^{k_1}$, $G_1 : \{0,1\}^{k_1} \rightarrow \{0,1\}^{k_0}$, $G_2 : \{0,1\}^{k_1} \rightarrow \{0,1\}^{k-k_0-k_1-1}$, and $F : \{0,1\}^k \rightarrow \{0,1\}^k$ be hash functions. The signing algorithm is as follows.*

SIGN(m)
   $r_1, r_2 \xleftarrow{R} \{0,1\}^{k_0}$
   $\bar{m}_1 \leftarrow$ SIGN2(m, r_1); $t_1 \xleftarrow{R} \{c \in \mathbb{Z}_N \mid c^2 = \pm\bar{m}_1 \pmod{N}\}$; $s_1 \leftarrow (t_1)^d \bmod N$
   $\bar{m}_2 \leftarrow$ SIGN2(m, r_2); $t_2 \xleftarrow{R} \{c \in \mathbb{Z}_N \mid c^2 = \pm\bar{m}_2 \pmod{N}\}$; $s_2 \leftarrow (t_2)^d \bmod N$
   $s \leftarrow$ ChooseAndShift(s_1, s_2)
   if $(s \bmod N = s_1)$ $r \leftarrow r_1$ else $r \leftarrow r_2$
   return (s, r)

where

   SIGN2(m, r)
      $w \leftarrow G_0(m||r)$; $r^* \leftarrow G_1(w) \oplus r$; $M \leftarrow 0||w||r^*||G_2(w)$; $\bar{m} \leftarrow M$
      while $\left(\left(\frac{\bar{m}}{N}\right) \neq 1\right)$ repeat $\bar{m} \leftarrow F(\bar{m})$
      return $\bar{m}$

CONF *(respectively* DENY*) is a non-interactive designated verifier proof which proves the knowledge of an integer e such that $g = h^e \pmod{N}$ and $s^{2e} = \pm$SIGN2$(m, r) \pmod{N}$ (resp. $g = h^e \pmod{N}$ and $s^{2e} \neq \pm$SIGN2$(m, r) \pmod{N}$). To construct such proofs, we first employ protocols similar to those in [14] by Galbraith, Mao, and Paterson. Then, we transform them to corresponding non-interactive designated verifier proofs by the method of Jakobsson, Sako, and Impagliazzo [15][2]. The equivalence class of this scheme is $EC(m, (s, r), pk) = \{(m, (\pm s' \pm uN, r)) \mid s' = s \bmod N \wedge u \in \lfloor (2^k - s')/N \rfloor\}$.*

In our scheme (and also the scheme by Galbraith and Mao), we have to use RSA moduli which are the products of safe primes for obtaining the anonymity property. Gennaro, Krawczyk, and Rabin [16] proposed the RSA-based undeniable signature schemes where RSA moduli are restricted to the products of safe primes, and the confirmation and denial protocols in [16] is more efficient than

---

[1] We need this restriction for proving anonymity.

[2] These proof transcripts must be encrypted when sent to the verifier if anonymity is to be preserved.

	Sampling Twice	Expanding [10]	Repeating
# of mod. exp. to sign (average / worst)	2 / 2	1 / 1	1.5 / k_1
# of computation of square root (average / worst)	2 / 2	1 / 1	1.5 / k_1
size of signatures	$k + k_0$	$2k + k_0$	$(k-1) + k_0$
# of random bits to sign (average / worst)	$k_0 + k + 5$ / $k_0 + k + 5$	$k_0 + k + 2$ / $k_0 + k + 2$	$1.5(k_0 + 2)$ / $k_1(k_0 + 2)$

Fig. 3. The comparison of the undeniable and confirmer signature schemes.

those by Galbraith, Mao, and Paterson [14]. Therefore, it seems better to use the protocols in [16]. However, if we use the protocols in [16], the prover will have to prove that her RSA modulo has the proper form (i.e. a product of safe primes) during the protocols, and it needs a costly proof. To avoid this, Galbraith, Mao, and Paterson [14] constructed different scheme where there is no restriction for the RSA moduli.

5.3 Analysis

We compare the four schemes with sampling twice, expanding, and repeating.

Security. Galbraith and Mao [10] proved that their scheme provides anonymity in the random oracle model under the assumption that the composite decision Diffie-Hellman problem is hard (Given $(g, h, u, v) \in (\mathbb{Z}_N^*)^4$, it is infeasible to determine whether the two equations $h = g^r \pmod{N}$ and $v = \alpha u^r \pmod{N}$ hold, where $r \in \mathbb{Z}_{\phi(N)}^*$ and $\mathrm{ord}(\alpha) = 2$. See [10] for details.). They also proved that their scheme is existential unforgeable in the random oracle model under the assumption that factoring integers which are products of safe primes is hard. We can prove that the scheme with sampling twice provides anonymity in the random oracle model under the assumption that the composite decision Diffie-Hellman problem is hard, and is existential unforgeable in the random oracle model under the assumption that factoring integers which are products of safe primes is hard. Noticing that the signature space changes, the proofs are similar to those for the Galbraith–Mao scheme (See Appendices B and C in [10].).

Efficiency. We show the number of modular exponentiations to sign, the number of computation of square root, the size of signatures, and the number of random bits to sign in Figure 3. We assume that N is uniformly distributed in $(2^{k-1}, 2^k)$.

6 Ring Signature

6.1 Definitions

In [12], Rivest, Shamir, and Tauman proposed the notion of ring signature, which allows a member of an ad hoc collection of users S to prove that a message is authenticated by a member of S without revealing which member actually produced the signature. Unlike group signature, ring signature has no group managers, no setup procedures, no revocation procedures, and no coordination.

Definition 11 (Ring Signature [12]). *One assumes that each user U_i (called a ring member) has received (via a PKI or a certificate) a public key P_i, for which the corresponding secret key is denoted by S_i. A ring signature scheme consists of the following algorithms.*

- **ring-sign**$(m, P_1, P_2, \cdots, P_r, s, S_s)$ *which produces a ring signature σ for the message m, given the public keys $P_1, P_2, \cdots, P_r$ of the r ring members, together with the secret key S_s of the s-th member (who is the actual signer).*
- **ring-verify**(m, σ) *which accepts a message m and a signature σ (which includes the public key of all the possible signers), and outputs either* valid *or* invalid.

The signer does not need the knowledge, consent, or assistance of the other ring members to put them in the ring. All he needs is knowledge of their regular public keys. Verification must satisfy the usual soundness and completeness conditions, but in addition the signature scheme must satisfy "signer-ambiguity," which is the property that the verifier is unable to determine the identity of the actual signer with probability greater than $1/r + \epsilon$, where r is the size of the ring and ϵ is negligible. Furthermore, the signature scheme must satisfy "existential unforgeability under adaptive chosen message attack."

The formal concept of ring signature can be related to an abstract concept called *combining functions*. In [12], Rivest, Shamir, and Tauman proposed a combining function based on a symmetric encryption scheme E modeled by a (keyed) random permutation

$$C_{k,v}(y_1, \cdots, y_r) = E_k(y_r \oplus E_k(y_{r-1} \oplus \cdots E_k(y_2 \oplus E_k(y_1 \oplus v))\cdots)).$$

For any k, v, z, any index s, and any fixed values of $\{y_i\}_{i \neq s}$, we can easily find y_s such that $C_{k,v}(y_1, \cdots, y_r) = z$ by using the following equation:

$$y_s = E_k^{-1}\big(y_{s+1} \oplus \cdots E_k^{-1}(y_r \oplus E_k^{-1}(z))\cdots\big) \oplus E_k\big(y_{s-1} \oplus \cdots E_k(y_1 \oplus v)\cdots\big).$$

6.2 Ring Signature with Sampling Twice

In this section, we propose a ring signature scheme with the sampling twice technique. To verify the signatures deterministically, we add some information c_i to the signature.

Definition 12. *Let ℓ, k be security parameters. Let E be a symmetric encryption scheme over $\{0,1\}^k$ using ℓ-bit keys, and let h be a hash function which maps strings of arbitrary length to ℓ-bit strings. Each user U_i has public key $P_i = (N_i, e_i, k)$ and secret key $S_i = (N_i, d_i, k)$ by running the key generation algorithm of* RSA *with security parameter k (i.e. the size of N_i is k). Let r be the number of ring members. The signing algorithm is as follows.*

ring-sign$(m, P_1, P_2, \cdots, P_r, s, S_s)$
  for each $i \in \{1, \cdots, s-1, s+1, \cdots, r\}$ do
    $x_i^1, x_i^2 \xleftarrow{R} \mathbb{Z}_{N_i}^*$
    $y_i^1 \leftarrow (x_i^1)^{e_i} \bmod N_i; \quad y_i^2 \leftarrow (x_i^2)^{e_i} \bmod N_i$
    $y_i \leftarrow \texttt{ChooseAndShift}(y_i^1, y_i^2)$
    if $(y_i \bmod N_i = y_i^1)$ $x_i \leftarrow x_i^1$ else $x_i \leftarrow x_i^2$
    if $(y_i \geq N_i)$ $c_i \leftarrow 1$ else $c_i \leftarrow 0$

  $v \xleftarrow{R} \{0,1\}^k$
  find y_s s.t. $C_{h(m),v}(y_1, \cdots, y_r) = v$
  if $(y_s \geq N_s)$ $c_s \leftarrow 1$ else $c_s \leftarrow 0$
  $x_s \leftarrow (y_s)^{d_s} \bmod N_s$
  return $\sigma = (P_1, P_2, \cdots, P_r, v, (x_1, c_1), (x_2, c_2), \cdots, (x_r, c_r))$

The verification algorithm ring-verify(m, σ) *computes* $y_i \leftarrow ((x_i)^{e_i} \bmod N_i) + c_i \cdot N_i$ *for each* (x_i, c_i) *and* $z \leftarrow C_{h(m),v}(y_1, \cdots, y_r)$. *It returns* valid *if and only if* $z = v$.

6.3   Analysis

We compare the four schemes with sampling twice, expanding, RSACD, and repeating.

Security. Rivest, Shamir, and Tauman [12] proved that their scheme is un-conditionally signer-ambiguous and provably secure in the ideal cipher model assuming RSA is one-way. Hayashi, Okamoto, and Tanaka [13] proved that their scheme is unconditionally signer-ambiguous and provably secure in the ideal cipher model assuming RSACD is one-way.

We can prove that our scheme is unconditionally signer-ambiguous, since for each k and v the equation $C_{h(m),v}(y_1, \cdots, y_r) = v$ has exactly $(2^{k-1})^{r-1}$ solutions, and all of them are chosen by the signature generation procedure with equal probability, regardless of the signer's identity.

	Sampling Twice	Expanding [12]	RSACD [13]	Repeating
# of mod. exp. to sign (average / worst)	$2r$ / $2r$	r / r	$1.5r$ / $2r$	$1.5r$ / kr
# of mod. exp. to verify (average / worst)	r / r	r / r	$1.5r$ / $2r$	r / r
size of signatures	$(3r+1)k + r$	$(3r+1)k$ $+160(r+1)$	$(3r+1)k$	$(3r+1)k - 1$
# of random bits to sign (average / worst)	$3(k+1)(r-1)+k$ / $3(k+1)(r-1)+k$	$(k+160)r$ / $(k+160)r$	kr / kr	$1.5k(r-1)+k-1$ / $k^2(r-1)+k-1$

Fig. 4. The comparison of the ring signature schemes ($|N_i| = k$).

We can also prove that our scheme is existential unforgeable under adaptive chosen message attack in the ideal cipher model assuming RSA is one-way. The proof is almost the same as that for the Rivest–Shamir–Tauman scheme. The difference is as follows.

In the proof of unforgeability for the Rivest–Shamir–Tauman scheme, given $y \in \mathbb{Z}_N^*$, one slips y as a "gap" between two consecutive E functions along the ring. Then, the forger has to compute the e-th root of y, and this leads one to obtain the e-th root of y.

In the proof for our scheme, given $y \in \mathbb{Z}_N^*$, we pick a random bit $t \in \{0, 1\}$, set $y' \leftarrow y + tN$. If $y' < 2^k$ then one slips y' as a "gap" between two consecutive E functions along the ring. The rest of the proof is the same as that for the Rivest–Shamir–Tauman scheme (See Section 3.5 in [12].).

Recently, Bresson, Stern, and Szydlo [17] improved the ring signature scheme of Rivest, Shamir, and Tauman. They showed that its security can be based on the random oracle model, which is strictly weaker than the ideal cipher model. Furthermore, this greatly simplified the security proof provided in [12]. We can apply their construction to the schemes with sampling twice and RSACD.

Efficiency. We show the number of modular exponentiations to sign and to verify, the size of signatures, and the number of random bits to sign in Figure 4. We assume that each N_i is uniformly distributed in $(2^{k-1}, 2^k)$.

In the schemes with sampling twice and RSACD, it is necessary for each ring member to choose her RSA modulo with the same length, and in the scheme with repeating, it is necessary for each ring member to choose her RSA modulo with almost the same length. In contrast to these schemes, in the scheme with expanding, there is no restriction on the lengths of users' moduli. However, if there is one ring member whose RSA modulo is much larger than the other member's moduli, then the size of the signature and the number of random bits depends on the largest modulo. For example, if there is a user whose RSA modulo has length $k + \ell$ and the other users' moduli have lengths k, then the size of signature is $(3r + 1)k + 160(r + 1) + \ell(r + 4)$ and the number of random bits to sign is $r(k + 160) + r\ell$.

7   Concluding Remarks

In this paper, we have proposed a new technique for obtaining the anonymity property of RSA-based cryptosystems, which we call "sampling twice." By applying the sampling twice technique, we have constructed the schemes for encryption, undeniable and confirmer signature, and ring signature.

In our analysis, we have observed that the scheme with sampling twice is efficient with respect to the sizes of ciphertexts and signatures, the computational costs to decrypt ciphertexts and to verify signatures in the average and worst cases, and the computational costs to encrypt messages and to sign messages in the worst case.

Acknowledgements

We thank the anonymous referees for valuable comments.

References

1. Bellare, M., Boldyreva, A., Desai, A., Pointcheval, D.: Key-Privacy in Public-Key Encryption. [18] 566–582 Full version of this paper, available via http://www-cse.ucsd.edu/users/mihir/.
2. Bellare, M., Rogaway, P.: Optimal Asymmetric Encryption – How to Encrypt with RSA. [19] 92–111
3. Fujisaki, E., Okamoto, T., Pointcheval, D., Stern, J.: RSA-OAEP is Secure under the RSA Assumption. In Kilian, J., ed.: Advances in Cryptology – CRYPTO 2001. Volume 2139 of Lecture Notes in Computer Science., Santa Barbara, California, USA, Springer-Verlag (2001) 260–274
4. Krawczyk, H.: SKEME: A Versatile Secure Key Exchange Mechanism for Internet. In: Proceedings of the 1996 Internet Society Symposium on Network and Distributed System Security, San Diego, CA, USA (1996) 114–127
5. Camenisch, J., Lysyanskaya, A.: Efficient Non-Transferable Anonymous Multi-Show Credential System with Optional Anonymity Revocation. In Pfitzmann, B., ed.: Advances in Cryptology – EUROCRYPT 2001. Volume 2045 of Lecture Notes in Computer Science., Innsbruck, Austria, Springer-Verlag (2001) 93–118
6. Sako, K.: An Auction Protocol Which Hides Bids of Losers. In Imai, H., Zheng, Y., eds.: Public Key Cryptography – PKC 2000. Volume 1751 of Lecture Notes in Computer Science., Melbourne, Victoria, Australia, Springer-Verlag (2000) 422–432
7. Chaum, D., Antwerpen, H.V.: Undeniable Signatures. In Brassard, G., ed.: Advances in Cryptology – CRYPTO '89. Volume 435 of Lecture Notes in Computer Science., Santa Barbara, California, USA, Springer-Verlag (1989) 212–217
8. Chaum, D.: Zero-Knowledge Undeniable Signatures. In Damgård, I., ed.: Advances in Cryptology – EUROCRYPT '90. Volume 473 of Lecture Notes in Computer Science., Aarhus, Denmark, Springer-Verlag (1990) 458–464
9. Chaum, D.: Designated Confirmer Signatures. [19] 86–91
10. Galbraith, S.D., Mao, W.: Invisibility and Anonymity of Undeniable and Confirmer Signatures. In Joye, M., ed.: Topics in Cryptology – CT-RSA 2003. Volume 2612 of Lecture Notes in Computer Science., San Francisco, CA, USA, Springer-Verlag (2003) 80–97
11. Desmedt, Y.: Securing traceability of ciphertexts: Towards a secure software escrow scheme. In Guillou, L.C., Quisquater, J.J., eds.: Advances in Cryptology – EUROCRYPT '95. Volume 921 of Lecture Notes in Computer Science., Saint-Malo, France, Springer-Verlag (1995) 147–157
12. Rivest, R.L., Shamir, A., Tauman, Y.: How to Leak a Secret. [18] 552–565
13. Hayashi, R., Okamoto, T., Tanaka, K.: An RSA Family of Trap-door Permutations with a Common Domain and its Applications. In Bao, F., Deng, R.H., Zhou, J., eds.: Public Key Cryptography – PKC 2004. Volume 2947 of Lecture Notes in Computer Science., Singapore, Springer-Verlag (2004) 291–304
14. Galbraith, S.D., Mao, W., Paterson, K.G.: RSA-based Undeniable Signatures for General Moduli. In Preneel, B., ed.: Topics in Cryptology – CT-RSA 2002. Volume 2271 of Lecture Notes in Computer Science., San Jose, CA, USA, Springer-Verlag (2002) 200–217

15. Jakobsson, M., Sako, K., Impagliazzo, R.: Designated Verifier Proofs and their Applications. In Maurer, U., ed.: Advances in Cryptology – EUROCRYPT '96. Volume 1070 of Lecture Notes in Computer Science., Saragossa, Spain, Springer-Verlag (1996) 143–154

16. Gennaro, R., Krawczyk, H., Rabin, T.: RSA-based Undeniable Signatures. In Kaliski, Jr., B.S., ed.: Advances in Cryptology – CRYPTO '97. Volume 1294 of Lecture Notes in Computer Science., Santa Barbara, California, USA, Springer-Verlag (1997) 132–149

17. Bresson, E., Stern, J., Szydlo, M.: Threshold Ring Signatures and Applications to Ad-hoc Groups. In Yung, M., ed.: Advances in Cryptology – CRYPTO 2002. Volume 2442 of Lecture Notes in Computer Science., Santa Barbara, California, USA, Springer-Verlag (2002) 465–480

18. Boyd, C., ed.: Advances in Cryptology – ASIACRYPT 2001. Volume 2248 of Lecture Notes in Computer Science., Gold Coast, Australia, Springer-Verlag (2001)

19. De Santis, A., ed.: Advances in Cryptology – EUROCRYPT '94. Volume 950 of Lecture Notes in Computer Science., Perugia, Italy, Springer-Verlag (1994)

From Fixed-Length to Arbitrary-Length RSA Encoding Schemes Revisited

Julien Cathalo[1], Jean-Sébastien Coron[2], and David Naccache[2,3]

[1] UCL Crypto Group,
Place du Levant 3, Louvain-la-Neuve, B-1348, Belgium
cathalo@dice.ucl.ac.be
[2] Gemplus Card International,
34 rue Guynemer, 92447 Issy-les-Moulineaux, France
{jean-sebastien.coron,david.naccache}@gemplus.com
[3] Royal Holloway, University of London,
Information Security Group,
Egham, Surrey TW20 0EX, UK
david.naccache@rhul.ac.uk

Abstract. To sign with RSA, one usually encodes the message m as $\mu(m)$ and then raises the result to the private exponent modulo N. In Asiacrypt 2000, Coron et al. showed how to build a secure RSA encoding scheme $\mu'(m)$ for signing arbitrarily long messages from a secure encoding scheme $\mu(m)$ capable of handling only fixed-size messages, without making any additional assumptions. However, their construction required that the input size of μ be larger than the modulus size. In this paper we present a construction for which the input size of μ does not have to be larger than N. Our construction shows that the difficulty in building a secure encoding for RSA signatures is not in handling messages of arbitrary length, but rather in finding a secure encoding function for short messages, which remains an open problem in the standard model.

1 Introduction

A common practice for signing with RSA is to first apply some encoding function μ to the message m, and then raise the result to the signature exponent modulo N. This is the basis of numerous standards such as ISO/IEC-9796-1 [7], ISO 9796-2 [8] and PKCS#1 v2.0 [11].

For digital signature schemes, the strongest security notion was defined by Goldwasser, Micali and Rivest in [6], as *existential unforgeability under an adaptive chosen message attack*. This notion captures the property that an attacker cannot produce a valid signature, even after obtaining the signature of (polynomially many) messages of his choice.

Many RSA encoding schemes have been designed and many have been broken (see [9] for a survey). The Full Domain Hash (FDH) scheme and the Probabilistic Signature Scheme (PSS) [3] were among the first practical and provably secure RSA signature schemes. Those schemes are provably secure in the random oracle

S. Vaudenay (Ed.): PKC 2005, LNCS 3386, pp. 234–243, 2005.

model [2], wherein the hash function is assumed to behave as a truly random function. However, security proofs in the random oracle model are not "real" proofs, and can be only considered as heuristic, since in the real world random oracles are necessarily replaced by functions which can be computed by all parties. A famous result by Canneti, Goldreich and Halevi [4] shows that a security proof in the random oracle model does not necessarily imply security in the "real world".

In this paper, we focus on the problem of finding a secure encoding scheme for arbitrarily long messages, given a secure encoding scheme for fixed-size messages. It is well known that this can be done using a collision-resistant hash function $H : \{0,1\}^* \rightarrow \{0,1\}^\ell$ for both signing and verifying, where ℓ is the input size of $\mu(m)$. A standard argument shows that if the original signature scheme is secure against existential forgery under a chosen-message attack, then so is the signature scheme with the hash.

In Asiacrypt 2000, Coron, Koeune and Naccache [5] showed that for RSA signatures, the same result can be obtained without assuming the existence of collision-resistant hash-functions. Namely, they construct an encoding scheme $\mu'(m)$ for messages in $\{0,1\}^*$, given an encoding scheme $\mu(m)$ for messages of fixed-size. They show that if RSA signature with $\mu(m)$ is secure against existential forgery under a chosen-message attack (in the standard model), then so is RSA with $\mu'(m)$ for messages of arbitrary size, without any additional assumptions.

However, their construction requires that the input size ℓ of $\mu(m)$ be larger than the size of N (hereafter denoted k). Several standards (for example the ISO/IEC 9796-1 standard [7]) fail to comply with this property. The authors left as an open problem the case $\ell \leq k$.

In this paper, we solve this open problem and provide a construction for any input size ℓ. A variant of this problem was already solved by Arboit and Robert in [1], who proposed a construction similar to [5] that works for any ℓ, but at the cost of a new security assumption, namely the division intractability of the encoding function $\mu(m)$. The advantage of our construction is that we do not make any additional assumptions, namely if RSA signature with $\mu(m)$ is secure against existential forgery under a chosen-message attack, then so is RSA with $\mu'(m)$ for messages of arbitrary size. As is the case for the constructions in [5] and [1], a practical advantage of our construction is that it allows to perform some pre-computations on partially received messages, e.g. on IP packets which are typically received in random order.

We believe that our result focuses more sharply the question of finding a secure encoding for RSA signatures, by showing that the difficulty is not in handling messages of arbitrary length, but rather in finding a securing encoding for short messages, which remains an open problem in the standard model.

2   Definitions

2.1   Signature Schemes

The digital signature of a message m is a string that depends on m and on some secret known only to the signer, in such a way that anyone can check the validity of the signature. The following definitions are based on [6].

Definition 1 (Signature Scheme). *A signature scheme is defined by the following:*

- *The key generation algorithm* Generate *is a probabilistic algorithm which given 1^k, outputs a pair of matching public and secret keys, (pk, sk).*
- *The signing algorithm* Sign *takes the message M to be signed and the secret key* sk *and returns a signature $x = \text{Sign}_{sk}(M)$. The signing algorithm may be probabilistic.*
- *The verification algorithm* Verify *takes a message M, a candidate signature x' and the public key* pk. *It returns a bit $\text{Verify}_{pk}(M, x')$, equal to one if the signature is accepted, and zero otherwise. We require that if $x \leftarrow \text{Sign}_{sk}(M)$, then $\text{Verify}_{pk}(M, x) = 1$.*

2.2   Security of Signature Schemes

The security of signature schemes was formalized in an asymptotic setting by Goldwasser, Micali and Rivest [6]. Here we use the definitions of [3] which provide a framework for the concrete security analysis of digital signatures. Resistance against adaptive chosen-message attacks is considered: a forger $\mathcal{F}$ can dynamically obtain signatures of messages of its choice and attempt to output a valid forgery. A *valid forgery* is a message/signature pair (M, x) such that $\text{Verify}_{pk}(M, x) = 1$ whilst the signature of M was never requested by $\mathcal{F}$.

Definition 2. *A forger $\mathcal{F}$ is said to $(t, q_{sig}, \varepsilon)$-break the signature scheme (Generate, Sign, Verify) if after at most $q_{sig}(k)$ signature queries and $t(k)$ processing time, it outputs a valid forgery with probability at least $\varepsilon(k)$ for any $k > 0$.*

Definition 3. *A signature scheme (Generate, Sign, Verify) is $(t, q_{sig}, \varepsilon)$-secure if there is no forger who $(t, q_{sig}, \varepsilon)$-breaks the scheme.*

2.3   The RSA Primitive

RSA [10] is the most widely used public-key cryptosystem. It can be used to provide both encryption schemes and digital signatures.

Definition 4 (The RSA Cryptosystem). *RSA is a family of trapdoor permutations. It is specified by:*

- *The RSA generator $\mathcal{RSA}$, which on input 1^k, randomly selects two distinct $k/2$-bit primes p and q and computes the modulus $N = p \cdot q$. It randomly picks an encryption exponent $e \in \mathbb{Z}_{\phi(N)}^*$ and computes the corresponding decryption exponent d such that $e \cdot d = 1 \bmod \phi(N)$. The generator returns $\{N, e, d\}$.*
- *The encryption function $f : \mathbb{Z}_N^* \to \mathbb{Z}_N^*$ defined by $f(x) = x^e \bmod N$.*
- *The decryption function $f^{-1} : \mathbb{Z}_N^* \to \mathbb{Z}_N^*$ defined by $f^{-1}(y) = y^d \bmod N$.*

2.4   RSA Encoding and Signature

Let μ be a encoding function taking as input a message of size ℓ bits and returning a k-bit integer. We consider in figure 1 the classical RSA signature scheme which signs fixed-length ℓ-bits messages.

```
System parameters
  - two integers k > 0 and ℓ > 0
   - a function μ : {0,1}ℓ → {0,1}k
Key generation: Generate
  - (N, e, d) ← RSA(1k)
  - public key: (N, e)
  - private key: (N, d)
Signature generation: Sign
  - let y ← μ(m)
  - return yd mod N
Signature verification: Verify
  - let y ← xe mod N
  - let y′ ← μ(m)
  - if y = y′ then return one else return zero.
```

Fig. 1. The Classical RSA Paradigm: Using μ for Signing Fixed-Length Messages.

3   The Coron-Koeune-Naccache Construction

We recall in figure 2 the construction proposed in [5]. It assumes that the encoding function μ can handle inputs of size $k + 1$ where k is the size of the modulus and allows to sign $2^a \cdot (k - a)$ bit messages where $0 \leq a \leq k - 1$. The construction can be recursively iterated to sign messages of arbitrary length. Throughout this paper, $m_1 \| m_2$ will denote the concatenation of m_1 and m_2.

It is shown in [5] that the scheme described in figure 2 is secure against existential forgery under a chosen message attack:

Theorem 1. *If the signature scheme* (Generate, Sign, Verify) *is* $(t, q_{sig}, \varepsilon)$ *secure, then the signature scheme* (Generate*, Sign*, Verify*) *which signs* $2^a \cdot (k - a)$ *bit messages is* $(t^*, q^*_{sig}, \varepsilon^*)$ *secure, where:*

$$t^*(k) = t(k) - 2^a \cdot q_{sig}(k) \cdot \mathcal{O}(k^2), \tag{1}$$

$$q^*_{sig}(k) = q_{sig}(k) - 2^{a+1}, \tag{2}$$

$$\varepsilon^*(k) = \varepsilon(k) . \tag{3}$$

4   Bimodular Encoding

The drawback of the previous construction is that the the input size ℓ of $\mu(m)$ needs to be larger than the size of the modulus N. In this section, we describe a

System parameters
- two integers $k > 0$ and $a \in [0, k-1]$
- a function $\mu : \{0,1\}^{k+1} \to \{0,1\}^k$

Key generation: Generate*
- $(N, e, d) \leftarrow RSA(1^k)$
- public key: (N, e)
- private key: (N, d)

Signature generation: Sign*
- Split the message m into $(k-a)$-bit blocks
  such that $m = m[1]\|\ldots\|m[r]$.
- let $\alpha = \prod_{i=1}^{r} \mu(0\|i\|m[i]) \bmod N$
  where i in $0\|i\|m[i]$ is an a-bit string representing i.
- let $y \leftarrow \mu(1\|\alpha)$
- return $y^d \bmod N$

Verification: Verify*
- let $y \leftarrow x^e \bmod N$
- let $\alpha = \prod_{i=1}^{r} \mu(0\|i\|m[i]) \bmod N$
- let $y' \leftarrow \mu(1\|\alpha)$
- if $y = y'$ then return one else return zero.

Fig. 2. Coron-Koeune-Naccache Encoding of Arbitrary Length Messages.

construction wherein the input size ℓ of the encoding function μ does not need larger than k. We denote by $\ell(k)$ the input size of the encoding function μ as a function of the security parameter k. In the following, we assume that $\ell(k)$ is an increasing function of k. For example, for the ISO/IEC 9796-1 standard [7], we have $\ell(k) \simeq k/2$.

The new signature scheme (Generate', Sign', Verify') is described in figure 3. The new signature scheme is parameterized by two security parameters k_1, k_2 such that $k_1 < k_2$. As the previous construction, it is a deterministic signature scheme. The construction uses the same encoding function μ with two distinct moduli N_1 and N_2 of sizes k_1 and k_2 bits, respectively. For the sake of clarity and since encoding functions take the modulus as a parameter, we will write μ_i when μ is used with modulus N_i. We denote by $\ell_1 = \ell(k_1), \ell_2 = \ell(k_2)$ the input sizes of μ_1, μ_2 respectively. Our construction requires that $\ell_2 \geq k_1$. Since by assumption $\ell(k)$ is an increasing function of k, this means that a sufficiently large security parameter k_2 must be selected in order to have $\ell_2 = \ell(k_2) \geq k_1$

Our construction enables to sign $2^a \cdot (\ell_1 - a)$ bit messages where $0 \leq a \leq \ell_1 - 1$. The maximum length that can be handled by the new construction is therefore $2^{\ell_1 - 1}$ bits for $a = \ell_1 - 1$ or $a = \ell_1 - 2$ and, as in [5], the construction can be recursively iterated so as to sign arbitrarily long messages.

A possible realization example is the following: assume that we are given an encoding function μ that takes as input $k/2$-bit messages and outputs k-bit strings, for signing with a k-bit RSA modulus. If we take for example $k_1 = 1024$, $k_2 = 2048$ and $a = 24$, then messages of size up to $2^{24} \cdot 488 \simeq 8.2 \cdot 10^9$ bits can

```
System parameters
   - two positive integers k₁, k₂ such that k₂ > k₁
   - an integer a ∈ [0, k₁ − 1]
   - two functions μᵢ : {0,1}^ℓᵢ → {0,1}^kᵢ for i = 1, 2
     such that ℓ₂ ≥ k₁.
Key generation: Generate'
   - (N₁, e₁, d₁) ← RSA(1^k₁)
   - (N₂, e₂, d₂) ← RSA(1^k₂)
   - public key: (N₁, N₂, e₂)
   - private key: (N₁, N₂, d₂)
Signature generation: Sign'
   - Split the message m into (ℓ₁ − a)-bit blocks
     such that m = m[1]|| ... ||m[r].
   - let α = ∏ᵢ₌₁ʳ μ₁(i||m[i]) mod N₁
     where i in i||m[i] is an a-bit string representing i.
   - let y ← μ₂(α)
   - return y^d₂ mod N₂
Verification: Verify'
   - y ← x^e₂ mod N₂
   - let α = ∏ᵢ₌₁ʳ μ₁(i||m[i]) mod N₁
   - let y' ← μ₂(α)
   - if y = y' then return one else return zero.
```

Fig. 3. Bimodular Encoding of Arbitrary Length Messages.

be signed. First, one applies the encoding function $\mu_1 : \{0,1\}^{512} \to \{0,1\}^{1024}$ to the 2^{24} blocks of 488 bits; then one multiplies together the resulting 1024-bit integers modulo N_1 and obtains a 1024-bit integer which is finally signed using the encoding function $\mu_2 : \{0,1\}^{1024} \to \{0,1\}^{2048}$ modulo N_2. Notice that d_1 is not used for signing and e_1 is not needed for the verification either; thus (e_1, d_1) is to be deleted after the generation of N_1.

The following theorem states that this construction preserves the resistance against chosen message attacks of the original signature scheme:

Theorem 2. *If the signature scheme* (Generate, Sign, Verify) *is* $(t, q_{sig}, \varepsilon)$ *secure, then the signature scheme* (Generate', Sign', Verify') *which signs* $2^a \cdot (\ell_1 - a)$ *bit messages is* $(t', q'_{sig}, \varepsilon')$ *secure, where:*

$$t'(k_1, k_2) = t(k_1) - q'_{sig} \cdot 2^a \cdot \left(T_\mu(k_2) + \mathcal{O}(k_2{}^3)\right), \tag{4}$$

$$q'_{sig}(k_1, k_2) = q_{sig}(k_1) - 2^{a+1}, \tag{5}$$

$$\varepsilon'(k_1, k_2) = 4 \cdot \varepsilon(k_1). \tag{6}$$

and $T_\mu(k_2)$ *is the time required to compute* $\mu(m)$ *for security parameter* k_2.

Proof. Without loss of generality, we can assume that $t(k)$, $q_{sig}(k)$ and $T_\mu(k)$ are increasing functions of k, and that $\varepsilon(k)$ is a decreasing function of k.

Let $\mathcal{F}'$ be a forger that breaks the signature scheme (Generate', Sign', Verify') for the parameters (k_1, k_2). We construct a forger $\mathcal{F}_1$ for the signature scheme (Generate, Sign, Verify) for the parameter $k = k_1$ and a forger $\mathcal{F}_2$ for same signature scheme with parameter $k = k_2$. When the same property holds for both $\mathcal{F}_1$ and $\mathcal{F}_2$, we write this property for a generic forger $\mathcal{F}$. The forger $\mathcal{F}$ will run $\mathcal{F}'$ in order to produce a forgery; it will answer the signature queries of $\mathcal{F}'$ by itself. $\mathcal{F}$ has access to a signing oracle $\mathcal{S}$ for (Generate, Sign, Verify).

First, we pick a random bit b. If $b = 1$, we construct a forger $\mathcal{F}_1$ for the parameter $k = k_1$. If $b = 0$, we construct a forger $\mathcal{F}_2$ for the parameter $k = k_2$.

$\mathcal{F}$ is first given as input (N, e) where N, e were obtained by running Generate for the parameter k defined previously. The forger $\mathcal{F}$ then starts running $\mathcal{F}'$ with the public key (N_1, N_2, e_2), where N_1, N_2, e_2 are defined as follows:

If $b = 1$, the forger $\mathcal{F}_1$ sets $N_1 \leftarrow N$, $e_1 \leftarrow e$ and runs $RSA(1^{k_2})$ to obtain (N_2, e_2, d_2). Otherwise (if $b = 0$) the forger $\mathcal{F}_2$ sets $N_2 \leftarrow N$, $e_2 \leftarrow e$ and runs $RSA(1^{k_1})$ to obtain (N_1, e_1, d_1).

We observe that the view of the forger $\mathcal{F}'$ in independent of the bit b, since in both cases the moduli N_1 and N_2 are generated using $RSA(1^{k_1})$ and $RSA(1^{k_2})$, either by $\mathcal{F}$ itself or through (N, e) given as input to $\mathcal{F}$.

When $\mathcal{F}'$ asks the signature of the j-th message m_j with $m_j = m_j[1]||\ldots|| m_j[r_j]$, $\mathcal{F}$ computes:

$$\alpha_j = \prod_{i=1}^{r_j} \mu_1(i||m_j[i]) \bmod N_1$$

If $b = 0$ then $\mathcal{F}_2$ requests the signature s_j of α_j from $\mathcal{S}$. If $b = 1$ then $\mathcal{F}_1$ can compute $s_j = \mu_2(\alpha_j)^{d_2} \bmod N_2$ directly since it knows d_2. Let q'_{sig} be the total number of signatures requested by $\mathcal{F}'$.

Eventually $\mathcal{F}'$ outputs a forgery (m', s') for the signature scheme (Generate', Sign', Verify') with $m' = m'[1]||\ldots||m'[r']$, from which $\mathcal{F}$ computes:

$$\alpha' = \prod_{i=1}^{r'} \mu_1(i||m'[i]) \bmod N_1 \tag{7}$$

We denote by β the probability that $\alpha' \notin \{\alpha_1, \ldots, \alpha_q\}$. Note that since the view of $\mathcal{F}'$ is independent of b, this event is independent of b as well. We distinguish three cases:

First Case: $\alpha' \notin \{\alpha_1, \ldots, \alpha_q\}$ and $b = 0$. From the remark above, this happens with probability $\beta/2$. In which case $\mathcal{F}_2$ outputs the forgery (α', s') and halts. This is a valid forgery for the signature scheme (Generate, Sign, Verify) since $s' = \mu_2(\alpha')^{d_2} \bmod N_2$ and the signature of α' was never asked to the signing oracle $\mathcal{S}$.

Second Case: $\alpha' \in \{\alpha_1, \ldots, \alpha_q\}$ and $b = 1$. This happens with probability $(1 - \beta)/2$. Let c be such that $\alpha = \alpha_c$. We write $m = m_c$, $\alpha = \alpha_c$ and $r = r_c$, which gives using (7):

$$\prod_{i=1}^{r'} \mu_1(i||m'[i]) \bmod N_1 = \prod_{i=1}^{r} \mu_1(i||m[i]) \bmod N_1 \tag{8}$$

We show that the previous equation leads to a multiplicative forgery for the modulus $N_1 = N$, which enables $\mathcal{F}_1$ to compute a forgery.

First, the message m' must be distinct from m because the signature of m has been requested by $\mathcal{F}'$ whereas the signature of m' was never requested by $\mathcal{F}$, since m' is the message for which a forgery was obtained. Consequently there exists an integer j such that either:

$$j||m'[j] \notin \{1||m[1], \ldots, r||m[r]\} \tag{9}$$

or:

$$j||m[j] \notin \{1||m'[1], \ldots, r'||m'[r']\} \tag{10}$$

We assume that condition (9) is satisfied (condition (10) leads to the same result). Therefore from (8) we can write:

$$\mu(j||m'[j]) = \left(\prod_i \mu(i||m[i])\right)\left(\prod_{i \neq j} \mu(i||m'[i])\right)^{-1} \bmod N_1 \tag{11}$$

Consequently, $\mathcal{F}_1$ asks the signing oracle $\mathcal{S}$ for the signatures x_i of the messages $i||m[i]$, $1 \leq i \leq r$, and for the signatures x_i' of the messages $i||m'[i]$, $1 \leq i \leq r'$, $i \neq j$. Using (11), $\mathcal{F}_1$ can compute the signature of $j||m'[j]$ from the other signatures:

$$x_j' = \mu(j||m'[j])^{d_1} = \left(\prod_i x_i\right)\left(\prod_{i \neq j} x_i'\right)^{-1} \bmod N_1$$

and $\mathcal{F}_1$ finally outputs the forgery $(j||m'[j], x_j')$. This is a valid forgery for the signature scheme (Generate, Sign, Verify) since the signature of $j||m'[j]$ was never asked to the signing oracle.

Third Case: $\alpha' \notin \{\alpha_1, \ldots, \alpha_q\}$ and $b = 1$, or $\alpha' \in \{\alpha_1, \ldots, \alpha_q\}$ and $b = 0$. In this case, $\mathcal{F}$ fails. This happens with probability $1/2$.

To summarize, from a forger $\mathcal{F}'$ that breaks the signature scheme (Generate', Sign', Verify') with probability $\varepsilon'(k_1, k_2)$ for the parameters (k_1, k_2), we construct a forger $\mathcal{F}$ that breaks the signature scheme (Generate, Sign, Verify) with probability $\varepsilon' \cdot \beta/2$ for the parameter k_2, and with probability $\varepsilon' \cdot (1 - \beta)/2$ for the parameter k_1, for some (unknown) β.

Therefore, if we assume that the signature scheme (Generate, Sign, Verify) cannot be broken in time $t(k)$ with probability greater than $\varepsilon(k)$ for all k, we must have:

$$\varepsilon'(k_1, k_2) \cdot \beta/2 \leq \varepsilon(k_2)$$

and

$$\varepsilon'(k_1, k_2) \cdot (1 - \beta)/2 \leq \varepsilon(k_1)$$

which implies using $\varepsilon(k_2) \leq \varepsilon(k_1)$ that:

$$\varepsilon'(k_1, k_2) \leq 4 \cdot \varepsilon(k_1)$$

which gives (6).

If $b = 0$, then for each of the q'_{sig} queries of $\mathcal{F}'$, the forger $\mathcal{F}_2$ makes at most 2^a multiplications modulo N_1 and one query to $\mathcal{S}$. Thus $\mathcal{F}_2$ runs in time

$$t(k_2) = t'(k_1, k_2) + q'_{sig} \cdot 2^a \cdot \left(T_\mu(k_1) + \mathcal{O}(k_1^{\ 2}) \right) \tag{12}$$

If $b = 1$ then for each query of $\mathcal{F}'$, the forger $\mathcal{F}_1$ makes at most 2^a multiplications modulo N_1 and one exponentiation modulo N_2. After it has received the forgery, it makes at most 2^{a+1} multiplications modulo N_1 to compute its own forgery. Thus $\mathcal{F}_1$ runs in time:

$$t(k_1) = t'(k_1, k_2) + q'_{sig} \cdot \left(2^a \cdot \left(T_\mu(k_1) + \mathcal{O}(k_1^{\ 2}) \right) + T_\mu(k_2) + \mathcal{O}(k_2^{\ 3}) \right) \tag{13}$$

From inequalities (12) and (13), and using $t(k_1) \leq t(k_2)$ and $T_\mu(k_1) \leq T_\mu(k_2)$ we obtain (4).

Finally, the forger $\mathcal{F}_2$ makes at most q'_{sig} queries to the signing oracle, and the forger $\mathcal{F}_1$ makes at most 2^{a+1} queries to the signing oracle. This gives $q_{sig}(k_2) \leq q'_{sig}(k_1, k_2)$ and $q_{sig}(k_1) \leq 2^{a+1}$. Using $q_{sig}(k_1) \leq q_{sig}(k_2)$, we obtain

$$q_{sig}(k_1) \leq 2^{a+1} + q'_{sig}(k_1, k_2),$$

which gives (5). $\square$

5   Conclusion

In this paper, we showed how to construct a secure RSA encoding scheme for signing arbitrarily long messages, given any secure encoding scheme for signing fixed-size messages. This solves a problem left open by Coron *et al.* in [5]. We believe that our work focuses the question of finding a secure encoding for RSA signatures, by showing that the difficulty in building secure encoding schemes for RSA is not in handling messages of arbitrary length, but rather in finding a secure redundancy function for short messages, which remains an open problem in the standard model.

References

1. G. Arboit and J.M. Robert, *From Fixed-Length to Arbitrary-Length Messages Practical RSA Signature Padding Schemes*, in LNCS 2020 – Topics in Cryptology CT-RSA 2001, Springer-Verlag, p. 44-51.
2. M. Bellare and P. Rogaway, *Random oracles are practical: a paradigm for designing efficient protocols*, proceedings of the First Annual Conference on Computer and Commmunications Security, ACM, 1993.
3. M. Bellare and P. Rogaway, *The exact security of digital signatures - How to sign with RSA and Rabin*, proceedings of Eurocrypt'96, LNCS vol. 1070, Springer-Verlag, 1996, pp. 399-416.
4. R. Canetti, O. Goldreich and S. Halevi, *The Random Oracle Methodology, Revisited*, STOC '98, ACM, 1998.

5. J.S. Coron, F. Koeune, D. Naccache, *From fixed-length to arbitrary-length RSA padding schemes*, Proceedings of Asiacrypt 2000, LNCS vol. 1976, Springer-Verlag, 2000.
6. S. Goldwasser, S. Micali and R. Rivest, *A digital signature scheme secure against adaptive chosen-message attacks*, SIAM Journal of computing, 17(2):281-308, april 1988.
7. ISO/IEC 9796, *Information technology - Security techniques - Digital signature scheme giving message recovery, Part 1: Mechanisms using redundancy*, 1999.
8. ISO/IEC 9796-2, *Information technology - Security techniques - Digital signature scheme giving message recovery, Part 2: Mechanisms using a hash-function*, 1997
9. J.F. Misarsky, *How (not) to design signature schemes*, proceedings of PKC'98, Lecture Notes in Computer Science vol. 1431, Springer Verlag, 1998.
10. R. Rivest, A. Shamir and L. Adleman, *A method for obtaining digital signatures and public key cryptosystems*, CACM 21, 1978.
11. RSA Laboratories, PKCS #1: *RSA cryptography specifications*, version 2.0, September 1998.

Tractable Rational Map Signature

Lih-Chung Wang[1,*], Yuh-Hua Hu[2], Feipei Lai[3],
Chun-Yen Chou[4,**], and Bo-Yin Yang[5,***]

[1] Department of Applied Mathematics,
National Donghwa University, Hualien 974, Taiwan
lcwang@mail.ndhu.edu.tw
[2] Department of Computer Science and Information Engineering,
National Taiwan University, Taipei 106, Taiwan
d92015@csie.ntu.edu.tw
[3] Departments of Electrical Engineering &
of Computer Science and Information Engineering,
National Taiwan University, Taipei 106, Taiwan
flai@ntu.edu.tw
[4] Department of Mathematical Education,
National Hualien Teachers College, Hualien 970, Taiwan
choucy@mail.nhltc.edu.tw
[5] Dept. of Mathematics, Tamkang University, Tamsui 251, Taiwan
by@moscito.org

Abstract. Digital signature schemes are crucial for applications in electronic commerce. The effectiveness and security of a digital signature scheme rely on its underlying public key cryptosystem. Trapdoor functions are central to public key cryptosystems. However, the modular exponentiation for RSA or the discrete logarithms for ElGamal/DSA/ECC, as the choice of the trapdoor functions, are relatively slow in performance. Some multivariate schemes has potentially much higher performance than other public key cryptosystems. We present a new multivariate digital signature scheme (TRMS) based on tractable rational maps. We also give some security analysis and some actual implementation data in comparison to some other signature schemes.

Keywords: multivariate, public key, digital signature, finite field, tractable rational maps

1 Introduction

Digital signature schemes are crucial for applications in electronic commerce. For example, to improve the efficiency and maintain the order of stock exchange, each on-line transaction needs to be verified to be validated. The effectiveness and security of a digital signature scheme rely on its underlying public key cryptosystem. Trapdoor functions are central to public key cryptosystems. Only a

* Partially supported by National Science Council Grant NSC-93-2115-M-259-003.
** Partially supported by National Science Council Grant NSC-93-2115-M-026-001.
*** Partially supported by National Science Council Grant NSC-93-2115-M-032-008.

S. Vaudenay (Ed.): PKC 2005, LNCS 3386, pp. 244–257, 2005.

handful of the many schemes attempted reached practical deployment. However, the modular exponentiation for RSA or the discrete logarithms for ElGamal/DSA/ECC, as the choice of the trapdoor functions, are relatively slow in performance. One main reason is the size of the single operand which (at the required security levels) tends to be huge, and this slows the performance.

Some multivariate schemes distinguish themselves from other public key cryptosystems by showing potential for higher performance. For example, Courtois, Goubin and Patarin proposed SFLASH, which has been selected by Nessie Consortium and recommended for low-cost smart cards. The newest version of this signature scheme, SFLASH^{v3} may be found in [12]. Also, Chen and Yang gave a class of signature (TTS) scheme based on tame transformations in [4, 5, 38]. The newest version of TTS, called Enhanced TTS, outperforms ([40]) all previously known digital signature schemes of comparable security levels, including SFLASH^{v3}. A summary of this newest instance may be found in [38].

Here we will present a new class of multivariate digital signature scheme (TRMS) based on tractable rational maps. TRMS has similar security and performance as Enhanced-TTS. However there is a small yet non-negligible chance (around 7%) that signing takes perceptibly longer in the newer versions of TTS. In contrast, the signing time for TRMS is constant, which can do no harm and may be an improvement.

Fix a finite field $\mathbb{K}$ and a natural number n. Tractable rational maps on $\mathbb{K}^n$ are invertible affine transformations or, after a rearrangement of indices if necessary, functions of the following form $\varphi : \mathbb{K}^n \to \mathbb{K}^n$,

$$
\begin{cases}
y_1 = r_1(x_1) \\
y_2 = r_2(x_2)\dfrac{p_2(x_1)}{q_2(x_1)} + \dfrac{f_2(x_1)}{g_2(x_1)} \\
\quad\vdots \\
y_k = r_k(x_k)\dfrac{p_k(x_1, x_2, \ldots, x_{k-1})}{q_k(x_1, x_2, \ldots, x_{k-1})} + \dfrac{f_k(x_1, x_2, \ldots, x_{k-1})}{g_k(x_1, x_2, \ldots, x_{k-1})} \\
\quad\vdots \\
y_n = r_n(x_n)\dfrac{p_n(x_1, x_2, \ldots, x_{n-1})}{q_n(x_1, x_2, \ldots, x_{n-1})} + \dfrac{f_n(x_1, x_2, \ldots, x_{n-1})}{g_n(x_1, x_2, \ldots, x_{n-1})}
\end{cases}
$$

where for $i = 2, 3, \ldots, n$, p_i, q_i, f_i, g_i are polynomials, and for $i = 1, 2, \ldots, n$, r_i is a permutation polynomial on $\mathbb{K}$. That is, r_i is a polynomial function which is also a bijection from $\mathbb{K}$ onto itself.

Let $S = \{(x_1, x_2, \ldots, x_n) \mid \prod_{j=2}^{n} p_j q_j g_j \neq 0\}$. For any point in the image set of S, it is very easy to find point-wise inverse for tractable rational maps: Given a point $(y_1, y_2, \ldots, y_n) \in \varphi(S)$, we can easily compute $(x_1, x_2, \ldots, x_n) \in \mathbb{K}^n$ such that $\varphi(x_1, x_2, \ldots, x_n) = (y_1, y_2, \ldots, y_n)$. When φ is an invertible affine transformation, we can easily write the inverse transformation φ^{-1} in an explicit and simultaneous way. That is, we have an explicit formula from which we can compute $x_1, x_2, \ldots, x_n$ simultaneously. When φ is not an invertible affine transformation, although it is computationally infeasible to write the inverse in an explicit and simultaneous way, given any point $(y_1, y_2, \ldots, y_n) \in \varphi(S)$, it is very easy to compute $x_1, x_2, \ldots, x_n$ in a sequential way. We simply apply a sequence of substitutions as follows. We refer to this as substitution property.

$$
\begin{cases}
x_1 = r_1^{-1}(y_1) \\
x_2 = r_2^{-1}\left((y_2 - \dfrac{f_2(x_1)}{g_2(x_1)}) \dfrac{q_2(x_1)}{p_2(x_1)} \right) \\
\quad \vdots \\
x_k = r_k^{-1}\left((y_k - \dfrac{f_k(x_1, x_2, \ldots, x_{k-1})}{g_k(x_1, x_2, \ldots, x_{k-1})}) \dfrac{q_k(x_1, x_2, \ldots, x_{k-1})}{p_k(x_1, x_2, \ldots, x_{k-1})} \right) \\
\quad \vdots \\
x_n = r_n^{-1}\left((y_n - \dfrac{f_n(x_1, x_2, \ldots, x_{n-1})}{g_n(x_1, x_2, \ldots, x_{n-1})}) \dfrac{q_n(x_1, x_2, \ldots, x_{n-1})}{p_n(x_1, x_2, \ldots, x_{n-1})} \right)
\end{cases}
$$

Note that, by Lagrange interpolation, any map over a finite field is a polynomial map. There are both computational and categorical reasons that we put our maps in rational form. For computational reasons, it is faster to compute the division between two function values by low degree polynomial maps than to compute a single function value by a much higher degree polynomial map. For example, it is much easier to compute $\dfrac{1}{x}$ than to compute x^{254} over $GF(256)$. And categorically, even given a tractable rational map without denominator, by the direct computation above, the inverse of that map is most naturally described as a rational map. Therefore we choose to put the map in the rational form. For details, see [36].

TRMS is the result of exploring the combination of substitution property of tractable rational maps and other mathematical ideas into application of digital signatures.

In [26], T. Moh invented a public key cryptosystem (TTM) based on tame automorphisms which also have the substitution property. It is easily seen that tame transformations are special cases of tractable rational maps with the term $r_k(x_k)\dfrac{p_k(x_1, x_2, \ldots, x_{k-1})}{q_k(x_1, x_2, \ldots, x_{k-1})}$ replaced by x_k. Therefore it is not surprising at all that TRMS based on tractable rational maps can achieve similar security and performance as TTS based on tame automorphisms. However, there are also substantial differences between TRMS and TTS with respect to other mathematical ideas and designs.

In section 2, we give the details of TRMS. In section 3, we give some actual implementation data. In section 4, we give some analysis and compare TRMS to other signature schemes, in particular, including TTS.

2   Details of TRMS

We show an implement scheme of TRMS. It can be seen that there are a variety of schemes of TRMS which are all based on tractable rational maps.

Let $\mathbb{K} = GF(2^8)$. We will construct 3 maps $\varphi_1 : \mathbb{K}^{28} \to \mathbb{K}^{28}$, $\varphi_2 : \mathbb{K}^{28} \to \mathbb{K}^{20}$, $\varphi_3 : \mathbb{K}^{20} \to \mathbb{K}^{20}$ where φ_1, φ_3 are invertible affine transformations, $\varphi_2 = \pi \circ \widetilde{\varphi_2} \circ i$

with π a projection, i an imbedding, and $\widetilde{\varphi_2}$ identified as a tractable rational map over some extension field over $\mathbb{K}$. All the details are given below.

The public key or the verification map V is the result of the composition map $\varphi_3 \circ \varphi_2 \circ \varphi_1$. Therefore the public key will only be seen as 20 quadratic polynomials in 28 variables whose size is about 8.7KB as shown below.

The private key or the key part in the signing map S is the triple $(\varphi_1, \varphi_2, \varphi_3)$ in some specified structured form whose size is about 0.4KB as shown below. As mentioned in the introduction, each φ_i gives direct instruction to find the point-wise inverse for any concrete instance. Therefore the private key holder or the signer can directly apply φ_i^{-1} point-wisely.

To sign a message M, first find its hash $\mathbf{z} = H(M) \in \mathbb{K}^{20}$ by a publicly agreed hash function. Then do $\mathbf{y} = \varphi_3^{-1}(\mathbf{z})$, where the indices of $\mathbf{y}$ is starting at 9. Then choose 8 nonzero random numbers $r_1, r_2, \ldots, r_8$. Then get $\mathbf{x}$ by identifying it with $(\widetilde{\varphi_2}^{-1} \circ i)(r_1, r_2, \ldots, r_8, \mathbf{y})$ which is computed by a sequence of substitutions. Then get the signature $\mathbf{w} = \varphi_1^{-1}(\mathbf{x})$.

To verify a signature $\mathbf{w}$, simply check if $V(\mathbf{w}) = (\varphi_3 \circ \varphi_2 \circ \varphi_1)(\mathbf{w}) = (\varphi_3 \circ \pi \circ \widetilde{\varphi_2} \circ i)(\mathbf{x}) = (\varphi_3 \circ \pi)(r_1, r_2, \ldots, r_8, \mathbf{y}) = \varphi_3(\mathbf{y}) = \mathbf{z} = H(M)$.

2.1 Details of φ_1 and φ_3

Since $GF(2^{32})$ is finite extension fields of $\mathbb{K}$ of degree 4, therefore we can identify an element in $\mathbb{K}^4$ as an element in $GF(2^{32})$. Furthermore, we can decompose $(x_1, x_2, \ldots, x_{28}) \in \mathbb{K}^{28}$ into seven groups: for $i = 1, 2, \ldots, 7$, $X_i = (x_{4i-3}, x_{4i-2}, x_{4i-1}, x_{4i})$ and identify $X_i \in GF(2^{32})$, $i = 1, 2, \ldots, 7$. Hence we can identify $\mathbb{K}^{28}$ with $GF(2^{32})^7$. Similarly, we can identify $\mathbb{K}^{20}$ with $GF(2^{32})^5$.

Let φ_1, φ_3 be invertible affine maps on $\mathbb{K}^{28}$ and $\mathbb{K}^{20}$ respectively such that $\varphi_1 = S_1 \circ T_1 \circ L_1 \circ D_1 \circ U_1$ and $\varphi_3 = T_3 \circ L_3 \circ D_3 \circ U_3 \circ S_3$ where

1. S_1 is a circular shift on $\mathbb{K}^{28}$ and S_3 is a circular shift on $\mathbb{K}^{20}$.
2. T_1 is a translation on $\mathbb{K}^{28}$ and T_3 is a translation on $\mathbb{K}^{20}$. T_3 is used to cancel the constant terms in the public key. Therefore T_3 is not chosen but determined.
3. L_1 is a 7×7 lower triangular matrix over $GF(2^{32})$ and L_3 is a 5×5 lower triangular matrix over $GF(2^{32})$ such that both with diagonal entries equal to $1 \in GF(2^{32})$.
4. D_1 is a 28×28 invertible upper triangular matrix over $\mathbb{K}$ and D_3 is a 20×20 invertible upper triangular matrix over $\mathbb{K}$ in the following form:

$$D_1 = \begin{pmatrix} d_1 & d_1^2 & d_1^3 & \ldots & d_1^{28} \\ 0 & d_2 & d_2^2 & \ldots & d_2^{27} \\ 0 & 0 & d_3 & \ldots & d_3^{26} \\ \vdots & \vdots & & \ddots & \vdots \\ 0 & 0 & 0 & \ldots & d_{28} \end{pmatrix}$$

5. U_1 is a 7×7 upper triangular matrix over $GF(2^{32})$ and U_3 is a 5×5 upper triangular matrix over $GF(2^{32})$ such that both with diagonal entries equal to $1 \in GF(2^{32})$.

Note that circular shifts on $\mathbb{K}^n$ are indeed linear transformations on $\mathbb{K}^n$ and each T_i above represents the translation part in the corresponding affine transformation. The LDU decomposition above covers quite a part of general invertible linear transformations. Moreover, our construction enjoys some benefits in key size. With L_1, U_1 linear on $GF(2^{32})^7$ and L_3, U_3 linear on $GF(2^{32})^5$, key size of the private key is reduced. Also, the calculation speed of additions is optimized on current 32-bit computer hardware structure. The diagonal entries in L's and U's are 1 implies that when we solve $L\mathbf{u} = \mathbf{v}$ or $U\mathbf{u} = \mathbf{v}$ we only have to do additions and multiplications and don't have to bother to do any division. Furthermore, with D_1 and D_3 both linear over $\mathbb{K}$ but not on $GF(2^{32})$, and also the circular shifts over $\mathbb{K}^n$, we can choose φ_1, φ_3 linear over $\mathbb{K}$, but not linear over $GF(2^{32})$. The purpose is to maintain security at the level over $\mathbb{K}$.

2.2   Details of φ_2

Let $\mathbb{L}, \mathbb{L}', \mathbb{L}''$ be the finite extension fields of $\mathbb{K}$ such that $\mathbb{K} \subset \mathbb{L}'' \subset \mathbb{L}' \subset \mathbb{L}$ and $[\mathbb{L}'' : \mathbb{K}] = 2$, $[\mathbb{L}' : \mathbb{L}''] = 3$, $[\mathbb{L} : \mathbb{L}'] = 3$. Therefore we can identify an element in $\mathbb{K}^2$ as an element in $\mathbb{L}' = GF(2^{16}) \subset \mathbb{L}' \subset \mathbb{L}$, an element in $\mathbb{K}^6$ as an element in $\mathbb{L}' = GF(2^{48}) \subset \mathbb{L}$, and an element in $\mathbb{K}^{18}$ as an element in $\mathbb{L} = GF(2^{144})$.

Decompose $(x_1, x_2, \ldots, x_{28}) \in \mathbb{K}^{28}$ into five groups: $X_1 = (x_1, x_2, \ldots, x_8)$, $X_2 = (x_9, x_{10}, x_{11}, x_{12}, x_{13}, x_{14})$, $X_3 = (x_{15}, x_{16})$, $X_4 = (x_{17}, x_{18}, x_{19})$ and $X_5 = (x_{20}, x_{21}, \ldots, x_{28})$. Identify X_1 with $(0, \ldots, 0, x_1, x_2, \ldots, x_8) \in \mathbb{L}$. Identify $X_2 \in \mathbb{K}^6$ as an element in $\mathbb{L}' \subset \mathbb{L}$. Identify $X_3 \in \mathbb{K}^2$ as an element in $\mathbb{L}'' \subset \mathbb{L}' \subset \mathbb{L}$ and $X_4 \in \mathbb{K}^3$ with $(0, x_{17}, 0, x_{18}, 0, x_{19}) \in \mathbb{L}'' \subset \mathbb{L}$. Identify $X_5 \in \mathbb{K}^9$ with $(0, x_{20}, 0, x_{21}, \ldots, 0, x_{28})$ as an element in $\mathbb{L}$. Hence we have a natural imbedding $i : \mathbb{K}^{28} \hookrightarrow \mathbb{L}^5$ by $i(x_1, x_2, \ldots, x_{28}) = (X_1, X_2, X_3, X_4, X_5)$. Similarly, decompose $(y_9, y_{10}, \ldots, y_{32}) \in \mathbb{K}^{20}$ into four groups: $Y_2 = (y_9, y_{10}, y_{11}, y_{12}, y_{13}, y_{14})$, $Y_3 = (y_{15}, y_{16})$, $Y_4 = (y_{17}, y_{18}, y_{19})$ and $Y_5 = (y_{20}, y_{21}, \ldots, y_{28})$ and identify them as elements in $\mathbb{L}$. For any $r_i \in \mathbb{K}$, $i = 1, 2, \ldots, 8$, identify $R_1 = (r_1, r_2, \ldots, r_8) \in \mathbb{K}^8$ with $(0, \ldots, 0, r_1, r_2, \ldots, r_8) \in \mathbb{L}$. Then we also have

$$i(r_1, r_2, \ldots, r_8, y_9, y_{10}, \ldots, y_{28}) = (R_1, Y_2, Y_3, Y_4, Y_5) \in \mathbb{L}^5.$$

Furthermore, since $\mathbb{K}^{20}$ is a subspace of $\mathbb{L}^5 = \mathbb{K}^{90}$, we have the projection $\pi : \mathbb{L}^5 \to \mathbb{K}^{20}$ such that $(\pi \circ i)(r_1, r_2, \ldots, r_8, y_9, y_{10}, \ldots, y_{28}) = (y_9, y_{10}, \ldots, y_{28})$

Let $\widetilde{\varphi_2} : \mathbb{L}^5 \to \mathbb{L}^5$ be a tractable rational map of the following form.

$$\begin{cases} R_1 = X_1 \\ Y_2 = X_2\, p_2(X_1)\, +\, f_2(X_1) \\ Y_3 = r_3(X_3)\, +\, f_3(X_1, X_2) \\ Y_4 = X_4\, p_4(X_1, X_2, X_3)\, +\, f_4(X_1, X_2, X_3) \\ Y_5 = X_5\, p_5(X_1, X_2, X_3, X_4)\, +\, f_5(X_1, X_2, X_3, X_4) \end{cases}$$

such that $\varphi_2 = \pi \circ \widetilde{\varphi_2} \circ i$, and we have the following in φ_2:

1. $R_1 = X_1$ induces $(r_1, r_2, \ldots, r_8) = (x_1, x_2, \ldots, x_8)$.
2. $Y_2 = X_2\, p_2(X_1)\, +\, f_2(X_1)$ induces

$$
\begin{pmatrix} y_9 \\ y_{10} \\ \vdots \\ y_{14} \end{pmatrix} = \begin{pmatrix} x_9 \\ x_{10} \\ \vdots \\ x_{14} \end{pmatrix} *_6 \begin{pmatrix} x_1 \\ x_2 \\ \vdots \\ x_6 \end{pmatrix} + \begin{pmatrix} c_1 x_1 x_2 \\ c_2 x_2 x_3 \\ \vdots \\ c_6 x_6 x_7 \end{pmatrix} + \begin{pmatrix} c_7 x_3 \\ c_8 x_4 \\ \vdots \\ c_{12} x_8 \end{pmatrix}
$$

where c_i's are constant parameters of user's choice and $\mathbf{u} *_n \mathbf{v}$ denotes first identifying $\mathbf{u}, \mathbf{v} \in \mathbb{K}^n$ in the extension field with degree n then carrying out the multiplication there. For details see Appendix.

3. $Y_3 = r_3(X_3) + f_3(X_1, X_2)$ induces

$$
\begin{pmatrix} y_{15} \\ y_{16} \end{pmatrix} = \begin{pmatrix} x_{15} \\ x_{16} \end{pmatrix}^2 + \begin{pmatrix} c_{13} x_1 x_2 + c_{14} x_3 x_4 + \cdots + c_{19} x_{13} x_{14} \\ c_{20} x_{14} x_1 + c_{21} x_2 x_3 + \cdots + c_{26} x_{12} x_{13} \end{pmatrix} + \begin{pmatrix} c_{27} x_1 \\ c_{28} x_2 \end{pmatrix}
$$

where $\begin{pmatrix} x_{15} \\ x_{16} \end{pmatrix}^2 = \begin{pmatrix} x_{15} \\ x_{16} \end{pmatrix} *_2 \begin{pmatrix} x_{15} \\ x_{16} \end{pmatrix}$ and c_i's are constant parameters of user's choice.

4. $Y_4 = X_4 \, p_4(X_1, X_2, X_3) + f_4(X_1, X_2, X_3)$ induces

$$
\begin{pmatrix} y_{17} \\ y_{18} \\ y_{19} \end{pmatrix} = \begin{pmatrix} x_{17} \\ x_{18} \\ x_{19} \end{pmatrix} *_3 \begin{pmatrix} x_8 \\ x_9 + x_{11} + x_{12} \\ x_{13} + x_{15} + x_{16} \end{pmatrix} + \begin{pmatrix} c_{29} x_4 x_{16} \\ c_{30} x_5 x_{10} \\ c_{31} x_{15} x_{16} \end{pmatrix} + \begin{pmatrix} c_{32} x_9 \\ c_{33} x_{10} \\ c_{34} x_{11} \end{pmatrix}
$$

where c_i's are constant parameters of user's choice.

5. $Y_5 = X_5 \, p_5(X_1, X_2, X_3, X_4) + f_5(X_1, X_2, X_3, X_4)$ induces

$$
\begin{pmatrix} y_{20} \\ y_{21} \\ \vdots \\ y_{28} \end{pmatrix} = \begin{pmatrix} x_{20} \\ x_{21} \\ \vdots \\ x_{28} \end{pmatrix} *_9 \begin{pmatrix} x_1 \\ x_2 + x_6 + x_{11} \\ x_3 + x_7 + x_{12} \\ x_4 + x_8 + x_{13} \\ x_5 + x_9 + x_{14} \\ x_{10} + x_{14} + x_{16} \\ x_{11} + x_{15} + x_{17} \\ x_{12} + x_{16} + x_{18} \\ x_{13} + x_{17} + x_{19} \end{pmatrix} + \begin{pmatrix} c_{35} x_{18} x_{19} \\ c_{36} x_{17} x_{13} \\ c_{37} x_{16} x_{14} \\ c_{38} x_{12} x_{13} \\ c_{39} x_{15} x_{14} \\ c_{40} x_{19} x_{12} \\ c_{41} x_{18} x_{10} \\ c_{42} x_{12} x_6 \\ c_{43} x_{13} x_5 \end{pmatrix} + \begin{pmatrix} c_{44} x_1 \\ c_{45} x_2 \\ \vdots \\ c_{52} x_9 \end{pmatrix}
$$

where c_i's are constant parameters of user's choice.

The reason why the formulas in the above assignments represents a permutation polynomial r_3 and polynomials $p_2, f_2, f_3, p_4, f_4, p_5, f_5$ is as follows.

1. We identify $X_3 = (x_{15}, x_{16})$ as an element in $\mathbb{L}'' = GF(2^{16})$ which is of characteristic 2. For any finite field of characteristic 2, $X \mapsto X^2$ is an automorphism. Hence let $r_3(X) = X^2$, then r_3 is an automorphism on $\mathbb{L}''$, hence a permutation polynomial. And $\begin{pmatrix} x_{15} \\ x_{16} \end{pmatrix} \mapsto \begin{pmatrix} x_{15} \\ x_{16} \end{pmatrix}^2$ surely represents r_3.

2. For polynomials $p_2, f_2, f_3, p_4, f_4, p_5, f_5$, simply notice that on a finite field, any map is a polynomial map. See [36] for details. For example, we show the case of p_2 for illustration. Consider a map $\mathcal{P}$ on $\mathbb{L}$ as follows

$$\mathcal{P}(X_1) = \begin{cases} \begin{pmatrix} 0 \\ \vdots \\ 0 \\ 0 \\ 0 \\ x_1 \\ x_2 \\ x_3 \\ x_4 \\ x_5 \\ x_6 \end{pmatrix} & \text{if } X_1 = \begin{pmatrix} 0 \\ \vdots \\ 0 \\ x_1 \\ x_2 \\ x_3 \\ x_4 \\ x_5 \\ x_6 \\ x_7 \\ x_8 \end{pmatrix}, \\ \\ \vec{0} & \text{otherwise.} \end{cases}$$

Simply let p_2 to be the polynomial representation for $\mathcal{P}$.

It is worth to mention the following.

1. For theoretical purpose we showed above that φ_2 is viewed as $\pi \circ \widetilde{\varphi_2} \circ i$ where $\widetilde{\varphi_2} : \mathbb{L}^5 \to \mathbb{L}^5$ is a tractable rational map with polynomials p_2, f_2, f_3, p_4, f_4, p_5, f_5 possibly very complicated. Computationally, we actually follow the other way around. That is, φ_2 is a computationally efficient representation for $\widetilde{\varphi_2}$ when restricted to the subspace $i(\mathbb{K}^{28})$. We get benefits on calculation speed due the following. The second assignment in φ_2 can be carried out in the subfield $GF(2^{48})$ instead of in $\mathbb{L} = GF(2^{144})$. For details see appendix. Similarly, the third assignment in φ_2 can be carried out in $\mathbb{L}'' = GF(2^{16})$ instead of in $\mathbb{L} = GF(2^{144})$. Both these contribute on calculation speed.
2. It is easily seen that our φ_2 representation is quadratic in x_i's. Since φ_1, φ_3 are affine maps, the public key is 20 general quadratic polynomials in 28 variables without constant terms.

2.3   Information on Keys

As shown above, $\varphi_1 = S_1 \circ T_1 \circ L_1 \circ D_1 \circ U_1$, $\varphi_3 = T_3 \circ L_3 \circ D_3 \circ U_3 \circ S_3$, and there are 52 parameters $c_1, c_2, \ldots, c_{52}$ for the private key user to choose in φ_2. Therefore the size for private key is $[0 + 28 + 4(1 + 2 + 3 + 4 + 5 + 6) + 28 + 4(6 + 5 + 4 + 3 + 2 + 1)] + [20 + 4(1 + 2 + 3 + 4) + 20 + 4(4 + 3 + 2 + 1) + 0] + 52 = 396$ Bytes. However, T_3 in φ_3 is not chosen but determined. Hence it is to choose 376 nonzero elements in $\mathbb{K}$ to generate the private key.

Also, since the public key is 20 general quadratic polynomials in 28 variables without constant terms, its size is $20 \cdot (\dfrac{28 \cdot 29}{2} + 28) = 8680$ bytes. In general, there are two ways to generate the public keys. One way is the method of undetermined coefficients, the other one is to make the composition by direct computation. Both have many optimized variants. Our major concern is on the structure of TRMS, therefore we did not put much effort in the optimization of the key generation.

3   Performance

Test Platform: CPU: P4 2.4GHz; RAM: 1024MB; OS: Linux + gcc 3.3;
ARG: gcc -O3 -march=pentium4 -fomit-frame-pointer

Scheme Name	Signature size (byte)	Public Key Size (byte)	Private Key Size (byte)	Sign (μs)	Verify (μs)	Key Generation (ms)
TTS(20,28)	28	8680	1399	7	20	2.2
TRMS(20,28)	28	8680	396	4.8	20	1.2

Table: NESSIE signature report, TTS and TRMS tested as above

Unit: $\begin{cases} \text{Signature/key size:Bytes,} \\ \text{Sign/Verify/Key Generation: cycles/invocation} \end{cases}$

Scheme Name	Signature size	Public Key Size	Private Key Size	Sign	Verify	Key Generation
ECDSA	48	48	24	1971K	5415K	1758K
ESgin	144	145	96	4434K	936K	269M
RSA-PSS	128	128	320	82M	1587K	3206M
SFLASH$_{v2}$	37	$\approx$ 15K	$\approx$ 28K	5106K	765K	2929M
SQARTZ	16	$\approx$ 71K	$\approx$ 4K	6261M	144K	3167M
ACESign	425	620	748	26M	20M	9645M
TTS(20,28)	28	$\approx$ 8.7K	$\approx$ 1.4K	16.8K	48K	5.28M
TRMS(20,28)	28	$\approx$ 8.7K	396	11.4K	48K	2.67M

4   Analysis and Comparison

4.1   Security Analysis

For brevity, we fix the following notations for our TRMS example:

- $m = 20$ denotes the dimension of the hash space.
- $n = 28$ denotes the dimension of the signature space.
- $q = 2^8$ denotes the size of the base field $GF(256)$.

There are several known attacks for multivariate cryptosystems.

Rank Attack: Goubin and Courtois shows that the MinRank attack for Tri-angular-Plus-Minus systems. Yang and Chen generalized the idea to Rank attack for multivariate systems in [38]. The complexity of the Rank attack is about $q^r \cdot \dfrac{(m^2(\frac{n}{2} - \frac{m}{6}) + mn^2)}{k}$ multiplications, where k is the number of linear combinations of the components of φ_2 which reach the minimal rank r. The minimal rank for our example is at least 12, and k is 6. Therefore the complexity is about 2^{107} multiplications or 2^{101} 3DES units (1 unit of 3DES $\approx 2^6$ multiplications).

Dual Rank Attack: Coppersmith et al first ([6]) used the Dual Rank attack against multivariate scheme of Shamir; Yang and Chen to generalize this attack to all tame-like multivariate systems in [38]. The complexity of the Dual Rank attack is about $q^u(un^2 + \frac{n^3}{6})$ multiplications where u is the minimal number of appearances in φ_2 for any variable x_i. When $u = 9$ for our sample scheme, the complexity is about 2^{86} multiplications or 2^{80} 3DES units.

Unbalanced Oil and Vinegar Attack: As in [38], Let an "oil-set" be any set of independent variables x_i, such that any of their cross-products never appears in any equation in φ_2. Suppose the maximum size of an oil set is k, then then we may determine in time $k^4 q^{n-2k-1}$ the "vinegar" and the "oil" subspaces. After that, several possible techniques may be used to find a solution. If case $k = 9$, so the time taken to identify the vinegar and oil subspaces is about 2^{86} multiplications, or 2^{80} 3DES units.

Patarin Relations Attack for C^* Family: In φ_2 of our TRMS example, there is no Patarin relation, which means the attack for C^* family is not feasible for our system.

Affine Parts Distillation: Geiselmann et al. in [19, 20] pointed out the possibility that if the middle portion of any multivariate system is homogeneous of degree two, then it is possible to find the constant parts of both affine mappings easily. The φ_2 in our TRMS example is not homogeneous.

XL Family and Gröbner Bases: Courtois et al proposed the XL method for solving overdetermined quadratic system (which can be viewed as a refinement of the relinearization method by Kipnis-Shamir, [24]) and its variant FXL in [11]. Faugère ([15, 16]) have been improving algorithms for computing Gröbner Bases, and the current state-of-the art variant is **F$_5$**, which was used as the critical equation solver in breaking the HFE challenge 1 ([17]). The consensus of current research ([1–3, 13, 39, 41]) is that Gröbner/XL-like equation solvers on generic equations are exponential in the number of variables. The best variant will be **FF$_5$** if $O(n^{2+\varepsilon})$ timing can be achieved, and FXL otherwise. The time complexity for the two methods on a system with $m = 20$ equations will be respectively 2^{74} and 2^{76} 3DES units, still better than RSA-1024 (see [29]). If $m = 24$, then we would get 2^{80} and 2^{81} respectively.

Remark: The speed estimates on nongeneric equations are still being debated, but the converse to Moh's lemma was proved in [39], which shows that it is likely that all Gröbner/XL-like equation solvers will run into trouble if the dimension of the projective solution set at infinity (denoted $\dim H_\infty$) is non-zero. It is not very easy to benefit from this, however, because the UOV attack means that the last stage of our sample TRMS scheme or something similar cannot be too large, and the dual rank attack dictates that it cannot be too small! Thus for $m = 20$, we cannot benefit $\dim H_\infty > 0$, because the last stage is forced to be 9 variables. For larger TRMS schemes, say $m = 28$ upwards, we can start to do better with optimal selection of parameters.

Finding Minus and Vinegar Variables: These are very specialized methods designed against what is generally called "Big-Field" multivariate schemes such as C^{*--}. They do not work against tame-like multivariates with non-constant central parts.

Patarin's IP Approach: Patarin et al proposed an attack method for fixed middle map schemes in [31, 32]. Since there are variable parameters in the middle map, the IP attack is not applicable.

Search Methods: Courtois et al proposed some search methods at PKC 2002 in [7]. However, they are mainly designed for small finite fields, and we may follow the computations of [4] to find a complexity of 2^{120} 3DES units.

4.2 Comparison to Enhanced-TTS

The structure of the latest version of TTS, Enhanced-TTS is as follows. Fix a finite field $\mathbb{K}$. Choose three natural numbers m, n, k such that $m < n$ and $k < n - m$. Let φ_1, φ_3 are invertible affine maps on $\mathbb{K}^n$ and $\mathbb{K}^m$ respectively. Let $\varphi_2 : \mathbb{K}^n \to \mathbb{K}^m$ be of the following form. (Below f_i's are all quadratic and $\mathbf{y} = (y_{n-m+1}, \ldots, y_n)$.)

$$
\begin{cases}
r_1 & = x_1 \\
r_2 & = x_2 \\
\vdots & \vdots \\
r_{n-m} & = x_{n-m} \\
\begin{pmatrix} y_{n-m+1} \\ y_{n-m+2} \\ \vdots \\ y_{n-k-j} \end{pmatrix} & = \begin{pmatrix} \text{invertible} \\ \text{matrix of} \\ \text{linear} \\ \text{expressions of} \\ x_1, \ldots, x_{n-m} \end{pmatrix} \begin{pmatrix} x_{n-m+1} \\ x_{n-m+2} \\ \vdots \\ x_{n-k-j} \end{pmatrix} + \begin{pmatrix} \text{column} \\ \text{vector of} \\ \text{quadratic} \\ \text{expressions of} \\ x_1, \ldots, x_{n-m} \end{pmatrix} \\
y_{n-k-j+1} & = x_{n-k-j+1} + f_{n-k-j+1}(x_1, x_2, \ldots, x_{n-k-j}) \\
\vdots & \vdots \\
y_{n-k} & = x_{n-k} + f_{n-k}(x_1, x_2, \ldots, x_{n-k-1}) \\
\begin{pmatrix} y_{n-k+1} \\ y_{n-k+2} \\ \vdots \\ y_n \end{pmatrix} & = \begin{pmatrix} \text{invertible} \\ \text{matrix of} \\ \text{linear} \\ \text{expressions of} \\ x_1, \ldots, x_{n-k} \end{pmatrix} \begin{pmatrix} x_{n-k+1} \\ x_{n-k+2} \\ \vdots \\ x_n \end{pmatrix} + \begin{pmatrix} \text{column} \\ \text{vector of} \\ \text{quadratic} \\ \text{expressions of} \\ x_1, \ldots, x_{n-k} \end{pmatrix}
\end{cases}
$$

The verification map V can be decomposed as $\mathbf{w} \in \mathbb{K}^n \overset{\varphi_1}{\mapsto} \mathbf{x} \overset{\varphi_2}{\mapsto} \mathbf{y} \overset{\varphi_3}{\mapsto} \mathbf{z} \in \mathbb{K}^m$. That is, $V = \varphi_3 \circ \varphi_2 \circ \varphi_1$, where $\mathbf{x} = \varphi_1(\mathbf{w}) = M_1\mathbf{w} + \mathbf{c}_1$, $\mathbf{z} = \varphi_3(\mathbf{y}) = M_3\mathbf{y} + \mathbf{c}_3$ and $(r_1, r_2, \ldots, r_{n-m}, \mathbf{y}) = \varphi_2(\mathbf{x})$.

To sign a message, Enhanced-TTS needs to solve two systems of equations for finding one inverse image point of the middle map. There is about $1/25$ chance of redoing the signing procedure for the implement in [38]. However, our TRMS example has constant signing time, since the non-zero element in a field is always invertible.

Regarding to signing time, TRMS is better than TTS. One reason is that TRMS utilizes special field extension structure to reduce the computation time for φ_2^{-1}, the details is in the Appendix, while TTS only uses the common method of Gaussian elimination. Another reason is that during computation of the affine transformations φ_1, φ_3, part of it is also carried out in a larger field, which will benefit the computation, too. We like to point out that there are a lot of ways to construct φ_1, φ_3. One reason for us to use the LU-decomposition is that it has advantages when implemented on smart cards.

The main external differences between TRMS(20,28) and Enhanced-TTS(20,28) can be tabulated as follows.

1. The private key size for TTS is 1.4KB, while for TRMS it is 396 bytes.
2. Regarding to signing time, TRMS is better than TTS.
3. TTS has at most 7% chance of redoing the signing procedure while the signing time for TRMS is constant.

5   Appendix: Implement of Field Extension

Firstly, $GF(2) = \{(0)_2, (1)_2\}$, where $(\cdot)_2$ means the binary representation. Then $t^2 + t + (1)_2$ is irreducible over $GF(2)$. Let $GF(4) = GF(2)[t]/(t^2 + t + (1)_2)$ and $(ab)_2$ denote the equivalent class of $at + b$. Then we have the following multiplication table.

	$(00)_2$	$(01)_2$	$(10)_2$	$(11)_2$
$(00)_2$	$(00)_2$	$(00)_2$	$(00)_2$	$(00)_2$
$(01)_2$	$(00)_2$	$(01)_2$	$(10)_2$	$(11)_2$
$(10)_2$	$(00)_2$	$(10)_2$	$(11)_2$	$(01)_2$
$(11)_2$	$(00)_2$	$(11)_2$	$(01)_2$	$(10)_2$

Similarly, we have $t^2 + t + (10)_2$ is irreducible over $GF(4)$. Let $GF(16) = GF(4)[t]/(t^2 + t + (10)_2)$ and $(abcd)_2$ denote the equivalent class of $(ab)_2 t + (cd)_2$. Then we can construct a multiplication table of size 16×16.

Similarly, we have $t^2 + t + (1000)_2$ is irreducible over $GF(16)$. Let $GF(256) = GF(16)[t]/(t^2 + t + (1000)_2)$ and $(abcdefgh)_2$ denote the equivalent class of $(abcd)_2 t + (efgh)_2$. Then we can construct a multiplication table of size 256×256.

Similarly, we have $t^2 + t + (1000, 0000)_2$ is irreducible over $GF(256)$. Let $\alpha_1 = (1000, 0000)_2$. Let $GF(2^{16}) = GF(256)[t_1]/(t_1^2 + t_1 + \alpha_1)$. However, we do not construct the multiplication table of $GF(2^{16})$. For $a, b, c, d \in GF(256)$, $(at_1 + b)(ct_1 + d) = act_1^2 + (ad + bc)t_1 + bd = ac(t_1 + \alpha_1) + (ad + bc)t_1 + bd = [(a + b)(c + d) + bd]t_1 + [ac\alpha_1 + bd]$.

Similarly, we have $t^2 + t + (1000, 0000, 0000, 0000)_2$ is irreducible over $GF(2^{16})$. Let $\alpha_2 = (1000, 0000, 0000, 0000)_2$. Let $GF(2^{32}) = GF(2^{16})[t_2]/(t_2^2 + t_2 + \alpha_2)$. For $A, B, C, D \in GF(2^{16})$, $(At_2 + B)(Ct_2 + D) = [(A + B)(C + D) + BD]t_2 + [AC\alpha_2 + BD]$.

Note that we now have a recursive definition for $GF((2^8)^{(2^i)})$. With a proper choice of α_i, we let $GF((2^8)^{(2^i)}) = GF((2^8)^{(2^{i-1})})[t_i]/(t_i^2 + t_i + \alpha_i)$. For $a, b, c, d \in GF((2^8)^{(2^{i-1})})$,

$$(at_i + b)(ct_i + d) = [(a + b)(c + d) + bd]t_i + [ac\alpha_i + bd]$$

where the addition is the bitwise XOR and the multiplication of expressions of a, b, c, d and α_i are done in $GF((2^8)^{(2^{i-1})})$.

To find the inverse of $at_i + b$, first we let $(at_i + b)(At_i + B) = 1$, that is, $(aA + aB + Ab)t_i + aA\alpha_i + bB = 1$ or, in vector form, by considering $\{t_i, 1\}$

as a basis, $\begin{pmatrix} a+b & a \\ a\alpha_i & b \end{pmatrix}\begin{pmatrix} A \\ B \end{pmatrix} = \begin{pmatrix} 0 \\ 1 \end{pmatrix}$. Hence $\begin{pmatrix} A \\ B \end{pmatrix} = \begin{pmatrix} a+b & a \\ a\alpha_i & b \end{pmatrix}^{-1}\begin{pmatrix} 0 \\ 1 \end{pmatrix} =$

$(ab + b^2 + a^2\alpha_i)^{-1}\begin{pmatrix} b & a \\ a\alpha_i & a+b \end{pmatrix}\begin{pmatrix} 0 \\ 1 \end{pmatrix} = (ab + b^2 + a^2\alpha_i)^{-1}\begin{pmatrix} a \\ a+b \end{pmatrix}$. Therefore

$(at_i + b)^{-1} = (at_i + a + b)(ab + b^2 + a^2\alpha_i)^{-1}$.

Here we give an example of field extension of degree 12 to illustrate how we can accelerate the computation of large field. We let $\mathbb{K} = GF(2^8)$ and $\mathbb{L}, \mathbb{L}', \mathbb{L}''$ be the finite extension fields of $\mathbb{K}$ such that $\mathbb{K} \subset \mathbb{L}'' \subset \mathbb{L}' \subset \mathbb{L}$ and $[\mathbb{L}'' : \mathbb{K}] = 2$, $[\mathbb{L}' : \mathbb{L}''] = 2$, $[\mathbb{L} : \mathbb{L}'] = 3$. Therefore $\mathbb{L}' = GF(2^{16})$, $\mathbb{L}' = GF(2^{32}) \subset \mathbb{L}$, and $\mathbb{L} = GF(2^{96})$ and we need to discuss the field extension of degree 3 below.

Since $t^3 + t + 1$ is irreducible over $GF(2^{32})[t]$, we can identify $GF(2^{96})$ with

$GF(2^{32})[t]/(t^3 + t + 1)$. If we use $\begin{pmatrix} a \\ b \\ c \end{pmatrix}$ to represent $at^2 + bt + c$, then

$$\begin{pmatrix} a \\ b \\ c \end{pmatrix} *_{12} \begin{pmatrix} x_1 \\ x_2 \\ x_3 \end{pmatrix} = \begin{pmatrix} (a+c) & b & a \\ (a+b) & (a+c) & b \\ b & a & c \end{pmatrix}\begin{pmatrix} x_1 \\ x_2 \\ x_3 \end{pmatrix}$$

where $*_{12}$ denotes the multiplication in $\mathbb{L}$ and the right hand side is just the usual matrix multiplication. In signing a message, we need to solve $\mathbf{ax} = \mathbf{y}$ for $\mathbf{x}$ in $\mathbb{L}$. That is, to solve

$$\begin{pmatrix} (a+c) & b & a \\ (a+b) & (a+c) & b \\ b & a & c \end{pmatrix}\begin{pmatrix} x_1 \\ x_2 \\ x_3 \end{pmatrix} = \begin{pmatrix} y_1 \\ y_2 \\ y_3 \end{pmatrix}$$

for x_1, x_2, x_3. Therefore, we have

$$\begin{pmatrix} x_1 \\ x_2 \\ x_3 \end{pmatrix} = \frac{1}{\Delta}\left[\mathbf{adj}\begin{pmatrix} (a+c) & b & a \\ (a+b) & (a+c) & b \\ b & a & c \end{pmatrix}\right]\begin{pmatrix} y_1 \\ y_2 \\ y_3 \end{pmatrix}.$$

Write out $\mathbf{adj}\begin{pmatrix} (a+c) & b & a \\ (a+b) & (a+c) & b \\ b & a & c \end{pmatrix}$ as $\begin{pmatrix} A_{11} & A_{12} & A_{13} \\ A_{21} & A_{22} & A_{23} \\ A_{31} & A_{32} & A_{33} \end{pmatrix}$, then

$$A_{31} = A_{12} = A_{23} = a^2 + bc$$
$$A_{11} = A_{22} = a(b+c) + c^2$$
$$A_{32} = A_{13} = ac + (a+b)^2$$
$$A_{21} = A_{31} + A_{13}$$
$$A_{33} = A_{22} + A_{32}$$
$$\Delta = aA_{31} + bA_{32} + cA_{33}$$

According to the calculation above, to solve $\mathbf{ax} = \mathbf{y}$, we need 21 multiplications and one inverse operation in $GF(2^{32})$, which is roughly 342 multiplications in $\mathbb{K}$. Comparing to TTS, doing the Gaussian elimination for two 9×9 matrices, it takes at least about $2 \times 9^3/3 \approx 500$ multiplications in $\mathbb{K}$.

Note: There will be a extended version at IACR eprint archive.

References

1. G. Ars and J.-C. Faugère, *Comparison of XL and Gröbner Bases Algorithms over Finite Fields*, preprint. Will appear as one half of an article at Asiacrypt 2004 and LNCS.

2. M. Bardet, J.-C. Faugère, and B. Salvy, *Complexity of Gröbner Basis Computations for Regular Overdetermined Systems*, INRIA Rapport de Recherche No. 5049; a slightly modified preprint is accepted by the International Conference on Polynomial System Solving.

3. M. Bardet, J.-C. Faugère, B. Salvy, and B.-Y. Yang, *Asymptotic Complexity of Gröbner Basis Algorithms for Semi-regular Overdetermined Systems over Large Fields*, manuscript in preparation.

4. J.-M. Chen and B.-Y. Yang, *Tame Transformations Signatures With Topsy-Turvy Hashes*, proc. IWAP 2002, Taipei.

5. J.-M. Chen and B.-Y. Yang, *A More Secure and Efficacious TTS Scheme*, ICISC 2003, LNCS v. 2971, pp. 320-338; full version at eprint.iacr.org/2003/160.

6. D. Coppersmith, J. Stern, and S. Vaudenay, *Attacks on the Birational Permutation Signature Schemes*, Crypto 1993, LNCS v. 773, pp. 435–443.

7. N. Courtois, L. Goubin, W. Meier, and J. Tacier, *Solving Underdefined Systems of Multivariate Quadratic Equations*, PKC 2002, LNCS v. 2274, pp. 211-227

8. N. Courtois, *Generic Attacks and the Security of Quartz*, PKC 2003, LNCS v. 2567, pp. 351-364.

9. N. Courtois, *Algebraic Attacks over $GF(2^k)$, Cryptanalysis of HFE Challenge 2 and SFLASH^{v2}*, accepted for PKC 2004.

10. N. Courtois, A. Klimov, J. Patarin, and A. Shamir, *Efficient Algorithms for Solving Overdefined Systems of Multivariate Polynomial Equations*, EUROCRYPT 2000, LNCS v. 1807, pp. 392-407.

11. N. Courtois and J. Patarin, *About the XL Algorithms over $GF(2)$*, CT-RSA 2003, LNCS v. 2612, pp. 141-157.

12. N. Courtois, L. Goubin, and J. Patarin, *SFLASH^{v3}, a Fast Asymmetric Signature Scheme*, preprint

13. C. Diem, *The XL-algorithm and a Conjecture from Commutative Algebra*, preprint (to appear Asiacrypt 2004 and LNCS) and private communication.

14. W. Diffie and M. Hellman, *New Directions in Cryptography*, IEEE Trans. Info. Theory, vol. IT-22, no. 6, pp. 644-654.

15. J.-C. Faugére, *A New Efficient Algorithm for Computing Gröbner Bases (F4)*, Journal of Pure and Applied Algebra, 139 (1999), pp. 61–88.

16. J.-C. Faugère, *A New Efficient Algorithm for Computing Gröbner Bases without Reduction to Zero (F5)*, Proc. ISSAC 2002, pp. 75-83, ACM Press 2002.

17. J.-C. Faugère and A. Joux, *Algebraic Cryptanalysis of Hidden Field Equations (HFE) Cryptosystems Using Gröbner Bases*, Crypto 2003, LNCS v. 2729, pp. 44-60.

18. M. Garey and D. Johnson, *Computers and Intractability, A Guide to the Theory of NP-completeness*, 1979, p. 251.

19. W. Geiselmann, R. Steinwandt, and T. Beth, *Attacking the Affine Parts of SFLASH*, 8th International IMA Conference on Cryptography and Coding, LNCS v. 2260, pp. 355-359.

20. W. Geiselmann, R. Steinwandt, and T. Beth, *Revealing the 441 Key Bits of SFLASH^{v2}*, Third NESSIE Workshop, 2002.
21. L. Goubin and N. Courtois, *Cryptanalysis of the TTM cryptosystem*, Asiacrypt 2000, LNCS v. 1976, pp. 44-57.
22. A. Kipnis and A. Shamir, *Cryptanalysis of the Oil and Vinegar Signature Scheme*, Crypto'98, LNCS v. 1462, pp. 257-266
23. A. Kipnis, J. Patarin, and L. Goubin, *Unbalanced Oil and Vinegar Sigature Schemes*, Crypto'99, LNCS v. 1592, pp. 206-222
24. A. Kipnis and A. Shamir, *Cryptanalysis of the HFE Public Key Cryptosystem by Relinearization*, Crypto'99, LNCS v. 1666, pp. 19-30
25. T. Matsumoto and H. Imai, *Public Quadratic Polynomial-Tuples for Efficient Signature-Verification and Message-Encryption*, EUROCRYPT'88, LNCS v. 330, pp. 419-453.
26. T. Moh, *A Public Key System with Signature and Master Key Functions*, Communications in Algebra, 27 (1999), pp. 2207-2222.
27. T. Moh and J. -M. Chen, *On the Goubin-Courtois Attack on TTM*, published electronically by Cryptology ePrint Archive (2001/072).
28. *New European Schemes for Signatures, Integrity, and Encryption*, project homepage at http://www.cryptonessie.org.
29. *Performance of Optimized Implementations of the NESSIE primitives, version 2.0* http://www.cryptonessie.org.
30. J. Patarin, *Cryptanalysis of the Matsumoto and Imai Public Key Scheme of Eurocrypt'88*, Crypto'95, LNCS v. 963, pp. 248-261.
31. J. Patarin, *Hidden Fields Equations (HFE) and Isomorphisms of Polynomials (IP) Two New Families of Asymmetric Algorithms*, EUROCRYPT'96, LNCS v. 1070, pp. 33-48.
32. J. Patarin, L. Goubin, N. Courtois, *Improved Algorithm for Isomorphisms of Polynomials*, EUROCRYPT'98, LNCS v. 1403, pp. 184-200.
33. J. Patarin, N. Courtois, and L. Goubin, *QUARTZ, 128-Bit Long Digital Signatures*, CT-RSA 2001, LNCS v. 2020, pp. 282-297. Updated version available at http://www.cryptonessie.org.
34. J. Patarin, N. Courtois, and L. Goubin, FLASH, *a Fast Multivariate Signature Algorithm*, CT-RSA 2001, LNCS v. 2020, pp. 298-307. Updated version available at http://www.cryptonessie.org.
35. A. Shamir and E. Tromer, *Factoring Large Numbers with the TWIRL Device*, Crypto 2003, LNCS v. 2729, pp. 1-26.
36. Lih-Chung Wang and Fei-Hwang Chang, *Tractable Rational Map Cryptosystem*, available at http://eprint.iacr.org/2004/046.
37. C. Wolf, *Efficient Public Key Generation for Multivariate Cryptosystems, preprint*, available at http://eprint.iacr.org/2003/089.
38. B.-Y. Yang and J.-M. Chen, *Rank Attacks and Defence in Tame-Like Multivariate PKC's*, see http://eprint.iacr.org/2004/061.
39. B.-Y. Yang and J.-M. Chen, *All in the XL Family: Theory and Practice*, to appear at ICISC 2004 and LNCS.
40. B.-Y. Yang, Y.-H. Chen, and J.-M. Chen, *TTS: High-Speed Signatures on a Low-End Smart Card*, Proc. CHES '04, LNCS v. 3156, pp. 371-385.
41. B.-Y. Yang, J.-M. Chen, and N. Courtois, *On Asymptotic Security Estimates in XL and Gröbner Bases-Related Algebraic Cryptanalysis*, ICICS 2004, LNCS v. 3269, pp. 401-413.

Cryptanalysis of the Tractable Rational Map Cryptosystem

Antoine Joux[1], Sébastien Kunz-Jacques[2],
Frédéric Muller[2], and Pierre-Michel Ricordel[2]

[1] SPOTI
Antoine.Joux@m4x.org
[2] DCSSI Crypto Lab 51, Boulevard de La Tour-Maubourg,
75700 Paris 07 SP France
{Sebastien.Kunz-Jacques,Frederic.Muller,Pierre-Michel.Ricordel}
@sgdn.pm.gouv.fr

Abstract. In this paper, we present the cryptanalysis of a public key scheme based on a system of multivariate polynomial equations, the "tractable rational map" cryptosystem. We show combinatorial weaknesses of the cryptosystem, and introduce a variant of the XL resolution algorithm, the Linear Method, which is able to leverage these weaknesses to invert in short time the trapdoor one-way function defined by the cipher using only the public key, and even rebuild a private key. We also interpret the behavior of the Linear Method on random instances of the scheme, and show that various generalizations of the cipher, as well as an increase of the security parameter, cannot lead to a secure scheme.

Keywords: Public Key Cryptography, Polynomial Systems, Tractable Rational Map Cryptosystem, XL, Gröbner Bases, Isomorphism of Polynomials

1 Introduction

Several recent public key cryptosystems use multivariate polynomial systems of equations instead of number-theoretic constructions. The "public" operation in such a system is to evaluate the system output on a given input value: this is a very simple operation even for devices with limited resources such as smart cards, although the system needs to be stored. The "private" operation is to find a preimage of a given value.

Determining whether a random system of n polynomial equations with n variables over any finite field has a solution is known to be a NP-complete problem, and thus seems to be a good starting point to build a cryptosystem. But the polynomial systems used in cryptographic applications must have a special form to make the solving operation possible given the knowledge of a secret backdoor. Thus the cryptanalyst does not have to solve random polynomial systems, but rather random instances of a special subfamily of polynomial systems.

The first cryptosystems based on polynomial equations were defeated. For example the Matsumoto-Imai scheme introduced in 1988 [6] was cryptanalyzed

S. Vaudenay (Ed.): PKC 2005, LNCS 3386, pp. 258–274, 2005.

by J. Patarin (Crypto 95, [14]). More recently, some attacks against stronger schemes, such as HFE (Eurocrypt 96, [15]) or SFLASH (RSA Conference 2001, [13]), have emerged. In addition, a 80-bit HFE challenge was broken by J.-C. Faugere in 2002 [4]. It was later described by Faugère and Joux how to attack HFE using an optimized Gröbner basis algorithm and a linear algebra approach (see [7]).

All these cryptosystems share some common properties:
- They use only quadratic equations on the ground field. We can however notice that, in general, an equation of degree more than 2 is equivalent to a quadratic system with more variables.
- Public and private keys are systems of equations related by a linear or affine masking: a composition with a linear or affine transformation on the left, and a linear or affine substitution of variables on the right is performed on the private key to hide its structure, and the result constitutes the public key.

Finding whether two random systems are equal under such a transformation is a difficult problem (it is referred to as the "Isomorphisms of Polynomials" (IP) problem, and is studied in [12]), thus the linear/affine masking seems a strong enough barrier between the public and the private key.

These cryptosystems also generally use the relation between n-variable polynomials over a field F, and univariate polynomials over an extension G of degree n of F: any system composed of n equations in n variables over F can be transformed into a unique 1-variable polynomial over G. For example, the HFE private key is a sparse polynomial over an extension of $GF(2^7)$; the function it defines can be inverted using the Berlekamp algorithm. But the system can also be expressed using several polynomials over the ground field $GF(2^7)$.

The Tractable Rational Map Cryptosystem (TRMC, [2]) also follows this framework: its private key comprises equations on various extensions of $GF(2^8)$. It is in a block triangular form: a subset of the equations can be solved, and then the result injected into other equations to further solve the system. We will show that this structure is not well hidden by a linear masking. In fact, an attacker can solve the public system using essentially the same resolution technique as the owner of the private key (of course, the resolution time will be higher, albeit still feasible in a reasonable time).

The outline of this paper is as follows: first, we present techniques used to solve systems of polynomial equations, and in particular the technique we implemented to break TRMC. Then, we introduce the cryptosystem and compute the complexity of finding preimages of some fixed values with the resolution method we have chosen. We then present our experimental results, and discuss the security of variants of the cryptostem that would use more unknowns and/or more equations. Finally, me discuss a method that can rebuild a "pseudo-private key", a system almost as easy to invert as the private key itself.

2   Algorithms for Solving Polynomial Systems

In this section, we review some known algorithms that allow to solve a system of multivariate polynomial equations. These algorithms fall into two categories:

special-purpose solving algorithms that only apply to systems having a unique solution (at least without further work), and Gröbner basis algorithms.

Since the method we used in the case of the TRMC is inspired by linear algebra solving techniques and not by Gröbner basis techniques, we will not discuss this second category of algorithms extensively. We will however make a quick review of the Buchberger algorithm, which is the historical Gröbner basis algorithm, and on more recent algorithms like F_4 and F_5. Reference material on Gröbner basis can be found in [1].

From now on, we will deal only with systems having a unique solution or "zero-dimensional ideals", and deal with Gröbner basis computation algorithms only in the case of such systems. Moreover, since systems of interest for us are quadratic, we will freely assume in the description of the algorithms that we deal with sets of quadratic polynomials.

2.1   Linearization, Relinearization

Linearization is the most simple and natural resolution technique. The idea behind linearization is to consider each quadratic monomial of the system as a new unknown. If the system has n variables, this introduces at most $n(n+1)/2$ unknowns. Each equation is then viewed as a line vector of a matrix, with higher degree monomials leftmost. Then Gaussian elimination is applied to the system. If there are enough linearly independent equations, this will hopefully yield new polynomials without quadratic terms. Since the size of the matrix is $O\left(n^2\right)$, the simplest reduction algorithm has a cost of $O\left(n^6\right)$ additions and multiplications in the finite field. Note that as soon as the number of linearly independent equations exceeds the total number of quadratic monomials present in the system, the gaussian elimination will yield at least one linear polynomial in the ideal, which will allow to eliminate one unknown in the original system and to iterate the method to finish the resolution.

Unfortunately, linearization requires approximately $n^2/2$ equations, which is not suitable for most practical situations (there are systems with n equations or more that have a unique solution, therefore linearization leaves many systems with a unique solution unsolved).

Relinearization is a method introduced by A. Kipnis and A. Shamir to cryptanalyze HFE in [8], and further analyzed (and compared to XL) in [11]. It is a generalization of the linearization method that works with less equations. In fact, there are several variants of the relinearization method, that are able to cope with various lower bounds for the ratio m/n^2, where n is the number of unknowns and m the number of equations.

The simplest relinearization technique, the *fourth degree relinearization*, goes as follows. Build the linearized matrix as in the linearization method. This time, we have less linearly independent polynomials than quadratic monomials in the system, thus the matrix has a non-trivial kernel. Parameter the kernel space by new unknowns $z_1, \ldots, z_k$ $(k = \frac{n(n+1)}{2} + n + 1 - m)$. Now, each quadratic monomial of the original system $x_i x_j = y_{ij}$ is viewed as a linear combination of the z_i. We can write quadratic equations on the z_i by writing compatibility equations on the y_{ij}:

$$x_i x_j x_k x_\ell = y_{ij} y_{k\ell} = y_{ik} y_{j\ell} = y_{i\ell} y_{jk}$$

We can write $2\binom{n}{4} = \dfrac{n(n-1)(n-2)(n-3)}{12}$ such equations. Thus we have about $n^4/12$ quadratic equations for the z_i. These equations can be proven to be linearly independent. If we linearize the new quadratic system, this gives us a new (relinearized) system with $n^4/12$ equations and $\left(n^2/2 - m\right)^2 / 2$ unknowns. This new system will have more equations than unknowns if

$$m > \left(\frac{1}{2} - \frac{1}{\sqrt{6}}\right) n^2 \approx 0.09 n^2$$

This degree 4 relinearization solves the original system if the above condition is met.

Higher degree relinearizations are able to cope with systems with less equations. They consist in writing higher degree consistency equations on the z_i, like for example for a degree 6 relinearization, $y_{ij} y_{k\ell} y_{pq} = y_{ik} y_{jp} y_{\ell q}$. Even for degree 6 relinearization, it is difficult to perfom a precise computation of the threshold m/n^2 above which systems become solvable. This is related to the fact that many consistency equations are linearly dependent, and we cannot precisely estimate the number of equations needed.

2.2   XL

XL was introduced by N. Courtois, A. Klimov, J. Patarin and A. Shamir in [11]. It relates to some works peformed by formal calculus researchers like D. Lazard (see, for example, [9]), aimed at improving the efficiency of Gröbner basis computation by using linear algebra and Gaussian reduction.

XL is partly inspired from an idea introduced to use the Buchberger algorithm to explicitly solve systems of equations having a unique solution. The Bucherger algorithm allows to eliminate monomials in the polynomials of an ideal, that is to find new polynomials of the ideal that are written using only a specific set of monomials. Thus to solve a system, one can try to eliminate all the monomials but the powers of a selected unknown of the system, say x_1. If this succeeds, this leads to at least one univariate polynomial in x_1 that is in the ideal. One can then use the Berlekamp algorithm to solve such a univariate polynomial equation, replace x_1 by its value in the original system, and run the algorithm again with the new system that has one unknown less than the original one.

Let S be a system of multivariate polynomial equations having a unique solution, I the ideal generated by the polynomials in S and $p \in I$. Since p is a sum of elements of S with polynomial coefficients, p is also a sum with scalar coefficients of all the multiples of elements of S by all monomials of degree $\leq d$, for some degree d. This applies in particular to the univariate polynomials of the ideal (we know there are such polynomials in I since S has a unique solution).

Following the preceding observations, XL looks for univariate polynomials built from the elements of S as follows. First, a monomial order is chosen where all the powers of some unkown, say x_1, come last. Then the matrix of all the polynomials that are multiple of some element in S by some monomial of degree d is built. The polynomials are mapped to lines in the matrix and each column gives the coefficient of the polynomials with respect to some particular monomial. Monomials that come first in the order are leftmost in the matrix. Then a Gaussian reduction is performed. If d is high enough, this step yields at least one non-zero univariate polynomial in x_1. The algorithm then loops as described above.

Note that at this point, there is no need for a combinatorial argument about the number of polynomials built and the number of monomials of a given degree to ensure that, for some d, we will find univariate polynomials. It suffices to see that such polynomials are in the ideal and that they can be written as polynomial combinations of elements of S.

In [11], it was proven that XL is more powerful than the relinearization algorithm, in the following sense: if a d-degree relinearization succeeds in solving a system S, then XL will also succeed by building the matrix of (total) degree d from S. Moreover, the system size of the matrix in XL will be lower than the relinearization matrix. Estimates of the complexity of XL are also given.

2.3   Gröbner Bases, Buchberger, F_4, F_5

In general, a system of polynomial equations does not have a unique solution thus "solving" it does not necessarily make sense. The relevant concept is the *Gröbner basis* of a polynomial system. A Gröbner basis of an ideal is a family of polynomials of the ideal that plays the same role in the multivariate case, than the polynomial generating an ideal in the univariate case. Indeed, with a Gröbner basis of an ideal I, it can be quickly decided whether a polynomial p belongs to I or not. This is done with an euclidian division algorithm generalized to the multivariate case that reduces p on the basis. The special property of Gröbner bases is that a polynomial reduces to 0 iff it belongs to the ideal. This is not true in general for a family $\mathcal{F}$ generating an ideal I: if a polynomial reduces to 0 on $\mathcal{F}$, it belongs to the ideal (since it is a sum of elements of $\mathcal{F}$), but the converse needs not to be true.

In the case of a system having a unique solution $x_1 = a_1, \ldots, x_n = a_n$, the family $X_1 - a_1, \ldots, X_n - a_n$ generates the ideal of the system and is a Gröbner basis. More generally, any (minimal) Gröbner basis of such a system will contain only degree 1 polynomials, and there will be sufficiently many of them to recover the solution of the system. Thus Gröbner basis algorithms are of interest for us.

In the univariate case, the euclidian division crucially uses the properties of the degree. The degree enables to totally order the monomials of a polynomial and then, by only considering the leading terms of two polynomials (p_1, p_2), one can decide whether p_1 can be reduced by p_2 or not. In a similar fashion, in the multivariate case, we use monomial orderings (total, well-funded, compatible with multiplication). These monomial orderings are at the heart of reduction algorithms because they associate to each polynomial a leading monomial in a consistent way, and reduction decisions are made only by considering leading monomials.

- **The Buchberger Algorithm**

  The central notion in the Buchberger algorithm is the *S-polynomial S* formed from a pair of polynomials (p_1, p_2). S is the simplest polynomial combination of p_1 and p_2 that has a leading term strictly smaller than the least common multiple of the leading terms of p_1 and p_2. It is formed by mutiplying p_1 and p_2 by appropriate monomials so that in the sum of the results, the two leading terms cancel each other.

  A Gröbner basis has the characteristic property that all S-polynomials built upon it reduce to zero on the base; this results from the special property of Gröbner bases since S-polynomials belong to the ideal. Based on this observation, the Buchberger algorithm works as follows: starting from a polynomial family F, one builds all the *S*-polynomials that can be formed from F, then reduces them on F. If all polynomials reduce to zero, F is a Gröbner basis. If not, non-zero polynomials that have been found after reduction are added to F. This yields new pairs to examine. This algorithm always terminates, but the execution time and the size of the resulting basis are hard to predict; in particular, the resulting family is not in general a minimal Gröbner basis. It usually contains many redundant polynomials and can be "cleaned up".

  One of the problems of the Buchberger algorithm is that once it has built a Gröbner basis of an ideal, there are usually many pairs left to examine and the algorithm will terminate only when all these pairs have been reduced to zero. This termination phase usually represents a significant part of the computation. It is possible to avoid reducing some pairs, but we will see that in F_5 or in linear algebraic approaches, an efficient criterion can be found to avoid considering polynomials trivially reducing to zero.

- **F_4 and F_5**

  Both of these algorithms were engineered by J.C. Faugère and his team. F_4 was introduced in [5] and F_5 in [3]. F_4 uses some ideas from the Buchberger algorithm combined with linear algebra. Its performance is roughly equivalent to XL for a system that has a unique solution.

  F_5 is built upon F_4 but has the additional property to avoid trivial reductions to zero. This is performed by maintaining a set of known generators G of the ideal, and avoiding to form polynomial relations $gh - hg = 0$ $(g, h \in G)$. Other trivial relations may also arise from the Frobenius map of the finite field, but F_5 avoids considering them too.

3   A Variant of XL: The Linear Method

In this section, we describe the variant of XL that we implemented. We call it the Linear Method. Just like XL tries to build univariate polynomials, our method looks for linear polynomials in the ideal. Once sufficiently many (linearly independent) linear polynomials have been built, the solution of the system can be found. This purely linear approach has provable properties that will be very useful to break TRMC, even if XL might be more efficient.

3.1 Principles of the Linear Method

Let S be a set of polynomials and $I =< S >$ the ideal it generates. The basic operation of the algorithm, for a target degree d, unfolds as follows. Consider $p \in S$, of degree $d' \le d$. Every multiple of p by a monomial m of degree $d' - d$ is in I, and of degree d. The algorithm builds a matrix description of all the polynomials of degree d obtained this way, for all $p \in S$ of degree $\le d$ and all suitable m. Each line in the matrix describes a polynomial, and each column gives the coefficient of a particular monomial in the polynomials. Monomials of lower degree correspond to rightmost columns in the matrix. Starting with m quadratic polynomials with n variables in S, the degree d matrix has $m \begin{pmatrix} n - 1 + d - 2 \\ d - 2 \end{pmatrix}$ rows and $\sum_{d'=0}^{d} \begin{pmatrix} n - 1 + d' \\ d' \end{pmatrix}$ columns.

The matrix can then be row reduced by the Gauss algorithm. Since this reduction cancels the coefficients of the higher degree monomials in the polynomials described by the matrix, it may yield new polynomials of degree $< d$. They are in I, since they are expressed as linear combinations of polynomials of I.

The aim of the algorithm is to build linear polynomials in the ideal by building and reducing degree d matrices for various values of d. Having built and reduced the degree d matrix, what degree should we analyze next? Since reducing degrees smaller than d is far less costly than reducing degree d, one could choose to always reduce degree d' when new polynomials of degree $d' < d$ have been found during the reduction of degree d, and reduce degree $d + 1$ otherwise. Another variant would be to go into degree d' as soon as one polynomial of degree $d' < d$ is found when reducing degree d. In general, it is difficult to find an optimal strategy. Moreover, the behavior of the algorithm is heavily dependent on the structure of the system solved. For random systems, the choice of strategy is usually not so important, because no fall of degree will happen before the *critical degree* for which the corresponding matrix has mores lines than columns.

We specialized our algorithm to solve TRMC, and since we wanted to explore in detail the combinatorial behavior of the system, we did not implement any particular stategy and rather opted for a manual sequencing.

- **Numerical Data for TRMC**
  With 40 variables such as in the case of the TRMC, and 48 polynomials in S, the degree 4 matrix is 39360×123410. It is only feasible to go to degree 4 or 5 on a typical 32-bit machine, e.g. a PC with 2 GB of RAM.
- **An Alternative to the Gauss Reduction: Sparse Matrix Algebra**
  Let A be the the degree d matrix before Gauss reduction. The columns of A represent monomials of degree $\le d$: split A horizontally in A_1, corresponding to monomials of degree d, and A_2, corresponding to monomials of degree $< d$. If v is a nontrivial kernel vector of ${}^t A_1$, then $v A_2$ represents a polynomial

of I of degree $< d$. Any such v can be found using sparse algebra resolution techniques like Lanczos or Wiedemann. Since lines in A are sparse, this technique saves memory for high values of d.

- **Room for Improvement**
    - Starting with degree 4, if the polynomials of the system have degree 2, the matrices that are built yield many polynomials trivially reducing to zero arising from the relations $fg - gf = 0$ (see section 5.1 for an example). This can be avoided by selectively removing some polynomial multiples when building the matrix.
    - When a linear polynomial ℓ has been found, it can be used to reduce the number of unknowns in the system by a direct susbstitution, instead of adding multiples of ℓ to the known polynomials. The same polynomials are found in both cases, but the first approach is faster and saves memory.

In the case of TRMC however, these optimizations are not relevant since they would save very little computation time.

3.2   Properties of the Linear Method

Here, we present two key properties of the Linear Method which enable it to break TRMC. The proofs are given in annex A.

In the course of the resolution of a system, we are interested in the number of linearly independent polynomials of degree $d' < d$ that appear when reducing the degree d matrix. These falls of degree are strongly related to the ability to solve a system. The number of falls of degree that appear at all degrees d and for all sequencing choices of the algorithm when solving a system S are what we call the **combinatorial properties** of S.

Independence from Linear-Affine Masking Two systems equal up to left linear and right affine invertible transformations have the same combinatorial properties w.r.t. the linear method.

Independence from Subfield Projection If the Linear Method is able to solve a system S expressed on a finite extension G of a field F by reducing degrees less than d, it will also be able to solve S expressed on F by reducing degrees less than d.

In the case of TRMC, these properties mean that the public key and private key systems have the same combinatorial properties. In particular, the Linear Method will give the same results on both systems.

4   The Tractable Rational Map Cryptosystem

The Tractable Rational Map Cryptosystem was introduced in [2] by F. Chang and L. Wang. Its private key is a system of 48 quadratic equations with 40 unknowns over $F = GF(2^8)$. In the public key, these equations are masked by affine transformations on the left (before the polynomial system) and on the right (after the polynomial system). Some equations of the private key are derived from extensions of F, $GF(2^{16})$, $GF(2^{32})$ and $GF(2^{128})$. As in [2], we will use the notation $x_{i,\dots,i+k-1}$ for a k-uple of elements $x_i, \dots, x_{i+k-1}$ of $GF(2^8)$ viewed as an element of the extension $GF(2^{8k})$ of $GF(2^8)$.

The input of the private system is $x_1, \dots, x_{40}$, and its output is $y_1, \dots, y_{48}$. The system can be written as follows:

$$y_{1,2} = q_1(x_{1,2}, x_{3,4}, x_{5,6}, x_{7,8}, x_{9,10}, x_{11,12}, x_{13,14}) \tag{1}$$

$$y_{3,4} = q_2(x_{1,2}, x_{3,4}, x_{5,6}, x_{7,8}, x_{9,10}, x_{11,12}, x_{13,14}) \tag{2}$$

$$y_{5,6} = q_3(x_{1,2}, x_{3,4}, x_{5,6}, x_{7,8}, x_{9,10}, x_{11,12}, x_{13,14}) \tag{3}$$

$$y_{7,8} = q_4(x_{1,2}, x_{3,4}, x_{5,6}, x_{7,8}, x_{9,10}, x_{11,12}, x_{13,14}) \tag{4}$$

$$y_{9,10} = q_5(x_{1,2}, x_{3,4}, x_{5,6}, x_{7,8}, x_{9,10}, x_{11,12}, x_{13,14}) \tag{5}$$

$$y_{11,12} = q_6(x_{1,2}, x_{3,4}, x_{5,6}, x_{7,8}, x_{9,10}, x_{11,12}, x_{13,14}) \tag{6}$$

$$y_{13,14} = q_7(x_{1,2}, x_{3,4}, x_{5,6}, x_{7,8}, x_{9,10}, x_{11,12}, x_{13,14}) \tag{7}$$

$$y_{15,16} = q_8(x_{1,2}, x_{3,4}, x_{5,6}, x_{7,8}, x_{9,10}, x_{11,12}, x_{13,14}) \tag{8}$$

$$y_{17,18} = q_9(x_{1,2}, x_{3,4}, x_{5,6}, x_{7,8}, x_{9,10}, x_{11,12}, x_{13,14}) \tag{9}$$

$$y_{19,20} = q_{10}(x_{1,2}, x_{3,4}, x_{5,6}, x_{7,8}, x_{9,10}, x_{11,12}, x_{13,14}) \tag{10}$$

$$y_{21,22} = q_{11}(x_{1,2}, x_{3,4}, x_{5,6}, x_{7,8}, x_{9,10}, x_{11,12}, x_{13,14}) \tag{11}$$

$$y_{23,\dots,26} = x_{15,\dots,18}(x_{2,\dots,5}^{256} + x_{2,\dots,5} + a) + b\,x_{6,\dots,9}x_{10,\dots,13} \tag{12}$$

$$y_{27} = x_{19} + f_1(x_1, \dots, x_{18}) \tag{13}$$

$$y_{28} = x_{20} + f_2(x_1, \dots, x_{19}) \tag{14}$$

$$y_{29} = x_{21} + f_3(x_1, \dots, x_{20}) \tag{15}$$

$$y_{30} = x_{22} + f_4(x_1, \dots, x_{21}) \tag{16}$$

$$y_{31} = x_{23} + f_5(x_1, \dots, x_{22}) \tag{17}$$

$$y_{32} = x_{24} + f_6(x_1, \dots, x_{23}) \tag{18}$$

$$y_{33,48} = x_{25,\dots,40}(x_{7,\dots,22}^{256} + x_{7,\dots,22} + c) + f_{7,\dots,22}(x_1, \dots, x_{24}) \tag{19}$$

where:

- a, b and c are random values in $GF(2^8)$,
- $f_1, \dots, f_6$ are random quadratic polynomials over $GF(2^8)$ (the number of variables of each polynomial ranges from 18 to 23),
- $f_{7,\dots,22}$ is a random system of 16 quadratic polynomials over $GF(2^8)$ with 24 variables,
- $q_1, \dots, q_{11}$ are random quadratic polynomials with 7 variables over $GF(2^{16})$.

Note that in any extension of $F = GF(2^8)$, viewed as a F-vector space, $x \mapsto x^{256}$ is linear, and each multiplication coordinate is a quadratic form. Therefore all equations, including equations 12 and 19, yield quadratic equations when expressed over F.

As far as our attack is concerned, we will only retain the following aspects of the structure of the system: it has a block triangular structure; it contains a random susbsystem of 11 equations with 7 variables over $GF(2^{16})$, that must be solved first. The next equations allow to retrieve one or several variables at a time (depending on the field on which they are written).

5   Combinatorial Properties
of the Public and Private Key of TRMC

By section 3.2, we know that the combinatorial properties of the public and private key of TRMC are the same. That means that the Linear Method is able to break TRMC without exploring a higher degree than the one needed to solve the private key system expressed over $GF(2^8)$. In this section, we show that the private key system can be solved by analyzing degrees ≤ 4.

We first review the behavior of the Linear Method on the subsystem of 11 equations with 7 variables over $GF(2^{16})$.

We do not have to consider the role of field equations ($x^{|k|} - x = 0$) since the maximum degree of the polynomials we will consider, 4, is less than the size of the smallest field considered, $GF(2^8)$.

5.1   Resolution of the Subsystem over $GF(2^{16})$

Let us compute the number of monomials of a given degree with 7 variables. There are $\binom{n-1+d}{d}$ monomials of degree d with n variables, thus we have

degree	1	2	3	4
monomials	7	28	84	210

We also need the number of polynomials of a given degree d that can be formed from the 11 original polynomials:

degree	2	3	4
polynomials	11	77	308

Suppose now we try to build linear polynomials by multiplying the original polynomials by quadratic polynomials. Will we find some? This is equivalent to saying that we are looking for linear combinations of the 11+77+308=396 polynomials of the preceding table, that are linear. We thus need to cancel 210+84+28=322 terms in these polynomials. Unfortunately, our 396 polynomials are not linearly independent, because there are $\binom{11}{2} = 55$ relations in degree 4 of the form $fg - gh = 0$ with $g \neq h$ belonging to the set of the original polynomials. This leaves us with 396-55-322=19 linear polynomials. They cannot be linearly independent. Indeed, since we only have 7 variables and since our system has a unique solution, the dimension of the linear polynomials in the system is 7. Thus we have 12 more cancellations, which are in fact caused by the redundancy of the original equations (with very high probability, not all of the equations of the original system are needed for the system to have a unique solution).

We know by section 3.2 that when translated over $GF(2^8)$, the subsystem, which becomes a system of 22 equations with 14 variables, is still solvable by exploring degrees 4, 3, 2 then 1.

These theoretical observations are confirmed when running our algorithm on such a system. Building and reducing the matrices of degrees 4, then 3, 2 and

1 of the system expressed over $GF(2^{16})$ yields the solution as expected. The total number of cancellations occuring during the computation is 67, which corresponds to the 55 "$fg - gh$" cancellations and the 12 redundancy cancellations. Over $GF(2^8)$, the system can be solved as well, but the number of cancellations observed (255) is higher than 2×67, because many parasistic redundant equations are induced by the projections.

5.2 Behavior of the Linear Method over the Full Private Key

Because of the results of section 5.1, when reducing degrees 4, 3, 2, then 1, we expect to find 14 linearly independent linear polynomials in the ideal. Then, by adding multiples of these polynomials to the degree 2 matrix (which amounts to using these relations to reduce the number of variables in the original system), and reducing degree 2 again, we expect to find 4 more linear polynomials (because once $x_1, \ldots, x_{14}$ have been found and their value substituted into the system, equation 12 becomes linear in $x_{15}, \ldots, x_{18}$). Substituting into the degree 2 polynomials and reducing will yield x_{19}, and so on. In our experiments, this phenomenon was observed as predicted. The only surprise is that we do not have to know $x_1, \ldots, x_{24}$ to get a partial information on $x_{25}, \ldots, x_{40}$. Indeed, once $x_1, \ldots, x_{22}$ are known, equation 19 becomes linear in $x_{25}, \ldots, x_{40}$, and thus equations 17, 18 and 19 form a set of 18 equations over $GF(2^8)$ with 18 linear terms and only 3 quadratic terms (x_{23}^2, $x_{23}x_{24}$, and x_{24}^2): their reduction gives 15 linear polynomials, among which there is x_{23}, one linear combination of $x_{24}, \ldots, x_{40}$ and 13 linear combinations of $x_{25}, \ldots, x_{40}$. The next step is identical except that x_{23} and x_{23}^2 are now constants; there is now only one quadratic term left, instead of 3, and thus reduction gives x_{24} and another linear combination of $x_{25}, \ldots, x_{40}$. The last step yields the last linear relation needed to compute the values of $x_{25}, \ldots, x_{40}$.

6   Experimental Results and Complexity Estimates

6.1 Linear Method Used over Instances of TRMC Public Keys

To be in a realistic cryptanalysis situation, we built a random public key with Magma [10], computed the image of a random vector by the public key, and built the system composed of the value obtained substracted to the key. We then tried to solve the resulting system using the Linear Method[1].

The resolution process follows exactly the steps described in subsection 5.2: reduction of degrees 4 downto 1 yields 14 linear polynomials, and then we only have to loop between degrees 1 and 2 to get 4, then 1, 1, 1, 1, 15, 2 and 1 linear equations. The longest step is the degree 4 reduction, which we have performed using a lanczos algorithm. The computation time of the lanczos algorithm is proportional to the number of vectors computed. Thus, instead of

---

[1] The resulting system is guaranteed to have at least one solution (the random vector) but combinatorial arguments show that this solution is very likely to be unique. Thus we can apply the Linear Method.

looking for degree 3 polynomials in the degree 4 matrix M, we tried to build directly quadratic polynomials: this gave us 23 polynomials instead of the 273 cubic polynomials that can be buit from M (these are experimental figures obtained from experiments on a system of 11 equations with 7 variables on $GF(2^{16})$ and expressed over $GF(2^8)$). Overall, the lanczos resolution took 5 hours on a cluster of 6 bi-pentium IV PCs and used 400MB of RAM on each machine (data was duplicated on every machine). In that case, a Gauss reduction would have probably been faster but broke the 2GB per process limit, and could not be implemented simply on a 32-bit PC.

The other steps are performed in a few minutes on an average PC.

6.2   Asymptotic Security of TRMC

Here, we estimate the computation time ratio between the legitimate user of the system and the cryptanalyst who tries to decrypt a message, first for the "plain" TRMC algorithm, and then in the asymtptotic limit of a generalized TRMC with more variables and equations.

The preimage computation method suggested by the authors of TRMC is to solve first the random subsystem using XL, and then to substitute the result into the other equations. Using the Linear Method instead of XL, solving the random subsystem S requires to build the degree 4 matrix from the 11 equations with 7 variables of S. The complexity of a legitimate inversion is thus roughly equal to the computation of the kernel of a $\left[11 * \binom{7-1+2}{2} = 308\right] \times \left[\binom{7-1+4}{4} = 210\right]$ matrix. On the other hand, the cryptanalyst must deal with 48 equations with 40 unknowns, and thus compute the kernel of a matrix of size 39360×123410. Suppose this computation is performed using a Gauss reduction, and that the cost of a reduction of a $a \times b$ matrix is $a^2 b$, then the complexity ratio between the cryptanalyst and the legitimate user is about 2^{23}.

Now, put TRMC in the following more general setting: suppose we have a random quadratic system of m equations with n variables that can be solved by building and reducing matrices of degree less than or equal to d with the Linear Method, and that this subsystem is embedded in a block triangular system of $m' > m$ equations with $n' > n$ variables. Then the Linear Method is able to solve the big system by iterative explorations of polynomials of degree $\leq d$ built from the m' equations with n' variables.

For the legitimate user, the biggest matrix that must be built is

$$m\binom{n-1+d-2}{d-2} \times \binom{n-1+d}{d} \approx mn^{d-2} \times n^d$$

For the cryptanalyst, it is

$$m'\binom{n'-1+d-2}{d-2} \times \binom{n'-1+d}{d} \approx m'n'^{d-2} \times n'^d.$$

At degree d since the systems can be solved, we have $mn^{d-2} \geq n^d$ and $m'n'^{d-2} \geq n'^d$. Thus with ♣

Note that since the system has more equations than unknowns, not every value has a preimage by the system; this is why we had to compute first an image value.a Gaussian elimination algorithm as before, the ratios of the running times is $\leq \left(\frac{m'n'^{d-2}}{n^d}\right)^3$. This rough estimate is sufficient to show that an increase in the number of variables of the big system, n', increases the overall security of the scheme at most polynomially in n'.

In this analysis, we did not consider the degrees of the field extensions involved as a security parameter. The idea to use extensions of variable degree is used, for instance, in HFE, and is analyzed in [7]. Although the authors of [2] do not explicitly state what the security parameter of TRMC is, the algorithm does not seem to be designed with extensions of variable degree in mind.

7   Computing a Pseudo-private Key

Here, we show that the knowledge of the combinatorial properties of the system of equations of the public key allows the attacker to build a system equivalent to the public or the private key and that has the block triangular form of the private key. Although this pseudo-private key is not necessarily equal to the private key, it enables the attacker to speed up further attacks.

As we saw in section 5.2 and 6.1, linear equations are computed in several passes during the course of the resolution. For example, the first group of linear equations obtained corresponds to the innermost subsystem hidden in the public key. This subsystem can be extracted from the public key in the following way. Let S bet the first group of 14 linear equations obtained during resolution, with their constant part removed. Complete S with other linear equations to obtain an invertible linear system with 40 variables. Apply the inverse of this change of variables to the public key. Let us call the new variables $z_1, \ldots, z_{40}$, with z_1 to z_{14} corresponding to elements of S. In the resulting system, there are 22 linear combinations of the equations that only depend on the $z_1, \ldots, z_{14}$. These equations can be computed by a Gaussian elimination on this system, by putting linear and quadratic monomials depending only on $z_1, \ldots, z_{14}$ leftmost.

Since $z_1, \ldots, z_{14}$ are only equal to $x_1, \ldots, x_{14}$ up to an invertible linear transformation, the resulting subsystem is not necessarily equal to the subsystem of the private key.

We can iterate this method to further mimic the structure of the original system, but the main interest of this technique is to recover the random subsystem up to a linear transform.

Each preimage computation now requires from the cryptanalyst to find the kernel of the degree 4 matrix built from 22 polynomials with 14 variables, a matrix that is 2310×2380. This computation is roughly 2^9 times slower than a legitimate preimage computation.

8   Conclusion

In this article, we performed a practical and full cryptanalysis of a public key scheme using sets of polynomial equations over finite field, the Tractable Rational

Map Cryptosystem. To do so, we used a variant of the XL algorithm which we call the Linear Method. Our cryptanalysis is two-staged. A first resolution step is performed using the Linear Method to find a preimage of some value; depending on the usage of TRMC, this might correspond for example to a signature forgery or to a decryption of some message. This operation has a cost of 2^{23} legitimate preimage computations. Using its result and additional information about the process of the computation, we can then build a pseudo-private key that reduces the cost of finding a new preimage to only 2^9 legitimate preimage computations.

We also showed that the very principle of TRMC is flawed in that its security parameter cannot be reasonably increased to make it secure.

The Linear Method behaves identically on a system whether it is masked by linear or affine transformations or not. These masking techniques are used to separate the public key from the private key not only in TRMC but also in well-known schemes such as HFE or sFLASH. As with other cryptanalysis techniques like relinearization ([8]), the difficulty in breaking HFE with the linear method comes from the combination of a projection on a subfield and a linear masking, and not from the linear masking alone.

References

1. W. Adams and P. Loustaunau. *An introduction to Gröbner Bases*, volume 3 of *Graduate Studies in Mathematics*. American Mathematical Society, 1994.
2. L. Wang F. Chang. Tractable Rational Map Cryptosystem. Cryptology ePrint archive, Report 2004/046, available at http://eprint.iacr.org.
3. J.-C. Faugère. A New Efficient Algorithm for Computing Gröbner Bases without reduction to zero (F_5). In T. Mora, editor, *ISSAC 2002*, pages 75–83, 2002.
4. J.-C. Faugère. Report on a Successful Attack of HFE Challenge 1 with Gröbner Basis Algorithm F5/2. Announcement on sci.crypt newsgroup, in April 19th 2002.
5. J.-C. Faugère. A New Efficient Algorithm for Computing Gröbner Bases (F_4). *Journal of Pure and Applied Algebra*, 139(1-3):61–88, 1999.
6. T. Matsumoto H. Imai. Public Quadratic Polynomial-tuples for Efficient Signature Verification and Message Encryption. In C. G. Günther, editor, *Advances in Cryptology - Eurocrypt'88*, volume 330 of *LNCS*, pages 419–453. Springer Verlag, 1988.
7. A. Joux J.-C. Faugère. Algebraic Cryptanalysis of Hidden Field Equation (HFE) Cryptosystems Using Gröbner Bases. In D. Boneh, editor, *Advances in Cryptology - Crypto'2003*, volume 2729 of *LNCS*, pages 44–60. Springer Verlag, 2003.
8. A. Kipnis and A. Shamir. Cryptanalysis of the HFE Public-key Cryptosystem. In M. Wiener, editor, *Advances in Cryptology - Crypto'99*, volume 1666 of *LNCS*, pages 19–30. Springer Verlag, 1999.
9. D. Lazard. Gröbner Basis, Gaussian Elimination and Resolution of Systems of Algebraic Equations. In J. A. van Hulzen, editor, *EUROCAL '83, European Computer Algebra Conference*, volume 162 of *LNCS*, pages 146–156. Springer Verlag, 1983.
10. The magma home page. http://www.maths.usyd.edu.au/u/magma.
11. J. Patarin N. Courtois, A. Klimov and A. Shamir. Efficient Algorithms for Solving Overdefined Systems of Multivariate Polynomial Equations. In B. Preneel, editor, *Advances in Cryptology - Eurocrypt'2000*, volume 180 of *LNCS*, pages 392–407. Springer Verlag, 2000.

12. J. Patarin N. Courtois, L. Goubin. Improved Algorithms for Isomorphisms of Polynomials. In K. Nyberg, editor, *Advances in Cryptology - Eurocrypt'98*, volume 1403 of *LNCS*, pages 184–200. Springer-Verlag, 1998.

13. J. Patarin N. Courtois, L. Goubin. Flash, a Fast Multivariate Signature Algorithm. In D. Naccache, editor, *The Cryptographers' Track at RSA Conference 2001*, volume 2020 of *LNCS*, pages 298–307. Springer-Verlag, 2001.

14. J. Patarin. Cryptanalysis of the Matsumoto and Imai Public Key Scheme of Eurocrypt'88. In D. Coppersmith, editor, *Advances in Cryptology - Crypto'95*, volume 963 of *LNCS*, pages 248–261. Springer Verlag, 1995.

15. J. Patarin. Hidden Fields Equations (HFE) and Isomorphisms of Polynomials (IP): Two New Families of Asymmetric Algorithms. In *Advances in Cryptology - Eurocrypt'96*, volume 1070 of *LNCS*, pages 33–48. Springer Verlag, 1996.

A   Proofs of the Properties of the Linear Method

In this section, we prove the two results stated in section 3.2.

A.1   Notions of d-Relations and Depth

Let $S = \{p_i\}$ be a finite set of polynomials. We are looking for the existence of d-*relations* of the form

$$\sum m_j e_j = p \quad (1)$$

where $\forall j$, $\deg(m_j e_j) \leq d$. p is the *result* of the relation. The polynomials e_j are either elements of S or results of other d-relations, thus relation results always belong to the ideal generated by S, denoted $< S >$. Note that substituting one d-relation into another yields a e-relation for $e > d$, that is not in general a d-relation. This means that such a relation can be found in two passes by exploring degrees at most d, but in one pass by exploring degree e. We introduce the notion of depth that captures the number of degree d explorations needed to compute a polynomial as element of $< S >$.

Let $p \in < S >$. The d-*depth* of p is defined recursively as follows: elements of S have d-depth 0. If p is obtained by a d-relation $\sum_j m_j e_j$,

$$\mathrm{depth}_d(p) = 1 + \max_j \mathrm{depth}_d(e_j)$$

If p is the multiple of a depth k polynomial by a monomial, then $\mathrm{depth}(p) = k$.

The depth of a polynomial p might not be uniquely defined. This is because there may be several sequences of reductions (relations) and multiplications that lead to p. In this case, we define the depth of p as the minimum of all depths of p.

The d-depth of a polynomial p is thus the minimal number of d-relations required to construct p as an element of $< S >$. Some polynomials p in $< S >$ might never be reached through d-relations, and for these p we set $\mathrm{depth}_d(p) = \infty$.

The depth is an useful tool to perform recursions on relations.

A.2   Behavior of the Linear Method with Respect to Linear of Affine Masking

Here we prove that two systems equal up to left linear and right affine invertible transformations, have the same combinatorial properties w.r.t. the Linear Method.

First, let us show that a change of variables has no influence on relations. Intuitively, this is clear because multiples of polynomials in the transformed system are just transformed of multiples of the original system. To prove the result formally, we show that there is a one-to-one depth-preserving correspondence between the d-relations of the two systems for any d.

We fix some value of d and perform a recursion on the relation depth.

Let $S = \{p_j\}$ and $T = \{q_j\}$ be two families of polynomials satisfying

$$\forall j, \quad q_j = p_j \circ A$$

where A is an invertible affine transformation of the variables. This exactly means that $\varphi : p \mapsto p \circ A$ is a one-to-one correspondence between depth 0 polynomials of $< S >$ and $< T >$.

Suppose that φ establishes a one-to-one correspondence between polynomials of d-depth k in $< S >$ and $< T >$, and that p is a polynomial of d-depth $k + 1$ w.r.t. S:

$$\sum m_j e_j = p$$

with $\forall j, \quad \deg(m_j e_j) \leq d$ and $\mathrm{depth}_d(e_j) \leq k$.

Then for T, $\mathrm{depth}_d(e_j \circ A) \leq k$, hence

$$\sum (m_j \circ A)(e_j \circ A) = p \circ A$$

is a d-relation. Since A is affine, $\forall j, \quad \deg((m_j \circ A)(e_j \circ A)) \leq d$, thus

$$\mathrm{depth}_d(p \circ A) \leq k + 1$$

Therefore we have shown that the right affine invertible transformations do not change the relations results. Similarily, left invertible linear transformations do not change at all relations results since they do not change the vector space spanned by a polynomial family.

Left affine transformations do change relations in general. Indeed, such an operation can even transform a system having a unique solution into a system that does not have this property. In TRMC or other cryptosystems, left affine transformations are used, but the systems to which we apply the linear resolution method are not masked systems, but *masked systems minus a masked image value*. Thus the constant of the affine transformation is cancelled, and we only have to consider left *linear* transformations.

A.3   Behavior of the Linear Method w.r.t Projection on a Smaller Field

Here, we prove that if the Linear Method is able to solve a system $S = \{p_j\}$ expressed on a finite extension G of a field F by reducing degrees less than d, it is also able to solve S expressed over F by reducing degrees no more than d. Roughly said, this is because the projected system contains all the projections of the relations of the original system.

Let $[G : F] = \ell$, and $p_k, 1 \le k \le \ell$, be the projections from G to F associated to some basis $\{b_1, \ldots, b_\ell\}$ of G over F. If q is a polynomial over G with u unknowns, it defines a function $f : F^{ul} \to G$ that can be composed with any p_k. $p_k(q)$ is the polynomial over F corresponding to the k-th coordinate of f (this polynomial is unique with some extra conditions on its degree). Each equation $e \in S$ is translated into ℓ equations $p_1(e), \ldots, p_\ell(e)$ over F. Thus the starting point of the Linear Method over F is the set $S' = \{p_k(e) | 1 \le k \le \ell, e \in S\}$.

We only have to prove that, for any d and $q \in <S>$, if the d-depth of q is n, then for $1 \le k \le \ell$, the d-depth of $p_k(q)$ is at most n.

Indeed, if that result holds, then by applying it to the case where q is linear, we get that as soon as the algorithm in G computes enough linear relations to solve the system, the algorithm running over F solves the system too.

For depth 0, the result is true because S' contains the $p_k(S)$, $1 \le k \le \ell$. Suppose it is true at depth n. Let $q \in <S>$ of depth $n+1$ output by the relation

$$\sum_j m_j e_j = q$$

with $\deg(m_j e_j) \le d$ and $\operatorname{depth}(e_j) \le n$.

$$p_k(q) = p_k\left(\sum_j m_j e_j\right) = \sum_j p_k(m_j e_j)$$

Since $\forall i, j$, $\operatorname{depth}(p_i(e_j)) \le n$, we only have to show that for all j, the $p_k(m_j e_j)$ can be written $\sum_i m_{ij} p_i(e_j)$, with $\forall i, j$, $\deg(m_{ij} p_i(e_j)) \le d$.

This is true because for any polynomial r over G, a projection of a multiple of r $p_k(mr)$ can be expressed as a sum of multiples of projections of r

$$\sum_i m_i p_i(r)$$

with m_i polynomials over F and $\forall i$, $\deg m_i \le \deg m$.

Let $\alpha_{ijk} \in F$ such that $\forall i, j$, $b_i b_j = \sum_k \alpha_{ijk} b_k$. Then since $r = \sum_i p_i(r) b_i$ and $m = \sum_j p_j(m) b_j$,

$$mr = \sum_{i,j} p_i(r) p_j(m) b_i b_j = \sum_k \left(\sum_{i,j} \alpha_{ijk} p_j(m) p_i(r)\right) b_k$$

thus

$$p_k(mr) = \sum_i \left(\sum_j \alpha_{ijk} p_j(m)\right) p_i(r)$$

Large Superfluous Keys
in $\mathcal{M}$ultivariate $\mathcal{Q}$uadratic Asymmetric Systems

Christopher Wolf and Bart Preneel

K.U.Leuven, ESAT-COSIC,
Kasteelpark Arenberg 10,
B-3001 Leuven-Heverlee, Belgium
{Christopher.Wolf,Bart.Preneel}@esat.kuleuven.ac.be
chris@Christopher-Wolf.de
http://www.esat.kuleuven.ac.be/cosic/

Abstract. In this article, we show that public key schemes based on multivariate quadratic equations allow many equivalent, and hence superfluous private keys. We achieve this result by investigating several transformations to identify these keys and show their application to Hidden Field Equations (HFE), C*, and Unbalanced Oil and Vinegar schemes (UOV). In all cases, we are able to reduce the size of the private – and hence the public – key space by at least one order of magnitude. We see applications of our technique both in cryptanalysis of these schemes and in memory efficient implementations.

Keywords: Multivariate Quadratic Equations, Public Key Schemes

1 Introduction

One way to achieve more variety in asymmetric cryptology are schemes based on the problem of solving $\mathcal{M}$ultivariate $\mathcal{Q}$uadratic equations ($\mathcal{MQ}$-problem). This is very important to have alternatives ready if large scale quantum computing becomes feasible. In particular, the existence of quantum computers in the range of 1000 bit would be a threat to systems based on factoring, *e.g.*, RSA, as there is a polynomial time factoring algorithm available for quantum computers [13]. The same algorithm would also solve the discrete log problem in polynomial time – and therefore defeat schemes based on elliptic curves.

In the last two decades, several such public key schemes were proposed, *e.g.*, [8, 11, 6]. All of them use the fact that the $\mathcal{MQ}$-problem, *i.e.*, finding a solution $x \in \mathbb{F}^n$ for a given system of m quadratic polynomial equations in n variables each

$$\begin{cases} y_1 = p_1(x_1, \ldots, x_n) \\ y_2 = p_2(x_1, \ldots, x_n) \\ \quad \vdots \\ y_m = p_m(x_1, \ldots, x_n), \end{cases}$$

for given $y_1, \ldots, y_m \in \mathbb{F}$ and unknown $x_1, \ldots, x_n$ is difficult, namely $\mathcal{NP}$-complete (cf [4, p. 251] and [12, App.] for a detailed proof)). In the above system of equations, the polynomials p_i have the form

S. Vaudenay (Ed.): PKC 2005, LNCS 3386, pp. 275–287, 2005.
© International Association for Cryptologic Research 2005

$$p_i(x_1, \ldots, x_n) := \sum_{1 \leq j \leq k \leq n} \gamma_{i,j,k} x_j x_k + \sum_{j=1}^{n} \beta_{i,j} x_j + \alpha_i \,,$$

for $1 \leq i \leq m; 1 \leq j \leq k \leq n$ and $\alpha_i, \beta_{i,j}, \gamma_{i,j,k} \in \mathbb{F}$ (constant, linear, and quadratic terms). This polynomial-vector $\mathcal{P} := (p_1, \ldots, p_m)$ forms the public key of these systems. Moreover, the private key consists of the triple $(S, \mathcal{P}', T)$ where $S \in \mathrm{AGL}_n(\mathbb{F}), T \in \mathrm{AGL}_m(\mathbb{F})$ are affine transformations and $\mathcal{P}' \in \mathcal{MQ}_m(\mathbb{F}^n)$ is a polynomial-vector $\mathcal{P}' := (p'_1, \ldots, p'_m)$ with m components; each component is a polynomial in n variables $x'_1, \ldots, x'_n$. Throughout this paper, we will denote components of this private vector $\mathcal{P}'$ by a prime $'$. In contrast to the public polynomial vector $\mathcal{P} \in \mathcal{MQ}_m(\mathbb{F}^n)$, the private polynomial vector $\mathcal{P}'$ does allow an efficient computation of $x'_1, \ldots, x'_n$ for given $y'_1, \ldots, y'_m$. At least for secure $\mathcal{MQ}$-schemes, this is not the case if the public key $\mathcal{P}$ alone is given. The main difference between $\mathcal{MQ}$-schemes lies in their special construction of the central equations $\mathcal{P}'$ and consequently the trapdoor they embed into a specific class of $\mathcal{MQ}$-problems.

Having a large private (and consequently public) key space is a desirable property for any public key scheme. In this paper, we will show that many schemes based on multivariate quadratic polynomial equations have a large number of "equivalent" private keys. Hence, they have many superfluous private keys and consequently a smaller private and public key space than initially expected. Our main tool for this purpose are so-called "sustaining transformations", which will be formally introduced in Sect. 2.

1.1   Related Work

In their cryptanalysis of HFE, Kipnis and Shamir report the existence of "isomorphic keys" [7]. A similar observation for Unbalanced Oil and Vinegar Schemes can be found in [6]. In both cases, there has not been a systematic study of the structure of equivalent key classes. In addition, Patarin observed the existence of some equivalent keys for C* [10] – however, his method is different from the one presented in this paper, as he concentrated on modifying the central monomial. Moreover, Toli observed that there exists an additive sustainer (cf Sect. 3.1) in the case of Hidden Field Equations [14]. In the case of symmetric ciphers, [1] used a similar idea in the study of S-boxes.

1.2   Outline

The remainder of this paper is organised as follows: first, we introduce the necessary mathematical background and concentrate on useful properties of linear and affine transformations. Second, we identify several candidates for sustaining transformations. Third, we apply these candidates to the Hidden Field Equations, the C* scheme, and Unbalanced Oil and Vinegar schemes. Sect. 5 concludes this paper.

2   Mathematical Background

After giving some basic definitions in the following section, we will move on to observations about affine transformations.

2.1   Basic Definitions

We start with a formal definition of the term "equivalent private keys":

Definition 1. *We call two private keys*

$$(T, \mathcal{P}', S), (\tilde{T}, \tilde{\mathcal{P}}', \tilde{S}) \in AGL_m(\mathbb{F}) \times \mathcal{MQ}_m(\mathbb{F}^n) \times AGL_n(\mathbb{F})$$

"equivalent" if they lead to the same public key, i.e., if we have

$$T \circ \mathcal{P}' \circ S = \mathcal{P} = \tilde{T} \circ \tilde{\mathcal{P}}' \circ \tilde{S}.$$

In order to find equivalent keys, we consider the following transformations:

Definition 2. *Let* $(S, \mathcal{P}', T) \in AGL_m(\mathbb{F}) \times \mathcal{MQ}_m(\mathbb{F}^n) \times AGL_n(\mathbb{F})$ *where* $\sigma, \sigma^{-1} \in AGL_n(\mathbb{F})$ *and* $\tau, \tau^{-1} \in AGL_m(\mathbb{F})$. *Moreover, let*

$$\mathcal{P} = T \circ \tau^{-1} \circ \tau \circ \mathcal{P}' \circ \sigma \circ \sigma^{-1} \circ S \qquad (1)$$

We call the pair $(\sigma, \tau) \in AGL_n(\mathbb{F}) \times AGL_m(\mathbb{F})$ *"sustaining transformations" for an* $\mathcal{MQ}$-system *if the "shape" of* $\mathcal{P}'$ *is invariant under the transformations* σ *and* τ. *For short, we write* $(\sigma, \tau) \bullet (S, \mathcal{P}', T)$ *for (1) and* (σ, τ) *sustaining transformations.*

Remark 1. In the above definition, the meaning of "shape" is still open. In fact, its meaning has to be defined for each $\mathcal{MQ}$-system individually. For example, in HFE (cf Sect. 4.1), it is the bounding degree $d \in \mathbb{N}$ of the polynomial $P'(X')$, while it is the fact that the oil-variables do not mix with other oil-variables, while vinegar-variables do, in the case of the UOV (cf Sect. 4.3). However, for σ, τ sustaining transformations, we are now able to produce equivalent keys for a given private key by $(\sigma, \tau) \bullet (S, \mathcal{P}', T)$. A trivial example of sustaining transformations is the identity transformation, *i.e.*, to set $\sigma = \tau = id$.

Lemma 1. *Let* (σ, τ) *be sustaining transformation. If* $G := (\sigma, \circ)$ *and* $H := (\tau, \circ)$ *form a subgroup of the affine transformations, they produce equivalence relations within the private key space.*

Proof. We prove the statement for $G := (\sigma, \circ)$. The proof for $H := (\tau, \circ)$ is analogous. First, we have reflexivity as the identity transformation is contained in G. Second, we have symmetry as a subgroup is closed under inversion. Third, we also have transitivity as a subgroup is closed under composition. Therefore, the groups G and H partition the private key space into equivalence classes.

Remark 2. We want to point out that the above proof does not use special properties of sustaining transformations, but the fact that these are a subgroup of the group of affine transformations. Hence, the proof does not depend on the term "shape" and is therefore valid even if the latter is not rigorously defined yet. In any case, instead of proving that sustaining transformations form a subgroup of the affine transformations, we can also consider normal forms of private keys.

After these initial observations over equivalent keys, we concentrate on bijections between ground fields and their extension fields. Let $\mathbb{F}$ be a finite field with $q := |\mathbb{F}|$ elements. Using a polynomial $i(t) \in \mathbb{F}[t]$, irreducible over $\mathbb{F}$, we generate an extension field $\mathbb{E} := \mathbb{F}[t]/i(t)$ of dimension n. This means we view elements of $\mathbb{E}$ as polynomials in t of degree less than n. Addition and multiplication are defined as for polynomials modulo $i(t)$. In addition, we can view elements from $\mathbb{E}$ as vectors over the vector-space $\mathbb{F}^n$. We will therefore view elements $a \in \mathbb{E}$ and $b \in \mathbb{F}^n$ as

$$a := \alpha_n t^{n-1} + \ldots + \alpha_2 t + \alpha_1 \text{ and } b := (\beta_1, \ldots, \beta_n),$$

for $\alpha_i, \beta_i \in \mathbb{F}$ with $1 \leq i \leq n$. Moreover, we define a bijection between $\mathbb{E}$ and $\mathbb{F}^n$ by identifying the coefficients $\alpha_i \leftrightarrow \beta_i$. We use this bijection throughout this paper.

2.2   Affine Transformations

In the context of affine transformations, the following lemma proves useful:

Lemma 2. Let $\mathbb{F}$ be a finite field with $q := |\mathbb{F}|$ elements. Then we have $\prod_{i=0}^{n-1} q^n - q^i$ invertible $(n \times n)$-matrices over $\mathbb{F}$.

Next, we recall some basic properties of affine transformations over the finite fields $\mathbb{F}$ and $\mathbb{E}$.

Definition 3. Let $M_S \in \mathbb{F}^{n \times n}$ be an invertible $(n \times n)$ matrix and $v_s \in \mathbb{F}^n$ a vector and let $S(x) := M_S x + v_s$. We call this the "matrix representation" of the affine transformation S.

Definition 4. Moreover, let $s_1, \ldots, s_n$ be n polynomials of degree 1 at most over $\mathbb{F}$, i.e., $s_i(x_1, \ldots, x_n) := \beta_{i,1} x_1 + \ldots + \beta_{i,n} x_n + \alpha_i$ with $1 \leq i, j \leq n$ and $\alpha_i, \beta_{i,j} \in \mathbb{F}$. Let $S(x) := (s_1(x), \ldots, s_n(x))$ for $x := (x_1, \ldots, x_n)$ as a vector over $\mathbb{F}^n$. We call this the "multivariate representation" of the affine transformation S.

Remark 3. The multivariate and the matrix representation of an affine transformation S are interchangeable. We only need to set the corresponding coefficients to the same values: $(M_S)_{i,j} \leftrightarrow \beta_{i,j}$ and $(v_S)_i \leftrightarrow \alpha_i$ for $1 \leq i, j \leq n$.

In addition, we can also use the "univariate representation" over the extension field $\mathbb{E}$ of the transformation S.

Definition 5. Let $0 \leq i < n$ and $A, B_i \in \mathbb{E}$. Moreover, let the polynomial $S(X) := \sum_{i=0}^{n-1} B_i X^{q^i} + A$ be an affine transformation. We call this the "univariate representation" of the affine transformation $S(X)$.

Lemma 3. An affine transformation in univariate representation can be transfered efficiently in multivariate representation and vice versa.

Remark 4. This lemma follows from [7, Lemmata 3.1 and 3.2] by a simple extension from the linear to the affine case.

3   Sustaining Transformations

In this section, we give several examples for sustaining transformations. In addition, we will consider their effect on the central transformation $\mathcal{P}'$. The authors are not convinced that the transformations stated here are the only ones possible but encourage the search for other and maybe more powerful sustaining transformations.

3.1   Additive Sustainer

For $n = m$, let $\sigma(X) := (X + A)$ and $\tau(X) := (X + A')$ for some elements $A, A' \in \mathbb{E}$. Moreover, as long as they keep the shape of the central equations $\mathcal{P}'$ invariant, they form sustaining transformations.

In particular, we are able to change the constant parts $v_s, v_t \in \mathbb{F}^n$ or $V_S, V_T \in \mathbb{E}$ of the two affine transformations $S, T \in \mathrm{AGL}_n(\mathbb{F})$ to zero, *i.e.*, to obtain a new key $(\hat{S}, \hat{\mathcal{P}}', \hat{T})$ with $\hat{S}, \hat{T} \in \mathrm{GL}_n(\mathbb{F})$.

Remark 5. This is a very useful result for cryptanalysis as it allows us to "collect" the constant terms in the central equations $\mathcal{P}'$. For cryptanalytic purposes, we therefore need only to consider the case of linear transformations $S, T \in \mathrm{GL}_n(\mathbb{F})$.

The additive sustainer also works if we interpret it over the vector space $\mathbb{F}^n$ rather than the extension field $\mathbb{E}$. In particular, we can also handle the case $n \neq m$ now. However, in this case it may happen that we have $a' \in \mathbb{F}^m$ and consequently $\tau : \mathbb{F}^m \to \mathbb{F}^m$. Nevertheless, we can still collect all constant terms in the central equations $\mathcal{P}'$.

If we look at the central equations as multivariate polynomials, the additive sustainer will affect the constants α_i and $\beta_{i,j} \in \mathbb{F}$ for $1 \leq i \leq m$ and $1 \leq j \leq n$. A similar observation is true for central equations over the extension field $\mathbb{E}$: in this case, the additive sustainer affects the additive constant $A \in \mathbb{E}$ and the linear factors $B_i \in \mathbb{E}$ for $0 \leq i < n$.

3.2   Big Sustainer

We now consider multiplication in the (big) extension field $\mathbb{E}$, *i.e.*, we have $\sigma(X) := (BX)$ and $\tau(X) := (B'X)$ for $B, B' \in \mathbb{E}^*$. Again, we obtain a sustaining transformation if this operation does not modify the shape of the central equations as $(BX), (B'X) \in \mathrm{AGL}_n(\mathbb{F})$.

The big sustainer is useful if we consider schemes defined over extension fields as it does not affect the overall degree of the central equations over this extension field.

3.3   Small Sustainer

We now consider multiplications over the (small) ground field $\mathbb{F}$, *i.e.*, we have $\sigma(x) := Diag(b_1, \ldots, b_n)x$ and $\tau(x) := Diag(b'_1, \ldots, b'_m)x$ for the coefficients $b_1, \ldots, b_n, b'_1, \ldots, b'_m \in \mathbb{F}^*$ and $Diag(b)$ the diagonal matrix on a vector $b \in \mathbb{F}^n$ and $b' \in \mathbb{F}^m$, respectively.

In contrast to the big sustainer, the small sustainer is useful if we consider schemes which define the central equations over the ground field $\mathbb{F}$ as it only introduces a scalar factor in the polynomials $(p'_1, \ldots, p'_m)$.

3.4 Permutation Sustainer

For the transformation σ, this sustainer permutes input-variables of the central equations while for the transformation τ, it permutes the polynomials of the central equations themselves. As each permutation has a corresponding, invertible permutation-matrix, both $\sigma \in S_n$ and $\tau \in S_m$ are also affine transformations. The effect of the central equations is limited to a permutation of these equations and their input variables, respectively.

3.5 Gauss Sustainer

Here, we consider Gauss operations on matrices, *i.e.*, row and column permutations, multiplication of rows and columns by scalars from the ground field $\mathbb{F}$, and the addition of two rows/columns. As all these operations can be performed by invertible matrices; they form a subgroup of the affine transformations and are hence a candidate for a sustaining transformation.

The effect of the Gauss Sustainer is similar to the permutation sustainer and the small sustainer. In addition, it allows the addition of multivariate quadratic polynomials. This will not affect the shape of some $\mathcal{MQ}$-schemes.

Remark 6. We want to point out that all five sustainers in this section form groups and hence partition the private key space into equivalence classes (cf Lemma 1).

4   Application to $\mathcal{M}$ultivariate $\mathcal{Q}$uadratic Schemes

In this section, we show how to apply the sustainers from the previous section to several $\mathcal{MQ}$-schemes. Due to space limitations in this paper, we will only outline some central properties of each scheme. In particular, we will not explain how they can be used to derive signatures but refer the reader to the original papers for this purpose. We want to stress that the reductions in size we achieve are only lower, no upper limits: as soon as new sustaining transformations are identified, they will reduce the key space of the schemes in questions. At present, we prefer not to attempt to give an upper limit for the reductions possible, as the subject is far too new.

4.1 Hidden Field Equations

The Hidden Field Equations (HFE) have been proposed by Patarin [11].

Definition 6. *Let* $\mathbb{E}$ *be a finite field and* $P(X)$ *a polynomial over* $\mathbb{E}$. *For*

$$P(X) := \sum_{\substack{0 \le i,j \le d \\ q^i + q^j \le d}} C_{i,j} X^{q^i + q^j} + \sum_{\substack{0 \le k \le d \\ q^k \le d}} B_k X^{q^k} + A$$

$$where \begin{cases} C_{i,j} X^{q^i + q^j} & for\ C_{i,j} \in \mathbb{E}\ are\ the\ quadratic\ terms, \\ B_k X^{q^k} & for\ B_k \in \mathbb{E}\ are\ the\ linear\ terms,\ and \\ A & for\ A \in \mathbb{E}\ is\ the\ constant\ term \end{cases}$$

and a degree $d \in \mathbb{N}$, *we say the central equations* $\mathcal{P}'$ *are in HFE-shape.*

Using a generalisation of the Kipnis-Shamir Theorem (cf Lemma 3), we see that we can express the univariate polynomial over $\mathbb{E}$ as multivariate polynomials over $\mathbb{F}$. Moreover, as the degree of the polynomial P is bounded by d, this allows efficient inversion of the equation $P(X) = Y$ for given $Y \in \mathbb{E}$. So the "shape" of HFE is in particular this degree d of the private polynomial P. Moreover, we observe that there are no restrictions on its coefficients $C_{i,j}, B_k, A \in \mathbb{E}$ for $i, j, k \in \mathbb{N}$ and $q^i, q^i + q^j \le d$. Hence, we can apply both the additive and the big sustainer (cf sect. 3.1 and 3.2) without changing the shape of this central equation.

Theorem 1. *For* $K := (S, P, T) \in AGL_n(\mathbb{F}) \times \mathbb{E}[X] \times AGL_n(\mathbb{F})$ *a private key in HFE, we have*

$$q^{2n} \cdot (q^n - 1)^2$$

equivalent keys. Hence, the key-space of HFE can be reduced by this number.

Proof. To prove this theorem, we consider normal forms of private keys: we first apply the additive sustainer to reduce the constant parts of the two affine transformations S and T to zero. Second, we apply the big sustainer on the univariate representation of S and T to reduce one of its coefficients to the neutral element of multiplication. W.l.o.g., let B_0 be the non-zero coefficient of the lowest power in the univariate representation of S. Applying $\sigma^{-1}(X) := B_0^{-1} X$ will reduce this coefficient to one. Similar, we can reduce one coefficient of the affine transformation T. Hence, we have now computed a unique normal form for any given private key. Moreover, we can "reverse" these computations and derive an equivalence class of size $q^{2n} \cdot (q^n - 1)^2$ this way as we have

$$(BX + A, B'X + A) \bullet (S, \mathcal{P}', T) \text{ for } B, B' \in \mathbb{E}^* \text{ and } A, A' \in \mathbb{E}.$$

Remark 7. The idea presented in this section also works against the variations HFEv (adding vinegar variables) and HFE- (removing public equations). However, for HFE- we have to take into account that some rows of the private matrix T do not influence the public key. Hence, the number of equivalent keys is even larger. Due to space limitations in this paper, we just point out this fact.

For the case $q = 2$ and $n = 107$, the number of redundant keys is 2^{428}. In comparison, the number of choices for S and T is $2^{22,894}$. This special choice of parameters has been used in a repaired version of Quartz [2, 15].

4.2   Class of C* Schemes

As HFE, the scheme C^*, due to Matsumoto and Imai [8], uses a finite field $\mathbb{F}$ and an extension field $\mathbb{E}$. However, the choice of the central equations is far more restricted than in HFE as we only have one monomial here.

Definition 7. *Let $\mathbb{E}$ be an extension field of dimension n over the finite field $\mathbb{F}$ and $\lambda \in \mathbb{N}$ an integer with $\gcd(q^n - 1, q^\lambda + 1) = 1$. We then say that the following central equation is of C^*-shape:*

$$P(X) := X^{q^\lambda + 1}.$$

The restriction $\gcd(q^n - 1, q^\lambda + 1) = 1$ is necessary first to obtain a permutation polynomial and second to allow efficient inversion of $P(X)$. In this setting, we cannot apply the additive sustainer, as this monomial does not allow any linear or constant terms. Moreover, the monomial requires a factor of one. Hence, we have to preserve this property. At present, the only sustainer suitable seems to be the big sustainer (cf Sect. 3.2). We use it in the following theorem.

Theorem 2. *For $K := (S, P, T) \in AGL_n(\mathbb{F}) \times \mathbb{E}[X] \times AGL_n(\mathbb{F})$ a private key in C^*, we have*

$$(q^n - 1)$$

equivalent keys. Hence, the key-space of C^* can be reduced by this number.

Proof. To prove this statement, we consider normal forms of keys in C^*. In particular, we concentrate on a normal form of the affine transformation S where S is in univariate representation. As for HFE and w.l.o.g., let B_0 be the non-zero coefficient of the lowest power in the univariate representation of S. Applying $\sigma^{-1}(X) := B_0^{-1}X$ will reduce this coefficient to one. In order to "repair" the monomial $P(X)$, we have to apply an inverse transformation to T. So let $\tau(X) := (B_0^{q^\lambda + 1})^{-1}X$. This way we obtain

$$\begin{aligned}
\mathcal{P} &= T \circ \tau^{-1} \circ \tau \circ P \circ \sigma \circ \sigma^{-1} \circ S \\
&= \tilde{T} \circ (B_0^{(q^\lambda + 1).(-1)}.B_0^{q^\lambda + 1}.X^{q^\lambda + 1}) \circ \tilde{S} \\
&= \tilde{T} \circ P \circ \tilde{S},
\end{aligned}$$

where $\tilde{S}$ has its coefficient B_0 reduced to one. In contrast to HFE (cf Thm. 1), we cannot chose the transformations σ and τ independently: each choice of σ implies a particular τ and vice versa. So we have

$$(BX, B^{-q^\lambda - 1}X) \bullet (S, P, T) \text{ where } B \in \mathbb{E}^*$$

and can hence compute a total of $(q^n - 1)$ equivalent keys for any given key. Since all these keys form equivalence classes, we reduced the private key space of C^* by this factor.

Remark 8. Patarin observed that it is possible to derive equivalent keys by changing the monomial P [10]. As the aim of this paper is the study of equivalent keys by chaining the affine transformations S, T alone, we did not make use of this property.

Moreover, we observed in this section that it is not possible for C* to change the transformations S, T from affine to linear. In this context, we want to point out that Geiselmann showed how to reveal the constant parts of these transformations [5]. Hence, having S, T affine instead of linear does not seem to enhance the overall security of C*.

Finally, we want to note that C* itself is insecure, due to a very efficient attack by Patarin [9]. However, due to space limitations in this paper, we will not investigate equivalent keys of the more secure version C*$^{--}$.

For $q = 128$ and $n = 67$, we obtain 2^{469} equivalent private keys per class. The number of choices for S, T is $2^{62,848}$ in this case. This particular choice of parameters has been used in Sflash^{v3} [3].

4.3 Unbalanced Oil and Vinegar Schemes

In contrast to the two schemes before, we now consider a class of $\mathcal{MQ}$-schemes which does not mix operations over two different fields $\mathbb{E}$ and $\mathbb{F}$ but only performs computations over the ground field $\mathbb{F}$. Moreover, Unbalanced Oil and Vinegar schemes (UOV) omit the affine transformation T but use $S \in \mathrm{AGL}_n(\mathbb{F})$. To fit in our framework, we set it to be the identity transformation, *i.e.*, we have $T = \tau = id$. UOV were proposed in [6].

Definition 8. *Let $\mathbb{F}$ be a finite field and $n, m \in \mathbb{N}$ with $n \geq 2m$. Moreover, let $\alpha'_i, \beta'_{i,j}, \gamma'_{i,j,k} \in \mathbb{F}$. We say that the polynomials below are central equations in UOV-shape:*

$$p_i(x'_1, \ldots, x'_n) := \sum_{j=1}^{m} \sum_{k=1}^{n} \gamma'_{i,j,k} x'_j x'_k + \sum_{j=1}^{n} \beta'_{i,j} x'_j + \alpha'_i.$$

In this context, the variables x'_i for $1 \leq i \leq n - m$ are called the "vinegar" variables and x'_i for $n - m < i \leq n$ the "oil" variables. Note that the vinegar variables are combined quadratically while the oil variables are only combined with vinegar variables in a quadratic way. Therefore, assigning random values to the vinegar variables, results in a system of linear equations in the oil variables which can than be solved, *e.g.*, using Gaussian elimination. So the "shape" of UOV is the fact that a system in the oil variables alone is linear. Hence, we may not mix oil variables and vinegar variables in our analysis but may perform affine transformations within one set of these variables. So for UOV, we can apply the additive sustainer and also the Gauss sustainer (cf sect. 3.1 and 3.5). However, in order to ensure that the shape of the central equations does not change, we have to ensure that the Gauss sustainer influences the vinegar and oil variables separately.

Theorem 3. *Let* $K := (S, P, id) \in AGL_n(\mathbb{F}) \times \mathcal{MQ}_m(\mathbb{F}^n) \times AGL_n(\mathbb{F})$ *be a private key in UOV. Then we have*

$$q^n \prod_{i=0}^{n-m-1} (q^{n-m} - q^i) \prod_{i=0}^{m-1} (q^m - q^i)$$

equivalent keys. Hence, the key-space of UOV can be reduced by this number.

Proof. As in the case of the schemes before, we compute a normal form for a given private key. First, applying the additive sustainer reduces the affine transformation S to a linear transformation. This gives us a factor of q^n in terms of equivalent keys. Second, applying the Gauss sustainer separately within vinegar and oil variables, we can enforce the following structure, denoted $R \in \mathbb{F}^{n \times n}$, on the matrix $M_S \in \mathbb{F}^{n \times n}$ of the (now only) linear transformation S:

$$R := \begin{pmatrix} I_m & 0 & A_m \\ 0 & I_{n-2m} & B_m^{n-2m} \\ I_m & C_{n-2m}^m & D_m \end{pmatrix}.$$

In this context, the matrices I_m, I_{n-2m} are the identity elements of $\mathbb{F}^{m \times m}$ and $\mathbb{F}^{(n-2m) \times (n-2m)}$, respectively. Moreover, we have the matrices $A_m, D_m \in \mathbb{F}^{m \times m}$, the matrix $B_m^{n-2m} \in \mathbb{F}^{(n-2m) \times m}$ and $C_{n-2m}^m \in \mathbb{F}^{m \times (n-2m)}$. For a given central equation $\mathcal{P}'$, each possible matrix R leads to the same number of equivalent keys. Let

$$E := \begin{pmatrix} G_{n-m} & 0 \\ 0 & H_m \end{pmatrix}$$

be an $(n \times n)$-matrix. Here, we require that the matrices $G_{n-m} \in \mathbb{F}^{(n-m) \times (n-m)}$ and $H_m \in \mathbb{F}^{m \times m}$ are invertible (cf Lemma 2). This way, we define the transformation $\sigma(x) := Ex$ where $x \in \mathbb{F}^n$. Note that these transformations σ form a subgroup within the affine transformations. So we have

$$(Ex + a, id) \bullet (S, \mathcal{P}', id) \text{ for } a \in \mathbb{F}^n \text{ and } E \text{ as defined above.}$$

As this choice of σ partitions the private key space into equivalence classes of equal size, and due to the restrictions on E, we reduced the size of the private key space by an additional factor of $\prod_{i=0}^{n-m-1}(q^{n-m} - q^i) \prod_{i=0}^{m-1}(q^m - q^i)$.

5   Conclusions

In this paper, we showed through the examples of Hidden Field Equations (HFE), C^* and Unbalanced Oil and Vinegar (UOV) that it is possible to reduce the number of keys in these multivariate quadratic public key schemes by at least one order of magnitude. For UOV, the reduction was the most drastic one as it allowed to reduce the number of possible keys by more than half of the number of possible affine transformations S, cf Table 1 and Table 2 for numerical examples.

Table 1. Summary of the Reduction Results of this Paper.

Scheme	Reduction
Hidden Field Equations	$q^{2n}(q^n - 1)^2$
C*	$q^n - 1$
Unbalanced Oil and Vinegar	$q^n \prod_{i=0}^{n-m-1}(q^{n-m} - q^i) \prod_{i=0}^{m-1}(q^m - q^i)$

Table 2. Numerical Examples for the Reduction Results of this Paper.

Scheme	Parameters	Choices for S, T (in $\log_2$)	Reduction (in $\log_2$)
HFE	$q = 2, n = 107$	22,894	428
C*	$q = 128, n = 67$	62,846	469
UOV	$q = 2, m = 64, n = 192$	36,862	20,668
	$q = 2, m = 64, n = 256$	65,534	41,212

The results in this paper can be used in various contexts. First, it is possible to employ them for implementing these schemes in a memory-efficient way: instead of storing the original private key, one can reduce the key to its normal form and omit storing the superfluous parts. Due to the fact that the sustaining transformations in this paper form sub-groups of the affine transformation, this reduction can be done without any loss of security. In addition, we can use the results of this paper in cryptanalysis by enforcing a special structure to either the affine transformations S, T (as done here), or on the central equations $\mathcal{P}'$. This way, it is possible to concentrate on the parts of the scheme which actually contribute to the security of multivariate quadratic schemes and neglect others, e.g., constant parts of the affine transformations in HFE or UOV. However, we want to point out that the key space for any of these schemes is still far larger than, e.g., in the case of RSA, cf Table 2 for the number of choices on S, T alone. So even with the results in this paper, we are not able to break any of these schemes by exhaustive key search. On the other hand, it is not clear at present if the sustainers presented in this paper are the only ones possible. Therefore, the existence of other sustaining transformations is stated as an open problem.

Finally, we want to remark that the techniques in this paper are quite general, see the list of possible sustaining transformations in Sect. 3. Hence, it is not only possible to apply them on HFE, C*, and UOV, but also on other multivariate quadratic schemes, such as enTTS [16]. However, due to space limitations in this paper, we needed to make a choice and decided to concentrate on HFE, C*, and UOV.

Acknowledgments

This work was supported in part by the Concerted Research Action (GOA) Mefisto-2000/06 of the Flemish Government.

Moreover, we want to thank An Braeken for helpful remarks and Micheal Quisquater for fruitful discussions (COSIC, KU Leuven, Belgium).

References

1. Alex Biryukov, Christophe De Cannière, An Braeken, and Bart Preneel. A toolbox for cryptanalysis: Linear and affine equivalence algorithms. In *Advances in Cryptology – EUROCRYPT 2003*, Lecture Notes in Computer Science, pages 33–50. Eli Biham, editor, Springer, 2003.
2. Nicolas Courtois, Louis Goubin, and Jacques Patarin. *Quartz: Primitive specification (second revised version)*, October 2001. https://www.cosic.esat.kuleuven.ac.be/nessie/workshop/submissions/quartzv21-b.zip, 18 pages.
3. Nicolas Courtois, Louis Goubin, and Jacques Patarin. *SFlash^{v3}, a fast asymmetric signature scheme – Revised Specificatoin of SFlash, version 3.0*, October 17th 2003. ePrint Report 2003/211, http://eprint.iacr.org/, 14 pages.
4. Michael R. Garay and David S. Johnson. *Computers and Intractability – A Guide to the Theory of NP-Completeness.* W.H. Freeman and Company, 1979. ISBN 0-7167-1044-7 or 0-7167-1045-5.
5. W. Geiselmann, R. Steinwandt, and Th. Beth. Attacking the affine parts of SFlash. In *Cryptography and Coding - 8th IMA International Conference*, volume 2260 of *Lecture Notes in Computer Science*, pages 355–359. B. Honary, editor, Springer, 2001.
6. Aviad Kipnis, Jacques Patarin, and Louis Goubin. Unbalanced oil and vinegar signature schemes. In *Advances in Cryptology – EUROCRYPT 1999*, volume 1592 of *Lecture Notes in Computer Science*, pages 206–222. Jacques Stern, editor, Springer, 1999.
7. Aviad Kipnis and Adi Shamir. Cryptanalysis of the HFE public key cryptosystem. In *Advances in Cryptology – CRYPTO 1999*, volume 1666 of *Lecture Notes in Computer Science*, pages 19–30. Michael Wiener, editor, Springer, 1999. http://www.minrank.org/hfesubreg.ps or http://citeseer.nj.nec.com/kipnis99cryptanalysis.html.
8. Tsutomu Matsumoto and Hideki Imai. Public quadratic polynomial-tuples for efficient signature verification and message-encryption. In *Advances in Cryptology – EUROCRYPT 1988*, volume 330 of *Lecture Notes in Computer Science*, pages 419–545. Christoph G. Günther, editor, Springer, 1988.
9. Jacques Patarin. Cryptanalysis of the Matsumoto and Imai public key scheme of Eurocrypt'88. In *Advances in Cryptology – CRYPTO 1995*, volume 963 of *Lecture Notes in Computer Science*, pages 248–261. Don Coppersmith, editor, Springer, 1995.
10. Jacques Patarin. Asymmetric cryptography with a hidden monomial. In *Advances in Cryptology – CRYPTO 1996*, volume 1109 of *Lecture Notes in Computer Science*, pages 45–60. Neal Koblitz, editor, Springer, 1996.
11. Jacques Patarin. Hidden Field Equations (HFE) and Isomorphisms of Polynomials (IP): two new families of asymmetric algorithms. In *Advances in Cryptology – EUROCRYPT 1996*, volume 1070 of *Lecture Notes in Computer Science*, pages 33–48. Ueli Maurer, editor, Springer, 1996. Extended Version: http://www.minrank.org/hfe.pdf.
12. Jacques Patarin and Louis Goubin. Trapdoor one-way permutations and multivariate polynomials. In *International Conference on Information Security and Cryptology 1997*, volume 1334 of *Lecture Notes in Computer Science*, pages 356–368. International Communications and Information Security Association, Springer, 1997. Extended Version: http://citeseer.nj.nec.com/patarin97trapdoor.html.

13. Peter W. Shor. Polynomial-time algorithms for prime factorization and discrete logarithms on a quantum computer. *SIAM Journal on Computing*, 26(5):1484–1509, October 1997.
14. Ilia Toli. Cryptanalysis of HFE, June 2003. arXiv preprint server, http://arxiv.org/abs/cs.CR/0305034, 7 pages.
15. Christopher Wolf and Bart Preneel. Asymmetric cryptography: Hidden field equations. In *European Congress on Computational Methods in Applied Sciences and Engineering 2004*. P. Neittaanmäki, T. Rossi, S. Korotov, E. Oñate, J. Périaux, and D. Knörzer, editors, Jyväskylä University, 2004. 20 pages, extended version: http://eprint.iacr.org/2004/072/.
16. Bo-Yin Yang and Jiun-Ming Chen. Rank attacks and defence in Tame-like multivariate PKC's. Cryptology ePrint Archive, Report 2004/061, 23rd March 2004. http://eprint.iacr.org/, 21 pages.

Cryptanalysis of HFEv
and Internal Perturbation of HFE

Jintai Ding[1] and Dieter Schmidt[2]

[1] Department of Mathematical Sciences,
University of Cincinnati, Cincinnati, OH, 45221, USA
ding@math.uc.edu
[2] Department of Electrical & Computer Engineering and Computer Science,
University of Cincinnati, Cincinnati, OH, 45221, USA
dieter.schmidt@uc.edu

Abstract. Hidden field equation (HFE) multivariable cryptosystems were first suggested by Patarin. Kipnis and Shamir showed that to make the cryptosystem secure, a special parameter D of any HFE cryptosystem can not be too small. Consequently Kipnis, Patarin and Goubin proposed an enhanced variant of the HFE cryptosystem by combining the idea of Oil and Vinegar construction with the HFE construction. Essentially they "perturb" the HFE system with some external variables. In this paper, we will first present a new cryptanalysis method for the HFEv schemes. We then use the idea of internal perturbation to build a new cryptosystem, an internally perturbed HFE cryptosystem (IPHFE).

Keywords: Public-key, multivariable, quadratic polynomials, Hidden field equation, internal perturbation.

1 Introduction

Since the invention of the RSA scheme, there has been great interest in constructing other public key cryptosystems. One of the directions is to use multivariable polynomials, in particular, quadratic polynomials. This construction relies on the proven theorem that solving a set of multivariable polynomial equations over a finite field is, in general, an NP-hard problem [GJ79]. Nevertheless, it is not enough to guarantee the security of such a cryptosystem.

One of the basic designs in this directions was started by Matsumoto and Imai [MI88]. They suggested to use a map F over a large field $\bar{K}$, which is a degree n extension of a smaller finite field k. By identifying $\bar{K}$ with k^n the map F produces a multivariable polynomial map from k^n to k^n, which is denoted by $\tilde{F}$. Then one "hides" this map $\tilde{F}$ by composing from the left and the right by two invertible affine linear maps L_1 and L_2 on k^n. This generates a quadratic map $\bar{F}$:

$$\bar{F} = L_1 \circ \tilde{F} \circ L_2$$

from k^n to k^n ($\circ$ means composition of two maps). Matsumoto and Imai suggested the map $F : X \longmapsto X^{1+q^i}$, where q is the number of elements in k, X is an

S. Vaudenay (Ed.): PKC 2005, LNCS 3386, pp. 288–301, 2005.

element in $\bar{K}$ and k is of characteristic 2. However Patarin [Pat95] showed that this scheme is insecure under an algebraic attack when linearization equations are used.

Since then, Patarin and his collaborators have made a great effort to find secure modifications of the Matsumoto-Imai system. These modified cryptosystems can be divided into two types:

1) Minus-Plus method [PGC98]: The Minus method was first suggested in [Sha98] and is the simplest idea among all. In the Minus method one removes a few of the components of $\bar{F}$, and in the Plus method one adds a few randomly chosen quadratic polynomials. It is possible to combine both methods. The main reason to take the "Minus" action is the necessity to make the corresponding equations more difficult to solve so that the linearization equations can no longer be used. Minus (only) method is well suited for signature schemes. One such scheme, Sflash^{v2} [ACDG03,PCG01], was last year accepted as one of the final selections in the New European Schemes for Signatures, Integrity, and Encryption: IST-1999-12324, although Patarin has now proposed that Sflash^{v2} should be replaced by the new version Sflash^{v3} [CGP03].

2) Hidden Field Equation Method (HFE) [Pat95]: Patarin believes that this construction is the strongest. The difference of this scheme to the original system of Matsumoto-Imai is that F is substituted by a new map (function)

$$F : X \longmapsto \sum_{0,0}^{D} a_{ij} X^{q^i + q^j} + \sum_{0}^{D} b_i X^{q^i} + c,$$

where the polynomial coefficients are randomly chosen. The total degree of F can not be too large, because the decryption process needs to solve the polynomial equation $F(X) = Y'$ for a constant Y'. However a new algebraic attack by Kipnis and Shamir [KS99] using both Minrank and relinearization shows that the number D can also not be too small. This is confirmed by [Cou01,FJ03].

Another direction Patarin and his collaborators have pursued is inspired by the linearization equations mentioned above. This type of construction includes Dragon [Pat96a], Little Dragon [Pat96a], Oil and Vinegar [Pat97], and Unbalanced Oil and Vinegar [KPG99]. From the point view of our paper, the interesting ones are the last two schemes, where the basic idea is that certain quadratic equations can be easily solved if we are allowed to guess a few variables. The key map is a map O from $k^n = k^{o+v}$ to k^o:

$$O(x_1, ..., x_o, x_1', ..., x_v') = (O_1(x_1, ..., x_o, x_1', ..., x_v'), ..., O_o(x_1, ..., x_o, x_1', ..., x_v')),$$

such that each O_i is a Oil and Vinegar polynomial in the form:

$$O_i(x_1, ..., x_o, x_1', ..., x_v') = \sum a_{ij} x_i x_j' + \sum b_{ij} x_i' x_j' + \sum c_i x_i + \sum d_i x_j' + e$$

where the x_i's are called Oil variables and the x_j''s Vinegar variables. One can see the similarity of the above formula with the linearization equations. This family of cryptosystems are designed specially for signature schemes, where we need only to find one solution of a given equation not a unique solution.

In order to enhance the security of the HFE system, Patarin and his collaborators proposed later a new scheme, which is a combination of the HFE system with the Unbalanced Oil and Vinegar system. They denote it by the Hidden Field Equation Vinegar (HFEv) schemes. The basic idea besides the HFE method is to add a few new (Vinegar) variables to make the system more complicated [Pat96b]. This method essentially replaces F with an even more complicated map from $\bar{K} \times k^r$ to $\bar{K}$ of the form:

$$F_v(X, x_1', \ldots, x_r') = \tag{1}$$

$$\sum_{0,0}^{D,D} a_{ij} X^{q^i+q^j} + \sum_0^D b_i X^{q^i} + \sum_0^D \Omega_i(x_1', \ldots, x_r') X^{q^i} + U_0(x_1', \ldots, x_r'),$$

where Ω_i is a randomly chosen k linear affine injective map from k^r to $\bar{K}$ and U_0 is a randomly chosen quadratic map from k^r to $\bar{K}$.

One can see that these new variables are mixed in a special way with the original variables (like oil and vinegar). The decryption process requires a search on these added small number of variables. For the signature case, the Vinegar variables can be selected at random. It has a good probability to succeed, otherwise another selection is made until a correct answer is found.

As far as we know, there does not exist any algebraic attack using the structure of HFEv. However, in this paper, we will show that it is possible that the attack in [KS99] can also be applied here to separate the Vinegar variables and attack the system if both D and r are small. The basic idea is to use the algebraic method to find a way to purge out the Vinegar variables. The complexity of such an attack is, however, exponential in term of r.

After all the papers mentioned above, it seems that all possible extensions and generalizations of the Matsumoto-Imai system are exhausted, but recently a new idea was proposed by Ding [Din04] to enhance the Matsumoto-Imai system. It is called internal perturbation and represents a very general idea.

In a very broad context the HFE and Oil-Vinegar methods can also be seen as an extension of a commonly used idea in mathematics and physics, namely perturbation. A good way to deal with a continuous system often is to "perturb" the system at a minimum scale. In terms of this view, the HFEv and Oil-Vinegar methods can be viewed as perturbations of the HFE method by the newly added Vinegar variables. However, the perturbation is in some sense more an "external" perturbation, as a few extra (external) variables (Vinegar) are introduced. The idea of internal perturbation is to use internal variables instead, which map to a small subspace of the original variables.

We call the new system an internally perturbed HFE (IPHFE) system. For a IPHFE system, this method essentially replaces F with a new function:

$$F : (X) \longmapsto$$

$$\sum_{0,0}^{D,D} a_{ij} X^{q^i+q^j} + \sum_0^D b_i X^{q^i} + \sum_{0,0}^{D,n-1} c_{i,j} X^{q^i} \tilde{X}_r^{q^j} + \sum_{0,0}^{n-1,n-1} \alpha_{ij} \tilde{X}_r^{q^i+q^j} + \sum_0^{n-1} \beta_i \tilde{X}_r^{q^i} + \gamma.$$

The new internal perturbation variable $\tilde{X}_r$ is given by $\tilde{X}_r = \sum_0^{n-1} a_i X^{q^i}$. The function $Z(X) = \sum_0^{n-1} a_i X^{q^i}$, when viewed as a linear map from k^n to k^n, has an image space of low dimension r, which we call the perturbation dimension.

This perturbation is performed through a small set of variables "inside" the space k^n (therefore they are "internal" variables) and one does **not** introduce any new variables. Namely given a quadratic multivariable system $\bar{F}$ over k^n, we randomly find a linear map Z from k^n to k^n with the image space of a small dimension r, then we try to "perturb" the system through the small number variables related to Z.

Although we use the same basic idea of internal perturbation as in [Din04], the perturbation here is done differently. In the original method only terms like U_0 were used, whereas here a mixing of the linear terms from the original and perturbation variables $Z(X)$ occurs, so that the perturbation variables and the original variables are fully mixed. This makes the system more complicated.

The motivation for our work came from our attack method to purge out the external perturbation. This lead us to construct new systems that are resistant to the algebraic attack [Pat95,KS99] and its extensions like XL, but without sacrificing much of the efficiency of the system. An additional advantage of the new systems is that the internal perturbation makes the process of elimination of unnecessary candidates in the decryption process much faster.

In the first section of the paper, we will introduce, in detail, our idea of how to attack an HFEv system. Then we will present the IPHFE system and a practical implementation example of an 89 bits cryptosystem system, where we choose the perturbation dimension to be 2. We will show that it should have a very high security level against all known attacking methods. We will analyze the security and efficiency of the system.

2   Cryptanalysis of HFEv Cryptosystem

2.1   The HFEv Cryptosystem

Let $\bar{K}$ be a degree n extension of a finite field k of characteristic 2 with q elements, and $\bar{K} \cong k[x]/g(x)$, where $g(x)$ is a degree n irreducible polynomial over k. That k has characteristic 2 is not essential here.

Let ϕ be the standard k-linear map that identifies $\bar{K}$ with k^n:

$$\phi : \bar{K} \longmapsto k^n,$$

such that

$$\phi(a_0 + a_1 x + a_2 x^2 + \cdots + a_{n-1} x^{n-1}) = (a_0, a_1, a_2, \cdots, a_{n-1}).$$

The idea of lifting a map over spaces of a small finite field [KS99] to a larger field is the key idea, which leads us to a new formulation of the HFEv explained in the introduction.

Lemma 1 *[KS99] Let* $Q(x_1, \ldots, x_n) = (Q_1(x_1, \ldots, x_n), \ldots, Q_n(x_1, \ldots, x_n))$ *be a linear map from* k^n *into* k^n. *Then there exist* $a_0, \ldots, a_{n-1}$ *in* $\bar{K}$, *such that*

$$\phi^{-1} \circ Q(x_1, \ldots, x_r) = \sum_{i=0}^{n-1} a_i X^{q^i},$$

where $X = \phi^{-1}(x_1, \ldots, x_n)$.

From this lemma, we have

Lemma 2 *Let* $Q(x'_1, \ldots, x'_r) = (Q_1(x'_1, \ldots, x'_r), \ldots, Q_n(x'_1, \ldots, x'_r))$ *be a linear map from* k^r *into* k^n. *Then there exist* $a_0, \ldots, a_{n-1}$ *in* $\bar{K}$, *such that*

$$\phi^{-1} \circ Q(x'_1, \ldots, x'_r) = \sum_{i=0}^{n-1} a_i \bar{X}_r^{q^i},$$

where $\bar{X}_r = \phi^{-1}(x'_1, \ldots, x'_r, 0, \ldots, 0)$.

This lemma is a simple corollary from Lemma 1 above from [KS99]. It allows us to reformulate the key function (1) and give an equivalent description:

$$F : (X, X_r) \longmapsto$$

$$\sum_{0,0}^{D,D} a_{ij} X^{q^i+q^j} + \sum_{0}^{D} b_i X^{q^i} + \sum_{0,0}^{D,n-1} c_{i,j} X^{q^i} \bar{X}_r^{q^j} + \sum_{0,0}^{n-1,n-1} \alpha_{ij} \bar{X}_r^{q^i+q^j} + \sum_{0}^{n-1} \beta_i \bar{X}_r^{q^i} + \gamma,$$

where $X_r = (x'_1, \ldots, x'_r)$ represents the new Vinegar variables. The first two terms are the same as in (1), the third term here is derived from the third term in (1), and the last three terms come from U_0.

This new formulation is the key to our attack. Let $\tilde{F}$ be a map from k^{n+r} to k^n and

$$\tilde{F}(x_1, \ldots, x_n, x'_1, \ldots, x'_r) = \phi \circ F \circ (\phi^{-1} \times Id)(x_1, \ldots, x_n, x'_1, \ldots, x'_r) =$$

$$(\tilde{F}_1(x_1, ..., x_n, x'_1, ..., x'_r), \tilde{F}_2(x_1, ..., x_n, x'_1, ..., x'_r), \cdots, \tilde{F}_n(x_1, ..., x_n, x'_1, ..., x'_r)).$$

Here $\tilde{F}_i(x_1, \ldots, x_r, x'_1, \ldots, x'_r)$ are quadratic polynomials of $n + r$ variables.

Let L_1 and L_2 be two randomly chosen invertible affine linear maps one over k^n and the other over k^{n+r}.

$$\bar{F}(x_1, \ldots, x_n, x'_1, \ldots, x'_r) = L_1 \circ \tilde{F} \circ L_2(x_1, \ldots, x_n, x'_1, \ldots, x'_r) =$$

$$(\bar{F}_1(x_1, ..., x_n, x'_1, ..., x'_r), \bar{F}_2(x_1, ..., x_n, x'_1, ..., x'_r), ..., \bar{F}_n(x_1, ..., x_n, x'_1, ..., x'_r))$$

is the cipher for the HFEv system. No effective algebraic attack method exists for it yet, which uses the properties of the map F.

2.2 Cryptanalysis for the Case $r = 1$

In this section, we will present a new attack method for the HFEv cryptosystem, which is an extension of an idea of Kipnis and Shamir. We will show how it works when $r = 1$, which we will assume throughout this section.

When $r = 1$, the map F from $\bar{K} \times k$ to $\bar{K}$, which is used to define the HFEv system, is:

$$F : (X, x_1') \longmapsto$$

$$\sum_{0,0}^{D} a_{ij} X^{q^i+q^j} + \sum_{0}^{D} b_i X^{q^i} + \sum_{0}^{D} c_i X^{q^i} T_1(x_1') + \alpha T_1(x_1')^2 + \beta T_1(x_1') + \gamma$$

where x_1' represents the new Vinegar variables, $\bar{X} = \phi^{-1}(x_1', 0, \ldots, 0)$ is the image of a k linear embedding map T_1 from k to $\bar{K}$: $T_1(x) = \phi^{-1}(x, 0, \ldots, 0)$.

Let $\hat{K}$ be the $n + 1$ dimensional k subspace in $\bar{K} \times \bar{K}$ such that for any element $\hat{X} = (X_1, X_2)$,

$$\phi(X_2) = (x_1', 0, \ldots, 0).$$

The map $F(X, x_1')$ can be reinterpreted as a map from $\hat{K}$ to K, so that we have

$$F : (X, \bar{X}) \longmapsto$$

$$\sum_{i,j}^{D} a_{ij} X^{q^i+q^j} + \sum_{0}^{D} b_i X^{q^i} + \sum_{i}^{D} c_i X^{q^i} \bar{X} + \alpha \bar{X}^2 + \beta \bar{X} + \gamma,$$

with

$$\phi(\bar{X}) = (x_1', 0, \ldots, 0).$$

We should recall that

$$\bar{X}^q = \bar{X},$$

and this is why the formula above has no high power terms of $\bar{X}$. Let P_1 be the projection such that

$$P_1(x_1, \ldots, x_n) = x_1.$$

Let $\phi_1 = \phi \times (P_1 \circ \phi)$ be the standard map from $\hat{K}$ to k^{n+1}, then

$$\tilde{F} = \phi \circ F \circ \phi_1^{-1}$$

and the cipher (public key) is given as

$$\bar{F} = L_1 \circ \tilde{F} \circ L_2,$$

where L_1 is an invertible affine linear map on k^n and L_2 is an affine linear map on k^{n+1}.

The public key consists of the polynomial components of $\bar{K}$. The private key is L_1, L_2 and F and its related field structure.

One way to attack the system is to find L_1 and L_2 such that if we compose from the two ends with their inverses we would recover F.

To attack, the first observation we have is that:

$$\hat{F} = \phi^{-1} \circ \bar{F} \circ \phi_1 = \phi^{-1} \circ L_1 \circ \tilde{F} \circ L_2 \circ \phi_1$$
$$= (\phi^{-1} \circ L_1 \circ \phi) \circ F \circ (\phi_1^{-1} \circ L_2 \circ \phi_1).$$

We know what $(\phi \circ L_1 \circ \phi^{-1})$ is like from Lemma 1 and for $\phi_1 \circ L_2 \circ \phi_1^{-1}$, we have the following lemma

Lemma 3 *Let* $Q(x_1, \ldots, x_n, x_1') = (Q_1(x_1, \ldots, x_1'), \ldots, Q_{n+1}(x_1, \ldots, x_1'))$ *be a linear map from* k^{n+1} *to* k^{n+1}. *Then there exist* $a_0, \ldots, a_{n-1}, a_0', a, b$ *in* $\bar{K}$, *such that*

$$\phi_1^{-1} \circ Q(x_1, \ldots, x_n, x_1') = (\sum_0^{n-1} a_i X^{q^i} + a_0' \bar{X}, b\bar{X} + \sum_0^{n-1} a^{q^i} X^{q^i}),$$

as a k *linear map over* $\hat{K}$, *where* $\bar{X} = \phi^{-1}(x_1', 0, \ldots, 0)$, $X = \phi^{-1}(x_1, \ldots, x_n)$ *and* $\phi(b) = (b, 0, \ldots, 0)$.

This can be proven with the same argument as the one for Lemma 1 in [KS99].

In order to simplify the presentation, from now on we will assume that L_1 and L_2 and F are homogeneous. Our attack works the same way for the non–homogeneous case, because we can simply drop all lower degree terms.

In this case,

$$F : (X, \bar{X}) \longmapsto \sum_{0,0}^{D} a_{ij} X^{q^i + q^j} + \sum_0^{D} c_i X^{q^i} \bar{X} + \alpha \bar{X}^2.$$

From the lemma above, we can set

$$\bar{L}_1(X) = \phi \circ L_1 \circ \phi^{-1}(X) = \sum_0^{n-1} l_{1i} X^{q^i},$$

as in Lemma 1;

$$\bar{L}_2(X, \bar{X}) = \phi_1 \circ L_2 \circ \phi_1^{-1}(X, \bar{X}) = (\sum_0^{n-1} l_{2i} X^{q^i} + l_{2,0}' \bar{X}, l_{2,1}' \bar{X} + \sum_0^{n-1} l_2^{q^i} X^{q^i}),$$

as in Lemma 3. This means that

$$\hat{F}(X, \bar{X}) = \sum_{0,0}^{n-1, n-1} \hat{a}_{ij} X^{q^i + q^j} + \sum_0^{D} \hat{c}_i X^{q^i} \bar{X} + \hat{\alpha} \bar{X}^2.$$

Once we have the public key, it is clear that $\hat{F}$ can be easily found by solving a set of a linear equations, once we fix the field structure of $\bar{K}$. Because all finite fields with the same size are isomorphic, any choice would work in this case as was pointed out in [KS99].

Our formulation changes the problem of finding L_1 and L_2 into a problem of finding $\bar{L}_1$ and $\bar{L}_2$.

Now we will use the same method as in [KS99], namely we treat the map $\hat{F}$ and F as a quadratic form, to which we associate a $(n + 1) \times (n + 1)$ matrix for a corresponding bilinear form.

In this case, we associate a symmetric matrix $\hat{A}$ with $\hat{F}$ such that

$$\hat{A} = \begin{pmatrix} 0 & \hat{a}_{0,1} + \hat{a}_{1,0} & \cdot & \cdot & \cdot & \hat{a}_{0,n-1} + \hat{a}_{n-1,0} & \hat{c}_0 \\ \hat{a}_{0,1} + \hat{a}_{1,0} & 0 & \cdot & \cdot & \cdot & \hat{a}_{1,n-1} + \hat{a}_{n-1,1} & \hat{c}_1 \\ \hat{a}_{0,2} + \hat{a}_{2,0} & \hat{a}_{1,2} + \hat{a}_{2,1} & \cdot & \cdot & \cdot & \hat{a}_{2,n-1} + \hat{a}_{n-1,2} & \hat{c}_2 \\ \cdot & \cdot & \cdot & \cdot & \cdot & & \cdot \\ \hat{a}_{0,n-1} + \hat{a}_{n-1,0} & \hat{a}_{0,n-1} + \hat{a}_{n-1,0} & \cdot & \cdot & \cdot & 0 & \hat{c}_{n-1} \\ \hat{c}_0 & \hat{c}_1 & \cdot & \cdot & \cdot & \hat{c}_{n-1} & 0 \end{pmatrix}.$$

We associate a matrix A to F as

$$A = \begin{pmatrix} 0 & a_{0,1} + a_{1,0} & \cdots & a_{0,D} + a_{D,0} & 0 & \cdots & 0 & c_0 \\ a_{0,1} + a_{1,0} & 0 & \cdots & a_{1,D} + a_{D,1} & 0 & \cdots & 0 & c_1 \\ a_{0,2} + a_{2,0} & a_{1,2} + a_{2,1} & \cdots & a_{2,D} + a_{D,2} & 0 & \cdots & 0 & c_2 \\ \cdot & \cdot & \cdots & \cdot & \cdot & \cdots & \cdot & \cdot \\ a_{0,D} + a_{D,0} & \cdot & \cdots & 0 & 0 & \cdots & 0 & c_D \\ 0 & \cdot & \cdots & \cdot & \cdot & \cdots & 0 & c_{D+1} \\ \cdot & \cdot & \cdots & \cdot & \cdot & \cdots & \cdot & \cdot \\ 0 & \cdot & \cdots & \cdot & \cdot & \cdots & 0 & c_{n-1} \\ c_0 & c_1 & \cdots & c_D & \cdot & \cdots & c_{n-1} & 0 \end{pmatrix}.$$

Then we can show that the matrix $\bar{A}$ associated to $F \circ \bar{L}_2$ is:

$$\bar{A} = B_2^t \, A \, B_2,$$

and

$$B_2 = \begin{pmatrix} l_{2,0} & l_{2,1} & \cdots & \cdot & l_{2,n-2} & l_{2,n-1} & l'_{2,0} \\ l_{2,n-1}^q & l_{2,0}^q & \cdots & \cdot & l_{2,n-3}^q & l_{2,n-2}^q & l'_{2,0}{}^q \\ l_{2,n-2}^{q^2} & l_{2,n-1}^{q^2} & \cdots & \cdot & l_{2,n-4}^{q^2} & l_{2,n-3}^{q^2} & l'_{2,0}{}^{q^2} \\ l_{2,1}^{q^{n-1}} & l_{2,2}^{q^{n-1}} & \cdots & \cdot & l_{2,n-4}^{q^{n-1}} & l_{2,n-3}^{q^{n-1}} & l'_{2,0}{}^{q^{n-1}} \\ l_2 & l_2^q & \cdots & \cdot & l_2^{q^{n-2}} & l_2^{q^{n-1}} & l'_{21} \end{pmatrix}.$$

The matrix $\tilde{A}$ associated to $\bar{L}_1 \circ F$ is:

$$\tilde{A} = l_{1,0}A + l_{1,1}A_1 + ... + l_{1,n-1}A_{n-1},$$

where A_l corresponding to the polynomial F^{q^l} and we can see that

$$(A_l)_{i,j} = A^{q^l}_{i-l(mod(n)),j-l(mod(n))}, \text{ for } 0 < i, j < n+1;$$

$$(A_l)_{n+1,j} = A^{q^l}_{n+1,j-l(mod(n))}, \text{ for } j < n+1;$$

$$(A_l)_{j,n+1} = A^{q^l}_{j-l(mod(n)),n+1}, \text{ for } j < n+1;$$

$$(A_l)_{n+1,n+1} = 0.$$

Therefore we have

$$\bar{A} = B_2^t(l_{1,0}A + l_{1,1}A_1 + \cdots + l_{1,n-1}A_{n-1})B_2.$$

What we know is $\bar{A}$, because the invertibility of L_1 and L_2, the problem to attack the system becomes a problem to find $\bar{L}_1^{-1}$ and $\bar{L}_2^{-1}$ or equivalently to find B_2^{-1} and $\bar{L}_1^{-1}(X) = \sum_0^{n-1} l'_{1i}X^{q^i}$. This will allow us to recover A because

$$A = (B_2^t)^{-1}(l'_{1,0}\bar{A} + l'_{1,1}\bar{A}_1 + \cdots + l'_{1,n-1}\bar{A}_{n-1})B_2^{-1}$$

where $\bar{A}_l$ is the matrix corresponding to $(\bar{F})^{q^l}$ similar to the case of A_l.

One more point we notice is that if we do a change of variable X by aX, it does not affect the rank of F at all, therefore this freedom allows us to assume that $l_2 = 1$, which we will assume now.

Now we can see that we have reduced our problem to exactly the same problem that was dealt with in [KS99], and we can apply the whole machinery developed in [KS99]. But here we suggest an improved method of applying the Minrank attack method for HFE in [Cou01], such that we first find $\bar{L}_1^{-1}$ and then find B_2^{-1}. We know that the rank of A is at most and in general $D + 1$. Using results in [Cou01], we know that recovering the secret key (or equivalent key) has a complexity of $(n+1)^{3(D+1)+O(1)}$. This means our attack is subexponential, and in general, if $D = 3$ and $n \leq 2^6$, the security is less than 2^{80}. We did some computer simulations with $n < 20$ and $D = 1, 2$ and the results are as predicted.

For the more general $r > 1$ case our method can be extended directly and our initial analysis shows that the attack complexity is $(n + r)^{3(D+r)+O(1)}$. But the details of the attack are much more complicated, and we will present them in the full version of this paper. This attack complexity depends on n, r and D and the exponent depends on D and r. It would be much better if we could find some attack such that r would not be in the exponent. But from a point view of symmetry, this is impossible. If we consider the case when r is large (bigger than n), then the property of the HFEv polynomial should be dominated by the r Vinegar variables and these polynomials are more or less than what can be treated with randomly chosen polynomials. From this point of view, we think that this attack complexity must include r in some way in the exponent and we speculate our attack method could be very close to what might be achieved in general.

In addition, we think our attack could lead to some new ways of attacking HFEv using the XL family of methods, see [Cou01].

3 Internal Perturbation of HFE

From the above, we can see that HFEv is indeed a cryptosystem derived through perturbation of HFE through some external variable. It is possible to purge the external variables using the method we proposed above. Now we will suggest a new cryptosystem through internal perturbation, which we will call an internally perturbed HFE cryptosystem – IPHFE.

In this section, we will present the new cryptosystem. The idea is very simple, namely we will not add new variables, but instead we will perturb the system by using some internal variables, such that the above attack can no longer be used.

3.1   The IPHFE Cryptosystem

Here we will use the same notations as in the section above, namely $\bar{K}$, a degree n extension of the finite field k of characteristic 2 with q elements. That k is of characteristic 2 is not essential. Let $\bar{K} \cong k[x]/g(x)$ and $\phi : \bar{K} \longmapsto k^n$ again be the standard k-linear map that identifies $\bar{K}$ with k^n. Let $D > 1$, $r \geq 1$ be two small integers.

Let $Z(X) = \sum_0^{n-1} z_i X^{q^i}$ be a randomly chosen k linear map from $\bar{K}$ to $\bar{K}$ such that the dimension of the image space of Z in k^n is r. We can also say that the linear map $\phi \circ Z \circ \phi^{-1}$ from k^n to k^n has a kernel of dimension $n - r$.

Let F be a map from $\bar{K}$ to $\bar{K}$, and

$$F : (X) \longmapsto$$

$$\sum_{0,0}^{D} a_{ij} X^{q^i + q^j} + \sum_0^D b_i X^{q^i} + \sum_{0,0}^{D,n-1} c_{i,j} X^{q^i} \tilde{X}_r^{q^j} + \sum_{0,0}^{n-1,n-1} \alpha_{ij} \tilde{X}_r^{q^i + q^j} + \sum_0^{n-1} \beta_i \tilde{X}_r^{q^i} + \gamma,$$

where the new internal perturbation variable $\tilde{X}_r$ is given as $\tilde{X}_r = \sum_0^{n-1} z_i X^{q^i}$.

Let L_1 and L_2 be two randomly chosen invertible affine linear maps on k^n and let $\bar{F} = L_1 \circ \phi \circ \tilde{F} \circ \phi^{-1} \circ L_2$.

For this public-key cryptosystem, $\bar{F}$, that is the set of n quadratic polynomials of $\bar{F}$ and the structure of the field k form the public key. L_1, L_2, the field structure of $\bar{K}$, F, and Z are the secret key.

To encrypt a message $(x_1', \ldots, x_n')$, one just finds the value of $\bar{F}(x_1', \ldots, x_n')$.

To decrypt a message, one just "inverts" each component of the composition. It is easy to invert everything except the function F. Here, by "inverting" F, we mean to solve the equation

$$F(x_1, \ldots, x_n) = (y_1', \ldots, y_n').$$

What we do is plug in all possible values of $\tilde{X}_r \in Z(\bar{K})$ into the equation, which consists of q^r elements, and then solve the corresponding degree q^{2D} polynomial equations. This is why both q and r must be small. It is possible for many of the cases, that there is no solution at all, but we should have at least one solution among all the possibilities. For each case of $\tilde{X}$, if we have any solution $X = (x_1, \ldots, x_n)$, we then have to make sure that the solution is consistent with the corresponding elements in $\bar{X} \in Z(\bar{K})$, namely the solution X must also satisfy the equation $\bar{X} = Z(X)$, otherwise the solution is discarded. This process helps us to eliminate efficiently most of the unwanted solutions.

In general, we should have a good chance to have only one solution, but due to the definition of F, we know that the map F is not necessarily injective, which requires us to add something extra just like in the case of HFE [Pat96b]. One can add hash functions or just add (Plus method) more randomly chosen quadratic polynomials.

Similarly we can apply the Minus method [Sha98] to build authentication schemes.

3.2   A Practical Realization of an IPHFE Cryptosystem

For a practical realization, we have chosen $\bar{K}$ to be a degree $n = 89$ extension of the finite field $k = Z_2$ with $q = 2$ elements. We use $D = 3$, and $r = 2$. In this case, we will choose the terms $X^{2^3+2^3}$ to be zero. In terms of key size, the public key is the largest, which is the size of about 400,000 bits (50 KBytes). This implementation is comparable with any of the existing multivariable cryptosystems.

In this case, the decryption process requires us to solve four times an equation of degree 16 over a finite field of size 2^{89}, which can be done easily.

3.3   Cryptanalysis

We will now show that existing algebraic attacking methods for multivariable cryptosystems can no longer be used efficiently against IPHFE. This includes the method, which was suggested above for attacking HFEv. The reason is that the internal perturbation is fully mixed with the original system and can no longer be distinguished.

We will take a careful look at two algebraic methods. We start first with the attack method of [KS99,Cou01] for HFE. From the formula for Z we can see that F, when described as a polynomial of X, looks far more complicated than F in the HFE system. Essentially it has all possible terms of $X^{q^i+q^j}$, and the corresponding symmetric matrix for its related bilinear form is expected to have a very high rank in general. In all of our computer simulations it turns out that the rank of this matrix is exactly $D + r + 1$. Therefore, we conjecture that the rank of this matrix is exactly $D + r + 1$, and we believe it is possible to actually prove this statement.

Let's now try to use the method of Kipnis-Shamir to attack our system. In the fist step, the Minrank method is used to recover part of the key L_1 and we know that for this step, the computational complexity for our implementation is $89^{3\times 6}$, which is bigger than 2^{120}. Let's now further assume that this can be done, and that we already have part of the key, namely L_1. In the case of the attack by Kipnis-Shamir, the second step is essentially trivial due to fact that we know that the symmetric matrix corresponding to the original $n \times n$ matrix has the shape:

$$\begin{pmatrix} \Omega & 0 \\ 0 & 0 \end{pmatrix}$$

where Ω is a submatrix of size $(D + 1) \times (D + 1)$, whose null space therefore is known to us and can be used to find the second part of the key L_2. However, in our case, even if we successful recover L_1, we have no idea what the matrix corresponding to the original polynomial is. As we mentioned above, it is far more complicated and we have no way of knowing what its null space is like and therefore we still can not recover L_2, which is what happened in our computer simulations. Therefore the Kipnis-Shamir method and the key part, the Minrank method, can not be used anymore to attack IPHFE efficiently.

Second, we look at the method we use in this paper to attack HFEv. In the case of "internal" perturbations we can no longer use our method to differentiate what are the perturbation variables, or put into a more intuitive term, internal perturbation allows the perturbation to be fully "mixed" with the original variables. This is unlike the Oil-Vinegar "mixing" of the HFEv. Therefore we can no longer use the attack method in this paper to attack the IPHFE.

The only possible attack method we can see is the XL method or the method of improved Gröbner basis. But we can not see any reason why they would perform well against our construction, especially after experimenting with some examples. In order to really check how our system can resist such attacks, we need to find out how the attack complexity changes as r changes with a fixed D. Computer simulations should give us some reasonable way of estimating it, but it is in general a rather daunting time consuming task. A referee of our paper pointed out, that the results in [AFI+04], to be presented in Asiacrypt'04, show that the new Gröbner basis algorithm is actually more powerful than the XL method. This implies that we will only need to find out how our new schemes behave under the attack by the new Gröbner basis algorithm. We are now using an implementation of the new Gröbner basis algorithm in Magma to study this problem and preliminary results seem to be very supportive of our speculation on the security of our new schemes.

Overall, in accordance with our own estimates the attack complexity of all existing methods should be at least 2^{80}. We believe that it could be much higher so that the best method to attack the IPHFE system might be brute force, that is, checking all possible answers one by one.

4   Conclusion

In this paper, we presented a new algebraic method to attack the HEFv cryptosystem. This is the first attack using the algebraic structure of the HFEv. The basic idea is to view the new Vinegar variables as an external perturbation and to try to separate them. This method allows us, for the cases when $D + r$ is small, to attack the system efficiently. However, the complexity of such an attack is indeed exponential in terms of r.

Then we used the method of internal perturbation developed by Ding [Din04] to improve the system such that this attack can no longer be applied. It gives us the internally perturbed HFE cryptosystem. This system, at this moment, seems to be very secure and can be implemented efficiently. However more work, in particular, large scale simulation should be done to study the explicit relation between the level of the security and the level of perturbation and confirm the claims in this paper. In general, it seems that internal perturbation is a method that can be used to improve substantially the security of multivariable cryptosystem without sacrificing much of the efficiency of such a system.

Acknowledgment

We would like to thank the anonymous referees for their suggestions. Jintai Ding would also like to thank Dingfeng Ye and Lei Hu for their useful discussions.

References

[ACDG03]   Mehdi-Laurent Akkar, Nicolas T. Courtois, Romain Duteuil, and Louis Goubin. A fast and secure implementation of Sflash. In *PKC-2003, LNCS*, volume 2567, pages 267–278. Springer, 2003.

[AFI⁺04]   Gwénolé Ars, Jean-Charles Faugère, Hideki Imai, Mitsuru Kawazoe, and Makoto Sugita. Comparison between XL and Gröbner basis algorithms, 2004. To be presented in *Asiacrypt-2004*.

[CGP03]   Nicolas Courtois, Louis Goubin, and Jacques Patarin. Sflash^{v3}, a fast asymmetric signature scheme, 2003. http://eprint.iacr.org.

[Cou01]   Nicolas T. Courtois. The security of hidden field equations (HFE). In C. Naccache, editor, *Progress in cryptology, CT-RSA, LNCS*, volume 2020, pages 266–281. Springer, 2001.

[Din04]   Jintai Ding. A new variant of the Matsumoto-Imai cryptosystem through perturbation. In F. Bao, R. Deng, and J. Zhou, editors, *Public Key Cryptosystems, PKC-2004, LNCS*, volume 2947, pages 305–318. Springer, 2004.

[FJ03]   Jean-Charles Faugère and Antoine Joux. Algebraic cryptanalysis of hidden field equation (HFE) cryptosystems using Gröbner bases. In Dan Boneh, editor, *Advances in cryptology – CRYPTO 2003, LNCS*, volume 2729, pages 44–60. Springer, 2003.

[GJ79]   M. R. Garey and D. S. Johnson. *Computers and intractability, A Guide to the theory of NP-completeness*. W.H. Freeman, 1979.

[KPG99]   Aviad Kipnis, Jacques Patarin, and Louis Goubin. Unbalanced oil and vinegar signature schemes. In *Eurocrypt'99, LNCS*, volume 1592, pages 206–222. Springer, 1999.

[KS99]   Aviad Kipnis and Adi Shamir. Cryptanalysis of the HFE public key cryptosystem by relinearization. In M. Wiener, editor, *Advances in cryptology – Crypto '99, LNCS*, volume 1666, pages 19–30. Springer, 1999.

[MI88]   T. Matsumoto and H. Imai. Public quadratic polynomial-tuples for efficient signature verification and message encryption. In C. G. Guenther, editor, *Advances in cryptology – EUROCRYPT '88, LNCS*, volume 330, pages 419–453. Springer, 1988.

[Pat95]   J. Patarin. Cryptanalysis of the Matsumoto and Imai public key scheme of Eurocrypt'88. In D. Coppersmith, editor, *Advances in Cryptology – Crypto '95, LNCS*, volume 963, pages 248–261, 1995.

[Pat96a]   J. Patarin. Asymmetric cryptography with a hidden monomial. In N. Koblitz, editor, *Advances in cryptology, CRYPTO '96, LNCS*, volume 1109, pages 45–60. Springer, 1996.

[Pat96b]   J. Patarin. Hidden field equations (HFE) and isomorphism of polynomials
           (IP): Two new families of asymmetric algorithms. In U. Maurer, editor,
           Eurocrypt'96, LNCS, volume 1070, pages 33–48. Springer, 1996.

[Pat97]   J. Patarin. The oil and vinegar signature scheme. *Dagstuhl Workshop on
           Cryptography, September 1997*, 1997.

[PCG01]   Jacques Patarin, Nicolas Courtois, and Louis Goubin. Flash, a fast mul-
           tivariate signature algorithm. In *LNCS*, volume 2020, pages 298–307.
           Springer, 2001.

[PGC98]   Jacques Patarin, Louis Goubin, and Nicolas Courtois. C^*_{-+} and HM: vari-
           ations around two schemes of T. Matsumoto and H. Imai. In K. Ohta
           and D. Pei, editors, *ASIACRYPT'98, LNCS*, volume 1514, pages 35–50.
           Springer, 1998.

[Sha98]   Adi Shamir. Efficient signature schemes based on birational permutations.
           In *LNCS, Advances in cryptology – CRYPTO '98 (Santa Barbara, CA,
           1998)*, volume 1462, pages 257–266. Springer, 1998.

A Generic Scheme
Based on Trapdoor One-Way Permutations
with Signatures as Short as Possible

Louis Granboulan[*]

École Normale Supérieure

Abstract. We answer the open question of the possibility of building a digital signature scheme with proven security based on the one-wayness of a trapdoor permutation and with signatures as short as possible. Our scheme is provably secure against existential forgery under chosen-message attacks (with tight reduction) in the ideal cipher model. It is a variant of the construction used in QUARTZ [11], that makes multiple calls to the trapdoor permutation to avoid birthday paradox attacks. We name our scheme the *generic chained construction* (GCC) and we show that the k-rounds GCC based on a k-bit one-way permutation with k-bit security generates k-bit signatures with almost k-bit security.

1   Introduction

The size of the signature is one of the measures of the efficiency of a digital signature scheme. In the security model where the threat is existential forgery, one obvious lower bound is that k-bit signatures cannot provide better than k-bit security, because the probability that a signature is valid is at least 2^{-k}.

The quest for short signatures is long and many schemes have been proposed. One approach to obtain signatures as short as possible for a given security level of k bits has been initiated by Boneh et al. [5, 4], who use pairing in elliptic curves to generate $2k$-bit signatures. This approach permits relatively fast signature generation and signature verification, its main drawback is that the signature have twice the minimal possible length. Other schemes with short signatures based on the hardness of the elliptic curve discrete logarithm have been proposed [17, 18] but they use message recovery and the signed message is not shorter than with Boneh et al.. The approach of Patarin, Courtois et al. [11, 9, 10] is to use new hard problems (based on multivariate equations or coding theory) to generate αk-bit signatures with $\alpha < 2$. But their security is based on ad hoc assumptions (see section 4.3 for more details). Granboulan [13] uses the ideal cipher model to generate k-bit signatures based on any trapdoor one-way permutation, but the main weakness of his technique is that these are signature schemes with message recovery. This result is extended in [14].

---

[*] This work is supported in part by the French government through X-Crypt, in part by the European Commission through ECRYPT.

S. Vaudenay (Ed.): PKC 2005, LNCS 3386, pp. 302–312, 2005.

In this paper, we introduce a new technique, which can be seen as a mix of [11, 9] and [13], that allows to have k-bit signatures with appendix with security based on the sole one-wayness of a permutation, in the ideal cipher model.

The next section recalls classical definitions and previous results. It includes well known results on Full Domain Hash schemes and emphasises the fact that its generic security proof is optimal. It describes the Chained Patarin (or Feistel-Patarin) construction for digital signature schemes and makes an overview of its known properties. The material of this section is similar to the one that introduces Courtois' study of Quartz [9].

The third section describes our new *generic chained construction* for digital signature schemes, and shows that it can have an optimal generic security proof and that it can be used to design schemes that are as close as needed to the theoretical lower bound on the length of signatures. Our chained construction is based on iterating a trapdoor permutation, and therefore can be linked to the techniques by Lysyanskaya et al. [16] that generate aggregate signatures.

The fourth section compares GCC with some other techniques, and gives some comments and open questions.

2 Preliminaries

2.1 Definitions

Digital Signatures Schemes. A digital signature scheme ("with appendix", not "with message recovery") is defined by the following sets and algorithms:

- $\mathcal{M}$ is the set of messages,
- $\mathcal{PK}$ is the set of public keys and $\mathcal{SK}$ the set of secret keys,
- for any $pk \in \mathcal{PK}$, $\mathcal{S}_{pk}$ is the (finite) set of possible signatures,
- Gen is a randomised key generation algorithm that outputs a pair $(pk, sk) \in \mathcal{PK} \times \mathcal{SK}$,
- $\mathsf{Sign}_{pk,sk} : \mathcal{M} \to \mathcal{S}_{pk}$ is the signature algorithm for the public key pk,
- $\mathsf{Ver}_{pk} : \mathcal{M} \times \mathcal{S}_{pk} \to \{0, 1\}$ is the corresponding verification algorithm.

The scheme is consistent if for all (pk, sk) generated by Gen and all m we have $\mathsf{Ver}_{pk}(m, \mathsf{Sign}_{pk,sk}(m)) = 1$.

Security of a Digital Signatures Scheme. The scheme is secure under chosen message attack with q_S queries if no attacker allowed to adaptively ask q_S signatures of chosen messages can with high success probability output a valid signature that was not one of the q_S answers. Such a machine is called an existential forger[1]. For $q_S = 0$ it is said that the scheme is secure under a no-message attack.

---

[1] A slightly less strong definition is more common in the literature, where the forgery needs to be with a new message. We prefer the stronger definition even if it may not be necessary [1].

Exact Security. The scheme is (t, ϵ)-secure if no forger is a (t, ϵ)-forger, where a (t, ϵ)-forger is a forger running in expected time at most t (where the unit for time measurement is e.g. the average time necessary to run Ver_{pk}) and with a probability of successfully outputting a forgery less than ϵ.

The scheme is said to have k-bit security if there is no (t, ϵ)-forger such that $t/\epsilon < 2^k$.

To avoid technical subtleties about the exact running time and success probability, we will introduce a new definition: a scheme is $[t, \epsilon]$-secure if it is $(\alpha_t t, \alpha_\epsilon \epsilon)$-secure for $1/\beta < \alpha_t, \alpha_\epsilon < \beta$, for a small β (typically 2 or 10). Another equivalent definition of $[t, \epsilon]$-security applies to the case where the scheme depends on a complexity parameter n (e.g. the size of the public key), and the condition is that β is a constant independent of n. $[k]$-bit security is defined in a similar way.

Trapdoor One-Way Permutations. For any $pk \in \mathcal{PK}$, let $\mathcal{S}_{pk}$ be a set of $2^{\ell_{pk}}$ elements. The family $\mathsf{f}_{pk} : \mathcal{S}_{pk} \to \mathcal{S}_{pk}$ is said to be a family of trapdoor one-way permutations if f_{pk} is easy to compute for any pk and if pk can be randomly generated by some algorithm Gen in such a way that it comes with a trapdoor sk that makes easy to compute f_{pk}^{-1}. It is (t, ϵ)-secure if any machine running in expected time t (the unit for time measurement is e.g. the average time necessary to compute f_{pk}) on a random input pk and $s \in \mathcal{S}_{pk}$ cannot compute f_{pk}^{-1} with better probability than ϵ. Such a machine is called an inverter. The permutation is said to have k-bit security if there is no (t, ϵ)-inverter such that $t/\epsilon < 2^k$.

It is obvious that an exhaustive search can be used to invert f_{pk}, therefore it is impossible to have k-bit security for $k > \ell$ where ℓ is the average value of ℓ_{pk} for random pk generated by Gen. It is an open problem whether if it is possible to reach this lower bound or not. The best candidates are some discrete logarithm-based functions, which apparently have $[\ell/2]$-bit security, and some specific functions (e.g. based on quadratic multivariate equations [11] or error correcting codes [10]) that may have $[\alpha\ell]$-bit security for $\alpha > 1/2$.

Another obvious property is that trapdoor one-way permutations that are random-self-reducible or based on claw-free functions have another upper bound for their security: an attack based on the birthday paradox shows that it is impossible to have k-bit security for $k > \ell/2$. It is the case for trapdoor one-way permutations based on classical number theoretical problems (factorisation or discrete logarithm).

A $[\ell]$-bit secure trapdoor one-way permutation is called *optimal trapdoor one-way permutation*.

2.2   Previous Results on Full Domain Hash

Full Domain Hash (FDH) has been named by Bellare and Rogaway [2] and is one of the most classical techniques to construct digital signature schemes.

Definition 1 (FDH). *Let $\mathsf{H}_{pk} : \mathcal{M} \to \mathcal{S}_{pk}$ be a family of cryptographic hash functions and $\mathsf{f}_{pk} : \mathcal{S}_{pk} \to \mathcal{S}_{pk}$ be a family of trapdoor one-way permutations. A valid signature s of a message m under the key pk is the unique value such that $\mathsf{H}_{pk}(m) = \mathsf{f}_{pk}(s)$. It can be generated using the trapdoor by $s = \mathsf{f}_{pk}^{-1} \circ \mathsf{H}_{pk}(m)$.*

Generic Attack by Birthday Paradox. The forger computes $2^{\ell_{pk}/2}$ hash on random messages and $2^{\ell_{pk}/2}$ images of random signatures. Birthday paradox[2] shows that there is probably a collision such that $H_{pk}(m) = f_{pk}(s)$.

Therefore FDH cannot have better than $\lceil \ell/2 \rceil$-bit security.

Security Proof. The classical security proof for FDH needs the random oracle model. This means that the forger is forced to use an external *oracle* when it wants to compute the hash function. The number of queries to this oracle is bounded by q_H. The security proof shows that if there exists a (t, ϵ) forger against FDH that makes q_S signature queries and q_H hash queries, then one can design an algorithm that uses this forger as a black box, that controls the oracle for H_{pk}, and that is a $[t, \epsilon/q_H]$-inverter for the trapdoor permutation.

Therefore FDH based on a k-bit secure trapdoor one-way permutation has at least $\lceil k/2 \rceil$-bit security.

Conclusion. If there exists an optimal family of trapdoor one-way permutations, then the security proof and the generic attack show that FDH based on this family has exactly $\lceil \ell/2 \rceil$-bit security. Therefore the previous security proof is optimal, because a better proof would imply the non-existence of optimal trapdoor one-way permutations. It can be improved only with additional properties of f_{pk}, e.g. claw-free function [7, 12].

2.3 Previous Results on Chained Patarin Construction

It has been introduced for the QUARTZ signature scheme [11], and is named The Chained Patarin Construction (CPC) [19] or Feistel-Patarin Construction [9]. It depends on an integer parameter r (the number of rounds). QUARTZ uses $r = 4$ and FDH is the special case where $r = 1$. Here we describe the basic CPC. QUARTZ uses a generalisation of CPC to trapdoor functions that are not permutations.

Definition 2 (CPC). *For any $pk \in \mathcal{PK}$ let $\mathcal{S}_{pk}$ be a set of $2^{\ell_{pk}}$ elements with a group operation $\oplus$. For $i = 1...r$ let $H_{pk,i} : \mathcal{M} \to \mathcal{S}_{pk}$ be a cryptographic hash function and $f_{pk,i} : \mathcal{S}_{pk} \to \mathcal{S}_{pk}$ be a trapdoor one-way permutation. A signature $s \in \mathcal{S}_{pk}$ for the message m under the key pk is checked with the following procedure: let $s_r = s$ and for $i > 0$ let $s_{i-1} = f_{pk,i}(s_i) \oplus H_{pk,i}(m)$, the signature is valid if $s_0 = 0$. The signature is generated using the trapdoors by $s_0 = 0$, for $i = 1...r$, $s_i = f_{pk,i}^{-1}(s_{i-1} \ominus H_{pk,i}(m))$ and $s = s_r$.*

Generic Attack by Birthday Paradox. The forger chooses $2^{\frac{r}{r+1}\ell_{pk}}$ random messages and computes $H_{pk,1}(m)$ and chooses $2^{\frac{r}{r+1}\ell_{pk}}$ random values x_1 and computes their images $y_1 = f_{pk,1}(x_1)$. Birthday paradox shows that there are

---

[2] Usually the birthday paradox is invoked when looking at collisions when randomly selecting a single set from a larger superset. Here collisions between two independently selected sets from the same superset are examined. The same principle applies, up to a small constant in the probability of collision ($1/\sqrt{2}$).

$2^{\frac{r-1}{r+1}\ell_{pk}}$ collisions such that $f_{pk,r}(x_1) = H_{pk,1}(m)$. After one round, we have $2^{\frac{r-1}{r+1}\ell_{pk}}$ candidate pairs (m, x_1). Then the forger chooses $2^{\frac{r}{r+1}\ell_{pk}}$ random values x_2 and computes their images $y_2 = f_{pk,2}(x_2)$. For each candidate pair, there is a probability $2^{-\frac{1}{r+1}\ell_{pk}}$ that $x_1 \ominus H_{pk,2}(m)$ is equal to some y_2. Therefore after 2 rounds we have $2^{\frac{r-2}{r+1}\ell_{pk}}$ candidate pairs (m, x_2). And after i rounds we have $2^{\frac{r-i}{r+1}\ell_{pk}}$ candidate pairs (m, x_i). After r rounds all candidate pairs (m, x_r) are valid signatures, and the expected number of such pairs is roughly one.

Therefore the r-rounds CPC cannot have better than $[\frac{r}{r+1}\ell]$-bit security.

Security Proof. The security proof of FDH applies to CPC. There is no known better security proof for CPC. The most comprehensive study of the security of CPC is by Courtois [9].

Conclusion. There is a gap between the security proof and the best generic attack known on CPC.

3   The Generic Chained Construction and Its Security

3.1   Introduction

The Generic Chained Construction (GCC) is a generalisation of CPC where a block encryption is used instead of just xoring the current value with the result of a hash function.

Definition 3 (GCC). *For any $pk \in \mathcal{PK}$ and let $\mathcal{S}_{pk}$ be a set of $2^{\ell_{pk}}$ elements. For $i = 1...r$ let $E_{pk,i} : \mathcal{M} \times \mathcal{S}_{pk} \to \mathcal{S}_{pk}$ be a block cipher and $f_{pk,i} : \mathcal{S}_{pk} \to \mathcal{S}_{pk}$ be trapdoor one-way permutations. A signature $s \in \mathcal{S}_{pk}$ for the message m under the key pk is generated using the trapdoors by $s = f_{pk,r}^{-1} \circ E_{pk,r}^{-1}[m] \circ ... \circ f_{pk,1}^{-1} \circ E_{pk,1}^{-1}[m](0)$. The signature verification computes $v = E_{pk,1}[m] \circ f_{pk,1} \circ ... \circ E_{pk,r}[m] \circ f_{pk,r}(s)$. The signature is valid if $v = 0$.*

The special case where $E_{pk,i}[m](x) = x \oplus H_{pk,i}(m)$ is exactly the chained Patarin construction.

The public key should contain the description of all $E_{pk,i}$ and of all $f_{pk,i}$. NB: the security proof of theorem 1 below shows that these r functions don't need to be distinct.

Generic Attack by Birthday Paradox. This is the same attack as the attack against CPC.

The forger chooses $2^{\frac{r}{r+1}\ell_{pk}}$ random messages and computes $E_{pk,1}^{-1}[m](0)$ and chooses $2^{\frac{r}{r+1}\ell_{pk}}$ random values x_1 and computes their images $y_1 = f_{pk,1}(x_1)$. Birthday paradox shows that there are $2^{\frac{r-1}{r+1}\ell_{pk}}$ collisions such that $f_{pk,1}(x_1) = E_{pk,1}^{-1}[m](0)$. After one round, we have $2^{\frac{r-1}{r+1}\ell_{pk}}$ candidate pairs (m, x_1). Then the forger chooses $2^{\frac{r}{r+1}\ell_{pk}}$ random values x_2 and computes their images $y_2 = f_{pk,2}(x_2)$. For each candidate pair, there is a probability $2^{-\frac{\ell_{pk}}{r+1}}$ that $E_{pk,2}^{-1}[m](x_1)$

is equal to some y_2. Therefore after 2 rounds we have $2^{\frac{r-2}{r+1}\ell_{pk}}$ candidate pairs (m, x_2). And after i rounds we have $2^{\frac{r-i}{r+1}\ell_{pk}}$ candidate pairs (m, x_i). After r rounds all candidate pairs (m, x_r) are valid signatures, and the expected number of such pairs is roughly one.

Therefore the r-rounds GCC cannot have better than $[\frac{r}{r+1}\ell]$-bit security.

3.2   Security Proof Against a Chosen Message Attack

Theorem 1. *If there exists a (t, ϵ)-forger against r-rounds GCC based on trapdoor one-way permutations of 2^ℓ elements that makes at most q_E cipher queries and q_S signature queries then one can design an algorithm that uses this forger as a black box, that controls the oracle for $E_{pk,i}$, and is a $[t, (q_E + q_S)^{-1/r}\epsilon]$-inverter against one of the trapdoor one-way permutations.*

Proof. The forger receives a public key and makes at most q_E cipher queries and q_S signature queries, corresponding to $N \leq q_E + q_S$ messages m. The algorithm that answers those queries should simulate the behaviour of an algorithm that knows the secret key, it is called the simulator. The challenge is pk and a value $\bar{x} \in S_{pk}$, and the simulator wins the game if it computes one of the $f_{pk,i}^{-1}(\bar{x})$.

We denote y_j the intermediate values that occur in the computation of the signature. They depend on the message, and are denoted $y_j[m]$. More precisely, for each message m that appear in some query, we let $y_0[m] = 0$ and for $j = 1...r$, let $x_j[m] = E_{pk,j}^{-1}[m](y_{j-1}[m])$ and $y_j[m] = f_{pk,j}^{-1}[m](x_j[m])$. The last value $y_r[m]$ is the signature.

- Simulation

  Game 0. For each m, the simulator chooses random values for $y_j[m]$, computes $x_j[m] = f_{pk,j}[m](y_j[m])$, and fixes $\mathsf{Sign}(m) = y_r[m]$ and $E_{pk,j}[m]$: $x_j[m] \mapsto y_{j-1}[m]$. All other cipher queries are answered with random values. All the answers to cipher queries are kept in a table, that restricts the choice of the random answers to the queries to the ones such that all $E_{pk,j}[m]$ are permutations. It is a perfect simulator.

  Game j, for $j = 1...r$. This game is similar to Game j-1, but the values $y_j[m]$ are not fixed in advance but only when needed. Therefore, $y_j[m]$ is fixed only if $\mathsf{Sign}(m)$ or $E_{pk,j}^{-1}[m](y_{j-1}[m])$ are queried.
  All values $y_{j+1}[m]$, ..., $y_r[m]$ are still fixed in advance. That means that all $x_{j+1}[m]$, ..., $x_r[m]$ are computed in advance, but that $x_j[m]$ is unknown. Therefore (unless $y_j[m]$ is fixed) the simulator does not know when a $E_{pk,j}[m]$ for $x_j[m]$ is made, and answers random values to all $E_{pk,j}[m]$ queries. Event Bad(j) happens when some $E_{pk,j}[m](\hat{x})$ query is answered $y_{j-1}[m]$ and afterwards the signature of m is queried, because the simulator needs to know the value of $y_j[m]$ hence needs to find $f_{pk,j}^{-1}(\hat{x})$. For each $E_{pk,j}[m]$ cipher query, the probability that the answer is $y_{j-1}[m]$ is $2^{-\ell}$.

- A study of Game r

  There are at most q_E queries that may cause some event Bad(j), therefore this failure happens with probability less than $q_E 2^{-\ell}$. But we can make the hypothesis that the forger is at least as efficient as the one based on the birthday paradox, therefore $(q_E + q_S) \leq 2^{\frac{r}{r+1}\ell}$. Game 0 and Game r can be distinguished with probability at most $2^{-\frac{\ell}{r+1}}$, which is less than $\frac{1}{2}$ if $r \leq l-1$.

Let $X(j)$ be the set of the messages such that $y_1[m], ..., y_j[m]$ are fixed by cipher queries. Let n_j be the size of $X(j)$.

If m is a random message in $X(j)$ with $j < r$, then with probability $\frac{n_{j+1}}{n_j}$ it is also an element of $X(j+1)$ and the simulator does not need to know $y_j[m]$ when answering $x_j[m]$ to the cipher query $E_{pk,j}[m](y_{j-1}[m])$, because it will learn it when $E_{pk,j}[m](y_j[m])$ is queried.

If m is a random message in $X(r)$, then with probability $\frac{1}{n_r}$ it is the message that is output by the forger and the simulator does not need to know $y_r[m]$ when answering $x_r[m]$ to the cipher query $E_{pk,r}[m](y_{r-1}[m])$, because it will learn it when the forger outputs its forgery.

- Inversion

  Game j' for $j = 1...r$. The simulator runs a game identical to Game j with the exception of one value $y_j[m]$ that is unknown to the simulator but fixed with $x_j[m] = \bar{x}$. Therefore with probability $\frac{n_{j+1}}{n_j}$ the simulator learns the value of $f_{pk,j}^{-1}(\bar{x})$.

  Last Game. The simulator runs at random one of the Games j'.

  One of the probabilities $\frac{n_2}{n_1}$, ..., $\frac{n_{j+1}}{n_j}$, ..., $\frac{n_r}{n_{r-1}}$, $\frac{1}{n_r}$ is greater than $n_1^{-1/r}$, which is greater than $(q_E + q_S)^{-1/r}$, therefore, if $r \leq l-1$, the probability of successfully learning one of the $f_{pk,j}^{-1}(\bar{x})$ is greater than $\frac{1}{2r}(q_E + q_S)^{-1/r}$. $\qquad \square$

This theorem shows that r-rounds GCC based on a $[t, \epsilon]$-bit secure trapdoor one-way permutation has $(t, (q_E + q_S)^{1/r}\epsilon)$-bit security in a chosen-message attack. This implies that for k-bit secure permutations the scheme is $[k - \frac{1}{r}\log_2(q_E + q_S)]$-secure. The running time of an attacker is necessarily greater than $q_E + q_S$, therefore $\log_2(q_E + q_S) \leq k - \frac{1}{r}\log_2(q_E + q_S)$ or equivalently $\log_2(q_E + q_S) \leq \frac{r}{r+1}k$, which means that the scheme is $[k - \frac{1}{r+1}k]$-secure.

Our theorem shows that r-rounds GCC based on a k-bit secure trapdoor one-way permutation has $[\frac{r}{r+1}k]$-bit security in a chosen-message attack. Therefore r-rounds GCC based on optimal trapdoor one-way permutations has at least $[\frac{r}{r+1}\ell]$-bit security, which is the efficiency of the generic attack by birthday paradox.

One surprising fact is that chosen-message attacks of GCC are not more powerful than no-message attacks.

4   Comments on GCC

4.1   Optimality

k-Round GCC Has Almost the Best Possible Security for a Generic Scheme Based on Trapdoor One-Way Permutations. If a scheme can be based on any k-bit secure trapdoor one-way permutation, then it should be secure in the case where there exist an algorithm that computes inverses of the permutation in time 2^k and with probability 1. Then, the forger that uses this algorithm to implement the signature algorithm runs in time $r2^k$ where r is the number of inverses needed to sign. This proves that a digital signature scheme based on a k-bit secure trapdoor one-way permutation cannot have better than $[k]$-bit security[3].

For any constant α, αk-round GCC has asymptotically $[k - \log k]$-bit security, which is almost the best possible result.

k-Round GCC Based on an Optimal Trapdoor One-Way Permutation Is a Digital Signature Scheme with the Shortest Possible Signatures. This is a consequence from the previous remark. If there exists an optimal trapdoor one-way permutation, we can obtain $[k]$-bit security with signature as short as $k + \log k$ bits.

This seems to contradict the result of Coron [8, annex E], which implies that a hash-and-sign digital signature with k-bit security cannot have shorter signature than $k + \log q_S$ bits. But our scheme is not a hash-and-sign scheme.

4.2   Implementation and Practical Use

The Ideal Cipher Model. The ideal cipher model is a technique to prove the security of a cryptographic scheme in an *idealised world* where an oracle exists which implements random permutations. It is similar to the random oracle model, where the oracle implements random functions. The random oracle model has been proven[4] to be impossible to instantiate in general [6], and it is very likely that this result extends to the ideal cipher model. However, there is no reason for a block cipher with no other properties than being a strong pseudo-random permutation generator to fail to instantiate the ideal cipher in GCC.

Choosing the Cipher. The key space of the cipher is the set of all possible messages. No cipher has such an infinite key space, but this problem can easily be solved. For k-bit security, we need a collision-resistant hash function H with a $2k$-bit output, and a block cipher C with $2k$-bit keys and, then $\mathsf{E}[m](x) = \mathsf{C}_{\mathsf{H}(m)}(x)$ can be used in GCC.

A more difficult problem is that the cipher should encrypt blocks that are in the set $\mathcal{S}_{pk}$ of $2^{\ell_{pk}}$ elements permuted by the $f_{pk,i}$. Current block cipher only handle the cases where $\ell_{pk} \in \{64, 128, 256\}$, while we may want to use arbitrary integer and non-integer values. There is some literature on the subject [3] but no well-established solution exist.

A problem may arise if the domain $\mathcal{S}_{pk}$ depends on pk, because implementing a block cipher depending on pk is costly.

---

[3] A scheme based on a k-bit secure trapdoor one-way permutation may have better than $[k]$-bit security if there is no such inverter for the permutation. For example if the best k-bit inverter runs in time 2^{k-1} and succeeds with probability $1/2$, the previous argument describes a forger that succeeds with probability 2^{-r}, which is a $[k + r]$-bit forger.

[4] The applicability of this proof to realistic cryptographic schemes is debatable [15], because it uses a specific ad hoc and unrealistic construction of a counter-example.

The Trapdoor One-Way Permutations. The description of the r-round scheme uses r trapdoor permutations $f_{pk,i}$. But the security proof does not make the hypothesis that these permutations are distinct ones. If the size of the public key matters, we recommend to use the same trapdoor permutation for all rounds. This is also true for CPC, and for example Quartz uses a unique $f_{pk,i}$.

However, if the attacker is able to easily invert one of the $f_{pk,i}$, then the effect is that one round of GCC is cancelled. Therefore the attack by birthday paradox is more efficient and the security proof is less efficient. The use of distinct permutations for $f_{pk,i}$ allows to combine their one-wayness without increasing the size of the signature.

4.3   Comparison with Some Other Schemes

Theoretical design	Message recovery	Signature length	Heuristic security	Proven security[5]	Based on
r-round GCC		k	$\frac{r}{r+1}k$	$\frac{r}{r+1}k$	one-way
r-round CPC [11]		k	$\frac{r}{r+1}k$	$k/2$	one-way
CFS-like scheme [10]		k	k	$k/2$	one-way
FDH		$2k$	k	k	one-way
Improved PSS [14]		$2k$	k	$k-1$	claw-free
OPSS-R [13, 14]	X	k	k	k	one-way
Boneh et al. [5, 4]		$2k$	k	k	pairing
Naccache-Stern [17]	X	$2.5k$	k	k	discrete log
Pintsov-Vanstone [18]	X	$2k$	k	k	discrete log

Quartz. Our security proof for GCC is different from the study of CPC made by Courtois, because the security proof in [9, section 4] is based on an additional assumption for the underlying one-way function: the assumption that the best algorithm that computes many inverses is the one that computes them independently. This assumption is likely to hold for optimal trapdoor one-way permutations, but does not hold in general.

Moreover, both the structure of Quartz and of the Differential Signature Scheme [9, annex A.4] are insecure if the underlying one-way function F is homomorphic (i.e. $F(x+y) = F(x)+F(y)$) while our structure makes no hypothesis other than the one-wayness.

It is an open problem to prove the security of the CPC construction under the hypothesis of non-homomorphism and one-wayness.

Code-Based Schemes [10]. The authors describe a scheme that generates 81-bit signatures and claims to have 83-bit security against no-message attacks. The scheme is constructed using a non-proven generalisation of FDH to trapdoor injective functions where $f_{pk} : \mathcal{S}_{pk} \to \mathcal{H}_{pk}$ where membership in $f_{pk}(\mathcal{S}_{pk})$ is difficult to test without the trapdoor. It is likely that a security proof for this scheme will suffer the same problem as the security proof of FDH: that it is not tight.

---

[5] If the underlying function is one-way.

4.4   Conclusion

We decribe a new technique that allows to generate digital signature schemes based on trapdoor one-way permutations, that are secure in the ideal cipher model and have a signature length as short as possible. However, their running time (for k-bit security) is k times the running time of Full Domain Hash.

An open question is whether it is possible to have short signatures with less than k calls to the trapdoor function or not. Another open question is whether it is possible to have signatures of similar length that are provably secure without an idealised model or not.

References

1. J. H. An, Y. Dodis, and T. Rabin, "On the security of joint signature and encryption." in *Proceedings of Eurocrypt'02* (L. R. Knudsen, ed.), no. 2332 in Lecture Notes in Computer Science, pp. 83–107, Springer-Verlag, 2002.
2. M. Bellare and P. Rogaway, "The exact security of digital signature – how to sign with RSA and Rabin." in *Proceedings of Eurocrypt'96* (U. Maurer, ed.), no. 1070 in Lecture Notes in Computer Science, pp. 399–416, Springer-Verlag, 1996. Revised version available at
   http://www-cse.ucsd.edu/users/mihir/papers/exactsigs.html.
3. J. Black and P. Rogaway, "Ciphers with arbitrary finite domains." in *Proceedings of CT-RSA'02* (B. Preneel, ed.), no. 2271 in Lecture Notes in Computer Science, pp. 114–130, Springer-Verlag, 2002.
4. D. Boneh and X. Boyen, "Short signatures without random oracles." in *Proceedings of Eurocrypt'04* (C. Cachin and J. Camenisch, eds.), no. 3027 in Lecture Notes in Computer Science, pp. 56–73, Springer-Verlag, 2004.
5. D. Boneh, B. Lynn, and H. Shacham, "Short signature from the Weil pairing." in *Proceedings of Asiacrypt'01* (C. Boyd, ed.), no. 2248 in Lecture Notes in Computer Science, pp. 514–532, Springer-Verlag, 2001.
6. R. Canetti, O. Goldreich, and S. Halevi, "The random oracle methodology, revisited." in *Proceedings of Symposium on Theory of Computing – STOC'98*, pp. 209–218, ACM Press, 1998.
7. J.-S. Coron, "On the exact security of Full Domain Hash." in *Proceedings of Crypto'00* (M. Bellare, ed.), no. 1880 in Lecture Notes in Computer Science, pp. 229–235, Springer-Verlag, 2000.
8. J.-S. Coron, "Optimal security proofs for PSS and other signature schemes." in *Proceedings of Eurocrypt'02* (L. R. Knudsen, ed.), no. 2332 in Lecture Notes in Computer Science, pp. 272–287, Springer-Verlag, 2002. Also available at
   http://eprint.iacr.org/2001/062/.
9. N. T. Courtois, "Generic attacks and the security of Quartz." in *Proceedings of Public Key Cryptography – PKC'03* (Y. Desmedt, ed.), no. 2567 in Lecture Notes in Computer Science, pp. 351–364, Springer-Verlag, 2003.
10. N. T. Courtois, M. Finiasz, and N. Sendrier, "How to Achieve a McEliece-Based Digital Signature Scheme." in *Proceedings of Asiacrypt'01* (C. Boyd, ed.), no. 2248 in Lecture Notes in Computer Science, pp. 157–175, Springer-Verlag, 2001.
11. N. T. Courtois, L. Goubin, and J. Patarin, "Quartz, 128-bit long digital signature." in *Proceedings of CT-RSA'01* (D. Naccache, ed.), no. 2020 in Lecture Notes in Computer Science, pp. 282–297, Springer-Verlag, 2001. See also
    http://www.minrank.org/quartz/.

12. Y. Dodis and L. Reyzin, "On the power of claw-free permutations." in *Proceedings of SCN'02* (S. Cimato, C. Galdi, and G. Persiano, eds.), vol. 2576 of *Lecture Notes in Computer Science*, Springer-Verlag, 2002. Also available at http://eprint.iacr.org/2002/103/.

13. L. Granboulan, "Short signatures in the random oracle model." in *Proceedings of Asiacrypt'02* (Y. Zheng, ed.), no. 2501 in Lecture Notes in Computer Science, pp. 364–378, Springer-Verlag, 2002.

14. J. Katz and N. Wang, "Efficiency improvements for signature schemes with tight security reductions." in *Proceedings of CCS'03*, ACM Press, 2003.

15. N. Koblitz and A. Menezes, "Another Look at 'Provable Security' ". 2004. Available at http://eprint.iacr.org/2004/152/.

16. A. Lysyanskaya, S. Micali, L. Reyzin, and H. Shacham, "Sequential aggregate signatures from trapdoor permutations." in *Proceedings of Eurocrypt'04* (C. Cachin and J. Camenisch, eds.), no. 3027 in Lecture Notes in Computer Science, pp. 74–90, Springer-Verlag, 2004.

17. D. Naccache and J. Stern, "Signing on a postcard." in *Proceedings of Financial Cryptography – FC'00* (Y. Frankel, ed.), no. 1962 in Lecture Notes in Computer Science, pp. 121–135, Springer-Verlag, 2000.

18. L. A. Pintsov and S. A. Vanstone, "Postal revenue collection in the digital age." in *Proceedings of Financial Cryptography – FC'00* (Y. Frankel, ed.), no. 1962 in Lecture Notes in Computer Science, pp. 105–120, Springer-Verlag, 2000.

19. NESSIE consortium, "NESSIE Security report." Deliverable report D20, NESSIE, 2002. Available from http://www.cryptonessie.org/.

Cramer-Damgård Signatures Revisited: Efficient Flat-Tree Signatures Based on Factoring

Dario Catalano[1] and Rosario Gennaro[2]

[1] CNRS – École normale supérieure, Laboratoire d'informatique,
45 rue d'Ulm, 75230 Paris Cedex 05, France
dario.catalano@ens.fr
[2] I.B.M. T.J.Watson Research Center, P.O.Box 704, Yorktown Heights, NY 10598
rosario@us.ibm.com

Abstract. At Crypto 96 Cramer and Damgård proposed an efficient, tree-based, signature scheme that is provably secure against adaptive chosen message attacks under the assumption that inverting RSA is computationally infeasible.

In this paper we show how to modify their basic construction in order to achieve a scheme that is provably secure under the assumption that factoring large composites of a certain form is hard.

Interestingly our scheme is as efficient as the original Cramer Damgård solution while relying on a seemingly weaker intractability assumption.

1 Introduction

Digital Signatures are arguably the most important primitive of public-key cryptography [10]. Using digital signatures the receiver of a message can be assured that the message originated with a specific sender, and even more importantly, she will be able to prove such thing to a third party (non-repudiation). Because of the centrality of this concept it is very important to find signature schemes which are provably secure and efficient.

The concept of provable security for signature schemes (i.e. forgery should be equivalent to the solution of a well-defined conjectured hard problem) was formalized in the seminal paper by Goldwasser *et al.* [14] where an exact definition of what "forgery" means is given.

Starting from the scheme described in [14], several other provably secure signature schemes have been proposed in the literature that follows their paradigm. An important line of research has been to try to identify the minimal assumption needed to construct provably secure signature schemes. The assumption used in [14] was the existence of *trapdoor claw-free permutations*. Later, Bellare and Micali [2] showed that any trapdoor permutation would suffice. A breakthrough result came with Naor and Yung [18] who showed that it is possible to construct provably secure signatures out of *one-way permutations*, disposing of the trapdoor assumption which was considered essential. Finally Rompel [23] relaxed the assumption to the mere existence of one-way functions (which is easily seen to be the minimal assumption required).

S. Vaudenay (Ed.): PKC 2005, LNCS 3386, pp. 313–327, 2005.

However, the schemes mentioned above fall short in terms of their *efficiency* (which is measured as of computing time needed to produce and verify signatures and as of signature length). For example the original scheme in [14] builds a binary tree of height d, and the signature lenght and the computing time is $O(d)$. The parameter d is chosen so that 2^d is larger than the number of messages that the signer will ever sign.

It is thus important to research if using the properties of *specific* number-theoretic problems (like Factoring, RSA or Discrete Log) it is possible to devise provably secure yet efficient signature schemes.

For the case of the RSA function, Dwork and Naor [11] propose such a scheme, which was later improved by Cramer and Damgård [7]. The idea proposed in [11, 7] is to use specific properties of the RSA function to modify the original scheme in [14] to work with a "flat"tree, i.e. a tree with large branching factor $l > 2$. In the [11, 7] schemes, computation time and signature length are still $O(d)$ but now d is much smaller because all we need is that l^d is larger than the total number of signed messages.

At the same time Cramer [5] extended the basic GMR [14] technique to work with a flat-tree. The resulting scheme allows to obtain signatures that are somewhat shorter than GMR. This however comes at the cost of requiring much larger keys and public parameters: for example the signer is required to keep $l + 1$ different "trapdoors" and users of the scheme must agree on a common list of l random numbers (the latter is required also in [11]). In particular this means that the private storage for the signer is larger by a factor of l with respect to [11, 7]. The computational efficiency of Cramer's scheme [5] is comparable to [14], which is less efficient than [7].

Thus from a purely computational point of view (i.e. regardless of the assumption used), the method presented in [7] is more desirable since it uses less time and space. The open question, then, is to see if one can achieve the same efficiency as [7], only relying on a factoring assumption.

OUR CONTRIBUTION. In this paper we give a positive answer to this question, by showing how to construct an efficient flat-tree signature scheme whose security is based on the assumption that factoring large RSA moduli of a special form is hard. The restriction on the moduli N is that we require that the product of the smallest l primes divides $\phi(N)$. This restriction does not seem to affect the security of the factoring assumption, nor does it seem to make finding these moduli any harder.

Some components of our scheme (particularly the basic authentication step) are identical to the ones proposed by Cramer and Damgård in [7]. The security reduction to factoring is achieved by changing the key generation protocol and the choice of the public parameters. Because the basic authentication step remains the same, however, the efficiency of our scheme is pretty much equivalent to the efficiency of the scheme proposed in [7], while relying on a seemingly weaker assumption.

1.1   Other Related Work

Besides the works already mentioned in the Introduction, we point out that efficient provably secure signature schemes have been proposed using a variation on the RSA assumption. These works [13, 8] present efficient, state-free (all the above schemes, including ours, require the signer to keep some state) signatures based on a stronger assumption on the inversion of the RSA function. Although these schemes are more efficient than ours we stress that our goal was to prove the security of a reasonably efficient signature scheme based on the weaker assumption about factoring large integers, which subsumes both the regular and the strong RSA Assumptions.

A different approach followed in the literature is to try to prove "as much as possible" the security of efficient signature schemes like traditional RSA and schemes of the ElGamal family [12]. Starting from the work of Bellare and Rogaway [3] several papers proved that these schemes are secure (according to the [14] definition) in an idealized model of computation where a *random oracle* (an oracle that returns the result of a random function) is available to all parties. The random oracle is used to model "complicated hash functions" on which the security of the scheme relies. Although a proof in the random oracle model is better than no proof at all, it should not be automatically construed as a proof of security in the real model of computation. Indeed this is not the case, as proven in a result by Canetti *et al.* [4]. Since our scheme does not use a random oracle, we do not further discuss the random oracle model in this paper.

2   Definitions and Notations

We start with some definitions and notations. Given a probability space C we indicate with $x \leftarrow C$ the algorithm which assigns to x a random element according to C. In the case in which C is a finite set, $x \leftarrow C$ indicates the algorithm which assigns to x a random (uniformly chosen) element of C.

We say that a function $\epsilon(\cdot)$ is *negligible* if for every constant $c \geq 0$ there exists an integer k_c such that for all $k > k_c$ $\epsilon(k) < k^{-c}$

In the rest of the paper we assume that N is an n-bit composite modulus obtained as the product of two *Blum* primes p and q (i.e. p and q are such that $p \equiv q \equiv 3 \bmod 4$). We denote such moduli as *Blum modului*. We denote with $\lambda(N) = lcm(p-1, q-1)$. It is well known that for all $x \in Z_N^*$ we have that $x^{\lambda(N)} = 1 \bmod N$.

Consider now l (small) odd primes $\rho_1, \ldots, \rho_l$ and let σ be their product. We are going to consider Blum moduli N, such that $\forall i \; \rho_i$ is a divisor of $\lambda(N)$, but ρ_i^2 is not, and moreover $N >> \sigma^4$. Let's denote then with $BLUM(k, \rho_1, \rho_2, \ldots, \rho_l)$ the set of such Blum moduli with the property that $\lambda(N)/\sigma$ is of length k, i.e.

$$BLUM(k, \rho_1, \rho_2, \ldots, \rho_l) = \{N = pq \; : \; p, q \equiv 3 \bmod 4 \,,$$
$$\rho_i | \lambda(N) \,, \; \rho_i^2 \nmid \lambda(N) \,, \; |\lambda(N)/(\rho_1 \cdots \rho_l)| = k\}$$

In the following we will assume that factoring such integers is hard even when given knowledge of the product σ of the small primes that divides $\lambda(N)$.

Assumption 1 (Factoring). *For every polynomial-time algorithm $\mathcal{A}$, and for every set of small primes $\rho_1, \ldots, \rho_l$, the following probability is negligible in k:*

$$Pr\left[\begin{array}{l} N \leftarrow BLUM(k, \rho_1, \rho_2, \ldots, \rho_l), \\ \mathcal{A}(N, \rho_1, \ldots, \rho_l) = (p, q) \quad : \quad N = pq \end{array} \right]$$

FAMILIES OF HASH FUNCTIONS. We consider families of hash functions mapping strings of arbitrary length to strings of fixed length. Namely we consider a family $\mathcal{H} = \{\mathcal{H}_k\}_k$ where each $\mathcal{H}_k$ is a collection of functions of the form $H : \{0,1\}^* \rightarrow \{0,1\}^k$ for some integer k. $\mathcal{H}_k$ is polynomially samplable. We will be interested in hash functions that are *collision intractable*. A family $\mathcal{H}$ of hash functions is said to be collision intractable if it is infeasible to find two different inputs that map to the same output for a randomly chosen member of the family.

Definition 1 (Collision Intractability [9]). *We say that $\mathcal{H}$ is collision intractable if, for every probabilistic polynomial time algorithm $\mathcal{A}$ there exists a negligible function $\epsilon(\cdot)$ such that*

$$Pr[H \leftarrow \mathcal{H}_k; \ \mathcal{A}(H) = (x_1, x_2) \ s.t. \ x_1 \neq x_2 \ and \ H(x_1) = H(x_2)] \leq \epsilon(k)$$

We now define digital signatures.

Definition 2 (Digital Signatures). *Let k be a security parameter, we define a digital signature as the triplet $(\mathcal{G}, \mathcal{SIG}, \mathcal{VER})$, where*

- *$\mathcal{G}$ is a polynomial time randomized algorithm that on input 1^k outputs a pair (PK, SK) of matching public and secret keys.*
- *$\mathcal{SIG}$ is the signing algorithm. It takes as input a message m, the keys PK, SK and possibly keeps some internal state. It produces as output a signature σ for m. This algorithm can be probabilistic.*
- *$\mathcal{VER}$ is the verification algorithm. It receives as input a message m, the public key PK and a signature σ, and checks if σ is valid according to m and PK. In other words $\mathcal{VER}(m, PK, \sigma) = 1$ if $\sigma = \mathcal{SIG}(m, PK, SK)$.*

The strongest notion of security for signature schemes was given by Goldwasser, Micali and Rivest [14]

Definition 3 (Secure Signatures). *A signature scheme $(\mathcal{G}, \mathcal{SIG}, \mathcal{VER})$ is existentially unforgeable against an adaptive chosen message attack if it is computationally infeasible for a forger, who knows just the public key, to produce a valid signature σ on a message m even after having obtained polynomially many signatures on messages m_i of his choice from the signer.*

More formally, for every probabilistic polynomial time algorithm $\mathcal{F}$, there exists a negligible function $\epsilon(\cdot)$ such that

$$Pr\left[\begin{array}{l} (PK, SK) \leftarrow \mathcal{G}(1^k) \\ for \ i = 1 \ldots n \\ \quad m_i \leftarrow \mathcal{F}(PK, m_1, \sigma_1, \ldots, m_{i-1}, \sigma_{i-1}) \\ \quad \sigma_i \leftarrow \mathcal{SIG}(m_i, PK, SK) \\ (m, \sigma) \leftarrow \mathcal{F}(PK, m_1, \sigma_1, \ldots m_n, \sigma_n); \\ m \neq m_i \ for \ i = 1 \ldots n, \ and \ \mathcal{VER}(m, PK, \sigma) = 1 \end{array} \right] \leq \epsilon(k)$$

3   The New Scheme

Our scheme will make use of a l-ary tree (i.e. with branching degree l), which we call the *signature tree*. The root of the tree will be a random value S included in the public key of the signer. The tree has depth $d+1$ with a branching degree of l in the first d levels and a branching degree of 1 in the last level. By this setting we will allow the signer to sign up to l^d messages (we are going to assume l^d to be polynomial in k the security parameter). We now introduce some terminology: The first d levels of the tree are denoted as *expanding* levels, since every parent node S_j at level j ($j \in \{1, \ldots, d\}$) has l children (we have the root as $S_0 = S$). We call these nodes *expanding nodes*. The remaining level, level $d+1$, is called, the *terminal* level. Every parent node belonging to this levels has exactly one child. The parent nodes at the terminal level are denoted as *terminal nodes*. As usual, each terminal node's only child is called a leaf of the tree. We call an *item* a parent together with all his children and an *arc* a parent with one of his children. This means that every item has l arcs. A *path* from a node A to a node B is is the sequence of arcs that connects A with B.

Informally the signature algorithm will start "filling up" this tree. To sign the ith message m_i, the signer will place m_i as the ith leaf and will output an authentication chain that links m_i to the root of the tree (which is part of the public key). The verifier, will follow this authentication chain and if the end result matches the value in the public key, accepts the signature. Formal details follow.

3.1   Formal Description on the Scheme

We now give a formal detailed description of our scheme.

KEY GENERATION. The signer chooses l odd distinct primes[1] $\rho_i < 2^v$ (for some small enough parameter v) and sets $\hat{p} = \prod_{i=1}^{l/2} \rho_i$, $\hat{q} = \prod_{i=l/2+1}^{l} \rho_i$ and $\sigma = \hat{p}\hat{q}$. He then randomly picks two (distinct) large primes p' and q' of length $k/2$ such that $p = 2p'\hat{p} + 1$ and $q = 2q'\hat{q} + 1$ are two $(k+\omega)/2$-bit primes (for some parameter ω that depends on v and l). Then he sets $N = pq$ as the public modulus.

Note that by this position we have that N is a Blum integer such that ρ_i (but *not* ρ_i^2) divides $\lambda(N)$, and of the appropriate length. Notice also that 2 (but *not* $2^2 = 4$) divides $\lambda(N)$.

Denote with $E = 2\sigma = 2\rho_1 \cdots \rho_l$. The signer chooses uniformly and at random two E-th residues h, S in $\mathbb{Z}_N^*$ and a function H from a family of collision intractable hash functions. We will assume that H outputs a value in $\{0,1\}^\ell$, for some security parameter ℓ. For technical reasons, that will become apparent in the proof of security, the signer sets $e = 2^{\ell+1}$ and for each $i = 1, \ldots, l$ sets $e_i = \rho_i^{\ell_i}$, where ℓ_i is the minimum integer such that $e_i > 2^\ell$. The signer publishes $(N, h, S, e, e_1, \ldots, e_l, H, d)$, where d represents the depth of the tree, as his public key and keeps private the factorization of the modulus. Note that this allows the signer to sign up to l^d messages.

---

[1] The choice of these primes needs not satisfy any special requirement. For efficiency reason these primes could be chosen as the first l odd primes.

Remark 1. The key generation algorithm is very similar to the one proposed by Naccache and Stern in [17]. They showed that the extra requirement on the choice of p, q in practice slows down the generation of N by around 9% with respect to the generation of a regular RSA modulus (see [17] for more details).

SIGNATURE ALGORITHM. The signer holds a tree of depth d with root S. All the nodes in the tree at the beginning are empty.

To sign the ith message m_i the signer proceeds as follows:

1. He visits the path on the tree from the root to the ith leaf, which is labeled with m_i. If a node j on this path has not been visited before, the signer labels it with a random E-residue S_j.
2. Let $(S, i_1, S_{i_1}, \ldots, i_d, S_{i_d})$ be the visited path (where each i_j is an index in $\{1, \ldots, l\}$). Then he solves the following equations

$$y_{i_1}^{e_{i_1}} = S \cdot h^{H(S_{i_1})} \bmod N$$

and for all $j = 2, \ldots, d$

$$y_{i_j}^{e_{i_j}} = S_{i_{j-1}} \cdot h^{H(S_{i_j})} \bmod N$$

To conclude the signature he computes a z_i such that

$$z_i^e = S_{i_d} \cdot h^{H(m_i)} \bmod N$$

3. The output signature on m_i is $\mathsf{sig}(m_i) = (z_i, y_{i_1}, i_1, \ldots, y_{i_d}, i_d)$.

SIGNATURE VERIFICATION. The receiver, given a message m, the public key $(N, h, S, e, e_1, \ldots, e_l, H, d)$ and a purported signature $\mathsf{sig}(m) = (z_i, y_{i_1}, i_1, \ldots, y_{i_d}, i_d)$, computes the following

$$S_{i_d} = z_i^e \cdot h^{-H(m_i)} \bmod N$$

followed by

$$S_{i_{j-1}} = y_{i_j}^{e_{i_j}} \cdot h^{-H(S_{i_j})} \bmod N$$

for all $j = d$ downto 1.

If the final value $S_0 \equiv S \bmod N$ the signature is accepted as valid.

Remark 2. Note that even though we perform iterated root extractions during the signing procedure we just need to assume that h and the S_j's above are E-th residues to make the above procedure work. Indeed we have that $gcd(e_i, \lambda(N)) = \rho_i$, so we can find α_i, β_i such that $\alpha_i e_i + \beta_i \lambda(N) = \rho_i$. This means that, in order to compute the $e_i = \rho_i^{\ell_i}$-th root of an E-residue x, the signer should first compute $\Delta = x^{\alpha_i}$ which by the above GCD computation is an e_i-root of x^{ρ_i} and then compute a ρ_i-root of Δ. A similar argument holds for e-roots.

Now let Δ be an E-residue and let δ_i one of its ρ_i-roots, i.e. $\delta_i^{\rho_i} = \Delta \bmod N$. In general the value δ_i can be computed in $O(\rho_i)$ time if we know the factorization of N (cf. [1]). Note that this is not a problem if one assumes that the primes ρ_i are all very small. However, if one wants to use slighly larger primes, the $O(\rho_i)$ solution may become too inefficient. In Appendix A we show a method to extract ρ_i-roots at the cost of a single modular exponentiation in Z_N^*.

The security of the scheme is stated in the following Theorem.

Theorem 1. *If Assumption 1 holds and H is a collision resistant hash function, then the digital signature scheme presented above is secure against an adaptive chosen message attack.*

The proof appears in the following Section 4. In the proof we use the following fact: Assume to have an algorithm $\mathcal{A}$ that on input N, e and an e-th residue y outputs an eth root of y. In Appendix B we prove that it is then possible to construct a different algorithm $\mathcal{B}$, having black box access to $\mathcal{A}$, that factors the modulus with probability $1 - 1/e$.

Remark 3. Our presentation of the scheme, and consequently the theorem statement, assume the existence of collision-resistant hash functions. However it should be noted that factoring does imply the existence of collision-resistant hashing, thus we are not introducing any extra computational assumption. Moreover, using techniques similar to the ones presented in [7], one can completely dispense with the hash function H in our scheme. Either solution (implementing a factoring-based hashed function or changing the scheme so not to need one) would be however much more expensive than using, say, SHA-1. In order to keep the presentation simple, we decided to present the scheme this way, since we believe it is also conceptually clearer to "separate" the role of the hash function from the number-theoretic authentication step. In the final version of the paper we will show how to adapt the techniques in [7] to our scheme to avoid using H altogether.

4   Proof of Security

The proof goes by *reductio ad absurdum*. We assume that the proposed scheme is not secure, meaning that there exists an adversary $\mathcal{A}$ that can forge signatures with some non-negligible probability ϵ. Then we prove that if such an adversary exists, then it is possible to construct a probabilistic polynomial time algorithm $\mathcal{B}$ (a simulator) that, using $\mathcal{A}$ as an oracle, can factor with non negligible probability, thus contradicting the hypothesis of the theorem.

If we assume that such $\mathcal{A}$ exists, then his interaction with the signer would be as follows. First $\mathcal{A}$ gets the public key. Then for $i = 1, \ldots, t$ (where t is the maximum number of signatures the adversary is allowed to ask) he asks for the signature on a message m_i and receives back a valid signature $\mathsf{Sig}(m_i) = (z_i, y_{i_1}, i_1, \ldots, y_{i_d}, i_d)$. Then he will output $m \neq m_i$ and a valid signature $\mathsf{Sig}(m_j) = (z_j, y_{j_1}, j_1, \ldots, y_{j_d}, j_d)$ on it.

We argue that the public key and the verification tests on a valid signature imply that the forged signature must satisfy one of the following (mutually exclusive) conditions (where with S_{i_0} we denote S the root of the tree contained in the public key):

Type I. For some $1 \le i \le t$, one has that $y_{j_k} = y_{i_k}$ for each $k = 1, \ldots, d$, $S_{i_d} = S_{j_d}$, but $z_j \ne z_i$.

Type II. For some $1 \le i \le t$, there exist an index $1 \le k' < d$ such that for all $k \le k'$, $y_{j_k} = y_{i_k}$, $S_{i_{k'}} = S_{j_{k'}}$ but $y_{j_{k'+1}} \ne y_{i_{k'+1}}$.

If there is a forger that succeeds with non negligible probability, then there must be a forger that can successfully produce either a Type I forgery, or a Type II forgery with non negligible probability.

In the rest of the proof we will distinguish two cases, depending on the type of expected forgery. Since these two cases are exhaustive, one of them must happen with probability at least $\epsilon/2$.

Forgery of Type I. The algorithm $\mathcal{B}$ (the simulator) is given as input a Blum modulus N of the appropriate form together with a set of l small primes $(\rho_1, \ldots \rho_l)$ such that for every ρ_i one has that $\rho_i | \lambda(N)$ but $\rho_i^2 \nmid \lambda(N)$. We want to show how $\mathcal{B}$ can use the forgery received from $\mathcal{A}$ to factor N. Let t be the maximum number of sign-queries the adversary is allowed to ask (for simplicity we will assume that $\mathcal{A}$ will ask *exactly* t queries). The simulator generates his public key as follows. First it generates the public exponents $e, e_1, \ldots e_l$ as a real signer would do. Next, it sets $F = 2 \cdot e_1 \cdots e_l$, choses α, β uniformly and at random in $\mathbb{Z}_N^*$ and sets $h = \alpha^F \bmod N$ and $S = \beta^F \bmod N$. Notice that we can take e_i-roots of h, S (for any i) but not e-roots (since $e = 2^{\ell+1}$).

All the internal node, except those of depht d are computed in a similar way. The simulator sets $S_k = x_k^F \bmod N$ (where, once again, the x_k's are chosen randomly in $\mathbb{Z}_N^*$) and stores the x_k's for future usage. Observe that all the nodes generated this way – as well as S and h – are random E-residues in $\mathbb{Z}_N^*$, so they are distributed exactly as in the real signing process (more details below).

The simulator can generate valid signatures as follows. To sign the i-th message m_i, it chooses z_i at random in $\mathbb{Z}_N^*$ and sets

$$S_{i_d} = z_i^e h^{-H(m_i)} \bmod N$$

All the remaining relations can be easily computed as follows. For each index i_k in the path of the signature, the simulator sets

$$y_{i_k} = x_{i_{k-1}}^{F/e_{i_k}} (\alpha^{F/e_{i_k}})^{H(S_{i_k})} \bmod N$$

Finally it outputs the signature

$$\mathsf{Sig}(m_i) = (z_i, y_{i_1}, i_1, \ldots, y_{i_d}, i_d)$$

Observe that the signatures produced by the simulator are *perfectly* indistinguishable with respect to the signatures a real signer would generate. As a matter of fact the only difference between a real signature and a simulated one is the following. In the first case all the nodes of the tree – as well as the root S and the public value h – are E-residues (recall that $E = 2 \cdot \rho_1 \cdots \rho_l$), whereas in the simulation they are F-residues (with $F = 2 \cdot e_1 \cdots e_l$). However, since $e_i = \rho_i^{\ell_i}$ (for each index $i = 1, \ldots, l$) and N is a Blum modulus, every ρ_i-th residue is *also* an $\rho_i^{\ell_i}$ power. Consequently any E-residue is also an F-residue. Moreover, notice that, according to the simulation method described so far, the value α is never revealed to the adversary. In the terminal levels the (simulated) authentication procedure does not involve *any* e-root extraction. On the other hand, in the expanding levels, the authentication method requires the simulator to extract e_i-roots, but it is always the case that $e_i \neq e$. In other words the simulation is information-theoretically independent from α.

Now let $\mathsf{Sig}(m_j) = (z_j, y_{j_1}, j_1, \ldots, y_{j_d}, j_d)$ be the forgery produced by the adversary on a (up to now) unsigned message m_j. Since we are assuming the adversary creates a Type I forgery, for some previously produced signature $\mathsf{Sig}(m_i) = (z_i, y_{i_1}, i_1, \ldots, y_{i_d}, i_d)$ we have that $y_{j_k} = y_{i_k}$ for each $k = 1, \ldots, d$ but $z_j \neq z_i$.

This yields to the following system of equations:

$$(z_j)^e = S_{i_d} h^{H(m_j)} \bmod N$$

$$(z_i)^e = S_{i_d} h^{H(m_i)} \bmod N$$

Moreover, since H is collision resistant $m_i \neq m_j$ implies that $H(m_i) \neq H(m_j)$ and we can write $H(m_i) - H(m) = 2^\omega q$ for some $\omega \leq \ell$ and an odd $q \geq 1$.

From the two equations above we can compute

$$\left(\frac{z_j}{z_i}\right)^e = (h^q)^{2^\omega} \bmod N = (\alpha^{qF/2})^{2^{\omega+1}} \bmod N$$

Recall now that $e = 2^{\ell+1}$ so we get that

$$\left(\frac{z_j}{z_i}\right)^{2^{\ell+1-\omega}} = h^q \bmod N$$

Now, h^q has two square roots, of which we already know one: $\alpha^{qF/2}$. From the above equation we get that $(z_j z_i^{-1})^{2^{\ell-\omega}}$ is also a square root of h^q. Notice that $\ell - \omega \geq 0$ so we can easily compute the value without computing square-roots.

Observe that the adversary has no information at all regarding the original α chosen by the simulator (in an information theorethic sense). Consequently the value $(z_j z_i^{-1})^{2^{\ell-\omega}}$ is a square root of h^q that is different from $\alpha^{qF/2}$ with probability $1/2$. This immediately allows to factor the modulus.

Forgery of Type II. The algorithm $\mathcal{B}$ is given as input a Blum modulus N of the appropriate form together with a set of l small primes $(\rho_1, \ldots \rho_l)$ such that for every ρ_i one has that $\rho_i | \lambda(N)$ but $\rho_i^2 \nmid \lambda(N)$.

The simulator starts generating the signing public key by choosing a random index $1 \leq \delta \leq l$. This random choice can be interpreted as the simulator "guessing" the value of $j_{k'+1}$, the index of the first child where the forgery and the regular signature path of the tree will differ.

Next it creates the public exponents $e, e_1, \ldots e_l$ as prescribed by the key generation algorithm. Then it chooses a random element $\alpha \in \mathbb{Z}_N^*$, computes $G = e \cdot e_1 \cdots e_{\delta-1} \cdot \rho_\delta \cdot e_{\delta+1} \cdots e_\tau$ and sets $h = \alpha^G \bmod N$.

The simulation proceeds by letting $\mathcal{B}$ precompute the authentication tree in order to be able to produce t valid signatures. This precomputation phase goes very similarly to the one described before. The main difference here is that the root and the internal nodes of the tree are computed in a bottom-up fashion (rather than top-down, as for the forgeries of type one).

For each node S_{i_d} (nodes of depth d) the simulator chooses a random element x_{i_d} and sets $S_{i_d} = x_{i_d}^G \bmod N$. Once the nodes of level d are prepared, one can construct the expanding nodes, item by item.

Here, for simplicity, we show the method for a generic item I. The basic idea is to construct the parent node S_{I_0} in terms of its δ-th child S_{I_δ}. In particular the simulator chooses a random value $x_I \in \mathbb{Z}_N^*$, sets

$$S_{I_0} = x_I^{G \cdot \rho_\delta^{\ell_\delta - 1}} h^{-H(S_{I_\delta})} \bmod N$$

and stores the values S_{I_0} and x_I (in the following, for each item I, we will refer to x_I as to the *basis* of S_{I_0}).

Using this methodology the simulator can (inductively) generate the entire tree. Each new level is obtained by combining the items of the previous level in a tree structure (the roots of the items of level k play the role of the leaves to construct the items of level $k-1$). At the end of this phase the simulator comes up with a global root S, which is included as part of the public key.

On top of this construction to sign the message m_i, the simulator does as follows. First he computes the path $(i_1, \ldots, i_d)$ from the root to the ith leaf of the tree. Then he proceeds according to the following procedure:

for $k = 1$ **to** d
    Assume S_{i_k} is the b-th child of $S_{i_{k-1}}$
    Let x_{i_k} be the basis of $S_{i_{k-1}}$
    if $b == \delta$
        Set $y_{i_k} = x_{i_k}^{G/\rho_\delta}$
    if $b \neq \delta$
        Set $y_{i_k} = x_{i_k}^{G/e_b \cdot \rho_\delta^{\ell_\delta - 1}} \cdot (\alpha^{G/e_b})^{H(S_{i_k})}$
    Set $z_i = x_{i_d}^{G/e}(\alpha^{G/e})^{H(m_i)}$
    Output the signature $\mathsf{Sig}(m_i) = (z_i, y_{i_1}, i_1, \ldots, y_{i_d}, i_d)$

In other words, the adversary easily computes e-roots and e_i-roots (for $i \neq \delta$) because all the values are G-residues and he knows G-roots of them. For the case $i = \delta$ it is not necessary to compute e_δ-roots thanks to the way in which the internal nodes have been prepared.

If the adversary produces a valid forgery $\mathsf{Sig}(m_j) = (z_j, y_{j_1}, j_1, \ldots, y_{j_d}, j_d)$, one can "use" it to break Assumption 1 as follows. Since we are dealing with a forgery of the second type, there exists and index k (such that $1 \leq k \leq d$) for which one has that $S_{i_{k-1}} = S_{j_{k-1}}$ but $y_{i_k} \neq y_{j_k}$. Moreover, since $\mathcal{B}$ simulates a real signer perfectly, with probability $1/l$ one has that S_{j_k} is the δ-th child of $S_{j_{k-1}}$. If this is the case we can then consider the following equations:

$$y_{j_k}^{e_\delta} = S_{i_{k-1}} h^{H(S_{j_k})} \bmod N$$

$$y_{i_k}^{e_\delta} = S_{i_{k-1}} h^{H(S_{i_k})} \bmod N$$

which dividing term by term become

$$Y^{e_\delta} = h^{\Delta H} \bmod N$$

where we set $Y = (y_{j_k}/y_{i_k})$ and $\Delta H = H(S_{j_k}) - H(S_{i_k})$.

Once again since H is collision resistant, from the fact that $S_{j_k} \neq S_{i_k}$ we can assume that $\Delta H \neq 0$. Therefor we can write $\Delta H = \rho_\delta^\omega q$ with $q \geq 1$, such that $\gcd(q, \rho_\delta) = 1$. Moreover $\omega < \ell_\delta$, because of the way we chose ℓ_δ.

The above equation can then be rewritten as

$$Y^{\rho_\delta^{\ell_\delta}} = \left(\alpha^{\frac{qG}{\rho_\delta}} \right)^{\rho_\delta^{\omega+1}} \bmod N$$

which implies that the value $Z = Y^{\rho_\delta^{\ell_\delta - \omega - 1}}$ is an ρ_δ root of h^q, that is different with respect to $\alpha^{\frac{qG}{\rho_\delta}}$ with probability $1 - 1/\rho_\delta$. Again notice that $\ell_\delta - \omega - 1 \geq 0$ so the value Z can be easily computed without computing ρ_δ-roots.

5   Security Analysis

For lack of space we cannot discuss in more details our intractability assumption. In the full version of this paper we give some evidence why assuming $N >> \sigma^4$ seems to be safe. We point out here, however, that the same analysis was already presented in [17]. The interested reader is referred to [17] for details.

5.1   Comparison with GMR

In [14] Goldwasser, Micali and Rivest proposed the first example of digital signature scheme secure against adaptive chosen message attack. The scheme relies on the existence of *claw free* permutations, but the authors propose a concrete implementation based on the hardness of factoring. The reader is referred to [14] for the technical details; here we compare the practical performance of our scheme with respect to the one presented in [14].

Their scheme is based on a binary tree. As we mentioned before the depth of the tree is $\hat{d} = \log K$. Let us denote with $\delta > 1$ the ratio $\hat{d}/d$.

The length of the signature is about $2\hat{d}n$ bits, i.e. $2n$ bits per level of the tree. Notice that this is a factor of 2δ longer than our signatures.

The basic authentication step, performed at each level of the tree, consists of taking repeated square roots. In the original scheme in [14] the number of square roots taken at each level is about $2n$, where n is the length of the modulus. This happens because the number of square roots taken is proportional to the length of the information being authenticated. However to obtain a fair comparison with our scheme, we should improve the scheme in [14] by introducing a separate collision-resistant hash function H, like we did in our scheme. If one hashes the information at each step, before applying the authentication step, we reduce the work to 2ℓ square-root computations per level of the tree. By using the speed-up trick suggested by Goldreich (cf. Section 10.2 of [14]) this is equivalent to one exponentiation with an ℓ bit exponent, and one full exponentiation $\mod N$, per level of the tree, i.e. roughly $1.5(\ell + n)$ multiplications. Thus the worst-case cost of computing a signature is $1.5\hat{d}(\ell + n)$ multiplications, which is a factor δ slower than ours.

To compute the amortized complexity of signatures in [14] we need to multiply the cost of the basic authentication step, by $2^{\hat{d}}$ (the number of nodes divided by two)[2] and then divide by $2^{\hat{d}}$ (the number of signatures). The net result is that the amortized cost is $1.5(\ell + n)$ multiplications per signature, the same as ours.

Similarly the verification of a signature requires the computation of about 2ℓ squarings at each level of the tree, for a total of $2\ell\hat{d}$ multiplications. Verification in [14] is thus a factor of $2\delta/3$ slower than in ours.

Let us consider a specific example in which $n = 1024$, $d = 80$, $l = 32$ (i.e. $\hat{d} = 16$) and $\ell = 160$. In this case $\delta = 5$ and we immediately obtain that our signatures are a factor of 10 shorter than the ones in [14]. The worst case complexity of computing a signature is also 5 times smaller in our scheme, while the amortized complexity is the same. Finally verification time is about three times as fast in our scheme.

5.2   Comparison with Cramer-Damgård

It is not hard to see that our scheme is very similar to the scheme proposed by Cramer and Damgård in [7]. Thus the efficiency of our scheme is identical to the one of the scheme proposed there, while relying on a weaker assumption.

6   Conclusions

We presented a new and efficient signature scheme, which is provably secure against adaptive chosen message attack under the assumption that factoring large composites of a certain form is infeasible.

Our scheme shows that the "flat-tree" approach can lead also to efficient signatures under a factoring assumption, while previous proposals relied either on the seemingly stronger RSA Assumption or were less efficient.

In terms of efficiency our scheme is equivalent to the RSA-based scheme presented in [7], and much better than the factoring-based ones in [14] and in [5].

Acknowledgements

We thank Pascal Paillier for helpful discussions.

---

[2] This is because a basic authentication step in [14] requires to authenticate an entire (binary) item.

References

1. E. Bach and J. Shallit. Algorithmic Number Theory. Vol.1 Efficient Algorithms. *MIT Press*. 1996.
2. M. Bellare and S. Micali How to sign given any trapdoor permutation *Journal of the ACM* no. 39(1), pages 214-233, 1992
3. M. Bellare and P. Rogaway Random Oracles are Practical: A paradigm for designing efficient protocols. *Proc. of First ACM Conference on Computer and Communications Security*, pages 62-73, 1993
4. R. Canetti, O. Goldreich and S. Halevi. The Random Oracle Methodology, Revisited. *Proc. 30th ACM Symposium on Theory of Computing*, 1998
5. R. Cramer Modular design of secure yet practical cryptographic protocols. Ph.D. Thesis, University of Amsterdam, 1996.
6. R. Cramer and I. Damgård. Secure signature schemes based on interactive protocols. *Proc. of Crypto '95* LNCS no. 963, pp.297-310.
7. R. Cramer and I. Damgård. New Generation of Secure and Practical RSA-based signatures. *Proc. of Crypto '96* LNCS no. 1109, pages 173-185.
8. R. Cramer and V. Shoup. Signature schemes based on the Strong RSA assumption. *Proc. of 6th ACM Conference on Computer and Communication Security 1999*.
9. I. Damgård. Collision free hash functions and public key signature schemes. *Proc. of Eurocrypt '87* LNCS no. 304, pages 203-216.
10. W. Diffie and M.E. Hellman. New Directions in Cryptography. *IEEE Transactions on Information Theory*, IT-22(6):644-654, November 1976.
11. C. Dwork and M. Naor. An efficient existentially unforgeable signature scheme and its applications. *J. of Cryptology* 11(3) 1998, pages 187-208.
12. T. ElGamal. A public key cryptosystem and a signature scheme based on discrete logarithms. *Proc. of Cryypto '84* LNCS no. 196, pages 10-18.
13. R. Gennaro, S. Halevi and T. Rabin. Secure Hash-and-Sign Signatures Without the Random Oracle. *Proc. of Eurocrypt '99* LNCS no. 1592, pages 123-139.
14. S. Goldwasser, S. Micali and R. Rivest. A digital signature scheme secure against adaptive chosen message attacks. *SIAM J. on Computing* 17(2):281-308 1988.
15. N. Koblitz *A course in number theory and cryptography*, 2nd ed., Springer Verlag
16. R. Merkle. A Digital Signature based on a Conventional Encryption Function. *Advances in Cryptology–Crypto'87*. LNCS, vol.293, pp. 369–378, Springer–Verlag, 1988.
17. D. Naccache and J. Stern. A new cryptosystem based on higher residues. *Proc. of the 5th ACM conference on on computer and communication security, ACM press (1998), pp.59-66*.
18. M. Naor, M. Yung. Universal one-way hash functions and their cryptographic applications *Proc. of 21st ACM STOC* pages 33-43, 1989.
19. B. Pfitzmann. Digital Signatures Schemes - General Framework and Fail-Stop Signatures. Lecture Notes in Computer Science no. 1100 Springer.
20. D. Pointcheval and J. Stern. Security Arguments for Digital Signatures and Blind Signatures. *J. of Cryptology*. 13(3):361–396. Springer. Summer 2000.
21. M. Rabin. Digital Signatures and Public Key Encryptions as Intractable as Factorization. MIT Technical Report no. 212, 1979
22. R. Rivest, A. Shamir and L. Adelman. A Method for Obtaining Digital Signature and Public Key Cryptosystems. *Comm. of ACM*, 21 (1978), pp. 120–126
23. J. Rompel. One-way functions are necessary and sufficient for secure signatures. *Proc. of 22nd STOC* 1990, pages 387-394.

A   Efficient Root Extractions

With the following lemma we show a simple method (taking advantage of the fact that the ρ_i's are all odd primes) to extract ρ_i-roots in a (asyntotically) more efficient way.

Lemma 1. *Let p be a Blum prime of size k. Let e be a prime such that $e|p-1$ but $e^2 \nmid p-1$. Then there exists an efficient algorithm, taking as input an e-residue a, that returns as output an e-root of a in time $O(k^3)$.*

Proof. First note that the prime p can be written as $p = 2em + 1$ where m is an odd integer such that $\gcd(e, m) = 1$. Since a is an e-residue in $\mathbb{Z}_p^*$ it must be true that

$$a^{\frac{p-1}{e}} \equiv 1 \bmod p$$

Now let B such that $\frac{p-1}{e} + B = Ae$ for some A over the integers. The equation above can the be rewritten as

$$a^{\frac{p-1}{e}} \cdot a^B \equiv a^{Ae} \bmod p$$

or better

$$a^{Ae} \equiv a^B \bmod p$$

Furthemore observe that since $\gcd(2m, e) = 1$ it has to be the case that $\gcd(B, e) = 1$. This means that, using the extended Euclidean algorithm, it is possible to compute two values λ and μ such that $\lambda B + \mu e = 1$ over the integers. Thus the equation above becomes

$$a^{\lambda B + \mu e} \equiv (a^A)^{e\lambda} \cdot a^{\mu e} \bmod p$$

and then

$$a \equiv \left(a^{A\lambda + \mu}\right)^e \bmod p$$

Thus $a^{A\lambda + \mu}$ is an e-root of a.

The cost of the described method is dominated by the cost of the Extended Euclidean Algorithm which requires $O(k^3)$ bit operations.

B   Two Simple Lemmas

The following two lemmas are invoked during the proof of security of the signature scheme.

Lemma 2. *Let $N = pq$ be the product of two primes. Let e be a divisor of $\lambda(N)$ with multiplicity one (i.e. e^2 does not divide $\lambda(N)$) such that e divides either $p-1$ or $q - 1$ but not both of them. Then every e-th residue has exactly e different e-th roots.*

Proof. It is a well known fact from number theory [15] that in every finite cyclic group G, the equation $x^d = a$ has $gcd(d, ord(G))$ different solutions. This fact, however, cannot be immediately applied to Z_N^* because it is not a cyclic group, but can be applied to the cyclic groups Z_q^* and Z_p^* having order, respectively, $\phi(q) = (q-1)$ and $\phi(p) = (p-1)$ (see [15] for details).

Without loss of generality assume that e divides $p-1$ but does not divide $q-1$. Now from the equation $y = x^e \bmod N$, we derive the equations

$$y = x^e \bmod p \tag{1}$$

and

$$y = x^e \bmod q \tag{2}$$

Equation 1 has then $gcd(e, (p-1)) = e$ different solutions and equation 2 has $gcd(e, (q-1)) = 1$ different solutions. Using the Chinese Remainder Theorem [15], these can be combined to yield e different solutions modulo N.

Lemma 3. *Let $N = pq$ be the product of two primes. Let e be a divisor of $p-1$ (resp. $q-1$) but not a divisor of $q-1$ (resp. $p-1$) with multiplicity one. Let a be an e-residue in Z_N^* and y_1, y_2 two distinct solutions of the equation $x^e = a \bmod N$. Then there is an efficient algorithm that on input y_1 and y_2 returns the factorization of N.*

Proof. Without loss of generality assume that e divides $p-1$. Since the equation $x^e = a \bmod q$ has only one solution, it must be the case that

$$y_1 \equiv y_2 \bmod q \tag{3}$$

On the other hand since $y_1 \neq y_2 \bmod N$ it has to be the case that

$$y_1 \not\equiv y_2 \bmod p \tag{4}$$

Equation 3 tells us that $y_1 - y_2 \equiv 0 \bmod q$ and thus, since $y_1, y_2 < N$, $gcd(y_1 - y_2, N)$ is a non trivial factor of N.

The two lemmas above have the following consequence. Assume to have an algorithm $\mathcal{A}$ that on input N, e and an e-th residue y outputs an eth root of y. From the lemmas above it is immediate to see that is then possible to construct a different algorithm $\mathcal{B}$, having black box access to $\mathcal{A}$, that factors the modulus with probability $1 - 1/e$ (just feed $\mathcal{A}$ with $y = x^e \bmod N$, where x is chosen randomly, and with probability $1 - 1/e$ $\mathcal{A}$ will return a root different than x).

The Security of the FDH Variant of Chaum's Undeniable Signature Scheme

Wakaha Ogata[1], Kaoru Kurosawa[2], and Swee-Huay Heng[3]

[1] Tokyo Institute of Technology,
2-12-1 O-okayama, Meguro-ku,Tokyo, 152-8552 Japan
wakaha@craft.titech.ac.jp
[2] Department of Computer and Information Sciences, Ibaraki University,
4-12-1 Nakanarusawa, Hitachi, Ibaraki 316-8511, Japan
kurosawa@cis.ibaraki.ac.jp
[3] Multimedia University,
Jalan Ayer Keroh Lama, 75450 Melaka, Malaysia
shheng@mmu.edu.my

Abstract. In this paper, we first introduce a new kind of adversarial goal called *forge-and-impersonate* in undeniable signature schemes. Note that forgeability does not necessarily imply impersonation ability. We then classify the security of the FDH variant of Chaum's undeniable signature scheme according to three dimensions, the goal of adversaries, the attacks and the ZK level of confirmation and disavowal protocols. We finally relate each security to some well-known computational problem. In particular, we prove that the security of the FDH variant of Chaum's scheme with NIZK confirmation and disavowal protocols is equivalent to the CDH problem, as opposed to the GDH problem as claimed by Okamoto and Pointcheval.

Keywords: Undeniable signature, security analysis

1 Introduction

1.1 Background

The notion of undeniable signature schemes was introduced by Chaum and van Antwerpen in 1989 [11]. Since then, there have been a wide range of research covering a variety of different schemes for undeniable signatures. The validity or invalidity of an undeniable signature can only be verified with the signer's consent by engaging interactively or non-interactively in a confirmation or disavowal protocol respectively, as opposed to a digital signature in which its validity is universally verifiable. Extended schemes possess variable degrees of security and additional features such as convertibility [6, 15, 23], designated-verifier technique [21], designated-confirmer technique [9], and so on. Among others, we also include [8, 12, 19, 18, 17].

Undeniable signatures have various applications in cryptography such as in licensing softwares, electronic voting and auctions. The most popular application is in licensing softwares. For example, software vendors might want to sign on

S. Vaudenay (Ed.): PKC 2005, LNCS 3386, pp. 328–345, 2005.

their products to provide authenticity to their paying customers. Nevertheless, they strictly disallow dishonest users who have illegally duplicated their softwares to verify the validity of these signatures. Undeniable signature scheme plays an important role here as it allows only legitimate users to verify the validity of the signatures on the softwares.

The first proposal of undeniable signature which is based on the intractability of the computational Diffie-Hellman (CDH) problem was due to Chaum and van Antwerpen [11] and it was further improved by Chaum [8]. It is a simple and nice scheme.

On the other hand, in general, each undeniable signature scheme may have three variants of confirmation and disavowal protocols, namely, the perfect zero-knowledge protocol (ZKIP), the 3-move honest-verifier zero-knowledge protocol (HVZK) and the non-interactive zero-knowledge protocol (NIZK) with designated-verifier technique.

However, the unforgeability of Chaum's undeniable signature scheme (under any types of confirmation and disavowal protocols) has been an open problem for a long time. Recently, Okamoto and Pointcheval [25] proved the security of the full-domain hash (FDH) [5, 13] variant of Chaum's scheme with NIZK confirmation and disavowal protocols. They proved that its security is equivalent to the gap Diffie-Hellman (GDH) problem in the random oracle model, where one is allowed to use the decisional Diffie-Hellman (DDH) oracle to solve the CDH problem.

1.2 Our Contributions

In this paper, we first introduce a new kind of adversarial goal called *forge-and-impersonate* in undeniable signature schemes. In the past, the main adversarial goal is *forging* and thus the most desirable security notion is the security against existentially forgery under adaptive chosen message attack [20]. In the new adversary model, the adversary not only attempts to forge but it also attempts to impersonate a legitimate signer. More precisely, an adversary first forges a message-signature pair and next executes a confirmation protocol with a verifier, trying to convince the verifier that the signature is indeed valid. Note that forgeability does not necessarily imply impersonation ability.

We then classify the security of the FDH variant of Chaum's undeniable signature scheme according to three dimensions, the adversarial goals, the attacks and the ZK level of confirmation and disavowal protocols. Finally, we prove the equivalence between each security and some well-known computational problem under various types of confirmation and disavowal protocols as shown in Table 1. However, we cannot solve the three cells marked "?" and it will be a further work to make them clear.

In our result, we also point out that the claim of Okamoto and Pointcheval as mentioned at the end of Section 1.1 is wrong. Following our result from Theorem 1 which is indicated in Table 1, we show that the unforgeability of the FDH variant of Chaum's scheme with NIZK confirmation and disavowal protocols is equivalent to the CDH problem, as opposed to the GDH problem as claimed by them (cf. Claim 1). Further comments on their flaw will be given in Section 3.1.

Table 1. The Equivalence.

	forge (F)		forge-and-impersonate (FI)	
	passive	active	passive	active
ZKIP	CDH (Theorem 2)		?	?
HVZK	CDH (Theorem 3)	?	DLOG (Theorem 4)	$\geq$ one-more DLOG (Theorem 6)
NIZK	CDH (Theorem 1)	–	DLOG or break PKS (Theorem 5)	–

*PKS denotes the verifier's public key system

Following is some explanation on Table 1. In the passive attack, the adversary does not interact with the prover. What the adversary does is eavesdropping and she is in possession of transcripts of conversations between the prover and the verifier. In the active attack, the adversary gets to play the role of a cheating verifier, interacting with the prover several times, in an effort to extract some useful information before the forgery or *forge-and-impersonate* attempt. We remark that if the scheme employs the NIZK confirmation and disavowal protocols then it is not necessary to consider the active attack.

Meanwhile, there exists another security notion for undeniable signatures called invisibility which was first introduced by Chaum et al. [12]. This notion is essentially the inability to determine whether a given message-signature pair is valid for a given user. We can prove the invisibility of the FDH variant of Chaum's scheme and show the similar result as in Table 1.

1.3   Organization

The remainder of this paper is organized as follows. In Section 2, we recall the definitions for some computational problems and the definition for undeniable signatures. We also describe the FDH variant of Chaum's scheme and all the confirmation and disavowal protocols associated with it. In Section 3, we explore the unforgeability of the FDH variant of Chaum's scheme with NIZK protocols. In particular, we point out the flaw in Okamoto and Pointcheval's claim in Section 3.1 and provide a correct formal proof in Section 3.2. In Section 4, we present a new adversary model for undeniable signatures. In Section 5, we analyze and discuss the security of the FDH variant of Chaum's scheme under various confirmation and disavowal protocols comprehensively. Finally, we conclude this paper in Section 6.

2   Preliminaries

2.1   Some Computational Problems

Let G be an Abelian group of prime order q, and let g be a generator of G. We say that (g, g^x, g^r, g^z) is a DH-tuple if $z = xr \bmod q$.

The DDH problem is to decide if (g, g^x, g^r, g^z) is a DH-tuple. The CDH problem is to compute g^{xr} from (g, g^x, g^r). The GDH problem is to solve the CDH problem with the help of a DDH oracle. (Informally, it means that the CDH problem is hard but the DDH problem is easy.) The DLOG problem is to compute x from g^x.

We also briefly define the one-more DLOG problem as follows [3, 4]: A one-more DLOG adversary is a randomized, polynomial time algorithm M that gets input g and has access to two oracles, namely, a *DLOG oracle* that given $y \in G$ returns $x \in Z_q$ such that $g^x = y$, and a *challenge oracle* that each time it is invoked (it takes no inputs), returns a random challenge point $y \in G$. We say that the adversary M wins if for arbitrary (polynomially bounded) t challenge oracle access, it can find the DLOGs of all the challenges with at most $t - 1$ (strictly less than t) DLOG oracle access.

2.2 Undeniable Signatures

We briefly review the concept of undeniable signatures introduced by Chaum and van Antwerpen [11].

Definition 1. *An undeniable signature scheme consists of the following two polynomial time algorithms and two possibly interactive polynomial time protocols (note that in some schemes confirmation and disavowal protocols can be combined as a single protocol and they are usually zero-knowledge protocols).*

- **Key Generation.** *On input the security parameter 1^k, the algorithm produces a pair of matching public and secret keys (pk, sk).*
- **Signing.** *On input a secret key sk and a message m, the algorithm returns a signature σ.*
- **Confirmation Protocol.** *A protocol between a signer and a verifier such that when given a message m, a signature σ and a public key pk, allows the signer to convince the verifier that σ is indeed a valid signature on m for a public key pk, with the knowledge of the secret key sk. If (m, σ) is invalid, then no signer can prove it with non-negligible probability.*
- **Disavowal Protocol.** *A protocol between a signer and a verifier such that when given a message m, a signature σ and a public key pk, allows the signer to convince the verifier that σ is an invalid signature on m for a public key pk, with the knowledge of the secret key sk. If (m, σ) is valid, then no signer can prove it with non-negligible probability.*

In the existing literature, the unforgeability for undeniable signatures is similar to the one for ordinary digital signatures, which is the notion of existential unforgeability against adaptive chosen message attack [20]. The only difference is that besides the signing oracle access, the forger of an undeniable signature is also allowed to access to the confirmation/disavowal oracle. The confirmation/disavowal oracle is simulated based on the types of attacks mounted, i.e. passive attack and active attack.

Informally speaking, the forger is given the public key, and after some adaptive signing queries and confirmation/disavowal queries, the forger attempts to produce a valid message-signature pair (m, σ) such that m has never been queried to the signing oracle and (m, σ) has never been queried to the confirmation/disavowal oracle earlier. We say that the forger is successful if it can output such a valid forgery.

2.3   The FDH Variant of Chaum's Undeniable Signature Scheme

The FDH variant of Chaum's scheme is described as follows. Let G be an Abelian group of prime order q, and let g be a generator of G.

- **Key Generation.** On input the security parameter 1^k, choose $x \in Z_q$ randomly and compute $y = g^x$. Choose a cryptographic hash function $H : \{0,1\}^* \to G$. Set the public key as (g, y, H) and the secret key as x.
- **Signing.** On input the public key (g, y, H), the secret key x and a message $m \in \{0,1\}^*$, the algorithm returns the signature as $\sigma = H(m)^x$.
- **Confirmation Protocol.** Given a message-signature pair (m, σ), the signer proves that $(g, y, H(m), \sigma)$ is a DH-tuple.
- **Disavowal Protocol.** Given a message-signature pair (m, σ), the signer proves that $(g, y, H(m), \sigma)$ is not a DH-tuple.

Confirmation and Disavowal Protocols. There are various confirmation and disavowal protocols associated with Chaum's scheme, each with variable degrees of zero-knowledgeness and efficiency. We make an effort to summarize the various confirmation and disavowal protocols as follows.

Zero-Knowledge Interactive Proof (ZKIP). The first proposal by Chaum and van Antwerpen was not zero-knowledge [11]. In [8], an improved version with *zero-knowledgeness* was proposed. The confirmation protocol is a 4-move ZKIP for language of DH-tuples. For brevity, we describe the complete protocol in Fig. 1-(a).

A somewhat inefficient ZKIP disavowal protocol which requires more than 4-move was also proposed in [8]. A single execution of the protocol is as depicted in Fig. 1-(b). In this figure, com(s) denotes the commitment of s and decom(s) denotes the revealing of s.

3-Move Honest-Verifier Zero-Knowledge Proof (HVZK). A 3-move honest-verifier zero-knowledge (HVZK) confirmation protocol is depicted in Fig. 2-(a). The corresponding 3-move HVZK disavowal protocol was shown by Camenisch and Shoup recently [7]. We describe the protocol in Fig. 2-(b).

Non-interactive Zero-Knowledge Proof (NIZK). In general, a 3-move honest-verifier zero-knowledge protocol can be transformed to a more efficient non-interactive zero-knowledge (NIZK) protocol by using the Fiat-Shamir transformation [16, 1], where we need to employ another random oracle H'. However, we cannot use the above solution as a confirmation protocol or a disavowal protocol because such NIZK proof is just an ordinary digital signature.

Signer		Verifier
		$a,b \xleftarrow{R} Z_q$
	$\xleftarrow{c}$	$c = g^a H(m)^b$
$r \xleftarrow{R} Z_q$		
$z_1 = cg^r$		
$z_2 = z_1^x$	$\xrightarrow{z_1,z_2}$	
	$\xleftarrow{a,b}$	
$c \overset{?}{=} g^a H(m)^b$	$\xrightarrow{r}$	
		$z_1 \overset{?}{=} g^{a+r} H(m)^b$
		$z_2 \overset{?}{=} y^{a+r}\sigma^b$

Signer		Verifier
		$s \xleftarrow{R} \{0,1,\ldots,k\}$
		$a \xleftarrow{R} Z_q$
		$c = g^a H(m)^s$
	$\xleftarrow{c,c'}$	$c' = y^a \sigma^s$
find s' s.t.		
$(c^x/c') = (H(m)^x/\sigma)^{s'}$	$\xrightarrow{com(s')}$	
	$\xleftarrow{a}$	
$c \overset{?}{=} g^a H(m)^{s'}$	$\xrightarrow{decom(s')}$	
		$s' \overset{?}{=} s$

(a) Confirmation protocol   (b) A single execution of disavowal protocol

Fig. 1. ZKIP protocols.

Signer		Verifier
$r \xleftarrow{R} Z_q$		
$z_1 = g^r$		
$z_2 = H(m)^r$	$\xrightarrow{z_1,z_2}$	
	$\xleftarrow{c}$	$c \xleftarrow{R} Z_q$
$d = r + cx \bmod q$	$\xrightarrow{d}$	
		$g^d \overset{?}{=} z_1 y^c$
		$H(m)^d \overset{?}{=} z_2\sigma^c$

Signer		Verifier
$s,r,r' \xleftarrow{R} Z_q$		
$w = (H(m)^x/\sigma)^s$		
$z_1 = g^r/y^{r'}$		
$z_2 = H(m)^r/\sigma^{r'}$	$\xrightarrow{w,z_1,z_2}$	$w \overset{?}{\neq} 1$
	$\xleftarrow{c}$	$c \xleftarrow{R} Z_q$
$d = r + cxs \bmod q$		
$d' = r' + cs \bmod q$	$\xrightarrow{d,d'}$	
		$g^d/y^{d'} \overset{?}{=} z_1$
		$H(m)^d/\sigma^{d'} \overset{?}{=} z_2 w^c$

(a) Confirmation protocol   (b) Disavowal protocol

Fig. 2. HVZK protocols.

To overcome this problem, designated-verifier technique was introduced in [21] by Jakobsson et al. In a designated-verifier confirmation proof, the signer proves that "$(g, y, H(m), \sigma)$ is a DH-tuple" or "he knows the verifier's secret key" (the signer knows the former, but not the latter). In other words, the verifier is able to produce such a valid proof himself using his secret key. By using the designated-verifier technique, one can thereby prevent illegal copies of the proof.

Using the technique shown in [14], a designated-verifier proof can be constructed for a public-secret key pair of any well-known public key system. The obtained NIZK proof is zero-knowledge in the random oracle model.

We do not give the concrete NIZK designated-verifier confirmation and disavowal protocols since different protocols are associated with different public key systems used by the verifier.

3   Unforgeability of NIZK Scheme

Chaum's original scheme (which does not employ a cryptographic hash function) is not secure as it is existentially forgeable. Most precisely, it succumbed to the basic multiplicative attack: suppose that an adversary has two message-signature pairs (m_1, σ_1) and (m_2, σ_2), where $\sigma_1 = m_1^x$ and $\sigma_2 = m_2^x$. Then it is obvious that $\sigma_1 \sigma_2$ is a signature of $m_1 m_2$.

Okamoto and Pointcheval [25] made the first attempt to analyze the security of Chaum's scheme by incorporating the full-domain hash (FDH) technique [5, 13]. In other words, they studied the security of the FDH variant of Chaum's scheme in the random oracle model by modeling the hash function H as a random oracle[1]. Okamoto and Pointcheval further claimed that they have solved the more than 10 years open problem, i.e. the security of the FDH variant of Chaum's scheme with NIZK protocols is equivalent to the GDH problem.

However, we are going to disprove their claim in this section. In the sequel, we first restate their claim and point out the major flaw in their proof. We then prove that the security of the FDH variant of Chaum's scheme with NIZK protocols is in fact equivalent to the CDH problem, a more difficult problem than GDH.

In the NIZK scheme, the public key is (g, y, H, H'), where H' is a hash function which is used for Fiat-Shamir transformation (which transforms a 3-move HVZK protocol to an NIZK proof).

3.1   The Flaw in Okamoto and Pointcheval's Claim

Their claim is as follows.

Claim 1. *[25, Theorem 9]. An existential forgery under adaptively chosen message attack for the FDH variant of Chaum's undeniable signature scheme is equivalent to the GDH problem in the random oracle model, where the confirmation and disavowal protocols are NIZK.*

The correctness of the above claim was shown by proving the following [25]:

(1) If there exists an algorithm M that solves the GDH problem, then one can construct a forger F that manage to forge a message-signature pair by running M as its subroutine.
(2) If there exists a forger F that forges a message-signature pair, then one can construct an algorithm M that can solve the GDH problem by running F as its subroutine.

The proof of (1) is wrong. In the proof, the forger F runs the algorithm M as follows. At first, the forger F is given the public key (g, y, H, H') (H' is used to transform HVZK to a non-interactive one). F then chooses m randomly and runs M on input $(g, y, H(m))$. If M submits $(g, y, H(m'), \sigma')$ to the DDH oracle,

---

[1] Another merit in the FDH variant is that messages may be arbitrary bit strings and do not need to be encoded as group elements as in the original scheme.

then F queries to its confirmation/disavowal oracle and returns the answer to M. M finally outputs $H(m)^x$ with non-negligible probability from our assumption. Therefore, F can forge the signature on m as $H(m)^x$ with non-negligible probability.

However, suppose that M submits $(g, y, H(m'), \sigma')$ to the DDH oracle. Then what F can query to its confirmation/disavowal oracle is (m', σ'), but not $(H(m'), \sigma')$. Since F cannot compute m' from $H(m')$, so it cannot query (m', σ'). More precisely, since a prover in the confirmation/disavowal protocol takes only the message m' and its signature σ' as input, simulating a DDH oracle would require to inverse the hash function H, which is obviously impossible! Therefore, F fails to simulate the DDH oracle correctly. This is indeed a critical flaw.

The proof of (2) is redundant. In the proof, the confirmation/disavowal oracle is simulated by the DDH oracle. More precisely, to decide whether the given (m, σ) is a valid pair or not, M asks $(g, y, H(m), \sigma)$ to the DDH oracle, and then simulates the confirmation/disavowal oracle by itself. However, notice that M can decide the validity of (m, σ), since it can simulate the signing oracle by itself and furthermore the signing algorithm is deterministic. Thus the DDH oracle is totally redundant here as it plays no function at all.

3.2   Correct Equivalence

Based on the above argument, we have indirectly proven Theorem 1, i.e. the existence of F is equivalent to the existence of M that solves the CDH problem (without the DDH oracle access). For clarity and completeness, we provide a formal proof for the theorem.

Theorem 1. *The security of the FDH variant of Chaum's undeniable signature scheme with NIZK confirmation and disavowal protocols is equivalent to the CDH problem in the random oracle model.*

Proof. Firstly, we show that if there exists an algorithm M that solves the CDH problem with advantage ϵ_M, then one can construct a forger F that can forge in the universal way with advantage ϵ_F, by running M as a subroutine. The forger F is given the public key (g, y, H, H') where $y = g^x$. For any message m, F computes $h = H(m)$ and gives the triple (g, y, h) as input to M. When M outputs h^x, F simply outputs the forgery as $(m, \sigma = h^x)$. It is clear that $\epsilon_F = \epsilon_M$. This completes the first half of our proof.

Secondly, we show that if there exists a forger F that manage to forge with advantage ϵ_F, then one can construct an algorithm M that can solve the CDH problem with advantage ϵ_M, by running F as a subroutine. Suppose the input to M is (g, g^x, g^r). M then starts running F by feeding F with the public key $(g, y = g^x, H, H')$ where H and H' are random oracles that will be simulated by M. M also simulates the signing oracle and the confirmation/disavowal oracle itself. Let q_S and q_H be the number of signing queries and H-queries that F issues respectively. We assume that when F makes a confirmation/disavowal query for a message-signature pair (m_i, σ'_i), it has already made the corresponding signing query on m_i. We also assume that when F requests a signature on a message m_i, it has already made the corresponding H-query on m_i.

When F makes a H-query for a message m_i, M responds with $h_i = H(m_i) = g^{\alpha_i}$ with probability δ and $h_i = H(m_i) = (g^r)^{\alpha_i}$ with probability $1 - \delta$, where α_i is chosen randomly from Z_q and δ is a fixed probability which will be determined later.

When F makes a H'-query for a new str, where str is the string that F would like to know its H' value. M always responds with a random number. In fact, M assigns some values to $H'(str)$ for some str in order to simulate the confirmation/disavowal oracle. When F makes a H'-query for such str, M returns $H'(str)$ to F.

When F makes a signing query for a message m_i, if $h_i = g^{\alpha_i}$ then M returns $\sigma_i = y^{\alpha_i}$ as the valid signature (since $y^{\alpha_i} = (g^x)^{\alpha_i} = h_i^x = H(m_i)^x$). Otherwise, M aborts and it fails to solve the CDH problem.

Next, we consider the case that F makes a confirmation/disavowal query for a message-signature pair (m_i, σ_i'). In this case, M has to do in two steps. In the first step, it checks the validity of (m_i, σ_i') using the signing oracle. From our assumption, F has already made a signing query for m_i, and M answered with a valid signature σ_i with probability δ (with probability $(1 - \delta)$ M aborts). Therefore, if $\sigma_i = \sigma_i'$ then it is valid, otherwise it is invalid. Remember that the signing algorithm is deterministic. In the second step, M does the following. If (m_i, σ_i') is a valid pair then M returns the transcript of the confirmation protocol. Otherwise, it returns the transcript of the disavowal protocol. As mentioned before, M can manipulate H'-oracle and thus it can generate a transcript of the confirmation or disavowal protocol. (In fact, it is possible that collision occurs for str, meaning that str is being asked to H'-oracle by F earlier before M assigns a value to $H'(str)$. However, this probability is negligible and thus it will not affect the overall success probability for M.)

Eventually, F halts and outputs a forgery (m, σ). We assume that F has queried the H-oracle on m and so $m = m_i$ for some i. If $h_i = (g^r)^{\alpha_i}$, then we have $\sigma = h_i^x = (g^{r\alpha_i})^x$. Consequently, M outputs $g^{xr} = \sigma^{1/\alpha_i}$ and thus it solves the CDH problem. Otherwise, M aborts and it fails to solve the CDH problem.

To complete the proof, it remains to calculate the probability that M does not abort. The probability that M answers to all the signing queries is δ^{q_S} and M outputs g^{xr} with probability $1 - \delta$. Therefore, the probability that M does not abort during the simulation is $\delta^{q_S}(1 - \delta)$. This value is maximized at $\delta_{opt} = 1 - 1/(q_S + 1)$. This shows that M's advantage ϵ_M is at least $(1/e(1 + q_S))\epsilon_F$, where e is the base of the natural logarithm. This is because the value $(1 - 1/(q_S + 1))^{q_S}$ approaches $1/e$ for large q_S. This completes our proof. $\qquad\square$

4   New Adversary Model

In this section, we present a new adversary model for undeniable signatures that incorporates a new adversarial goal called *forge-and-impersonate*. In the past, the main adversarial goal is *forging*, i.e. one considers an undeniable signature scheme to be secure if it is existentially unforgeable against adaptive chosen message attack. In our new proposal, the adversary not only attempts to forge but it also attempts to impersonate a legitimate signer.

It is clear that forgeability does not necessarily imply impersonation ability. Hence the new adversarial goal is stronger. (On the other hand, the latter implies the former because if (m, σ) is invalid, then any signer can convince the verifier with only negligible probability in the confirmation protocol. See Section 2.2.)

Now, we present our proposal and explain what motivates us to consider this new adversarial goal.

4.1   Adversarial Goals

As usual, we classify adversaries by their ultimate adversarial goals. Normally, an adversary with the motive to forge a new message-signature pair (m, σ) is given the name *forger*. As mentioned earlier, this is the traditional security notion.

Now, we introduce a new type of adversary. The new adversarial goal is to forge a message-signature pair (m, σ) and further convincing a (honest) verifier that σ is indeed a valid signature on m, by executing the confirmation protocol with the verifier. To avoid confusion, we stick to the following notation. We denote the former type of adversary as *forge* (F) and the latter as *forge-and-impersonate* (FI).

It is pretty hard for this new adversary to gain a success, but let us look at the motivation for the adversary. As noted earlier in the introduction part, the most common application of undeniable signatures is in licensing softwares. If an adversary succeeds in forging a signature (but not in convincing the verifier by executing a confirmation protocol), no doubt it would cause some damage to the legitimate signer (e.g. Microsoft). On the other hand, if an adversary succeeds in forging as well as in impersonating, then it can sell its own softwares by impersonating an agent of Microsoft. In this case, it can actively earn some fast money through its wicked deed. This is the motivation behind the attack.

Intuitively, the security against a FI adversary is equivalent to a problem which is no easier than the problem which is equivalent to the security against a F adversary. We shall exemplify this with some security analyses in the next section.

On the other hand, we also remark that the security against FI does not imply unforgeability from the definitions. From the definition of FI adversary, the adversary forges (m, σ) and succeeds in the confirmation protocol. However, notice that there is a possibility that even if (m, σ) is invalid, the adversary succeeds in the confirmation protocol. Hence, the security against FI adversary does not imply unforgeability. We also note that if we use a ZKIP confirmation protocol, then the security against FI adversary does imply unforgeability, due to the soundness of the ZKIP protocol.

4.2   Types of Attacks

We can also classify adversaries by their capabilities or types of attacks. More precisely, there exist two types of attacks, namely, passive attack and active attack. Obviously, passive attack is a weaker attack.

Both the passive and active adversaries have access to the signing oracle as well as the confirmation/disavowal oracle. The signing oracle plays the role similar to those in the ordinary signature scheme. We highlight the difference between a passive attack and an active attack below.

Whenever an adversary submits a confirmation/disavowal query (m, σ), the oracle responds based on whether a passive attack or an active attack is mounted. In a passive attack, the confirmation/disavowal oracle first checks the validity of (m, σ) using the signing oracle. If it is a valid pair, then the oracle returns "yes" and a transcript of confirmation protocol. Otherwise, the oracle returns "no" and a transcript of disavowal protocol. In an active attack, the confirmation/disavowal oracle first checks the validity of (m, σ) using the signing oracle. If it is a valid pair, then the oracle returns "yes" and proceeds with the execution of the confirmation protocol with the adversary (acting as a cheating verifier). Otherwise, the oracle returns "no" and executes the disavowal protocol with the adversary accordingly.

4.3   Formal Security Definitions

In this section, we provide the formal security definitions by considering the two adversarial goals, namely forge (F) and forge-and-impersonate (FI) and the two types of attacks mounted by the adversary.

Definition 2 (Unforgeability). *An undeniable signature scheme is said to be existential unforgeable under adaptive chosen message attack if no probabilistic polynomial time (PPT) forger F has a non-negligible advantage in the following game:*

1. *Let pk be the input to F.*
2. *The forger F is permitted to issue a series of queries:*
   - *Signing queries: F submits a message m and receives a signature σ on m. (We consider adaptive queries here – subsequent queries is made based on previously obtained signatures.)*
   - *Confirmation/disavowal queries: F submits a message-signature pair (m, σ), and the oracle responds based on whether a passive attack or an active attack is mounted.*
     In a passive attack, the confirmation/disavowal oracle first checks the validity of (m, σ) using the signing oracle. If it is a valid pair, then the oracle returns "yes" and a transcript of confirmation protocol. Otherwise, the oracle returns "no" and a transcript of disavowal protocol.
     In an active attack, the confirmation/disavowal oracle first checks the validity of (m, σ) using the signing oracle. If it is a valid pair, then the oracle returns "yes" and proceeds with the execution of the confirmation protocol with the forger F (acting as a cheating verifier). Otherwise, the oracle returns "no" and executes the disavowal protocol with F accordingly.
3. *At the end of this attack game, F outputs a message-signature pair (m, σ) such that m has never been queried to the signing oracle and that (m, σ) has never been queried to the confirmation/disavowal oracle earlier.*

The forger F wins the game if σ is a valid signature on m. F's advantage in this game is defined to be $Adv(F) = \Pr[F\,wins]$.

Definition 3 (Unforgeability-and-Unimpersonation). *An undeniable signature scheme is said to be secure against forgery and impersonation under adaptive chosen message attack if no PPT adversary A has a non-negligible advantage in the following game:*

1. *Let pk be the input to A.*
2. *The adversary A enters the learning phase where it performs a series of queries: signing queries and confirmation/disavowal queries as in the previous definitions (based on whether a passive attack or an active attack is mounted). At the end of this forgery phase, A outputs a forged message-signature pair (m, σ) such that m has never been queried to the signing oracle and that (m, σ) has never been queried to the confirmation/disavowal oracle earlier.*
3. *In the impersonation phase, A proceeds to execute the confirmation protocol with a verifier on input (m, σ), trying to convince the verifier that (m, σ) is a valid pair.*

The adversary A wins the game if it can convince the verifier that (m, σ) is a valid message-signature pair. A's advantage in this game is defined to be $Adv(A) = \Pr[A\,wins]$.

4.4   FI-Security in NIZK

For undeniable signature schemes with designated-verifier NIZK proofs, we have to carefully define the security against FI attack. This is because in such scheme, besides breaking the undeniable signature scheme, an adversary can also impersonate by breaking the public key system of a verifier.

   Therefore, we first specify the key generation algorithm of the public key system PKS of the target verifier. We denote the FI attack in this situation with FI^{PKS} attack. We then adopt the following adversary model.

1. As usual, after making some oracle queries, the adversary A outputs a forged message-signature pair (m, σ).
2. Now, A is given a public key of a verifier randomly.
3. Next, it outputs a non-interactive non-transferable confirmation transcript corresponding to the given public key.

   We say that A succeeds in FI^{PKS} attack if the proof is accepted with non-negligible probability, where the probability is taken over the key generation algorithm of PKS as well.

5   The Equivalence

5.1   Our Objective

Following from the previous section, it is thus clear that we need to consider four types of adversaries, namely, the passive F, the active F, the passive FI and the active FI.

There are various confirmation and disavowal protocols associate with the FDH variant of Chaum's scheme, namely, ZKIP, 3-move HVZK and 1-move NIZK.

We intend to explore further on the equivalence between the security of the scheme (with various confirmation and disavowal protocols) and some computational problems, under the various types of adversaries. In other words, our objective is to fill up Table 1.

We remark that if the scheme employs the non-interactive confirmation and disavowal protocols (NIZK), then it is not necessary to consider active attack.

In what follows, a xxx scheme denotes the scheme with xxx confirmation and disavowal protocols, where xxx is ZKIP, HVZK or NIZK.

5.2   On F Attacks

First of all, recall that in Theorem 1 of Section 3.1, we have shown that the passive F attack to the scheme with NIZK protocols is equivalent to the CDH problem.

Theorem 2. *The ZKIP scheme is secure against each of passive/active F attack in the random oracle model if and only if the CDH problem is hard.*

Proof. The *only if* part is trivial. The *if* part can be shown almost similarly to Theorem 1. However, notice that M does not need to simulate the H'-oracle here. The signing oracle, H-oracle and the first step of the confirmation/disavowal oracle are simulated similarly (see the proof of Theorem 1). The only difference is in the second step of the confirmation/disavowal oracle simulation. Please refer to the full version of this paper [24] for the concrete simulation of confirmation/disavowal oracle in an active attack. Intuitively, the zero-knowledge property of the protocols assures that M can simulate the confirmation/disavowal oracle. Therefore, it is also clear that M can simulate the confirmation/disavowal oracle in a passive attack, since passive attack is weaker than active attack.   □

Theorem 3. *The HVZK scheme is secure against passive F attack in the random oracle model if and only if the CDH problem is hard.*

Proof. The *only if* part is trivial. The *if* part can be shown almost similarly to Theorem 2 except in the confirmation/disavowal oracle simulation. Please refer to [24] for the concrete perfect simulation of the transcripts of confirmation/disavowal protocol.   □

5.3   On Passive FI Attacks

Theorem 4. *The passive FI attack on the HVZK scheme is equivalent to the DLOG problem in the random oracle model.*

Proof. Firstly, we show that if there exists an algorithm M that solves the DLOG problem, then an adversary A can succeed in FI attack by running M as a subroutine. The adversary A is given the public key (g, y, H) where $y = g^x$. Since A can obtain the secret key x by feeding y to algorithm M, it can succeed in the FI attack. This completes the first half of the proof.

Secondly, let A be a passive FI adversary. We show that one can construct an algorithm M that can solve the DLOG problem by running A as a subroutine. Suppose that the input to M is (g, g^x), M then starts running A by feeding A with the public key $(g, y = g^x, H)$, where H is a random oracle that will be simulated by M. M also simulates the signing oracle and the confirmation/disavowal oracle itself. We assume that when A makes a confirmation/disavowal query for a message-signature pair (m_i, σ'_i), it has already made the corresponding signing query on m_i. We also assume that when A requests a signature on a message m_i, it has already made the corresponding H-query on m_i.

When A makes a H-query for a message m_i, M responds with $h_i = g^{\alpha_i}$, where α_i is chosen randomly from Z_q. When A makes a signing query for a message m_i, M returns $\sigma_i = y^{\alpha_i}$ as the valid signature (since $y^{\alpha_i} = (g^x)^{\alpha_i} = h_i^x = H(m_i)^x$).

When A makes a confirmation/disavowal query for a message-signature pair (m_i, σ'_i), A can distinguish between a valid pair and an invalid pair by checking the signing queries record. Further, M can simulate the confirmation/disavowal oracle perfectly since the views of the honest-verifier zero-knowledge protocols are simulatable (see [24]).

Eventually, A outputs a forgery (m, σ). It then proceeds to prove that σ is indeed a valid signature by executing the confirmation protocol with the honest-verifier. Since the confirmation protocol is a proof of knowledge of x, thus M can extract x by using the reset technique [2]. Please refer to [24] for the details. □

The following theorem states the security of the scheme against passive FI attack when non-interactive zero-knowledge proofs are used.

Theorem 5. *The passive* FI^{PKS} *attack on the NIZK scheme is equivalent to "solving the DLOG problem" or "breaking* PKS*" in the random oracle model. Here, "breaking* PKS*" means that the adversary obtains the secret key corresponding to the given public key which is chosen randomly in* PKS.

Proof. Consider an algorithm M whose input is $((g, y), Pk)$ where y is a random element of G and Pk is a randomly chosen public key in PKS. If M outputs x such that $y = g^x$ or Sk such that (Pk, Sk) is a public-secret key pair in PKS, then we can say that M succeeds in "solving the DLOG problem or breaking PKS". Clearly, if there exists such algorithm M, then an adversary A can succeed in FI^{PKS} attack by running M as a subroutine. Thus the first half of the proof was shown.

Secondly, let A be a passive FI^{PKS} adversary. We show that one can construct an algorithm M that can solve the DLOG problem or can break PKS by running A as a subroutine. Suppose that the input to M is $((g, y), Pk)$. At first, M starts running A by feeding A with the public key (g, y, H, H'). We assume that when A makes a confirmation/disavowal query for a message-signature pair (m_i, σ'_i), it has already made the corresponding signing query on m_i. We also assume that when A requests a signature on a message m_i, it has already made the corresponding H-query on m_i.

The simulation of the H-oracle and the signing oracle are the same as in the previous proof. The simulation of the H'-oracle is the same as the proof of Theorem 1. The simulation of the confirmation/disavowal oracle is also almost the same as those in the proof of Theorem 1, except that now when A makes a signing query for m_i, M answered with a valid signature σ with probability 1.

Eventually, A outputs a forgery (m, σ) and requests a verifier's public key. M then hands Pk to A. A next generates a non-interactive non-transferable confirmation transcript corresponding to Pk and returns the transcript to M. After that, M resets A. Unlike in the previous proof, M has to rewind A to the point that it has made the H'-query for str where $H'(str)$ is used as a random challenge in the confirmation transcript. Using the same argument of forking lemma [26], if A outputs a NIZK confirmation transcript with non-negligible probability, then rewinding A with a different H' value will result M in getting two confirmation transcripts for a common input (m, σ), with non-negligible probability. From these two transcripts, M can obtain a witness W. At last M outputs W. Remember that the designated-verifier confirmation transcript is a proof of knowledge of x (the signer's secret key) or the verifier's secret key Sk. Therefore, we have $W = x$ or $W = Sk$, that is, M succeeds in solving the DLOG problem or breaking PKS. □

From the above theorem, if the target verifier uses ElGamal cryptosystem, then the passive FI attack on NIZK scheme is equivalent to the DLOG problem. If the target verifier uses RSA cryptosystem, then the passive FI attack on NIZK scheme is equivalent to "solving the DLOG problem" or "factoring the RSA modulus N" [22].

5.4   On Active FI Attacks

Finally, we consider the last case, the active FI attack. In the active FI attack, the adversary has additional power, i.e. to execute confirmation and disavowal protocols interactively with the signer. M plays the role of the signer in this scenario, interacting with the adversary whenever it receives a confirmation/disavowal query.

The proof of the following theorem is given in [24].

Theorem 6. *The HVZK scheme is secure against active* FI *attack in the random oracle model if the one-more DLOG problem is hard.*

5.5   Discussion

We have analyzed the security of the FDH variant of Chaum's scheme under various types of confirmation/disavowal protocols using the newly proposed adversary model. Their equivalence with some known computational problems are proven. In conclusion, the results we obtained are as summarized in Table 1, which follows from Theorem 1 to Theorem 6.

The three cells marked "?" are still unsolved at the moment due to the following reasons. In the proofs of Theorem 4 and Theorem 5, M can extract x from $y = g^x$ because the confirmation protocol is a proof of *knowledge* of x, thus there exists a knowledge extractor for x. On the other hand, the perfect zero-knowledge confirmation protocol shown in Fig. 1-(a) is a proof of *language* and not a proof of *knowledge*. Therefore, it is impossible for us to construct such a knowledge extractor. This is the reason why we are unable to prove the equivalence between FI attack and and some well-known computational problem by using the same approach. May be there exist some other approaches to prove the equivalence, however we are yet to discover it at the moment.

However, we conjecture that the problem which should be equivalent to the security against passive FI and active FI attacks when ZKIP protocols are employed and the problem which should be equivalent to the security against active F attack when HVZK protocols are employed, should be no easier than the CDH problem. We anticipate the solution in the near future and we encourage more attempts on them.

There exists another security notion for undeniable signatures called invisibility which was first introduced by Chaum et al. [12]. This notion is essentially the inability to determine whether a given message-signature pair is valid for a given signer. We can prove the invisibility of the FDH variant of Chaum's scheme and show the similar results as in Table 1. Due to the space limitation, the details will be given in the final paper.

6   Conclusion

In this paper, we introduced another new adversarial goal called *forge-and-impersonate* in undeniable signature schemes, and this leads to a new adversary model which is slightly stronger than the existing one. We also classified the security of the FDH variant of Chaum's undeniable signature scheme according to three dimensions, the attacks, the adversarial goals and the ZK level of confirmation and disavowal protocols, and then related each security to some well-known computational problem. In addition, we also pointed out the flaw in Okamoto and Pointcheval's claim, i.e. we proved that the unforgeability of the FDH variant of Chaum's scheme with NIZK confirmation and disavowal protocols is equivalent to the CDH problem, as opposed to the GDH problem as claimed by them.

References

1. M. Abdalla, J. An, M. Bellare and C. Namprempre. From identification to signatures via the Fiat-Shamir transform: minimizing assumptions for security and forward-security. *Advances in Cryptology – EUROCRYPT '02*, LNCS 2332, pp. 418–433, Springer-Verlag, 2002.
2. M. Bellare and A. Palacio. GQ and Schnorr identification schemes: proofs of security against impersonation under active and concurrent attacks. *Advances in Cryptology – CRYPTO '02*, LNCS 2442, pp. 162–177, Springer-Verlag, 2002.
3. M. Bellare, C. Namprempre, D. Pointcheval and M. Semanko. The power of RSA inversion oracles and the security of Chaum's RSA-based blind signature scheme. *Financial Cryptography '01*, LNCS 2339, pp. 319–338, Springer-Verlag, 2002.

4. M. Bellare, C. Namprempre, D. Pointcheval and M. Semanko. The one-more-RSA-inversion problems and the security of Chaum's blind signature scheme. *Journal of Cryptology*, vol. 16, no. 3, pp. 185–215, Springer-Verlag, 2003.

5. M. Bellare and P. Rogaway. The exact security of digital signatures – how to sign with RSA and Rabin. *Advances in Cryptology – EUROCRYPT '96*, LNCS 1070, pp. 399–416, Springer-Verlag, 1996.

6. J. Boyar, D. Chaum, I. Damgård and T. Pedersen. Convertible undeniable signatures. *Advances in Cryptology – CRYPTO '90*, LNCS 537, pp. 189–208, Springer-Verlag, 1990.

7. J. Camenisch and V. Shoup. Practical verifiable encryption and decryption of discrete logarithms. *Advances in Cryptology – CRYPTO '03*, LNCS 2729, pp. 126–144, Springer-Verlag, 2003.

8. D. Chaum. Zero-knowledge undeniable signatures. *Advances in Cryptology – EUROCRYPT '90*, LNCS 473, pp. 458–464, Springer-Verlag, 1990.

9. D. Chaum. Designated confirmer signatures. *Advances in Cryptology – EUROCRYPT '94*, LNCS 950, pp. 86–91, Springer-Verlag, 1995.

10. T. Chaum and T. P. Pedersen. Wallet databases with observers. *Advances in Cryptology – CRYPTO '92*, LNCS 740, pp. 89–105, Springer-Verlag, 1993.

11. D. Chaum and H. van Antwerpen. Undeniable signatures. *Advances in Cryptology – CRYPTO '89*, LNCS 435, pp. 212–216, Springer-Verlag, 1989.

12. D. Chaum, E. van Heijst and B. Pfitzmann. Cryptographically strong undeniable signatures, unconditionally secure for the signer. *Advances in Cryptology – CRYPTO '91*, LNCS 576, pp. 470–484, Springer-Verlag, 1991.

13. J. Coron. On the exact security of full domain hash. *Advances in Cryptology – CRYPTO '00*, LNCS 1880, pp. 229–235, Springer-Verlag, 2000.

14. R. Cramer, I. Damgård and B. Schoenmakers. Proofs of partial knowledge and simplified design of witness hiding protocols. *Advances in Cryptology – CRYPTO '94*, LNCS 839, pp. 174–187, Springer-Verlag, 1994.

15. I. Damgård and T. Pedersen. New convertible undeniable signature schemes. *Advances in Cryptology – EUROCRYPT '96*, LNCS 1070, pp. 372–386, Springer-Verlag, 1996.

16. A. Fiat and A. Shamir. How to prove yourself: practical solutions to identification and signature problems. *Advances in Cryptology – CRYPTO '86*, LNCS 263, pp. 186–194, Springer-Verlag, 1987.

17. S. Galbraith and W. Mao. Invisibility and anonymity of undeniable and confirmer signatures. *Topics in Cryptology – CT-RSA '03*, LNCS 2612, pp. 80–97, Springer Verlag, 2003.

18. S. Galbraith, W. Mao and K. G. Paterson. RSA-based undeniable signatures for general moduli. *Topics in Cryptology – CT-RSA '02*, LNCS 2271, pp. 200–217, Springer Verlag, 2002.

19. R. Gennaro, H. Krawczyk and T. Rabin. RSA-based undeniable signatures. *Advances in Cryptology – CRYPTO '97*, LNCS 1294, pp. 132–149, Springer-Verlag, 1997.

20. S. Goldwasser, S. Micali and R. Rivest. A digital signature scheme secure against adaptive chosen-message attacks. *SIAM Journal of Computing*, vol. 17, no. 2, pp. 281–308, 1988.

21. M. Jakobsson, K. Sako and R. Impagliazzo. Designated verifier proofs and their applications. *Advances in Cryptology – EUROCRYPT '96*, LNCS 1070, pp. 143–154, Springer-Verlag, 1996.

22. A. May. Computing the RSA secret key is deterministic polynomial time equivalent to factoring. *Advances in Cryptology – CRYPTO '04*, LNCS 3152, pp. 213–219, Springer-Verlag, 2004.
23. M. Michels and M. Stadler. Efficient convertible undeniable signature schemes. *Selected Areas in Cryptography – SAC '97*, pp. 231–244, Springer-Verlag, 1997.
24. W. Ogata, K. Kurosawa and S.-H. Heng. The security of the FDH variant of Chaum's undeniable signature scheme. The full version of this paper. Available from the *Cryptology ePrint Archive*, http://www.iacr.org/.
25. T. Okamoto and D. Pointcheval. The gap-problems: a new class of problems for the security of cryptographic schemes. *Public Key Cryptography – PKC '01*, LNCS 1992, pp. 104–118, Springer-Verlag, 2001.
26. D. Pointcheval and J. Stern. Security proofs for signature schemes. *Advances in Cryptology – EUROCRYPT '96*, LNCS 1070, pp. 387–398, Springer-Verlag, 1996.

Efficient Threshold RSA Signatures
with General Moduli and No Extra Assumptions

Ivan Damgård and Kasper Dupont*

Dept. of Computer Science, Aarhus University

Abstract. We propose techniques that allow construction of robust threshold RSA signature schemes that can work without a trusted dealer using known key generation protocols and is as efficient as the best previous schemes. We do not need special conditions on the RSA modulus, extra complexity or set-up assumptions or random oracles. An "optimistic" variant of the scheme is even more efficient in case no faults occur. Some potential more general applications of our basic idea are also pointed out.

1 Introduction

In a threshold public-key system we have a standard public key (for the RSA system, for instance), while the private key is shared among a set of servers, in such a way that by collaborating, these servers can apply the private key operation to a given input, to decrypt it or sign it, as the case may be. If there are l servers, such schemes typically ensure that even if an active adversary corrupts less than $l/2$ servers, he will not learn additional information about the private key, and will be unable to force the network to compute incorrect results. Thus threshold cryptography is an important concept because it can improve substantially the reliability and security of applications in practice of public-key systems.

The most efficient known robust threshold RSA signature scheme was proposed by Shoup [25] (see [9] for some of the first work in this direction and [18] for a more efficient solution in case of passive attacks). Shoup's scheme needs the RSA modulus n to be a product of *safe primes*, that is, besides $n = pq$ where p, q are prime, we require $p = 2p' + 1$, $q = 2q' + 1$ and p', q' are also primes. When Shoup proposed his scheme, it was not known how to generate efficiently such an RSA key in a *distributed* way, i.e., such that the servers generate the key from scratch without the secret key ever becoming known to a single entity. Shoup's scheme therefore assumed a trusted dealer generating the keys – although a distributed key generation would of course have been more satisfactory since it completely avoids any single points of attack.

---

* Both authors supported BRICS, Basic Research in Computer Science, Center of the Danish National Research Foundation, and FICS, Foundations in Cryptography and Security, Center of the Danish Science Research Council.

S. Vaudenay (Ed.): PKC 2005, LNCS 3386, pp. 346–361, 2005.

It was already known how to generate *general* (random) RSA keys via a distributed protocol [2, 10], but such keys are safe prime products with only negligible probability. Later, in [1], Algesheimer, Camenisch and Shoup propose a RSA key generation protocol that can also generate safe prime products in a reasonable amount of time, in the sense that their method will be much faster than employing generic multiparty computation methods.

Despite this result, there are good reasons for considering threshold RSA schemes that can use general RSA keys: we do not know if there are infinitely many safe primes, and in any case, safe prime products constitute a small fraction of the possible RSA keys. Thus it could in principle be the case that safe prime products are easy to factor, while the general RSA assumption is still true. We stress that nothing is known to suggest that this is the case, but in general most experts agree that the most sound approach is to use RSA keys with as few special constraints as possible. Furthermore, generating safe primes is slower than generating random primes, simply because there are so few of them: to generate a random k-bit prime, we need to examine $O(k)$ candidates before finding a prime, but (from heuristic arguments) we need $O(k^2)$ candidates before finding a safe prime. Most candidates can be ruled out using trial division, so the extra cost for safe primes may not be so significant in a traditional scenario where a single party generates keys. But it is much more painful in a distributed key generation protocol, since here even a simple trial division costs communication.

It is in fact possible to use more general RSA moduli: in [8], Damgård and Koprowski propose a threshold RSA scheme which is as efficient as Shoup's and which can use a much more general class of moduli. However, this comes at the expense an extra and non-standard intractability assumptions, on top of the basic RSA assumption (which is of course necessary). Independently, Fouque and Stern [14] suggested a different approach that is based only on the RSA assumption, but is significantly less efficient than [25, 8]. All these schemes need the random oracles to make the signing protocol be non-interactive. One can do without them at the expense of extra interaction, but doing it in a constant number of rounds requires extra set-up assumptions.

More recently, Cramer and Damgård propose a technique known as secret-key zero-knowledge[5]. They suggest applying this to threshold RSA, this way one obtains non-interactive protocols without random oracles. On the other hand, the modulus is restricted in the same way as for Shoup's scheme and extra key set-up assumptions are needed.

In this paper, we propose new threshold RSA schemes which are as efficient as [25, 8], they do not need the extra intractability assumptions introduced in [8], nor extra key set-up assumptions. To understand how this is possible, recall that in virtually any proposed threshold RSA scheme, each server must contribute a partial result computed from its own share of the private key, plus it must prove in zero-knowledge to the client requesting the signature that this partial result is correct. We then observe that a minor change in the algorithm that computes the signature from all contributions allows us to make do with a much larger (non-negligible) error probability for the zero-knowledge proofs. This is a very generic idea that can be applied to most known threshold RSA schemes. Now, since the restrictions on the RSA moduli in previous schemes were typically nedeed to have a negligible error probability, we no longer need these restrictions.

Working out the details of this can be more or less straightforward, depending on which of the previous RSA schemes we start from. For instance, if we start from Shoup's scheme, there are indeed a few technicalities to sort out, and we do this in detail in the last part of the paper. Since we want to avoid random oracles and extra set-up assumptions, we cannot get a protocol that is always non-interactive, but we can get one that requires at most 3 moves, and only 1 if servers behave correctly (as they would most of the time in practice). Note that this would not have been possible if we had used zero-knowledge proofs in the standard way. In any case, the total communication and computational complexity is comparable to that of [25, 8]. Our schemes comes in several variants:

- The most efficient variant can be proved secure, based on an assumption that implies the RSA assumption. We conjecture that they are in fact equivalent (and we can prove this in the random oracle model). The modulus $n = pq$ must satisfy that $(p-1)/2, (q-1)/2$ have no prime factors smaller than $3t^2$, where t is the maximal number of corrupted severs.
- A slightly more complex version that is slower than the basic one by a constant factor, but can be proved secure under the RSA assumption. It uses the same clas of moduli as the basic one.
- A variant that can use *any* RSA modulus and is secure under the RSA assumption. Its complexity is higher than the basic one by a factor of $\log_2 3 + 2\log_2 t$ – in practice, this is usually a rather small price to pay.

In the last section of the paper, we point out some more general applications of our basic idea, in particular, any threshold signature scheme, but also threshold cryptosystems based on polynomial secret sharing could benefit from our technique.

2   Model

Here we describe the model for threshold signature schemes we use, rather informally, due to space limitations. In the type of schemes we consider there are l *servers* and one *client*. In the *generation phase* on input a security parameter k the public key pk and *secret key shares* $s_1, ..., s_l$ are created, where s_i belongs to server number i. There is a *signing protocol* defined for the servers and the client, which takes a message M as input and outputs (publically) a signature σ.[1] Finally, there is a *verification predicate* V, which is efficiently computable, takes pk, message M and signature σ as inputs, and returns *accept* or *reject*. Both

---

[1] Thus, we are in fact asuming (as usual in threshold signature schemes) that the client and servers agree on which message is to be signed. In practice, the implementation or application will have to ensure this. This is reflected in the model by not allowing the adversary to send inconsistent signing requests to servers, even if the client is corrupted.

the signing protocol and the verification predicate may make use of a random oracle (although most of the schemes we consider here do not).

To define security, we assume a polynomially bounded static and active adversary $\mathcal{A}$, who corrupts initially $t < l/2$ of the l servers, and possibly the client. Thus, the adversary always learns pk and the s_i's of corrupted servers. As the adversary's algorithm is executed, he may issue two types of requests:

- An *oracle request*, where he queries the random oracle used, he is then given the oracle's answer to the query he specified. Of course, this is only relevant if the protocol uses a random oracle.
- A signature request, where the adversary specifies a message M. This causes the signing protocol to be executed on input M, where the adversary controls the behaviour of corrupted servers and of the client if he is corrupt. The adversary will of course see whatever information is made public by honest servers.

At the end, $\mathcal{A}$ outputs a message M_0 and a signature σ_0.

We say the scheme is secure if the following two conditions hold for any adversary A:

Robustness: If the client is honest, each signature request results in the client computing a correct signature on M in expected polynomial time.

Unforgeability: The following happens with probability negligible in k: A outputs M_0, σ_0 such that M_0 was not used in a previous signature request, and $V(pk, M_0, \sigma_0) = accept$

3 Some Observations on Error Probabilities

Our first observations can be understood without bothering about the lower level details of threshold RSA schemes. So assume we start from the schemes of [25] or [8] which on a high level are completely similar: we are given as RSA public key n, e, and each of the l servers hold a share of the private key, s_i for the i'th server. In addition, there are some public verification keys, a global one v and a special verification key v_i for each server. These are used to verify that servers behave correctly. It is assumed that an adversary may initially corrupt up to $t < l/2$ servers and make them behave as he likes.

Given an input x to sign. We assume that x is the message as it looks after possible hashing and padding, so that the purpose is simply to compute the correct RSA root of x. We denote by H whatever process that leads from the actual message M to x, so that $x = H(M)$. Now, server i computes a signature share x_i, and gives a zero-knowledge proof $proof_i$, that x_i was correctly computed. Now, computing the signature takes place in two steps: First we discard all x_i corresponding to proofs that were rejected, leaving a set $\{x_i|\ i \in S_0\}$ of signature shares, where $S_0 = \{i|\ proof_i$ was accepted$\}$. We have $|S_0| \geq t + 1$, since at least $t + 1$ servers are honest. Second, we run an algorithm *Combine* on inputs $\{x_i|\ i \in S_0\}, m, n, e$ which is guaranteed to output the correct signature on m, if $|S_0| \geq t + 1$ and all shares in $\{x_i|\ i \in S_0\}$ are correct. This last condition is satisfied except with negligible probability since in [8, 25] the proofs are designed such that the adversary can give an acceptable proof for an incorrect x_i with only negligible probability.

Now, an initial observation – first made in [23] – is that since one can always verify if the output from R is correct, one can always compute the signature, even if no proofs were available:

- For every subset $S \subset \{1, 2, ..., l\}$ of size $t + 1$, do: Compute $sig := R(\{x_i| i \in S\}, m, n, e)$. If sig is a correct signature on m w.r.t. public key n, e, output sig and stop.

The problem with this algorithm is of course that it is inefficient for large l, t, in fact it takes exponential time in l, if $t \approx l/2$ because there are exponentially many subsets to try, so this may be unpleasant already for moderately large t, l.

However, a similar idea might still work, if we first use the proofs to reduce the number of incorrect signature shares from t down to something "sufficiently close" to 0. Our main point is that this can be done, even if there is a *non-negligible* chance of giving an acceptable proof for a bad signature share. We do the following:

Algorithm **Extended-Combine**

- For all $i = 1..l$ receive signature share x_i from server i, and let server i give a proof $proof_i$ that x_i is correct. Let $S_0 = \{i| proof_i$ was accepted$\}$.
- For every subset $S \subset S_0$ of size $t + 1$, do: Compute $sig := Combine(\{x_i| i \in S\}, m, n, e)$, where $Combine$ is the algorithm mentioned above. If sig is a correct signature on m w.r.t. public key n, e, output sig and stop.

Assume a worst case situation, where t is maximal, so that we have only $t+1$ honest servers, and furthermore all corrupt servers supply incorrect signature shares. Let $p(t)$ be the soundness error for the interactive proofs that servers use to prove correctness of signature shares. In other words, if a signature share x_i is incorrect, then the proof given by server i is accepted with probability at most $p(t)$ (we assume we can control this error probability so that it is some function of t). Then, for any $i \in \{0, 1, ..., t\}$, the probability that i of the t proofs for incorrect signature schares are accepted is at most $\binom{t}{i}p(t)^i(1 - p(t))^{t-i}$. If i proofs are accepted, S_0 contains $t + 1 + i$ signature shares, and we need to find the subset of size $t+1$ corresponding to the $t+1$ correct signature shares. Hence, the expected time spent to compute the signature using the algorithm sketched above is proportional to (at most)

$$E(t) := \sum_{i=0}^{t} \binom{t+1+i}{t+1}\binom{t}{i}p(t)^i(1 - p(t))^{t-i}$$

Lemma 1. *If $p(t) \leq 1/ct^2$ for some constant $c > 2$, then (as a function of l and and t), the expected number of subsets tested by $Extended - Combine$ is in $O(1)$.*

Proof. It is sufficient to show that $E(t)$ is in $O(1)$. Choose a c' such that $2 < c' < c$, then for any $t > 1/(c' - 2)$:

$$E(t) = \sum_{i=0}^{t} \binom{t+1+i}{t+1} \binom{t}{i} p(t)^i (1 - p(t))^{t-i} \tag{1}$$

$$\leq \sum_{i=0}^{t} \binom{t+1+i}{t+1} \binom{t}{i} p(t)^i \tag{2}$$

$$\leq \sum_{i=0}^{t} (t+1+i)^i t^i p(t)^i \tag{3}$$

$$\leq \sum_{i=0}^{t} (c't)^i t^i p(t)^i \tag{4}$$

$$= \sum_{i=0}^{t} (c't^2 p(t))^i \tag{5}$$

$$\leq \sum_{i=0}^{t} (c't^2 \frac{1}{ct^2})^i \tag{6}$$

$$= \sum_{i=0}^{t} (\frac{c'}{c})^i \tag{7}$$

$$= \frac{1 - (c'/c)^{t+1}}{1 - c'/c} \tag{8}$$

$$\leq \frac{1}{1 - c'/c} \tag{9}$$

In (3) we use the fact that $\binom{a}{b} \leq a^b$. In (4) we use the assumption about t and the fact $i \leq t$. In (6) we use the assumption about $p(t)$ In (8) we use the well known formula $\sum_{i=0}^{n} x^i = \frac{1-x^{n+1}}{1-x}$ for $x \neq 1$.

We remark that concrete caluations suggest that it may be possible to prove this lemma assuming $p(t) \leq 1/ct^a$ for a slightly smaller than 2, but that $a = 1$ would not work.

4   A Threshold RSA Scheme

The scheme we describe in this section follows to a large extent the approach of [8, 25]. The new ingredient is the way in which signatures shares are verified, where we use the observations we made in the previous section. Concretely, this means that the zero-knowledge proofs given for correctness of signature shares are interactive, using 3 moves. But on the other hand, since we can make do with a non-negligible soundness error, we only need short random challenges from the verifier, and this means that the proofs can be shown to be zero-knowledge and sound in the standard model without using random oracles.

4.1 Key Set-Up

We describe here the setup of keys as a trusted dealer D would do it. However, this dealer can be replaced by any of the known distributed RSA key generation protocols. Using a particular such protocol may affect slightly the way the secret sharing of the secret exponent is done (see below). Any such change can easily be accomodated, however.

1. D chooses a k-bit RSA modulus $n = pq$ where the primes p, q satisfy that $(p-1)/2, (q-1)/2$ have no prime factors less than $3t^2$, where t is the maximal number of corrupted servers we want to tolerate. Let l be the total number of servers, and $\Delta = l!$. In addition, $\phi(n)$ must be prime to the public exponent e, which must be a prime such that $e > l$. We set $d = e^{-1} \bmod \phi(n)$.
2. D chooses a random polynomial $f(x)$ of degree at most t with integer coefficients, such that $f(0) = d$;

$$f(x) = d + c_1 x + ... + c_t x^t$$

where the c_i's are random independent integers chosen from the interval $[0..\Delta n 2^t 2^L]$, where L is a secondary security parameter. The secret share of the i'th server is $s_i = f(i)$. With the given choice of coefficients, it can be shown that, if we compare the distribution of any t shares resulting from sharing d with the one resulting from sharing any other d', the statistical distance between the two is at most 2^{-L} [19].
3. D chooses a random square v modulo n. For the i'th server, the verification key v_i is $v_i = v^{\Delta s_i} \bmod n$.
4. The public information is now $n, e, v, v_1, ..., v_l$, while each server i has s_i as its private information.

Note that by construction of n, any square modulo n has order not divisible by any prime less than $3t^2$.

4.2 An Auxiliary Protocol

Suppose we are given elements in Z_n^*, v, w, α, β. Also given is an integer B of size polynomial in k, the security parameter. We assume it is guranteed that the orders of v, w, α and β are not divisible by any prime less than B. Finally, a prover P is given an integer s such that $v^s = w \bmod n$, and now P wants to convince us that $\alpha^s = \beta \bmod n$. We use the following variant of a standard protocol (a similar protocol was used in [13, 8, 25]):

1. P chooses r, a random integer of bitlength $\log_2(s) + \log_2(B) + L$. and sends $a = v^r, b = \alpha^r$.
2. The verifier chooses a random challenge c, with $0 \le c < B$.
3. P replies by sending $z = r + cs$
4. To check the proof, one verifies that $v^z = aw^c$ and $\alpha^z = b\beta^c$.

It is trivial to see that if $\alpha^s = \beta$ and P follows the protocol, the verifier will always accept. Moreover, a standard rewinding argument shows that the protocol is statistical zero-knowledge, since the number of challenges is polynomial and r is chosen to be exponentially (in L) larger than cs. For the soundness part, we have the following result, which asserts that if the claim is wrong, then the prover can only have the verifier accept with unusually large probability if he can solve a supposedly hard problem:

Lemma 2. *Let $n, v, w, \alpha, \beta, s, B$ be given as described above, and suppose $\alpha^s \neq \beta \bmod n$. Let P^* be any prover in the above protocol, and fix any set of random coins for P^*. If the probability (given these random coins) that the verifier accepts is larger than $1/B$, then: using P^* as oracle, one can easily compute either a μ'th root of v modulo n , $1 < \mu < B$, or a multiple of the order of v in Z_n^*.*

Remark 1. A very similar protocol and analysis was presented in [13]. The difference is that here, we are satisfied with a non-negligible error probability and hence we can use small challenges. This is what implies that to break the soundness, the adversary must find a root of v with "public exponent" in a very small set (between 1 and B). We can therefore base security essentially on the standard RSA assumption, rather than the strong RSA assumption as in [13].

Proof. The claimed algorithm will simply send all possible challenges to P^* (rewinding in between) and record all answers. Since the number of possible challenges is B and the accept probability was larger than $1/B$, we must get good answers to at least 2 distinct challenges c, c'. So we have values a, b, c, c', z, z' such that $v^z = aw^c$, $\alpha^z = b\beta^c$, $v^{z'} = aw^{c'}$ and $\alpha^{z'} = b\beta^{c'}$ (all equations modulo n). It follows that

$$v^{z-z'} = w^{c-c'}, \quad \alpha^{z-z'} = \beta^{c-c'}.$$

Now, let $d = gcd(z - z', c - c') < B$. By assumption on the orders of v, w, α, β

$$v^{(z-z')/d} = w^{(c-c')/d}, \quad \alpha^{(z-z')/d} = \beta^{(c-c')/d}.$$

Now, if $d < c - c'$, take integers γ, δ such that $1 = \gamma(z - z')/d + \delta(c - c')/d$. Using the relation we just derived, we get:

$$v = v^{\gamma(z-z')/d + \delta(c-c')/d} = (w^\gamma v^\delta)^{(c-c')/d}$$

which is, as promised, a non trivial μ'th root of v, where $\mu = (c - c')/d$. On the other hand, if $d = c - c'$, we have in fact that

$$v^{(z-z')/(c-c')} = w, \quad \alpha^{(z-z')/(c-c')} = \beta.$$

It must be the case that $s \neq (z - z')/(c - c')$ since otherwise we get a contradiction with $\alpha^s \neq \beta$, so this and $v^s = w$ implies that the order of v divides $s - (z - z')/(c - c')$.

4.3   Signing a Message

We can now describe how the threshold RSA scheme will work. We give first a basic version, which we later show how to modify to get a more practical scheme or to reduce the necessary assumptions.

- When a client requests that message $x = H(M)$ be signed, server i will compute a signature share as $x_i = x^{2\Delta s_i} \bmod n$.
- The server then proves that x_i is correct. This proof will consist of proving in ZK that the discrete log of x_i^2 base x^4 equals the discrete log of v_i base v (namely Δs_i), although the proof will have a non-negligible error probability. For this we may use the auxiliary protocol given above, with parameters $n, B = 3t^2, v, w = v_i, \alpha = x^4 \bmod n, \beta = x_i^2 \bmod n$ and $s = \Delta s_i$. It is easy to see that with our choices of n, v, this will satisfy the conditions we stated for the auxiliary protocol.
- The client now attempts to find a $t + 1$-subset of signature shares with accepted proofs that leads to the correct signature being computed, i.e., we use the $Extended - Combine$ from the previous section. Concretely, let S be a $t + 1$-subset of the indices $1, .., l$, and define interpolation coefficients

$$\lambda_{0,j}^S = \Delta \prod_{i \in S \setminus \{j\}} \frac{i}{i - j}$$

These are integers, and we have $d\Delta = f(0)\Delta = \sum_{j \in S} \lambda_{0,j}^S s_j$. If for all signature shares in S, it is indeed the case that server's claim about x_i is true, i.e., $(x^4)^{\Delta s_i} = x_i^2 \bmod n$, then we can compute

$$\omega = \prod_{j \in S} x_j^{2\lambda_{0,j}^S} = x^{4\Delta^2 d} \bmod n$$

- Note that $\omega^e = x^{4\Delta^2} \bmod n$. But since e is prime to $4\Delta^2$, we can take integers a, b such that $a4\Delta^2 + be = 1$. It now follows easily that $y = \omega^a x^b \bmod n$ is the desired RSA signature, provided the subset we tried consisted of correct signature shares. If the signature does not verify, we try the next subset.

We base the security on the following assumptions. First a variant of the standard RSA assumption:

Conjecture 1. Let a k-bit RSA modulus n and t chosen as described above be given, and let $w \in Z_n^*$ be uniformly chosen. Given this input, any probabilistic polynomial time algorithm computes a μ'th root of $w \bmod n$, where $1 < \mu < 3t^2$, with negligible probability (in k).

The only difference to standard RSA is that the public exponent is not fixed to a single value but must be in a small given set. This is in contrast to the *strong* RSA assumption, where the adversary can choose an arbitrary public exponent.

Conjecture 2. Let n, e, t be chosen as described above be given and let $w \in Z_n^*$ be uniformly chosen. Suppose an oracle is also given that on input message M will return y such that $y^e = H(M) \bmod n$. Given this input and oracle, any probabilistic polynomial time algorithm computes a μ'th root of $w \bmod n$, where $1 < \mu < 3t^2$, with negligible probability.

The second assumption is clearly at least as strong as the first, but they may well be equivalent, namely if access to the e'th root oracle does not help to compute μ'th roots. This seems reasonable since e is by assumption prime to any allowed μ-value, and the adversary cannot even choose freely the numbers on which e'th roots are computed. Indeed, if we model H as a (full domain)random oracle, the assumptions are provably equivalent since then, using standard tricks, the e'th root oracle is easy to implement without knowing the factors of n.

The basic variant of the threshold RSA scheme that we already presented can be proved secure under Conjecture 2. Before doing this, we need two auxiliary lemmas:

Lemma 3. *Let n, e, distributed as the honest dealer chooses them, be given. Furthermore, let w, a random square in Z_n^* be given. Based on this, the information the adversary learns from the honest dealer initially can be simulated efficiently with a statistically close distribution, and with $v = w^e \bmod n$.*

Proof. Note that the information seen by the adversary is n, e, v, the shares of corrupted players, and the public verification values v_i of all players.

We begin by setting $v = w^e \bmod n$, and so we have $w = v^d \bmod n$. Without loss of generality, assume the adversary corrupts the first t players. Perform now a sharing of an arbitrary value d' (say, $d' = 1$) according to the algorithm used by the dealer, and let $s_1, ..., s_t$ be the shares for the corrupted players resulting from this. By the privacy of the secret sharing, this is statistically close to the distribution resulting from sharing the correct d. Hence, except with negligible probability, there exists a polynomial $f(x)$ of degree at most t and with coefficients in the correct range, such that $f(0) = d$ and $f(i) = s_i, i = 1...t$. So we have $w = v^d = v^{f(0)} \bmod n$. Define $S = \{0, 1, ..., t\}$. Recall that we earlier defined $\lambda_{i,j}^S$, the standard Lagrange interpolation coefficients multiplied by Δ. We can now compute, for honest plyer i:

$$w \cdot \prod_{j=1}^{t}(v^{s_j})^{\lambda_{i,j}^S} = \prod_{j=0}^{t}(v^{f(j)})^{\lambda_{i,j}^S} = v^{\Delta f(i)}$$

which is by definition exactly the public verification values that results for honest players when the dealer chooses $f(x)$ for the sharing of d. We can therefore output $n, e, s_1, ..., s_t, v, v^{\Delta f(1)}, ..., v^{\Delta f(l)}$.

Lemma 4. *Assume we are given a set of values distributed by the honest dealer to the adversary, i.e., $n, e, v, v_1, v_2, ..., v_l$ and the s_i's sent to the corrupt servers. Let also a message M, and the signature $H(M)^d \bmod n$ be given. Based on this, the contributions from honest servers in the protocol where M is signed can be simulated efficiently with the correct distribution.*

Proof. Let $f(x)$ be the polynomial used by the dealer to share d. Since we are given $H(M)^d = H(M)^{f(0)} \bmod n$, and we know the shares of corrupted players, we can compute what we need by interpolation "in the exponent" similarly to the proof of the previous lemma. Assume without loss of generality that the first t players are corrupt. We then compute, for honest player i:

$$\prod_{j=0}^{t}(H(M)^{f(j)})^{\lambda_{i,j}^{S}} = H(M)^{\Delta f(i)}$$

which is by definition the signature share contributed by this player.

Theorem 1. *The threshold RSA scheme defined in this section is secure under Conjecture 2 and assuming the underlying RSA signature scheme is chosen message attack secure. In the random oracle model, we can replace Conjecture 2 by Conjecture 1.*

Proof. We will show that if there exists an adversary A that breaks the above threshold RSA scheme, there exists an expected poly-time adversary A' that either breaks the underlying RSA signature scheme under a chosen message attack, or contradicts Conjecture 2.

Our claimed adversary A' will be given just public key n, e and access to an e'th root oracle, or equivalently, a chosen message attack on the underlying signature scheme. Then A' will start a copy of A, choose w as a random square modulo n and run the simulation from Lemma 3 and in this way produce values v, v_i for everyone, and s_i for those t servers A wanted to corrupt.

When A wants to have some x signed, A' uses the chosen message attack to get a signature on x, uses Lemma 4 to compute the x_i of honest servers and the zero-knowledge property to simulate their proofs. Note that if the client is corrupt, this involves simulating the proofs of honest servers where A acts as verifier. If the client is honest, A' just executes the normal client algorithm. In this way, A' simulates an entire execution of A and outputs whatever A outputs.

Note that to break the threshold scheme, A must either violate robustness or unforgeability. Since A' does a statistically close simulation of A's attack, either event happens with essentially the same probability in A''s execution as in real life.

Assume first that A violates robustness. Since the client by definition keeps going until it finds a correct signature (and eventually it will always succeed), A can only violate this property by creating a situation whete the expected time spent by the client is larger than specified. By Lemma 1, this can only happen, if at least one incorrect signature share is accepted with probability larger than $1/ct^2$, which is $1/3t^2$ in this particular case. By Lemma 2, this implies that either that we can find a μ'th root of v where $1 < \mu < 3t^2$, and hence of w since $w = v^e \bmod n$ and e is guaranteed to be prime to μ. Or we can find a multiple of the order of v and hence of w. Note that instead of choosing w, A' could take a random input and use this as w. Such an input will be a square with large probability $(1/4)$. Hence, in the first case, we can directly break Conjecture 2, in the second case we note that ability to find the order of random elements in Z_n^* implies we can factor n using a well known reduction, and so we can in particular break Conjecture 2.

Now, assume A violates unforgeability and not robustness. This clearly means that A' runs in expected polynomial time, and produces with non-negligible probability a new message with valid signature. Since A' runs only with access to a chosen message attack on the underlying signature scheme, we have broken this scheme.

4.4   An "Optimistic" Variant

We show how to modify the basic scheme so it becomes more efficient and also non-interactive in case the severs behave correctly, which in a practical scenario is likely to be the case almost all the time.

The client will send requests to the servers to sign x. Each server returns x_i, a_i where a_i is the first message in the proof of correctness for x_i. Moreover, the randomness used in computing a_i is computed by applying a pseudorandom function on x. That is, the random coins are computed as $\phi_{K_i}(x)$ where K_i is a secret key server i stores together with its secret share s_i, and $\phi.(\cdot)$ is a pseudorandom function (say, built from AES encryption). The client tries to compute the signature, assuming all servers sent correct x_i's. If it fails, it sends requests to the servers for proofs that the x_i's were correct, including x, x_i and challenge e in the request to server i. The servers can verify that indeed $x_i = x^{2\Delta s_i} \bmod n$, and if so, recompute a_i using the pseudorandom function. The proofs can then be completed exactly as in the original scheme.

Note that servers do not need to remember anything from the intial request to sign x, the proof can be conducted only from the public data, x, x_i and the private values s_i, K_i. This idea can also be used with the two variants given below.

4.5   A Variant Based on Reduced Assumptions

In this subsection, we present a variant that can be proved secure, only from Conjecture 1, without relying on random oracles. It is less efficient than the basic one, but only by a constant factor. We only sketch the solution informally.

The idea is to use 2 RSA moduli n, n', chosen independently but of the same form as in previous sections. The public exponent e is defined w.r.t. n, the secret key is shared as before, and signature shares are still computed as $x_i = x^{2\Delta^2 s_i} \bmod n$.

The change applies to the way in which we verify the signature shares. We generate a public key modulo n' for the integer commitment scheme of [6], i.e., $h, g \in Z_{n'}^*$, such that h is random square modulo n' and $g = h^z \bmod n'$ for secret z. Then the verification key v_i is a commitment to s_i under public key n', g, h, i.e., $v_i = g^{s_i} h^{r_i} \bmod n'$ for random r_i of suitable size, given to server i initially. This commitment scheme is unconditionally hiding, and is binding relative to the RSA assumption.

Note that since commitments are always random elements in the group generated by h (no matter the value committed to) it is easy to simulate the v_i's without knowing the s_i's. Therefore results analogous to Lemmas 3,4 also hold in this scenario.

Now, in [6], a protocol of the standard 3-move form is presented for proving knowledge of how to open a commitment. An easy modification of this protocol also allows proving that the contents of a commitment is the same as a given discrete log, for instance the one defined by input x and a signature share x_i.

Soudness of this protocol is proved in [6] relative to the strong RSA assumption. However, in our scenario, we can make do with a larger error probability, in particular, challenges for this protocol are chosen between 0 and B. Therefore, the proof of soundness from [6] now works relative to Conjecture 1 (w.r.t n'). We can therefore prove security of this new scheme following the same strategy as for the basic one. In particular, if we are given an adversary that breaks robustness, this implies we can break Conjecture 1 w.r.t. n', assuming we are given an oracle that generates signatures w.r.t. n. But we can then do a reduction that it takes n' as input, generates n with known factors, and does the generation of secret exponent and secret shares itself. This means that requests to sign messages can be handled without any oracle access, and so security follows from Conjecture 1 alone.

4.6   A Variant Using Any RSA Modulus

The basic scheme imposes some restrictions on the RSA moduli that can be used. In this section we describe a variant that can use a completely arbitrary RSA modulus and can be proved secure assuming only that the underlying RSA signature scheme is secure.

This is done using the basic scheme we already described, with only one difference: in the proofs of correctness of a signature share, we use the auxiliary protocol from Section 4.2 with a 1-bit challenge, instead of choosing it in $[0..B[$. The protocol is then repeated in parallel $\log B$ times (where we choose as before $B = 3t^2$, and t is the number of corruptible servers). More precisely, given x_i that is to be verified against x, v, v_i, the server starts $\log B$ copies of the auxiliary protocol, sends the initial messages $a_i^{(1)}, ..., a_i^{(\log B)}$, the client sends a random $\log B$-bit challenge $b_1, ..., b_{\log B}$ and the server answers this, using b_j as challenge in the j'th instance of the protocol.

Now, if a server can answer more than one challenge, there is at least one instance j where it can answer both $b_j = 0$ and $b_j = 1$. It is now trivial to see from the proof of Lemma 2 that given such answers, and if the server's claim is false, one can find a multiple of the order of v, and hence factor n, without assuming anything about the form of n, except that it is a valid RSA modulus. Hence the proof of security of this modified scheme goes through in exactly the same way as before. The only difference is that in this case we know that if the verification of the signature shares fail, the adversary can factor n, and hence also break the underlying signature scheme (in the basic scheme, we can only prove he can break Conjecture 2). We obtain:

Theorem 2. *The modified threshold RSA scheme defined in this section is secure no matter how the RSA modulus is chosen, assuming the underlying RSA signature scheme is chosen message attack secure.*

Note that it is not known how to use arbitrary RSA moduli for threshold RSA unless 1-bit challenge proofs are used. Furthermore, without the observations we made earlier about the required error probability, one would need to repeat the 1-bit challenge protocol enough times to make the error probability be negligible, e.g., k repetitions where k is the security parameter. Being able able to do with $\log B = \log 3 + 2 \log t$ iterations will be a significant advantage in most practical cases.

5   General Applications of the Main Idea

Let us try to generalize the basic idea from this paper to other threshold cryptosystems or signature schemes. Let the input be x, and suppose server i contributes string x_i that hopefully enables decryption or signing of x. We will assume that we have $t + 1$ honest servers and at most t corrupt ones. Suppose finally that the servers prove interactively that each x_i is correct, that the soundness error for these proofs satisfy the bound stated in Lemma 1, and that from any set of $t + 1$ correct contributions, we can easily decrypt or sign x.

Lemma 1 now guarantees us that we can compute the correct output efficiently, by searching exhaustively through all $t + 1$-subsets of the accepted contributions; *assuming, however, that we can recognize the correct subset when we get to it during the exhaustive search.*

For a signature scheme, this is easy because we can tentatively assume that the subset is correct, attempt to produce a signature, and verify the output value using the public verification key. The same is true for most RSA encryption schemes, namely those that map a message m to some number $y(m,r) \in Z_n$ where r denotes some random coins chosen internally by the decryption process, n is the modulus, and where the ciphertext is $x = y(m,r)^e \bmod n$. In such a case, each guess at a subset will produce a candidate value for $y(m,e)$ which can be checked by verifying the relation $x = y(m,r)^e \bmod n$.

For a probabilistic encryption scheme such as El-Gamal, however, the situation is less clear. The problem is that for El Gamal and related encryption schemes, one cannot easily check whether a given plaintext is contained in a given ciphertext. Simply encrypting the suggested plaintext m under the public key most likely results in a ciphertext different from x even if m was the correct answer.

However, if $t < l/3$ where l is the total number of servers, there is an alternative way to recognize the set of correct contributions: for threshold El-Gamal, like for most threshold cryptosystems, we have for a correct contribution x_j that $x_j = x^{s_j}$ where s_j is a secret exponent held by server i, and where in fact $s_j = f(j)$ where f is a polynomial of degree at most t over some finite field, typically $GF(q)$ for a prime q in case of threshold El-Gamal encryption.

Now, by the assumption $t < l/3$ we have in the worst case t incorrect contributions and $2t + 1$ correct ones. Some of the incorrect contributions will be discarded by the proofs of correctness, and among the remaining ones, we can search for a subset of $2t + 1$ values x_j, such that all x_j's in the subset are of form $x_j = x^{f'(j)}$ for a polynomial f' of degree at most t. This can be verified by Lagrange interpolation: assume without loss of generality that $\{x_i | i = 1...2t+1\}$ is the set we are checking. Then, for $i > t + 1$, and any polynomial f' of degree at most t, we have $f'(i) = \sum_{j=1}^{t+1} \alpha_{i,j} f'(j)$ for fixed and public coefficients $\alpha_{i,j}$. We can therefore verify for all $i = t+2, ..., 2t+1$ that $x_i = \prod_{j=1}^{t+1} x_j^{\alpha_{i,j}}$. Assuming this verifies for all $i = t+2, ..., 2t+1$, we know that the subset is of the required form. It is now easy to see that since $t < l/3$, the polynomial f' we implicitly define here must agree with the polynomial f defined by the honest players in at least t+1 points, hence $f = f'$ and therefore the plaintext suggested by this subset is correct.

For this situation, we can do a computation similar to the one for Lemma 1. We obtain that is this case, the expected number of subsets to test is in $O(1)$ if the soundness error of the correctness proofs is at most $1/ct^2$ where $c > 3$.

References

1. Algesheimer, Camenisch and Shoup: *Efficient computations modulo a shared secret with applications to generation of shared safe-prime products*, proc. of Crypto 2002.
2. D. Boneh and M. Franklin *Efficient generation of shared RSA keys*, Proc. of Crypto' 97, Springer-Verlag LNCS series, nr. 1233.
3. R. Canetti, *Security and Composition of Multiparty Cryptographic Protocols*, Journal of Cryptology, vol.13, 2000. On-line version at http://philby.ucsd.edu/cryptolib/1998/98-18.html.
4. R.Canetti, *A unified framework for analyzing security of protocols*, Cryptology Eprint archive 2000/67, http://eprint.iacr.org/2000/067.ps
5. Cramer and Damgård: *Secret-Key Zero-Knowledge*, Proc. of TCC 2003, Springer Verlag LNCS.
6. Damgård and Fujisaki: *A statistically hiding integer commitment scheme based on groups with hidden order*, proc. of AsiaCrypt 2002.
7. Damgård and Jurik: *A Generalization and some Applications of Paillier's Probabilistic Public-key System*, to appear in Public Key Cryptography 2001.
8. Damgård and Koprowski: *Practical threshold RSA signatures without a trusted dealer*, Proc. of EuroCrypt 2001.
9. Alfredo De Santis, Yvo Desmedt, Yair Frankel, Moti Yung: *How to share a function securely*, STOC 1994: 522-533
10. Yair Frankel, Peter Gemmell, Philip D. MacKenzie and Moti Yung *Optimal-Resilience Proactive Public-Key Cryptosystems* Proc. of FOCS 97.
11. Yair Frankel, Philip D. MacKenzie and Moti Yung *Robust Efficient Distributed RSA-Key Generation*, Proc. of STOC 98.
12. P. Fouque, G. Poupard, J. Stern: *Sharing Decryption in the Context of Voting or Lotteries*, Proceedings of Financial Crypto 2000.
13. E. Fujisaki and E. Okamoto: *Statistical Zero-Knowledge Protocols to prove Modular Polynomial Relations*, proc. of Crypto 97, Springer Verlag LNCS series 1294.
14. Pierre-Alain Fouque and Jacques Stern: *Fully Distributed Threshold RSA under Standard Assumptions*, IACR Cryptology ePrint Archive: Report 2001/008, February 2001
15. Gennaro, Jarecki, Krawczyk and Rabin: *Secure Distributed Key Generation for Discrete-Log Based Cryptosystems*, Proc. of EuroCrypt 99, Springer Verlag LNCS series, nr. 1592.
16. Gennaro, Rabin, Jarecki and Krawczyk: *Robust and Efficient Sharing of RSA Functions*, J.Crypt. vol.13, no.2.
17. Shingo Miyazaki, Kouichi Sakurai and Moti Yung *On Threshold RSA-Signing with no Dealer*, Proc. of ICISC 1999, Springer Verlag LNCS series, nr.1787.
18. Brian King: *Improved Methods to Perform Threshold RSA.*, ASIACRYPT 2000, pp.359-372, Springer Verlag LNCS.
19. M. Koprowski: *Threshold Integer Secret Sharing*, manuscript, 2003.

20. P.Pallier: *Public-Key Cryptosystems based on Composite Degree Residue Classes,* Proceedings of EuroCrypt 99, Springer Verlag LNCS series, pp. 223-238.
21. Pedersen: *A Threshold cryptosystem without a trusted third party,* proc. of Euro-Crypt 91, Springer Verlag LNCS nr. 547.
22. T.Rabin: *A Simplified Approach to Threshold and Proactive RSA,* proc. of Crypto 98, Springer Verlag LNCS 1462.
23. M.K.Reiter and K.P.Birman: *How to securely replicate services,* ACM Transactions on programming languages and systems 1994, vol 16, nr.3, pp.986–1009.
24. J. B. Rosser and L. Schoenfeld: *Approximate formulas for some functions of prime numbers,* Ill. J. Math. 6 (1962), 64–94.
25. Victor Shoup *Practical Threshold Signatures,* Proceedings of EuroCrypt 2000, Springer Verlag LNCS series nr. 1807.

Improved Identity-Based Signcryption

Liqun Chen[1] and John Malone-Lee[2]

[1] Hewlett-Packard Laboratories, Filton Road,
Stoke Gifford, Bristol, BS34 8QZ, UK
liqun.chen@hp.com
[2] University of Bristol, Department of Computer Science,
Woodland Road, Brsitol, BS8 1UB, UK
malone@cs.bris.ac.uk

Abstract. Identity-based cryptography is form of public-key cryptography that does not require users to pre-compute key pairs and obtain certificates for their public keys. Instead, public keys can be arbitrary identifiers such as email addresses. This means that the corresponding private keys are derived, at any time, by a trusted private key generator. The idea of signcryption is to provide a method to encrypt and sign data together in a way that is more efficient than using an encryption scheme combined with a signature scheme.

We present an identity-based signcryption solution that we believe is the most efficient, provably-secure scheme of its type proposed to date. Our scheme admits proofs of security in the random oracle model under the bilinear Diffie-Hellman assumption using the definitions proposed by Boyen.

1 Introduction

Two of the most important services offered by cryptography are those of providing private and authenticated communications. Much research has been done into creating encryption schemes to meet highly developed notions of privacy [3, 16]. Similarly, designing unforgeable signature schemes to give authenticity and non-repudiation is also a well studied problem [10]. It is possible to combine encryption schemes and signature schemes, using methods such as those described in [1], to obtain private and authenticated communications.

In 1997, Zheng proposed a primitive that he called *signcryption* [20]. The idea of a signcryption scheme is to combine the functionality of an encryption scheme with that of a signature scheme. It must provide privacy; signcryptions must be unforgeable; and there must be a method to settle repudiation disputes. This must be done in a more efficient manner than a composition of an encryption scheme with a signature scheme. Along with the concept, Zheng also proposed an efficient, discrete logarithm based scheme.

The first formal security treatment for signcryption appeared in [1]. This work formalised notions of privacy and unforgeability. Subsequently, several provably secure signcryption schemes have been designed, for example [12].

S. Vaudenay (Ed.): PKC 2005, LNCS 3386, pp. 362–379, 2005.

The concept *identity-based cryptography* was proposed by Shamir in 1984 [18]. The idea of an identity-based system is that public keys can be derived from arbitrary strings. This means that if a user has a string corresponding to its identity, this string can be used to derive the user's public key. For this to work there is a *trusted authority* (TA henceforth) that generates private keys using some master key related to the global parameters for the system. In [18] Shamir proposed an identity-based signature scheme, but for many years identity-based encryption remained an open problem. The problem was solved nearly two decades after it was originally proposed [5,9]. In [9] Cocks proposed a solution based on quadratic residuosity and in [5] Boneh and Franklin gave a scheme using bilinear pairings on elliptic curves. It is pairings on elliptic curves that have become the most popular building block for identity-based cryptography and many schemes have been designed using this primitive.

The idea of *identity-based signcryption* was first proposed by Malone-Lee in [13] along with a security model. This model dealt with notions of privacy and unforgeability. A weakness in the scheme from [13] was subsequently pointed out by Libert and Quisquater in [11] where a new scheme was proposed. The new scheme came with proofs of security in the model of [13]. This model was developed by Boyen in [6]. Three new security notions were added: *ciphertext unlinkability*, *ciphertext authentication* and *ciphertext anonymity*. We discuss these notions in Section 3. Boyen also proposed a scheme in [6] and analysed it in the enhanced model.

We take the model from [6] as the starting point for this work. We describe a scheme that admits security proofs in this model. We show that our scheme compares favourably with other provably-secure signcryption schemes in the literature.

The paper proceeds as follows. In Section 2 we formally define what we mean by identity-based signcryption. Section 3 recalls the security model from [6]. We present our scheme in Section 4 and provide security results for it in Section 5. A comparison is made with existing schemes in Section 6. The paper ends with some concluding remarks.

2   Identity-Based Signcryption

Before formally defining what we mean by identity-based signcryption we describe the notation that we will use throughout the paper.

Notation. Let S be a set. We write $v \leftarrow S$ to denote the action of sampling from the uniform distribution on S and assigning the result to the variable v. If S contains one element s we use $v \leftarrow s$ as shorthand for $v \leftarrow \{s\}$. If $\mathcal{A}$ is an algorithm we denote the action of running $\mathcal{A}$ on input I and assigning the resulting output to the variable v by $v \leftarrow \mathcal{A}(I)$.

If E is an event defined in some probability space, we denote the probability that E occurs by $\mathbf{Pr}[E]$ (assuming the probability space is understood from the context). Let $\mathbb{Z}_q$ denote the non-negative integers modulo q and let $\mathbb{Z}_q^*$ denote the corresponding multiplicative group.

An identity-based signcryption scheme consists of the following six algorithms: **Setup**, **Extract**, **Sign**, **Encrypt**, **Decrypt** and **Verify**. We describe the functions of each below.

- **Setup:** On input of a security parameter 1^k the TA uses this algorithm to produce a pair (params, s), where params are the global public parameters for the system and s is the master secret key. The public parameters include a global public key Q_{TA}. We will assume that params are publicly known so that we do not need to explicitly provide them as input to other algorithms.
- **Extract:** On input of an identity ID_U and the master secret key s, the TA uses this algorithm to compute a secret key S_U corresponding to ID_U.
- **Sign:** User A with identity ID_A and secret key S_A uses this algorithm with input (m, S_A) to produce a signature σ on m valid under the public key derived from ID_A. It also produces some ephemeral data r.
- **Encrypt:** On input of $(S_A, ID_B, m, \sigma, r)$, ID_A uses this algorithm to produce a ciphertext c. This is the encryption of m, and ID_A's signature on m, which can be decrypted using the secret key of the user with identity ID_B.
- **Decrypt:** User B with identity ID_B and secret key S_B uses this algorithm with input (c, S_B) to produces (m, ID_A, σ) where m is a message and σ is a purported signature by ID_A on m.
- **Verify:** On input of (m, ID_A, σ), this algorithm outputs $\top$ if σ is ID_A's signature on m and it outputs $\bot$ otherwise.

The above algorithms have the following consistency requirement. If

$$(m, \sigma, r) \leftarrow \textbf{Sign}(m, S_A), \ c \leftarrow \textbf{Encrypt}(S_A, ID_B, m, \sigma, r) \text{ and}$$

$$(\hat{m}, I\hat{D}_A, \hat{\sigma}) \leftarrow \textbf{Decrypt}(c, S_B),$$

then we must have

$$I\hat{D}_A = ID_A, \ m = \hat{m} \text{ and } \top \leftarrow \textbf{Verify}(\hat{m}, I\hat{D}_A, \hat{\sigma}).$$

Note that in some models for signcryption [20] and identity-based signcryption [13,11], the **Sign** and **Encrypt** algorithms are treated as one "signcryption" algorithm, as are the **Decrypt** and **Verify** algorithms. Our scheme supports a separation and so we stick with the above definition as in [6]. One advantage of this approach, where it is possible, is that it makes non-repudiation of messages a straightforward consequence of unforgeability. This follows from the fact that after decryption there is a publicly verifiable signature that can be forwarded to a third party.

3   Security Notions

In this section we review the security model for identity-based signcryption proposed in [6]. This model uses the notions of *insider security* and *outsider security* from [1]. Informally insider security is security against a legitimate user of the scheme while outsider security is security against an outside third party. Where appropriate, this makes insider security a stronger notion. We will comment on the significance of the distinction at relevant points in this section.

3.1   Ciphertext Authentication

A scheme offering ciphertext authentication provides the guarantee to the recipient of a signed and encrypted message that the message was encrypted by the same person who signed it. This means that the ciphertext must have been encrypted throughout the transmission and so it cannot have been the victim of a successful man-in-the-middle attack. It also implies that the signer chose the recipient for its signature.

We define this notion via a game played by a challenger and an adversary.

Game

- **Initial:** The challenger runs **Setup**(1^k) and gives the resulting **params** to the adversary. It keeps s secret.
- **Probing:** The challenger is probed by the adversary who makes the following queries.
  - **Sign/Encrypt:** The adversary submits a sender identity, a receiver identity and a message to the challenger. The challenger responds with the signature of the sender on the message, encrypted under the public key of the receiver.
  - **Decrypt/Verify:** The adversary submits a ciphertext and a receiver identity to the challenger. The challenger decrypts the ciphertext under the secret key of the receiver. It then verifies that the resulting decryption is a valid message/signature pair under the public key of the decrypted identity. If so the challenger returns the message, its signature and the identity of the signer, otherwise it returns $\perp$.
  - **Extract:** The adversary submits an identity to the challenger. The challenger responds with the secret key of that identity.
- **Forge:** The adversary returns a recipient identity ID_B and a ciphertext c. Let (m, ID_A, σ) be the result of decrypting c under the secret key corresponding to ID_B. The adversary wins if $ID_A \neq ID_B$; **Verify**(m, ID_A, σ) = $\top$; no extraction query was made on ID_A, or ID_B; and c did not result from a sign/encrypt query with sender ID_A and recipient ID_B.

Definition 1. *Let $\mathcal{A}$ denote an adversary that plays the game above. If the quantity $\mathbf{Adv}[\mathcal{A}] = \mathbf{Pr}[\mathcal{A} \text{ wins}]$ is negligible we say that the scheme in question is existentially ciphertext-unforgeable against outsider chosen-message attacks, or AUTH-IBSC-CMA secure.*

Here we have an example of outsider security since the adversary is not able to extract the secret key corresponding to ID_B. This models the true adversarial scenario where an attack would be re-encrypting a signed message using a public key with unknown secret key.

3.2   Message Confidentiality

The accepted notion of security with respect to confidentiality for public key encryption is *indistinguishability of encryptions under adaptive chosen ciphertext attack*, as formalised in [16]. The notion of security defined in the game below is a natural adaptation of this notion to the identity-based signcryption setting.

Game

- **Initial:** The challenger runs **Setup**(1^k) and gives the resulting **params** to the adversary. It keeps s secret.
- **Phase 1:** The challenger is probed by the adversary who makes queries as in the game of Section 3.1. At the end of Phase 1 the adversary outputs two identities $\{ID_A, ID_B\}$ and two messages $\{m_0, m_1\}$. The adversary must not have made an extract query on ID_B.
- **Challenge:** The challenger chooses a bit b uniformly at random. It signs m_b under the secret key corresponding to ID_A and encrypts the result under the public key of ID_B to produce c. The challenger returns c to the adversary.
- **Phase 2:** The adversary continues to probe the challenger with the same type of queries that it made in Phase 1. It is not allowed to extract the private key corresponding to ID_B and it is not allowed to make a decrypt/verify query for c under ID_B.
- **Response:** The adversary returns a bit b'. We say that the adversary *wins* if $b' = b$.

Definition 2. *Let $\mathcal{A}$ denote an adversary that plays the game above. If the quantity* $\mathbf{Adv}[\mathcal{A}] = |\mathbf{Pr}[b' = b] - \frac{1}{2}|$ *is negligible we say that the scheme in question is semantically secure against adaptive chosen-ciphertext attack, or IND-IBSC-CCA2 secure.*

Note that Definition 2 deals with insider security since the adversary is assumed to have access to the private key of the sender of a signcrypted message. This means that confidentiality is preserved even if a sender's key is compromised.

3.3   Signature Non-repudiation

A signcryption scheme offering non-repudiation prevents the sender of a signcrypted message from disavowing its signature. Note that non-repudiation is not as straightforward for signcryption as it is for digital signature schemes since we are dealing with encrypted data. As a consequence, by default, only the intended recipient of a signcryption can verify.

We define the notion of non-repudiation via the following game played by a challenger and an adversary.

Game

- **Initial:** The challenger runs **Setup**(1^k) and gives the resulting **params** to the adversary. It keeps s secret.
- **Probing:** The challenger is probed by the adversary who makes queries as in the game of Section 3.1.
- **Forge:** The adversary returns a recipient identity ID_B and a ciphertext c. Let (m, ID_A, σ) be the result of decrypting c under the secret key corresponding to ID_B. The adversary wins if $ID_A \neq ID_B$; **Verify**$(m, ID_A, \sigma) = \top$; no extraction query was made on ID_A; no sign/encrypt query $(m, ID_A, ID_{B'})$ was responded to with a ciphertext whose decryption under the private key of $ID_{B'}$ is (m, ID_A, σ).

This model is a natural adaptation of existential unforgeability (EUF) under adaptive chosen message attack, the accepted notion of security for digital signature schemes [10].

Definition 3. *Let $\mathcal{A}$ denote an adversary that plays the game above. If the quantity $\mathbf{Adv}[\mathcal{A}] = \mathbf{Pr}[\mathcal{A}\ wins]$ is negligible we say that the scheme in question is existentially unforgeable against insider chosen-message attacks, or EUF-IBSC-CMA secure.*

In Definition 3 we allow the adversary access to the secret key of the recipient of the forgery. It is this that gives us insider security. Also note that the adversary's advantage is with respect to its success in forging the signature within the ciphertext. This is indeed the correct definition for non-repudiation in this context because it is the signature and not the ciphertext that contains it that is forwarded to a third party in the case of a dispute.

3.4   Ciphertext Anonymity

Ciphertext anonymity is the property that ciphertexts contain no third-party extractable information that helps to identify the sender of the ciphertext or the intended recipient. It is defined via the following game.

Game

- **Initial:** The challenger runs **Setup**(1^k) and gives the resulting **params** to the adversary. It keeps s secret.
- **Phase 1:** The challenger is probed by the adversary who makes queries as in the game of Section 3.1. At the end of Phase 1 the adversary outputs a message m; two sender identities $\{ID_{A_0}, ID_{A_1}\}$; and two recipient identities $\{ID_{B_0}, ID_{B_1}\}$. The adversary must not have made an extract query on either of $\{ID_{B_0}, ID_{B_1}\}$.
- **Challenge:** The challenger chooses two bits $(b, \hat{b})$ uniformly at random. It signs m under the secret key S_{A_b} corresponding to ID_{A_b}. It then encrypts the result under the public key of $ID_{B_{\hat{b}}}$ to produce a ciphertext c. The challenger returns c to the adversary.
- **Phase 2:** The adversary continues to probe the challenger with the same type of queries that it made in Phase 1. It is not allowed to extract the private key corresponding to ID_{B_0} or ID_{B_1} and it is not allowed to make a decrypt/verify query for c under ID_{B_0} or under ID_{B_1}.
- **Response:** The adversary returns two bits $(b', \hat{b}')$. We say that the adversary wins if $b = \hat{b}$ or $b' = \hat{b}'$.

Definition 4. *Let $\mathcal{A}$ denote an adversary that plays the game above. If the quantity $\mathbf{Adv}[\mathcal{A}] = |\mathbf{Pr}[b' = b \vee \hat{b}' = \hat{b}] - \frac{3}{4}|$ is negligible we say that the scheme in question is ciphertext-anonymous against insider adaptive chosen-ciphertext attack, or ANON-IBSC-CCA2 secure.*

Note that in the equivalent definition from [6] the adversary only wins if $b = \hat{b}$ and $b' = \hat{b}'$. It is stated there that the scheme is ANON-IBSC-CCA2 secure if the quantity $\mathbf{Adv}[\mathcal{A}] = |\mathbf{Pr}[b' = b \wedge \hat{b}' = \hat{b}] - \frac{1}{4}|$ is negligible. The two definitions are clearly equivalent. We prefer our formulation because it explicitly states that the adversary should not be able to guess either of the bits. The intuition is that it gains no information about the sender of a message or the intended recipient. Definition 4 follows from the fact that the adversary is always able to guess at least one of the bits correctly with probability 3/4.

An additional security definition dubbed ciphertext unlinkability is described in [6]. Informally this notion means that Alice is able to deny having sent a given ciphertext to Bob, even if the ciphertext decrypts under Bob's secret key to a message bearing Alice's signature. This property is demonstrated for the scheme in [6] by showing that given a message signed by Alice, Bob is able to create a valid ciphertext addressed to himself for that message. It is easily verified that our scheme also has this property.

4   The Scheme

In this section we describe how our identity-based signcryption scheme works. We will refer to the scheme as IBSC henceforth.

Before explaining our scheme we must briefly summarise the mathematical primitives necessary for pairing based cryptography. We require two groups $\mathbb{G}_1$ and $\mathbb{G}_2$ of large prime order q. These groups must be such that there exists a non-degenerate, efficiently computable map $\hat{e} : \mathbb{G}_1 \times \mathbb{G}_1 \to \mathbb{G}_2$. This map must be bilinear i.e. for all $P_1, P_2 \in \mathbb{G}_1$ and all $a, b \in \mathbb{Z}_q^*$ we have $\hat{e}(aP_1, bP_2) = \hat{e}(P_1, P_2)^{ab}$. A popular construction for such groups uses supersingular elliptic curves over finite fields. The bilinear map is realised using a modification of the Tate pairing or the Weil pairing. For details of such instantiations see [2, 5].

We also require three hash functions $H_0 : \{0,1\}^{k_1} \to \mathbb{G}_1$, $H_1 : \{0,1\}^{k_0+n} \to \mathbb{Z}_q^*$ and $H_2 : \mathbb{G}_2 \to \{0,1\}^{k_0+k_1+n}$. Here k_0 is the number of bits required to represent an element of $\mathbb{G}_1$; k_1 is the number of bits required to represent an identity; and n is the number of bits of a message to be signed and encrypted.

Setup
Establish parameters $\mathbb{G}_1$, $\mathbb{G}_2$, q, $\hat{e}$, $H_0 : \{0,1\}^{k_1} \to \mathbb{G}_1$, $H_1 : \{0,1\}^{k_0+n} \to \mathbb{Z}_q^*$ and $H_2 : \mathbb{G}_2 \to \{0,1\}^{k_0+k_1+n}$ as described above; choose P such that $\langle P \rangle = \mathbb{G}_1$; choose $s \leftarrow \mathbb{Z}_q^*$ and compute the global public key $Q_{TA} \leftarrow sP$.

Extract
To extract the private key for user U with $ID_U \in \{0,1\}^{k_1}$: Compute the public key $Q_U \leftarrow H_0(ID_U)$ and the secret key $S_U \leftarrow sQ_U$.

Sign
For user A with identity ID_A to sign $m \in \{0,1\}^n$ with private key S_A corresponding to public key $Q_A \leftarrow H_0(ID_A)$: Choose $r \leftarrow \mathbb{Z}_q^*$; compute $X \leftarrow rQ_A$, $h_1 \leftarrow H_1(X\|m)$ and $Z \leftarrow (r + h_1)S_A$; return the signature (X, Z) and forward (m, r, X, Z) to **Encrypt**.

Encrypt
For user A with identity ID_A to encrypt m using r, X, Z output by **Sign** for receiver ID_B: Compute $Q_B \leftarrow H_0(ID_B)$, $w \leftarrow \hat{e}(rS_A, Q_B)$ and $y \leftarrow H_2(w) \oplus (Z||ID_A||m)$; return ciphertext (X, y).

Decrypt
For user B with identity ID_B to decrypt (X, y) using $S_B = sH_0(ID_B)$: Compute $w \leftarrow \hat{e}(X, S_B)$ and $Z||ID_A||m \leftarrow y \oplus H_2(w)$; forward message m, signature (X, Z) and purported sender ID_A to **Verify**.

Verify
To verify user A's signature (X, Z) on message m where A has identity ID_A: Compute $Q_A \leftarrow H_0(ID_A)$ and $h_1 \leftarrow H_1(X||m)$; if $\hat{e}(Z, P) = \hat{e}(Q_{TA}, X + h_1 Q_A)$, return $\top$; else, return $\bot$.

Note that, as was the case in [6], the key setup used by our scheme is that proposed in [17], and the signing algorithm is that proposed in [7]. Also, the encryption is done in a manner similar to the BasicIdent scheme from [5]. The integrity checking necessary for security against adaptive adversaries comes from the signature in our case.

5   Security Results

In this section we state our security results. Owing to space constraints, we only provide a proof of the ciphertext authentication property here. The proofs of the other properties may be found in the full version of the paper [8].

All our results are relative to the *bilinear Diffie-Hellman* (BDH) problem. Informally, using the notation of Section 4, this is the problem of computing $\hat{e}(P, P)^{abc}$ from (P, aP, bP, cP) where a, b, c are chosen at random from $\mathbb{Z}_q^*$ and P generates $\mathbb{G}_1$. For further details see [5].

To prove our results we model H_0, H_1 and H_2 as random oracles [3]. We assume that the adversary makes q_i queries to H_i for $i = 0, 1, 2$. The number of sign/encrypt and decrypt/verify queries made by the adversary are denoted q_s and q_d respectively.

Ciphertext Authentication

Theorem 1. *If there is an AUTH-IBSC-CMA adversary $\mathcal{A}$ of IBSC that succeeds with probability ϵ, then there is a simulator $\mathcal{B}$ running in polynomial time that solves the BDH problem with probability at least*

$$\epsilon \cdot \left(1 - \frac{q_s(q_1 + q_2 + 2q_s)}{q}\right) \cdot \frac{1}{q_0(q_0 - 1)(q_s + q_d)(q_2 + q_s)}.$$

Proof. We will show how an AUTH-IBSC-CMA adversary $\mathcal{A}$ of IBSC may be used to construct a simulator $\mathcal{B}$ that solves the BDH problem for (P, aP, bP, cP).

We now describe the construction of the simulator $\mathcal{B}$. The simulator runs $\mathcal{A}$ with trusted third party public key $Q_{TA} \leftarrow cP$. It also creates algorithms to respond to queries made by $\mathcal{A}$ during its attack. To maintain consistency between queries made by $\mathcal{A}$, the simulator keeps the following lists: L_i for $i = 0, 1, 2$ of data for query/response pairs to random oracle H_i; L_s of signcryptions generated by the simulator; and L_d of some of the queries made by $\mathcal{A}$ to the decrypt/verify oracle. We will see in the construction of the sign/encrypt simulator that the list L_s stores other information that will be useful to $\mathcal{B}$. Its use will become apparent in the subsequent analysis, as will the use of L_d.

Simulator: $H_0(ID_U)$
At the beginning of the simulation choose i_a, i_b uniformly at random from $\{1, \ldots, q_0\}$ ($i_a \neq i_b$). We respond to the i-th query made by $\mathcal{A}$ as follows (assuming $\mathcal{A}$ does not make repeat queries).

- If $i = i_a$ then respond with $H_0(ID_U) \leftarrow aP$ and set $ID_A \leftarrow ID_U$.
- If $i = i_b$ then respond with $H_0(ID_U) \leftarrow bP$ and set $ID_B \leftarrow ID_U$.
- Else choose $x \leftarrow \mathbb{Z}_q^*$; compute $Q_U \leftarrow xP$; compute $S_U \leftarrow xQ_{TA}$; store (ID_U, Q_U, S_U, x) in L_0 and respond with Q_U.

Simulator: $H_1(X\|m)$

- If $(X\|m, h_1) \in L_1$ for some h_1, return h_1.
- Else choose $h_1 \leftarrow \mathbb{Z}_q^*$; add $(X\|m, h_1)$ to L_1; return h_1.

Simulator: $H_2(w)$

- If $(w, h_2) \in L_2$ for some h_2, return h_2.
- Else choose $h_2 \leftarrow \{0,1\}^{k_0+k_1+n}$; add (w, h_2) to L_2; return h_2.

Simulator: Extract(ID_U)
We assume that $\mathcal{A}$ queries $H_0(ID_U)$ before it makes the extraction query ID_U.

- If $ID_U = ID_A$ or $ID_U = ID_B$, abort the simulation.
- Else search L_0 for the entry (ID_U, Q_U, S_U, x) corresponding to ID_U and return S_U.

Simulator: Sign/Encrypt(m, ID_1, ID_2)
We will assume that $\mathcal{A}$ makes the queries $H_0(ID_1)$ and $H_0(ID_2)$ before it makes a sign/encrypt query using these identities. We have five cases to consider.

Case 1: $ID_1 \neq ID_A$ and $ID_1 \neq ID_B$

- Find the entry (ID_1, Q_1, S_1, x) in L_0; choose $r \leftarrow \mathbb{Z}_q^*$; compute $X \leftarrow rQ_1$; compute $h_1 \leftarrow H_1(X\|m)$ (where H_1 is the simulator above); compute $Z \leftarrow (r + h_1)S_1$; compute $Q_2 \leftarrow H_0(ID_2)$ (where H_0 is the simulator above); compute $w \leftarrow \hat{e}(rS_1, Q_2)$; compute $y \leftarrow H_2(w) \oplus (Z\|ID_1\|m)$ (where H_2 is the simulator above); return (X, y).

Case 2: $ID_1 = ID_A$, $ID_2 \neq ID_A$ and $ID_2 \neq ID_B$

- Choose $r, h_1 \leftarrow \mathbb{Z}_q^*$; compute $X \leftarrow rP - h_1 Q_A$; compute $Z \leftarrow rQ_{TA}$; add $(X||m, h_1)$ to L_1; find the entry (ID_2, Q_2, S_2, x) in L_0; compute $w \leftarrow \hat{e}(X, S_2)$; compute $y \leftarrow H_2(w) \oplus (Z||ID_A||m)$ (where H_2 is the simulator above); return (X, y).

Case 3: $ID_1 = ID_B$, $ID_2 \neq ID_A$ and $ID_2 \neq ID_B$
Use the simulation of **Case 2** replacing (ID_A, Q_A) with (ID_B, Q_B).

Case 4: $ID_1 = ID_A$ and $ID_2 = ID_B$

- Follow the first four steps of **Case 2**; choose $h_2 \leftarrow \{0, 1\}^{k_0+k_1+n}$; compute $y \leftarrow h_2 \oplus Z||ID_A||m$; add $(ID_A, ID_B, X, y, Z, m, r, h_1, h_2)$ to L_s; return (X, y).

Case 5: $ID_1 = ID_B$ and $ID_2 = ID_A$
Use the simulation of **Case 4** swapping (ID_A, Q_A, ID_B) with (ID_B, Q_B, ID_A).

Decrypt/Verify:$(X, y), ID_2$
We assume that $\mathcal{A}$ makes the query $H_0(ID_2)$ before making a decryption query for ID_2. We have the following three cases to consider.

Case 1: $ID_2 \neq ID_A$ and $ID_2 \neq ID_B$

- Find the entry (ID_2, Q_2, S_2, x) in L_0; compute $w = \hat{e}(X, S_2)$; initialise $b \leftarrow 1$.
- If $w \in L_2$, compute $Z||ID_1||m \leftarrow y \oplus H_2(w)$, else $b \leftarrow 0$.
- If $b = 1$ and $ID_1 \in L_0$, let $Q_1 \leftarrow H_0(ID_1)$, else $b \leftarrow 0$.
- If $b = 1$ and $X||m \in L_1$, let $h_1 \leftarrow H_1(X||m)$, else $b \leftarrow 0$.
- If $b = 1$ and $\hat{e}(Z, P) = \hat{e}(Q_{TA}, X + h_1 Q_1)$, return m, (X, Z) and ID_1, else step through the list L_s as follows.
  - If the current entry has the form $(ID_A, ID_B, X', y, Z, m', r, h'_1, h_2)$ then test if $\hat{e}(X', Q_B) = \hat{e}(X, xP)$. If so continue, else move on to the next element of L_s and begin again.
  - Else if the current entry has the form $(ID_B, ID_A, X', y, Z, m', r, h'_1, h_2)$ then test $\hat{e}(X', Q_A) = \hat{e}(X, xP)$. If so continue, else move on to the next element of L_s and begin again.
  - Compute $Z||ID_1||m \leftarrow y \oplus h_2$.
  - If $ID_1 = ID_2$ move to the next element in L_s and begin again.
  - If $ID_1 \in L_0$ let $Q_1 \leftarrow H_0(ID_1)$, else move to the next element in L_s.
  - If $X||m \in L_1$ let $h_1 \leftarrow H_1(X||m)$, else move to the next element in L_s.
  - Check that $\hat{e}(Z, P) = \hat{e}(Q_{TA}, X + h_1 Q_1)$, if so return m, (X, Z) and ID_1, if not move on to the next element in L_s and begin again.
- If no message has been returned, return $\perp$.

Case 2: $ID_2 = ID_B$

- If $(ID_A, ID_B, X, y, Z, m, r, h_1, h_2) \in L_s$ for some m, return m, (X, Z), ID_A.

- Else, add $(X, y), ID_B$ to L_d and step through the list L_2 with entries (w, h_2) as follows.
  - Compute $Z||ID_1||m \leftarrow y \oplus h_2$.
  - If $ID_1 = ID_A$ or $ID_1 = ID_B$, move to the next element in L_2 and begin again.
  - If $ID_1 \in L_0$ let $Q_1 \leftarrow H_0(ID_1)$ and find S_1 in L_0, else move to the next element in L_2 and begin again.
  - If $X||m \in L_1$ let $h_1 \leftarrow H_1(X||m)$, else move on to the next element in L_2 and begin again.
  - Check that $w = \hat{e}(Z - h_1 S_1, Q_B)$ and if not move on to the next element in L_2 and begin again.
  - Check that $\hat{e}(Z, P) = \hat{e}(Q_{TA}, X + h_1 Q_1)$, if so return $m, (X, Z)$ and ID_1, else move on to the next element in L_2 and begin again.
- If no message has been returned after stepping through the list L_2, step through the list L_s as follows.
  - If the current entry has the form $(ID_A, ID_B, X', y, Z, m', r, h_1', h_2)$ then check that $X' = X$. If so continue, else move on to the next element of L_s and begin again.
  - Else if the current entry has the form $(ID_B, ID_A, X', y, Z, m', r, h_1', h_2)$ then check that $\hat{e}(X', Q_A) = \hat{e}(X, Q_B)$. If so continue, if not move on to the next element of L_s and begin again.
  - Compute $Z||ID_1||m \leftarrow y \oplus h_2$.
  - If $ID_1 = ID_B$, move to the next element in L_s and begin again.
  - If $ID_1 \in L_0$ let $Q_1 \leftarrow H_0(ID_1)$, else move to the next element in L_s.
  - If $X||m \in L_1$ let $h_1 \leftarrow H_1(X||m)$, else move to the next element in L_s.
  - Check that $\hat{e}(Z, P) = \hat{e}(Q_{TA}, X + h_1 Q_1)$, if so return $m, (X, Z)$ and ID_1, else move on to the next element in L_s and begin again.
- If no message has been returned, return $\perp$.

Case 3: $ID_2 = ID_A$
Use the simulation of Case 2 replacing (ID_B, Q_B, ID_A) with (ID_A, Q_A, ID_B).

Once $\mathcal{A}$ has been run, $\mathcal{B}$ does one of two things.

1. With probability $q_s/(q_s+q_d)$ choose a random element from L_s and a random element (w, h_2) from L_2. We call this event Ch_1 in the analysis below (Ch for choice). The significance of the probability will become apparent in the subsequent analysis we only mention here that we are assuming $|L_s| = q_s$ at the end of our simulation. This is the worst case scenario.
   - If the chosen element has form $(ID_A, ID_B, X, y, Z, m, r, h_1, h_2)$, compute
   $$B = (w/\hat{e}(rbP, cP))^{-1/h_1}.$$
   - If the chosen element has form $(ID_B, ID_A, X, y, Z, m, r, h_1, h_2)$, compute
   $$B = (w/\hat{e}(raP, cP))^{-1/h_1}.$$

2. With probability $q_d/(q_s + q_d)$ choose a random element from L_d and a random element (w, h_2) from L_2. We call this event Ch_2 in the analysis below. Again, the significance this probability will become apparent in the subsequent analysis. As above, we are assuming $|L_d| = q_d$ at the end of our simulation. This is the worst case scenario.

- If the chosen element from L_d has the form $(X, y), ID_B$ compute $y \oplus h_2$. If $y \oplus h_2$ has the form $Z||ID_A||m$ for some Z, m, compute

$$B = \left(w/\hat{e}(Z, bP)\right)^{-1/h_1}.$$

  If $y \oplus h_2$ does not have this form B has failed.
- If the chosen element from L_d has the form $(X, y), ID_A$ compute $y \oplus h_2$. If $y \oplus h_2$ has the form $Z||ID_B||m$ for some Z, m, compute

$$B = \left(w/\hat{e}(Z, aP)\right)^{-1/h_1}.$$

  If $y \oplus h_2$ does not have this form B has failed.

The rational for these probabilities and computations will become apparent in the discussion of equations (1), (2), (4) and (5) below.

Let us now analyse our simulation. The simulations for the random oracles and the extraction queries are trivial. The simulation of the sign/encrypt queries uses standard techniques. We make some remarks about the decrypt/verify simulation since this is less obvious. We will treat each case separately.

Case 1: In this case the simulator B knows the secret key of the receiver and so it is able to compute the correct ephemeral encryption key. The first six steps in this case are therefore those that would be followed in genuine decryption and verification. The reason that it does not stop at this point is that the sign/encrypt simulator implicitly defines $H_2(w)$ for values of w that are unknown to the simulator. It must check that the ephemeral encryption key w that it has computed is not one of these values. For example, suppose that there is an entry of the form $(ID_A, ID_B, X', y, Z, m, r, h'_1, h_2)$ in L_s. Referring back to the construction of the sign/encrypt simulator, it needs to know if

$$\hat{e}(X', S_B) = \hat{e}(X, S_2).$$

The simulator knows that $S_2 = xQ_{TA} = xcP$ and it know $S_B = bQ_{TA} = bcP = cQ_B$ so this test becomes

$$\hat{e}(X', Q_B) = \hat{e}(X, xP).$$

Case 2: In this case the simulator B does not know the secret key of the receiver and so it is unable to compute the ephemeral encryption key $\hat{e}(X, S_B)$. The first loop, through the list L_2, determines whether the H_2 value of the ephemeral encryption key is in L_2 itself i.e. for each w in L_2 it wants to know if $w =$

$\hat{e}(X, S_B)$. Since by construction $Q_{TA} = cP$ this test becomes $w = \hat{e}(cX, Q_B)$ and, under the assumption that the ciphertext is correctly formed, it becomes $\hat{e}(Z - h_1 S_1, Q_B)$. Note that if the ciphertext is not correctly formed the simulator does not care whether the value of $H_2(w)$ is defined since it is correct to reject. The final test in this loop is just the standard test for verification.

The second loop, through L_s, determines whether the value of $H_2(w)$ that $\mathcal{B}$ is looking for has been determined by the sign/encrypt simulator. If it is searching L_s for an entry of form $(ID_A, ID_B, X', y, Z, m, r, h'_1, h_2)$ then the receiver identities are the same in this entry and in the decrypt/verify query that we are trying to respond to. The check is then simply on the values of X and X'.

If $\mathcal{B}$ is looking at an entry of L_s of the form $(ID_B, ID_A, X', y, Z, m, r, h'_1, h_2)$ then the receivers identities are not the same in this entry and in the decrypt/verify query that it is trying to respond to. The check that it wishes to perform is $\hat{e}(X', S_A) = \hat{e}(X, S_B)$. This is clearly equivalent to the check $\hat{e}(X', Q_A) = \hat{e}(X, Q_B)$.

Case 3: The analysis is identical to that of **Case 2** with A and B reversed.

Let us now consider how our simulation could fail i.e. describe events that could cause $\mathcal{A}$'s view to differ when run by $\mathcal{B}$ from its view in a real attack. We call such an event an error and denote it ER.

It is clear that the simulations for H_0 and H_1 are indistinguishable from real random oracles. Let us now consider the H_2 simulator. The important point here is that H_2 is not only defined at points where the H_2 simulator is called by $\mathcal{A}$ or by the simulator itself. It is also defined at certain points implicitly by the sign/encrypt simulator. For example, suppose that the sign/encrypt simulator responds to a query m, ID_A, ID_B. In this case it adds an entry $(ID_A, ID_B, X, y, Z, m, r, h_1, h_2)$ to L_s. This implicitly defines $H_2(\hat{e}(X, S_B)) = h_2$ although it is not actually able to compute $\hat{e}(X, S_B)$. If the H_2 simulator is subsequently called with $w = \hat{e}(X, S_B)$ it will not recognise it and so it will not return h_2. We denote such events H-ER. However, if such an event occurs we have

$$w = \hat{e}(X, S_B) = \hat{e}(rP - h_1 Q_A, S_B)$$

from which it is possible to compute

$$\hat{e}(P, P)^{abc} = \hat{e}(Q_A, S_B) = \left(w / \hat{e}(rQ_B, Q_{TA})\right)^{-1/h_1} = \left(w / \hat{e}(rbP, cP)\right)^{-1/h_1}. \quad (1)$$

Similarly if the H_2 simulator is called with w that is implicitly defined by an entry $(ID_B, ID_A, X, y, Z, m, r, h_1, h_2) \in L_s$ we can compute.

$$\hat{e}(P, P)^{abc} = \hat{e}(Q_B, S_A) = \left(w / \hat{e}(rQ_A, Q_{TA})\right)^{-1/h_1} = \left(w / \hat{e}(raP, cP)\right)^{-1/h_1}. \quad (2)$$

Let us now consider how the simulation for sign/encrypt could fail. We denote such an event S-ER. The most likely failure will be caused by the sign/encrypt simulator responding to a query of the form Case 4 or Case 5 (see simulator).

Since we do not know how often each case will occur we will be conservative and assume that each query will be one of these, 4 say. The only possibilities for introducing an error here are defining $H_1(X||m)$ when it is already defined or defining $H_2(\hat{e}(X, S_B))/H_2(\hat{e}(X, S_A))$ when it is already defined. Since X takes its value uniformly at random in $\langle P \rangle$, the chance of one of these events occurring is at most $(q_1 + q_2 + 2q_s)/q$ for each query. The $2q_s$ comes from the fact that the signing simulator adds elements to L_1 and L_2. Therefore, over the whole simulation, the chance of an error introduced in this way is at most

$$q_s(q_1 + q_2 + 2q_s)/q. \tag{3}$$

We now turn our attention to the decrypt/verify simulator. An error in this simulator is denoted D-ER. It is clear that this simulator never accepts an invalid encryption. What we have to worry about is the possibility that it rejects a valid one. This can only occur with non-negligible probability in Case 2 or Case 3. Suppose that we are trying to decrypt $(X, y), ID_B$ (i.e. Case 2). An error will only occur if while stepping through L_2 there is an entry (w, h_2) such that $Z||ID_A||m \leftarrow y \oplus h_2$ and (X, y) is a valid encryption of m from ID_A to ID_B. In this case we must have

$$w = \hat{e}(Z - h_1 S_A, Q_B) = \hat{e}(Z, Q_B) \cdot \hat{e}(-h_1 S_A, Q_B) = \hat{e}(Z, bP) \cdot \hat{e}(-h_1 acP, bP),$$

where $h_1 = H_1(X||m)$. From the above we can compute

$$\hat{e}(P, P)^{abc} = \left(w/\hat{e}(Z, bP) \right)^{-1/h_1}. \tag{4}$$

Suppose now that we are trying to decrypt $(X, y), ID_A$ (i.e. Case 3). An error will only occur if while stepping through L_2 there is an entry (w, h_2) such that $Z||ID_B||m \leftarrow y \oplus h_2$ and (X, y) is a valid encryption of m from ID_B to ID_A. In this case we must have

$$w = \hat{e}(Z - h_1 S_B, Q_A) = \hat{e}(Z, Q_A) \cdot \hat{e}(-h_1 S_B, Q_A) = \hat{e}(Z, aP) \cdot \hat{e}(-h_1 bcP, aP),$$

from which we can compute

$$\hat{e}(P, P)^{abc} = \left(w/\hat{e}(Z, aP) \right)^{-1/h_1}. \tag{5}$$

The final simulator is the extract simulator. Note that the adversary will only succeed in its task with non-negligible probability if it queries H_0 with the two identities under which the encrypted and signed message it produces is supposed to be valid. Looking at the H_0 simulator we see that it chooses two H_0 queries made by the adversary and responds to these with group elements from the BDH instance that it is trying to solve. The simulator hopes that these will be the identities for the adversary's encrypted and signed message. This will be the case with probability at least

$$1/q_0(q_0 - 1). \tag{6}$$

If this is not the case we say that an error has occurred in the extract simulator because, if the adversary tried to extract the private key for these identities, the simulator would abort. An error in the extract simulator is denoted E-ER.

Once $\mathcal{A}$ has been run by the simulator $\mathcal{B}$, there are two courses of action: Ch_1 and Ch_2 (as described above). If Ch_1 has been chosen, we denote the event that $\mathcal{B}$ selects the correct elements to solve the BDH problem from L_s and H_2 by CG_1 (under the assumption that there are such correct elements in the lists at the end of the simulation). Likewise if Ch_2 has been chosen, we denote the event that $\mathcal{B}$ selects the correct elements from L_d and H_2 by CG_2.

With the events described above we have

$$\mathbf{Adv}[\mathcal{B}] \geq \mathbf{Pr}[\neg\mathsf{E\text{-}ER} \wedge \mathsf{H\text{-}ER} \wedge \neg\mathsf{S\text{-}ER} \wedge \mathsf{Ch}_1 \wedge \mathsf{CG}_1]$$
$$+ \mathbf{Pr}[\mathsf{D\text{-}ER} \wedge \neg\mathsf{E\text{-}ER} \wedge \neg\mathsf{H\text{-}ER} \wedge \neg\mathsf{S\text{-}ER} \wedge \mathsf{Ch}_2 \wedge \mathsf{CG}_2]. \qquad (7)$$

Also,

$$\mathbf{Pr}[\neg\mathsf{E\text{-}ER} \wedge \mathsf{H\text{-}ER} \wedge \neg\mathsf{S\text{-}ER} \wedge \mathsf{Ch}_1 \wedge \mathsf{CG}_1]$$
$$= \mathbf{Pr}[\neg\mathsf{E\text{-}ER} \wedge \neg\mathsf{S\text{-}ER}] \cdot \mathbf{Pr}[\mathsf{Ch}_1 \wedge \mathsf{CG}_1] \cdot \mathbf{Pr}[\mathsf{H\text{-}ER}], \qquad (8)$$

and,

$$\mathbf{Pr}[\mathsf{D\text{-}ER} \wedge \neg\mathsf{E\text{-}ER} \wedge \neg\mathsf{H\text{-}ER} \wedge \neg\mathsf{S\text{-}ER} \wedge \mathsf{Ch}_2 \wedge \mathsf{CG}_2]$$
$$= \mathbf{Pr}[\mathsf{D\text{-}ER}] \cdot \mathbf{Pr}[\neg\mathsf{E\text{-}ER} \wedge \neg\mathsf{H\text{-}ER} \wedge \neg\mathsf{S\text{-}ER}] \cdot \mathbf{Pr}[\mathsf{Ch}_2 \wedge \mathsf{CG}_2]. \qquad (9)$$

Note that, in the event $\neg\mathsf{E\text{-}ER} \wedge \neg\mathsf{H\text{-}ER} \wedge \neg\mathsf{S\text{-}ER}$, the adversary $\mathcal{A}$ is run by $\mathcal{B}$ in exactly the same way that it would be run in a real attack until the event D-ER occurs. Moreover, in the event $\neg\mathsf{E\text{-}ER} \wedge \neg\mathsf{H\text{-}ER} \wedge \neg\mathsf{S\text{-}ER}$, $\mathcal{A}$ winning and D-ER are equivalent. This means that (9) becomes

$$\mathbf{Pr}[\mathsf{D\text{-}ER} \wedge \neg\mathsf{E\text{-}ER} \wedge \neg\mathsf{H\text{-}ER} \wedge \neg\mathsf{S\text{-}ER} \wedge \mathsf{Ch}_2 \wedge \mathsf{CG}_2]$$
$$= \epsilon \cdot \mathbf{Pr}[\neg\mathsf{E\text{-}ER} \wedge \neg\mathsf{S\text{-}ER}] \cdot \mathbf{Pr}[\mathsf{Ch}_2 \wedge \mathsf{CG}_2] \cdot \mathbf{Pr}[\neg\mathsf{H\text{-}ER}]. \qquad (10)$$

From the definitions of Ch_1, CG_1, Ch_2 and CG_2 above it is clear that

$$\mathbf{Pr}[\mathsf{Ch}_1 \wedge \mathsf{CG}_1] = \frac{q_s}{q_s + q_d} \cdot \frac{1}{q_s(q_2 + q_s)} = \frac{1}{(q_s + q_d)(q_2 + q_s)} \text{ and} \qquad (11)$$

$$\mathbf{Pr}[\mathsf{Ch}_2 \wedge \mathsf{CG}_2] = \frac{q_d}{q_s + q_d} \cdot \frac{1}{q_d(q_2 + q_s)} = \frac{1}{(q_s + q_d)(q_2 + q_s)}. \qquad (12)$$

Note that we are assuming a worst case scenario here i.e. $|L_s| = q_s$ and $|L_d| = q_d$. We will make this assumption throughout the remaining analysis without further comment. From the fact that $\mathbf{Pr}[\mathsf{H\text{-}ER}] + \mathbf{Pr}[\neg\mathsf{H\text{-}ER}] = 1$, (7), (8), (10), (11) and (12) we have

$$\mathbf{Adv}[\mathcal{B}] \geq (\mathbf{Pr}[\mathsf{H\text{-}ER}] + \epsilon \cdot \mathbf{Pr}[\neg\mathsf{H\text{-}ER}]) \cdot \mathbf{Pr}[\neg\mathsf{E\text{-}ER} \wedge \neg\mathsf{S\text{-}ER}] \cdot \frac{1}{(q_s + q_d)(q_2 + q_s)}$$

$$\geq \epsilon \cdot (\mathbf{Pr}[\mathsf{H\text{-}ER}] + \mathbf{Pr}[\neg\mathsf{H\text{-}ER}]) \cdot \mathbf{Pr}[\neg\mathsf{E\text{-}ER} \wedge \neg\mathsf{S\text{-}ER}] \cdot \frac{1}{(q_s + q_d)(q_2 + q_s)}$$

$$= \epsilon \cdot \mathbf{Pr}[\neg\mathsf{E\text{-}ER} \wedge \neg\mathsf{S\text{-}ER}] \cdot \frac{1}{(q_s + q_d)(q_2 + q_s)}. \qquad (13)$$

Finally, by the independence of E-ER and S-ER, using (3), (6) and (13) we have

$$\mathbf{Adv}[\mathcal{B}] \geq \epsilon \cdot \left(1 - \frac{q_s(q_1 + q_2 + 2q_s)}{q}\right) \cdot \frac{1}{q_0(q_0 - 1)(q_s + q_d)(q_2 + q_s)}. \tag{14}$$

$\square$

Message Confidentiality

Theorem 2 describes the security of our scheme under Definition 2. We provide a proof in the full version of the paper[8].

Theorem 2. *If there is an IND-IBSC-CCA2 adversary $\mathcal{A}$ of IBSC that succeeds with probability ϵ, then there is a simulator $\mathcal{B}$ running in polynomial time that solves the BDH problem with probability at least*

$$\epsilon \cdot \left(1 - \frac{q_s(q_1 + q_s)}{q}\right) \cdot \frac{1}{q_0 q_2}.$$

Signature Non-repudiation

In Theorem 3 we state the security result for our scheme under Definition 3. The proof will be found in the full version of the paper[8].

Theorem 3. *If there is an EUF-IBSC-CMA adversary $\mathcal{A}$ of IBSC that succeeds with probability ϵ, then there is a simulator $\mathcal{B}$ running in polynomial time that solves the BDH problem with probability at least*

$$\epsilon \cdot \left(1 - \frac{q_s(q_1 + q_s)}{q}\right)^2 \cdot \frac{1}{4q_0^2(q_1 + q_s)^2}.$$

Ciphertext Anonymity

Our final security result is Theorem 4. This deals with security under Definition 4. The proof appears in the full version of the paper[8].

Theorem 4. *If there is an ANON-IBSC-CCA2 adversary $\mathcal{A}$ of IBSC that succeeds with probability ϵ, then there is a simulator $\mathcal{B}$ running in polynomial time that solves the BDH problem with probability at least*

$$\epsilon \cdot \left(1 - \frac{q_s(q_1 + q_2 + 2q_s)}{q}\right) \cdot \frac{1}{q_0(q_0 - 1)(2 + q_s)(q_2 + q_s)}.$$

6 Performance and Security Comparison

We compare our scheme with other schemes appearing in the literature in Table 1. We assume that all schemes are implemented with the same $\mathbb{G}_1$, $\mathbb{G}_2$, $\hat{e}$ and q as defined in Section 4.

Table 1. A comparison between various schemes in the literature.

scheme	security				ciphertext size	sign/encrypt ops.			decrypt/verify ops.		
	1	2	3	4		$\mathbb{G}_1$	$\mathbb{G}_2$	$\hat{e}$	$\mathbb{G}_1$	$\mathbb{G}_2$	$\hat{e}$
[6]	y	y	y	y	$2n_1 + n_{id} + m$	3	1	1	2	0	4
[11]	?	y	y	n	$n_1 + n_q + m$	2	2	2	0	2	4
[13]	y	n	y	n	$2n_1 + m$	3	0	1	0	1	4
[14]	?	?	?	n	$3n_1 + m$	3	1	0	1	0	2
[15]	?	?	?	n	$2n_1 + m$	2	1	1	0	1	3
[19]	?	y	y	?	$2n_1 + n_{id} + m$	4	0	1	1	0	3
ours	y	y	y	y	$2n_1 + n_{id} + m$	3	0	1	1	0	3

The 1, 2, 3 and 4 in the "security" column refer to security under Definition 1, 2, 3 and 4 respectively. A y means that the scheme provably meets the definition, a n means that the scheme is not secure under the definition, and a ? means that the status is unknown.

In the "ciphertext size" column we let n_1 be the number of bits required to represent an element of $\mathbb{G}_1$, n_q be the number of bits required to represent an element of $\mathbb{F}_q$, n_{id} be the number of bits required to represent an identity, and m be the number of bits in the message being signcrypted. The ciphertext size is therefore measured in bits.

In the "sign/encrypt ops." and "decrypt/verify ops." columns, the subcolumns $\mathbb{G}_1$, $\mathbb{G}_2$ and $\hat{e}$ hold the number of multiplications in $\mathbb{G}_1$, exponentiations in $\mathbb{G}_2$ and computations of $\hat{e}$ respectively.

Note that the scheme in [14] has a slight computational overhead for computing public keys when compared to the other schemes we have mentioned. This is not reflected in the table above.

7   Conclusions

We have proposed an identity-based signcryption scheme that is the most efficient among the provably secure schemes of its type proposed to date. Our scheme admits a full security analysis in the model of Boyen [6].

Our security analysis, like the security analysis for all provably secure identity-based signcryption schemes, requires the random oracle model [3]. Techniques have recently been developed for designing identity-based encryption schemes with provable security in the standard model [4]. It would be interesting to know if these, or other, techniques can be applied to identity based signcryption.

References

1. J. H. An, Y. Dodis, and T. Rabin. On the security of joint signature and encryption. In *Advances in Cryptology - EUROCRYPT 2002*, volume 2332 of *LNCS*, pages 83–107. Springer-Verlag, 2002.
2. P. S. L. M. Barreto, H. Y. Kim, B. Lynn, and M. Scott. Efficient algorithms for paring-based cryptosystems. In *Advances in Cryptology - CRYPTO 2002*, volume 2442 of *LNCS*, pages 354–368. Springer-Verlag, 2002.

3. M. Bellare and P. Rogaway. Random oracles are practical: A paradigm for designing efficient protocols. In 1st *ACM Conference on Computer and Communications Security*, pages 62–73, 1993.

4. D. Boneh and X. Boyen. Secure identity based encryption without random oracles. In *Advances in Cryptology - CRYPTO 2004*, volume 3152 of *LNCS*, pages 443–459. Springer-Verlag, 2004.

5. D. Boneh and M. Franklin. Identity-based encryption from the Weil pairing. In *Advances in Cryptology - CRYPTO 2001*, volume 2139 of *LNCS*, pages 213–229. Springer-Verlag, 2001.

6. X. Boyen. Multipurpose identity-based signcryption: A swiss army knife for identity-based cryptography. In *Advances in Cryptology - CRYPTO 2003*, volume 2729 of *LNCS*, pages 382–398. Springer-Verlag, 2003.

7. J. C. Cha and J. H. Cheon. An identity-based signature from gap Diffie-Hellman groups. In *Public Key Cryptography - PKC 2003*, volume 2567 of *LNCS*, pages 18–30. Springer-Verlag, 2003.

8. L. Chen and J. Malone-Lee. Improved identity-based sincryption. Cryptology ePrint Archive, Report 2004/114, 2004. http://eprint.iacr.org/.

9. C. Cocks. An identity-based encryption scheme based on quadratic residues. In *Cryptography and Coding*, volume 2260 of *LNCS*, pages 360–363. Springer-Verlag, 2001.

10. S. Goldwasser, S. Micali, and R. Rivest. A digital signature scheme secure against adaptive chosen-message attacks. *SIAM Journal on Computing*, 17(2):281–308, 1988.

11. B. Libert and J. J. Quisquater. New identity-based signcryption schemes from pairings. In *IEEE Information Theory Workshop 2003*. Full version available at http://eprint.iacr.org/2003/023/.

12. B. Libert and J. J. Quisquater. Efficient signcryption with key privacy from gap Diffie-Hellman groups. In *Public Key Cryptography - PKC 2004*, volume 2947 of *LNCS*, pages 187–200. Springer-Verlag, 2004.

13. J. Malone-Lee. Identity-based signcryption. Cryptology ePrint Archive, Report 2002/098, 2002. http://eprint.iacr.org/.

14. Noel McCullagh and Paulo S. L. M. Barreto. Efficient and forward-secure identity-based signcryption. Cryptology ePrint Archive, Report 2004/117, 2004. http://eprint.iacr.org/.

15. D. Nalla and K. C. Reddy. Signcryption scheme for identity-based cryptosystems. Cryptology ePrint Archive, Report 2003/066, 2003. http://eprint.iacr.org/.

16. C. Rackoff and D. Simon. Non-interactive zero-knowledge proof of knowledge and chosen ciphertext attack. In *Advances in Cryptology - CRYPTO '91*, volume 576 of *LNCS*, pages 433–444. Springer-Verlag, 1992.

17. R. Sakai, K. Ohgishi, and M. Kasahara. Cryptosystems based on pairings. In *Symposium on Cryptography and Information Security*, 2000.

18. A. Shamir. Identity-based cryptosystems and signature schemes. In *Advances in Cryptology - CRYPTO '84*, volume 0193 of *LNCS*, pages 47–53. Springer-Verlag, 1984.

19. T. H. Yuen and V. K. Wei. Fast and proven secure blind identity-based signcryption from pairings. Cryptology ePrint Archive, Report 2004/121, 2004. http://eprint.iacr.org/.

20. Y. Zheng. Digital signcryption or how to achieve cost(signature & encryption) $<<$ cost(signature) + cost(encryption). In *Advances in Cryptology - CRYPTO '97*, volume 1294 of *LNCS*, pages 165–179. Springer-Verlag, 1997.

Efficient Multi-receiver Identity-Based Encryption and Its Application to Broadcast Encryption

Joonsang Baek, Reihaneh Safavi-Naini, and Willy Susilo

Centre for Information Security Research,
School of Information Technology and Computer Science,
University of Wollongong,
Wollongong NSW 2522, Australia
{baek,rei,wsusilo}@uow.edu.au

Abstract. In this paper, we construct an efficient "multi-receiver identity-based encryption scheme". Our scheme only needs one (or none if precomputed and provided as a public parameter) pairing computation to encrypt a single message for n receivers, in contrast to the simple construction that re-encrypts a message n times using Boneh and Franklin's identity-based encryption scheme, considered previously in the literature. We extend our scheme to give adaptive chosen ciphertext security. We support both schemes with security proofs under precisely defined formal security model. Finally, we discuss how our scheme can lead to a highly efficient public key broadcast encryption scheme based on the "subset-cover" framework.

Keywords: Multi-Receiver Identity-Based Encryption, Formal Security Analysis, Public Key Broadcast Encryption

1 Introduction

Motivation. Assume that there are n receivers, numbered $1, \ldots, n$, and that each of them keeps a private and public key pair denoted by (sk_i, pk_i). A sender then encrypts a message M_i directed to receiver i using pk_i for $i = 1, \ldots, n$ and sends $(C_1, \ldots, C_n)$ as a ciphertext. Upon receiving the ciphertext, receiver i extracts C_i and decrypts it using its private key sk_i. This setting of public key encryption is generally referred to as "multi-receiver (recipient) public key encryption" in the literature [2, 3, 16].

Now consider a situation where "Identity-Based Encryption (IBE)" [7, 10] is incorporated to the above setting. In this setting, the public key pk_i is replaced by receiver i's identifier information (identity) ID_i, which will be used as encryption key. Receiver i has a private key associated with ID_i, obtained from the trusted Private Key Generator (PKG), so that it can correctly decrypt C_i. This setting, which we call "multi-receiver identity-based encryption", is a main theme of this paper.

As one can easily see, any multi-receiver public key encryption scheme can be transformed into a natural *broadcast encryption* scheme: Receivers are given

S. Vaudenay (Ed.): PKC 2005, LNCS 3386, pp. 380–397, 2005.

private/public key pairs which may be generated by the sender. A *single* message M is then encrypted by running the multi-receiver encryption algorithm with all messages M_i for $i = 1, \ldots, n$ set to M to produce a ciphertext which is sent to all receivers.

In the non-identity-based setting, the above broadcast encryption has received a great attention from the research community, while relatively little research has been done on the identity-based setting. One may, however, argue that the natural construction of a broadcast encryption scheme derived from the multi-receiver public key encryption scheme can trivially be transformed into the one in the identity-based setting. That is, a single message M is encrypted n times using ID_i for $i = 1, \ldots, n$ and the resulting ciphertext $(C_1, \ldots, C_n)$ is sent to the receivers. However, what one should not overlook here is that when the most widely used IBE scheme proposed by Boneh and Franklin [7] is employed to realize such scheme, we need at least n bilinear pairing computations, which is very expensive. (In fact, this was suggested in [18] and [11]).

Our Contributions. Following the above discussion, a natural question one can ask is how to design a multi-receiver identity-based encryption scheme that broadcasts a message with a high-level of computational efficiency while retaining security. In this paper, we answer this question affirmatively, providing an *efficient* multi-receiver IBE scheme that only requires "one" (or "none" if precomputed) pairing computation to encrypt a single message for multiple receivers. We provide formal security notions for multi-receiver IBE schemes based on the "selective identity attack" model in which an attacker outputs ahead of time the identities of multiple receivers that it wishes to challenge [8, 4]. We then prove that our schemes are secure against chosen plaintext attack (CPA) and adaptive ciphertext attack ("CCA2 [5]") in the random oracle model [6] assuming the standard assumptions related to the Bilinear Diffie-Hellman problems [7] are computationally hard. Finally, we show how our schemes lead to very efficient public key broadcast encryption schemes based on the "subset-cover" framework [18]. As an independent interest, we discuss in Section 5 how the selective identity attack model plays an important role in obtaining an efficient reduction in the security analysis of our efficient multi-receiver IBE schemes.

Related Work. The concept of multi-receiver public key encryption was independently formalized by Bellare, Boldyreva, and Micali [2], and Baudron, Pointcheval, and Stern [1]. Their main result is that the security of public key encryption in the single-receiver setting implies the security in the multi-receiver setting. Hence, for example, one can construct a semantically secure multi-receiver public key encryption scheme by simply encrypting a message under n different public keys of a semantically secure single-receiver public key encryption scheme. Later, Kurosawa proposed a technique called "randomness re-use" to improve the computational efficiency and bandwidths of an ElGamal [13] version of multi-receiver public key encryption scheme. Kurosawa's work was refined in [3] in a sense that a general test to determine whether a given public key encryption scheme permits the randomness re-use to build up an efficient multi-receiver encryption scheme.

To our knowledge, identity-based encryption in the multi-receiver setting has not been much treated in the literature. Chen, Harrison, Soldera, and Smart [9], and Smart [21] considered the problem of "conjunction" and "disjunction" of private keys associated with multiple identities in Boneh and Franklin's IBE scheme. In terms of conjunction, a user who has all the private keys associated with the identities that were used to encrypt a message can decrypt the ciphertext. Regarding disjunction, a user who possesses one of the private keys associated with identities that were used to create the ciphertext can decrypt. The authors of [9] and [21] showed how Boneh and Franklin's IBE scheme can be modified to solve the conjunction and disjunction problems efficiently. Especially, Smart presented a scheme that realizes the general logic formula called "conjunctive-disjunctive normal form (CDNF)" and showed how it can be used in access control to broadcast encrypted data. However, one criticism about the work of [9] and [21] is that their schemes are not supported by appropriate formal security model and proofs. Although our motivation is somewhat similar to those of [9] and [21] in terms of realizing "disjunction" in identity-based encryption, our constructions are different from theirs and importantly, we provide formal model and security proofs for our schemes.

Our work is also related to broadcast encryption [14] based on the "subset-cover" framework proposed by Naor, Naor, and Lotspiech [18]. In Section 6, we discuss it in detail.

2 Definitions for Multi-receiver Identity-Based Encryption

Model. We present a generic model for multi-receiver IBE schemes. Note that in the multi-receiver IBE setting, either a single message or multiple messages can be encrypted. However, *throughout the rest of the paper including the following definition, we assume that a single message is broadcast to the multiple receivers*, which leads to interesting schemes and applications.

Definition 1 (Multi-receiver IBE). A generic multi-receiver IBE scheme for broadcasting a single message, denoted by Π, consists of the following algorithms.

- PKG's key generation algorithm KeyGen: The PKG runs this algorithm to generate a PKG's master key and a common parameter, denoted by mk_{PKG} and cp_{PKG} respectively. Note that cp_{PKG} is given to all interested parties while mk_{PKG} is kept secret.
- PKG's private key extraction algorithm Extract: Providing an identity ID received from a user and its master key mk_{PKG} as input, the PKG runs this algorithm to generate a private key associated with ID, denoted by sk_{ID}. We write $S_{\text{ID}} = \text{Extract}(mk_{\text{PKG}}, \text{ID})$.
- Encryption algorithm Encrypt: Providing multiple identities $(\text{ID}_1, \ldots, \text{ID}_n)$ of the receivers, the PKG's common parameter cp_{PKG}, and a plaintext message M as input, the sender runs this algorithm to generates a ciphertext C which is an encryption of M under $(\text{ID}_1, \ldots, \text{ID}_n)$. We write $C = \text{Encrypt}(cp_{\text{PKG}}, (\text{ID}_1, \ldots, \text{ID}_n), M)$.

- Encryption algorithm Encrypt: Providing multiple identities $(\text{ID}_1, \ldots, \text{ID}_n)$ of the receivers, the PKG's common parameter cp_{PKG}, and a plaintext message M as input, the sender runs this algorithm to generates a ciphertext C which is an encryption of M under $(\text{ID}_1, \ldots, \text{ID}_n)$. We write $C = \text{Encrypt}(cp_{\text{PKG}}, (\text{ID}_1, \ldots, \text{ID}_n), M)$.
- Decryption Algorithm Decrypt: Providing its private key sk_{ID_i}, the PKG's common parameter cp_{PKG}, and a ciphertext C as input, the receiver numbered i runs this algorithm to get a decryption D, which is either a certain plaintext message or a "*Reject*" message. We write $D = \text{Decrypt}(cp_{\text{PKG}}, sk_{\text{ID}_i}, C)$

Security Notions. We present security notions for multi-receiver IBE schemes. In these notions, we consider the "selective identity attack" [8] in which an attacker commits ahead of time the identity that it intends to attack, which is slightly weaker than the model proposed in [7], where the attacker adaptively chooses the identity that will be challenged on rather than outputting it at the beginning.

We assume that this type of attacker outputs ahead of time a number of identities (of the receivers) that it wishes to attack, which we call a "*selective multi-ID attack* ". We then define "indistinguishability of encryptions under selective multi-ID, chosen plaintext attack", which we refer to as "IND-sMID-CPA" as follows.

Definition 2 (IND-sMID-CPA). Let A denote an attacker. Let Π be a generic multi-receiver IBE scheme. Consider the following game in which A interacts with the "Challenger":

Phase 1: A outputs target multiple identities, denoted by $(\text{ID}_1^*, \ldots, \text{ID}_n^*)$.

Phase 2: The Challenger runs the PKG's key generation algorithm $\text{KeyGen}_{\text{PKG}}(k)$ to generate a master key and a common parameter $(mk_{\text{PKG}}, cp_{\text{PKG}})$. The Challenger gives cp_{PKG} to A while keeps mk_{PKG} secret from A.

Phase 3: A issues a number of private key extraction queries, each of which is denoted by ID. Upon receiving ID, the Challenger runs the private key extraction algorithm to get $S_{\text{ID}} = \text{Extract}(mk_{\text{PKG}}, \text{ID})$. A restriction here is that $\text{ID} \neq \text{ID}_i^*$ for $i = 1, \ldots, n$.

Phase 4: A outputs a target plaintext pair (M_0, M_1). Upon receiving (M_0, M_1), the Challenger picks $\beta \in \{0, 1\}$ at random and creates a target ciphertext $C^* = \text{Encrypt}(cp_{\text{PKG}}, (\text{ID}_1^*, \ldots, \text{ID}_n^*), M_\beta)$. The Challenger returns C^* to A.

Phase 5: A issues a number of private key extraction queries as in Phase 3.

Phase 6: A outputs its guess $\beta' \in \{0, 1\}$.

We define A's guessing advantage $\mathbf{Adv}_{\Pi}^{\text{IND-sMID-CPA}}(A) = |\Pr[\beta' = \beta] - \frac{1}{2}|$. A breaks IND-sMID-CPA of Π with (t, q_{ex}, ϵ) if and only if the guessing advantage of A that makes q_{ex} private key extraction queries is greater than ϵ within running time t. The scheme Π is said to be (t, q_{ex}, ϵ)-IND-sMID-CPA secure if there is no attacker A that breaks IND-sMID-CPA of Π with (t, q_{ex}, ϵ).

We now define "indistinguishability of encryptions under selective multi-ID, *adaptive* chosen ciphertext attack", which we refer to as "IND-sMID-CCA".

Definition 3 (IND-sMID-CCA). Let A denote an attacker. Let Π be a generic multi-receiver IBE scheme. Phases 1, 2, 4, and 6 of the attack game for IND-sMID-CCA are identical to those of IND-sMID-CPA. We only describe Phase 3 and 5 in the following:

Phase 3: A issues private key extraction queries as in Phase 3 of IND-sMID-CPA. Additionally, it issues decryption queries for target identities, each of which is denoted by (C, ID_i^*) for some $i \in [1, n]$. Upon receiving this, the Challenger generates a private key associated with ID_i^*, which is denoted by $sk_{\mathrm{ID}_i^*}$, and returns $D = \mathsf{Decrypt}(cp_{\mathrm{PKG}}, S_{\mathrm{ID}_i}, C)$ to A.

Phase 5: As in Phase 3, A issues a number of private key extraction and decryption queries for target identities. However, this time, A is not allowed to issue a target ciphertext C^* as a decryption query.

We define A's guessing advantage $\mathbf{Adv}_{\Pi}^{\mathrm{IND-sMID-CCA}}(A) = |\Pr[\beta' = \beta] - \frac{1}{2}|$. A breaks IND-sMID-CCA of Π with $(t, q_{ex}, q_d, \epsilon)$ if and only if the guessing advantage of A that makes q_{ex} private key extraction queries and q_d decryption queries is greater than ϵ within running time t. The scheme Π is said to be $(t, q_{ex}, q_d, \epsilon)$-IND-sMID-CCA secure if there is no attacker A that breaks IND-sMID-CCA of Π with $(t, q_{ex}, q_d, \epsilon)$.

3   Bilinear Pairing and Related Computational Problems

As preliminaries, we review the bilinear pairing and related computational problems on which our efficient multi-receiver IBE schemes are based.

Definition 4 (Bilinear Pairing). An admissible bilinear pairing [7], which we denote by "$\hat{e}$", is defined over two groups of the same prime-order q denoted by $\mathcal{G}$ and $\mathcal{F}$ in which the Computational Diffie-Hellman problem is intractable. We will use an additive notation to describe the operation in $\mathcal{G}$ while we will use a multiplicative notation for the operation in $\mathcal{F}$. In practice, the group $\mathcal{G}$ is implemented using a group of points on certain elliptic curves, each of which has a small MOV exponent [17], and the group $\mathcal{F}$ will be implemented using a subgroup of the multiplicative group of a finite field. The admissible bilinear map has the following properties. 1) Bilinear: $\hat{e}(aP_1, bP_2) = \hat{e}(P_1, P_2)^{ab}$, where $P_1, P_2 \in \mathcal{G}$ and $a, b \in \mathbb{Z}_q^*$; 2) Non-degenerate: $\hat{e}$ does not send all pairs of points in $\mathcal{G} \times \mathcal{G}$ to the identity in $\mathcal{F}$. (Hence, if P is a generator of $\mathcal{G}$ then $\hat{e}(P, P)$ is a generator of $\mathcal{F}$).; 3)Computable: For all $P_1, P_2 \in \mathcal{G}$, the map $\hat{e}(P_1, P_2)$ is efficiently computable.

We now review the "Bilinear Decision Diffie-Hellman (BDDH)" problem, which is a "decisional" version of the Bilinear Diffie-Hellman problem on which Boneh and Franklin's IBE scheme [7] is based.

Definition 5 (BDDH). Let $\mathcal{G}$ and $\mathcal{F}$ be two groups of the same prime order q. Let P be a generator of $\mathcal{G}$. Suppose that there exists a bilinear map $\hat{e} : \mathcal{G} \times \mathcal{G} \to \mathcal{F}$. Let A be an attacker. A tries to solve the following problem: *Given (P, aP, bP, cP, κ) for uniformly chosen $a, b, c \in \mathbb{Z}_q^*$ and $\kappa \in \mathcal{F}$, decide whether $\kappa = \hat{e}(P, P)^{abc}$.*

We define A's guessing advantage $\mathbf{Adv}_{\mathcal{G}}^{\mathrm{BDDH}}(A)$ by

$$\Pr[A(P, aP, bP, cP, \hat{e}(P, P)^{abc}) = 1] - \Pr[A(P, aP, bP, cP, \gamma) = 1],$$

where $\gamma \in \mathcal{F}$ is chosen uniformly at random. A solves the BDDH problem with (t, ϵ) if and only if the guessing advantage of A is greater than ϵ within running time t. The BDDH problem is said to be (t, ϵ)-intractable if if there is no attacker A that solves the BDDH problem with (t, ϵ).

It is widely believed that the BDDH problem is computationally hard [4, 8]. Hence, we can define a Gap-Bilinear Diffie-Hellman (Gap-BDH) problem which belongs to the new class of computational problems, called "Gap Problems" proposed by Okamoto and Pointcheval [19]. Informally, the intractability of the Gap-BDH means that it is hard to compute a Bilinear Diffie-Hellman key $\hat{e}(P, P)^{abc}$ of (P, aP, bP, cP) although one has access to a BDDH oracle that, given a tuple (P, aP, bP, cP, κ), decides whether $\kappa = \hat{e}(P, P)^{abc}$. A formal definition follows.

Definition 6 (Gap-BDH). Let $\mathcal{G}$ and $\mathcal{F}$ be two groups of order the same prime order q. Let P be a generator of $\mathcal{G}$. Suppose that there exists a bilinear map $\hat{e} : \mathcal{G} \times \mathcal{G} \to \mathcal{F}$. Let A be an attacker. A tries to solve the following problem: Given (P, aP, bP, cP), compute a Bilinear Diffie-Hellman key $\hat{e}(P, P)^{abc}$ with the help of the Bilinear Decisional Diffie-Hellman (BDDH) oracle, which, given (P, aP, bP, cP, κ), outputs 1 if $\kappa = \hat{e}(P, P)^{abc}$ and 0 otherwise.

We define A's advantage $\mathbf{Adv}_{\mathcal{G}}^{\mathrm{Gap-BDH}}(A) = \Pr[A(P, aP, bP, cP) = \hat{e}(P, P)^{abc}]$. A solves the Gap-BDH problem with (t, q_o, ϵ) if and only if the guessing advantage of A that makes q_o BDDH-oracle queries is greater than ϵ within running time t. The Gap-BDH problem is said to be (t, q_o, ϵ)-intractable if if there is no attacker A that solves the Gap-BDH problem with (t, q_o, ϵ).

4 Proposed Schemes

CPA Secure Scheme. We present our efficient multi-receiver IBE scheme based on the bilinear pairing. Our scheme is motivated by the binary-tree scheme of Canetti, Halevi, and Katz [8], which bears some similarities to Gentry and Silverberg's [15], and Boneh and Boyen's [4] hierarchical IBE schemes. However, the purpose and structure of our scheme are different from those of all the previous ones.

- KeyGen$_{\mathrm{PKG}}$: Choose two groups $\mathcal{G} = \langle P \rangle$ and $\mathcal{F}$ of the same prime order q. Construct a bilinear pairing $\hat{e} : \mathcal{G} \times \mathcal{G} \to \mathcal{F}$. Choose $Q \in \mathcal{G}^*$ uniformly at random. Choose $s \in \mathbb{Z}_q^*$ uniformly at random and compute $T = sP$. Also, select a hash function $H_1 : \{0, 1\}^* \to \mathcal{G}^*$. Return $cp_{\mathrm{PKG}} = (q, \mathcal{G}, \mathcal{F}, \hat{e}, P, Q, T, H_1)$ and $mk_{\mathrm{PKG}} = (q, \mathcal{G}, \mathcal{F}, \hat{e}, P, s)$ as a PKG's common parameter and a master key respectively.
- Extract$(mk_{\mathrm{PKG}}, \mathrm{ID})$: Compute $S_{\mathrm{ID}} = sH_1(\mathrm{ID})$. Return S_{ID} as a private key associated with identity ID.
- Encrypt$(cp_{\mathrm{PKG}}, (\mathrm{ID}_1, \ldots, \mathrm{ID}_n), M)$: Choose $r \in \mathbb{Z}_q^*$ uniformly at random and compute $C = (U, V_1, \ldots, V_n, W, \mathcal{L})$ such that

$$(U, V_1, \ldots, V_n, W, \mathcal{L}) = (rP, rH_1(\mathrm{ID}_1) + rQ \ldots, rH_1(\mathrm{ID}_n) + rQ, \hat{e}(Q, T)^r M, \mathcal{L}),$$

where $\mathcal{L}$ is a label that contains information about how "V_i" is associated with each receiver. Return C as a ciphertext. (Notice that $\hat{e}(Q, T)$ can be precomuted and provided as a PKG's common parameter. In this case, there is no need for the sender to perform a pairing computation).

- Decrypt($cp_{\text{PKG}}, S_{\text{ID}_i}, C$) for some $i \in [1, n]$: Parse C as $(U, V_1, \ldots, V_n, W, \mathcal{L})$. Using $\mathcal{L}$, find appropriate V_i. Then, compute

$$M = \frac{\hat{e}(U, S_{\text{ID}_i})}{\hat{e}(T, V_i)} W$$

and return M as a plaintext.

It is easy to see that the above decryption algorithm is consistent. Indeed, if C is a valid ciphertext,

$$\frac{\hat{e}(U, S_{\text{ID}_i})}{\hat{e}(T, V_i)} W = \frac{\hat{e}(rP, sH_1(\text{ID}))}{\hat{e}(sP, rH_1(\text{ID}_i) + rQ)} W = \frac{\hat{e}(rP, sH_1(\text{ID}))}{\hat{e}(rP, sH_1(\text{ID}_i) + sQ)} W$$

$$= \frac{\hat{e}(rP, sH_1(\text{ID}))}{\hat{e}(rP, sH_1(\text{ID}_i))\hat{e}(rP, sQ)} \hat{e}(Q, T)^r M = M.$$

Security Analysis. We now prove that the hardness of the BDDH problem (Definition 5) is sufficient for the above scheme to be IND-sMID-CPA secure in the random oracle model [6].

Theorem 1. *The above scheme is $(t, q_{H_1}, q_{ex}, \epsilon)$-IND-sMID-CPA secure in the random oracle model assuming that the BDDH problem is (t', ϵ')-intractable, where $t' > t + q_{H_1} O(\tau_1)$. ($\tau_1$ denotes the computing time for an exponentiation in $\mathcal{G}$).*

Proof. Assume that an attacker A breaks IND-sMID-CPA of the above scheme with probability greater than ϵ within time t making q_{ex} private key extraction queries. We show that using A, one can construct an attacker B for solving the BDDH problem (Definition 5).

Suppose that B is given $(q, \mathcal{G}, \mathcal{F}, P, aP, bP, cP, \kappa)$ as an instance of the BDDH problem. By ϵ' and t', we denote B's winning probability and running time respectively. B can simulate the Challenger's execution of each phase of IND-sMID-CPA game for A as follows.

[Simulation of Phase 1] Suppose that A outputs target multiple identities (ID_1^*, ..., ID_n^*).

[Simulation of Phase 2] B sets $Q = bP$ and $T = cP$, and gives A ($q, \mathcal{G}, \mathcal{F}, \hat{e}, P, T, Q, H_1$) as the PKG's common parameter, where H_1 is a random oracle controlled by B as follows.

Upon receiving a random oracle query ID_j to H_1:
- If there exists (ID_j, l_j, L_j) in H_1List, return L_j. Otherwise, do the following:
  * If $\text{ID}_j = \text{ID}_i^*$ for some $i \in [1, n]$, compute $L_j = l_j P - Q$.
  * Else choose $l_j \in \mathbb{Z}_q^*$ uniformly at random and compute $L_j = l_j P$.
  * Put (ID_j, l_j, L_j) in H_1List and return L_j as answer.

[Simulation of Phase 3] B answers A's private key extraction queries as follows.

Upon receiving a private key extraction query ID_j (Note that by the assumption of the IND-sMID-CPA game, $\text{ID}_j \neq \text{ID}_i^*$ for $i = 1, \ldots, n$).:
- If (ID_j, l_j, L_j) exists in $\mathsf{H_1List}$, compute $S_{\text{ID}_j} = l_j T$. Otherwise do the following:
  * Choose $l_j \in \mathbb{Z}_q^*$ uniformly at random and compute $S_{\text{ID}_j} = l_j T$.
  * Put (ID_j, l_j, L_j) in $\mathsf{H_1List}$ and return S_{ID_j} as answer. (Note that $S_{\text{ID}_j} = l_j T = l_j cP = cl_j P = cH_1(\text{ID}_j)$ for all $j \neq i$).

[Simulation of Phase 4] B creates a target ciphertext C^* as follows.

Upon receiving (M_0, M_1):
- Choose $\beta \in \{0, 1\}$ at random.
- Search $\mathsf{H_1List}$ to get l_i that corresponds to ID_i^* for $i = 1, \ldots, n$.
- Compute $l_i aP$ for $i = 1, \ldots, n$ and κM_β.
- Return $C^* = (aP, l_1 aP, \ldots, l_n aP, \kappa M_\beta)$ as a target ciphertext. Note here that.

[Simulation of Phase 5] B answers A's random oracle/private key extraction queries as in Phase 3.

[Simulation of Phase 6] A outputs its guess β'. If $\beta' = \beta$, B outputs 1. Otherwise, it outputs 0.

[Analysis] We note that if $\kappa = \hat{e}(P, P)^{abc}$, $\kappa M_\beta = \hat{e}(bP, cP)^a M_\beta = \hat{e}(Q, T)^a M_\beta$. Note also that $l_i aP = l_i aP - aQ + aQ = a(l_i P - Q) + aQ = aH_1(\text{ID}_i^*) + aQ$ for $i = 1, \ldots, n$. Hence C^* is a valid ciphertext. On the other hand, if κ is uniform and independent in $\mathcal{F}$, so is κM_β. It is clear that from the construction above, B perfectly simulates the random oracle H_1 and the key private key extraction in Phase 3 and 5. Hence, we get $\Pr[B(P, aP, bP, cP, \hat{e}(P, P)^{abc}) = 1] = \Pr[\beta' = \beta]$, where $|\Pr[\beta' = \beta] - \frac{1}{2}| > \epsilon$, and $\Pr[B(P, aP, bP, cP, \gamma) = 1] = \Pr[\beta' = \beta] = \frac{1}{2}$, where γ is uniform in $\mathcal{F}$. Consequently, we get

$$| \Pr[B(P, aP, bP, cP, \hat{e}(P, P)^{abc}) = 1] - \Pr[B(P, aP, bP, cP, \gamma) = 1]|$$
$$> \left| (\frac{1}{2} \pm \epsilon) - \frac{1}{2} \right| = \epsilon.$$

Note that $t' > t + q_{H_1} O(\tau_1)$, where τ_1 denotes the computing time for an exponentiation in $\mathcal{G}$.   □

CCA Secure Scheme. In order to enhance security, we modify our scheme to provide (adaptive) chosen ciphertext security. Considering efficiency and simplicity, we employ the technique used in the REACT scheme proposed by Okamoto and Pointcheval' [20].

- $\mathsf{KeyGen_{PKG}}$: Choose two groups $\mathcal{G} = \langle P \rangle$ and $\mathcal{F}$ of the same prime order q. Construct a bilinear pairing $\hat{e} : \mathcal{G} \times \mathcal{G} \rightarrow \mathcal{F}$. Choose $Q \in \mathcal{G}^*$ uniformly at random. Choose $s \in \mathbb{Z}_q^*$ uniformly at random and compute $T = sP$. Also, select hash functions $H_1 : \{0,1\}^* \rightarrow \mathcal{G}$, $H_2 : \mathcal{F} \rightarrow \{0,1\}^{k_1}$, and $H_3 : \mathcal{G} \times \cdots \times \mathcal{G} \times \mathcal{F} \times \{0,1\}^{k_1} \rightarrow \{0,1\}^{k_2}$. Return $cp_{\text{PKG}} = (q, \mathcal{G}, \mathcal{F}, \hat{e}, q, P, Q, T, H_1, H_2, H_3)$ and $mk_{\text{PKG}} = (q, \mathcal{G}, \mathcal{F}, \hat{e}, P, s)$ as PKG's common parameter and master key respectively.

- Extract(mk_{PKG}, ID): Compute $S_{\text{ID}} = sH_1(\text{ID})$. Return S_{ID} as a private key associated with identity ID.
- Encrypt(cp_{PKG}, $(\text{ID}_1, \ldots, \text{ID}_n), M$) where $M \in \{0,1\}^{k_1}$: Choose $R \in \mathcal{F}$ and $r \in \mathbb{Z}_q^*$ at random and compute compute $C = (U, V_1, \ldots, V_n, W_1, W_2, \mathcal{L}, \sigma)$ such that

$$(U, V_1, \ldots, V_n, W_1, W_2, \mathcal{L}, \sigma)$$
$$= (rP, rH_1(\text{ID}_1) + rQ \ldots, rH_1(\text{ID}_n) + rQ, \hat{e}(Q,T)^r R, M \oplus H_2(R),$$
$$H_3(R, M, U, V_1, \ldots, V_n, W_1, W_2, \mathcal{L}))$$

Return C as a ciphertext. (Notice that the "tag" σ guarantees the integrity of entire sequence of a ciphertext.)
- Decrypt(cp_{PKG}, S_{ID_i}, C, ID_i) for some $i \in [1, n]$: Parse C as $(U, V_1, \ldots, V_n, W_1, W_2, \mathcal{L}, \sigma)$. Using $\mathcal{L}$, find appropriate V_i. Then, subsequently compute $R = \frac{\hat{e}(U, S_{\text{ID}_i})}{\hat{e}(T, V_i)} W_1$, $M = W_2 \oplus H_2(R)$, and $\sigma' = H_3(R, M, V_1, \ldots, V_n, W_1, W_2, \mathcal{L})$. If $\sigma' = \sigma$, return M as a plaintext and "Reject" otherwise.

Security Analysis. We prove that the hardness of the Gap-BDH problem (Definition 6) is sufficient for the above scheme to be IND-sMID-CCA secure in the random oracle model. (The proof is given in Appendix A).

Theorem 2. *The above scheme is $(t, q_{H_1}, q_{H_2}, q_{H_3}, q_{ex}, q_d, \epsilon)$-IND-sMID-CCA secure in the random oracle model assuming that the Gap-BDH problem is (t', q_o, ϵ')-intractable, where $\epsilon' > \epsilon - \frac{q_d}{2^{k_2}}$ and $t' > t + (q_{H_1} + q_{ex})O(\tau_1) + q_d O(\tau_2) + (q_{H_2} + q_{H_3})O(1)$, $q_o = q_{H_2} + q_{H_3}$ (τ_1 and τ_2 respectively denote the computing time for an exponentiation in $\mathcal{G}$ and a pairing $\hat{e}$).*

5   Discussions on Efficiency and Security of Our Scheme

Efficiency Gains. We compare the major computational overhead and transmission rate (the length of the ciphertext) of our scheme with those of the obvious construction of multi-receiver IBE that simply re-encrypt a message M n times using Boneh and Franklin's IBE scheme, which we call "n-sequential composition of BF-IBE". In this scheme, M is encrypted to $(r_1 P, M \oplus H_2(\hat{e}(H_1(\text{ID}_1), T)^{r_1}))$, $\ldots, (r_n P, M \oplus H_2(\hat{e}(H_1(\text{ID}_n), T)^{r_n}))$, where $r_1, \ldots, r_n \in \mathbb{Z}_q^*$ are uniformly chosen at random and $(s, T = (sP)$ is the PKG's master key and common parameter respectively. As one can see, it is clear that our scheme provides much better performance: To encrypt a message M, our scheme only needs one pairing computation (none if $\hat{e}(Q,T)$ is precomputed), n additions in group $\mathcal{G}$ (to compute $H_1(\text{ID}_i) + Q$), $n + 1$ scalar multiplications with elements from $\mathcal{G}$ (to compute rP and $r(H_1(\text{ID}_i) + Q) = rH_1(\text{ID}_i) + rQ$), and 1 exponentiation in group $\mathcal{F}$ (to compute $\hat{e}(Q,T)^r$). The transmission rate is $(n+1)l_1 + l_2$ where l_1 and l_2 denote the bit-length of the element in $\mathcal{G}$ and $\mathcal{F}$ respectively. On the other hand, the n-sequential composition of BF-IBE needs n pairing computations (to compute $\hat{e}(H_1(\text{ID}_i), T)$, n scalar multiplications with elements in $\mathcal{G}$ (to compute $r_i P$), n exponentiations in group $\mathcal{F}$ (to compute $\hat{e}(H_1(\text{ID}_i), T)^{r_i}$). The transmission rate of this scheme is $nl_1 + nl_3$ where l_3 denotes the bit-length of the message.

In the following table, we summarize the above comparison.

	Pairings	Add. in $\mathcal{G}$	Mult. in $\mathcal{G}$	Exp. in $\mathcal{F}$	Trans. Rate
Our scheme	1 (or 0)	n	$n+2$	1	$(n+1)l_1 + l_2$
n-seq. comp. of BF-IBE	n	0	n	n	$nl_1 + nl_3$

One might argue, however, that the randomness re-use technique [16, 3] can be employed to reduce the number of multiplications in group $\mathcal{G}$. This indeed helps, but the n pairings and n exponentiations in group $\mathcal{F}$ still cannot be removed.

Fully Adaptive Multi-ID Attack. We notice that our scheme can also be proven secure in the "fully adaptive multi-ID attack" model where the attacker adaptively chooses which identity to attack and outputs target multiple identities in the challenger phase after it sees public parameters (rather than ahead of time). Unfortunately, the reduction is not very tight in that it introduces q_{ex}^n factor, where n denotes the number of receivers. The difficulty in getting an efficient reduction for our scheme stems from the difficulty in simulating a target ciphertext while handling the random oracle and key extraction queries.

To get a feeling for this, we sketch a security proof for our scheme in the fully adaptive multi-ID attack model. Let B be a BDDH attacker which is given (P, aP, bP, cP, κ), where κ is either $\hat{e}(P, P)^{abc}$ or a random element in $\mathcal{F}$, as an instance. Let A be a CPA attacker for our scheme in the fully adaptive multi-ID attack model. B first sets $Q = bP$ and $T = cP$, which will serve as the PKG's public key. Upon receiving a query ID to the random oracle H_1, B generates a random coin δ such that $\Pr[\delta = 0] = \rho$ and responds to the query with lP, where $l \in \mathbb{Z}_q^*$ is chosen at random, if $\delta = 0$, and $lP - Q$ otherwise. B puts $(\mathtt{ID}, l, \delta)$ in H_1List, and if the same query is asked, B searches this list to respond to it. Upon receiving a private key extraction query ID, B runs the above algorithm for simulating H_1 to get $(\mathtt{ID}, l, \delta)$ and answers with lT if $\delta = 0$, and aborts the simulation otherwise. Upon receiving target multiple identities $(\mathtt{ID}_1^*, \ldots, \mathtt{ID}_n^*)$ and target plaintexts (M_0, M_1), B runs the above algorithm for simulating H_1 to get $(\mathtt{ID}_1^*, l_1, \delta_1), \ldots, (\mathtt{ID}_n^*, l_n, \delta_n)$. Unless $\delta_1 = \cdots = \delta_n = 1$, B aborts the simulation, otherwise, creates a target ciphertext as follows: $C^* = (aP, l_1 aP, \ldots, l_n aP, \kappa M_\beta)$ for a random $\beta \in \{0, 1\}$. The rest of the simulation are the same as the proof of Theorem 1.

As long as B does not abort the game, A's view in the simulation is identical to the view in the real attack from the same argument given in the proof of Theorem 1. The probability that B does not abort the simulation is $\rho^{q_{ex}}(1 - \rho)^n$, which is maximized at $1 - \frac{n}{q_{ex}+n}$. Consequently, this introduces q_{ex}^n factor in the reduction cost. In the *selective* multi-ID attack model, we do not have this problem as $H_1(\mathtt{ID}_i^*)$ values can be "programmed" *at the beginning*.

On the other hand, we notice that one can get an efficient reduction for the security of the n-sequential composition of BF-IBE in the fully adaptive multi-ID attack model, due to its structural property which results in more pairing computations.

Trading off between security and efficiency is subjective. However, as seen from the beginning of this section, the efficiency gain in our scheme is huge, especially when there are a large number of receivers. In the following section, we show this is indeed a merit when our scheme is applied to broadcast encryption.

6   Application to Public Key Broadcast Encryption Based on Subset-Cover Framework

Broadcast Encryption Based on the Subset-Cover Framework. "Broadcast encryption" [14] deals with the problem of one party transmitting data to a large group of receivers so that only qualified subsets can decrypt the data. There are a number of applications of such scheme, e.g. pay-TV applications, distribution of copyright material, streaming audio/video, and etc. Since its introduction [14], broadcast encryption has been extensively studied in the literature. However, in this paper, we only focus on the "stateless receiver" case for broadcast encryption in the *public key* setting [18]. (Note that "stateless receiver" means that each user is given a fixed set of keys that cannot be changed through the lifetime of the system).

In the symmetric setting of broadcast encryption, only the trusted designer of the system, which we refer to as "Center", can broadcast a message. On the other hand, in the public key setting, the Center publishes a short public key which enables any party to broadcast data. Formally, a generic broadcast encryption scheme in the public key setting can be defined as follows [11].

Definition 7 (Public Key Broadcast Encryption). A public key broadcast encryption scheme consists of the following algorithms.

- Center's key generation algorithm $\mathsf{KeyGen}_{\mathrm{CTR}}$: Providing possibly a revocation threshold z (the maximum number of users that can be revoked) as input, the Center runs this algorithm to generate the Center's private key and public key, denoted by sk_{CTR} and pk_{CTR} respectively.
- Registration algorithm Reg: Providing the Center's private key and an index i associated with a user as input, the Center runs this algorithm to generate the secret initialization data, denoted by sk_i, to be delivered to a new user when he subscribes to the system. We write $sk_i = \mathsf{Reg}(sk_{\mathrm{CTR}}, i)$.
- Encryption algorithm $\mathsf{Encrypt}$: Providing the Center's public key, a session key K, and a set $\mathcal{R}$ of revoked users (with $|\mathcal{R}| \leq z$ if a threshold was specified to the Center's key generation algorithm) as input, the sender runs this algorithm to generate a ciphertext C to be broadcast. We write $C = \mathsf{Encrypt}(pk_{\mathrm{CTR}}, K, \mathcal{R})$.
- Decryption algorithm $\mathsf{Decrypt}$: Providing the secret data sk_i of a user and c ciphertext C, the user runs this algorithm to generate a decryption D, which is either a certain plaintext or a *"Reject"* message. We write $D = \mathsf{Decrypt}(sk_i, C)$.

Subset-Cover Framework. In brief, the basic idea behind the "subset-cover" framework for broadcast encryption (in the symmetric setting) proposed by Naor, Naor, and Lotspiech [18] is to define a family $\mathcal{S}$ of subsets of the set $\mathcal{N}$ of users, and to assign a key to each subset. Note that all the users in the subset have access to the assigned key. If the Center wants to broadcast a message to all the "non-revoked" users, it first determines a partition of $\mathcal{N}/\mathcal{R}$, where $\mathcal{R}$ denotes the set of "revoked" users, and then encrypts the session key used to masquerade the message with all the keys associated to the subsets in the partition, which are elements of $\mathcal{S}$.

In [18], two specific methods that realize the above subset-cover framework: The "Complete Subtree (CS)" method and "Subset Difference (SD)" method. Since our scheme is well applicable to the CS method, we review it in detail as follows. In the CS scheme, users are organized in a full binary tree, denoted by $\mathcal{T}$: For simplicity, assume that there are $N = 2^h$ users in the system. Then, associate each user to a leaf of the full binary tree $\mathcal{T}$ of height h. The Subset-Cover family $\mathcal{S}$ is now the collection of all the full *subtrees* of $\mathcal{T}$. That is, if v_i is a node in $\mathcal{T}$, $S_i \in \mathcal{S}$ is the set of all the leaves of the full subtree of $\mathcal{T}$ rooted at v_i. To associate a key with each element of $\mathcal{S}$, the Center simply assigns a random number k_i to each node v_i. k_i is then be used as encryption/decryption key for the subset S_i. Since each user needs to know the keys corresponding to all the subsets he/she belongs to, during the registration step, the Center gives the user all the keys k_i assigned to each node v_i in the path from the root to the leaf representing the user. Hence, each user is required to store $O(\log N)$ keys. Note that the Center needs to keep track of all these keys given to each user. However, it was suggested in [18] that the Center derive all the $2N - 1$ keys from some short seed using a pseudo-random function.

A New Public Key Broadcast Encryption from Our Efficient Multi-receiver IBE Scheme. The CS method described above can also be realized in the public key setting as envisioned in [18]. Namely, one can assign a public key pk_i to each node v_i. However, as already mentioned in [18], this is very inefficient in that total $2N - 1$ public keys should explicitly be stored in some directory. To overcome this deficiency, the authors of [18] suggest that the IBE scheme be employed, which requires only $O(1)$ space. According to Dodis and Fazio [11], this can be explained as follows: First, assign an identifier $\text{ID}(S_i)$ to each subset S_i of the family $\mathcal{S}$. As an example, assign each edge of the full binary tree $\mathcal{T}$ with 0 or 1 depending on whether the edge connects the node with its left or right child, and assign to the subset S_i rooted at v_i the bit-string obtained reading off all the labels in the path from the root down to v_i. Then, the Center runs the key generation algorithm of IBE scheme to generate public parameters and the description of the mapping used to assign an identifier to each subset. Namely, the Center plays the role of the PKG in the IBE scheme. For each subset $S_i \in \mathcal{S}$, the Center generates a private key associated with it by running the private key extraction algorithm of the IBE scheme with the identifier $\text{ID}(S_i)$. The Center then distributes the private data needed to decrypt the broadcast ciphertext, as in the symmetric key setting. Now, when a party wants to broadcast a message, it encrypts the session key used to protect the message under the public keys $\text{ID}(S_{j_i})$ relative to all the subsets that cover all the non-revoked users. Note that this party only needs to know the public key of the Center and the description of the mapping $\text{ID}(\cdot)$.

As a concrete instantiation, Dodis and Fazio apply the simple sequential composition of Boneh and Franklin's [7] IBE scheme to realize the above. More precisely, one can encrypt a session key K as follows: $(r_1 P, K \oplus H_2(\hat{e}(H(\text{ID}(S_1)), T)^{r_1})), \ldots, (r_t P, K \oplus H_2(\hat{e}(H(\text{ID}(S_t)), T)^{r_t}))$ where $S_1, \ldots, S_t$ denote the subsets that cover $\mathcal{N}/\mathcal{R}$ and $(s, T = (sP))$ is the Center's private and public key pair. Note that $t = \mu \log \frac{N}{\mu}$ where $\mu = |\mathcal{R}|$ and $N = |\mathcal{N}|$. Hence, at least t pairing computations are needed.

Our Proposal. In contrast, using our multi-receiver IBE scheme presented in Section 4, one can design a very efficient public key broadcast encryption scheme that realizes the CS mechanism. In this new scheme, a session key K is encrypted as follows:

$$(rP, rH_1(\text{ID}(S_1)) + rQ \ldots, rH_1(\text{ID}(S_t)) + rQ, \hat{e}(Q, T)^r K),$$

where $(P, Q, T(= sP))$ and s are the Center's public and private keys respectively, and $r \in \mathbb{Z}_q^*$ is uniformly chosen at random.

Note that in the above scheme, the length of the broadcast message remains the same as that of the original scheme of [18]. That is, $t = \mu \log \frac{N}{\mu}$. The main advantage of our scheme over those considered in [18,11], however, is that it is computationally much more efficient as we just need to compute t additions in group $\mathcal{G}$ instead of t pairings. Note also that compared with the scheme based on the SD method, which is proposed in [11], our scheme turns out to be more efficient in that the hierarchical IBE scheme [15] adopted in [11] results in expansion of the length of the encryption proportional to the depth in the hierarchy and more pairing computations proportional to the number of subset covers.

The above scheme can also be extended to provide chosen ciphertext security using our CCA scheme proposed in Section 4. More precisely, the security of the this scheme is relative to the following notion, which is weaker than the (public key version of) security notion for broadcast encryption presented in [18] in a sense that the the attacker outputs a set of revoked user before it sees a public key *but stronger* in a sense that it provides adaptive chosen ciphertext security. Note that the security notion given in [18] only considers non-adaptive chosen ciphertext attack, sometimes referred to as "CCA1 [5]".

Definition 8 (IND-sREV-CCA). Let A denote an attacker. Consider the following game in which A interacts with the "Challenger":

Phase 1: A outputs a set of revoked users denoted by $\mathcal{R}$.
Phase 2: The Challenger runs the Center's key generation algorithm $\text{KeyGen}_{\text{CTR}}$ to generate a private and public key pair $(sk_{\text{CTR}}, pk_{\text{CTR}})$ of the Center. The Challenger gives cp_{CTR} to A while keeps sk_{CTR} secret from A.
Phase 3: A requests the private data relative to the revoked users. Upon receiving each request, the Challenger runs the registration algorithm $\text{Reg}(sk_{\text{CTR}}, i)$ to give A the private data relative to the revoked users. A also queries arbitrary ciphertexts to see any non-revoked users decrypt them. Upon receiving each decryption query, the Challenger runs $\text{Decrypt}(sk_i, C)$ and give the resulting decryption to A.

Phase 4: A outputs a target session key pair (K_0, K_1). Upon receiving (K_0, K_1), the Challenger picks a coin $\beta \in \{0, 1\}$ at random and returns a target ciphertext $C^* = \mathsf{Encrypt}(pk_{\mathrm{CTR}}, K_\beta, \mathcal{R})$.

Phase 5: A issues a number of decryption queries C as in Phase 3 with a restriction that $C \neq C^*$.

Phase 6: A outputs its guess $\beta' \in \{0, 1\}$.

The reduction from IND-sMID-CCA (Definition 3) of our CCA-version of multi-receiver IBE scheme presented in Section 4 to IND-sREV-CCA of the public key broadcast scheme described above is almost obvious: When the attacker A for the above broadcast encryption scheme outputs the set $\mathcal{R}$ of revoked users, the attacker B for the multi-receiver IBE scheme computes subsets $S_1, \ldots, S_1$ that cover $\mathcal{N}/\mathcal{R}$ and then outputs $\mathtt{ID}_1(S_1), \ldots, \mathtt{ID}_t(S_1)$ as a target multiple identities. B then gives A the obtained PKG's common parameter as the Center's public key. B proceeds to answer A's queries in Phase 3 by querying its private key extraction and decryption oracles. When A outputs a target key pair (K_0, K_1) in Phase 4, B forwards it to its Challenger to get an encryption of K_0 or K_1 under the target multiple identities $\mathtt{ID}_1(S_1), \ldots, \mathtt{ID}_t(S_1)$. B gives this as a target ciphertext to A and proceeds to answer A's decryption queries, which are different from the target ciphertext. When A outputs $\beta' \in \{0, 1\}$ in Phase 6, B returns it as its final guess.

7 Concluding Remarks

In this paper, we proposed provably secure multi-receiver IBE schemes that broadcast encrypted data with a high-level of efficiency. We also discussed how the proposed schemes can be used to enhance the efficiency of public key broadcast encryption schemes for stateless receivers, based on the subset-cover framework.

Acknowledgement

The authors are grateful to anonymous referees for their helpful comments.

References

1. O. Baudron, D. Pointcheval, and J. Stern, *Extended Notions of Security for Multicast Public Key Cryptosystems*, In ICALP 2000, LNCS 1853, pp. 499–511, Springer-Verlag, 2000.
2. M. Bellare, A. Boldyreva, and S. Micali, *Public-key Encryption in a Multi-User Setting: Security Proofs and Improvements*, In Eurocrypt 2000, LNCS 1807, pp. 259–274, Springer-Verlag, 2000.
3. M. Bellare, A. Boldyreva, and D. Pointcheval, *Multi-Recepient Encryption Schemes: Security Notions and Randomness Re-Use*, In PKC 2003, LNCS 2567, pp. 85–99, Springer-Verlag, 2003.

4. D. Boneh and X. Boyen, *Efficient Selective-ID Secure Identity Based Encryption Without Random Oracles*, In Eurocrypt 2004, LNCS 3027, pp. 223–238, Springer-Verlag, 2004.

5. M. Bellare, A. Desai, D. Pointcheval, and P. Rogaway, *Relations Among Notions of Security for Public-Key Encryption Schemes*, In Crypto '98, LNCS 1462, pp. 26–45, Springer-Verlag, 1998.

6. M. Bellare and P. Rogaway, *Random Oracles are Practical: A Paradigm for Designing Efficient Protocols*, In ACM CCCS '93, pp. 62–73, 1993.

7. D. Boneh and M. Franklin, *Identity-Based Encryption from the Weil Pairing*, Advances in Cryptology - In Crypto 2001, LNCS 2139, pp. 213–229, Springer-Verlag, 2001.

8. R. Canetti, S. Halevi, and J. Katz, *A Forward-Secure Public-Key Encryption Scheme*, Advances in Cryptology - In Eurocrypt 2003, LNCS 2656, pp. 255–271, Springer-Verlag, 2003.

9. L. Chen, K. Harrison, D. Soldera, and N. P. Smart: *Applications of Multiple Trust Authorities in Pairing Based Cryptosysems*, In InfraSec 2002, LNCS 2437, pp. 260–275, Springer-Verlag, 2002.

10. C. Cocks, *An Identity Based Encryption Scheme Based on Quadratic Residues*, In IMA 2001, LNCS 2260, pp. 360–363, Springer-Verlag, 2001.

11. Y. Dodis and N. Fazio, *Public Key Broadcast Encryption for Stateless Receivers*, In ACM-DRM, 2002.

12. Y. Dodis and N. Fazio, *Public Key Trace and Revoke Scheme Secure against Adaptive Chosen Ciphertext Attack*, In Public Key Cryptography 2003 (PKC 2003), LNCS 2567, pp. 100–115, Springer-Verlag 2002.

13. T. ElGamal: *A Public Key Cryptosystem and a Signature Scheme Based on Discrete Logarithms*, IEEE Transactions on Information Theory, Vol. 31, pp. 469–472, IEEE, 1985.

14. A. Fiat and M. Naor, *Broadcast Encryption*, In Crypto '94, LNCS 773, pp. 480–491, Springer-Verlag, 1994.

15. C. Gentry and A. Silverberg, *Hierarchical ID-Based Cryptography*, In Asiacrypt 2002, LNCS 2501, pp. 548–566, Springer-Verlag, 2002.

16. K. Kurosawa, *Multi-Recepient Public-Key Encryption with Shortened Ciphertext*, In PKC 2002, LNCS 2274, pp. 48–63, Springer-Verlag, 2002.

17. A. J. Menezes, T. Okamoto, and S. A. Vanstone: *Reducing Elliptic Curve Logarithms to a Finite Field*, IEEE Tran. on Info. Theory, Vol. 31, pp. 1639–1646, IEEE, 1993.

18. D. Naor, M. Naor, and J. Lotspiech, *Revocation and Tracing Schemes for Stateless Receivers*, In Crypto 2001, LNCS 2139, pp. 41-62, Springer-verlag, 2001.

19. T. Okamoto and D. Pointcheval, *The Gap-Problems: A New Class of Problems for the Security of Cryptographic Schemes*, In PKC 2001, LNCS 1992, pp. 104–118, Springer-Verlag, 2001.

20. T. Okamoto and D. Pointcheval, *REACT: Rapid Enhanced-security Asymmetric Cryptosystem Transform*, In CT-RSA 2001, LNCS 2020, pp. 159–174, Springer-Verlag, 2001.

21. N. P. Smart, *Access Control Using Pairing Based Cryptography*, In CT-RSA 2003, LNCS 2612, pp. 111–121, Springer-Verlag, 2003.

A Proof of Theorem 2

Proof. We first define a normal public key encryption (non-IBE) scheme, which we call *"Bilinear ElGamal"* as follows.

- KeyGen: Choose two groups $\mathcal{G} = \langle P \rangle$ and $\mathcal{F}$ of the same prime order q. Construct a bilinear pairing $\hat{e} : \mathcal{G} \times \mathcal{G} \to \mathcal{F}$. Choose $Q \in \mathcal{G}^*$ uniformly at random. Choose $s \in \mathbb{Z}_q^*$ uniformly at random and compute $T = sP$. Return $pk = (q, \mathcal{G}, \mathcal{F}, \hat{e}, P, Q, T)$ and $sk = (q, \mathcal{G}, \mathcal{F}, \hat{e}, P, T, s)$ as a public key and a private key key respectively.
- Encrypt(pk, M): Choose $r \in \mathbb{Z}_q^*$ at random and compute $C = (U, W)$ such that $(U, W) = (rP, \hat{e}(Q, T)^r M)$ for $M \in \mathcal{F}$. Return C as a ciphertext.
- Decrypt(sk, C): Parse C as (U, W), compute $M = W/\hat{e}(U, Q)^s$, and return M as a plaintext.

In [20], a security notion for public key encryption called "One-Way-ness under Plaintext Checking Attack (OW-PCA)" is defined. Informally, a public key encryption scheme is (t', q_o, ϵ')-OW-PCA secure if for any t'-time attacker B making q_o queries to the *Plaintext Checking (PC) oracle*, which, given a ciphertext-plaintext message pair (C, M), outputs 1 if C encrypts M and 0 otherwise, B's advantage that finds a pre-image of a given ciphertext is less than ϵ'.

It is easy to see that the above Bilinear ElGamal scheme is OW-PCA secure assuming that the Gap-BDH problem (Definition 6) is intractable: Taking a public key (P, Q, T), a ciphertext (U, W), and a certain plaintext M' as input, the PC oracle checks whether $(P, U, Q, T, W/M')$ is a Bilinear Diffie-Hellman tuple. Hence, the running time and advantage of the OW-PCA attacker is exactly the same as those of Gap-BDH attacker.

Now, assume that an attacker A breaks IND-sMID-CCA of the proposed scheme in Section 4 with probability greater than ϵ within time t making q_{H_1}, q_{H_2} and q_{H_3} random oracle queries and q_{ex} private key extraction queries and q_d decryption queries. We show that using this A, one can construct an OW-PCA attacker B for the Bilinear ElGamal Scheme.

Suppose that B is given $(q, \mathcal{G}, \mathcal{F}, \hat{e}, P, Q, T)$ as a public key, and $(U^*, W^*) = (r^*P, \hat{e}(Q, T)^{r^*} R^*)$ as a target ciphertext of the *Bilinear ElGamal* Scheme. Suppose also that B's makes q_o queries to the PCA oracle of the Bilinear ElGamal scheme within time t'. We denote B's winning probability by ϵ', which will be determined later. B can simulate the Challenger's execution of each phase of IND-sMID-CCA game for A as follows.

[Simulation of Phase 1] Suppose that A outputs target multiple identities (ID$_1^*$, ..., ID$_n^*$).

[Simulation of Phase 2] B gives A $(q, \mathcal{G}, \mathcal{F}, \hat{e}, P, Q, T, H_1, H_2, H_3)$ as the PKG's common parameter, where H_1, H_2, and H_3 are random oracles controlled by B as follows.

Upon receiving a query ID$_j$ to the random oracle H_1 for some $j \in [1, q_{H_1}]$:
- If (ID_j, l_j, L_j) exists in H_1List, return L_j. Otherwise do the following:
  * If ID$_j$ = ID$_i^*$ for some $i \in [1, n]$, compute $L_j = l_j P - Q$.
  * Else choose $l_j \in \mathbb{Z}_q^*$ uniformly at random and compute $L_j = l_j P$.
  * Put (ID_j, l_j, L_j) in H_1List and return L_j as answer.

Upon receiving a query R_j to the random oracle H_2 for some $j \in [1, q_{H_2}]$:
- If (R_j, K_j) exists in H_2List, return L_j. Otherwise do the following:
  * Check whether (U^*, W^*) encrypts R_j using the PC oracle. If it is, return R_j and terminate the game. (In this case, B has achieved its goal as the pre-image of (U^*, W^*) has been found). Otherwise, do the following:
    · Pick $K_j \in \{0,1\}^{k_1}$ uniformly at random.
    · Put (R_j, K_j) in H_2List and return K_j as answer.

Upon receiving a query $(R_j, M_j, U_j, V_{j_1}, \ldots, V_{j_n}, W_{j_1}, W_{j_2}, \mathcal{L}_j)$ to the random oracle H_3 for some $j \in [1, q_{H_3}]$:
- If $((R_j, M_j, U_j, V_{j_1}, \ldots, V_{j_n}, W_{j_1}, W_{j_2}, \mathcal{L}_j), \sigma_j)$ exists in H_3List, return σ_j. Otherwise do the following:
  * Check whether (U^*, W^*) encrypts R_j using the PC oracle. If it is, return R_j and terminate the game. (In this case, B has achieved its goal as the pre-image of (U^*, W^*) has been found). Otherwise, do the following:
    · Pick $\sigma_j \in \{0,1\}^{k_2}$ uniformly at random.
    · Put $((R_j, M_j, U_j, V_{j_1}, \ldots, V_{j_n}, W_{j_1}, W_{j_2}, \mathcal{L}_j), \sigma_j)$ in H_3List and return σ_j as answer.

[Simulation of Phase 3] B then answers A's queries in Phase 3 as follows.

Upon receiving a private key extraction query ID_j for some $j \in [1, q_{ex}]$ (By assumption, $\text{ID}_j \neq \text{ID}_i^*$ for $i = 1, \ldots, n$).:
- If (ID_j, l_j, L_j) exists in H_1List, compute $S_{\text{ID}_j} = l_j T$. Otherwise do the following:
  * Choose $l_j \in \mathbb{Z}_q^*$ uniformly at random and compute $S_{\text{ID}_j} = l_j T$.
  * Put (ID_j, l_j, L_j) in H_1List and return S_{ID_j} as answer.

Upon receiving a decryption query (C_j, ID_i^*) for some $i \in [1, n]$ and $j \in [1, q_d]$, where $C_j = (U_j, V_{j_1}, \ldots, V_{j_n}, W_{j_1}, W_{j_2}, \mathcal{L}_j, \sigma_j)$:
- If $((R_j, M_j, U_j, V_{j_1}, \ldots, V_{j_n}, W_{j_1}, W_{j_2}, \mathcal{L}_j), \sigma_j)$ exists in H_3List do the following:
  * Compute $H_2(R_j)$ using the simulation of H_2 above and check whether $H_2(R_j) \oplus M_j = W_{j_2}$. If not, return "Reject", otherwise do the following:
    · Check whether (U_j, W_{j_1}) encrypts R_j using the PC oracle,
    · Check $\hat{e}(U_j, H_1(\text{ID}_i^*) + Q) = \hat{e}(P, V_{j_i})$.
    · If both of the above equations hold, return M_j and "Reject" otherwise.
- Else return "Reject".

[Simulation of Phase 4] Using the target ciphertext $(U^*, W^*) = (r^* P, \hat{e}(Q, T)^{r^*} R^*)$ of the Bilinear ElGamal scheme, B creates a target ciphertext C^* as follows.

Upon receiving (M_0, M_1):
- Choose $\beta \in \{0,1\}$ at random and search H_1List to get l_i that corresponds to ID_i^* for $i = 1, \ldots, n$. Then, compute $l_i U^*$ for $i = 1, \ldots, n$.
- Choose $K^* \in \{0,1\}^{k_1}$ uniformly at random and set $K^* = H_2(R^*)$. Also, create a label $\mathcal{L}^*$.
- Choose $\sigma^* \in \{0,1\}^{k_2}$ uniformly at random and set

$$\sigma^* = H_3(R^*, M_\beta, U^*, l_1 U^*, \ldots, l_n U^*, W^*, K^* \oplus M_\beta, \mathcal{L}^*).$$

- Return $C^* = (U^*, l_1 U^*, \ldots, l_n U^*, W^*, K^* \oplus M_\beta, \mathcal{L}^*, \sigma^*)$ as a target ciphertext.

[Simulation of Phase 5] B answers A's random oracle, decryption and private key extraction queries as before. Note that, this time, if $(R^*, M_\beta, U^*, l_1U^*, \ldots, l_nU^*, W^*, K^* \oplus M_\beta, \mathcal{L}^*)$ is asked to the the random oracle H_3, the value σ^* created in Simulation of Phase 4 is returned. (The value R^* can be detected with the help of the PC oracle).

[Simulation of Phase 6] A outputs its guess β'. If $\beta' = \beta$, B outputs 1. Otherwise, it outputs 0.

[Analysis] Note first that the private keys associated with each $\mathrm{ID}_j (\neq \mathrm{ID}_i^*)$ created in Simulation of Phase 3 are identically distributed as those in the real attack since $S_{\mathrm{ID}_j} = l_jT = l_jsP = sl_jP = sH_1(\mathrm{ID}_j)$. The simulations of the random oracle H_2 and H_3 are also perfect *unless* R^* has been asked to one of the random oracles H_2 and H_3. However, if these event happen, B breaks the OW-PCA of the Bilinear ElGamal scheme.

Note also that the distribution of the simulated target ciphertext is identical to that of the target ciphertext in the real attack since $l_iU^* = l_ir^*P = l_ir^*P - r^*Q + r^*Q = r^*(l_iP - Q) + r^*Q = r^*H_1(\mathrm{ID}_i^*) + r^*Q$ for all $i = 1, \ldots, n$.

The simulation of the decryption oracle is nearly perfect but there are cases when a valid ciphertext is rejected since, in the simulation of decryption oracle, if $(R, M, U, V_1, \ldots, V_n, W_1, W_2, \mathcal{L})$ has not been queried to H_3, the ciphertext is rejected straight way. Note that this leads to two cases: 1) A uses the value σ^* which is a part of a target ciphertext as a part its decryption query; 2) A has guessed a right value for the output of H_3 without querying it. However, in the first case, since $(U^*, l_1U^*, \ldots, l_nU^*, W^*, K^* \oplus M_\beta, \mathcal{L}^*)$ as well as (R^*, M_β) is provided as input to H_3, the decryption query A would ask is the same as the target ciphertext which is not allowed to query. The second case may happen but with a negligible probability $1/2^{k_2}$.

Following the above discussion, if B does not correctly guess the output of H_3, the view of A in the simulation is identical to the view in the real attack. Hence, we have $\Pr[B(P, aP, bP, cP) = \hat{e}(P, P)^{abc}] = \Pr[\beta' = \beta | \neg\mathsf{GuessH_3}] - \frac{1}{2}|$, where $\mathsf{GuessH_3}$ denotes an event that A correctly guesses the output of H_3. In the mean time, by definition of A, we have $|\Pr[\beta' = \beta] - \frac{1}{2}| > \epsilon$. Consequently, we have $|\Pr[\beta' = \beta | \neg\mathsf{GuessH_3}] - \frac{1}{2}| > |\Pr[\beta' = \beta] - \Pr[\mathsf{GuessH_3}] - \frac{1}{2}| > \epsilon - \Pr[\mathsf{GuessH_3}]$.

Since A makes total q_d decryption queries during the attack $\Pr[\mathsf{GuessH_3}] \leq q_d/2^{k_2}$. Thus, we have $\epsilon' > \epsilon - \frac{q_d}{2^{k_2}}$. The running time t' and the number q_o of PC oracle queries of B are readily checked. $\qquad\square$

CBE from CL-PKE:
A Generic Construction and Efficient Schemes

Sattam S. Al-Riyami and Kenneth G. Paterson

Information Security Group,
Royal Holloway, University of London,
Egham, Surrey, TW20 0EX,
United Kingdom
sattam@gmail.com, kenny.paterson@rhul.ac.uk

Abstract. We present a new Certificateless Public Key Encryption (CL-PKE) scheme whose security is proven to rest on the hardness of the Bilinear Diffie-Hellman Problem (BDHP) and that is more efficient than the original scheme of Al-Riyami and Paterson. We then give an analysis of Gentry's Certificate Based Encryption (CBE) concept, repairing a number of problems with the original definition and security model for CBE. We provide a generic conversion showing that a secure CBE scheme can be constructed from any secure CL-PKE scheme. We apply this result to our new efficient CL-PKE scheme to obtain a CBE scheme that improves on the original scheme of Gentry.

Keywords: Certificateless Public Key Encryption, CL-PKE, Certificate based Encryption, CBE, pairings.

1 Introduction

Gentry introduced the concept of Certificate Based Encryption (CBE) in [7]. His concept provides an efficient implicit certification mechanism for PKI and allows a form of automatic revocation. Independently, [2] introduced and developed the notion of certificateless public key cryptography (CL-PKC). CL-PKC is designed to overcome the key-escrow limitation of identity-based cryptography [9] without introducing certificates and the management overheads that this entails. CL-PKC is a model for the use of public key cryptography that is intermediate between the identity-based and traditional PKI approaches.

On the surface, CBE and CL-PKC appear to be quite different. In [2], it was recognized, though not explored in any detail, that the two concepts of CBE and certificateless public key encryption (CL-PKE) are in fact related. In this paper, we revisit the work of [2] and [7], providing more efficient schemes and exploring the connections between the concepts of CBE and CL-PKE.

Our first contribution is a new certificateless public key encryption (CL-PKE) scheme that improves on the main scheme of [2] in two ways. Firstly our scheme is more efficient than the scheme in [2]. Secondly, we show that the security of the new scheme rests on the hardness of the Bilinear Diffie-Hellman Problem (BDHP), rather than the non-standard generalized BDHP that was the basis of

S. Vaudenay (Ed.): PKC 2005, LNCS 3386, pp. 398–415, 2005.

security for the scheme in [2]. Our security result is proved in the full security model of [2].

Our second contribution is to provide a detailed analysis of the CBE concept of [7]. We point out a number of shortcomings in the definition of CBE as given in [7]. We repair these and then examine Gentry's security model for CBE. Comparing it to the model for CL-PKE given in [2] justifies us in making small changes to Gentry's security model. These still allow the security model to capture the kinds of attacks seen in real-world applications.

The small changes we make to Gentry's model also allow us to make our third contribution: a generic conversion that takes any CL-PKE scheme as input and produces from it a CBE scheme. The security of the CBE scheme in our adaptation of Gentry's model is tightly related to that of the CL-PKE scheme in the security model of [2]. Our result shows that the two concepts – CBE and CL-PKE – are indeed closely connected. We go on to explain why a generic construction going in the opposite direction, starting with a secure CBE scheme and yielding a secure CL-PKE scheme, is unlikely to be forthcoming.

Finally, we apply the generic conversion with our new CL-PKE scheme as input. The result is a secure CBE scheme that is more efficient than the original concrete scheme of [7].

1.1 Related Work

Kang, Park and Hahn [8] considered the signature analogue of certificate-based encryption. Since any certifying information can always be sent along with the actual signature, this concept seems less useful than that of CBE. Yum and Lee [11] gave a generic construction or a certificateless signature scheme from an ID-based signature scheme, proving the former to be secure (in an appropriate model) if the latter is. These authors also considered a generic construction for CL-PKE from identity-based encryption (IBE) [10] and the relationships between IBE, CBE and CL-PKE [12]. However, none of the results concerning the security of CL-PKE schemes proved in [10, 12] actually establishes security in the full security model developed in [2]: certain additional restrictions are always placed on the adversaries. For example, the Type I CL-PKE adversaries in [10, 12] are never permitted to extract the partial private key for the challenge identity. This restriction limiting the power of the adversary was not imposed in [2]. Moreover, no attempt is made in [10, 12] to properly handle decryption queries for identities whose public keys have been changed by the adversary. This issue was dealt with in [2] for concrete schemes by developing novel knowledge-extraction techniques. Thus the generic construction of CL-PKE schemes, secure in the full model of [2], from IBE or CBE schemes, remains an open problem. We return to this issue in Section 5.1.

2 Certificateless Public Key Encryption

In this section, we review the definition and security model for CL-PKE from [2]. We also provide some criticisms of the scheme in [2].

Definition 1. *[2] A CL-PKE scheme is specified by seven algorithms* (Setup, Partial-Private-Key-Extract, Set-Secret-Value, Set-Private-Key, Set-Public-Key, Encrypt, Decrypt) *such that:*

- Setup *is a probabilistic algorithm that takes security parameter k as input and returns the system parameters* params *and* master-key. *The system parameters includes a description of the message space $\mathcal{M}$ and ciphertext space $\mathcal{C}$.*
- Partial-Private-Key-Extract *is a deterministic algorithm that takes* params, master-key *and an identifier for entity A,* $ID_A \in \{0,1\}^*$, *as inputs. It returns a partial private key D_A.*
- Set-Secret-Value *is a probabilistic algorithm that takes as input* params[1] *and outputs a secret value x_A.*
- Set-Private-Key *is a deterministic algorithm that takes* params, D_A *and x_A as input. The algorithm returns S_A, a (full) private key.*
- Set-Public-Key *is a deterministic algorithm that takes* params *and x_A as input and outputs a public key P_A.*
- Encrypt *is a probabilistic algorithm that takes* params, $M \in \mathcal{M}$, P_A *and* ID_A *as inputs and returns either a ciphertext $C \in \mathcal{C}$ or the null symbol $\perp$ indicating an encryption failure[2].*
- Decrypt *is a deterministic algorithm that takes as inputs* params, $C \in \mathcal{C}$ *and S_A. It returns a message $M \in \mathcal{M}$ or a message $\perp$ indicating a decryption failure.*

Naturally, an output M should result from applying algorithm Decrypt *with inputs* params, S_A *on a ciphertext C generated by using algorithm* Encrypt *with inputs* params, P_A, ID_A *on message M.*

Algorithms Set-Private-Key and Set-Public-Key are normally run by an entity A for itself, after running Set-Secret-Value. Usually, A is the only entity in possession of S_A and x_A. Algorithms Setup and Partial-Private-Key-Extract are usually run by a trusted third party, called a key generating centre (KGC) [2].

2.1   Security Model for CL-PKE

The full IND-CCA security model for CL-PKE of [2] is an extension of the IND-ID-CCA model for IBE described in [4]. Below, we list the actions that an IND-CCA adversary $\mathcal{A}$ against a CL-PKE scheme may carry out and discuss how each action should be handled by the challenger for that adversary.

1. **Extract Partial Private Key of Entity A:** Challenger $\mathcal{C}$ responds by running algorithm Partial-Private-Key-Extract to generate D_A for entity A.

---

[1] Note that the original definition of this algorithm in [2] also takes ID_A as input; however this string is not used in defining x_A in any concrete schemes, so we omit it here.

[2] The concrete encryption schemes in [2] could fail because the public key fails to have the correct structure. A general encryption algorithm could fail because the public key is not in the right group, for example.

2. **Extract Private Key for Entity A:** If A's public key has not been replaced then C can respond by running algorithm Set-Private-Key to generate the private key S_A for entity A. It is assumed, as in [2], that the adversary does not make such queries for entities whose public keys have been changed.

3. **Request Public Key of Entity A:** C responds by running algorithm Set-Public-Key to generate the public key P_A for entity A (first running Set-Secret-Value for A if necessary).

4. **Replace Public Key of Entity A:** Adversary $\mathcal{A}$ can repeatedly replace the public key P_A for any entity A with any value P'_A of its choice. The current value of an entity's public key is used by C in any computations or responses to $\mathcal{A}$'s requests.

5. **Decryption Query for Ciphertext C and Entity A:** In the model of [2], adversary $\mathcal{A}$ can issue a decryption query for any entity and any ciphertext. It is assumed in [2] that C should properly decrypt ciphertexts, even for those entities whose public keys have been replaced. This is a rather strong property for the security model (after all, the challenger may no longer know the correct private key). However, it ensures that the model captures the fact that changing an entity's public key to a value of the adversary's choosing may give that adversary an advantage in breaking the scheme. For further discussion of this feature, see [2].

The IND-CCA security model of [2] distinguishes two types of adversary. A Type I adversary is able to change public keys of entities at will, but does not have access to the master-key. A Type II adversary is equipped with master-key but is not allowed to replace public keys. This adversary models security against an eavesdropping KGC. The security game proceeds in three phases; in the middle challenge phase, the adversary selects a challenge identifier ID_{ch} and corresponding public key P_{ch}, and is given a challenge ciphertext C^*. We provide a detailed description of the two adversary types and the security game next.

CL-PKE Type I IND-CCA Adversary: Adversary $\mathcal{A}_I$ does not have access to master-key. However, $\mathcal{A}_I$ may request public keys and replace public keys with values of its choice, extract partial private and private keys and make decryption queries, all for identities of its choice. $\mathcal{A}_I$ cannot extract the private key for ID_{ch} at any point, nor request the private key for any identifier if the corresponding public key has already been replaced. $\mathcal{A}_I$ cannot both replace the public key for the challenge identifier ID_{ch} before the challenge phase and extract the partial private key for ID_{ch} in some phase. Furthermore, in Phase 2, $\mathcal{A}_I$ cannot make a decryption query on the challenge ciphertext C^* for the combination $(\mathsf{ID}_{ch}, P_{ch})$ that was used to encrypt M_b.

CL-PKE Type II IND-CCA Adversary: Adversary $\mathcal{A}_{II}$ does have access to master-key, but may not replace public keys of entities. Adversary $\mathcal{A}_{II}$ can compute partial private keys for itself, given master-key. It can also request public keys, make private key extraction queries and decryption queries, all for identities of its choice. The restrictions on this type of adversary are that it cannot replace public keys at any point, nor extract the private key for ID_{ch} at any point.

Additionally, in Phase 2, $\mathcal{A}_{II}$ cannot make a decryption query on the challenge ciphertext C^* for the combination $(\mathsf{ID}_{ch}, P_{ch})$ that was used to encrypt M_b.

Definition 2. *A CL-PKE scheme is said to be IND-CCA secure if no polynomially bounded adversary $\mathcal{A}$ of Type I or Type II has a non-negligible advantage in the following game:*

Setup: $\mathcal{C}$ takes a security parameter k as input and runs the Setup algorithm. It gives $\mathcal{A}$ the resulting system parameters params. If $\mathcal{A}$ is of Type I, then $\mathcal{C}$ keeps master-key to itself, otherwise, it gives master-key to $\mathcal{A}$.

Phase 1: $\mathcal{A}$ issues a sequence of requests described above. These queries may be asked adaptively, but are subject to the rules on adversary behaviour defined above.

Challenge Phase: Once $\mathcal{A}$ decides that Phase 1 is over it outputs the challenge identifier ID_{ch} and two equal length plaintexts $M_0, M_1 \in \mathcal{M}$. Again, the adversarial constraints given above apply. $\mathcal{C}$ now picks a random bit $b \in \{0, 1\}$ and computes C^*, the encryption of M_b under the current public key P_{ch} for ID_{ch}. Then C^* is delivered to $\mathcal{A}$.

Phase 2: Now $\mathcal{A}$ issues a second sequence of requests as in Phase 1, again subject to the rules on adversary behaviour above.

Guess: Finally, $\mathcal{A}$ outputs a guess $b' \in \{0, 1\}$. The adversary wins the game if $b = b'$. We define $\mathcal{A}$'s advantage in this game to be $Adv(\mathcal{A}) := 2|\Pr[b = b'] - \frac{1}{2}|$.

2.2 The Concrete Scheme of Al-Riyami and Paterson

In [2], we presented a concrete IND-CCA secure CL-PKE scheme, named FullCL-PKE. The scheme is an adaptation of the pairing-based IBE scheme of [4]; we do not replicate it here. Instead we list three drawbacks of the scheme FullCL-PKE:

1. FullCL-PKE requires three pairing calculations for each encryption (though two of these are required to check the structure of the public key and all three can be eliminated for any subsequent encryptions to the same party). It would be preferable to have a less computationally intensive CL-PKE scheme.
2. Each public key in FullCL-PKE consists of two elements of a group $\mathbb{G}_1$. Shorter keys would be preferable.
3. The security of FullCL-PKE rests on the hardness of the Generalized Bilinear Diffie-Hellman Problem (GBDHP). This problem is less well-established and no harder than the BDHP introduced in [4]. It would be preferable to have a CL-PKE scheme with a more solid security foundation. We will comment further on this point in Section 3.3.

3   A New CL-PKE Scheme

In this section we present a new CL-PKE scheme and study its security. The scheme can be regarded as resulting from the optimization of a double encryption construction for CL-PKE, using the IBE scheme of [4] and the ElGamal public key encryption scheme [5] as components. This immediately suggests a generic construction for a CL-PKE scheme from the combination of an IBE scheme and a (normal) public key encryption (PKE) scheme. Indeed such a construction is possible (and was first suggested to us by Boneh), but it seems to be difficult to prove the resulting scheme secure in the full model of [2] using standard security assumptions about the component IBE and PKE schemes. For that reason we have concentrated here on the concrete scheme and its proof of security.

Before we give our new scheme, we provide some background on pairings and a related computational problem.

3.1   Review of Pairings

Let $\mathbb{G}_1$ denote an additive group of prime order q and $\mathbb{G}_2$ a multiplicative group also of order q. We let P denote a generator of $\mathbb{G}_1$. A pairing is a map $\hat{e} : \mathbb{G}_1 \times \mathbb{G}_1 \to \mathbb{G}_2$ with the following properties:

1. Bilinear: given any $Q, W \in \mathbb{G}_1$ and $a, b \in \mathbb{Z}_q$, we have

$$\hat{e}(aQ, bW) = \hat{e}(Q, W)^{ab} = \hat{e}(abQ, W) \text{ etc.}$$

2. Non-degenerate: $\hat{e}(P, P) \neq 1_{\mathbb{G}_2}$.
3. Efficiently computable.

The map $\hat{e}$ is usually derived from either the Weil or Tate pairing on an elliptic curve over a finite field; see [2, 4] for further details and references. The following computational problem was introduced in [4]:

Bilinear Diffie-Hellman Problem (BDHP): Let $\mathbb{G}_1$, $\mathbb{G}_2$, P and $\hat{e}$ be as above. The BDHP in $\langle \mathbb{G}_1, \mathbb{G}_2, \hat{e} \rangle$ is as follows: Given $\langle P, aP, bP, cP \rangle$ with uniformly random choices of $a, b, c \in \mathbb{Z}_q^*$, find $\hat{e}(P, P)^{abc} \in \mathbb{G}_2$.

BDH Parameter Generator: As in [4], a randomized algorithm $\mathcal{IG}$ is a BDH parameter generator if $\mathcal{IG}$: (1) takes as input security parameter $k \geq 1$, (2) runs in polynomial time in k, and (3) outputs the description of groups $\mathbb{G}_1$, $\mathbb{G}_2$ of prime order q and a pairing $\hat{e} : \mathbb{G}_1 \times \mathbb{G}_1 \to \mathbb{G}_2$. Formally, the output of the algorithm $\mathcal{IG}(1^k)$ is $\langle \mathbb{G}_1, \mathbb{G}_2, \hat{e} \rangle$.

3.2   The New Scheme

The algorithms for our new CL-PKE scheme FullCL-PKE* are:

Setup: This algorithm runs as follows:

1. Run $\mathcal{IG}$ on input k to generate output $\langle \mathbb{G}_1, \mathbb{G}_2, \hat{e} \rangle$.
2. Choose an arbitrary generator $P \in \mathbb{G}_1$.
3. Select a random master-key $s \in \mathbb{Z}_q^*$ and set $P_0 = sP$.
4. Choose cryptographic hash functions $H_1 : \{0, 1\}^* \to \mathbb{G}_1^*$, $H_2 : \mathbb{G}_2 \to \{0, 1\}^n$, $H_3 : \{0, 1\}^n \times \{0, 1\}^n \to \mathbb{Z}_q^*$, $H_4 : \{0, 1\}^n \to \{0, 1\}^n$ and $H_5 : \mathbb{G}_1 \to \{0, 1\}^n$. Here n will be the bit-length of plaintexts.

The system parameters are params= $\langle \mathbb{G}_1, \mathbb{G}_2, \hat{e}, n, P, P_0, H_1, H_2, H_3, H_4, H_5 \rangle$. The master-key is $s \in \mathbb{Z}_q^*$. The message space is $\mathcal{M} = \{0,1\}^n$ and the ciphertext space is $\mathcal{C} = \mathbb{G}_1 \times \{0,1\}^{2n}$.

Partial-Private-Key-Extract: This algorithm takes as input an identifier $\mathsf{ID}_A \in \{0,1\}^*$ for entity A, and carries out the following steps to construct the partial private key for A:

1. Compute $Q_A = H_1(\mathsf{ID}_A) \in \mathbb{G}_1^*$.
2. Output the partial private key $D_A = sQ_A \in \mathbb{G}_1^*$.

Set-Secret-Value: This algorithm takes as inputs params and an identifier ID_A. It selects a random $x_A \in \mathbb{Z}_q^*$ and outputs x_A as A's secret value.

Set-Private-Key: This algorithm takes as inputs params, entity A's partial private key D_A and A's secret value $x_A \in \mathbb{Z}_q^*$. The output of the algorithm is the pair $S_A = \langle D_A, x_A \rangle$. So the private key for A is just the pair consisting of the partial private key and the secret value.

Set-Public-Key: This algorithm takes params and entity A's secret value $x_A \in \mathbb{Z}_q^*$ as inputs and constructs A's public key as $P_A = x_A P$.

Encrypt: To encrypt $M \in \mathcal{M}$ for entity A with identifier $\mathsf{ID}_A \in \{0,1\}^*$ and a public key P_A, perform the following steps:

1. Check that P_A is in $\mathbb{G}_1^*$, if not output $\perp$.
2. Compute $Q_A = H_1(\mathsf{ID}_A) \in \mathbb{G}_1^*$.
3. Choose a random $\sigma \in \{0,1\}^n$.
4. Set $r = H_3(\sigma, M)$.
5. Compute and output the ciphertext:

$$C = \langle rP, \sigma \oplus H_2(\hat{e}(Q_A, P_0)^r) \oplus H_5(rP_A), M \oplus H_4(\sigma) \rangle.$$

Notice that $H_2(\hat{e}(Q_A, P_0)^r)$ is identical to the mask used in the IBE scheme in [4], while $H_5(rP_A)$ is a mask computed using the term rP_A used in the ElGamal encryption scheme.

Decrypt: Suppose $C = \langle U, V, W \rangle \in \mathcal{C}$. To decrypt this ciphertext using the private key $S_A = \langle D_A, x_A \rangle$:

1. Compute $V \oplus H_2(\hat{e}(D_A, U)) \oplus H_5(x_A U) = \sigma'$.
2. Compute $W \oplus H_4(\sigma') = M'$.
3. Set $r' = H_3(\sigma', M')$ and test if $U = r'P$. If not, output $\perp$ and reject the ciphertext. Otherwise, output M' as the decryption of C.

When C is a valid encryption of M using P_A and ID_A, it is easy to see that decrypting C will result in an output $M' = M$. This concludes the description of FullCL-PKE*.

Theorem 1. *Let hash functions* H_i, $1 \leq i \leq 5$, *be random oracles. Suppose further that there is no polynomially bounded algorithm that can solve the BDHP with non-negligible advantage. Then* FullCL-PKE* *is IND-CCA secure.*

A sketch of the proof of this result is given in Appendix A. A full proof can be found in [1].

3.3   Comparing FullCL-PKE* to FullCL-PKE

The scheme FullCL-PKE of [2] is in many ways superseded by our new scheme FullCL-PKE*:

1. The new scheme only requires one pairing computation per encryption. The only test of validity for public keys P_A in FullCL-PKE* is a simple group membership test $P_A \in \mathbb{G}_1^*$, while testing validity in FullCL-PKE requires two pairing computations. As with FullCL-PKE, the single pairing computation can be replaced with an exponentiation in $\mathbb{G}_2$ if repeated encryption to the same recipient is performed. Decryption costs for the two schemes are similar.
2. Public keys in FullCL-PKE* consist of only one element of $\mathbb{G}_1$ rather than the two required in FullCL-PKE.
3. FullCL-PKE* has better security guarantees as its security is related to the BDHP, rather than the GBDHP (in which the output is a pair $\langle Q, \hat{e}(P, Q)^{abc} \rangle$ for input aP, bP, cP). The GBDHP is an easier problem than the BDHP, in that an algorithm to solve the latter can be used to solve the former simply by setting $Q = P$. Note also that there do exist triples $\langle \mathbb{G}_1, \mathbb{G}_2, \hat{e} \rangle$ for which the GBDHP is trivial, but the BDGHP is presumed to be hard. For example, if the order q of $\mathbb{G}_1$ and $\mathbb{G}_2$ is not prime, but instead divisible by a small prime q_0, then to solve the GBDHP with non-negligible probability $1/q_0$, we can select $Q = \frac{q}{q_0}P$ and guess a solution $\langle Q, \hat{e}(P, Q)^x \rangle$, where x is picked at random from $\{0, 1, \ldots, q_0 - 1\}$. It would be interesting to determine if the BDHP and GBDHP are of equal hardness of in the groups of prime order usually selected for applications.

There is one further difference between FullCL-PKE and FullCL-PKE* that we note here. The public keys in the scheme FullCL-PKE, being of the form $\langle X_A = x_A P, Y_A = x P_0 \rangle$, are constructed with reference to a specific P_0 and hence a particular KGC. Therefore, the decrypting party can mandate a particular centralised point of control (that is, a particular KGC) from whom its partial private keys will be obtained. On the other hand, the public keys in the scheme FullCL-PKE* do not have this restriction. This means that an encrypting party can select an arbitrary KGC (so long as it uses the same group $\mathbb{G}_1$ in its params as the decrypting party does – though this restriction can be removed using a slightly less efficient scheme) and force the decrypting party to obtain its partial private key from that KGC. The merits and demerits of this property are discussed further in [1].

4   Certificate-Based Encryption

We now turn to a discussion of Certificate-Based Encryption (CBE), as introduced in [7]. In certificate-updating CBE, a Certification Authority (CA) is responsible for pushing fresh certificates to clients in each time period. Informally, a client needs to be in possession of its current certificate in order to be able to decrypt ciphertexts sent to it by other parties during that time period.

We begin by noting some incompatibilities between the generic definition of CBE and the concrete CBE schemes in [7]. We then present a simplified and corrected definition for CBE.

1. As can be seen from the first property in [7, Definition 1], combining an IBE scheme with a standard public key encryption (PKE) scheme is *explicitly* required when building a CBE scheme. This limits the ways in which CBE schemes can be constructed and, as we shall see, is an unnecessary restriction.
2. The first property of [7, Definition 1] requires that PK_{IBE} be an identifiable element of the IBE scheme's parameters that can be labelled as a public key (notice that PK_{IBE} is also used as a distinct computational element during encryption). Given that not every IBE scheme need have this property, this definition limits the IBE schemes that can be used to build CBE schemes. Again, the limitation is unnecessary.
3. Although the combination of IBE and PKE is required by the generic definition of CBE, none of the concrete CBE schemes in [7] actually makes use of explicitly defined IBE or PKE schemes in their construction. It is fairly clear how the concrete CBE schemes have evolved from the IBE scheme of [4], but strictly speaking, none of them meet the generic definition in [7, Definition 1].
4. The generic definition of CBE in [7, Definition 1] uses six algorithms $\mathsf{Gen_{IBE}}$, $\mathsf{Gen_{PKE}}$, Upd1, Upd2, Enc and Dec, while the concrete schemes in [7, Section 3] use instead five algorithms Setup, Certification, Encryption and Decryption. Essentially algorithms Upd1 and Upd2 are combined to yield algorithm Certification, but there are no explicit key generation algorithms in the concrete schemes.

To summarize, there are incompatibilities in [7] between the definition of CBE on the one hand and the concrete CBE schemes on the other, as well as a number of unnecessary restrictions in the CBE definition. We now provide an alternative definition for CBE. The concrete schemes in [7] are compatible with our simplified definition.

Definition 3. *A (certificate-updating) CBE scheme is defined by six algorithms* (Setup, Set-Key-Pair, Certify, Consolidate, Enc, Dec) *such that:*

- Setup *is a probabilistic algorithm taking as input a security parameter k. It returns SK_{CA} (the certifier's master-key) and public parameters* params *that include the description of a string space Λ. Usually, this algorithm is run by the CA.*
- Set-Key-Pair *is a probabilistic algorithm that takes* params *as input. When run by a client, it returns a public key PK and a private key SK.*
- Certify *is a deterministic certification algorithm that takes as input $\langle SK_{CA}$,* params*, τ, $\lambda \in \Lambda$, $PK \rangle$. It returns* Cert'_τ*, which is sent to the client. Here τ is a string identifying a time period, while λ contains other information needed to certify the client such as the client's identifying information, and PK is a public key.*

- Consolidate *is a deterministic certificate consolidation algorithm taking as input* $\langle$params, τ, λ, Cert$'_\tau\rangle$, *and optionally* Cert$_{\tau-1}$. *It returns* Cert$_\tau$, *the certificate used by a client in time period* τ.
- Enc *is a probabilistic algorithm taking as inputs* $\langle\tau$, λ, params, PK, $M\rangle$, *where* $M \in \mathcal{M}$ *is a message. It returns a ciphertext* $C \in \mathcal{C}$ *for message* M[3].
- Dec *is a deterministic algorithm taking* $\langle$params, Cert$_\tau$, SK, $C\rangle$ *as input in time period* τ. *It returns either a message* $M \in \mathcal{M}$ *or the special symbol* $\perp$ *indicating a decryption failure.*

Naturally, we require that if C *is the result of applying algorithm* Enc *with input* $\langle\tau$, λ, params, PK, $M\rangle$ *and* $\langle SK, PK\rangle$ *is a valid key-pair, then* M *is the result of applying algorithm* Dec *on input* $\langle$params, Cert$_\tau$, SK, $C\rangle$, *where* Cert$_\tau$ *is the output of the* Certify *and* Consolidate *algorithms on input* $\langle SK_{CA}$, params, τ, $\lambda \in \Lambda$, $PK\rangle$. *We write:*

$$\mathsf{Dec}_{\mathsf{Cert}_\tau, SK}(\mathsf{Enc}_{\tau, \lambda, PK}(M)) = M.$$

We note that a concrete CBE scheme need not involve certificate consolidation – see [7, Section 3] for examples. In this situation, algorithm Consolidate will simply output Cert$_\tau$ = Cert$'_\tau$.

4.1   Security Model for CBE

In this section, we present an amended security model for CBE, in accordance with our new definition for CBE. We will comment later on how this model can be further strengthened; however it is not our intention here to completely overhaul the work of [7].

As in [7], security for CBE is defined using two different games and the adversary chooses which game to play. In Game 1, the adversary models an uncertified entity and in Game 2, the adversary models the certifier in possession of the master-key SK_{CA} attacking a fixed entity's public key.

CBE Game 1: The challenger runs Setup, gives params to the adversary $\mathcal{A}_1$ and keeps SK_{CA} to itself. The adversary then interleaves certification and decryption queries with a single challenge query. These queries are answered as follows:

- On certification query $\langle\tau, \lambda, PK, SK\rangle$, the challenger checks that $\lambda \in \Lambda$ and that $\langle PK, SK\rangle$ is a valid key-pair. If so, it runs Certify on input $\langle SK_{CA}$, params, τ, λ, $PK\rangle$ and returns Cert$'_\tau$; else it returns $\perp$.
- On decryption query $\langle\tau, \lambda, PK, SK, C\rangle$, the challenger checks that $\lambda \in \Lambda$ and that $\langle PK, SK\rangle$ is a valid key-pair. If so, it generates Cert$_\tau$ by using algorithms Certify and Consolidate with inputs $\langle SK_{CA}$, params, τ, λ, $PK\rangle$, and outputs $\mathsf{Dec}_{\mathsf{Cert}_\tau, SK}(C)$; else it returns $\perp$.
- On challenge query $\langle\tau_{\mathrm{ch}}, \lambda_{\mathrm{ch}}, PK_{\mathrm{ch}}, SK_{\mathrm{ch}}, M_0, M_1\rangle$, where $M_0, M_1 \in \mathcal{M}$ are of equal length, the challenger checks that $\lambda_{\mathrm{ch}} \in \Lambda$ and that $\langle PK_{\mathrm{ch}}, SK_{\mathrm{ch}}\rangle$ is a valid key-pair. If so, it chooses a random bit b and returns $C^* = \mathsf{Enc}_{\tau_{\mathrm{ch}}, \lambda_{\mathrm{ch}}, PK_{\mathrm{ch}}}(M_b)$; else it returns $\perp$.

---

[3] We assume that Enc might also output $\perp$ if PK is not a valid public key.

Finally, $\mathcal{A}_1$ outputs a guess $b' \in \{0, 1\}$. The adversary wins the game if $b = b'$ and $\langle \tau_{ch}, \lambda_{ch}, PK_{ch}, SK_{ch}, C^* \rangle$ was not the subject of a decryption query after the challenge, and $\langle \tau_{ch}, \lambda_{ch}, PK_{ch}, SK_{ch} \rangle$ was not the subject of any certification query. We define $\mathcal{A}_1$'s advantage in this game to be $\text{Adv}(\mathcal{A}_1) := 2|\Pr[b = b'] - \frac{1}{2}|$.

CBE Game 2: The challenger runs Setup, gives params and SK_{CA} to the adversary $\mathcal{A}_2$. The challenger then runs Set-Key-Pair to obtain a key-pair $\langle PK_{ch}, SK_{ch} \rangle$ and gives PK_{ch} to the adversary $\mathcal{A}_2$. The adversary then interleaves certification and decryption queries with a single challenge query. These queries are answered as follows:

- On decryption query $\langle \tau, \lambda, C \rangle$, the challenger checks that $\lambda \in \Lambda$. If not, it returns $\perp$. If so, it generates Cert_τ by using algorithms Certify and Consolidate with inputs $\langle SK_{CA}, \text{params}, \tau, \lambda, PK_{ch} \rangle$. It then outputs $\text{Dec}_{\text{Cert}_\tau, SK_{ch}}(C)$.
- On challenge query $\langle \tau_{ch}, \lambda_{ch}, M_0, M_1 \rangle$, the challenger checks that $\lambda_{ch} \in \Lambda$. If so, it chooses random bit b and returns $C^* = \text{Enc}_{\tau_{ch}, \lambda_{ch}, PK_{ch}}(M_b)$; else it returns $\perp$.

Finally, $\mathcal{A}_2$ outputs a guess $b' \in \{0, 1\}$. The adversary wins the game if $b = b'$ and $\langle \tau_{ch}, \lambda_{ch}, C^* \rangle$ was not the subject of a decryption query after the challenge. We define $\mathcal{A}_2$'s advantage in this game to be $\text{Adv}(\mathcal{A}_2) := 2|\Pr[b = b'] - \frac{1}{2}|$.

Definition 4. *A certificate-updating CBE scheme is said to be secure against adaptive chosen ciphertext attack (or IND-CBE-CCA secure) if no probabilistic polynomial-time adversary has non-negligible advantage in either CBE Game 1 or CBE Game 2.*

Let us now analyse the CBE security model, and compare it to Gentry's original model in [7]. The only technical difference between our CBE security model and that of [7] is in Game 2. In Gentry's model, the Game 2 adversary is allowed to specify a fresh params in each of its queries. It also supplies the CBE master-key SK_{CA} in decryption queries, so that the challenger is able to provide decryptions. In our model, params and the master-key SK_{CA} are fixed at the beginning of Game 2, and are supplied to the adversary. In both models, the Game 2 adversary attacks a fixed key-pair that is specified by the challenger. We argue that, while the model of [7] is more flexible in Game 2, our adaptation accurately models the kinds of attacks that might be attempted by a CA. One would not expect a CA to change its public parameters on a frequent basis; rather it is more natural to model a CA with fixed public parameters and in possession of the master-key.

In the next section, we will show a generic conversion from CL-PKE to CBE that preserves security. Essentially, this conversion maps CL-PKE to CBE by using extended identifiers in the CL-PKE scheme, while the certificates in the CBE scheme are obtained from the partial private keys in the CL-PKE scheme. The conversion process naturally highlights some strengths and weaknesses in the CBE security model of [7]:

1. A CBE Game 1 adversary must provide a private key SK along with the corresponding public key PK in all of its queries. This enables the challenger to handle decryption queries. By contrast, in CL-PKE, a Type I adversary is

allowed to change an entity's public key without needing to show the private key. This gives the adversary more flexibility. For example, the adversary can replace the public key of one entity with that of another (without knowing the corresponding private key). The proofs of security for CL-PKE schemes in [3] and the full version of this paper handle decryption queries using special purpose knowledge extractors. The proof of security for the concrete scheme FullCBE in [7] is also able to remove the requirement of showing the private key.

2. A CBE Game 2 adversary does not get to choose a challenge public key to attack. Instead, it is given a specific public key by the challenger at the start of the game. This is unlike a CL-PKE Type II adversary, who has the freedom to work with multiple public keys and to select any one of them for the challenge query.

3. By contrast, the CBE Game 2 adversary in [7] is allowed to work with multiple values of params and the master-key. So this adversary can change the CBE scheme in *each* query. Both our CBE Game 2 adversary and a Type II CL-PKE adversary are given a fixed params and the master-key at the start of the game. This allows the adversary to 'break' that part of the scheme which the trusted third party is always able to break. We have already justified our making this restriction in CBE above.

5   CBE from CL-PKE

In this section, we present a construction for a CBE scheme using the algorithms of a generic CL-PKE scheme as components. After providing the construction, we prove that the resulting CBE scheme is IND-CBE-CCA secure (according to Definition 4), provided the CL-PKE scheme is IND-CCA secure (in the sense of Definition 2).

Suppose then that Π^{CL} is a CL-PKE scheme with algorithms $\mathsf{Setup}^{\mathrm{CL}}$, Partial-Private-Key-Extract, Set-Secret-Value, Set-Private-Key, Set-Public-Key, Encrypt and Decrypt. We define a CBE scheme Π^{CBE} by defining the six CBE algorithms ($\mathsf{Setup}^{\mathrm{CBE}}$, Set-Key-Pair, Certify, Consolidate, Enc, Dec) in terms of the CL-PKE algorithms.

– $\mathsf{Setup}^{\mathrm{CBE}}$: This algorithm takes a security parameter k and returns SK_{CA} and public parameters $\mathsf{params}^{\mathrm{CBE}}$ that includes the description of a string space Λ. We run algorithm $\mathsf{Setup}^{\mathrm{CL}}$ to obtain master-key^{CL} and $\mathsf{params}^{\mathrm{CL}}$. We set SK_{CA} of Π^{CBE} to be master-key^{CL}. We allow Λ to be any subset of $\{0,1\}^*$. We then define $\mathsf{params}^{\mathrm{CBE}}$ by extending $\mathsf{params}^{\mathrm{CL}}$ to include a description of Λ.

– Set-Key-Pair: For a client A, this algorithm takes $\mathsf{params}^{\mathrm{CBE}}$ as input. We extract $\mathsf{params}^{\mathrm{CL}}$ from $\mathsf{params}^{\mathrm{CBE}}$ then run Set-Secret-Value and then Set-Public-Key of Π^{CL} to obtain values x_A and then P_A. The output $\langle PK, SK \rangle$ is defined to be the pair $\langle P_A, x_A \rangle$.

- Certify: This algorithm takes as input $\langle SK_{CA}, \mathsf{params}^{\mathrm{CBE}}, \tau, \lambda, PK \rangle$. We extract $\mathsf{params}^{\mathrm{CL}}$ from $\mathsf{params}^{\mathrm{CBE}}$ and obtain master-key^{CL} from SK_{CA}. We then set $\mathsf{ID}'_A = \mathsf{params}^{\mathrm{CBE}} \| \tau \| \lambda \| PK$ and run algorithm Partial-Private-Key-Extract of Π^{CL} on input $\langle \mathsf{params}^{\mathrm{CL}}, \mathsf{master\text{-}key}^{\mathrm{CL}}, \mathsf{ID}'_A \rangle$ to obtain a partial private key D_A. The output Cert'_τ is defined to be D_A.
- Consolidate: This algorithm takes as input $\langle \mathsf{params}^{\mathrm{CBE}}, \tau, \lambda, \mathsf{Cert}'_\tau \rangle$. It simply outputs the value Cert'_τ.
- Enc: This algorithm takes $\langle \tau, \lambda, \mathsf{params}^{\mathrm{CBE}}, PK, M \rangle$ as input. Here, we assume $M \in \mathcal{M}$, the message space for Π^{CL}. We extract $\mathsf{params}^{\mathrm{CL}}$ from $\mathsf{params}^{\mathrm{CBE}}$. We set $\mathsf{ID}'_A = \mathsf{params}^{\mathrm{CBE}} \| \tau \| \lambda \| PK$ and use the Encrypt algorithm of Π^{CL} with input $\langle \mathsf{params}^{\mathrm{CL}}, M, PK, \mathsf{ID}'_A \rangle$ to obtain a ciphertext $C \in \mathcal{C}$. The output of Enc is defined to be C.
- Dec: This algorithm takes $\langle \mathsf{params}^{\mathrm{CBE}}, \mathsf{Cert}_\tau, SK, C \rangle$ as input in time period τ. We extract $\mathsf{params}^{\mathrm{CL}}$ from $\mathsf{params}^{\mathrm{CBE}}$, set $D_A = \mathsf{Cert}_\tau$, set $x_A = SK$, and run algorithm Set-Private-Key of Π^{CL} on input $\langle \mathsf{params}^{\mathrm{CL}}, D_A, x_A \rangle$ to obtain a private key S_A. Finally, we run algorithm Decrypt of Π^{CL} on input $\langle \mathsf{params}^{\mathrm{CL}}, C, S_A \rangle$ to obtain the output of algorithm Dec.

It is evident from the construction that the message and ciphertext spaces of Π^{CBE} are the same as those of Π^{CL}. It's also clear that partial private keys in Π^{CL} are (roughly speaking) transformed into certificates in Π^{CBE}. In the CBE scheme, we allow Λ to be any subset of $\{0,1\}^*$ for maximum flexibility, while identifiers of the form $\mathsf{params}^{\mathrm{CBE}} \| \tau \| \lambda \| PK$ where $\lambda \in \Lambda$ are used in the CL-PKE scheme.

Next is our main theorem about the IND-CBE-CCA security of the CBE scheme constructed using a CL-PKE scheme as above.

Theorem 2. *Suppose that Π^{CL} is an IND-CCA secure CL-PKE scheme, and suppose that Π^{CL} is used to build a CBE scheme Π^{CBE} as above. Then Π^{CBE} is IND-CBE-CCA secure.*

Proof. The proof can be found in Appendix B. The proof demonstrates a tight relationship between the advantage of a CBE adversary against Π^{CBE} and that of a CL-PKE adversary against Π^{CL}.

It can be seen from examining Appendix B that the security argument used there to prove the CBE scheme secure does not require the use of private keys SK from the CBE scheme in answering any queries. It is therefore possible to prove that Π^{CBE} is secure in a somewhat stronger security model than we have developed in Section 4.1. In the stronger model, the adversary is not required to show any private keys when making queries. As well as being stronger, this seems like a more natural model of real adversarial behaviour. The original model of [7] can also be strengthened in the same way. Thus we see that the CL-PKE concept can lead to improvements in the security of CBE schemes.

5.1 CL-PKE from CBE?

By composing the generic constructions of an IBE scheme from a CBE scheme and a CL-PKE scheme from an IBE scheme in [12], it is possible to use the six algorithms of a generic CBE scheme to construct a CL-PKE scheme. The overall construction uses the encryption and decryption algorithms of the IBE scheme twice in defining the corresponding algorithms of the CL-PKE scheme. The KGC is responsible for setting the keys and parameters for one pair of encryption and decryption algorithms, while individual users control the setting for the other pair. This ensures that the key-escrow property of the IBE scheme is overcome. Note, however, that the security results of [12] only establish the security of the CL-PKE scheme in a security model that is significantly weaker than the full CL-PKE security model developed in [2] and reproduced here in Section 2.1. So the generic construction of a secure CL-PKE scheme from a CBE scheme remains an open problem.

One might consider the direct construction of a CL-PKE scheme from a single instance of a generic CBE scheme, that is, without going via an intermediate IBE scheme and using the algorithms of the CBE scheme only once in defining the CL-PKE scheme. In a generic construction, the Partial-Private-Key-Extract algorithm of the CL-PKE scheme would presumably need to be constructed from the Certify algorithm of the CBE scheme. Then one obstacle to a generic construction is that a CBE scheme requires certain parameters (namely τ and PK) to be included in the inputs to the Certify algorithm, while these are not provided as inputs to the Partial-Private-Key-Extract algorithm in a CL-PKE scheme. This would mean that the necessary parameters would not in general be available as inputs to the Certify algorithm. This implies an important functional difference between the CBE and CL-PKE concepts: in CBE, the algorithm Set-Key-Pair needs to be run before Certify, while in CL-PKE, the corresponding algorithm Partial-Private-Key-Extract can be run before *or* after algorithm Set-Public-Key. In this respect, CL-PKE is more flexible than CBE.

We note that if one is prepared to consider only the special class of CL-PKE schemes in which identifiers include public keys, then one can construct a (special) CL-PKE scheme generically from a single instance of a CBE scheme. One trick needed in the construction is to set τ to a fixed value for every CBE certification query. This kind of CL-PKE scheme was considered in [2], where it was shown that the binding technique allows the CL-PKE scheme to attain a level of trust closer to that of a traditional PKI. Even so, to prove this scheme secure, one must further modify the CBE security model to remove the requirement on the adversary to supply private keys SK in queries. One must also restrict the CL-PKE Type I adversary to not extract the partial private key for the challenge identifier, to prevent a corresponding CBE adversary from having to make a disallowed certification query. This means that the proof would not be in the full security model of [2].

It may well be possible to modify any particular concrete CBE scheme to produce a CL-PKE scheme that can be proven secure. For example, one might omit certain inputs to the Certify and Consolidate algorithms in order to define Partial-Private-Key-Extract. This is certainly true of the scheme FullCBE of [7]. However, this is not the same as obtaining a truly generic, security-preserving construction of one primitive from the other. Our discussion in this section points to the fact that, while similar in many respects, CBE and CL-PKE are not equivalent concepts. Indeed, we suspect that the generic construction of a fully secure CL-PKE scheme from a CBE scheme may be impossible. We reiterate that this does not contradict the result of Yum and Lee in [12], because they did not use the full security model of [2] when studying the security of their CL-PKE constructions.

5.2   A New CBE Scheme

Our generic construction in Section 5 applies to any CL-PKE scheme and produces an IND-CBE-CCA secure CBE scheme. For example, it can be applied to FullCL-PKE of [2] or to the scheme FullCL-PKE* developed in Section 3. Let us denote the CBE scheme obtained from FullCL-PKE* by FullCBE*. We do not give this scheme explicitly here. Instead we merely note that FullCBE* is more computationally efficient than the scheme FullCBE of [7], requiring only one pairing computation for encryption compared to the two needed in FullCBE.

6   Summary

In this paper, we have examined the relationship between the separate but related concepts of CBE [7] and CL-PKE [2]. We have given a generic construction producing a secure CBE scheme from a secure CL-PKE scheme. In order to obtain this construction, we have had to analyze and repair the CBE definition and security model. We have also given a new, secure CL-PKE scheme FullCL-PKE* that improves on the scheme FullCL-PKE of [2]. The generic construction applied to FullCL-PKE* produces the scheme FullCBE*, which is computationally superior to the scheme FullCBE of [7].

References

1. S.S. Al-Riyami, *Cryptographic schemes based on elliptic curve pairings*, Ph.D. thesis, University of London, 2004.
2. S.S. Al-Riyami and K.G. Paterson. Certificateless public key cryptography. In *Advances in Cryptology – ASIACRYPT 2003*, LNCS vol. 2894, pp. 452–473. Springer, 2003.
3. S.S. Al-Riyami and K.G. Paterson. Certificateless public key cryptography. Cryptology ePrint Archive, Report 2003/126, 2003. http://eprint.iacr.org/.
4. D. Boneh and M. Franklin. Identity-based encryption from the Weil pairing. In J. Kilian, editor, *Proc. CRYPTO 2001*, LNCS vol. 2139, pp. 213–229. Springer, 2001.
5. T. ElGamal A public key cryptosystem and a signature scheme based on Discrete logarithm In G.R. Blakley and D. Chaum, editor, *Proc. CRYPTO 1984*, LNCS vol. 196, pp. 10–18. Springer, 1985.
6. E. Fujisaki and T. Okamoto. Secure integration of asymmetric and symmetric encryption schemes. In M. J. Wiener, editor, *Proc. CRYPTO 1999*, LNCS vol. 1666, pp. 537–554. Springer, 1999.

7. C. Gentry. Certificate-based encryption and the certificate revocation problem. In E. Biham, editor, *Proc. EUROCRYPT 2003*, LNCS vol. 2656, pp. 272–293. Springer, 2003.
8. G. Kang, J.H. Park and S.H. Hahn. A certificate-based signature scheme. In *CT-RSA 2004*, LNCS vol. 2964, pp. 99–111, 2004.
9. A. Shamir. Identity-based cryptosystems and signature schemes. In *Proc. CRYPTO 1984*, LNCS vol. 196, pp. 47–53. Springer, 1984.
10. D.H. Yum and P.J. Lee. Generic construction of certificateless encryption. In *ICCSA 2004*, LNCS vol. 3043, pp. 802–811, 2004.
11. D.H. Yum and P.J. Lee. Generic construction of certificateless signature. In *ACISP 2004*, LNCS vol. 3108, pp. 200–211, 2004.
12. D.H. Yum and P.J. Lee. Identitiy-based cryptography in public key management. In *EuroPKI 2004*, LNCS vol. 3093, pp. 71–84, 2004.

A   Sketch Proof of Theorem 1

We provide a sketch of the main ideas in the proof of Theorem 1; the details can be found in [1]. We need to introduce five intermediate encryption schemes. The first, BasicCL-PKE*, is a simpler version of FullCL-PKE* which omits the Fujisaki-Okamoto hybridisation technique [6]. We also make use of the schemes BasicPub and BasicPub^{hy} from [4], and we introduce two ElGamal-like schemes called ElG-BasicPub and ElG-HybridPub. The second of these is obtained from the first by applying the technique of [6]. A key-pair in ElG-BasicPub is of the form $\langle P_A, x_A \rangle$ and the encryption of message M is defined to be $C = \langle rP, M \oplus H_5(rP_A) \rangle$ for r selected at random from $\mathbb{Z}_q^*$.

As in [3], the proof of the theorem is performed in two parts. We relate the advantage of a Type I or Type II attacker against FullCL-PKE* to that of an algorithm to solve BDHP or CDHP respectively. We first consider a Type I adversary.

Type I Adversary: We provide a reduction relating the IND-CCA security of FullCL-PKE* to the IND-CPA security of the standard PKE schemes ElG-HybridPub and BasicPub^{hy}. The reduction is similar to the one provided in [3], but simulates H_5 in a special way to ensure that it behaves consistently in the course of the attack. This reduction also makes use of a special-purpose knowledge extraction algorithm to handle decryption queries. Furthermore, in order for this knowledge extractor to have a high success probability, we require (and prove) that the scheme BasicCL-PKE is OWE secure if the BDHP is hard. Thereafter, we use a series of fairly standard results to reduce the security of ElG-HybridPub and BasicPub^{hy} to the hardness of the CDHP in $\mathbb{G}_1$ or BDHP in $\langle \mathbb{G}_1, \mathbb{G}_2, \hat{e} \rangle$, respectively.

Type II Adversary: We show that the IND-CCA security of FullCL-PKE* can be reduced to the usual IND-CCA security of a related (normal) public key encryption scheme ElG-HybridPub. The security of ElG-HybridPub is reduced to that of a second public key encryption scheme ElG-BasicPub against OWE adversaries using results of [6]. Finally, we relate the security of ElG-BasicPub to the hardness of the CDHP in $\mathbb{G}_1$.

Since any algorithm to solve the CDHP in $\mathbb{G}_1$ (output by $\mathcal{IG}(k)$) can be used to solve the BDHP in $\langle \mathbb{G}_1, \mathbb{G}_2, \hat{e} \rangle$, we finally have that the security of FullCL-PKE* is related to the hardness of the BDHP. For the concrete relationship we refer the reader to the full version of this paper.

B   Proof of Theorem 2

We begin by considering in detail the case of a Game 1 adversary against Π^{CBE}.

Let $\mathcal{A}_1$ be a Game 1 IND-CCA adversary against Π^{CBE} with advantage ϵ. We show how to construct from $\mathcal{A}_1$ a Type I IND-CCA adversary $\mathcal{B}_I$ against Π^{CL}. Let $\mathcal{C}$ denote a Π^{CL}-challenger against $\mathcal{B}_I$. $\mathcal{C}$ begins by supplying $\mathcal{B}_I$ with the parameters of Π^{CL}. $\mathcal{B}_I$ mounts an IND-CCA attack on Π^{CL} using help from $\mathcal{A}_1$ as follows.

Adversary $\mathcal{B}_I$ simulates the algorithm $\mathsf{Setup}^{\mathrm{CBE}}$ of Π^{CBE} for $\mathcal{A}_1$. This is done by $\mathcal{B}_I$ setting Λ to be an arbitrary subset of $\{0,1\}^*$ and $\mathsf{params}^{\mathrm{CBE}}$ to be an extension of $\mathsf{params}^{\mathrm{CL}}$ which includes a description of Λ. $\mathcal{B}_I$ then gives $\mathsf{params}^{\mathrm{CBE}}$ to $\mathcal{A}_1$. Now $\mathcal{A}_1$ launches its attack, and $\mathcal{B}_I$ launches Phase 1 of its attack. $\mathcal{A}_I$ interleaves queries of three types, during which $\mathcal{B}_I$ transitions from Phase 1 to the Challenge Phase and on to Phase 2 in a manner to be specified below. These queries are handled by $\mathcal{B}_I$ as follows:

- On certification query $\langle \tau, \lambda, PK, SK \rangle$, adversary $\mathcal{B}_I$ makes a replace public key query for the entity with identifier $\mathsf{ID}'_A = \mathsf{params}^{\mathrm{CBE}} \| \tau \| \lambda \| PK$, replacing the public key with the value PK. Then $\mathcal{B}_I$ makes a partial-private-key extract query to $\mathcal{C}$ for the identifier ID'_A and returns the resulting partial private key to $\mathcal{B}_I$.
- On decryption query $\langle \tau, \lambda, PK, SK, C \rangle$, $\mathcal{B}_I$ makes a replace public key query for the entity with identifier $\mathsf{ID}'_A = \mathsf{params}^{\mathrm{CBE}} \| \tau \| \lambda \| PK$, replacing the public key with the value PK. Then $\mathcal{B}_I$ makes a decryption query on ciphertext C for the entity with identifier ID'_A to $\mathcal{C}$. $\mathcal{B}_I$ relays $\mathcal{C}$'s response to $\mathcal{A}_1$.
- On receiving a challenge query $\langle \tau_{\mathrm{ch}}, \lambda_{\mathrm{ch}}, PK_{\mathrm{ch}}, SK_{\mathrm{ch}}, M_0, M_1 \rangle$, adversary $\mathcal{B}_I$ makes a replace public key query for the entity with identifier $\mathsf{ID}'_{\mathrm{ch}} = \mathsf{params}^{\mathrm{CBE}} \| \tau_{\mathrm{ch}} \| \lambda_{\mathrm{ch}} \| PK_{\mathrm{ch}}$, replacing the public key with the value PK_{ch}. Then $\mathcal{B}_I$ terminates Phase 1 of its attack and enters the challenge phase, sending $\mathsf{ID}'_{\mathrm{ch}}$ and messages M_0, M_1 to $\mathcal{C}$. Challenger $\mathcal{C}$ responds with a challenge ciphertext C^* which is the encryption of message M_b (for some bit b) for identifier $\mathsf{ID}'_{\mathrm{ch}}$ and public key PK_{ch} in the scheme Π^{CL}. Then $\mathcal{B}_I$ forwards C^* to $\mathcal{A}_1$ as the response to $\mathcal{A}_1$'s challenge query and begins Phase 2 of its attack. It is easy to see from the definition of Π^{CBE} that C^* is equal to the output of algorithm Enc of Π^{CBE} on input $\langle \tau_{\mathrm{ch}}, \lambda_{\mathrm{ch}}, \mathsf{params}^{\mathrm{CBE}}, PK_{\mathrm{ch}}, M_b \rangle$.

We further insist that, if $\mathcal{B}_I$ is forced during the course of its simulation to replace the public key for $\mathsf{ID}'_{\mathrm{ch}}$ before the challenge phase and make a partial-private-key extract query on $\mathsf{ID}'_{\mathrm{ch}}$ in some phase, then $\mathcal{B}_I$ aborts. Likewise, we insist that if $\mathcal{B}_I$ is in Phase 2 and is forced to relay a decryption query on ciphertext C^* for identifier $\mathsf{ID}'_{\mathrm{ch}}$ and public key PK_{ch}, then $\mathcal{B}_I$ aborts. Since $\mathsf{ID}'_{\mathrm{ch}}$ is the challenge identifier relayed to $\mathcal{B}_I$'s challenger and C^* is the challenge ciphertext, these abort conditions ensure that $\mathcal{B}_I$ is a well-behaved CL-PKE Type I adversary whenever it does *not* abort.

Guess: Eventually, $\mathcal{A}_1$ should make a guess b' for b. Then $\mathcal{B}_I$ outputs b' as its guess for b.

Analysis: We now analyze the behaviour of $\mathcal{B}_I$ and $\mathcal{A}_1$ in this simulation. We claim that if algorithm $\mathcal{B}_I$ does not abort during the simulation then algorithm $\mathcal{A}_1$'s view is identical to its view in the real attack. Moreover, if $\mathcal{B}_I$ does not abort then $2|\Pr[b = b'] - \frac{1}{2}| = \epsilon$. We justify this claim as follows. Adversary $\mathcal{B}_I$'s responses to decryption and certification queries are as seen by $\mathcal{A}_1$ in a real attack, provided of course that $\mathcal{B}_I$ does not abort. Furthermore, the challenge ciphertext C^* is a valid Π^{CBE} encryption of M_b where $b \in \{0,1\}$ is random. Thus, by definition of algorithm $\mathcal{A}_1$ we have that $2|\Pr[b = b'] - \frac{1}{2}| = \epsilon$.

The probability that $\mathcal{B}_I$ does not abort during the simulation remains to be calculated. $\mathcal{B}_I$ can abort for two reasons. The first reason is that $\mathcal{B}_I$ may be forced to replace the public key for $\mathsf{ID}'_{\mathrm{ch}}$ before the challenge phase and make a partial-private-key extract query on $\mathsf{ID}'_{\mathrm{ch}}$ in some phase. This combination of replace public key query and partial-private-key extract query can only arise from $\mathcal{A}_1$ making a Certify query on an input $\langle \tau_{\mathrm{ch}}, \lambda_{\mathrm{ch}}, PK_{\mathrm{ch}}, SK_{\mathrm{ch}} \rangle$. But this is exactly the certification query which $\mathcal{A}_1$ is forbidden from making. So this event never occurs in $\mathcal{B}_I$'s simulation. The second reason is that $\mathcal{B}_I$ may be forced to relay a decryption query on ciphertext C^* for identifier $\mathsf{ID}'_{\mathrm{ch}}$ and public key PK_{ch} in Phase 2. Because of the way that $\mathcal{B}_I$ relays ciphertexts, this event happens only if $\mathcal{A}_1$ makes a decryption query on input $\langle \tau_{\mathrm{ch}}, \lambda_{\mathrm{ch}}, PK_{\mathrm{ch}}, SK_{\mathrm{ch}}, C^* \rangle$ after having received its challenge ciphertext. However, $\mathcal{A}_1$ is forbidden from making precisely this decryption query. So this event never occurs in $\mathcal{B}_I$'s simulation.

To summarize, Algorithm $\mathcal{B}_I$ never aborts, provides a perfect simulation of $\mathcal{A}_1$'s challenger and has an advantage ϵ in guessing bit b. Thus we have shown that a Game 1 CBE adversary against Π^{CBE} with advantage ϵ can be used to construct a CL-PKE Type I adversary against Π^{CL} with an identical advantage. Since Π^{CL} is secure against CL-PKE Type I adversaries, we can deduce the Π^{CBE} is secure against CBE Game 1 adversaries.

Using similar ideas, we can also show that a CBE Game 2 adversary against Π^{CBE} can be used to construct a CL-PKE Type II adversary against Π^{CL}. Since Π^{CL} is secure against CL-PKE Type II adversaries, we can deduce that Π^{CBE} is secure against CBE Game 2 adversaries. This completes the proof.

A Verifiable Random Function
with Short Proofs and Keys

Yevgeniy Dodis[1,*] and Aleksandr Yampolskiy[2,**]

[1] Department of Computer Science, New York University,
251 Mercer Street, New York, NY 10012, USA
dodis@cs.nyu.edu
[2] Department of Computer Science, Yale University,
51 Prospect Street, New Haven, CT 06511, USA
aleksandr.yampolskiy@yale.edu

Abstract. We give a simple and efficient construction of a verifiable random function (VRF) on bilinear groups. Our construction is direct. In contrast to prior VRF constructions [14, 15], it avoids using an inefficient Goldreich-Levin transformation, thereby saving several factors in security. Our proofs of security are based on a decisional bilinear Diffie-Hellman inversion assumption, which seems reasonable given current state of knowledge. For small message spaces, our VRF's proofs and keys have constant size. By utilizing a collision-resistant hash function, our VRF can also be used with arbitrary message spaces. We show that our scheme can be instantiated with an elliptic group of very reasonable size. Furthermore, it can be made distributed and proactive.

1 Introduction

The notion of a **verifiable random function** (VRF) was introduced by Micali, Rabin, and Vadhan [15]. A VRF is a pseudo-random function that provides a non-interactively verifiable proof for the correctness of its output. Given an input value x, the knowledge of the secret key SK enables computing the function value $y = F_{SK}(x)$ together with the proof of correctness π_x. This proof convinces every verifier that the value $y = F_{SK}(x)$ is indeed correct with respect to the public key of the VRF. We can thus view a VRF as a commitment to an exponential number of random-looking bits.

Since their introduction, VRFs have found useful applications in protocol design. To give a few examples, in [16], VRFs were used to reduce the number of rounds for resettable zero-knowledge proofs to three in the bare model. Micali and Rivest [17] used VRFs to construct a non-interactive lottery system employed in micropayments. Recently, Jarecki and Shmatikov [12] constructed

---

* Supported in part by NSF CAREER award CCR-0133806 and NSF grant CCR-0311095.
** Supported by NSF grants CCR-0098078, ANI-0207399, CNS-0305258, and CNS-0435201.

a verifiable transaction escrow scheme, which preserves users' anonymity while enabling automatic de-escrow, again with the help of VRFs.

Unfortunately, despite their utility, VRFs are not very well studied. As of this moment, there exist only a handful of constructions in the standard model: [8, 14, 15]. With the exception of [8], these works first construct a **verifiable unpredictable function** (VUF), whose output is hard to predict but does not necessarily look random. Then, they use an inefficient Goldreich-Levin hardcore bit [10] to convert a VUF into a VRF, thereby losing a factor in security. The size of proofs and keys of VRFs in [8,14] is linear in the input size, which may be undesirable in resource-constrained environments. Meanwhile, the VRF of Micali-Rabin-Vadhan [15] operates over a large multiplicative group $\mathbb{Z}_n^*$ which has to be very large to achieve reasonable security. Before the VRF value can be computed, it requires inputs to be mapped to primes in a complicated fashion.

In this paper, we construct a simple VRF on groups equipped with bilinear maps. Our construction is direct; it does not use a Goldreich-Levin hardcore bit, saving several factors in security. The inputs need not be primes or codewords of some special encoding. For small inputs, our VRF has constant size proofs and keys. We show that by utilizing a collision-resistant hash function, we can use our VRF with arbitrary inputs as well. Our VRF can be made distributed and proactive.

We begin in Section 2 by formalizing the notions of a VRF and a VUF. We also review the definition of bilinear groups, which are used in our constructions. These groups, recently discovered by Joux and Nguyen [13], have the property that decisional Diffie-Hellman (DDH) assumption (given g, g^a, and g^b, distinguish g^{ab} from random) becomes easy, but computational Diffie-Hellman (CDH) assumption (given g, g^a, and g^b, compute g^{ab}) still remains hard. This fact gives us many useful properties like verifiability.

Our proofs of security rely on two assumptions, which we describe in Section 3. Informally, they are:

- **q-Diffie-Hellman inversion assumption** (q-DHI) states that no efficient algorithm can compute $g^{1/x}$ on input $\left(g, g^x, \ldots, g^{(x^q)}\right)$ [18];
- **q-decisional bilinear Diffie-Hellman inversion assumption** (q-DBDHI) states that no efficient algorithm can distinguish $e(g, g)^{1/x}$ from random even after seeing $\left(g, g^x, \ldots, g^{(x^q)}\right)$ [3]. (Here $e(\cdot, \cdot)$ is a bilinear map, which we define later.)

In Section 4, we give our constructions and analyze their efficiency.

First, in Section 4.1, we consider a signature due to Boneh and Boyen [4]. On input x and a secret key SK, the signature is $\text{SIGN}_{SK}(x) = g^{1/(x+SK)}$. Boneh and Boyen proved this signature to be existentially unforgeable against **non-adaptive** adversaries. By restricting inputs to have slightly superlogarithmic size (in security parameter), we are able to prove security against **adaptive** adversaries. As a result, our proof is more involved, but necessarily less tight than the proof of [4]. We thus obtain a VUF, which is secure for small inputs. This VUF can then be converted into a VRF using the approach of prior works [14,15]. Specifically, we could use the Goldreich-Levin hardcore bit [10] to convert it into a VRF with output size 1, amplify the output size to match the size of the input, and then follow a tree-based construction to get a VRF with arbitrary input size. Needless, to say this is rather inefficient.

Instead, we prefer to construct a VRF directly (Section 4.2), saving several factors in security. We give a simple direct VRF construction for small inputs, which is secure under the q-DBDHI assumption. On input x and a secret key SK, our VRF computes $(F_{SK}(x), \pi(x))$, where $F_{SK}(x) = e(g, g)^{1/(x+SK)}$ is the VRF value and $\pi(x) = g^{1/(x+SK)}$ is the proof of correctness. We can apply a collision-resistant hash function to large inputs to transform our VRF into a VRF with unrestricted input length. By making the group size sufficiently large, we can construct a VRF with inputs of size roughly 160 bits, which is the length of SHA-1 digests. In theory, we do not have to assume existence of collision-resistant hash functions, and could also apply a variant of a generic tree transformation to amplify the input size. Even though keys and proofs no longer have constant size, they are still shorter than the keys and proofs in constructions of [14,15]. We analyze how large the group has to be and how our VRF compares with other constructions in Section 4.4.

Evaluating the VRF at a single server is a performance bottleneck and a single point of failure. Naturally, in Section 5, we sketch how to make our VRF distributed and proactive.

In Section 6, we analyze the q-DBDHI assumption in the generic group model à la Shoup [21]. We show that if the adversary can distinguish $e(g, g)^{1/x}$ from random with probability $\frac{1}{2} + \epsilon$, he will need to perform (at least) $\Omega(\sqrt{\epsilon p/q})$ generic group operations in a group of size p.

We conclude in Section 7.

2   Definitions

Before presenting our results, we review some basic definitions and assumptions.

Let k be a security parameter. As customary, we model the protocol participants by probabilistic Turing machines whose running time is polynomial in k (abbreviated as PPTs). Hereafter, we use $negl(k)$ to refer to a negligible function in the security parameter k.[1]

2.1   VRFs and VUFs

Let $a : \mathbb{N} \mapsto \mathbb{N} \cup \{*\}$ and $b : \mathbb{N} \mapsto \mathbb{N}$ be any functions for which $a(k)$ and $b(k)$ are computable in $poly(k)$ time (except when a takes the value $*$).[2].

Intuitively, a **verifiable random function (VRF)** behaves like a pseudorandom function, but also provides proofs of its outputs' correctness.

Definition 1. *A function family* $F_{(\cdot)}(\cdot) : \{0,1\}^{a(k)} \mapsto \{0,1\}^{b(k)}$ *is a family of VRFs if there exists a PPT algorithm* GEN *and deterministic algorithms* PROVE

---

[1] A function $negl(k) : \mathbb{N} \mapsto (0,1)$ is **negligible** if for every $c > 0$, for all sufficiently large k, $negl(k) < 1/k^c$. See any standard reference, such as [11], for details.

[2] When $a(k)$ takes the value of $*$, it means the VRF is defined for inputs of all length.

and VER *such that* GEN(1^k) *outputs a pair of keys* (PK, SK); PROVE$_{SK}(x)$ *computes* $\left(F_{SK}(x), \pi_{SK}(x)\right)$, *where* $\pi_{SK}(x)$ *is the proof of correctness; and* VER$_{PK}(x, y, \pi)$ *verifies that* $y = F_{SK}(x)$ *using the proof* π. *Formally, we require:*

1. **Uniqueness:** *no values* $(PK, x, y_1, y_2, \pi_1, \pi_2)$ *can satisfy* VER$_{PK}(x, y_1, \pi_1)$ $=$ VER$_{PK}(x, y_2, \pi_2)$ *when* $y_1 \neq y_2$.
2. **Provability:** *if* $(y, \pi) =$ PROVE$_{SK}(x)$, *then* VER$_{PK}(x, y, \pi) = 1$.
3. **Pseudorandomness:** *for any PPT algorithm* $\mathcal{A} = (A_1, A_2)$, *who does not query its oracle on* x *(see below),*

$$
\Pr\left[b = b' \left|
\begin{array}{c}
(PK, SK) \leftarrow \text{GEN}(1^k); (x, st) \leftarrow A_1^{\text{PROVE}(\cdot)}(PK); \\
y_0 = F_{SK}(x); y_1 \leftarrow \{0,1\}^{b(k)}; \\
b \leftarrow \{0,1\}; b' \leftarrow A_2^{\text{PROVE}(\cdot)}(y_b, st)
\end{array}
\right. \right] \leq \frac{1}{2} + negl(k)
$$

A **verifiable unpredictable function (VUF)** is a close relative of a VRF. Essentially, it is a signature scheme, whose verification algorithm accepts at most one signature for every public key and message.

Definition 2. *A function family* $F_{(\cdot)}(\cdot) : \{0,1\}^{a(k)} \mapsto \{0,1\}^{b(k)}$ *is a family of VUFs, if it satisfies the same syntax, uniqueness and provability properties of the VRFs, except the pseudorandomness property is replaced by the following weaker property:*

3'. **Unpredictability:** *for any PPT algorithm* $\mathcal{A}$, *who does not query its oracle on* x *(see below),*

$$
\Pr\left[y = F_{SK}(x) \middle| (PK, SK) \leftarrow \text{GEN}(1^k); (x, y) \leftarrow \mathcal{A}^{\text{PROVE}(\cdot)}(PK) \right] \leq negl(k)
$$

For exact security bounds, we will occasionally say that $F_{(\cdot)}(\cdot)$ is an $(s'(k), \epsilon'(k))$ secure VRF (*resp.*, VUF) if no adversary $\mathcal{A}$, running in time $s'(k)$, can break the pseudorandomness (*resp.*, unpredictability) property with $\epsilon'(k)$ advantage.

2.2   Bilinear Groups

Our constructions utilize bilinear maps. We briefly review their properties below.

Let $\mathbb{G}$ and $\mathbb{G}_1$ be two (multiplicative) cyclic groups of prime order p. Let g be a generator of $\mathbb{G}$. We shall call a mapping **bilinear** if it is linear with respect to each of its variables. Formally:

Definition 3. *An (admissible) bilinear map* $e : \mathbb{G} \times \mathbb{G} \mapsto \mathbb{G}_1$ *is a map with the following properties:*

1. **Bilinear:** *for all* $u, v \in \mathbb{G}$ *and* $x, y \in \mathbb{Z}$, *we have* $e(u^x, v^y) = e(u, v)^{xy}$.
2. **Non-degenerate:** $e(g, g) \neq 1$.
3. **Computable:** *there is an efficient algorithm to compute* $e(u, v)$ *for all* $u, v \in \mathbb{G}$.

We say that a group $\mathbb{G}$ is **bilinear** if the group action in $\mathbb{G}$ is efficiently computable and there exists a group $\mathbb{G}_1$ and an admissible bilinear map $e : \mathbb{G} \times \mathbb{G} \mapsto \mathbb{G}_1$. Henceforth, we shall use $\mathbb{G}^*$ to stand for $\mathbb{G} \backslash \{1_{\mathbb{G}}\}$.

Bilinear maps provide an algorithm for solving the decisional Diffie-Hellman problem (DDH) in $\mathbb{G}$;[3] this property comes in handy for constructing a verification algorithm for our VRF. Such maps can be constructed from Weil and Tate pairings on elliptic curves or abelian varieties [5, 9, 13].

3   Complexity Assumptions

We now state the hardness assumptions on which our constructions are based. In what follows, we let $\mathbb{G}$ be a bilinear group of prime order p, and let g be its generator.

3.1   Diffie-Hellman Inversion Assumption

Our VUF construction relies on the Diffie-Hellman inversion (DHI) assumption, which was originally proposed in [18].

The q-DHI problem in $\mathbb{G}$ asks: given the tuple $\left(g, g^x, \ldots, g^{(x^q)}\right) \in (\mathbb{G}^*)^{q+1}$ as input, compute $g^{1/x}$. An algorithm $\mathcal{A}$ has advantage ϵ in solving q-DHI in $\mathbb{G}$ if

$$\Pr\left[\mathcal{A}(g, g^x, \ldots, g^{(x^q)}) = g^{1/x}\right] \geq \epsilon,$$

where probability is taken over the coin tosses of $\mathcal{A}$ and the random choice of $x \in \mathbb{Z}_p^*$.[4]

Definition 4. *(q-DHI Assumption). We say that (t, q, ϵ)-DHI assumption holds in $\mathbb{G}$ if, no t-time algorithm $\mathcal{A}$ has advantage at least ϵ in solving the q-DHI problem in $\mathbb{G}$.*

Boneh and Boyen [3] pointed out that the q-DHI assumption implies the $(q + 1)$-generalized Diffie-Hellman assumption (GDH), on which many cryptographic constructions are based (*e.g.*, [6, 19, 22] as well as the VUF in [14]). Therefore, security of our VUF rests on an equivalent complexity assumption to the one made before.

3.2   Decisional Bilinear Diffie-Hellman Inversion Assumption

In order to construct a VRF directly, we need to make a decisional bilinear Diffie-Hellman inversion assumption (DBDHI). It was previously used in [3] to construct a selective-ID secure identity based encryption scheme.

---

[3] Specifically, to determine whether (g, g^x, g^y, g^z) is a DDH tuple, we can check if $e(g^x, g^y) = e(g, g^z)$.

[4] To simplify the notation, from now on, we assume that algorithms implicitly get a description of the bilinear group $(\mathbb{G}, \circ, p)$, on which they operate, as input.

The q-DBDHI problem asks: given the tuple $\left(g, g^x, \ldots, g^{(x^q)}\right)$ as input, distinguish $e(g, g)^{1/x}$ from random. Formally, an algorithm $\mathcal{A}$ has advantage ϵ in solving the q-DBDHI problem if

$$\left| \Pr\left[\mathcal{A}(g, g^x, \ldots, g^{(x^q)}, e(g, g)^{1/x}) = 1\right] - \Pr\left[\mathcal{A}(g, g^x, \ldots, g^{(x^q)}, \Gamma) = 1\right]\right| \leq \epsilon,$$

where the probability is taken over the internal coin tosses of $\mathcal{A}$ and choices of $x \in \mathbb{Z}_p^*$ and $\Gamma \in \mathbb{G}_1$.

Definition 5. *(q-DBDHI Assumption). We say that the (t, q, ϵ)-DBDHI assumption holds in $\mathbb{G}$ if no t-time algorithm $\mathcal{A}$ has advantage at least ϵ in solving the q-DBDHI problem in $\mathbb{G}$.*

Clearly, q-DBDHI is a stronger assumption than q-DHI. To provide more confidence in its validity, we analyze this assumption in the generic group model in Section 6.

4   Our Constructions

In Section 4.1, we show that a signature scheme due to Boneh and Boyen [4] is in fact a VUF for small inputs. We could then use a Goldreich-Levin hardcore bit to convert the resulting VUF into a VRF. However, the generic transformation is rather inefficient, so we choose to forego it. Instead, in Section 4.2, we construct our VRF directly for inputs of small size. We then show how to extend the VRF input size in Section 4.3. Finally, we evaluate our construction's efficiency in Section 4.4.

Fix input length $a(k)$, output length $b(k)$, and security $s(k)$. For notational convenience, we will usually omit the security parameter k, writing, for example, a or s, instead of $a(k)$ or $s(k)$. Let $\mathbb{G}$ ($|\mathbb{G}| = p$) be a bilinear group, whose order p is a k-bit prime. Let g be a generator of $\mathbb{G}$. Throughout, we shall assume that messages can be encoded as elements of $\mathbb{Z}_p^*$.

4.1   A Verifiable Unpredictable Function

In order to build the intuition for our next proof, we first describe how to construct a simple VUF (GEN, SIGN, VER), which is secure for small (superlogarithmic) inputs.

Algorithm Gen(1^k): Chooses a secret $s \in_r \mathbb{Z}_p^*$ and sets the secret key to $SK = s$ and a public key to $PK = g^s$.

Algorithm Sign$_{SK}(x)$: Outputs the signature $\text{SIGN}_{SK}(x) = g^{1/(x+SK)}$. Note that the proof is embedded in the output value so we do not need to include it explicitly.

Algorithm Ver$_{PK}(x, y)$: Outputs 1 if $e(g^x \cdot PK, y) = e(g, g)$; otherwise, outputs 0. Indeed, if the VRF value y was correctly computed, we have:

$$e(g^x \cdot PK, y) = e(g^x g^s, g^{1/(x+s)}) = e(g, g).$$

Boneh and Boyen [4] proved this scheme to be existentially unforgeable against **non-adaptive adversaries** for inputs of arbitrary size. In our proof, we restrict inputs to have slightly superlogarithmic size in k (just like [15] do); that is, we set $a(k) = \log s(k) = \Omega(\log k)$. This enables us to enumerate all possible messages in $s(k)$ time and to respond to adversary's queries **adaptively**. Further, the proof of [4] is based on a q-strong Diffie-Hellman assumption (q-SDH), which is implied by a weaker q-DHI assumption used in our proof. Correspondingly, our proof is more involved but necessarily less tight than the proof of [4].

Theorem 1. *Suppose the $(s(k), 2^{a(k)}, \epsilon(k))$-DHI assumption holds in a bilinear group $\mathbb{G}$ ($|\mathbb{G}| = p$). Let the input size be $a(k)$ and output size be $b(k) = \log_2 p$. Then $(\text{GEN}, \text{SIGN}, \text{VER})$ is a $(s'(k), \epsilon'(k))$ verifiable unpredictable function, where $s'(k) = s(k)/(2^{a(k)} \cdot poly(k))$ and $\epsilon'(k) = \epsilon(k) \cdot 2^{a(k)}$.*

Proof. It is easy to see that uniqueness and provability properties of Definition 2 are satisfied. We thus concentrate on residual unpredictability.

We shall use a shortcut and write $q = 2^{a(k)}$. Suppose there exists an adversary $\mathcal{A}$, running in time $s'(k)$, which guesses the value of the function at an unseen point with non-negligible probability $\epsilon'(k)$. We shall construct an algorithm $\mathcal{B}$ that by interacting with $\mathcal{A}$ breaks the q-DHI assumption with non-negligible probability.

Input to the Reduction: Algorithm $\mathcal{B}$ is given a tuple $\left(g, g^\alpha, \ldots, g^{(\alpha^q)}\right) \in (\mathbb{G}^*)^{q+1}$, for some unknown $\alpha \in \mathbb{Z}_p^*$. Its goal is to compute $g^{1/\alpha}$.

Key Generation: We guess that $\mathcal{A}$ will output a forgery on message $x_0 \in_r \{0,1\}^{a(k)}$. We are right with probability $1/2^{a(k)}$; error probability can be decreased by repeating the algorithm sufficiently many times. Let $\beta = \alpha - x_0$.[5] We don't know what β is because α is secret. However, we can use the Binomial Theorem to compute $\left(g^\beta, \ldots, g^{(\beta^q)}\right)$ from $\left(g^\alpha, \ldots, g^{(\alpha^q)}\right)$. Because $a(k) = \log(s(k))$, we can enumerate all possible inputs in $s(k)$ time. Let $f(z)$ be the polynomial

$$f(z) = \prod_{w \in \{0,1\}^a, w \neq x_0} (z + w) = \sum_{j=0}^{q-1} c_j z^j \text{ (for some coefficients } c_0, \ldots, c_{q-1}).$$

We can compute

$$h = g^{f(\beta)} = \prod_{j=0}^{q-1} \left(g^{(\beta^j)}\right)^{c_j} \text{ and } h^\beta = \prod_{j=1}^{q} \left(g^{(\beta^j)}\right)^{c_{j-1}}.$$

Finally, we set h to be the generator and give $PK = h^\beta$ to $\mathcal{A}$. The secret key is $SK = \beta$, which we don't know ourselves.

Responding to Oracle Queries: Without loss of generality, we assume that $\mathcal{A}$ never repeats a query. Consider the ith query ($1 \leq i < q$) on message x_i. If

---

[5] For the sake of readability, we slightly abuse the notation. We should really have written $\beta = \alpha - \psi(x_0)$, where $\psi : \{0,1\}^{a(k)} \mapsto \mathbb{Z}_p^*$.

$x_i = x_0$, then we fail. Otherwise, we must compute $\mathrm{SIGN}_{SK}(x_i) = h^{1/(x_i+\beta)}$. Let $f_i(z)$ be the polynomial

$$f_i(z) = f(z)/(z+x_i) = \sum_{j=0}^{q-2} d_j z^j \text{ (for some coefficients } d_0, \ldots, d_{q-2}).$$

We can compute

$$g^{f_i(\beta)} = \prod_{j=0}^{q-2} \left(g^{(\beta^j)}\right)^{d_j} = h^{1/(x_i+\beta)}$$

and return it as the signature.

Outputting the Forgery: Eventually, $\mathcal{A}$ outputs a forgery (x^*, σ^*). If $x^* \neq x_0$, then our simulation failed. Because the signature is unique, we must have $\sigma^* = h^{1/(x_0+\beta)} = g^{f(\beta)/(x_0+\beta)}$. Compute

$$f(z)/(z+x_0) = \sum_{j=0}^{q-2} \gamma_j z^j + \frac{\gamma_{-1}}{z+x_0},$$

where $\gamma_{-1} \neq 0$. Hence,

$$\left(\sigma^* \cdot \prod_{j=0}^{q-2} \left(g^{(\beta^i)}\right)^{-\gamma_i}\right)^{1/\gamma_{-1}} = g^{1/(x_0+\beta)} = g^{1/\alpha}.$$

Let $\epsilon'(k) = \epsilon(k) \cdot 2^{a(k)}$ and $s'(k) = s(k)/(2^{a(k)} \cdot \mathrm{poly}(k))$. To finish the proof, note that algorithm $\mathcal{B}$ succeeds with probability $\epsilon'(k)/2^{a(k)} = \epsilon(k)$. Its running time is dominated by answering oracle queries, and each query takes $(2^{a(k)} - 2) \cdot \mathrm{poly}(k)$ time to answer. Therefore, $\mathcal{B}$ will run in roughly $s'(k) \cdot 2^{a(k)} \mathrm{poly}(k) = s(k)$ time.   □

Remark 1. The security reduction of Theorem 1 is not tight. It allows to construct VUFs with input roughly $a(k) = \Omega(\log s(k))$. In theory, this means that the input size we can achieve might be only slightly superlogarithmic in k (similar to [15]). First, it might be reasonable to assume subexponential hardness of the q-DHI assumption which will immediately allow one to support input of size $k^{\Omega(1)}$. Also, by utilizing a collision-resistant hash function, we will anyway only need to construct VUFs with relatively small input size such as 160 bits. Indeed, in Section 4.4, we show that our construction seems to yield a practical and secure VUF for inputs of arbitrary length already when $k = 1,000$ bits.

4.2   A Verifiable Random Function

Our main contribution is a direct construction of a verifiable random function from a slightly stronger q-DBDHI assumption. The VRF ($\mathrm{GEN}, \mathrm{PROVE}, \mathrm{VER}$) is as follows.

Algorithm Gen(1^k): Chooses a secret $s \in_r \mathbb{Z}_p^*$ and sets the secret key to $SK = s$ and the public key to $PK = g^s$.

Algorithm Prove$_{SK}(x)$: We let $\text{PROVE}_{SK}(x) = \left(F_{SK}(x), \pi_{SK}(x)\right)$ where $F_{SK}(x) = e(g,g)^{1/(x+SK)}$ is the VRF output and $\pi_{SK}(x) = g^{1/(x+SK)}$ is the proof of correctness.

Algorithm Ver$_{PK}(x, y, \pi)$: To verify whether y was computed correctly, check if $e(g^x \cdot PK, \pi) = e(g,g)$ and whether $y = e(g, \pi)$. If both checks succeed, output 1; otherwise, output 0.

We can prove this scheme to be secure (in the sense of Definition 1) for small inputs (superlogarithmic in k). We then show how to convert it into a VRF with unrestricted input size.

Theorem 2. *Suppose the $(s(k), 2^{a(k)}, \epsilon(k))$-decisional BDHI assumption holds in a bilinear group $\mathbb{G}$ ($|\mathbb{G}| = p$). Let the input size be $a(k)$ and the output size be $b(k) = \log_2 p$. Then $(\text{GEN}, \text{PROVE}, \text{VER})$, as defined above, is a $(s'(k), \epsilon'(k))$ verifiable random function, where $s'(k) = s(k)/(2^{a(k)} \cdot poly(k))$ and $\epsilon'(k) = \epsilon(k) \cdot 2^{a(k)}$.*

Proof. It is trivial to show that uniqueness and provability properties of Definition 1 are satisfied. We thus concentrate on the pseudorandomness property.

We shall use $q = 2^{a(k)}$ as a shortcut. For sake of contradiction, suppose there exists an algorithm $\mathcal{A} = (A_1, A_2)$, which runs in time $s'(k)$, and can distinguish between $F_{SK}(x) = e(g,g)^{1/(x+s)}$ (for some x) and a random element in $\mathbb{G}_1$ with probability at least $1/2 + \epsilon'(k)$. We shall construct an algorithm $\mathcal{B}$ that uses $\mathcal{A}$ to break the q-DBDHI assumption in $\mathbb{G}$.

Input to the Reduction: Algorithm $\mathcal{B}$ is given a tuple $(g, g^\alpha, \ldots, g^{(\alpha^q)}, \Gamma) \in (\mathbb{G}^*)^{q+1} \times \mathbb{G}_1$, where Γ is either $e(g,g)^{1/\alpha} \in \mathbb{G}_1$ or a random element in $\mathbb{G}_1$. Its goal is to output 1 if $\Gamma = e(g,g)^{1/\alpha}$ and 0 otherwise.

Key Generation: We guess that $\mathcal{A}$ will choose to distinguish the VRF value on message $x_0 \in \{0,1\}^{a(k)}$. Let $\beta = \alpha - x_0$ (see footnote 5). We generate the public and private keys for algorithm $\mathcal{A}$ as in the proof of Theorem 1. Using the Binomial Theorem, we compute the tuple $(g^\beta, \ldots, g^{(\beta^q)})$. We define

$$f(z) = \prod_{w \in \{0,1\}^a, w \neq x_0} (z + w) = \sum_{j=0}^{q-1} c_j z^j.$$

This enables us to compute the new base

$$h = g^{f(\beta)} = \prod_{j=0}^{q-1} \left(g^{(\beta^j)}\right)^{c_j}.$$

Finally, we give $PK = h^\beta = \prod_{j=1}^{q} \left(g^{(\beta^j)}\right)^{c_{j-1}}$ as the public key to $\mathcal{A}$. The secret key is $SK = \beta$, which we don't know.

Responding to Oracle Queries: Consider the ith query $(1 \leq i < q)$ on message x_i. If $x_i = x_0$, we fail. Otherwise, we must respond with the corresponding proof $\pi_{SK}(x_i)$ and a VRF value $F_{SK}(x_i)$.
As in Theorem 1, we define

$$f_i(z) = f(z)/(z + x_i) = \sum_{j=0}^{q-2} d_j z^j \text{ (for some coefficients } d_0, \ldots, d_{q-2}).$$

We can thus compute

$$\pi_{SK}(x_i) = \prod_{j=0}^{q-2} \left(g^{(\beta^j)}\right)^{d_j} = h^{1/(\beta+x_i)}$$

and

$$F_{SK}(x_i) = e(h, \pi_{SK}(x_i)) = e(h, h)^{1/(\beta+x_i)},$$

and return them to algorithm $\mathcal{A}$.

Challenge: Eventually, $\mathcal{A}$ outputs a message x^* on which it wants to be challenged. If $x^* \neq x_0$, then we fail. Otherwise, $\mathcal{A}$ claims to be able to distinguish $e(h, h)^{1/(\beta+x_0)} = e(h, h)^{1/\alpha}$ from a random element in $\mathbb{G}_1$. Recall that

$$f(z) = \sum_{i=0}^{q-1} c_i z^i.$$

Because $f(z)$ is not divisible by $(z + x_0)$, we have:

$$f'(z) = f(z)/(z + x_0) - \frac{\gamma}{z + x_0}$$
$$= \sum_{j=0}^{q-2} \gamma_j z^j \text{ (for some } \gamma \neq 0 \text{ and coefficients } \gamma_0, \ldots, \gamma_{q-2}).$$

Let Γ_0 be

$$\Gamma_0 = \left(\prod_{i=0}^{q-1} \prod_{j=0}^{q-2} e\left(g^{(\beta^i)}, g^{(\beta^j)}\right)^{c_i \gamma_j}\right) \cdot \left(\prod_{m=0}^{q-2} e\left(g, g^{(\beta^t)}\right)^{\gamma \cdot \gamma_m}\right)$$
$$= e\left(g^{f(\beta)}, g^{f'(\beta)}\right) \cdot e\left(g^\gamma, g^{f'(\beta)}\right) \tag{1}$$
$$= e(g, g)^{(f(\beta)^2 - \gamma^2)/\alpha}.$$

Set $\Gamma^* = \Gamma^{(\gamma^2)} \cdot \Gamma_0$. Notice that if $\Gamma = e(g, g)^{1/\alpha}$, then $\Gamma^* = e(g^{f(\beta)}, g^{f(\beta)/\alpha})$ $= e(h, h)^{1/\alpha}$. Meanwhile, if Γ is uniformly distributed, then so is Γ^*. We give Γ^* to algorithm $\mathcal{A}$.

Note: It may seem as though computing Γ_0 is very expensive. However, from Equation (1), we see that the computation only takes two bilinear map evaluations.

Guess: Algorithm $\mathcal{A}$ makes some more queries to which we respond as before. Finally, $\mathcal{A}$ outputs a guess $b \in \{0, 1\}$. We return b as our guess as well.

The running time of the reduction is dominated by simulating oracle queries. Per every query, we must perform one bilinear map evaluation (this takes $\mathrm{poly}(k)$ time) and $(2^a - 2)$ multiplications and exponentiations (this takes $2^a \cdot \mathrm{poly}(k)$ time). Because $\mathcal{A}$ can make at most $s'(k)$ queries, the running time of $\mathcal{B}$ is altogether $s'(k)(2^{a(k)} \cdot \mathrm{poly}(k))$. The advantage of $\mathcal{B}$ in this experiment is $\epsilon'(k)/2^{a(k)}$. Setting $s'(k) = s(k)/(2^{a(k)} \cdot \mathrm{poly}(k))$ and $\epsilon'(k) = \epsilon(k) \cdot 2^{a(k)}$ completes the proof. $\square$

4.3 Extending the Input Size

We constructed a VRF (GEN, PROVE, VER), which is provably secure for inputs of small size $a(k) = \Omega(\log(k))$. We now explain how to handle inputs of arbitrary size.

Hashing the Input. Notice that if we have a VRF $\mathrm{PROVE}_{SK}(\cdot) : \{0,1\}^{a(k)} \mapsto \{0,1\}^{b(k)}$ and a collision-resistant hash function $H(\cdot) : \{0,1\}^* \mapsto \{0,1\}^{a(k)}$, then their composition $\mathrm{PROVE}_{SK}(H(\cdot)) : \{0,1\}^* \mapsto \{0,1\}^{b(k)}$ is trivially secure. Although our security reduction is relatively loose, we can make the size of a bilinear group large enough (we give exact numbers in Section 4.4) to have inputs of length roughly $a(k) = 160$ bits, the length of SHA-1 digests. Restriction to small inputs is therefore not limiting because we can always hash longer inputs.

Tree Construction. Although, we recommend using the previous construction (by making the group large enough), in theory, we could always use the (inefficient) generic tree construction to extend the input length. Then, we do not have to assume the existence of a collision-resistant hash function; having a universal hash function suffices.

We shall use the following proposition:

Proposition 1 ([15]). *If there is a VRF with input length $a(k)$, output length 1, and security $s(k)$, then there is a VRF with unrestricted input length, output length 1 and security at least $\min(s(k)^{1/5}, 2^{a(k)/5})$.*

The construction first converts a VRF with output length 1 into a VRF with output length $(a-1)$. This transformation loses a factor of a in security. Because our VRF has output length much larger than 1, we can omit this step. Instead, we apply a universal hash function to VRF's output and let the VRF's value be the first $(a-1)$ bits of hash function's output (it is easily seen that these bits will be pseudo-random as well).

The rest of the transformation proceeds as usual. We construct a binary trie whose nodes are labeled with strings of length $(a-1)$. The root is labeled with 0^{a-1} and the children of node y are labeled with VRF values on inputs $(y \circ 0)$ and $(y \circ 1)$. Computing the VRF value on input $x \in \{0,1\}^*$ amounts to tracing a path through the trie to the leaf corresponding to x. The VRF value is the label of the leaf, and the proof of correctness is a tuple of VRF proofs – one proof per each node on the path traced by x.[6]

---

[6] The inputs have to be prefix-free for this tree construction to work. This can be accomplished using techniques of [15].

We also note that both of the aforementioned techniques can be used to convert the VUF in Section 4.1 into a VUF with unrestricted input length.

4.4 Efficiency

We now compare the efficiency of our construction with that of prior VRF constructions. We fix inputs to be $a(k) = 160$ bits, the length of SHA-1 digests, and let $q = 2^{a(k)}$.

Our VRF. According to Theorem 2, if $(s(k), q, \epsilon(k))$-DBDHI holds on $\mathbb{G}$, then our VRF is secure against adversaries running in time $s'(k) = s(k)/(2^{a(k)} \cdot \text{poly}(k))$ that have advantage $\epsilon'(k) = \epsilon(k) \cdot 2^{a(k)}$. To be generous, we instantiate $\epsilon'(k) = 2^{-80}$, $s'(k) = 2^{80}$, and $\text{poly}(k) = 2^{30}$. Then, we have: $\epsilon(k) = 2^{-240}$ and $s(k) = 2^{270}$. Suppose no better algorithm exists for breaking the q-DBDHI assumption than a generic group algorithm. Then, by Theorem 3 (which we prove in Section 6), for these security parameters a bilinear group must have size:

$$p \geq \frac{2(s(k) + q + 3)^2 q}{\epsilon(k)}$$

$$= \frac{2\left(2^{270} + 2^{160} + 3\right)^2 2^{160}}{2^{-240}}$$

$$\approx 2^{940}.$$

Therefore, making the group size be a 1,000 bit prime seems sufficient to guarantee security of the VRF that takes 160 bit inputs. Proofs and keys consist of a single group element and will roughly be 125 bytes each. We can generate such groups using the standard parameter generator of [5].

VRF by Micali-Rabin-Vadhan [15]. This VRF operates over a multiplicative group $\mathbb{Z}_n^*$, where $n = pq$ is a k-bit RSA modulus. The fastest general-purpose factoring algorithm today is the number field sieve [7]; it takes approximately $O\left(e^{1.9223(k^{1/3}(\log k)^{2/3})}\right)$ time to factor a k bit number. The RSA based VUF (not even a VRF) constructed in [15] has security $s'(k) = s(k)/(2^{a(k)} \cdot \text{poly}(k))$ where $s(k)$ is hardness of RSA. Letting $s'(k) = 2^{80}$ and $\text{poly}(k) = 2^{30}$ as before, we obtain an RSA security lower bound $s(k) = 2^{80} \cdot (2^{160} \cdot 2^{30}) = 2^{270}$. Because RSA is only secure as long as we cannot factor n, to get 270 bits of security, we need n to be a k-bit number, where

$$1.9223k^{1/3}(\log k)^{2/3} = 270.$$

Hence, n must be at least $14,383$ bits long if we want to use this VUF on 160 bit inputs. After following the tree construction, proofs for 160 bit inputs will have size 280 kilobytes.

VRF by Dodis [8] and VUF by Lysyanskaya [14]. These constructions work on elliptic curve groups, whose size is usually a 160 bit prime. At the bare minimum, 160 bit messages yield keys and proofs of size $160 \cdot 160 = 25,600$ bits, which is about 3.2 kilobytes. In fact, they will probably have larger size due to use of error-correcting codes and other encoding expansions.

To summarize, none of the prior VRF constructions come close to the 1,000 bit proofs and keys of our construction. If our VRF is used with the generic tree construction, its keys and proofs consist of $|x|$ group elements (one group element per input bit) when the input is $x \in \{0,1\}^*$. This is less than the $|x|^2$ group elements ($|x|$ group elements per input bit) needed by the VRF of [14].

5 Distributed VRF

We point out that our VUF/VRF constructions can be easily made distributed (or even proactive). Indeed, both of the constructions simply amount to a secure computation of the function $\pi_{SK}(x) = g^{1/(x+SK)}$ when the servers have shares of the secret SK. Because it is well known how to do multiparty addition, inversion, and exponentiation [1,2], this extension follows immediately. We notice however that unlike the construction of Dodis [8], our distributed VUF/VRF is interactive.

6 Generic Security of the q-DBDHI Assumption

In this section, we examine the q-DBDHI assumption in the generic group model of Shoup [21]. We proceed to derive a lower bound on the computational complexity of a generic adversary who breaks this assumption.

In the generic group model, elements of $\mathbb{G}$ and $\mathbb{G}_1$ are encoded as unique random strings. We define an injective function $\theta : \mathbb{Z}_p \mapsto \{0,1\}^*$, which maps $a \in \mathbb{Z}_p$ to the string representation $\theta(g^a)$ of $g^a \in \mathbb{G}$. Similarly, we define a function $\theta_1 : \mathbb{Z}_p \mapsto \{0,1\}^*$ for $\mathbb{G}_1$. The encodings are such that non-group operations are meaningless. There exist three oracles which compute the group action in $\mathbb{G}$, the group action in $\mathbb{G}_1$, and the bilinear pairing $e : \mathbb{G} \times \mathbb{G} \mapsto \mathbb{G}_1$ from elements' encodings.

Theorem 3. *Let $\mathcal{A}$ be an algorithm that solves the q-DBDHI problem. Assume both $x \in \mathbb{Z}_p^*$ and the encoding functions θ, θ_1 are chosen at random. If $\mathcal{A}$ makes at most q_G queries to oracles computing the group action in $\mathbb{G}, \mathbb{G}_1$ and the bilinear mapping $e : \mathbb{G} \times \mathbb{G} \mapsto \mathbb{G}_1$, then*

$$\left| \Pr \left[\begin{array}{c} \mathcal{A}\left(p, \theta(1), \theta(x), \dots, \theta(x^q), \\ \theta_1(\Gamma_0), \theta_1(\Gamma_1)\right) = b \end{array} \middle| \begin{array}{c} b \xleftarrow{r} \{0,1\}; \\ \Gamma_b \leftarrow 1/x; \Gamma_{1-b} \xleftarrow{r} \mathbb{Z}_p^* \end{array} \right] - \frac{1}{2} \right|$$
$$\leq \frac{2(q_G + q + 3)^2 q}{p}.$$

Proof. Instead of letting $\mathcal{A}$ interact with the actual oracles, we play the following game.

We maintain two lists: $L = \{(F_i, s_i) : i = 0, \ldots, t - 1\}$ and $L' = \{(F'_i, s'_i) : i = 0, \ldots, t' - 1\}$. Here $s_i, s'_i \in \{0, 1\}^*$ are encodings and $F_i, F'_i \in \mathbb{Z}_p[X, \Gamma_0, \Gamma_1]$ are multivariate polynomials in X, Γ_0, and Γ_1. The total length of lists at step $\tau \leq q_G$ in the game must be

$$t + t' = \tau + q + 3. \tag{2}$$

In the beginning of the game, we initialize the lists to $F_0 = 1, F_1 = X, \ldots, F_q = X^q$ and $F'_0 = \Gamma_0, F'_1 = \Gamma_1$. The corresponding encodings are set to arbitrary distinct strings in $\{0, 1\}^*$. The lists have length $t = q + 1$ and $t' = 2$.

We start the game by providing $\mathcal{A}$ with encodings $(s_0, \ldots, s_q, s'_0)$. Algorithm $\mathcal{A}$ begins to issue oracle queries. We respond to them in the standard fashion:

Group Action: Given a multiply/divide bit and two operands s_i and s_j ($0 \leq i, j < t$), we compute $F_t = F_i \pm F_j$ accordingly. If $F_t = F_l$ for some $l < t$, we set $s_t = s_l$. Otherwise, we set s_t to a random string in $\{0, 1\}^* \setminus \{s_0, \ldots, s_{t-1}\}$, and increment t by 1. Group action in G_1 is computed similarly, except we operate on list L'.

Bilinear Pairing: Given two operands s_i and s_j ($0 \leq i, j < t$), we compute the product $F_{t'} = F_i F_j$. If $F_{t'} = F_l$ for some $l < t'$, we set $s_{t'} = s_l$. Otherwise we set it to a random string in $\{0, 1\}^* \setminus \{s_0, \ldots, s_{t'-1}\}$. We then increment t' by 1.

After making at most q_G queries, $\mathcal{A}$ halts with a guess $\hat{b} \in \{0, 1\}$. We now choose $x, y \xleftarrow{r} \mathbb{Z}_p^*$ and consider $\Gamma_b \leftarrow 1/x, \Gamma_{1-b} = y$ for both choices of b. Our simulation is perfect and reveals nothing to $\mathcal{A}$ about b unless the values that we chose for indeterminates give rise to some non-trivial equality relation. Specifically, algorithm $\mathcal{A}$ wins the game if for any $F_i \neq F_j$ or any $F'_i \neq F'_j$, either of these hold:

1. $F_i(x, 1/x, y) - F_j(x, 1/x, y) = 0$
2. $F_i(x, y, 1/x) - F_j(x, y, 1/x) = 0$
3. $F'_i(x, 1/x, y) - F'_j(x, 1/x, y) = 0$
4. $F'_i(x, y, 1/x) - F'_j(x, y, 1/x) = 0$

Notice that $\mathcal{A}$ can never engineer an encoding of an element whose corresponding polynomial would have a $1/X$ term unless he is explicitly given it. Therefore, we can only get a non-trivial equality relation as a result of numerical cancellation.

For all i, $\deg(F_i) \leq q$ and $\deg(F'_i) \leq 2q$. We can use the Schwartz-Zippel Theorem [20] to bound the probability of a cancellation. It tells us that for all i, j, $\Pr[F_i - F_j = 0] \leq q/p$ and $\Pr[F'_i - F'_j = 0] \leq 2q/p$. Thus $\mathcal{A}$'s advantage is

$$\epsilon \leq 2 \cdot \left(\binom{t}{2} \frac{q}{p} + \binom{t'}{2} \frac{2q}{p} \right)$$

$$< 2(q_G + q + 3)^2 \frac{q}{p} \quad \text{(plugging into (2))}$$

$$= O\left(\frac{q_G^2 q + q^3}{p} \right).$$

$\square$

It turns out that in a generic group model algorithm $\mathcal{A}$ that solves the q-DBDHI problem has advantage, which is roughly twice as much as an advantage of an algorithm solving the q-SDH problem (see [4], Section 5). The asymptotic complexities are the same.

The following corollary is immediate.

Corollary 1. *Any adversary that breaks the q-DBDHI assumption with probability $\frac{1}{2} + \epsilon$ ($0 < \epsilon < 1/2$) in generic groups of order p such that $q < o(\sqrt[3]{p})$ requires $\Omega(\sqrt{\epsilon p / q})$ generic group operations.*

7   Conclusion

We have presented a simple and efficient construction of a verifiable random function. Our VRF's proofs and keys have constant size regardless of the size of the input. Our proofs of security are based on a decisional bilinear Diffie-Hellman inversion assumption, which seems reasonable given current state of knowledge. We also demonstrated that our scheme can be instantiated with elliptic groups of very reasonable size which makes our constructions quite practical.

Acknowledgments

The authors would like to thank James Aspnes, Dan Boneh, Salil Vadhan, and the anonymous referees for their helpful comments.

References

1. Judit Bar-Ilan and Donald Beaver. Non-cryptographic fault-tolerant computing in a constant number of rounds. In *Proceedings of the ACM Symposium on Principles of Distributed Computation*, pages 201–209, 1989.
2. Michael Ben-or, Shafi Goldwasser, and Avi Wigderson. Completeness theorems for non-cryptographic fault-tolerant distributed computing. In *Proceedings of the 20th Annual ACM Symposium on the Theory of Computing*, pages 1–10, 1988.
3. Dan Boneh and Xavier Boyen. Efficient selective-ID secure identity based encryption without random oracles. In *Advances in Cryptology – EUROCRYPT 2004*, volume 3027 of *Lecture Notes in Computer Science*, pages 223–238. Berlin: Springer-Verlag, 2004.
4. Dan Boneh and Xavier Boyen. Short signatures without random oracles. In *Advances in Cryptology – EUROCRYPT 2004*, volume 3027 of *Lecture Notes in Computer Science*, pages 56–73. Berlin: Springer-Verlag, 2004.
5. Dan Boneh and Matt Franklin. Identity-based encryption from the Weil pairing. *Lecture Notes in Computer Science*, 2139:213–229, 2001.
6. Dan Boneh and Alice Silverberg. Application of multilinear forms to cryptography. Cryptology ePrint Archive, Report 2002/080, 2002. http://eprint.iacr.org/2002/080/.
7. Johannes A. Buchmann, J. Loho, and J. Zayer. An implementation of the general number field sieve. *Lecture Notes in Computer Science*, 773:159–166, 1994.

8. Yevgeniy Dodis. Efficient construction of (distributed) verifiable random functions. In *Proceedings of 6th International Workshop on Theory and Practice in Public Key Cryptography*, pages 1–17, 2003.

9. Steven D. Galbraith. Supersingular curves in cryptography. *Lecture Notes in Computer Science*, 2248:495–513, 2001.

10. Oded Goldreich and Leonid Levin. A hard-core predicate for all one-way functions. In *Proceedings of the 21th Annual ACM Symposium on the Theory of Computing*, pages 25–32, 1989.

11. S. Goldwasser and M. Bellare. Lecture notes on cryptography. Summer Course "Cryptography and Computer Security" at MIT, 1996–1999, 1999.

12. Stanislaw Jarecki and Vitaly Shmatikov. Handcuffing big brother : an abuse-resilient transaction escrow scheme. In *Advances in Cryptology - Proceedings of EUROCRYPT 2004*, volume 3027 of *Lecture Notes in Computer Science*, pages 590–608. Springer-Verlag, 2004.

13. Antoine Joux and Kim Nguyen. Separating Decision Diffie-Hellman from Diffie-Hellman in cryptographic groups. Cryptology ePrint Archive, Report 2001/003, 2001. http://eprint.iacr.org/2001/003/.

14. Anna Lysyanskaya. Unique signatures and verifiable random functions from DH-DDH separation. In *Proceedings of the 22nd Annual International Cryptology Conference on Advances in Cryptology*, pages 597–612, 2002.

15. Silvio Micali, Michael O. Rabin, and Salil P. Vadhan. Verifiable random functions. In *Proceedings of the 40th IEEE Symposium on Foundations of Computer Science*, pages 120–130, 1999.

16. Silvio Micali and Leonid Reyzin. Soundness in the public-key model. *Lecture Notes in Computer Science*, 2139:542–565, 2001.

17. Silvio Micali and Ronald L. Rivest. Micropayments revisited. In *CT-RSA*, pages 149–163, 2002.

18. Shigeo Mitsunari, Ryuichi Sakai, and Masao Kasahara. A new traitor tracing. *IEICE Trans. Fundamentals*, pages 481–484, 2002.

19. Moni Naor and Omer Reingold. Number-theoretic constructions of efficient pseudo-random functions. In *Proceedings of the 38th IEEE Symposium on Foundations of Computer Science*, pages 458–467, 1997.

20. Jacob T. Schwartz. Fast probabilistic algorithms for verification of polynomial identities. *Journal of the Association for Computing Machinery*, 27:701–717, 1980.

21. Victor Shoup. Lower bounds for discrete logarithms and related problems. *Lecture Notes in Computer Science*, 1233:256–266, 1997.

22. Michael Steiner, Gene Tsudik, and Michael Waidner. Diffie-Hellman key distribution extended to group communication. In *Proceedings of the 3rd ACM Conference on Computer and Communications Security*, pages 31–37, 1996.

Author Index

Lecture Notes in Computer Science

For information about Vols. 1–3262

please contact your bookseller or Springer

Vol. 3312: A.J. Hu, A.K. Martin (Eds.), Formal Methods in Computer-Aided Design. XI, 445 pages. 2004.

Vol. 3311: V. Roca, F. Rousseau (Eds.), Interactive Multimedia and Next Generation Networks. XIII, 287 pages. 2004.

Vol. 3309: C.-H. Chi, K.-Y. Lam (Eds.), Content Computing. XII, 510 pages. 2004.

Vol. 3308: J. Davies, W. Schulte, M. Barnett (Eds.), Formal Methods and Software Engineering. XIII, 500 pages. 2004.

Vol. 3307: C. Bussler, S.-k. Hong, W. Jun, R. Kaschek, D.. Kinshuk, S. Krishnaswamy, S.W. Loke, D. Oberle, D. Richards, A. Sharma, Y. Sure, B. Thalheim (Eds.), Web Information Systems – WISE 2004 Workshops. XV, 277 pages. 2004.

Vol. 3306: X. Zhou, S. Su, M.P. Papazoglou, M.E. Orlowska, K.G. Jeffery (Eds.), Web Information Systems – WISE 2004. XVII, 745 pages. 2004.

Vol. 3305: P.M.A. Sloot, B. Chopard, A.G. Hoekstra (Eds.), Cellular Automata. XV, 883 pages. 2004.

Vol. 3303: J.A. López, E. Benfenati, W. Dubitzky (Eds.), Knowledge Exploration in Life Science Informatics. X, 249 pages. 2004. (Subseries LNAI).

Vol. 3302: W.-N. Chin (Ed.), Programming Languages and Systems. XIII, 453 pages. 2004.

Vol. 3300: L. Bertossi, A. Hunter, T. Schaub (Eds.), Inconsistency Tolerance. VII, 295 pages. 2004.

Vol. 3299: F. Wang (Ed.), Automated Technology for Verification and Analysis. XII, 506 pages. 2004.

Vol. 3298: S.A. McIlraith, D. Plexousakis, F. van Harmelen (Eds.), The Semantic Web – ISWC 2004. XXI, 841 pages. 2004.

Vol. 3296: L. Bougé, V.K. Prasanna (Eds.), High Performance Computing - HiPC 2004. XXV, 530 pages. 2004.

Vol. 3295: P. Markopoulos, B. Eggen, E. Aarts, J.L. Crowley (Eds.), Ambient Intelligence. XIII, 388 pages. 2004.

Vol. 3294: C.N. Dean, R.T. Boute (Eds.), Teaching Formal Methods. X, 249 pages. 2004.

Vol. 3293: C.-H. Chi, M. van Steen, C. Wills (Eds.), Web Content Caching and Distribution. IX, 283 pages. 2004.

Vol. 3292: R. Meersman, Z. Tari, A. Corsaro (Eds.), On the Move to Meaningful Internet Systems 2004: OTM 2004 Workshops. XXIII, 885 pages. 2004.

Vol. 3291: R. Meersman, Z. Tari (Eds.), On the Move to Meaningful Internet Systems 2004: CoopIS, DOA, and ODBASE, Part II. XXV, 824 pages. 2004.

Vol. 3290: R. Meersman, Z. Tari (Eds.), On the Move to Meaningful Internet Systems 2004: CoopIS, DOA, and ODBASE, Part I. XXV, 823 pages. 2004.

Vol. 3289: S. Wang, K. Tanaka, S. Zhou, T.W. Ling, J. Guan, D. Yang, F. Grandi, E. Mangina, I.-Y. Song, H.C. Mayr (Eds.), Conceptual Modeling for Advanced Application Domains. XXII, 692 pages. 2004.

Vol. 3288: P. Atzeni, W. Chu, H. Lu, S. Zhou, T.W. Ling (Eds.), Conceptual Modeling – ER 2004. XXI, 869 pages. 2004.

Vol. 3287: A. Sanfeliu, J.F. Martínez Trinidad, J.A. Carrasco Ochoa (Eds.), Progress in Pattern Recognition, Image Analysis and Applications. XVII, 703 pages. 2004.

Vol. 3286: G. Karsai, E. Visser (Eds.), Generative Programming and Component Engineering. XIII, 491 pages. 2004.

Vol. 3285: S. Manandhar, J. Austin, U.B. Desai, Y. Oyanagi, A. Talukder (Eds.), Applied Computing. XII, 334 pages. 2004.

Vol. 3284: A. Karmouch, L. Korba, E.R.M. Madeira (Eds.), Mobility Aware Technologies and Applications. XII, 382 pages. 2004.

Vol. 3283: F.A. Aagesen, C. Anutariya, V. Wuwongse (Eds.), Intelligence in Communication Systems. XIII, 327 pages. 2004.

Vol. 3282: V. Guruswami, List Decoding of Error-Correcting Codes. XIX, 350 pages. 2004.

Vol. 3281: T. Dingsøyr (Ed.), Software Process Improvement. X, 207 pages. 2004.

Vol. 3280: C. Aykanat, T. Dayar, İ. Körpeoğlu (Eds.), Computer and Information Sciences - ISCIS 2004. XVIII, 1009 pages. 2004.

Vol. 3279: G.M. Voelker, S. Shenker (Eds.), Peer-to-Peer Systems III. XI, 300 pages. 2004.

Vol. 3278: A. Sahai, F. Wu (Eds.), Utility Computing. XI, 272 pages. 2004.

Vol. 3275: P. Perner (Ed.), Advances in Data Mining. VIII, 173 pages. 2004. (Subseries LNAI).

Vol. 3274: R. Guerraoui (Ed.), Distributed Computing. XIII, 465 pages. 2004.

Vol. 3273: T. Baar, A. Strohmeier, A. Moreira, S.J. Mellor (Eds.), <<UML>> 2004 - The Unified Modelling Language. XIII, 454 pages. 2004.

Vol. 3272: L. Baresi, S. Dustdar, H. Gall, M. Matera (Eds.), Ubiquitous Mobile Information and Collaboration Systems. VIII, 197 pages. 2004.

Vol. 3271: J. Vicente, D. Hutchison (Eds.), Management of Multimedia Networks and Services. XIII, 335 pages. 2004.

Vol. 3270: M. Jeckle, R. Kowalczyk, P. Braun (Eds.), Grid Services Engineering and Management. X, 165 pages. 2004.

Vol. 3269: J. Lopez, S. Qing, E. Okamoto (Eds.), Information and Communications Security. XI, 564 pages. 2004.

Vol. 3268: W. Lindner, M. Mesiti, C. Türker, Y. Tzitzikas, A. Vakali (Eds.), Current Trends in Database Technology - EDBT 2004 Workshops. XVIII, 608 pages. 2004.

Vol. 3267: C. Priami, P. Quaglia (Eds.), Global Computing. VIII, 377 pages. 2004.

Vol. 3266: J. Solé-Pareta, M. Smirnov, P.V. Mieghem, J. Domingo-Pascual, E. Monteiro, P. Reichl, B. Stiller, R.J. Gibbens (Eds.), Quality of Service in the Emerging Networking Panorama. XVI, 390 pages. 2004.

Vol. 3265: R.E. Frederking, K.B. Taylor (Eds.), Machine Translation: From Real Users to Research. XI, 392 pages. 2004. (Subseries LNAI).

Vol. 3264: G. Paliouras, Y. Sakakibara (Eds.), Grammatical Inference: Algorithms and Applications. XI, 291 pages. 2004. (Subseries LNAI).

Vol. 3263: M. Weske, P. Liggesmeyer (Eds.), Object-Oriented and Internet-Based Technologies. XII, 239 pages. 2004.